Conservation
of Natural Resources

Young whooping crane "canus" rescued by the Canadian Wildlife Service after an injury on the nesting grounds in the Northwest Territories. Whooping cranes are an endangered North American bird now estimated to number approximately 50 individuals. (Photo by C. Eugene Knoder. Courtesy of the U.S. Department of the Interior, Bureau of Sport Fisheries and Wildlife.)

Conservation of Natural Resources

Fourth Edition

EDITOR: Guy-Harold Smith

The Ohio State University

CONTRIBUTORS:

ROBERT M. BASILE

MARION CLAWSON

JOHN H. GARLAND

H. BOWMAN HAWKES

LAWRENCE A. HOFFMAN

LEE M. JAMES

LOWRY B. KARNES

DONALD W. LEWIS

HAROLD H. MCCARTY

E. WILLARD MILLER

WILLIAM A. ROCKIE

HAROLD M. ROSE

FRANK SEAWALL

GUY-HAROLD SMITH

JAMES A. SPENCER

CARL H. STRANDBERG

HALENE HATCHER VISHER

WARREN C. WHITMAN

LOUIS A. WOLFANGER

THE LATE CHARLES A. DAMBACH

THE LATE HERBERT C. HANSON

THE LATE STEPHEN S. VISHER

JOHN WILEY & SONS, INC.

New York · London · Sydney · Toronto

Copyright © 1971 by John Wiley & Sons, Inc.

Copyright, 1950 © 1958, 1965 by John Wiley & Sons, Inc.

Library of Congress Catalogue Card Number: 71-129661

ISBN 0-471-80192-5

Printed in the United States of America

10 9 8 7 6 5 4 3 2 1

In memory of E. B. S.

Preface

When this book was first published in 1950 the knowledgeable people of the United States had developed a renewed interest in preserving and enhancing the resource base of the national economy. World War II (1939–1945) had been fought and won by the Allies over aggressive forces in central Europe and the western Pacific. The United States entered the war as an active partner in 1941 and made a decisive contribution of man power and material strength. Many people had hoped that the years immediately after the war could be used to re-establish a peacetime economy and lessen the drain on the nation's natural resources. They were to be disappointed.

It became evident almost immediately that the material and economic strength of the United States and other countries would be required to restore and rehabilitate the war-devastated areas of western and central Europe, of Greece, Turkey, Japan, and the Philippines. Before President Truman could commit the United States to this major responsibility the Secretary of the Interior, J. A. Krug, was called upon to report on the capacity of the national economy to undertake the momentous task of underwriting, with the assistance of other countries of the free world, the reconstruction programs needed to lift the devastated and defeated nations out of the despair and the sense of helplessness that followed the war.

Secretary Krug's report issued in 1947 entitled, *National Resources and Foreign Aid,* recognized the inadequacies of the resource base by noting the dependence of the United States on foreign areas for tropical products such as natural rubber, vegetable oils, coffee, and sugar, and for a number of products such as aluminium, nickel, chromium, manganese, and other minerals. The report also encouraged President Truman and others in the federal government to undertake this rehabilitation project.

George C. Marshall, Secretary of State, speaking at a commencement convocation at Harvard University on June 5, 1947, made a statement which in effect was a call for support of foreign aid. His proposal became what is known as the Marshall Plan. The United States continues its financial aid to a number of foreign countries but at a reduced rate.

The 20-year period between 1950 and 1970 witnessed the involvement of the United States in the Korean conflict (1950–1953) and the Vietnam War (since the middle 1950's). In this same period the population increased to more than 200,000,000; employment increased to nearly 76,000,000 in 1968; and the gross national product attained a level of $865,701,000,000 in 1968. Affluent America made heavy demands on the economy for both capital and consumer goods, and the use of resources on a large scale became a characteristic of American life. The President's Materials Policy Commission, in a report entitled, *Resources for Freedom* (1952), generally supported the use of resources for both national needs and foreign aid, but emphasis was placed on deficiencies and the need for conservation.

In the second year of President Kennedy's administration he convened a White House Conference on Resources (May 24–25, 1962) to re-examine the resource situation. A distinguished list of officials in the administration, members of the Congress, four Governors, and others attended. At this conference there were repeated calls for cleaning up the atmosphere and the polluted waters and for the conservation of the wasting resources. Three years later the Environmental Pollution Panel of the President's Science Advisory Committee presented its report on *Restoring the Quality of Our Environment* (1965), but still the problems remain to plague us.

The several reports on the resource situation by federal, state, and other public agencies were matched by an abundant literature published by Resources for the Future, Inc., The Conservation Foundation, and many other organizations and by private persons who had become greatly concerned with the wasteful use of resources and the deterioration of the environment.

As we enter the decade of the 1970's, President Nixon has called for a concerted attack on the problems of the environment. He has named Russell E. Train, initially Under-Secretary of the Department of the Interior, as Chairman of the Council on Environmental Quality. The President has asked Congress for $4 billion for clean waters and has called on the states to contribute $6 billion over a five-year period. Students in the colleges and universities have become involved in the thrust to clean up the environment. Teach-ins have been organized. A new interest in the old science of ecology has developed. Private industries have recognized their responsibilities, and many companies are now processing their waste products instead of discharging them into the lakes, rivers, and atmosphere.

The twenty contributors to this edition, seven of them new, have pooled their talents to bring to the reader, whether he be a student, a scholar, a scientist, a professional conservationist, a public servant, or a concerned citizen, the challenge of the 1970's. It is their hope that the many problems related to the adequacy of the resource base to support the economy and the security of the nation will be better understood. All citizens are called upon to become informed about the resource situation and to become involved conservationists.

Since my retirement as an active member of the staff of the Department of Geography at The Ohio State University in 1965, I have been provided with a desk and office space shared by an editorial assistant and usually one other person. The University celebrates the one-hundredth anniversary of its founding this year (1870–1970), and it is a pleasure to acknowledge the continued services provided working members of the emeritus staff. Secretarial service has been available to handle all correspondence, which at times has been heavy.

The editor has enjoyed the unfailing assistance of the personnel of the University Libraries. I wish to commend particularly the staff of the Reference Department who, because of their knowledge of sources and their commitment to their responsibilities, have eased my work as editor and as an author.

I wish to acknowledge the unfailing help of Mrs. Vera Luczka Herman who has served as my editoral assistant during the preparation of the third and fourth editions of this book. Her contribution is unseen but very real and much appreciated.

GUY-HAROLD SMITH
Editor

The Ohio State University
Columbus, Ohio, 1970

Contents

Part 8

Conservation
of Natural Resources

Part 1

HAROLD M. ROSE
University of Wisconsin-Milwaukee

CHAPTER 1

Conservation in the United States

The quest for security is an ongoing, universal phenomenon. Whether it's social, economic, physical, or spiritual in form, it is not always assured within the time spectrum that an individual or group actually occupies an area or can envision its occupancy by its progeny. Because of the uncertainty that has been associated historically with efforts to secure the basic necessities of life, men have been led to engage in activity that would minimize this uncertainty. Such behavior characterized primitive man, as well as modern man, and is destined to continue in the postmodern period. Although the basic need to engage in security-ensuring activity is universal, operational strategies have differed in various times and places. The conservation philosophy, and the programs and activity which have sprung from it, might be thought of as one such effort which has received support in the United States as a means of eliminating the insecurity surrounding the nation's ability to support itself now and in the future, and at some predetermined level.

Conservation, as a formal philosophy, is as American as Jeffersonian Democracy, and at times has proved to be no more flexible.

Great difficulty has been encountered in attempts to resolve the conflict inherent in many of the formal definitions of conservation. Much of the difficulty can be attributed to oversimplification, limited focus, and conflicting interests. The problem of a satisfactory definition most often arises when one attempts to move from the philosophical level to the operational level, and this should therefore be anticipated. The definitional problem becomes more acute as the issues to which the conservationist philosophy is applied become more complex. Each year, it seems, the list of issues grows longer.

NATIONAL DEVELOPMENT AND THE PRECONSERVATION ERA

Land, the Basic Resource. Land is frequently hailed as the basic contributing factor to the rapid and successful development of the nation. If land served as the basis for development, a land policy which permitted easy transfer of land from federal to individual ownership served as a catalyst. The land factor and all its productive powers, which are commonly referred to as natural resources, represented the nation's potential for development.

Once the Appalachian barrier had been penetrated, the frontier was swiftly and continuously pushed westward until the nation's land was inhabited by Americans from the Atlantic to the Pacific. During settlement there was much evidence of land-use mismanagement, which gave rise to the subsequent threat of scarcity and the despoliation of facets of nature's bounty, two factors which later led to dualisms in conservation philosophy. The dualisms that emerged revolved around the objectives that natural resources were thought to satisfy. This led very early in the twentieth century to the evolution of one group of conservationists who promoted natural resource development or use and another group who promoted preservation or nonuse. These basic value differences, which were early assigned to natural resources or the natural environment, have been passed on through time.

By the time of the transcendentalist writers Ralph Waldo Emerson and Henry David Thoreau, the frontier had been pushed to the base of the Rockies and mountain men were paving the way for settlement beyond the mountains.[1] These writers did much to focus attention on the man-nature relationship,[2] and their influence on both the ethical and aesthetic school of conservation thought has been pervasive.

Early Conservationist Thought. George P. Marsh is often considered the principal forerunner of the modern conservationist in the United States. Marsh, a naturalist, politician, and government servant, had the opportunity to observe man's relationship with nature in both Europe and the Middle East, areas that have been settled for a long time. He concluded that the abuse that was evident on

these continents would soon prevail in America if some attempts were not made to study the man-nature relationship. Marsh's thesis was that "man disrupts the fundamental harmony or balance of nature."[3] This thinking led to the eventual rise of the ecological philosophy of conservation. Marsh has been referred to as the "fountainhead of the conservation movement,"[4] even though conservation as a formal movement did not get underway until after his death.

Legislative Action and Natural-Resource Management. By the close of the Civil War the nation had acquired the entire territory that now constitutes the forty-eight contiguous states. The Homestead Act of 1862 had been passed to accelerate settlement on this newly acquired land. Within the next 30 years the frontier was steadily pushed westward, until at last more than just a series of isolated settlements existed west to the shores of the Pacific. It was from this generation that the nation's future conservation leaders were to originate, both native-born Americans and persons of European origin whose training in resource management prepared them well for the task ahead. These men observed with great clarity the problems that had evolved out of the passing of the frontier and their possible effects on the future of the nation's development.

It was during the latter part of the nineteenth century that the battle lines were drawn, which were to lead eventually to the dualisms that were to pervade conservation philosophy from its very beginnings to the present. The growing concern over natural-resource abuse has previously been attributed to the intense interest in these matters by naturalists and naturalist-philosophers. These individuals can be hailed as the promoters of what was to become the ecological school of conservation.

---

[1] Ray Allen Billington, *The Far Western Frontier, 1830–1860,* New York, 1962, pp. 41–68.

[2] Arthur A. Ekrich, Jr., *Man and Nature in America,* New York, 1963, pp. 47–69.

[3] *Ibid.,* p. 75.

[4] Quoted by Stewart L. Udall, *The Quiet Crisis,* New York, 1963, p. 94.

Another group of individuals, frequently representing persons trained in some area of natural-resource management, was also to come to the fore and promote efficiency in resource utilization. The emergence of this group, represented by Gifford Pinchot, has resulted in Hays identifying the period in which they exerted the dominant influence as one of maximum efficiency.[5] These were the forerunners of what might be thought of as economic and technologic conservationists.

THE ROLE OF THE FRONTIER IN CONSERVATION THOUGHT

There is very little serious writing on the conservation movement in the United States that does not attempt to relate the rise of the movement to the expansion of the frontier. The frontier hypothesis of Frederick Jackson Turner has done much to promote the idea of the rise of institutions west of the Alleghenies that were peculiarly American. The environment allegedly created men who exhibited strong individualistic traits and who resented seemingly senseless social controls. Thus the character of the frontiersmen promoted unregulated use of the natural resources of the Mississippi Valley. More recent explanations of the influence of the frontier on economic and social development in the West do much to refute the validity of the Turner hypothesis which leans heavily toward environmental determinism. It was recently stated that "the frontier was more than an area or a process; it was, in its deepest sense, an interaction of space as nature and of society as an evolutionary organism to produce those virtues upon which Americans prided themselves most."[6]

The Frontier Concept. The fear of declining abundance associated with the passage of

Turner's frontier is held by some to be invalid. A recent definition of a frontier is that it is "the edge of the unused,"[7] and therefore "science has its frontiers, technology its frontiers, and that so long as Americans can advance their standards of living and maintain the fluidity of their lives and their capacity for change along these frontiers, the disappearance of the agrarian frontier is not at all critical."[8] This change in thought has given rise to the concept of a vertical frontier, which might be as valid in explaining the availability and development of natural resources as the concept of a horizontal frontier was during a previous period.

The Horizontal versus the Vertical Frontier. It is now possible to link the two frontiers with the dualism that pervades the conservation philosophy. Those whose orientation is still the concept of the dominance of the horizontal frontier tend to represent individuals whose conservation views are principally ecological, ethical, and aesthetic. Much writing supports these views, including works by Samuel H. Ordway, Jr., Aldo Leopold, Paul B. Sears, F. Frazier Darling, William Vogt, and Fairfield Osborn, although the chief proponent and one of the earlier and most active conservationists was John Muir.

The recent rise of the concept of a vertical frontier and its focus on economic production factors has not resulted in developing as large a body of supporters in the resource area as there is for the horizontal frontier. But the writings of Allen V. Kneese, Orris C. Herfindahl, Joseph L. Fisher, Harold J. Barnett, and Chandler Morse have done much to create a formal awareness of this point of view. What seems most imperative at this time, however, is the necessity of reconciling the horizontal frontier and vertical frontier.

During much of the twentieth century the overriding emphasis has been placed on the

[5] Samuel P. Hays, *Conservation and the Gospel of Efficiency*, Cambridge, Massachusetts, 1959, p. 2.
[6] Robert F. Berkhofer, Jr., "Space, Time, Culture and the New Frontier," *Agricultural History*, Vol. 38, 1964, p. 24.

[7] David M. Potter, *People of Plenty*, Chicago, 1954, p. 157.
[8] *Ibid.*

goods-producing qualities of the environment, without giving due consideration to the feedback effect associated with the rise of the vertical frontier. Problems associated with feedback are currently very real and give indications of again raising the question of the meaningfulness of the concept of a horizontal frontier within the realm of conservation. The need for the reconciliation of these concepts can be observed in a recent statement by Joseph L. Fisher:

We shall have to examine the natural environment and its several parts more comprehensively and systematically, looking further ahead, and paying more attention to the interrelations between that environment on the one hand and the cultural environment of research, technology, economic development, and human welfare on the other hand.[9] The problems call for solutions now.

EVOLUTION OF THE CONSERVATION MOVEMENT

Conservation as a social movement in the United States was not initiated before the turn of the twentieth century, although there was much sporadic action and emphasis on resource abuse growing out of a land policy that had as its principal objective the acceleration of settlement west of the Mississippi. By 1890 it was realized that much of the legislation passed during the latter half of the nineteenth century had created problems that were unanticipated at the time of its passage. Some of the earlier laws, such as the Timber Culture Act of 1873, the Pre-emption Act, and the Desert Land Act of 1877, were eventually repealed or in the case of the last-named Act strengthened to prevent further dummy sales

that were being promoted by special-interest groups.[10]

The germinal concepts that later were identified with conservation were embodied in the writings of an early group of naturalists, teachers, and public servants, such as Louis Agassiz, Arnold Guyot, Nathaniel S. Shaler, George P. Marsh, and Major J. W. Powell, the first director of the United States Geological Survey. Agassiz and Shaler taught at Harvard University; Guyot was on the faculty at Princeton University. Major Powell,[11] a disabled veteran of the Civil War, appraised with keen perception the dry lands of the West. All were familiar with the emerging problems related to the use and abuse of the rich resources of the nation. All were pathfinders at a time when leadership was required.

While public land continued to be disposed of, some land was being withdrawn from private entry and set aside so that it could be protected and freed from possible abuse. Thus by the turn of the century the stage was set for the initiation of a formal social movement that would focus attention on the situation surrounding the nation's natural resources, which were thought to represent the key to continued national development.

Conservation Under Theodore Roosevelt. The initial phase of the conservation movement in the United States was associated with the administration of President Theodore Roosevelt, who himself was an active outdoors man. The idea of promoting a conscious effort to produce change in the area of natural-resource management was Gifford Pinchot's, a professional forester (Fig. 1). It was Pinchot who was to become a great influence in the nation's first attempt at organized conservation. Pinchot chose the term "conservation" to

[9] Joseph L. Fisher, "Natural Resources—Wise Use of the World's Inheritance," William R. Ewald, editor, *Environment and Policy*, Bloomington, Indiana, 1968, p. 332.

[10] Paul W. Gates, "The Homestead Law in an Incongruous Land System," Vernon R. Carstensen, editor, *The Public Lands*, Madison, Wisconsin, 1962, pp. 315–348.

[11] J. W. Powell, *Lands of the Arid Regions of the United States*, Washington, D.C., 1879.

Fig. 1 Gifford Pinchot, at one time Chief of the Division of Forestry (now the Forest Service) and later Governor of the Commonwealth of Pennsylvania, was one of the leading conservationists in the United States. For many years he was closely associated with President Theodore Roosevelt who reserved for public use large areas of forest land. (U. S. Forest Service.)

describe the movement in 1907. He had been informed that government forests in India were known as Conservancies,[12] and this term interested him, thus leading him to employ a form of it to describe his own favored program. Conservation is a meaningful term though difficult to define.

The primary emphasis during this period was focused on the problems associated with forestry. Pinchot was opposed to establishing forest reserves which would result only in their preservation rather than their conservation. To Pinchot the concept of conservation connoted use under systematic management. This belief was later to cause him to sever his

[12] Udall, *op. cit.*, p. 106.

friendship with another noted personality, John Muir (Fig. 2), whose interest was principally in nature for nature's sake. These two individuals were later to represent the conservation giants of the era, with Pinchot on the inside directing the government's program and Muir on the outside promoting his own following through his many writings on the subject and the organization of the Sierra Club. John Muir is still held in high esteem by natural beauty enthusiasts.

During much of the period 1901–1909, the conservation movement was characterized by much propaganda designed to focus attention on declining resources. Most authorities today agree that the greatest contribution to come

Fig. 2 John Muir, a scientist and nature lover, was a pioneer in the promotion of the esthetic and the ethical philosophy embodied in the conservation movement. The thinking of Muir continues to influence a number of the nation's leaders in conservation. (Department of the Interior.)

out of this era was that of pointing up the problems that characterize the nation's storehouse of natural resources.

One of the last major efforts of the Theodore Roosevelt period was the calling of the governors of each state to the White House Conference of 1908 in Washington to discuss the resource problems existing within their own states. Before Roosevelt could spread his influence further afield, and into the international area of conservation, he was out of public office. Even though many of Roosevelt's plans for conservation were eclipsed as a result of his leaving presidential politics, he left a legacy to resource-conscious individuals and groups that should not be minimized. The Reclamation Act of 1902, which fostered western development; the concept of multiple-purpose resource development; scientific forestry; a mineral policy for the public lands; and the development of the Inland Waterways Commission represented some of the lasting effects of the Theodore Roosevelt era that have had more far-reaching effects on national-resource development than the much publicized propaganda aspect of his program.

The influence of Roosevelt policy makers was to extend into the administration of President William Howard Taft. But the voices of such individuals as Frederick Newell, W. J. McGee, and Charles R. Van Hise were to be less frequently heard and only Pinchot, the giant of the previous administration, was to make his influence felt for another decade.

The Second Phase of the Conservation Movement. The initial phase of the conservation movement is generally regarded as having terminated in 1909. In the following decade there was no strong personality within the group in power who could promote the nation's conservation program. This does not mean that no attempts were made to promote conservation, but much of the period was given over to controversy arising out of policy differences between the Taft administration and the previous administration. The growing

conflict on the international scene did much to divert the nation's attention from national resource development to the war in Europe. Thus the latter half of the second decade of the century did not lend itself to the promotion of conservation. World War I required the use of man power and natural resources to bring the conflict to an early end.

The apparent waning of Pinchot's influence in conservation circles was evidenced by the passage of the Water Power Act of 1920, which did not promote the type of multiple-purpose policy to which he was committed. "By 1921 the way had been cleared for the rapid expansion of resource development on the public lands of the United States, and a new stage in Conservation history had begun." [13]

The second phase of the conservation movement saw three individuals occupying the position of central authority in the national government: Presidents Warren Harding, Calvin Coolidge, and Herbert Hoover. During their era no single personality dominated the scene or provided the type of leadership typical of the previous phase.

The natural resource on which most attention was focused during this period was petroleum. Petroleum had reached new heights in popularity, for it was the fuel that powered allied armies to victory in Europe. The growing automobile market created new demands for this power source in the years following the war, even to the extent that it was thought that the nation's limited reserves might soon be exhausted. The Bureau of Mines promoted a program that attempted to eliminate waste in petroleum production and to increase efficiency in drilling techniques. A petroleum experimental station was opened at Bartlesville, Oklahoma, in 1920 to aid in promoting the Bureau's policy.[14]

The Teapot Dome scandal, which occurred

[13] Donald C. Swain, *Federal Conservation Policy, 1921–1933*, Berkeley, California, 1963, p. 4.

[14] *Ibid.*, p. 57.

during the Harding administration, did little to create a favorable conservation atmosphere. The Teapot Dome was a formation containing petroleum on public land in Wyoming. It was to play a major role in weakening the conservation efforts of this period. The appointment of a Federal Oil Conservation Board by President Coolidge was an attempt to overcome the image created during the administration of his predecessor.

The last four years of the second phase of the movement were the most promising in regard to conservation. President Herbert Hoover had the opportunity to introduce a number of the programs to which he had given attention as Secretary of Commerce during the administrations of Presidents Harding and Coolidge. Hoover's contributions are not too frequently hailed in the general conservation literature, but his zeal for efficiency and his water-resource planning program must be recognized as valid contributions.

President Hoover, first as Secretary of Commerce and later as Chief Executive, had a vital interest in the orderly development and control of the water resources of the country. The Flood Control Act of 1928 passed in the Coolidge administration was strongly endorsed by Secretary Hoover. The great dam on the Colorado River which now bears his name was originally known as the Boulder Canyon Project, and the name Hoover Dam was belated recognition of his interest in, and support of, the project (Fig. 3). It was in his administration that the Federal Power Commission was reorganized and established as an agency that was to play a dominant role in the development of the water-power resources of the country. The Commission's jurisdiction has been increased by Congressional action.

Hoover's distaste for federal regulation and his dependence on voluntary cooperation and action was to reduce the effectiveness of his program. "In certain instances he achieved considerable success by means of cooperation. His oil policy is a good example. But on the whole, cooperative tactics failed in the face of strong opposition from resource users."[15] This era saw a movement away from complete dependence on the federal government for developing conservation programs. This was a break with the Roosevelt-Pinchot theme of conservation as a governmental function.[16]

Conservation and the New Deal. The period 1933–1939 might be thought of as the "golden age of conservation" in the United States. The state of the nation's economic situation did much to remove some of the obstacles to an effective conservation program that prevailed during the earlier period. Thus the stage was set for a strong personality to take over while conservation was on the wane. The problems to be corrected were both far-reaching and complex, since they related not only to land but also to man.

Franklin D. Roosevelt, unlike Theodore Roosevelt, was not overshadowed by any individual in his administration as the guiding force in the development of his administration's conservation program. Although Franklin D. Roosevelt did enlist a strong professional bureaucracy of experts in bringing about solutions to these multifarious problems the responsibility for leadership was his, and he accepted the role.

The primary emphasis during this period was on land planning, with a special focus on soil-improvement programs. Up to that time, the major conservation emphasis had been on a single natural resource. But it was then realized that the disharmony in the economy prevailing throughout most of the nation represented a failure in man-land relationships within an institutional frame of reference. Thus it was necessary to introduce the type of machinery that would result in the realignment of these discordant relations.

The F.D.R. program was characterized by

---

[15] *Ibid.*, p. 162.

[16] H. Bowman Hawkes, "The Paradoxes of the Conservation Movement," *Bulletin of the University of Utah*, Vol. 51, February 1960, p. 19.

Fig. 3 The Hoover Dam, in the Boulder Canyon section of the Colorado River, is concrete evidence of President Hoover's leadership in the development of the water resources of the dry Southwest. (Bureau of Reclamation.)

the passage of much legislation and the creation of numerous bureaus and agencies to transform legislation into meaningful action at the grassroots level. Some of the more far-reaching legislations were those acts allowing for the establishment of the Tennessee Valley Authority, the Civilian Conservation Corps, the National Resources Board, the Soil Conservation Service, and the Resettlement Administration.

The enthusiasm for soil conservation, both official and personal, was in large measure related to the leadership of Hugh Hammond

Bennett. The Soil Conservation Act of 1933 was the legal basis for establishing demonstration projects across the nation, particularly in those states where soil erosion had already greatly reduced the productivity of the land. Few people in the past century attracted a larger following of devoted conservationists than did Bennett, the long-time Chief of the Soil Conservation Service.

It was also during this period that the indiscriminate giveaway of land was terminated. The passage of the Taylor Grazing Act in 1934 resulted in the withdrawal from entry the remaining unreserved area of public domain, although at the same time tax-delinquent land within individual states was being ceded to the national government for the purpose of creating National Forests and other public holdings.

These various measures enabled the nation to start back on the road to economic recovery, with full recovery following on the heels of the outbreak of war in Europe, for the second time in a single generation. Thus once more the nation's interest was turned from the domestic scene to the international scene and the exigencies of war resulted in turning one's back on problems of a conservational nature which had existed only a short time before, but now seemed to have disappeared.

CONSERVATION IN THE POSTWAR ERA

The years following World War II found the nation deeply committed and active in the area of international economic recovery. The problems of recovery required much in the way of both financial assistance and the temporary employment of many of the nation's top resource specialists. Thus the Point Four Program, the Marshall Plan, and other such programs overshadowed the need to reappraise the domestic-resource situation and the problems that were later to evolve.

No Single Overriding Issue. The advent of the Korean crisis, occurring on the heels of the period of readjustment, did much to hamper strong government participation in sponsoring a unified conservation effort. This does not mean that the government was ignoring its responsibility, for numerous uncoordinated bits of legislation were passed that indicated resource consciousness. The "Paley Report," which was the nation's first postwar effort to appraise the status of its natural resources, is frequently hailed as the first attempt to take careful stock of the situation of resource adequacy.

The 1950's saw the nation becoming more and more urban, with employment operating at a high level and with an apparent absence of threat to material security. The conditions of the times made it difficult to generate much public interest of an emotional type in conservation, which was characteristic of a previous era.

Professional public bureaucrats were active in promoting the passage of legislation that supported their own specific interests. "The professional forester, engineer, conservationist, and economist are vital to the success of modern government. That hardly seems debatable, but we should raise an issue or two concerning the role of the professional public bureaucrat." [17] It is now apparent that, because of their complexity, many of the nation's resource programs do not originate at the grass-roots level, but are recommendations made by a group of specialists who desire to initiate some positive change. What is lacking is a central governmental authority that would look at the total field of natural resources as an area of policy and subject it to vigorous analysis as a means of coordinating it with other principal areas of national policy.[18]

The Expanding Role of Private Organizations. This period also saw the beginning of more participation by private organizations in the area of resource management and development. The Conservation Foundation and Resources for the Future, evolving in 1948 and 1952, respectively, are the most active in promoting research and education in this area. The former organization is ecologically oriented, whereas the latter is the chief proponent of the economic-engineering approach to resource problems. Other conservation organi-

[17] Ross B. Talbot, "The Political Forces," Howard W. Ottoson, editor, *Land Use Problems and Policy in the United States,* Lincoln, Nebraska, 1963, pp. 149–150.
[18] Charles M. Hardin, "Can We Afford a Separate Resources Policy," Henry Jarrett, editor, *Perspectives on Conservation,* Baltimore, 1958, p. 227.

zations generally represent special-interest groups that are frequently guilty of associating conservation solely with their own special interest. Resources for the Future, on the other hand, has supported numerous outstanding resource studies since its inception in 1952 and tends to focus on the larger resources picture, rather than confining its interest to a narrow spectrum. Much of the research relating to specific resource problems undertaken in the past 10 years has been sponsored by Resources for the Future. The Conservation Foundation recently sponsored a conference from which emanated a valuable contribution to the resource question, entitled *Future Environments of North America,* [19] reflecting both the ecological and economic points of view.

CONSERVATION TODAY

Today we find that the embryonic conservationist thought of George P. Marsh, which is now more than a century old, has reached maturity. The America of Marsh's day or even Theodore Roosevelt's day is a far cry from the America of today, with its concrete landscape, materialistic orientation, and metropolitan dominance. These changes in the nature of the landscape and in its settlement pattern have provided the necessary impetus for a reappraisal of the conservation concept and the subsequent policies and actions that are described or identified as conservational in nature.

The Technological Revolution. The problem of growing unemployment which made itself felt in the latter part of the 1950's, occurring at a time when the nation's standard of living was at a peak, was a bit difficult to understand. It was quite apparent, however, that this situation was not a replication of the situation that confronted Herbert Hoover or

[19] F. Fraser Darling and John P. Milton, editors, *Future Environments of North America,* Garden City, New York, 1966.

Franklin D. Roosevelt. This was an outgrowth of the technological revolution, its associated minimizing of land as a factor of production, and its expanded emphasis on the role of capital, both physical and human, in national development.

The technological revolution has left most Americans richer in material comforts than ever before during man's history on earth. Man's faith in technology has led to a lessening of demand for conservation programs based on the theme of "running out of resources." Although the technological revolution has assured against the possibility of abrupt depletion of any given resource, it has been responsible in no small measure for the emergence of a new set of problems that has had a direct and pervasive impact on the resource complex, which involves both man and environment.

Conservation and the Kennedy Administration. By 1960 the problems produced by the technological revolution had become more pervasive. Solutions to these problems became a major political issue during the presidential campaign of 1960. The election of John F. Kennedy to the highest position in the country is frequently thought to be a reflection of his ability to project a strong personal image, an element that had been missing since the administration of Franklin D. Roosevelt. On the basis of this assumption and subsequent Kennedy involvement in attempts to eliminate the multiplicity of resource problems that confronted the nation, it might be said that a fourth phase of the conservation movement had emerged.

The fourth phase of the conservation movement which got underway in the early 1960's was incipient in nature. But it was clearly evident that it was to have its initial focus on man. The fact that a small segment of the American population remained in a state of poverty at a time when the nation was at its economic zenith was distressing (Fig. 4). Attempts to alter this situation might be consid-

Fig. 4 Deep in the mountain recesses of Appalachia, poor people have managed to eke out a living as coal miners, woodsmen, truckers, or hunters. Notice in the foreground the plowing of a small garden area. When the vegetation is in full leaf the starkness of this scene will be softened. (*U.S. News & World Report.*)

ered the signal contribution of the Kennedy administration.

Attempts to solve the problems of the recent era are reflected in the passage of pertinent legislative acts and the growing role of private enterprise in the arena of public responsibility.

The Area Redevelopment Act of 1961 and the man-power Redevelopment Act of 1962 are among the major instruments designed to reduce the effects of the high rate of unemployment. A number of private firms have been similarly active in promoting job retraining experiences. The proposed Youth Employment Act is an administration attempt to solve an urban problem by employing a technique that is a throwback to a former period.

Although man is now receiving increased emphasis as a means of minimizing internal friction, problems of urban living continue to mount. The demand for land for outdoor recreation, the problems of traffic congestion and slum clearance, and rehabilitation are also receiving much-increased attention. The work of O.R.R.R.C. in the outdoor recreation field, increasing numbers of transportation studies, and the continued amending of the Housing Act of 1954 are evidence of attempts to relieve the nation of the problems that have emerged only recently.

Although there has been an increase in the current emphasis on man, this has in no way diminished concern for those elements that have traditionally served as the bases for economic and social development—natural resources. One of the first tasks undertaken by President Kennedy in the conservation arena was to request the National Academy of Sciences to evaluate the research that had been conducted "on behalf of conservation and the development of America's natural resources." [20]

In the spirit of Theodore Roosevelt, a White House Conference on conservation was held in Washington in May 1962. Five hundred of the leading conservationists in the nation convened at the White House to draw up plans that would aid in facilitating the minimization and elimination of resource problems in some seventeen specific areas of development.

Conservation and Resource Problems in the Post-Kennedy Era. The untimely death of John F. Kennedy brought to the presidency

[20] Herbert L. Schiller, "The Natural Resource Base: Where Do We Stand?" *World Politics,* Vol. XVI, July 1964, p. 669.

an individual who has his roots in the land. Lyndon B. Johnson, a native of the southwest, with an early rural orientation, very early made known his concern for order in nature by promoting a beauty in nature program, a laudable act considering the many more pressing issues that this president had to come to grips with. Mr. Johnson indicated further interest in nature by supporitng a wilderness bill that was passed during the early years of his administration. Although Mr. Johnson indicated a strong enthusiasm for beauty in nature, there are some problems in this area from which, for political reasons, he has remained aloof.[21]

A review of the record will show that Lyndon B. Johnson made his greatest contribution not in the area of outdoor recreation, but in the more difficult area of urban problems (Fig. 5). Much of the legislation in this area that had been recommended by his predecessor was pushed through by the new chief executive. President Johnson's contributions in the area of human resource development, which received its initial impetus from Kennedy, will not soon be viewed as the valuable contributions that history might prove them to be. The nation's involvement in what many consider to be an "extra-legal" war and the new national mood aimed at repressing urban unrest has already detracted from the value of the Johnson contribution.

By the mid-sixties a new focus on resource problems was clearly apparent. The earlier interest during the Kennedy administration in the quality of life experienced by a small segment of the American population had been translated into an interest in the actual and potential quality of life possible in a country in which it was generally conceded that environmental quality itself was rapidly deteriorating (Fig. 6). Thus it is quite clear that the central focus of the fourth phase of the conservation movement is environmental quality.

[21] Frank E. Smith, *The Politics of Conservation*, New York, 1966, p. 290.

Fig. 5   The crowded ghetto areas in the large cities are most unpleasant places to live. Playgrounds are not available or are inaccessible, and children must play in the alleys and streets. The quality of the urban environment has so deteriorated that remedial action is desperately needed. (*U.S. News & World Report.*)

Since 1965 a vast volume of literature has been published which is devoted to both describing and analyzing the problems for which we are showing increasing concern. The extent and diversity of these efforts were recently reviewed by Ian Burton, who categorized them generically.[22] He pointed up the underlying motivation for such studies, but

[22] Ian Burton, "The Quality of the Environment: A Review," *Geographical Review*, Vol. 58, July 1968, pp. 472–480.

Fig. 6 The high concentration of smog in the environs of the nation's Capitol is dramatic evidence of declining environmental quality in a once-beautiful governmental city. The photo was taken from the Virginia side of the Potomac River. (*Washington Post.*)

indicated that "the term 'environment' signifies a concept but does not convey much information." [23]

Besides the various approaches employed in conservation and resource management already mentioned, another has emerged as a result of the recent interest in environmental quality. This might be described as the psychic approach and is basically an outgrowth of the efforts of Gilbert F. White and his students to resolve some of the problems of environmental perception. In White's words the problem might be viewed as follows: "At the heart of managing a natural resource is the manager's perception of the resource and

of the choices open to him in dealing with it. At the heart of decisions on environmental quality are a manager's views of what he and others value in the environment and can preserve or cultivate." [24]

As an outgrowth of the expanded scope of interest in the area of resource management Robert Kates has presented the view that there now exists a "New Conservation." [25] So it seems that regardless of the nature of the problems that man is confronted with in the

[24] Gilbert F. White, "Formation and Role of Public Attitudes," Henry Jarrett, editor, *Environmental Quality*, Baltimore, 1966, p. 105.
[25] Robert Kates, "The Pursuit of Beauty in the Environment," *Landscape*, Vol. 16, Winter 1966–1967, pp. 21–22.

[23] *Ibid.*, p. 473.

realm of resources, the concept of conservation still has applicability. Attempts to resolve problems of environmental quality are promoting greater cooperation between those who were previously avowed ecologists or economists in resource orientation. The weaknesses of the previous single-minded approaches have been acknowledged recently by leading proponents of both the ecological and economic-technologic schools of thought. Today there appears to be a greater general interest in investigating and developing a general systems approach as a means of evaluating the resource complex.

References

Barnett, Harold J. and Chandler Morse, *Scarcity and Growth, The Economics of Natural Resource Availability,* Resources for the Future, The Johns Hopkins University Press, Baltimore, 1963.

Berkhofer, Robert F., Jr., "Space, Time, Culture and the New Frontier," *Agricultural History,* Vol. 38, 1964, pp. 21–30.

Billington, Ray Allen, *The Far Western Frontier, 1830–1860,* Harper and Row, New York, 1962.

Burton, Ian, "The Quality of the Environment: A Review," *Geographical Review,* Vol. 58, July 1968, pp. 472–480.

Carstensen, Vernon R., editor, *The Public Domain,* University of Wisconsin Press, Madison, Wisconsin, 1962.

Duncan, Craig, "Resource Utilization and the Conservation Concept," *Economic Geography,* Vol. 38, 1962, pp. 113–121.

Ekirch, Arthur A., Jr., *Man and Nature in America,* Columbia University Press, New York, 1963.

Fisher, Joseph L., "Natural Resources—Wise Use of the World's Inheritance," William R. Ewald, editor, *Environment and Policy,* Indiana University Press, Bloomington, 1968.

Gates, Paul W., "The Homestead Law in an Incongruous Land System," Vernon R. Carstensen, editor, *The Public Lands,* University of Wisconsin Press, Madison, 1962, pp. 315–348.

Hawkes, H. Bowman, "The Paradoxes of the Conservation Movement," *Bulletin of the University of Utah,* Vol. 51, 1960.

Hays, Samuel P., *Conservation and the Gospel of Efficiency,* Harvard University Press, Cambridge, Massachusetts, 1959.

Jarrett, Henry, editor, *Perspectives on Conservation,* Resources for the Future, The Johns Hopkins Press, Baltimore, 1958.

Kates, Robert, "The Pursuit of Beauty in the Environment," *Landscape,* Vol. 16, Winter 1966–1967, pp. 21–22.

Landsberg, Hans H., Leonard L. Fischman, and Joseph L. Fisher, *Resources in America's Future: Patterns of Requirements and Availabilities, 1960–2000,* Resources for the Future, The Johns Hopkins Press, Baltimore, 1963.

Noggle, Burl, *Teapot Dome: Oil and Politic in the 1920's,* Louisiana State University Press, Baton Rouge, Louisiana, 1962.

Ottoson, Howard W., *Land Use Policy and Problems in the United States,* University of Nebraska Press, Lincoln, Nebraska, 1963.

Potter, David M., *People of Plenty*, University of Chicago Press, Chicago, 1954.

Powell, J. W., *Lands of the Arid Regions of the United States*, U.S. Geographical and Geological Survey of the Rocky Mountain Region, Washington, D.C., 1879.

Schiller, Herbert L., "The Natural Resource Base: Where Do We Stand?" *World Politics*, Vol. XVI, July 1964, pp. 668–676.

Smith, Frank E., *The Politics of Conservation*, Pantheon Books, New York, 1966.

Swain, Donald C., *Federal Conservation Policy 1921–1933* (University of California Publications in History, Vol. 76), University of California Press, Berkeley, California, 1963.

Udall, Stewart L., *The Quiet Crisis*, Holt, Rhinehart and Winston, New York, 1963.

White, Gilbert F., "Formation and Role of Public Attitudes," Henry Jarrett, editor, *Environmental Quality*, The Johns Hopkins Press, Baltimore, 1966, pp. 105–127.

STEPHEN S. VISHER *

Indiana University

HALENE HATCHER VISHER

Formerly, Specialist for Geography and Conservation, U.S. Office of Education

CHAPTER 2

The Public Domain

The term "public domain" as here used applies to the land owned by the federal government, or formerly belonging to the people as a whole.

Acquisition of Areas. At the end of the American Revolution, the victorious thirteen original colonies received from England by the Treaty of Paris (1783) rights to all of her lands east of the Mississippi River. Shortly after the adoption of the Constitution, the thirteen original states ceded to the federal government all or nearly all of their claims to land beyond their borders. Thus the public domain soon consisted of most of the land between the original states (Fig. 1) and the Mississippi River, except the following new states created out of territory not ceded to the federal government: Vermont, 1791; Kentucky, 1792; Maine, 1820; West Virginia, 1863; and parts of Tennessee. The public domain, established for the common benefit of all the people, contained by 1802 more than 200 million acres.

As Figure 1 shows, other vast areas were acquired (1) by the Louisiana Purchase, (2)

from Mexico, (3) by the Oregon Compromise, and (4) by the purchase of Alaska. Smaller areas were purchased from Spain, Texas, and Mexico.

Figure 2 summarizes broadly the chief additions to the public domain. It reveals that, of the total land acquired, that ceded by the original states comprised nearly one-sixth, the Louisiana Purchase and Alaska each about one-fourth, the land acquired directly from Mexico about one-fifth, and the Oregon Compromise about one-tenth. The land purchased from Texas (to the north of that state's present boundary) made up 4 percent; the purchase of Florida added about 2 percent to the total public domain; and land purchased from Mexico added approximately 1 percent.

These lands were purchased at low prices. The Louisiana Purchase cost about 6.5 cents an acre; Florida, 20 cents; the tract purchased from Texas, 21 cents; the Gadsden Purchase, acquired from Mexico, 68 cents; and Alaska, about 2 cents an acre.

Disposal of Areas. THEIR TYPES AND GENERAL DISTRIBUTION. Slightly more than a billion acres have become private or state property. This is about three-fifths of the approximately

* Deceased, October 25, 1967

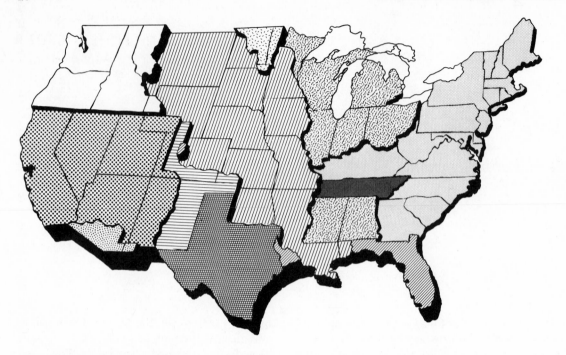

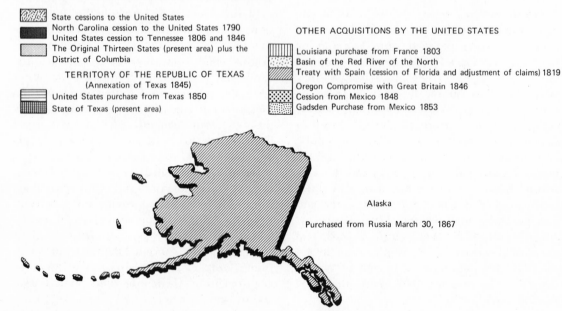

TERRITORY OF THE ORIGINAL THIRTEEN STATES

- State cessions to the United States
- North Carolina cession to the United States 1790
- United States cession to Tennessee 1806 and 1846
- The Original Thirteen States (present area) plus the District of Columbia

TERRITORY OF THE REPUBLIC OF TEXAS
(Annexation of Texas 1845)

- United States purchase from Texas 1850
- State of Texas (present area)

OTHER ACQUISITIONS BY THE UNITED STATES

- Louisiana purchase from France 1803
- Basin of the Red River of the North
- Treaty with Spain (cession of Florida and adjustment of claims) 1819
- Oregon Compromise with Great Britain 1846
- Cession from Mexico 1848
- Gadsden Purchase from Mexico 1853

Alaska

Purchased from Russia March 30, 1867

Fig. 1 Acquisitions of territory by the United States. (Bureau of Land Management, Department of the Interior.)

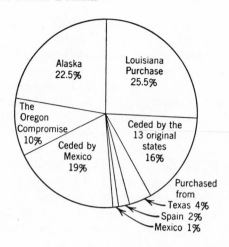

The Public Domain

Fig. 2 Sources, percentages.

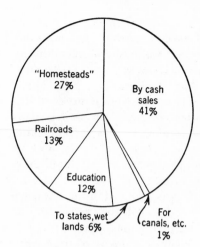

Fig. 3 How disposed of, percentages.

1,800,000,000 acres (almost 3,300,000 square miles) which at one time or another were owned by the federal government. About half of the remaining two-fifths is in Alaska.

The chief methods of disposal of the land are summarized in Fig. 3 which reveals that about 41 percent of the alienated land was sold; about 27 percent was disposed of under the homestead laws; about 12 percent was granted to the states in aid of education or for other purposes; and 13 percent was granted in aid of the railroads, most of which was given directly to railway corporations.

The land sold, except that sold under the Timber and Stone Act (1878), was located largely east of the Mississippi River or in Iowa, Missouri, and Arkansas. The land sold under the Timber and Stone Act was, however, largely in fine timber tracts of the Pacific states or northern Idaho and Minnesota.

Since the first homestead law was not passed until 1862, most of the more accessible land had already been disposed of by sale or grant. The land disposed of under the various homestead laws was therefore mostly in the second and third tiers of states west of the Mississippi River. Almost no land was homesteaded in Ohio, Indiana, Illinois, or Iowa, and none in Kentucky, Tennessee, or Texas. Under the several Desert Acts, which were modified homestead laws, nearly 2,000,000 acres were disposed of in Montana; nearly half as many in Wyoming; and about a fourth to a third as many in Colorado, California, and Utah; with small acreages in the other western states.

The land granted to the states in aid of education was distributed throughout the former public domain, with, however, larger acreages in the less fortunate states. The amount, Alaska being excepted, totaled about 120,000,000 acres, nearly 200,000 square miles, an area nearly four times as large as New England. During the earlier decades of the nineteenth century only one section (640 acres) of each township was reserved for schools. After 1848, however, two sections to the township were set aside. In 1850 four sections (2, 16, 32, and 36) were reserved for the schools of New Mexico and Utah. In 1864 the same provisions were made for Arizona. Moreover, liberal grants for institutions of higher learning were made after 1852. For example, "agricultural college scrip" (certificates entitling the

holder to specified acreages of public land) totaled 8,000,000 acres, a tract about one-fourth
as large as Pennsylvania. In addition, about
5,000,000 acres were given to state universities.
The educational grants to New Mexico were
greater than those to any other state, and totaled 9,600,000 acres, an area nearly half as
large as Indiana. The next in declining order
are Arizona, Utah, California, and Montana.
Twelve other states in the Middle West and
West received about 3,000,000 acres each, and
twelve others received from 1,000,000 to 2,-
000,000 acres. All the remaining states received smaller grants, mostly in the form of
scrip, chiefly in support of their agricultural
colleges.

The land granted to the states for canals
was mostly in Indiana, Ohio, and Michigan;
grants for river improvement were largely in
Iowa, Alabama, and Wisconsin; Oregon received 2,500,000 acres for roads; and Indiana
and Ohio received small grants. The total
grants to the states for canals, roads, and river
improvement were about 10,000,000 acres, an
area almost half as large as Ohio. In addition,
almost 65,000,000 acres of land classed as
"swamp and overflowed land" were ceded to
fourteen states. Florida received most, about
20,000,000 acres; Arkansas and Louisiana each
received about 8,000,000 acres (roughly one-
fourth of these states); and Michigan, Minnesota, Wisconsin, Missouri, and Mississippi
each got from 3,000,000 to 6,000,000 acres. Illinois, Iowa, Indiana, and California were
each granted 1,000,000 to 2,000,000 acres, and
Oregon and Alabama were granted small
acreages. A considerable share of the proceeds
from the sale of this "swamp land" (much of
it well-forested) was added by the states to
their endowment for public schools.

Figure 4 shows approximate limits in which
the railroads received their land grants. The
grants in aid of railroads, totaling 38,000,000
acres (60,000 square miles or an area almost as
large as New England), were also made chiefly
to the states bordering the Mississippi River.

However, a few other states—Michigan, Kansas, Alabama, and Florida—each received between 2,000,000 and 5,000,000 acres. Minnesota received most, 8,000,000 acres.

The grants to the railroad corporations,
totaling 94,000,000 acres (an area almost as
large as the East North Central states), were
made in the Rocky Mountain and Pacific
states and in North Dakota, Nebraska, and
Kansas. Two-fifths went to the Northern Pacific Railway, one-fourth to the Union Pacific,
about one-seventh to the Southern Pacific,
and nearly as much to the Santa Fe. Because
of the large grants to the Northern Pacific
Railway, the states through which this line
chiefly extends—Montana, North Dakota,
and Washington—contained the largest
acreages of railroad grants, from 6,000,000 to
9,000,000 acres each. Nebraska, Kansas, and
California each had about 5,000,000 acres.

Partly because of the nature of the type of
area involved, but also illustrating perhaps a
twentieth-century point of view, total land
grants to Alaska involve more than 104,-
700,000 acres, of which some 102,550,000 acres
were provided under the Statehood Act of
1958 for general state purposes.

Remaining Public Land. TYPES AND DISTRI-
BUTION. The public domain of the late 1960's
consists of three main types: (1) Land reserved
for specific purposes and presumably to be
held permanently for such uses. Chief among
these is the national forests; smaller areas
comprise the national parks, national monuments, and wildlife and recreation areas. (2)
The Indian reservations. (3) The lands which
were withdrawn (1934–1936) pending classification and further consideration of what
should be done with them. This type (nearly
all of it arid or semiarid) includes land
usually classed as "unappropriated public
land." All three of these principal types of
public land are located chiefly in the Rocky
Mountain and Pacific states, and in Alaska
(Fig. 5).

The states with the greatest percentage of

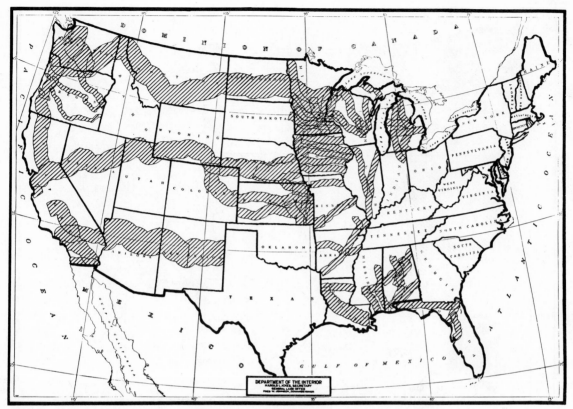

Fig. 4 Land grant limits. The shading shows the approximate limits of the areas in which the railroads received their land grants. (Bureau of Land Management, Department of the Interior.)

their land in federal ownership in 1968 are Alaska, 97.9; Nevada, 86.7; Utah, 66.8; Idaho, 64.3; and Oregon, 52.2. As with most public domain lands, the predominant use is for forests, wildlife, and grazing (Fig. 6). Because of the multiple-use management on federally owned lands, there is marked overlapping as to usage. For example, grazing extends considerably beyond the 52 "grazing districts," encompassing more than 156,000,000 acres, onto many suitable pasture areas in the national forests.

Indian lands, although largely in private holdings of individual Indians or Indian tribes, are subject to special restrictive provisions of the federal law administered by the Bureau of Indian Affairs. These lands have been set aside for Indian use by treaties, Congressional acts, and executive orders. Of the Indian lands, the largest areas in 1968 (in millions of acres) were in Arizona, 19.7; New Mexico, 7.1; Montana, 5.3; South Dakota, 5.0; Alaska, 4.2; Washington, 2.5; Utah, 2.3; Wyoming, 1.9; Oklahoma, 1.5; Nevada, 1.2; North Dakota, 0.9; Idaho, 0.8; Colorado, 0.8; Minnesota, 0.8; Oregon, 0.7; and California, 0.5.

A fourth type of public land consists chiefly of submarginal tracts formerly privately owned which have been purchased by the federal government to "withdraw them from agriculture," and for reforestation, range control, soil conservation, watershed protection,

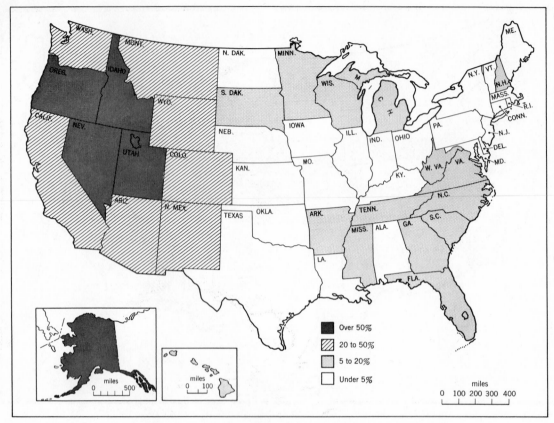

Fig. 5 Percent of the total area of each state in federal ownership. (*Statistical Abstract of the United States, 1968.*)

and wild animal refuges. Many areas of excellent land were acquired for military purposes in 1941–1945; vast expanses of former public domain were closed to entry during the same period and used for proving grounds, bombing ranges, and other military purposes.

Many tracts which had been patented became tax delinquent. These areas have become the properties of the local political subdivisions (the counties and states). Part of this land has been re-ceded to the federal government. Small increases in the public domain are the result of gifts of land, mostly to be incorporated into national parks, recreation areas, and wildlife refuges.

Types of Land Involved. The public do-

main has included almost all the various types of land in the United States. Choice agricultural land was well represented; forest land included most of the fine forests of the Middle West as well as the superb Pacific forests; mineral lands included most of the metals of the Far West, iron and copper of the Lake Superior region, and also the coal and oil fields of the Interior, the West, and Alaska. Grazing lands have been widely represented ever since the acquisition of the Louisiana Purchase, which included much of the Great Plains. The better agricultural, forest, and mineral lands passed out of federal ownership first. Since about 1900 most of the fairly accessible public domain has been grazing land, less val-

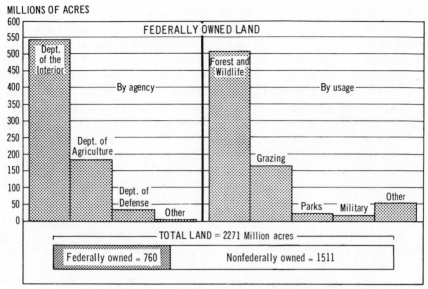

MILLIONS OF ACRES

Fig. 6 Land in federal ownership, distributed according to agency and to usage. (*Statistical Abstract of the United States, 1968.*)

uable forest land (including cut-over and burned-over areas), and wasteland.

CHANGES IN THE POPULAR ATTITUDE TOWARD PUBLIC LANDS

At a time when the seriousness of the problems facing the American people is being widely, though vaguely, realized, it is desirable to consider what should be the program concerning the remaining public domain. A preliminary step may properly be a survey of the chief historic changes in opinion as to various types of land.

The popular attitude toward the public domain has varied as a result of five chief influences: (1) the growth of population; (2) the spread of the people made possible partly by improvements in transportation; (3) the conspicuous consequences of the exploitation of the land, especially deforestation, depletion of minerals and game animals, and, more recently, the striking effects of soil erosion; and

(4) the growing realization that natural resources are limited in amount and many are being used up rapidly. (5) A fifth influence is the growing sense of responsibility concerning the welfare of the people of the future.

Programs concerning the American public domain have varied widely with changes in the popular interest in agriculture, forests, minerals, and outdoor recreation, and with concern for the distant future. Wild land was long considered to have little value. For example, Franklin was criticized by many prominent citizens for extending the national boundary as far west as the Mississippi River when he negotiated the treaty at the close of the Revolutionary War. Similarly, Jefferson's purchase of the Louisiana Territory was widely condemned, and Seward's purchase of Alaska was often called "sheer folly."

Similarly, trees were for a long time inadequately appreciated. The man who cleared the most land was the popular hero, and he who did not completely clear his land was called lazy. The statement, made by those less blind than their fellows, that there would soon be a timber shortage was widely ridiculed. Benjamin Harrison was the first president who felt strongly enough about the necessity of forest conservation to carve forest reserves out of the public domain (1892). Not until Theodore Roosevelt's terms (1901–1909), however, were large tracts reserved. He withdrew nearly 150,000,000 acres, in contrast to a total of about 45,000,000 acres withdrawn by all his predecessors. He included in national forests substantially all the forest lands then remaining in public ownership. Franklin D. Roosevelt (1933) was the first president to encourage effectively extensive reforestation by means of the Civilian Conservation Corps.

Minerals, too, except gold and silver, salt, perhaps lead, and possibly iron, meant little to most Americans until after 1850. Thus mineral reservations, except those made by Theodore Roosevelt, were rare. However, substantial income has been obtained from minerals on or under the public lands since the passage of the Mineral Leasing Act of 1920. In the recent period, offshore oil and gas production has provided large funds, as may prove to be the case with oil and gas on the north slope in Alaska and the oil shale resources of the mountain area.

Agriculture was the predominant source of livelihood of Americans until the 1920's. As late as 1880 two-thirds of the people lived on farms. Consequently, the public land was generally evaluated in terms of its agricultural utility. The population spread westward year by year, creating tens of thousands of new farms and pushing back the frontier. Nevertheless several great westward surges were prominent. The first of these followed the Revolutionary War, when the better lands of Kentucky and Tennessee were occupied. From 1810 to 1850, during the steamboat and canal period, the large families of the first frontier generations, supplemented by many migrants from the area from Pennsylvania to the Caro-

linas, crossed the Ohio and Mississippi rivers in large numbers. A third great surge into the public domain involved many people from New England and New York. It followed the completion of the Erie Canal (1825), the establishment of Great Lakes navigation, and the early railroad extension, to 1861. This wave was the first to spread over the prairies. After the Civil War there was a fourth great westward movement, facilitated by the railroads and encouraged by the free homesteads offered by the homestead law (1862). From 1870 to 1886 hundreds of thousands of people, mostly descendants of pioneers or immigrants, moved into the prairie plains and eastern Great Plains. The dry years of the late 1880's and early 1890's checked the spread; indeed, many Great Plains counties were almost depopulated. But starting about 1900, a series of wetter years, the enactment of legal provisions for enlarged homesteads, and the development of various inventions helpful to farmers led to another great increase in the interest in new farms.

Ten million acres of homesteads were patented in 1910—an area twice as large as New Jersey. Dry years, beginning in 1910, checked the spread, but the high prices for agricultural products associated with World War I again greatly increased popular interest in agriculture. However, since the land capable of adequately supporting a family on a half-section was "gone," the homestead unit was increased to 640 acres in 1916 for "stockraising" land. Almost a frenzy of filing on land followed, partly because military service reduced the residence requirements for homesteading. The collapse of farm prices after the close of the war chilled the popular enthusiasm for farming, and the droughts and low prices for farm products during 1930–1936 put an end to the frenzied interest in homesteading. Moreover, in November 1934 and February 1935, all the remaining unreserved and unappropriated land was withdrawn by executive order.

CHANGES IN THE OFFICIAL ATTITUDE TOWARD PUBLIC LANDS

The popular attitude toward the public domain, just sketched, influenced profoundly the official attitude. Nevertheless the opinions of governmental officials had sufficient independent influence so that a sketch of changes is desirable.

George Washington bought and sold unoccupied lands in New York, Virginia, Pennsylvania, and Kentucky to good effect. Many later government officials similarly considered that the unoccupied lands provided opportunities for personal gain. Alexander Hamilton and numerous other financiers of the early years thought of the public lands as potential sources of federal revenue. Many state officials were also interested in having their states receive grants of lands for both the foregoing reasons. Most of the vast tracts granted to states were sold promptly, often to members of the legislature or their friends, many of whom resold at large profits. The funds obtained by the states were used partly to reduce the immediate tax burdens.

Allied to the concept that the sale of public land should help support the government was the realization that such lands could help supply desirable improvements. The first important utilization of public land for this purpose was in 1803, when Ohio was admitted as a state. One full section of each township was set aside toward support of public schools. Other tracts were given, during the early decades of the nineteenth century, to aid in canal and road construction. Before long, increases in the grants for schools were made, and there were also grants for colleges. When many railroads were projected into sparsely settled or vacant regions (1865–1885), vast areas were granted to assist in their construction.

A similar use of public lands was the grant-

ing of scrip for 65,000,000 acres as partial compensation for military services. This scrip, which in many instances was sold, may be compared with the bonus payments after World War I.

The sales of public land, however, yielded only relatively small sums—only $60,000,000 during the first half-century of the nation's history and approximately $160,000,000 during the second half-century, and a total to June 30, 1967, of about $450,000,000—a striking contrast to the $2,074,000,000 collected as taxes on tobacco for 1966. Yet the total yield from sales of public lands is nearly six times as much as was paid for the land purchased from France, Spain, Mexico, Texas, and Russia. Indeed, a competent authority has concluded that most of the land sold by the federal government yielded only a small fraction of what it was then worth (that is, readily salable for). Almost none of it, even the choicest timberlands, brought more than $2.50 an acre. Sales or lease of the resources on or under the public lands have been more rewarding. Sales of timber through June 30, 1967, yielded more than $533,000,000; mineral leases, $1,612,000,000; and Outer Continental Shelf leases, $1,776,000,000. Fees, commissions, and miscellaneous bring the grand total for the period of 1785 through mid-1967 to about $4,816,000,000.

Similarly, the grants in aid of internal improvements, although locally and immediately helpful, nevertheless yielded disappointing results in many ways. For example, the 350,000 acres granted to Wisconsin in aid of the state university actually yielded less than $600,000, a pittance as compared with the more than $81,000,000 appropriated by the State Legislature for the University in 1967–1968.

The strong individualism encouraged by frontier life and the conspicuous emphasis placed on real estate, partly as a result of the fact that for generations it was readily possible for any ambitious person to own land, also strengthened the conviction that private ownership was better than public ownership. The fact that public land yielded no local taxes and supported almost no population increased the strong local desire to have all public land pass into private ownership as soon as it was feasible to do so.

The desire for the alienation of public land grew until it became a firm conviction of most of the influential people in America. Numerous steps were taken to facilitate the disposal of public land, and little was done to retard its disposal. An example of this attitude is the fact that when land was sold it was almost always disposed of at the minimum price set by law, regardless of its true value. Similarly, for homesteading, the requirements were the minimum legal conditions in respect to residence and improvements; little concern was shown as to whether or not the man receiving the title was a bona fide settler or merely the dummy of some grasping corporation or individual.

The demand for decentralization of government and for state control tended to bring about extensive gifts of public land to the states for no specified purpose. The feeling was that the states could dispose of certain public lands to better advantage than the more remote federal government. The gift of 65,000,000 acres of "swampland" to the states in 1850 was an example of this policy.

The several homestead laws with their increasingly generous provisions reflect this popular desire to dispose of the public domain. When the famous homestead law sponsored by Lincoln was passed in 1862, the unit was 160 acres; nevertheless settlers were soon permitted to obtain also a "pre-emption" of another 160 acres. From 1873 to 1891 in states then being rapidly settled, a "tree claim" was also possible, giving a possible total of 480 acres. The repeal, because of graft, of the pre-emption and tree claim acts in 1891 was offset in a way by increases in the homestead unit itself. This was increased to 320 acres for "desert" land in 1877 and for "dry farming" land

in 1910; it was increased still further to 640 acres for all land classified as "stock-raising homesteads" in 1916. An earlier act in 1904 provided for 640-acre homesteads in the "sand-hill country" of Nebraska.

The successive liberalizing of the homestead laws was in accord with the prevailing idea that the public domain ought to be given to bona fide settlers who would make a permanent home on the homestead. That larger acreage of poorer land than of good land is required in order to yield a livelihood should have been obvious, but it was largely ignored until it was seen that few of the homesteads of the poorer agricultural land continued to be the homes of people. It is difficult to overcome the handicap of poor land.

In the 1820's Congress first considered proposals to cede all public lands to the states in which they lay; somewhat similar proposals were before almost every Congress thereafter. Cession proposals reached their peak with the recommendations of the Garfield Report in 1931. Fortunately, however, there were enough congressmen whose states would have received no such gifts of land to prevent this. However, at almost every session of Congress, efforts are made to have some land now reserved made available for exploitation by lumbermen, cattlemen, miners, or others who are seeking additional personal wealth.

After nearly a century during which prompt disposal was the aim, some public land was finally set aside for permanent federal ownership. The establishment of Yellowstone National Park in 1872 was a momentous event in the history of the public domain and an example to other forward-looking countries. Since then 263 national parks and monuments have been created; and since the establishment of the first federal wildlife refuge in 1903, the world's largest system of wildlife reserves has evolved, with a total of 323 in 1968. Most of these were created from the remaining public domain. Notable was the establishment during the 1960's of several fine

United States Census Bureau, *Statistical Atlas,* 1903, 1914, 1924, and *Statistical Abstract,* Annual, Government Printing Office, Washington, D.C.

United States Department of the Interior, *Community Recreation and the Public Domain,* Washington, D.C., May 1963.

————, *Room to Roam, A Recreation Guide to Public Lands,* 1968.

Velie, Lester, "The Great Western Land Grab," *Reader's Digest,* Vol. 51, 1947, pp. 109–113.

Wooten, H. H., *The Land Utilization Program, 1934 to 1964: Origin, Development, and Present Status,* Agricultural Economic Report, No. 85, U.S. Department of Agriculture, E.R.S., Washington, D.C., 1965.

HAROLD H. McCARTY
The University of Iowa

CHAPTER 3

Economics and Conservation

The student of conservation soon learns that the subject or concept has been of interest to a great variety of people. He finds it appearing very often in the literature of geography, political science, sociology, and economics, as well as in the writings of the various physical sciences dealing with the earth and its resources. One of the first of these disciplines to become concerned with the problems of conservation was the science of economics. Over a period of almost two centuries writers in the field of economics and political economy have been concerned with problems involving the depletion, the disappearance, or the wise use of man's resources.

Emphasis on the economic aspects of the conservation problem has been especially strong in the United States and in the other countries of the world that have been devoted traditionally to free-enterprise types of economic systems. In these countries the tendency to view the conservation problem as essentially one of managing resources in order to produce a maximum of satisfaction of human wants has frequently been very strong. Not only have the average citizen and public official commonly expressed the problem in economic terms, but they have also tended to advocate the use of economic measures to bring about those reforms they consider most important.

Wants and Resources. Traditionally, the student of economics has taken as one of his special problems the apparently endless conflict between unlimited human wants and the limited means of satisfying them. To him, indeed, the economic drama has seemed to revolve around this conflict. On the one hand, he has looked at human nature and discovered that man's effort to satisfy his wants never ends—as soon as man satisfies one batch of wants, he immediately conjures up a whole set of new ones. Under these circumstances it soon became obvious that the means of satisfying those wants can never be adequate. A man's effort must always be directed toward acquiring more and more resources that can be converted into means of want satisfaction. Thus the economist reasoned that any organized society must give primary consideration to the manner in which the use of its resources shall be allocated among its people.

Human wants have been difficult to incorporate into a scientific decision-making framework, not only because human evaluations change from time to time, but also because many of them tend to defy quantitative expression. The economist has always defined wants in rather common sense ways, to include all kinds of expressions of desire. Complications appear, however, just as soon as one begins to rank those wants, whether they are individual wants, group wants, wants of the present, or of the future. Much of the literature of economics is devoted to problems encountered in measuring the intensity of individual wants and trying to discover the extent to which the wants of individuals agree with or differ from those of other individuals in the groups to which they belong. Since economics has long been committed to devising solutions that will provide the "greatest good to the greatest number" by showing how a maximum of wants can be satisfied with a given quantity of resources, the difficulty of measuring wants has always made computations difficult. In addition, the fact that wants change from time to time has made it particularly difficult to apply economic reasoning to problems of conservation in which a projection of wants into the future is essential to a solution that would maximize human welfare. The evolution of economic thought in these matters provides us with an excellent background for considering modern trends of thinking among economists who are concerned with conservation problems.

Early Economic Thought; The Scarcity Principle. Pioneer economists, such as Thomas Malthus and David Ricardo, tended to view the wants-resources problem essentially as a conflict between a continuous expansion of basic human wants, as evidenced by a rapidly growing world population, and a strictly static supply of natural resources that could be used in satisfying them.[1] Specifically,

1 An excellent review of the development of economic thought in these matters appears in Harold J. Barnett and Chandler Morse, *Scarcity and Growth*, Baltimore, 1963, Chapters 2 and 3.

their concern was centered on the simple problem of obtaining enough food, clothing, and shelter to satisfy those expanding human needs. As a result, their major emphasis was on the available supply of land, and their thinking was in terms of its capacity to produce food, fibers, fuel, forest products, minerals, and related goods required by man to satisfy his basic needs.

To attack these problems, early economists found it necessary to simplify their analyses by introducing certain basic assumptions as to the nature of the phenomena. One of these assumptions—that basic human needs will continue to expand as population increases—has already been specified. Their other assumption—that the fund of resources that may be used to satisfy those needs is specifically limited—merits further examination.

In particular, the limited resources concept is based on the assumption that man's ultimate source of livelihood is the physical earth. The earth can provide only a limited quantity of the items, such as minerals, rainfall, and the components of soil fertility, that can be used to provide sources of livelihood. When those stocks are exhausted, as in nonrenewable resources such as minerals, man is simply going to be deprived of goods and services whose production depends on their use. Or, in renewable resources, such as the sunshine and rain employed in agriculture, deprivation will begin whenever annual increments are exceeded by human demands. Little wonder that speculations based on these assumptions led people of that day to refer to economics as the "dismal science."

The mechanisms by which these scarcities were to be brought about are worthy of comment. Thomas Malthus, who was among the first to develop and popularize the scarcity concept, felt that man would go ahead willy-nilly utilizing available land until one day, perhaps rather suddenly, he would come to the end of that conquest and would be faced with the necessity of reducing per capita food and clothing inputs for his growing numbers. And, since Malthus saw no way of halting the then-existing "population explosion," the ultimate consequences to the human population certainly appeared to be disastrous.

The Malthus thesis achieved widespread acceptance among both economists and laymen, although it was modified considerably by later writers. David Ricardo, in particular, who appeared to have somewhat greater confidence in man's perspicacity, felt that the day of ultimate diminishing returns would be foreseen and that there would be a gradual, rather than a sudden, downward adjustment of levels of living that would be spread over a considerable period of time. John Stuart Mill modified further the hypothesis by introducing the notion that man might substitute one source of satisfaction for another and thus alter considerably the process of adjustment to the foreseen condition of scarcity.

In all these speculations of the classical economists, however, there was no provision for the admission of changes in technology or in the general institutional organization of society into the hypothesis. In other words, their world was essentially a world of unchanging patterns of demand and unchanging human abilities to utilize resources more effectively to satisfy those demands. Under those circumstances, a state of diminishing returns, in which man would continue to receive less and less in return for his efforts to satisfy his wants, was inevitable.

Early American Experience. The village economies of Colonial New England had a relatively simple way of handling the wants-resources problem. Members of these communities earned money and spent it bidding against each other for the limited supplies of available goods and services. In such a free-enterprise economy the allocation of resources to individuals was accomplished through the pricing system. Thus it could be assumed that those who had more intense desires for particular resources would gain possession of them

simply because they were willing to part with more purchasing power in order to get them. Money was rather evenly distributed among members of these Colonial communities, so that one member had about as much ability to command resources as another, and each one had an opportunity to obtain the goods and services he wanted most.

Despite these early circumstances, however, the pioneer economies did not always produce socially desirable ends. Resource allocation became especially unwieldy in the later years of this period, when some people obtained possession of more purchasing power than others and were willing to use it to gain possession of larger quantities of resources. Often these persons used those resources in ways that were felt to be detrimental to the welfare of the group. And so it came about, in the very early considerations of economic welfare, that restrictions were placed on many of the practices by which resources were utilized (Fig. 1).

Early attitudes concerning the wise use of resources are vividly portrayed in the notions commonly held by the Puritans and many of the later pioneers about "saving for a rainy day." The pioneer family, faced with the rigors of life on the frontier, quickly learned to avoid waste because daily living was so difficult. Saving was a virtue that was nurtured assiduously. Members of the family who did not use resources wisely were chastised, and these virtues became deeply ingrained into the mores of the American people. It is easy to see how such notions were transplanted into the national culture.

Who was to decide just what kinds of acts would endanger the "welfare" of the group? In the small communities of Colonial New England these questions were easily answered. The groups themselves were small, needs were easily apparent to all members, and consensus concerning the group welfare was quickly obtained. By the same token, the organized group, in town meetings or in other ways,

Fig. 1 Three combines harvesting and threshing the grain in a single operation. In the western Great Plains where extensive grain farming is characteristic of the agricultural economy mechanization has reduced the labor force substantially. Restrictions on wheat production are a feature of current agricultural practices. (John Deere and Company.)

could very easily impose penalties or take other steps to insure conformance by individual members. The idea of husbanding resources for the long, cold winter that was sure to come was readily incorporated into the cultural heritage of the American people.

Social Evolution. We can see in these early attitudes some of the ingredients from which the later conservation movement was made. The movement appeared slowly because there was little realization until near the end of the nineteenth century that unwise use might endanger the future social welfare. Growth and territorial expansion had occupied the energies of the American people, and the rapidly expanding frontier society rarely gave much thought to the future of its resources. These conditions persisted for several generations,

but by the decade of the 1890's it had become apparent to many that the conditions of life had changed enormously. The American people still believed in thrift and hard work, and they also retained their faith in a price-directed economy. But they began to see that preservation of the public welfare was going to require both a more precise definition of the conservation problem and a program of positive measures. It had become evident that wants were both individual and social.

Individual and Social Wants. Economics, which had long recognized the dual nature of these wants, found it easy to incorporate the more social of the human wants into its analyses of the wants-resources problem. Soon it became common for economists to include in their computations items such as the need for protection from one's enemies and the desire that one's children and grandchildren have enough food and clothing. Wants, said the economist, are not just the day-to-day items that arise out of ordinary biological needs; they also include education, recreation, health, and a wide variety of other items that are readily identified with social welfare.

The end of the nineteenth century also brought a considerable increase in the number of questions concerning whether the process by which an individual tries to satisfy his own wants necessarily produces a maximum of satisfaction for all the people. There was an increasing tendency to doubt the wisdom of permitting the man with the most money to acquire the most resources. Great attention came to be devoted to questions of how to regulate the acquiring of resources in ways that would promote the general public welfare. In this situation, the economist became a particularly valuable adviser because he was able to bring all the considerations together and evaluate them in terms of their monetary cost. Thus it occurred that the economic aspects of conservation were brought before the American people at a relatively early date.

Benefits and Costs. We have seen that much of the content of economic analysis consists of a comparison of inputs and outputs. We have traced some of the early developments that underlie the complex pattern of wants which the economist can consider as defining a certain set of goals. We shall soon find it desirable to examine those want patterns in greater detail, but in the meantime let us pause long enough to remind ourselves that the identification of goals is only part of the economist's task—he is equally concerned with the costs of attaining those goals. In conservation, as in other social affairs, the economist does not tell us what we should want, but he is presumed to be able to tell us how much it will cost, so that we may choose wisely between different means of want satisfaction. He must, however, know what we

want before he can tell us how much it will cost and what benefits may be expected (Fig. 2).

Changing Wants. The twentieth century has witnessed many changes in human wants. By 1900, the danger of starvation was no longer a serious threat to the American people. Mechanization had brought tremendous increases in farm productivity, and improvements in transportation had made foods and related products accessible to all sections of the country. It began to appear that the greatest dangers to the public welfare would arise from the shortages of metals and of fuels to operate machines rather than of food to nourish the population. These changes in needs were reflected by the placing of metals and fuels higher on the priority list of needed resources. Thus we came to a further realization of the fact that resources cannot be evaluated solely in physical terms but must also be considered in the light of human wants.

Immediate and Future Goals. Perhaps the matter of defining and measuring human wants would not give us very much trouble if we were concerned only with immediate wants and not with those that are going to appear in the future. Resources, of course, must be defined as items that are wanted, and the intensity with which they are wanted will govern the value that we place on the resources. So it is somewhat disconcerting to realize that human wants change considerably from time to time. And since these wants do change, it is difficult indeed to forecast a schedule of wants so that an adequate program of resource provision may be constructed.

All of us know that the structure of human wants is the product of a great variety of forces. Some of these forces are strictly biological and are concerned with the maintenance of man as a human being. Some of the foods we eat and some of the clothes we wear fall in this category, although probably most of our demands for food and clothing arise out of the culture in which we live rather than the

Fig. 2 An aerial view of the docks at Beaumont, Texas, showing the facilities for loading sulfur, some of it molten, into cargo boats for coastwise commerce and into barges destined for movement along the Intracoastal Canal and up the Mississippi River. Transporting the sulfur in molten form eliminates the necessity of reheating the sulfur. A net economic benefit is derived from this method of transportation. (Texas Gulf Sulphur Company.)

biological needs associated with merely staying alive. The culture, on the other hand, changes constantly. We want many things because other people want them, and we do not want the same things that our fathers and grandfathers wanted, nor do we expect to want the same things 10 years from today that we want today. So the person who would develop a schedule of wants is faced with a prospect of a very difficult forecast of their characteristics in future years. There is, for example, the whole matter of modern advertising which does a great deal to stimulate various kinds of wants. Other uncertainties are introduced into any forecast by the changing age composition of a population and unforeseeable events, such as wars, droughts, and economic depressions.

Yet we would not want to conclude that the forecasting of wants is entirely a matter of guesswork. Certainly we feel that all of us are going to continue to eat. We are going to continue to demand transportation and a considerable amount of recreation, religion, education, and numerous other services. We also know that, regardless of considerable changes in the characteristics of individual items, such as food, clothing, shelter, machines, and other things, the materials from which they will be made have a great deal in common; so that when one gets down to the actual natural resources which lie at the base of the economic process he discovers a rather basic group of chemicals and physical materials that must be considered as essential to the satisfaction of human wants.

The Role of Scientific Progress. This is not to say, however, that we have any very good basis for establishing the relative importance of these basic elemental resources. Who is to say what the relative importance of the various metals, iron, copper, aluminum, and many others, will be 100 years from now; and who is to decide whether it will be best to conserve petroleum at the expense of coal, or vice versa? These are the changes which constantly beset the economist or any other analyst who tries to set down a list of things that are going to be needed in the distant future.

The student of wants and resources soon discovers that these considerations apply to even such fundamental needs as food and clothing and to such basic resources as soil and timber supplies. Advances in soil chemistry have brought many changes in the older economist's definition of land as the "inherent and indestructible properties of the soil." Much of our older conservation practice was based on the assumption that such properties of the soil persist. But students of soils point out that a rich soil is basically one that provides water and minerals in the right proportions to sustain plant growth and that neither water nor chemicals are indestructible in any sense of the term. In other words, we have come to think of soil increasingly as a "manufactured" product, a medium on which plants stand as they absorb sunshine and air, and from which their root systems take water and needed minerals. Man, in short, is capable of producing resources as well as destroying them; and many economists list technology as

a resource along with the natural elements that have commanded attention for so many decades (Fig. 3).

Role of Diminishing Returns. Modifications in economic thinking that have marked the twentieth-century period in the United States have given increasingly greater weight to socio-technical variables in the solution of the resources problem. In particular, economists have been troubled by the fact that diminishing returns have appeared only very rarely in the century and a quarter since Malthus first formulated the scarcity principle, and when they have appeared it has been only in very restricted sectors of the economy. Recent studies have shown that in the United States, for example, during the period since 1870, evidences of diminishing returns have appeared only in the forest products industries among all types of production based on natural resources; and even in the forest industries there is good evidence that a substitution of products based on other resources (especially minerals) is rapidly alleviating such conditions of scarcity as may have appeared. In other sectors of the American economy, the per capita availability of suitable goods to meet expanding demands has consistently increased rather than declined in the period of rapidly increasing population that has marked recent decades of American history. Limited evidence points to existence of these same long-run trends in other parts of the world.[2]

Since economists are always eager to modify their models to bring them closer to the conditions of reality, their concern over the assumptions that underlay their classical scarcity model has been mounting. Among these assumptions, the most vulnerable seems to have been the notion of technological constancy, the idea that man does not "discover" new resources, does not have the ability to devise new and more economical ways of satisfying his wants. As a consequence, special ef-

[2] *Ibid.*, Chapter 1.

Fig. 3 A view of grain land near Melfort, eastern Saskatchewan. Moldboard plows are not used in this area. Fields are worked with stubble on top, to cut down on wind erosion. Anhydrous ammonia is being placed directly in the stubble without prior working of the soil. (George Marvin Mfg. Co.)

forts have been made to revise the classical scarcity model in ways that would include technology as a variable rather than a constant factor in economic growth.

Historical Evidence. Recognition of the importance of technological change in social decision making is one of the major features that differentiate the more recent thinking of economists in conservation matters from those of earlier periods of American history. One is impressed with the fact, however, that public acceptance of the relevance of technological change to matters of conservation policy has often been slow to materialize. In spite of the convincing mass of evidence to the contrary, there remains in the economic thinking of many people a strong conviction that absolute general scarcity of resources is inevitable, that diminishing returns must certainly occur in

the light of the world's rapidly expanding population, and that within the foreseeable future the dire predictions of Malthus and the other early economists that population will outrun its means of subsistence will come to pass. It is clear that this sort of reasoning is not supported by the facts in a world in which hundreds of millions of people have continued to live better and better, rather than worse and worse, in recent decades and in which there is no sound basis for predicting a reversal of that trend. Students of world food problems were particularly pleased to learn in the late 1960's that, for the first time in recent history, India and adjacent areas of south Asia not only had produced enough wheat and rice for their own needs, but even foresaw an export surplus of those grains. The shift from deficits and near-famine conditions

Fig. 4 An aerial view of the Weyerhaeuser lumber mill at Snoqualmie Falls near Seattle. Note the use of a circular water area for the storage of the timber awaiting processing at the mill. The timber already cut is protected from rapid decay by this method of storage. (Northern Pacific Railway Company.)

ingly, and diminishing waste as much as possible.

PETROLEUM CONSERVATION. The changing nature of needs and resources and their puzzling economic consequences are exemplified in the petroleum industry. In the early days of this industry, need for petroleum products was extremely limited, being confined largely to uses for household illumination. Later, petroleum became an essential feature of a new era of transportation that revolutionized human existence. Modern nations would be ineffective in peace or war without gasoline and other liquid fuels. Thus the need has expanded enormously and every modern nation is constantly searching for better ways to ensure itself of a future supply of this commodity.

Petroleum has long been considered one of the fund resources—it is exhaustible and nonrenewable. But note what has happened to the fund! An early textbook in conservation quoted the prediction that "at present rates of consumption, petroleum reserves will be exhausted by the year 1925." What has happened? The estimate was authoritative, the best obtainable in 1910. But at no time do estimators have a way of reckoning with future technological changes that are destined to expand the fund of proven petroleum reserves. Progress has been so steady that we have almost stopped talking about the need for substituting coal and other fuels for petroleum in the interests of conservation. Military experts have virtually abandoned plans to store oil for use in future emergencies—and the only peacetime restrictions on the use of gasoline encountered by the American motorist are those imposed by the amount of money that is in his pocketbook when he arrives at the filling station.

Incentives to Invention and Exploration. The mechanisms employed by a price-directed economy to promote conservation in cases such as these are worthy of careful study. In the case of petroleum, for example, the expanding needs mentioned previously were reflected in increases in price. Higher prices attracted capital and labor to the petroleum industry and encouraged the development of a great variety of technological improvements that expanded the fund of petroleum reserves enormously. Oil men confidently predicted that they would continue to find more oil as long as the price 'was high enough to pay them for taking the risks involved in exploration and development. Their predictions came true, and in this fashion the price-directed economy created an ample supply of these resources, enough to care for the expanding needs of the people.

But suppose that the search for new sources of oil had not been successful. How would the economy have reacted? We know that, before this new era of discovery, good progress had already been made in the development of substitutes, so that as soon as the price of petroleum rises to a certain level, a rapid development of industries devoted to the extraction of oil from oil shale, the transformation of coal into liquid fuel, and the application of atomic energy to tasks now performed by petroleum products will take place. The development of substitutes has served either to increase the availability or to diminish the need for nearly all the fund resources. In a price-directed economy these developments are presumed to appear automatically whenever scarcity and expanding demand combine to raise prices to levels at which the risk of developing new products appears to be worth taking.

Petroleum is a prime example of a resource for which the fund has been increased at a faster rate than the need has expanded. We are not at all sure that equivalent expansion can be attained in the funds of other minerals, such as tin, lead, copper, and iron. In all these cases, however, the drive to find new sources and to develop substitutes will become strong whenever prices rise high enough. Our experience promises success along these lines.

The Renewable Resources. We have already observed that the primary problem of conserving the flow resources involves measures designed to assure the maintenance of those resources. Some of the simplest examples of the economic aspects of resource utilization of these resources may be found in the studies of problems arising from the needs for supplying present-day societies with water.

WATER. We are familiar with the fact that needs for water have varied enormously, both geographically and historically. Inhabitants of arid lands have generally valued water very highly, whereas the peoples of humid lands have ordinarily considered it either a nuisance or, at best, a "free good," so abundant that it could be used in unlimited amounts by all the people. But in recent years the uses of water have expanded so much that modern nations must now consider how available supplies shall be allocated among a large number of competing users.

Water is a prime example of a renewable resource. There is, in fact, little that we could do to keep our supplies from being renewed through the processes of precipitation. Furthermore, these supplies are mostly free from contamination, so that the product as received has a uniformly high quality. But, except in agriculture, very little rain water is used directly by man, who depends almost exclusively for his supplies of this commodity on water that is stored on or near the earth's surface. Such storage areas are rather easily contaminated or destroyed, so that the natural product is easily rendered useless to the hordes of nonagricultural users who have developed important needs for it. Thus the flow of this resource continues, but its availability is diminished, and a condition of scarcity has arisen. Some means must therefore be found to determine how these scarce resources shall be allocated to the competing uses and what steps shall be taken to maintain supplies at optimum levels. Students of water problems have shown, for example, that irrigation of fields in dry areas uses enormous amounts of water. Many of them have suggested that it might be more economical to abandon farming in such areas and use fertilizers to build up the productivity of soils in humid areas, which could produce equivalent tonnages of foods and fibers without the addition of water, thus releasing large quantities of water for other uses. Economists find it relatively easy to evaluate such alternatives in quantitative terms.

Measurement and Implementation. The techniques of measurement that have become familiar to students of general economics have demonstrated their usefulness in attacking specific conservation problems. The first task is seen as one of producing a satisfactory estimate of the structure of human wants in the area over which the benefits of a particular project are presumed to be spread. To this end, hierarchies of wants are constructed out of results obtained in opinion polls, and in this type of work recent advancements in survey techniques and the analysis of findings

have given material aid to those who must weigh the desires of diverse individuals and groups in order to determine what the presumed beneficiaries *really* want. Once those wants are ordered and ranked, the analyst is ready to estimate the costs of various possible solutions. Complex problems, such as those that arise from designing a new dam to provide varying degrees of benefit for navigation, flood control, and recreation, can be formulated and, through the use of modern data-processing equipment, actual dollars-and-cents cost figures for alternative structures can be secured. In this manner, the economist can perform one of his most valuable functions: informing the decision makers how much it will cost to fulfill various combinations of their expressed desires. His activities thus promote rational decisions where these types of questions are involved. In this manner, summations of social needs may be related to lists of resources and the whole matter translated into public policy by governmental agencies. After these needs have been defined and means for satisfying them have been decreed, however, an important question must still be answered: "How shall these measures be enforced?"

Bonuses, Subsidies, and Benefit Payments. We have already intimated that many of the activities demanded in the public interest cannot be performed at a profit by the private owners of the various resources. We also know that the American people have shown great preference for an economic system in which resources are owned and managed by private individuals. Government ownership and management have been selected in a very few instances, notably in the attempt to care for recreational needs in the National Park system and in a variety of defense activities. Government supervision of leases to private individuals for exploitation has been utilized in connection with national forests and government range lands, but, for most of the translation of public demands into conservation practices, the American people have relied on devices that make the desired practices appear more profitable—and therefore more attractive—to the private owners of those resources. Among these private owners, the largest and most significant group has been in agriculture.

Soil Conservation. Farmers of America have been plagued by many problems, most of which are concerned with low prices for their products and high costs of production. But the farmers are also the owners of the soil— one of the resources that public policy insists must be conserved in the interests of future generations. Soil conservation has therefore become a major interest of federal, state, and local governments in the United States.

We have indicated that the soils problem is complicated by the fact that soils represent both fund and flow resources. The soils "fund" may be completely destroyed through erosion, or the "flow" may merely be reduced by depletion through poor soils management practices. Both aspects of the problem have been attacked by governmental agencies, and in both instances the procedure has been to stimulate conservation practices by making them appear more profitable than alternative practices to the individual farmer.

In implementing these programs, several kinds of subsidies have been provided. In their attempts to reduce erosion, governmental agencies have given extensive financial aid to farmers who would install dams and other preventive devices. They have also given financial encouragement to local agencies that would promote conservation and take steps to enforce locally approved conservation measures by legal means. In the attack on soil depletion, the whole program has been complicated by the generally accepted thesis that overproduction has kept prices low. There nevertheless has been a consistent effort to pay bonuses to farmers who devote part of their lands to those crops that will not induce erosion and that will also arrest depletion. The same result has been sought very often by price-fixing schemes in which the government undertakes to maintain prices at higher levels for soil-conserving crops than for those that have harmful effects on the soil. In all these schemes, however, the primary emphasis has been on making conservation practices appear profitable to the individual landholding farm operator.

OTHER INCENTIVES. Similar incentives are common in other aspects of the conservation program. In forested areas, for example, it is an accepted practice to keep yearly taxes at low levels and substitute a heavy severance tax when the trees are actually harvested. Many states follow this practice in taxing mineral lands. Government services in policing fisheries, forests, and other areas, to promote better conservation practices, are well known. The subsidy is a well-established aspect of the American conservation program.

OTHER INDUCEMENTS. The economist is always anxious to point to the fact that the payment of subsidies is not always the most successful or even the most economical way to bring about the adoption of conservation measures by the owners of private properties. He will point out, for example, that in many cases these owners could actually enhance their incomes by practicing conservation and are kept from doing so by sheer ignorance. Under these circumstances the payment of subsidies would be a social waste, and society certainly could get much more for its money if it were to spend it to educate those property holders.

There is also much evidence that wasteful exploitation often occurs because of lack of security on the operator's part. Farm tenants are often led to mismanage the soil so that they can make as much money as possible in a short time and then move to another farm. Renters of mineral claims often behave in the same way. It seems that means taken to lengthen the period of tenancy and to increase the security and level of living of the operators might be very effective in promoting the acceptance of conservation practices. These same effects could also be produced in many cases by reducing other costs of ownership, especially interest rates. All these alternatives must be considered by the economist as he prepares his estimations of how the desired goals may be achieved at minimum social cost.

SUMMARY

By way of summary, we see the interaction of economics and conservation operating at two different levels. On one of these levels, we find the economist defining conservation in terms of the identification of human needs and the allocation of resources to satisfy those needs. On the other level, the economist is concerned with finding the most economical ways of attaining social goals, which have been established to resolve the means-resources problems that were discovered in the earlier phases of his investigations. In these ways the science of economics serves first to help people define conservation problems in ways that will provide a basis for the formulation of intelligent public policies; and second, to determine the relative costs of alternative methods of carrying out those policies. In all instances the economist seeks to serve essentially as an adviser to those who must determine the content of public policy concerning conservation and all other matters involving conflicts between public and private interests.

References

Adelman, Irma and Cynthia Morris, "An Econometric Model of Socio-Economic and Political Change in Underdeveloped Countries," *American Economic Review,* Vol. 57, No. 5, 1968, pp. 1184–1219.

Barnett, Harold J. and Chandler Morse, *Scarcity and Growth,* The Johns Hopkins Press, Baltimore, 1963.

Barnett, Harold J., and Chandler Morse, *Scarcity and Growth: The Economics of Natural Resource Availability,* The Johns Hopkins Press, Baltimore, 1966 (Paperback).

Bunce, Arthur C., *The Economics of Soil Conservation,* Iowa State College Press, Ames, Iowa, 1942.

Burton, T. L. and Margaret Fulcher, "Measurement of Recreation Benefits—a Survey," *Journal of Economic Studies,* Vol. 3, No. 2, 1968, pp. 35–48.

Carlin, Alan, "The Grand Canyon Controversy: Lessons in Federal Cost-Benefit Practices," *Land Economics,* Vol. 44, No. 2, 1968, pp. 219–227.

Ciriacy-Wantrup, S. V., *Resource Conservation, Economics and Policies,* University of California Press, Berkeley and Los Angeles, 1963.

Clawson, Marion, "The Resource Economist of Tomorrow," *Journal of Soil and Water Conservation,* Vol. 23, No. 6, 1968, pp. 212–215.

Crocker, Thomas D., "Some Economics of Air Pollution Control," *Natural Resources Journal,* Vol. 8, No. 2, 1968, pp. 236–258.

Dowd, Douglas F., "Some Issues in Economic Development and Developmental Economics," *Journal of Economic Issues,* Vol. 1, No. 3, 1967, pp. 149–160.

Ely, Richard T., Ralph H. Hess, Charles K. Leith, and Thomas Nixon Carver, *The Foundations of National Prosperity,* The Macmillan Co., New York, 1918.

Heady, Earl O., *Economics of Agricultural Production and Resource Use,* Prentice-Hall, Englewood Cliffs, New Jersey, 1952.

————, *Principles of Conservation Economics,* Iowa Agricultural Experimental Station, Research Bull. 382, Ames, Iowa, 1951.

————, *Capacity and Trends in the Use of Land Resources,* Iowa State University, Ames, Iowa, 1968.

Jarrett, Henry, editor, *Perspectives on Conservation,* The Johns Hopkins Press, Baltimore, 1959.

Kneese, Allen V., "Economics and the Quality of the Environment—Some Empirical Experiences," a reprint from *Social Sciences and the Environment,* Resources for the Future, Washington, 1968.

Kneese, Allen V. and Orris C. Herfindahl, *Quality of the Environment,* The Johns Hopkins Press, Baltimore, 1965.

Krutilla, John V., "Conservation Reconsidered," *American Economic Review,* Vol. 57, No. 4, 1967, pp. 777–786.

Landsberg, Hans H., Leonard L. Fischman, and Joseph L. Fisher, *Resources in America's Future: Patterns of Requirements and Availabilities, 1960–2000,* The Johns Hopkins Press, Baltimore, 1963.

Lovejoy, W. F. and P. T. Homan, *Economic Aspects of Oil Conservation Legislation,* The Johns Hopkins Press, Baltimore, 1967.

Malthus, Thomas, *An Essay on Population* (various editions, 1798 to 1816), Ward, Lock and Company, London.

Mill, John Stuart, *Principles of Political Economy,* Longmans, Green, London, 1929.

Proceedings of the Inter-American Conference on Conservation of Renewable Resources, Denver, Colorado, September 7–20, 1948.

Raushenbush, Stephen, "Economic Considerations in Conservation and Development," UNSCCUR, Vol. 1: Plenary Meeting, New York, 1951, pp. 202–212; "Discussion," pp. 213–216.

Ricardo, David, *Principles of Political Economy and Taxation,* G. Bell and Sons, Ltd., London, 1922.

Scott, Anthony, *Natural Resources: The Economics of Conservation,* University of Toronto Press, Toronto, 1955.

Spengler, Joseph J., editor, *Natural Resources and Economic Growth,* Committee on Economic Growth of the Social Science Research Council, Resources for the Future, Washington, D.C., 1961.

Van Hise, Charles R. and Loomis Havemeyer, *The Conservation of Natural Resources in The United States,* Revised Edition, The Macmillan Co., New York, 1935.

Wolozin, Harold, *The Economics of Air Pollution,* W. W. Norton and Co., New York, 1966.

Woolman, Nathaniel, *The Water Resources of Chile,* The Johns Hopkins Press, Baltimore, 1968.

Zimmermann, Erich W., *Introduction to World Resources,* Henry L. Hunker, editor, Harper and Row, New York, 1964 (paperback).

————, *World Resources and Industries,* Revised Edition, Harper and Brothers, New York, 1951.

Part 2

Fig. 6 Windbreaks of willow to protect mint fields on muck land against wind erosion when the soil dries out. (USDA—Soil Conservation Service.)

rectly upon limestone or marl, with thickness varying from 12 to over 100 inches.

Large areas have been cleared, drained, and used for sugar cane, winter vegetable production, some citrus fruit, and improved pasture (Fig. 7). Part of the area is included in the Everglades National Park to assist in preserving its unique aquatic and bird life.

The Coastal Marshlands which form the Mississippi Delta include both mineral soils containing high amounts of organic matter, and dark brown to black mucks and peats containing from 30 percent to more than 85 percent organic matter.

These mucks and peats range from 2 feet to more than 12 feet in thickness. They occupy broad, level, and shallow concave areas. The area as a whole is used for recreation, hunting, fishing, and trapping. Easily accessible areas are used for grazing.

The Okefenokee Swamp is noted for its cypress. The land is used primarily for wildlife and recreation. A limited amount of timber is cut around the edges and on some islands within the swamp.

INCEPTISOLS [20]

Unlike the recently formed Entisols, these soils have made an appreciable start toward

[20] Latin *inceptum*, beginning. Young soils. Ando, Brown Forest, Brown Podzolic, Gray-Brown Podzolic, Sols Bruns Acides, Subarctic Brown Forest, and Tundra soils, with associated Regosols, Lithosols, Humic Gleys, and Low-Humic Gleys.

Fig. 7 A field of celery on Saprists (muck) in the Everglades south of Lake Okeechobee, Florida. The ditch is used for irrigation as well as drainage. The control of water levels is a major management problem. (USDA—Soil Conservation Service.)

acquiring some of the basic characteristics which distinguish soils from other earthlike formations that are popularly called soils.

Changes beyond relatively freshly formed or accumulated soil materials are evident, although the soils have not as yet acquired the more fully developed characteristics that are the product of long-acting soil-forming processes, such as breakdown of complex mineral constituents, or the formation of well-defined argillic, or other horizons. Horizons are only weakly differentiated. The soils are usually moist, although they may dry out during part of the warm season.

Characteristics which Inceptisols may exhibit include variations (1) in color (some ho-

rizons become darker colored, owing to accumulation of organic matter, or the horizon may show gleying), (2) in structure (if texture is fine enough to permit formation of granules and other aggregates), (3) in the presence or absence of compact horizons (fragipans) or indurated horizons (duripans), and others.

Five suborders reflect the influence of various soil-forming factors.

ANDEPTS [21] (IIS) VOLGANIC INCEPTISOLS. These "beginning" soils include or were weathered

[21] From Ando, a contraction of An-Katsu-Shoku-do, coined to designate certain dark-colored, volcanic ash soils of Japan. Includes Ando soils and some Reddish Brown, Brown Podzolic, Gray-Brown, and Tundra soils.

chiefly from volcanic materials. The silt, sand, and gravels composing the soils contain high percentages (60 percent and more) of fragments of volcanic origin: vitric or glasslike ash, pumice, cinders, and other pyroclastic materials.

The surface horizons are generally dark reddish-brown to near black in color, indicated in the name of the suborder. They are relatively high in organic matter. The soils are commonly acid and low in available phosphorus. They have a high water-holding capacity and are porous and permeable.

Forest Lands. The soils' characteristics seem to commend them for agricultural use, but this use is generally limited by acidity, fertility, topography, and climatic conditions. However, some less acid areas of these soils, or those properly managed, are quite productive.

Andepts mantle the fog-shrouded Aleutian Island chain of southwestern Alaska, a great submerged volcanic range, with a cool, rainy, severe climate (I1S). Steep, rocky slopes dominate, often descending to the water's edge. Only a small part of the land is level or near-level and covered with grasslands suitable for grazing.

The Cascade Mountains of western Oregon and Washington have long been famous for their volcanic peaks, heavy winter snows, and great stands of Douglas fir that have been heavily lumbered. Most of the land is still forested. Open areas are in pasture. Alpine meadows provide summer range (I1S).

Andepts mantle the rugged, forested Rockies of northern Idaho, northeastern Washington and northwestern Montana. Both the Cascades and northern Rockies have open areas of grasses and shrubs, however, which provide grazing for domestic livestock as well as good habitat for an abundance of wildlife.

The Hawaiian Islands, which still experience some active vulcanism from time to time, have the most agriculturally developed Andepts. These soils have thick dark-colored surface horizons. Their fame lies in their great

sugar cane (irrigated) and pineapple crops.

AQUEPTS [22] (I2) WET-LAND INCEPTISOLS. Aquepts occupy floodplains, basins, and other depressional or basinlike areas that are subject to seasonal saturation with water. Saturation may extend to depths of 3 feet or more. These Inceptisols are mineral soils, however, and should not be confused with the Histosols, which are primarily organic.

Some of the effects of poor drainage on soils, such as mottling, were noted in our discussion of Aqualfs. We may add that water-logging also promotes the accumulation of abnormal proportions of organic matter, as among the Histosols, since oxidation and activities of soil organisms of decomposition are retarded.

The Aquepts comprise one of our more highly productive suborders. The location of only two more extensive areas are shown on the map: (1) the Lower Mississippi Alluvial Plain, including several adjacent valleys and coastal lowlands, and (2) the Lake Huron Plains.

The Mississippi Plain. The Lower Mississippi Plain interjects a large body of highly productive land into a region of relatively "old" soils, the Ultisols (discussed later). These Aquepts are formed in comparatively fresh soil materials relatively recently carried into the Lower Mississippi Valley by floodwaters from far distant regions—the enormous upper basin of the Mississippi River system lying between the Rocky Mountains on the west and the Appalachians on the east. The soils are high in organic matter, in plant nutrients, and in weatherable minerals.

The upper part of the Valley is now generally drained, making high-yielding cotton, corn, and soybean lands (Fig. 8). A large part of the lower Valley, including neighboring smaller river valleys, is still undrained and in woodland. The Delta is in sugar cane.

The Lake Plains bordering the southern

[22] Alluvial soils and some Low-Humic Gleys.

Fig. 8 Skip row cotton (two rows planted and one row skipped) on better drained alluvial soils which occupy the natural levees parallel to the stream channel of the lower Mississippi. (USDA—Soil Conservation Service.)

end of Lake Huron are dark-colored clay loam soils with occasional overlays of sands. Although natural drainage is restricted because of flatness and moderately fine-textured soils, they are now generally drained artificially, using both tile and open ditches.

Nearly all of these soils are in crops. Principal uses are for dairying and production of cash crops, chiefly wheat, corn, sugar beets, pea (navy) beans, and potatoes (Fig. 9).

AQUEPTS (I2P) INCEPTISOLS WITH CONTINUOUS OR SPORADIC PERMAFROST. Except for land in relatively close proximity to the Pacific Ocean, the soils of Alaska are variously impregnated with permafrost as a result of their long, cold winters or previous glaciation.

Lands within one or two hundred miles of

the Pacific and Bering Sea experience frost only sporadically. The Arctic Plains have continuous permafrost; the Yukon-Tanana Valley is more or less variable, as will be explained on the following page.

The vegetation of the treeless Arctic Plains is a complex of various grasses and mosses, including both tall and short grasses. Plant growth is slow. Decomposition of organic matter produced by the "treeless" tundra cover is very slow. A thick mass of fibrous, peaty material bound together by woody stems and underground roots mantles the surface. In summer, the thick carpet remains saturated, preventing thaw of more than a few inches, leaving the under horizons permanently frozen within very shallow depths. The sur-

Fig. 12 The flat basin of former Lake Agassiz, which comprises one of the largest bodies of level land in the world. Slow surface drainage and early spring wetness are major limitations, but with adequate drainage the soils are highly productive. (USDA—Soil Conservation Service.)

their area constitutes our chief flaxseed lands and includes an appreciable acreage of rye and potatoes.

UDOLLS [29] (M3) HUMID MOLLISOLS. Udolls mantle our level interior uplands lying immediately west of the Humid Alfisols. They spread broadly westward from Indiana through Illinois, Iowa, and southern Minnesota into eastern Nebraska and southward through eastern Kansas into eastern Oklahoma.

This suborder has the most favorable agricultural climate—a humid continental type reflected in the name, Udoll. Precipitation averages 30 to 45 inches annually. Surface horizons are not quite as dark-colored as the Borolls, owing to the warmer climate which results in somewhat greater oxidation of organic matter. But soil temperatures average higher (very important to plant growth), and the soils enjoy long growing seasons with warm summer rains. There are occasional summer deficits, which do not, however, impose major limitations upon year-to-year productivity.

Although the Udolls comprise one of our most naturally fertile soils, they were scorned by many of the first comers migrating westward from the forested Alfisols to the east. Treeless lands were deemed poor for crops, even though rainfall was essentially the same

[29] Latin *udus,* humid. Brunizem or Prairie soils and associated intrazonal soils.

Fig. 13 The "Prairie Region" is really a combination of Udolls (regionally) and Udalfs (locally). The region is crossed in many places by streams which reduce the level surface to broad, rolling valleys. Hillsides and valley floors were occupied by oak, elm, hickory, and other trees, giving rise to the formation of Alfisols that finger through the region. (USDA—Soil Conservation Service.)

and the land was invitingly level. The early settlers preferred the local "islands" of forest uplands scattered through the prairies or the wooded valleys and river bottoms (Fig. 13).

When settlement finally got under way, however, the pioneers found themselves in a manifold paradise. They were spared the labor of clearing forest. They were able to plant crops into easily worked lands with very friable, naturally rich, and very durable agricultural soils.

The Udolls now embody the heart of the Corn Belt. Its fields of corn, oats, and soybeans, and hay and pasture lands sweep from horizon to horizon. Men can grow bumper crops and fatten many animals on this good land.

Now that the natural prairie grasses are gone, the soils are no longer enriched by their humus, or rejuvenated by the annual return of nutrients. Commercial fertilizers, manure, and soil-building crops, such as tame grasses and legumes, must now be their substitutes. A few decades ago, most people regarded the Udolls as inexhaustible, although no soils are so blessed. One of the striking revolutions in recent years has been the use and skilled application of mineral fertilizers, which have not only "restored" the soils, but have also increased their productivity to breath-taking heights.

USTOLLS [30] (M4) (M4S) SUBHUMID-SEMIARID MOLLISOLS. Westward beyond the 96th meridian, precipitation gradually decreases from ap-

[30] Latin *ustus*, burnt, indicative of dry or low-rain conditions. Includes Chernozems, Chestnut, and some Brown soils.

they consist principally of hydrated oxides of iron and aluminum, or both, kaolin (a white clay), and quartz sand.

The soils are low in plant nutrients, in weatherable minerals, and require heavy fertilization. They vary greatly in organic matter, from low to moderately high. They also range appreciably in soil moisture between suborders, from low to moderately high.

Oxisols are found on the Hawaiian Islands but are too small in individual area to note on our map.[50] They occur on Kaui, Oahu, Lanai, and Hawaii. Use is chiefly for pineapples, sugar cane, and pasture.

A BRIEF OVER VIEW

What may we now conclude, following this broad review of our soils?

Briefly re-examine the soil map legend with

[50] Their location is shown on a larger-scale map "Distribution of Principal Kinds of Soils: Orders, Suborders, and Great Groups," published in color by the U.S. Geological Survey, 1969.

its short description of each soil order, and note their varied character and utility.

Our review supports our introductory statements appraising our soil resources. We are richly endowed, more so than any other nation. We have a great diversity of soils of high inherent capability to serve our many interests. We have them in quantity. And they are generally coupled with favorable or useful climates and topography. The three go hand in hand.

With the technology in soil use and management that we have developed, we are able to produce both basic and luxury foods and organic raw materials in never-before-known quantities and qualities. This is especially evident when we examine the many subgroups which make up our broad soil orders.

We still have much to learn and practice in managing and protecting this basic component of our natural environment. Chapters which follow examine some of these problems.

Within which soil order and suborder do you live? What are the good things about them? What are their limitations?

References

Journal of Soil and Water Conservation, Soil Conservation Society of America, Des Moines. A bi-monthly periodical; includes excellent articles on soils and land use.

Kellogg, Charles E., "Why a New System of Soil Classification," *Soil Science,* Vol. 96, 1963, pp. 1–5.

Land Resource Regions and Major Land Resource Areas, Government Printing Office, Washington, D.C., 1965.

Selected Papers in Soil Formation and Classification, Special Publication Series 1, Soil Science Society, Madison, Wisconsin, 1967.

Smith, Guy D., Lectures on Soil Classification, *Pedologie,* Special Number 4, 1965.

——, "Objectives and Basic Assumptions of the New Soil Classification Scheme," *Soil Science,* Vol. 96, 1963, pp. 6–16.

Soil Classification, A Comprehensive System, 7th Approximation, Soil Survey Staff, Soil Conservation Service, Government Printing Office, Washington, D.C., 1960.

Soil Survey Reports, 1899—. United States Department of Agriculture. These reports, usually by counties, provide excellent detailed studies of local soils and their utilization.

Soils of the North Central Region of the United States, North Central Regional
    Publication 76, Agricultural Experiment Station, University of Wisconsin,
    Madison, 1960.

Soils of the Western United States, Western Land Grant Universities and Col-
    leges, with cooperation of Soil Conservation Service, Washington State Uni-
    versity, Pullman, 1964.

Supplement to Soil Classification System, 7th Approximation, Soil Survey Staff,
    Soil Conservation Service, Government Printing Office, Washington, D.C.,
    1967.

Travernier, René, "The 7th Approximation: Its Application to Western Europe,"
    Soil Science, Vol. 96, 1963, pp. 35–39.

WILLIAM A. ROCKIE

Soil Conservationist Emeritus
U.S. Department of Agriculture

CHAPTER 5

Soil Conservation

Soil erosion has been an enemy of every civilization since man began to use the land, more especially since he began to cultivate that land for the growing of crops. Now that agricultural use of land is being applied to an ever-increasing proportion of the earth's surface, combined with usually increased intensity of use, soil deterioration of many kinds is becoming ever more serious. Still further emphasis to the problem comes from the rapid increase in the world population, with its constantly growing need for more of everything.

Soil conservation is man's first concerted effort to protect the world's land resource. This science was born during the current century, although its conception stems from earlier happenings. Although its major objective is to minimize accelerated erosion of the soil, it has many other goals. This new applied science is already accepted by the scientific community all over the world, despite its recent recognition.

Man's failure to control soil erosion, which includes both the washing and the blowing away of soil, has caused the downfall of many of the nations of the past, and it is a real threat to the land resource in most countries.

Other common types of land damage resulting from the careless use of the land include the development of excessive salinity and alkalinity. Lowered soil fertility is an inevitable result of land use unless the user returns to the soil as much plant foods as his crops and erosion together have removed. Inadequate drainage, inadequate aeration, loss of soil structure, and other factors all contribute to the over-all problem of soil deterioration, with the accompanying decreased crop yields. Maximum yields from the land are imperative if the hunger of the billions of people on the earth today is to be satisfied. If we accept the current prediction that the world population may reach 6 billion by the year 2000, the urgency will have doubled.

HISTORY OF LAND USE

Whenever and wherever man and his activities use the land, he generally removes or destroys either part or all of the native plant cover by burning, cultivating, logging, or his animals eating it. As long as nature's plant cover is not changed, the land presents no special problem, for only the normal amount of geological erosion proceeds. This is not injurious to the land. Man creates the problem of accelerated erosion and the other types of land damage whenever he removes, destroys, or materially reduces nature's protective vegetation.

The farming methods and practices which have been developed and perfected by the farmers of the world during the several thousand years since the early beginnings of agriculture are almost innumerable. They have been created because of the infinite number of local variations in climate, soil, topography, drainage, and probably most of all, in people, and their habits and customs.

The principles of better land use require that the specific conditions which exist in any particular tract of land be managed by whatever practices and methods are best suited to that tract and to the crops being grown on it. Individual treatment of each field gives best results. Soil conditions vary just as much as do people, and no two people have ever been found to be exactly alike in every respect.

Man's agricultural use of the land has always been primarily to produce food, feed, fiber, and any other plants which he considers useful. Some crops involve cultural methods and practices which result in tremendously increased erosion or some other type of land damage. Other crops can be grown with no material damage to the land. Some crops even improve the land on which they are grown. The methods and practices by which each crop is grown can be improved or they can be made worse. Under certain conditions some crops are classed as soil-building, others as soil-conserving, and still others as soil-depleting. Changes in the methods and practices of growing a certain crop may be sufficiently different as to change it from one class to another. In such an instance, the methods and practices become more important to the land problem than the crop itself. A rotation system that combines the right crop with the best practices would be ideal.

AMERICA'S PIONEER SOIL CONSERVATIONISTS

Although ancient history provides many records which tell that soil erosion has long been recognized as one of man's enemies, we find relatively little evidence that the principles of soil conservation—or better land use generally—were either recognized or followed. Land deterioration has been all too universally accepted as the inevitable result of man's use of the land.

In America, Presidents George Washington and Thomas Jefferson both recommended practices and methods of farming which would minimize soil washing, making them our first leaders working for better land use. The first American book on the subject was by George P. Marsh in 1864, entitled *The Earth as Modified by Human Action*. The principles he included in his recommendations for better land use are as valid today as when he wrote the book. Although President Theodore Roosevelt did not single out the soil, his efforts and accomplishments in the conservation of all natural resources mark him as one of our most conservation-minded presidents.

SOIL CONSERVATION REVOLUTION

The first governmental recognition of the erosion problem in America occurred in 1903 when the United States Department of Agriculture began some field studies in "hillside erosion." In 1914, investigation of field terraces for the prevention of "hillside erosion" was begun. In 1915, the Department began studies in Utah, under the direction of Arthur Sampson, to determine the soil losses from forestland. The writer first studied the effectiveness of field terraces in Louisiana, Texas, and Georgia from 1915 to 1917. The Missouri Ag-

terials centers have achieved unbelievable accomplishments in this field.

In the early days of the Center at Pullman, Washington, Secretary of Agriculture Henry A. Wallace, agronomist and plant geneticist in his own right, came to the center for a 1-day study of its thousands of plant strains. He became so intrigued with what he found that he asked the writer to send telegrams to the San Francisco and Los Angeles chambers of commerce, where he had speaking engagements, that he was unable to keep those appointments. Instead, he spent those days crawling along on his knees inspecting the sensational developments underway in the fields at that Center.

Soil Survey. Detailed mapping of the soils of America is one phase of the work of the SCS which makes no direct contribution to erosion control. The resulting soil maps are in general use today, not only by the landowners whose lands they cover, but by all of the land-loaning agencies in the nation, including the Federal Land Bank, the entire banking industry, realtors, and everyone else who needs to know about the land (Fig. 21). They are the "land bible" of the community which they cover. The highway departments over the nation have found their contents indispensible in highway construction. They are probably used as widely as any other technical bulletins. They even inform the city dweller regarding the soil problems on his own city lot and can be the means of preventing flooded basements.

Soil and Water Conservation Needs Inventory. This nationwide study of the capabilities and the needs of all the nation's lands, insofar as erosion control is involved, is an SCS product, completed with the cooperation and approval of all the bureaus in the USDA. It was made so that a Soil and Water Diagnosis can be quickly computed for any land area in the entire country. The study was more than 20 years in the making, involving thousands of man-years.

Fig. 21 This Michigan homeowner has the soil scientist examining the soil profile of his septic tank drain field to be certain the drain field is adequate. (Soil Conservation Service.)

Snow Surveys. In the western part of America especially, much of the streamflow comes from melting snow in the high mountainous watersheds. To forecast accurately the amount of the streamflow during the summer irrigation season, the farmers of the many millions of irrigated acres in the country must know in advance of planting the year's crops the quantity of water they will have. Then they can gauge their planting to fit the water available. To supply these data to the irrigation farmers, snow samples are measured at key locations as to depth of snow and percentage of water content. They have proved extremely valuable to the millions of farmers involved in planning what crops and what acreages of each the farmer can plant with assurance that water will be available to bring the crop to successful maturity (Fig. 22).

Great Plains Conservation Program. The Great Plains has soil conservation problems peculiar to that particular part of the country

Fig. 22 The snow surveyor has become an integral part of the soil conservation picture, because he predicts scientifically the amount of water which will be available to the irrigation farmer during the succeeding crop season. (Soil Conservation Service.)

which require especially rigid controls. The area frequently has extremely dry years, commonly has high winds when the land has little or no plant cover, has inadequate protection from soil blowing, and therefore has inordinately great need for intensive land management practices. This special program was established to strengthen the regular soil conservation work by adding more practices in this area than are generally needed in other sections of the country. The additional practices are partially financed by the federal government. With this help, the risk of serious wind erosion damage is considered equalized with that of the remainder of the coun-try, thereby making it possible for the farmer in this region to protect more adequately his land from the type of excessive damage that it suffered during, and occasionally since, the drought of the 1930's. Measures which are eligible for cost sharing from federal funds include planting permanent cover, strip cropping, contour cultivation, improvement of range cover, planting windbreaks, establishing grassed waterways, building terrace systems, chiseling or pitting rangeland, building dams or ponds for irrigation, drilling wells for livestock, water pipelines, fencing, and controlling inroads of brush. Under present authority, this subsidized program terminates in

1971, but if it appears that its termination would be followed by a worsening of conditions, it is probable that its life would be extended.

Resource Conservation and Development Projects. Primary objectives of this activity of the SCS include (1) making America's beauty and recreational facilities available to all people by improving local recreation facilities for every community, and (2) to aid in the establishment of such facilities for those communities that are not blessed naturally with good recreational advantages. Secondary objectives may well include better wildlife habitat, watershed protection, flood retardation, improved markets for the products of the land, and even jobs for local people in the accomplishment of these multiple objectives.

Although most of the soil conservation work in America today is centered in the Soil Conservation Service, the Agricultural Stabilization and Conservation Service is currently expending government funds on SCS-approved conservation practices on privately owned farmlands, and other federal departments than Agriculture are doing soil conservation work on lands under the jurisdiction of the respective departments, notably Interior and Defense.

SOIL CONSERVATION IN FOREIGN LANDS

Scores of other nations are actively engaging in research or control, or both, of the different types of problems in soil conservation. One type of erosion may be the problem in one country, whereas another country is not bothered by that problem at all but by an entirely different one. Every country has its own special types of land problems, and a few have every type of land problem of which we know. Most of this work in soil conservation has been started as a direct result of the beginning of such work in the United States about 40 years ago. At least 40 foreign nations have sent their technical conservationists, or trainees for such positions, to this country to work with our field men for more complete training and for a better understanding of the worldwide problems of land damage.

Land deterioration has been almost universal under man's agricultural land use, not only in regard to erosion but to all types of damage which can occur to land. With the ever-increasing area of land being so used and also the generally increasing intensity of that use, the seriousness of the problem is steadily growing greater and more important to the future of our current civilization.

References

Bennett, Hugh Hammond, *Elements of Soil Conservation,* Second Edition, McGraw-Hill Book Co., New York, 1955.

Black, C. A., *Soil-Plant Relationships,* John Wiley & Sons, Inc., New York, 1957.

Bunting, Brian T., *The Geography of Soil,* Aldine Publishing Co., Chicago, 1966.

Cook, Ray L., *Soil Management for Conservation and Production,* John Wiley & Sons, Inc., New York, 1962.

Graham, Edward H., *Natural Principles of Land Use,* Oxford University Press, New York, 1944.

Held, R. Burnell and Marion Clawson, *Soil Conservation in Perspective,* Resources for the Future, Inc., The Johns Hopkins Press, Baltimore, 1965.

Jacks, G. V. and R. O. Whyte, *The Rape of the Earth,* Faber and Faber, Ltd.,

London, 1939. The American edition is entitled *Vanishing Lands: A World Survey of Soil Erosion,* Doubleday, Doran and Company, New York, 1939.

Journal of Soil and Water Conservation, Soil Conservation Society of America, Ankeny, Iowa. A bimonthly magazine.

Kellogg, Charles E., *The Soils that Support Us,* The Macmillan Co., New York, 1941.

Lutz, Harold J. and Robert F. Chandler, Jr., *Forest Soils,* John Wiley & Sons, Inc., New York, 11th Printing, May 1966.

Marsh, G. P., *The Earth as Modified by Human Action,* Charles Scribner's Sons, New York, 1907. First Edition, 1864.

Mickey, Karl B., *Man and the Soil,* International Harvester Company, Chicago, 1945.

Morgan, Robert J., *Governing Soil Conservation,* Resources for the Future, Inc., The Johns Hopkins Press, Baltimore, 1965.

Sears, Paul B., *Deserts on the March,* University of Oklahoma Press, Norman, Oklahoma, 1935. Second Edition, 1947.

Sharpe, C. F. Stewart, *What Is Soil Erosion?* Misc. Pub. 286, U.S. Department of Agriculture, Washington, D.C., 1938.

Shepard, Ward, *Food or Famine: the Challenge of Erosion,* The Macmillan Co., New York, 1945.

Soil Conservation, United States Soil Conservation Service, Washington, D.C. A monthly service magazine.

Stallings, J. H., *Soil Conservation,* Prentice-Hall, Englewood Cliffs, New Jersey, 1957.

———, *Soil; Use and Improvement,* Prentice-Hall, Englewood Cliffs, New Jersey, 1957.

Stern, Arthur C., editor, *Sources of Air Pollution and Their Control,* Vol. 3, Second Edition, Academic Press, New York, 1969.

United States Department of Agriculture, *Climate and Man, The 1941 Yearbook of Agriculture,* Washington, D.C.

———, *Crops in Peace and War, The 1950–51 Yearbook of Agriculture,* Washington, D.C.

———, *Grass, The 1948 Yearbook of Agriculture,* Washington, D.C.

———, *Land, The 1958 Yearbook of Agriculture,* Washington, D.C.

———, *Soils, The 1957 Yearbook of Agriculture,* Washington, D.C.

———, *Soils and Man, The 1938 Yearbook of Agriculture,* Washington, D.C.

———, *Water, The 1955 Yearbook of Agriculture,* Washington, D.C.

Vogt, William, *Road to Survival,* William Sloane Associates, New York, 1948.

ROBERT M. BASILE
University of Toledo

CHAPTER 6

Conservation of the Atmosphere

The atmosphere, a thin gaseous shell surrounding the rock and water portions of the earth, has a depth of about 6 miles at the poles; this increases to about 10 miles at the equator. In addition to the approximate 78 percent nitrogen and 21 percent oxygen, the atmosphere contains carbon dioxide, rare gases in small amounts, water vapor, and dust. Man has forced a change in this relationship by using the atmosphere as a disposal—a dump —for the many wastes of combustion. Although such contaminants as smoke, dust, odors, mists, and gases of various sorts may be from natural sources, man has poured increasing quantities into the atmosphere from the beginnings of the industrial revolution to the present by his burning of carbonaceous material for power and space heating.

The Los Angeles Basin had its pollution problem as long ago as 1542. A note in a diary indicates that even though the mountains surrounding the basin were visible, the valley was obscured by smoke from Indian fires. Cannel coal, used as a fuel in some early manufacturing processes, was the culprit in

smoke pollution of London atmosphere in the mid-seventeenth century.[1]

These pollution incidents are as numerous as there are towns and villages to report them. Established industries cannot be easily relocated. Were this possible the air pollution problem might be abated briefly, but certainly it would not be solved. As population centers have grown, so have the contributors to air pollution. The amounts of debris discarded into the atmosphere through smokestacks, exhaust pipes, and open fires have become so great that every citizen should be deeply concerned enough to accept certain responsibilities necessary to curb atmospheric pollution. The Public Health Service's National Center for Air Pollution Control in

---

[1] Reported by H. E. Landsberg in *Air Over Cities*, a symposium, Health, Education, and Welfare, Public Health Service, Taft Sanitary Engineering Center, Cincinnati, November 6–7, 1961 [from J. Evelyn (1661), *Fumifugium; The Inconvenience of the Air, and Smoke of London Dissipated*, Oxford; reprinted by National Smoke Abatement Society. Manchester, 1933, 18 pp.].

1967 noted these metropolitan areas within the United States where air pollution was most severe. Among the top contenders for this dubious honor were New York City, Chicago, Philadelphia, Los Angeles, Long Beach, Cleveland, Pittsburgh, and Boston.[2] However, the problem is far more widespread than these few metropolitan areas named would indicate.

It is estimated by the Public Health Service that more than 50 percent of Americans breathe polluted air constantly. All communities add to the total load of atmospheric pollutants, and because air is mobile, one city's problem of today may become a concern of serious proportions to another community tomorrow. Urban areas have spread so rapidly that industries once outside city boundaries now are well within city limits. Although industrial activities do contribute to the air pollution problem, the automobile is a far worse offender. In the United States industry contributes about 17 percent of the pollutants to the atmosphere, the automobile about 60 percent, power plants about 14 percent, and space heating and refuse burning about 9 percent.

Not only do atmospheric contaminants create a nuisance by restricting visibility, they also affect man's health through the air he breathes, as shown by the increase in respiratory diseases, such as emphysema. Plant and animal life and property are affected adversely as well, often to the extent that crops are destroyed, or at least their productivity is reduced. Sickness and even death have occurred in animals. Economic loss to property through discoloration and corrosion, and to business through absenteeism, is extensive. These constitute the air pollution problem, a problem that has been getting worse with each passing year. President Johnson, when he signed the Air Quality Act into law in 1967, said, "We are pouring 130 million tons of poi-

son into the air each year. That is two-thirds of a ton for every man, woman, and child in America."

We must act quickly, or the severe atmospheric pollution episodes which some communities have experienced will become universal. The deterioration of the air we breathe must be stopped (we have the necessary technology) and the process reversed, or the future will be one of an intolerably dirty and smelly existence for all. Not merely a local problem, pollution is interstate and national as well. In fact, it is of international concern since the atmosphere is no respecter of boundaries; pollutants have been and are being carried in the air across them for great distances and even around the world.

Air pollution may be endured today as it has been endured in the past; however, worsening as rapidly as it is, the problem must be attacked by an aroused citizenry in all areas, urban and rural. Although this action is beginning to gather momentum, the people must demand action at all government levels to abate air pollution if the rising rate is to be slowed and the trend reversed.

ATMOSPHERIC POLLUTANTS

Atmospheric pollutants fall into three major categories: gaseous, liquid, and particulate. These may be primary pollutants—those emitted directly to the atmosphere as products of combustion without change, or they may be secondary pollutants—those which through some reaction in the atmosphere catalyzed by sunlight form other substances or compounds. These are photochemical reactions important in the formation of the smog prevalent in the Los Angeles Basin.

Nature itself contributes some gases and particulate matter to the atmosphere. On one occasion in 1883 Krakatau, a small volcanic island in Indonesia, sent a cloud of dust high into the atmosphere following a series of violent explosions. The finest of the dust parti-

[2] *Newsweek,* August 14, 1967.

cles remained in the atmosphere for months and were carried around the world. Numerous volcanoes contribute sulfurous as well as other gasses to the atmosphere. Forest fires and dust storms contribute to atmospheric pollution, as does pollen from plants at certain times of the year.

Gaseous Pollutants. Whenever energy conversion takes place, whether it be in the wood-burning fireplace in the home or the most up-to-date factory complex, numerous gases are emitted to the atmosphere. Two of these gases, only rarely regarded as pollutants, are water vapor condensing from stack gases over a relatively limited area, and carbon dioxide, a product of complete combustion of organic fuels. From the latter part of the nineteenth century to about 1900 atmospheric carbon dioxide increased rather slowly; however, since 1900 it has been increasing at a relatively rapid rate (Fig. 1). It is increasing in

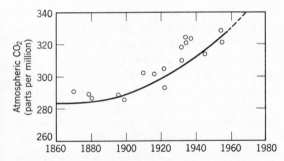

Fig. 1 The rising carbon dioxide content of the atmosphere, as shown here, is primarily a result of man's increased consumption of fossil fuels. ("Carbon Dioxide and Climate," *Scientific American,* Vol. 201, July 19, 1959.)

the atmosphere from industrial sources at about 4 percent per year and is expected to continue at about this rate through 1985.[3]

[3] F. A. Rohrman, B. J. Steigerwald, and J. H. Ludwig, "Industrial Emissions of Carbon Dioxide in the United States: A Projection," *Science,* May 19, 1967, p. 932.

Carbon dioxide affects the heat balance of the earth positively, so that global climate has been warming slightly. In the past 100 years atmospheric concentration of carbon dioxide has increased by about 13 percent, and the average temperature of the earth has been raised by 1 degree.[4]

Carbon monoxide, a product of incomplete combustion, is of greater concern as a pollutant. Although other sources of carbon monoxide exist, much of it originates in the atmosphere largely from incomplete combustion of fuels in the internal combustion engine, and it reaches its highest levels of concentration in the streets of our cities. In New York City's most congested areas the carbon monoxide concentrations up to about 5 feet above the pavement have exceeded the New York standard of 15 parts per million for 8 hours.[5] If combustion were complete the end products would be carbon dioxide and water, far less harmful emittants.

Oxides of sulfur, particularly sulfur dioxide, become part of the atmospheric pollutant load whenever coals and oils of high sulfur content are burned. Sulfur dioxide in the air and in the presence of moisture becomes sulfuric acid mist, and this is thought to be in part, if not largely, responsible for the deaths in the severe air pollution episodes in London, England, and in Donora, Pennsylvania. The obvious way of reducing these sulfur emissions to the atmosphere is to cease using high-sulfur coals and oils, a step that is being taken in many metropolitan areas.

Hydrogen sulfide, a gas having a highly objectionable odor, generally enters the atmosphere from bogs and slack water where compounds of sulfur are reduced by bacterial action, as well as from some industrial activities. Luckily, emissions of hydrogen sulfide are localized to relatively few areas. In one in-

[4] Gilbert N. Plass, "Carbon Dioxide and Climate," *Scientific American,* Vol. 201, July 1959, p. 46.

[5] J. M. Campbell, "A Breath of New York," *Science,* February 16, 1968, p. 693.

stance a pulp mill and its power-generating facilities were known to emit to the atmosphere every day "25,090 pounds of particulates, 1,663 pounds of hydrogen sulfide . . . from 44 pounds of sulfur dioxide in the summer up to 1,950, pounds in the winter, and more than 15 million pounds of water vapor."[6] Seldom is the gas found in objectionable quantities over wide areas, however.

The oxides of nitrogen are of considerable importance and interest because of their participation in photochemical reactions. Nitric oxide is formed by combustion at high temperatures, or when combustion occurs under high pressure, such as would be found in the internal combustion engine. It is the automobile that is responsible for the high concentrations of nitric oxide in the atmosphere of city environments. In bright sunlight nitric oxide is eventually oxidized to form nitrogen dioxide, which, because of its reddish brown color, effectively reduces visibility.

Hydrogen fluoride is localized in those areas where iron and nonferrous ores are smelted, and where phosphatic fertilizers, aluminum, and ceramics are produced. It is taken up by, and concentrated in, plants, which become highly toxic to the animal life consuming them.

Ozone, formed through a series of reactions, is a highly irritating oxidizing gas causing eye irritation as well as crop damage. It is the most important oxidizer in photochemical reactions and is formed by photochemical reaction on the exhaust gases of automobiles and in the vicinity of lightning discharges in the atmosphere.

Formaldehyde and acrolein, organic gases that irritate the eyes and mucous membranes, are produced by photochemical reaction and by incineration of some organic materials.

Ethylene, also a by-product of incomplete

[6] B. Nelson, "Air Pollution: The 'Feds' Move to Abate Idaho Pulp Mill Stench," *Science*, September 1, 1967, p. 1019.

combustion, is found in the exhaust gases of the automobile.

Particulate Matter. Particulate matter consists of finely divided materials, both liquid (mist, fog, spray) and solid (dust, smoke, soot). An example of the former is sulfuric acid mist, mentioned earlier; fly ash, fibers, and pollens are examples of the latter. The largest sizes of particulate matter will be deposited quickly from the atmosphere under gravitational pull. The smallest particles may remain suspended in the atmosphere indefinitely.

Dust from various metallic industries including arsenic (copper smelting), lead (lead and zinc foundries), molybdenum (steel plants), and fluorine (phosphatic fertilizer manufacture) has been responsible for serious injury or death to a variety of farm animals grazing within the proximity of the plant emitting the dust.

Radioactive materials in the atmosphere come from research activities, power plants using nuclear fuel, and from nuclear warheads. Although every attempt has been made to keep the radioactive gases and materials at low levels, certain amounts have reached the atmosphere and can become a serious problem if uncontrolled by all the nations responsible for their emission. Standards of radiation dosage are difficult to set since too little is known about the "safe" limit to radiation exposure by all forms of life. Radiation protection guides of the Federal Radiation Council recommend 0.5 rem (roentgen equivalent in man) as a maximum; however, the Atomic Energy Commission uses 3.9 rem per year in its Nevada test site.

To these should be added insecticides, used to protect crops from insects, and herbicides to remove undesirable plants. Even though used sparingly on quite restricted areas, traces of them have shown up at great distances from the source of emission.

The very descriptive word "smog" is a combination of the words "smoke" and "fog." Actually all atmospheric pollution cannot be termed "smog" as it contains neither the smoke nor the fog. There are, however, two major smog types, the London type and the photochemical type prevalent in Los Angeles Basin.

The London smog is often found in congested areas where incomplete combustion of fossil fuel forms smoke which is not dissipated but instead is concentrated and hangs over the city like a pall. It often occurs in still air when temperatures are relatively low and fogs prevalent, reducing visibility and causing bronchial irritation.

The Los Angeles smog results from the action of sunlight on the nitrogen oxides and hydrocarbon emissions of automobiles. It is irritating to the eyes and mucous membranes and causes damage to some plants, paints, and fabrics.

THE METEORLOGICAL ASPECTS OF AIR POLLUTION

The absorption of solar radiation by the atmosphere and by the earth's surface is the primary source of energy driving the atmosphere and keeping it in motion. Although some of incident solar radiation is scattered and reflected, much is absorbed by the earth, later to be re-radiated to, and absorbed by, the atmosphere. The amount absorbed depends upon the cloud cover, the carbon dioxide, and dust content of the atmosphere at the time. The climatological conditions in the city atmosphere are modified by the city itself —of this there is little doubt.

There are many differences between city and rural climates. In the city the contaminants as a whole include a considerably higher proportion of carbon monoxide; mean annual temperatures and winter minima are higher; the cloud cover, the precipitation, and the fog days are increased. On the other hand, the relative humidity and wind speeds are lessened as is solar radiation intensity (Table 1). In the latter instance the lessening of the solar

Table 1. Climatic Changes Produced by Cities

Element	Comparison with Rural Environs
Contaminants:	
Dust particles	10 times more
Sulfur dioxide	5 times more
Carbon dioxide	10 times more
Carbon monoxide	25 times more
Radiation:	
Total on horizontal surface	15 to 20% less
Ultraviolet, winter	30% less
Ultraviolet, summer	5% less
Cloudiness:	
Clouds	5 to 10% more
Fog, winter	100% more
Fog, summer	30% more
Precipitation:	
Amounts	5 to 10% more
Days with 0.2 inches	10% more
Temperature:	
Annual mean	1 to 1.5°F more
Winter minima	2 to 3°F more
Relative Humidity:	
Annual mean	6% less
Winter	2% less
Summer	8% less
Wind Speed:	
Annual mean	20 to 30% less
Extreme gusts	10 to 20% less
Calms	5 to 20% more

[Source: *Air Over Cities,* Public Health Service, Cincinnati, Ohio, 1961.]

radiation received may upset the heat balance of the earth and force climatic change.

Absorption of solar radiation by buildings and pavement in urban areas is high. The loss of terrestrial radiation at night to the outer atmosphere is retarded as it is reflected from pavement to building and building to building before reaching the atmosphere above, unimpeded except for the clouds, the dust and smoke, and carbon dioxide laden urban atmosphere. The carbon dioxide particularly is a

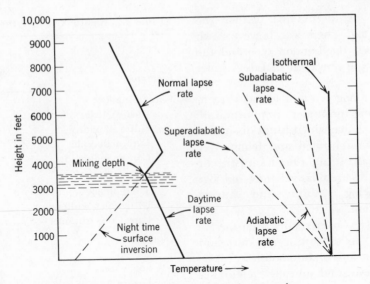

Fig. 2 The temperature lapse rates and inversion conditions within the atmosphere.

great absorber of terrestrial radiation and is generated within the city itself in high amounts through the consumption of organic fuels. City temperature may be generally higher than that of the surrounding countryside because of the capacity of its atmosphere to obtain and retain heat; the relative humidity of its atmosphere is lowered as a direct result of this higher temperature. Because of the greater numbers of condensation nuclei, cloud cover and precipitation increase. The wind velocities are lessened by the many obstructions in the form of buildings and structures of various sorts. In short, there is a city climate that is distinctly different from the climate of the surrounding rural areas.

Atmospheric temperature generally will decrease with increasing altitude. This lapse rate is usually given as a 3.5 degrees F difference for each 1000 feet of change in altitude; however, the lapse rate will vary from day to day. The lapse rate existing at any one time will affect the concentration of pollutants (Fig. 2).

The Adiabatic Lapse Rate. The rate of cooling within an air mass forced to rise over some obstruction, such as a row of buildings,

or rising above a stack is somewhat greater than the normal lapse rate. This greater rate of temperature change, about 5.4 degrees F for each 1000 feet of altitude change, is the adiabatic lapse rate. It is a temperature change downward within an expanding parcel of gas rising through an atmosphere of steadily decreasing pressure. For example, the air within a weather balloon, expanding as it rises through the steadily lessening pressure of the troposphere, will cool at 5.4 degrees F for each 1000 feet it rises. Should the parcel of air descend, as from the mountain slope to the valley bottom, the temperature will increase in that parcel of air at the same rate.

Temperature Inversion. Occasionally there will be a reversal of this trend, and an increase in temperature with height (a temperature inversion) will occur. This is often a nighttime phenomenon, although it is by no means confined to this period.

Within a relatively clear atmosphere during the daytime solar radiation is absorbed by the earth's surface at a maximum rate. The earth will in turn warm the lower atmosphere by conduction, by radiation, and by the convection currents set up by the warmer earth. A typical curve to illustrate this is shown by the normal lapse rate curve in Figure 2. At night rapid radiation of terrestrial energy results in the earth cooling more rapidly than the lower atmosphere. The heat exchange is then from the warmer atmosphere to the cooler earth, with a resultant decrease in temperature in the lower layers of the atmosphere. A typical nighttime surface inversion of the radiation type will occur in the lower few thousand feet of the atmosphere, as illustrated in Figure 2.

Should the inversion develop as a direct result of air movement over a colder surface, it is known as the advection type; or the inversion might develop as a subsidence inversion aloft where adiabatically warmed air comes in contact with cooler surface air. Inversions are a major cause of concentration of atmospheric pollutants. If the inversion is a few hundred feet deep the concentration of pollutants will be greater than if the inversion is a few thousand feet deep, all other things being equal.

Stability of the Atmosphere. If the lapse rate in the ambient air at a particular time is greater than the adiabatic rate (when there is no condensation or precipitation) the air is unstable. A parcel of air forced upward in this air by a mountain slope, for example, will cool at the adiabatic rate of 5.4 degrees F, yet will always be warmer than the surrounding air and will continue to rise through the atmosphere.

Air is stable if the lapse rate is less than the adiabatic rate. If a parcel of air is forced upward, such as gases within a stack of some power plant, it will continue to move upward only so long as the adiabatically cooling stack gas has a temperature greater than the air through which it is rising.

If with increasing altitude there is no temperature change in the atmosphere it is said to be isothermal. This condition is represented in the graph by a perpendicular line (Fig. 2). Where isothermal conditions exist the air is in a state of equilibrium.

Atmospheric Circulation. Meridional cells of atmospheric circulation exist in the approximate latitude of 0 to 30 degrees, 30 to 65 degrees, and 65 to 90 degrees. Atmospheric circulation is in part vertical from the earth's surface to the top of the troposphere on the poleward and equatorward margins, horizontal on the earth's surface, and aloft between the bounding latitudes of each cell. These circulations result in belts of prevailing winds that flow on the earth's surface as the "trades," "westerlies," and "polar easterlies."

The initial meridinal flow of air at the earth's surface is deflected to the left of the direction of motion in the southern hemisphere and to the right of the direction of motion in the northern hemisphere by the Coriolis force. The Coriolis force is proportional to the wind velocity and increases with latitude. As a result of this deflective force the "trades" of the northern hemisphere become northeasterly winds and the "prevailing westerlies" become southwesterly winds.

Of more importance locally to the air pollution problem are the winds of a lesser magnitude shifting about migrating pressure centers or varying as thermally induced pressure centers between land and sea, mountain and valley, and local fields wax and wane.

Air Masses and Fronts. Bodies of air are generally classified as to their origin, continental if originating over land and maritime if originating over the ocean; and further, if developed in a high latitude as polar or arctic air masses, and if from low latitudes as tropical air masses. Since continental polar (cP) air has temperature, moisture, and density characteristics that are quite different from maritime tropical (mT) air, the common boundary of contact between them separates air of sharply contrasting characteristics, and the air masses do not mix. The boundary of the advancing cold air mass is the Polar Front. A wave developing at the frontal zone gives rise to a migrating low-pressure cell of ascending air, a "cyclone," and the "warm" and "cold" fronts associated with it so often in evidence on the daily synoptic weather map.

The anticyclone or "high" weather system is an area of slowly descending, and adiabatically warming, air, usually indicative of clear weather; however, it has been responsible for subsidence inversion development and the concentration of atmospheric pollutants under stagnating conditions. The "low" is an area of converging and ascending air which will carry any pollutants that are in the air to high levels and disperse them widely.

The surface over which the air masses move may sufficiently modify the air mass so that vertical air movements will be suppressed. For example, a warm air mass moving over a colder surface causes a surface inversion to develop and thus stable conditions. Conversely cool air moving over a warmer surface causes a steepening of the lapse rate and unstable surface atmospheric conditions in which air will readily rise.

The Dispersion of Atmospheric Pollutants. The extent of atmospheric pollution is dependent upon direction, speed, and variability of wind. A point downwind of a pollutant source generally will receive greater amounts of the pollutant at slower wind speeds than at higher wind speeds and lesser amounts should the wind be variable. Wind variability may be affected by surface roughness, whether it be of a topographic nature or due to vegatation or man-made structures of various sorts. Surface roughness will affect air turbulence and potential air pollution in the lower atmosphere. When thermal turbulence is high, pollutants are dispersed. Thermal turbulence will decrease as stability of the air increases, with a resultant increase in the concentration of pollutants in the lower atmosphere, other factors being equal. The long-time averaging of wind conditions and other variables, including sources of pollutants, has enabled the construction of an isoline map showing the total number of days of high air pollution potential for the United States. When such con-

ditions, conducive to the occurence of high concentrations of air pollutants, exist locally, pollutants tend to accumulate until the conditions responsible for the reduced ventilation are modified. The industrialized valleys and urban areas of the eastern United States and the mountain basin areas of the West stand out as areas of frequent to persistent smog (Fig. 3).

Light winds may channel pollutants into a valley and in a stable atmosphere can result in the accumulation of pollutants in valley bottoms. Areas adjacent to the major cyclonic storm tracks and flat plains areas are least likely to develop stagnating conditions. Other areas may be more susceptible to atmospheric stagnation. These are major considerations in delineating atmospheric areas for pollution studies.

The depth through which pollutants are mixed in the atmosphere is of importance in potential air pollution. The maximum mixing depth, is of course, from the earth's surface to the top of the troposphere; however, when severe atmospheric pollution does occur the mixing depth may be only a few hundred feet under an inversion (Fig. 2). Under such an inversion air is stable and turbulence is greatly reduced, resulting in a concentration of pollutants below the inversion layer. Figure 4 of downtown Los Angeles provides an excellent example.

Should unstable atmospheric conditions develop, turbulence will be increased and pollutants dispersed. The change from a subadiabatic lapse rate to a superadiabatic lapse rate can result from strong warming of the earth by the sun with subsequent warming of the air immediately above creating a turbulence and a temperature drop in the turbulent area that is greater than the adiabatic rate. How effective this is is dependent on the kind of surface as well as the season of the year. In autumn, for example, with its relatively long nights and passage of relatively few cyclonic storms, conditions tend to reduce

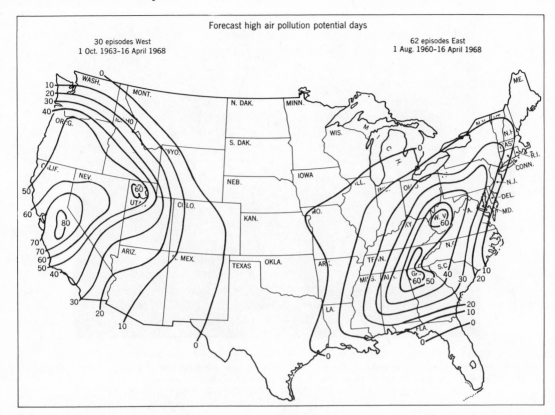

Fig. 3 Isarithms indicate the number of days that advisories of high air pollution potential have been in effect. (Environmental Science Services Administration.)

vertical motion and a stable atmosphere will occur under the inversion almost nightly.

Within a city the added heat by day is given off at night, reducing the possibility of a surface inversion within the city, although it may exist in rural areas and aloft over the city itself. Should the inversion occur aloft, a "lid" is formed over the city, concentrating the city-generated pollutants below it (Fig. 4). This envelope or "dust dome," as it has been called, is another factor that will affect the city climate (Fig. 5).

Many of the air pollution incidents in urban areas have occurred under a stagnating cold air mass. With the lack of wind and the formation of a temperature inversion aloft, the pollutants remain over a city, become con-

centrated, and aided by the city-generated nuclei condensation increases and persistent fogs develop. Only when the stagnant air mass is removed and the inversion destroyed is the atmosphere cleared.

The Removal of Pollutants. Rain and snow wash out great quantities of pollutants, both particulate and gaseous, from the atmosphere. Vegetation takes in carbon dioxide from the air in its growth processes (but releases it to the atmosphere upon decay) and causes some atmospheric turbulence, thus lessening wind velocities and carrying power of the wind. Vegetation also acts somewhat as a filter to collect particulate matter from the atmosphere. An estimation of dustfall removed by all means in various cities is given in Table 2.

Fig. 4 The depth to which mixing occurs is clearly evident in these photos of Los Angeles. As the inversion rises, the mixing depth rises and, as in these illustrations of Los Angeles, indicates the concentration of atmospheric pollutants has reached a point where buildings a relatively short distance away are almost obscured. Once the inversion

Table 2. Mean Monthly Dustfall in Various Localities

Place	Tons/Square Mile
Detroit	72
New York	68
Chicago	61
Pittsburgh	46
Cincinnati	34
Los Angeles	33

[Source: H. Landsberg, *Physical Climatology*, Gray Printing Co., Dubois, Pennsylvania, 1960.]

Oxidation of many pollutants aids in their removal. Carbon monoxide and methane gas are oxidized to carbon dioxide, and large quantities of the carbon dioxide are absorbed by the oceans. Eventually some of the carbon dioxide is removed from the oceans, in carbonate rocks, or given back to the atmosphere directly.

Oxidation of nitric oxide to nitrogen dioxide and the formation of sulfuric acid from sulfur dioxide are combinations that are part of the natural cleansing processes in the atmosphere. As these substances form they are easily washed out of the atmosphere by rain and snow.

Particulate matter will flocculate and fall to earth through the action of gravity and may also be washed out by rain and snowfall. The total self-cleansing activities of the atmosphere are inadequate, however, to cope with the enormous amounts of pollutants discharged into the atmosphere daily. The apathy of the public in general has not helped. However, through concerted governmental action, programs have been set in motion that hopefully

is destroyed, as would occur under superadiabatic lapse rates, unstable atmospheric conditions occur, resulting in greater air turbulence and a clearing of the atmosphere or, at least, in a dispersal of pollutants through a much deeper mixing depth. (Los Angeles County Air Pollution District.)

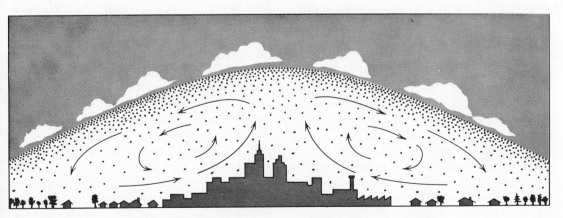

Fig. 5 Over a city a dust dome will form that is mainly the result of the emission of the products of combustion and the circulatory system is set up over the city, a product of the unique city climate. It may persist under a stagnating "high" and will be destroyed by heavy rainfall or strong wind. (After *Scientific American*.)

will stabilize, and in time reduce, air pollution.

Air Pollution Incidents of Note. In 1930, in the industrial Meuse Valley, Belgium, 63 persons died and 6000 became ill from breathing pollutants emitted by industrial activities within the valley and concentrated by a temperature inversion and fog. In 1948, in Donora, Pennsylvania, 20 died and close to 6000 others became ill from a similar concentration of chemical pollutants under an inversion of 4 days duration. Smog was blamed for many deaths in New York City in 1966. In Yokohama during the winter of 1946 many military personnel required treatment for lung congestion, supposedly caused by heavy air pollution. These incidents and others are a result of man's seeming unconcern or carelessness in allowing incomplete combustion of the fuel he uses in his furnaces, mills, and homes. They might not have occurred had he been more aware of those atmospheric conditions that cause pollutants to build up. Today even though much more needs to be learned concerning cause and effect relationships, such disastrous incidents should not recur. Nevertheless, air pollution is still a nationwide problem.

With the trend toward urbanization and technological change, air quality has continued to deteriorate across the nation. The smog problem in the Los Angeles Basin became prominent in the 1940's and continued to worsen even though the coal commonly thought to be the cause of smog was not consumed in the Los Angeles Basin. The problem became so universal in the State of California that in 1947 legislation was passed giving local and regional authorities the responsibility for control of air pollution within the areas under their jurisdiction. The Los Angeles County Air Pollution Control District was established and began operating the same year; it has done outstanding work in attacking the atmospheric pollution problem. It was about that time, some 2 decades ago, that the

nation as a whole awoke to the fact that it was running out of fresh air, especially in the urban areas, and that some serious thought must be given and action toward solving the dilemma. Evidence, although inconclusive, indicates that a health hazard does exist from polluted air and that urbanization is a factor. If for no other reason than the threat to national health, the pollution of the atmosphere must be slowed and existing pollution reduced quickly. It may be too late if we wait for conclusive evidence that indeed air pollution is a major cause of respiratory disease and death.

The tendency on the part of most of us not to become involved is strong. We are not greatly disturbed unless the problem, whatever its nature, directly concerns us. This attitude must be challenged and the citizenry must be apprised of the insidious character of air pollution—how it destroys human and animal life and the destruction it causes to material things. When the economics of the problem becomes more widely known, the interest in reducing pollution in the atmosphere will be much greater than it is at present.

POLLUTION CONTROL

The Clean Air Act of 1963. The Clean Air Act of 1963 was a major step by Congress toward effective pollution control. It provided for increased federal participation in research in air pollution caused by the automobile and sulfur dioxides arising from combustion of organic fuels. Although it does not set up air quality criteria relative to the effects of air pollution on health and property, it does recognize the need for research in, and the establishment of, such criteria. It further provides for technical assistance and training programs and matching grants to states and local governments for development of control programs, and federal action to abate pollution in instances where pollution problems are interstate.

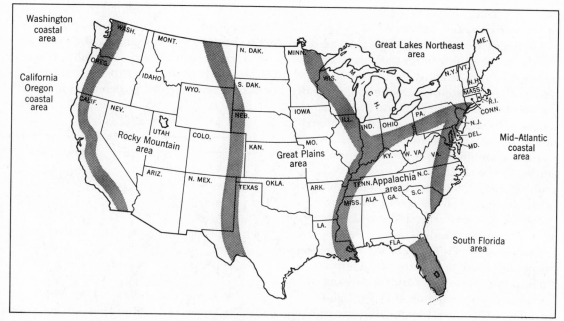

Fig. 6 The atmospheric areas of the United States as delineated by the Secretary of Health, Education, and Welfare. (Senate Document No. 92, 90th Congress, 2nd session, 1968.)

State and local programs were developed, as were programs of mass education on the effects of air pollution on health and property. Courses were and are offered by the Public Health Service on a regular basis to interested individuals. With the cooperation of interested local groups, the universities, and the mass media much information concerning air pollution has been disseminated to the public, yet the air pollution problem has continued to worsen. The problem was recognized more generally but little was done towards its solution.

The Air Quality Act of 1967. Because control activities under the Clean Air Act of 1963 were weak, the Air Quality Act of 1967 was passed, giving procedures and methods of action at all levels of government and among all segments of industry. It calls for a coordinated attack on air pollution on a regional basis, and toward that end requires the Department of

Health, Education, and Welfare to "delineate broad atmospheric areas of the Nation." Throughout these areas the meteorological, topographic, and climatological conditions affecting diffusion of air pollutants are of a similar nature. The United States has been subdivided into eight such regions (exclusive of Alaska and the Hawaiian Islands), as shown in Figure 6. The Air Quality Act also provides that standards of air quality be established within the state, and relative to these standards the extent to which air pollution affects health and property. It suggests research into possible measures for controlling air pollution, as well as the costs involved. Research studies are being done on particulate matter, sulfur oxides, photochemical oxidants, carbon monoxide, and atmospheric fluorides. Later studies will include criteria on lead, berillium, hydrogen sulfides, odors, certain heavy metals, asbestos, organic carcinogens, aldehydes, ethylene, pesticides, and rocket fuel components and their combustion products.[7]

Air quality regions within each atmospheric area are to be set up within states as approved by the Secretary of HEW. Although primary responsibility for control of pollution is within the jurisdiction of state and local governments, the Secretary of HEW has the authority to step in and initiate abatement action if the State's efforts are insufficient to abate the problem, and to intervene at once when air pollution problems are interstate. Provisions are also made for special studies concerning specific problems that may arise, and advisory groups are formed when needed.

Control of Air Pollution in the Los Angeles Basin. As stated previously, the Los Angeles County Air Pollution Control District was established and operating in 1947 following enabling legislation passed by the state legislature. The Los Angeles County Air Pollution Control District has been very active in the regulation of old industry as well as new and is recognized internationally as the leading agency of its kind. During World War II regulation measures to control emissions from a synthetic rubber plant reduced eye-irritating emissions sufficiently that the complaints ceased. However, a similar complaint was widespread following the war. In addition to the complaints of eye irritation, there were others of crop damage and the cracking and disintegration of rubber products. The usual controls for industrial emissions of dust and sulfur did no good. Upon further investigation it was found that oxidation, with ozone the major oxidizing agent, of the hydrocarbon exhaust emissions of the automobile in the presence of strong sunlight (not the reducing reaction common with sulfur dioxide) was the rule in the Los Angeles Basin. In fact, only

relatively small amounts of the reducing agents are to be found in the Los Angeles atmosphere.

The automobile was, and is, the major offender; consequently every automobile-driving citizen is a contributor to the total air-pollution problem (Fig. 7). When all sources of

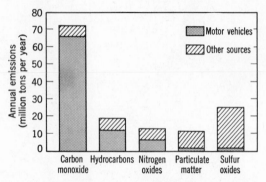

Fig. 7 The motor vehicle's contribution to five major air contaminants. (Senate Document No. 92, 90th Congress, 2nd session.)

pollution are considered, the total pollutants emitted by all sources other than transportation is about half that of transportation. In Los Angeles County about 88 percent of all uncontrolled emissions today are of automotive origin.[8]

The major pollutants being emitted daily from all sources are hydrocarbons, carbon monoxide, oxides of nitrogen, oxides of sulfur, and aerosols. On a weight basis the sulfur dioxide emissions from the automobile are very low. For the April 15th to November 15th period, emitted sulfur dioxide is 180 tons per day on the average compared to a total of 13,820 tons per day for all pollutants; about 1.3 percent of the total is sulfur dioxide (Table 3). For the November 16th to April 14th period, sulfur dioxide is only 2.2 percent of the total atmospheric pollutant load (Table 4).

---

[7] *Progress in the Prevention and Control of Air Pollution.* First Report of the Secretary of Health, Education, and Welfare to the U.S. Congress Pursuant to Public Law 90–148, The Air Quality Act of 1967, U.S. Government Printing Office, Washington, D.C., 1968.

[8] L. J. Fuller, *Air Pollution in Los Angeles,* Air Pollution Control District, County of Los Angeles, January 1968.

Table 3. Contaminants, in Tons per Day, from Major Sources Within Los Angeles County, April 15th to November 15th

Major Source	Organic Gases Reactivity			Aerosols	NO_x	SO_2	CO	Total (Rounded)
	High	Low	Total					
Gasoline-powered motor vehicles	1300	490	1790	45	585	35	9775	12,230
Organic solvent usage	300	160	460	8	–	–	–	470
Petroleum	55	175	230	3	40	30	75	380
Combustion of fuels	–	9	9	13	235	35	–	290
Aircraft	18	19	40	20	19	–	190	270
Chemical	15	45	60	9	–	75	–	145
Other	–	3	3	15	11	3	5	35
Total (rounded)	1690	900	2590	115	890	180	10,045	13,820

[Source: Los Angeles County Air Pollution Control District, 1968.]

Table 4. Contaminants, in Tons per Day, from Major Sources Within Los Angeles County, November 16th to April 14th

Major Source	Organic Gases Reactivity			Aerosols	NO_x	SO_2	CO	Total (Rounded)
	High	Low	Total					
Gasoline-powered motor vehicles	1300	490	1790	45	585	35	9775	12,230
Organic solvent usage	300	160	460	8	–	–	–	470
Petroleum	55	175	230	3	40	30	75	380
Combustion of fuels	–	9	9	20	280	165	1	475
Aircraft	18	19	40	20	19	–	190	270
Chemical	15	45	60	9	–	75	–	145
Other	–	3	3	15	11	3	5	35
Total (rounded)	1690	900	2590	120	935	310	10,045	14,000

[Source: Los Angeles County Air Pollution Control District, 1968.]

This fact is shown to be true nationally as well.

Today with certain controls in effect, the Los Angeles County Air Pollution Control District (APCD), "prevents the emission of about 5560 tons of air pollution daily. Another 1680 tons of air pollution are being controlled by the installation of crankcase and exhaust control devices on motor vehicles."[9]

In the day-to-day operations, nine completely automated air-monitoring stations are operated by the Los Angeles APCD. If, during an inversion and stagnating air condition, contamination of the atmosphere increases to dangerous levels, a warning alert is issued. What constitutes an alert has been established by a group of public health officials, medical men, chemists, and other scientists (Table 5).

There are three stages to the alert system:

First Alert: Close approach to maximum allowable concentration of pollutants for the population-at-large. Still considered to be at

[9] *Ibid.*, p. 3

Table 5. The Three Levels of Warning Alerts for Various Gases (Parts per Million)

	First Alert	Second Alert	Third Alert
Carbon monoxide	100	200	300
Nitrogen oxides	3	5	10
Sulfur oxides	3	5	10
Ozone	0.5	1.0	1.5

[Source: Air Pollution Control District, County of Los Angeles.]

safe levels but approaching a point where preventive action is required.

Second Alert: Air contamination is at a level where a health menace exists in a preliminary stage.

Third Alert: Air contamination level is at the point at which a dangerous health menace exists.

On the first alert unnecessary driving must cease and industry is directed to prepare to close down in case the second alert is sounded. If a second alert stage is reached, industry responsible for the contamination is ordered to shut down; all automotive vehicles with the exception of emergency vehicles are ordered to stop. Should a third alert stage be reached, the Governor of the State of California will declare a state of emergency, in which case pre-arranged procedures set forth in a Disaster Act become effective.[10] The alerts to date have been based on ozone alone and the number of such alerts ranges from a high of fifteen in 1955 to a low of one in 1968.

The controlling agency is constantly attempting to improve its program, and today its activity affects in some way every industry, business, and homeowner. Although natural gas is the major industrial fuel, occasional use of fuel oil for electrical generation is necessary when natural gas supplies are low, such as when the demand for home heating is high.

[10] Air Pollution Control District, County of Los Angeles, *The Alert System*, mimeographed.

Because fuel oils of lower sulfur content are used, the sulfur dioxide pollution resulting from the burning of fuel oil is low in the Los Angeles Basin. At no time from 1960 to 1967 has sulfur dioxide emission been greater than the standard of 0.3 ppm for a 8-hour period. Through the promotion of means for the removal of sulfur from petroleum in the late 1940's and the restriction requiring only the use of low sulfur fuels and natural gas in the mid-1950's, the emission of oxides of sulfur has decreased from a high of about 700 tons per day to about half of that amount today in Los Angeles County (Fig. 8).

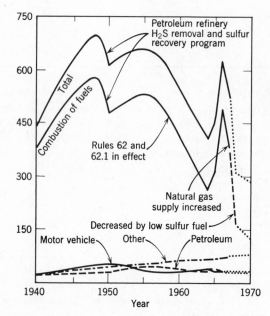

Fig. 8 The average emissions of oxides of sulfur in tons per day from major contributing sources in Los Angeles County. Rules 62 and 62.1 require the use of natural gas and other low-sulfur fuels. (Los Angeles County Air Pollution Control District.)

Stringent controls have been set for automotive emissions by the Secretary of Health, Education, and Welfare. Those emission standards proposed were adopted in March 1966 and applied to all autos and light trucks beginning with the 1968 model year. The 1970 standards as proposed allow for even less automotive emissions than in 1968, as is shown in Table 6. However, since the average life of an

Table 6. Proposed 1970 Vehicle Exhaust Emission Standards (Grams per Vehicle Mile)

	Typical Uncontrolled Vehicle	1968 Standard	Proposed 1970 Standard
Pollutant			
Carbon monoxide	71.0	33.0	23.0
Hydrocarbons	9.7	3.2	2.2

[Source: Senate Document No. 92, 90th Congress, 2nd Session, 1968, p. 197.]

automobile is 10 years and most of the automobiles on the road today have no pollution control device installed, it will be another 10 years, using 1970 standards, before automotive emissions will be reduced to approximately 30 percent of what they are today. This presumes no increase in the number of automobiles.

In 1960, under laws then in existence, automotive emissions were being controlled in the State of California. Crankcase emission control devices installed on new cars sold in California since 1961 were greatly improved in 1964. Since 1963 American-made automobiles have come equipped with such devices for crankcase emission control, and steady progress is being made in the control of exhaust emissions as well. California law requires that 1966 and later models be equipped to reduce exhaust emissions of hydrocarbons and carbon monoxide. Although the cost to the motorist has run into the tens of millions of dollars, the reduction in carbon monoxide and hydrocarbons has been dramatic, and can be even more so if projections prove to be correct (Fig. 9).

Although the Secretary of HEW by law prescribes emission standards for the nation, it is possible where conditions warrant for states to establish more stringent emission standards. A waiver of the federal law must be obtained if this is done. California applied for such a waiver in January 1968, since it was considered that stricter controls were necessary to maintain the status quo and further reduce atmospheric pollutants in the state. Although great progress has been made, the continued success of automotive emission control depends upon the continued application of the existing controls, the development of better devices, and even the administration of stricter controls as the number of automobiles increases. The combustion of gasoline to form carbon dioxide and water, the two innocuous emissions, is not impossible. If this is accomplished, less carbon monoxide and hydrocarbons will be released to the atmosphere.

Atmospheric Pollution Control Measures in Pennsylvania. The State of Pennsylvania may be used as an example of the extent to which the action under the Air Quality Act of 1967 has progressed. It is probably one of the first states whose Air Pollution Commission has taken on the task of developing the provisions called for in the act. After some preliminary work started in 1964 Pennsylvania, through a council of technical advisers from government and industry, developed air quality criteria for air basins as well as for single point emitting sources. These were adopted in 1967. These criteria consider total suspended pollutants and settled particulate matter for 30-day maximum values within the air basin. For single point measurement, particulate matter, both suspended and settled; lead; beryllium; sulfates; sulfuric acid mist; fluorides; sulfur dioxide; nitrogen dioxide; oxidants; hydrogen sulfide; and carbon monoxide are given for 30-day, 24-hour, and 1-hour values.

These criteria, under constant review, aid in the evaluation of studies of the Department of Health and serve as a basis for control reg-

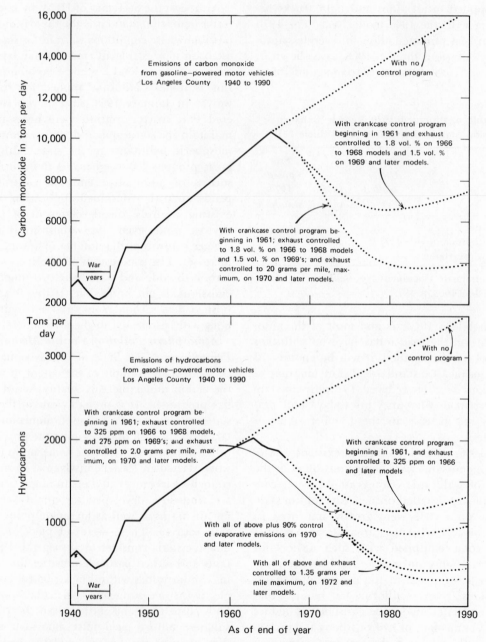

Fig. 9 Although the cost to the motorist has run high, the reduction in carbon monoxide and hydrocarbons, has been dramatic, and can be even more so if projections prove to be correct. (Los Angeles County Air Pollution Control District.)

ulations. They are believed to be the most comprehensive in the country.[11]

Continuing its work the Pennsylvania Air Pollution Commission set up regulations to control air pollution in specifically designated air basins. (The air basin is defined as an area influenced by common meteorological and topographical characteristics and of a scale of river basin or a portion of a river basin in size.) It is a subdivision of the Atmospheric Areas called for by, and subject to, the approval of the Secretary of HEW in the Air Quality Act of 1967. In its regulations the Air Pollution Commission set up the boundaries of a number of air basins in Pennsylvania and the blueprint for air pollution control within each. One of these basins is the Southeast Pennsylvania Air Basin. It extends westward from the west bank of the Delaware River and the Pennsylvania-Delaware state line to Valley Forge and the headwaters of the many small streams flowing into the Delaware, and includes parts of Delaware, Montgomery, and Bucks counties, and all of Philadelphia County.

The Southeast Pennsylvania Air Basin would be enlarged to include all of the foregoing counties, plus Chester County in Pennsylvania and the six counties adjacent to the Delaware River in the states of New Jersey and Delaware, in a federal proposal submitted in October 1968 by the Secretary of HEW. This area, to be called the "Metropolitan Philadelphia Area Interstate Air Quality Control Region," would encompass most present and future sources of pollution in a rapidly developing metropolitan area, as well as fostering "unified and cooperative governmental administration of the air resource throughout the region." [12] Pursuant to the Air Quality Act of 1967, within 90 days the governors of the states involved in the air basin must indi-

cate their intent to adopt the ambient air quality standards within a period of 180 days and within another 180 days adopt plans for implementation and enforcement of the standards for the region.

In July 1968, the Governor of Pennsylvania signed a measure appropriating $250,000 of state funds for automatic air monitoring equipment. To this was added $150,000 of a $699,222 federal grant made available under the Clean Air Act for a total of $400,000 for the purchase of 20 automatic air monitoring stations. Two of these fully equipped field stations have been installed in southeastern Pennsylvania.[13]

All field stations are equipped for continuous automatic transmission of data to the Department of Health's central office at Harrisburg. The data thus obtained will aid in spotting increases in pollution levels that may signal the need for an alert warning to be issued to the public. Figure 10 gives the numbers of manual monitoring stations for particulate matter and automatic instrumentation for monitoring gaseous pollutants for 1967 by state throughout the United States.

State Air Pollution Control Legislation. Some states and communities have not felt the pressing need for air pollution control measures that have been established in others. As of 1967 some control legislation has been in effect in all states with the exception of Alabama, Maine, South Dakota, and Vermont. Except for those noted, most states allow for some local control as well, and about half offer a tax incentive for pollution control at the source. Under the Air Quality Act of 1967, each state is to set up air quality regions and air quality standards within its boundaries. Should the state not do so the Secretary of HEW can get an injunction to abate pollution in any state where pollution may endanger health and property, as has been done already in Montana. Consequently, nationwide

[11] Air Pollution Commission, *Clean Air,* Harrisburg, Pennsylvania, September 1967.

[12] *Idem,* December, 1968, pp. 1 and 3.

[13] *Ibid.,* p. 2.

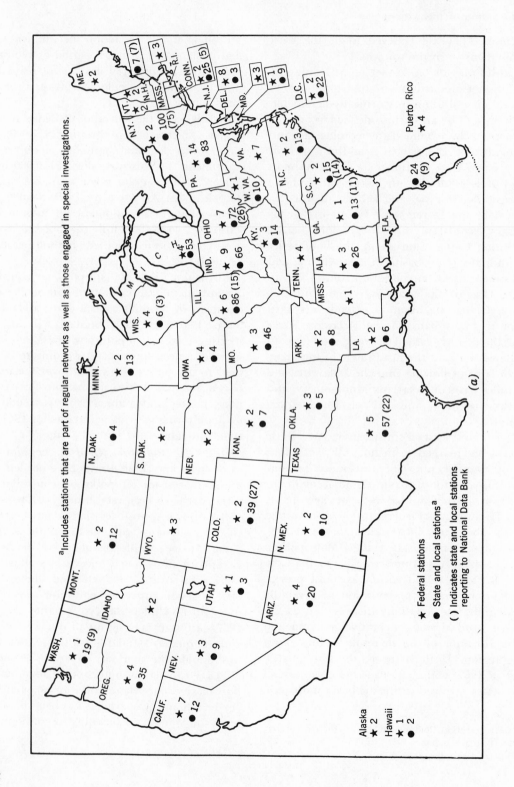

Includes stations that are part of regular networks as well as those engaged in special investigations.

★ Federal stations

● State and local stations[a]

( ) Indicates state and local stations reporting to National Data Bank

ME. ★ 2

VT. ★ 2
N.H. ★ 2

MASS. ★ 3
R.I.

CONN. 7 (7)

N.J. ★ 2 ● 25 (5)

DEL. ★ 8 ● 3

MD. ★ 3

★ 1 ● 9

D.C. ★ 2 ● 22

Puerto Rico ★ 4

N.Y. ★ 100 (75)

PA. ★ 14 ● 83

VA. ★ 1 ● 7

N.C. ★ 2 ● 13

S.C. ★ 2 ● 15 (14)

GA. ★ 1 ● 13 (11)

FLA. ● 24 (9)

OHIO ★ 7 ● 72 (26)

W. VA. ★ 1 ● 10

KY. ★ 3 ● 14

C ★ 4 ● 53

IND. ★ 9 ● 66

TENN. ★ 4

ALA. ★ 3 ● 26

ILL. ★ 6 ● 86 (15)

MISS. ★ 1

LA. ★ 2 ● 6

WIS. ★ 4 ● 6 (3)

MO. ★ 3 ● 46

ARK. ★ 2 ● 8

MINN. ★ 2 ● 13

IOWA ★ 4 ● 4

KAN. ★ 2 ● 7

OKLA. ★ 3 ● 5

N. DAK. ● 4

S. DAK. ★ 2

NEB. ● 2

TEXAS ★ 5 ● 57 (22)

WYO. ★ 3

COLO. ★ 2 ● 39 (27)

N. MEX. ★ 2 ● 10

MONT. ★ 2 ● 12

UTAH ★ 1 ● 3

ARIZ. ★ 4 ● 20

IDAHO ★ 2

WASH. ★ 1 ● 19 (9)

OREG. ★ 4 ● 35

NEV. ★ 3 ● 9

CALIF. ★ 7 ● 12

Alaska ★ 2

Hawaii ★ 1 ● 2

(a)

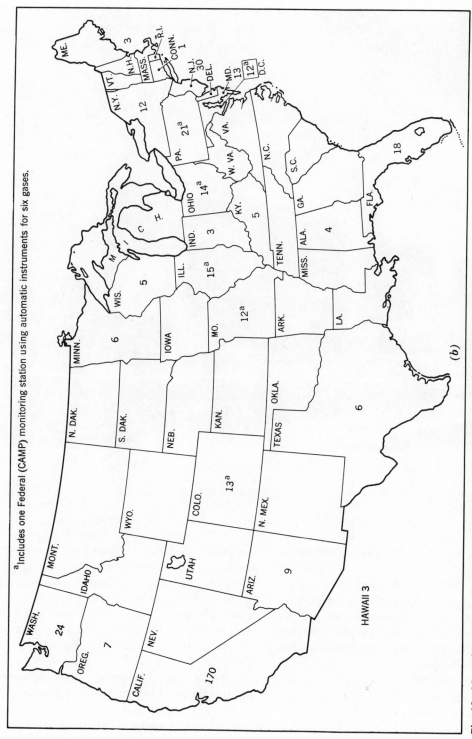

^aIncludes one Federal (CAMP) monitoring station using automatic instruments for six gases.

(b)

Fig. 10 Manual monitoring stations for particulate matter and continuous automatic instruments for monitoring gaseous pollutants. (a) Manual monitoring stations for particular air pollutants—1967. (b) Continuous automatic instruments for monitoring gaseous pollutants—1967. (Senate Document No. 92, 90th Congress, 2nd session, 1969.)

153

Fig. 11 The scrubber in operation at the Armco Steel Plant in Houston, Texas. During its operation, dirty gas is mixed with a wetting agent, usually water, and the dust particles are captured and removed with the water. (Research-Cottrell, Inc., and Armco Steel Corporation.)

controls of air pollution are essentially in effect.

Pollution Control Equipment. Once the parameters of a particular problem are defined, very efficient control equipment can and has been designed to cope with the problem. Several types of control equipment are defined in general terms below.

ELECTRICAL PRECIPITATORS. The electrical precipitator contains charged plates placed in the air or gas stream. Particulate matter in the flowing air stream is charged oppositely to

the plates as it flows through the equipment and hence is attracted to the plates of the precipitator. Periodically the particulate material is washed from the precipitator plates.

BAG HOUSES. These collect particulate matter from the gas stream in fabric bags in much the same way as does the home vacuum cleaner.

FUME BURNERS. Operating under high temperatures, fume burners consume combustible materials in a waste gas fed to the equipment.

SETTLING CHAMBERS. These collect the heavier particles from a gas stream, the velocity of which is sufficiently reduced in the chamber so that the particles settle out under gravity action.

SCRUBBERS AND WASHERS. Particulate laden gas is sprayed with water as it is passed through a chamber, and the particulate material is removed; or it is removed as the gas is bubbled through a water-filled tank.

VAPOR COLLECTION EQUIPMENT. Such equipment collects volatile products and compresses them to a liquid or incinerates them in fume burners.

ABSORBERS. These separate one gas from another by selective dissolving within cylindrical towers.

ADSORBERS. Activated carbon in a suitable container captures gas or liquid molecules passed through it.

Figures 11 and 12 are illustrations of two pieces of air pollution control equipment. Figure 13 shows that little or no air pollution reaches the atmosphere when proper measures for abatement are taken.

The Cost of Air Pollution. Control equipment for specific industrial use in the Los Angeles area has cost anywhere from a few hundred dollars to over $1,500,000. The steel

Fig. 12 The bag filter collector installed at the General Electric Plant at Pittsfield, Massachusetts. The dirty gas routed through the bag filter is cleansed of dust. The dust collected on the inside of the bag is removed by the agitation of the bag. (Research-Cottrell, Inc., and the General Electric Company.)

Fig. 13 Humble Oil and Refining Company's Bayway Refinery at Linden, New Jersey, as viewed from the general petroleum products process area. (Humble Oil and Refining Co.)

industry alone spent in 1968 or later $102,-000,000 for new control facilities across the nation. The industry's expenditure for air pollution control in 1967 was $39,400,000, an increase of $1,700,000 over its expenditure on such controls in 1966.[14] To control air pollution is costly. Although estimates have been made, just what the total annual bill is nationwide is difficult to say.

Only a rough estimate can be made of the real cost to health in respiratory diseases, eye irritations, and even deaths that have been attributed to the various air pollutants. Carbon monoxide probably has been studied more than any other pollutant with regard to its effects on human health. Recent studies show that carbon monoxide taken in by the bloodstream impairs oxygen transport by the blood. Hemoglobin has an affinity for carbon monoxide 210 times greater than it has for oxy-

gen; since its preference for carbon monoxide over oxygen is so great, the capacity of the blood to carry oxygen throughout the body is greatly reduced.[15] Not only is less oxygen carried throughout the body, but the hemoglobin where carbon monoxide is present releases oxygen less readily than it otherwise would. Carboxyhemoglobin, as it is called, is highly concentrated in the blood of cigarette smokers and may account for the higher mortality from cardiovascular disease among them. However, this problem is not the concern of the cigarette smoker alone. High concentrations of carboxyhemoglobin have also been found among nonsmokers within cities, strong evidence that the carbon monoxide laden city air is dangerous to health.[16]

[14] *Steel Facts,* October–November 1968, p. 5.

[15] John R. Goldsmith and S. A. Landow, "Carbon Monoxide and Human Health," *Science,* December 20, 1968, pp. 1352–1359.
[16] *Ibid.,* p. 1359.

There is mounting evidence that sulfur dioxide, fluorine, ozone, ethylene, chlorine, ammonia, hydrogen chloride, hydrogen sulfide, and others are taking a heavy toll in vegetation.[17] Agricultural crops "alfalfa, cotton, and lettuce have been . . . injured by sulfur dioxide . . . gladiolus, azalea, and vaccinium are most sensitive to fluorine; ozone produces weather fleck in tobacco; ethylene ruins orchid blooms . . . photochemical smog from Los Angeles has reduced the citrus fruit . . . south of the city by 20 to 25 percent in the past 15 years." [18] Across the nation the bill to agriculture is "at least five hundred million dollars a year." Of this $325,000,000 was attributed to crop damage and $175,000,000 to livestock, all of which the consumer eventually must pay.[19]

Sulfur dioxide and fluoride have injured coniferous trees in widespread areas. White pine in test plots failed to grow to the lee of an iron sintering plant for a distance of over thirty miles.[20] Many species of trees were drastically harmed south of the Trail smelter in British Columbia and in the vicinity of the smelter near Anaconda, Montana. The Ducktown, Tennessee, area of copper smelting is a classic example of such forest damage, in which 17,000 acres were denuded of forests and 30,000 acres of forest damaged.[21]

The visible effects of some air pollutants on material things is often readily noticeable. Lead-based paints discolor rapidly where hydrogen sulfide is present. Silver tarnishes; fabrics and buildings soil readily, requiring frequent cleaning and painting; fabrics and

rubber disintegrate and require replacement. These are a few of the observable effects of polluted air, the cost of which is almost impossible to determine.

Farm animals have been poisoned from arsenic, lead, molybdenum, and fluorides in the vicinity of smelters. A very recent incident in Montana involved a granulated texture in milk, a result of fluorine intake from grazing by the dairy herd on pastures downwind from the fertilizer plant using phosphate rock of high fluorine content. In this case the pollution problem was abated by federal intervention and is the first instance of such federal action under the Clean Air Act within the boundaries of one state.[22]

The cost of damage from polluted air to health, vegetation, paints, fabrics, and so forth, is estimated at $850 per year per family in Manhattan and somewhat less in the other boroughs of New York City. If all control measures were taken by the polluters and the cost passed on to the consumer, the cost to each family in Manhattan would be $50 per year—an $800 saving to the head of the household—and he and his family would breathe clean air once more.[23]

On the national level the cost of dirty air is estimated at $12,000,000,000 per year—about $60 per man, woman, and child.

If the best abatement techniques were utilized by all polluters, the pollution would be reduced very appreciably and for between $15 and $16 per capita per year we would have clean air.[24] Assuming the latter two estimates to be correct, if we spent the money necessary to clean the air, it would cost each of us only one quarter of what we now pay for polluted air.

[17] George H. Heping, "Damage to Forests from Air Pollution," *Journal of Forestry,* September 9, 1964, pp. 630–634.

[18] *Ibid.,* p. 631.

[19] William M. Blair, "Dirty Air Found Costly to Crops," *New York Times,* October 1, 1967.

[20] Heping, *op. cit.,* p. 631.

[21] C. R. Hursh, "Local Climate in the Copper Basin of Tennessee, as Modified by the Removal of Vegetation, *USDA Circular 774,* 1948, 38 pages.

[22] Nelson, *op. cit.,* pp. 1018–1021.

[23] New York City Department of Air Pollution Control, *What Does Air Pollution Cost You?* brochure.

[24] E. K. Faltermayer, "We Can Afford Clean Air," *Fortune,* November 1965; reprint, United States Department of Health, Education, and Welfare, p. 8.

References

A Digest of State Air Pollution Laws, 1967 Edition, U.S. Department of Health, Education, and Welfare, Public Health Service Publication No. 711, U.S. Government Printing Office, Washington, D.C.

Air Conservation, Report of the Air Conservation Commission of the A.A.A.S. Publ. No. 80, Washington, D.C., 1965.

Air Pollution, World Health Organization Monograph Series No. 6, Geneva, 1961.

Air Pollution in Los Angeles, Los Angeles Air Pollution Control District, Los Angeles, 1968.

Boffey, Philip M., "Smog: Los Angeles Running Hard, Standing Still," *Science,* Vol. 161, September 6, 1968, pp. 990–992.

Brady, Nyle C., *Agriculture and the Quality of Our Environment,* A.A.A.S. Publ. No. 85, Washington, D.C., 1967.

Bryson, Reid A. and John E. Kutzbach, *Air Pollution,* Association of American Geographers, Resource Paper No. 2, Washington, D.C., 1968.

Clean Air, The Air Pollution Commission, Commonwealth of Pennsylvania. Issued quarterly.

Heimann, Harry, M.D., *Air Pollution and Respiratory Disease,* U.S. Public Health Service Publication No. 1257, U.S. Government Printing Office, Washington, D.C., 1964.

Hepting, George H., "Damage to Forests from Air Pollution," *Journal of Forestry,* Vol. 62, No. 9, September 1964, pp. 630–634.

Magill, P. L., F. R. Holden, and C. Ackley, editors, *Air Pollution Handbook,* McGraw-Hill Book Co., New York, 1966.

Pack, Donald H., "Meteorology of Air Pollution," *Science,* Vol. 146, November 27, 1964, pp. 1119–1128.

Progress in the Prevention and Control of Air Pollution, First Report of the Secretary of Health, Education, and Welfare to the United States Congress, Senate Document No. 92, U.S. Government Printing Office, Washington, D.C., 1968.

Smoking and Health: Report of the Advisory Committee to the Surgeon General of the Public Health Service, U.S. Department of Health, Education, and Welfare, U.S. Government Printing Office, Washington, D.C., 1964.

Stern, Arthur C., editor, *Air Pollution,* Second Edition, Vol. I, *Air Pollution and Its Effects,* Vol. II, *Analysis, Monitoring, and Surveying,* Vol. III, *Sources of Air Pollution and Their Control,* Academic Press, New York, 1968.

Sutton, Sir Graham, "Micrometeorology," *Scientific American,* Vol. 211, October 1964, pp. 62–70, 75–76.

Wolman, Abel, "Air Pollution: Time for Appraisal," *Science,* Vol. 159, March 29, 1968, pp. 1437–1440.

GUY-HAROLD SMITH
The Ohio State University

CHAPTER 7

The Land We Possess

The development of agriculture in the United States has been marked by an increasing control over a rich land resource and conversely by a wasteful exploitation of the soils. The frontier of settlement, in a little more than two centuries, advanced across the mountains and the plains, across the forests and the prairies, and across the steppe lands and the deserts from the Atlantic seaboard to the Pacific. Progress was not steady or uniform but was characterized by surges of rapid movement alternating with filling in and consolidating the farmlands requisitioned from nature and the aborigines. Changes in the agricultural scene have reflected the progress of scientific advancement, the stultifying effect of depression, the uneasy peace between wars, the cataclysm of war itself, and the challenging opportunities of the postwar period of readjustment. Peaceful developments were interrupted by military action in Korea (1950–1953) and in Vietnam in the 1960's.

Agriculture in the United States, both as an industry and as a way of life, is related to a variety of conditions. In the utilization and conservation of the land resources the agricultural prospect is linked inextricably with:

1. The trends and changing character of the population, both rural and urban.

2. The area of land available, its productivity, and its suitability for the various purposes for which land is required.

3. The level of living, both of the farm population and the nonfarm population who purchase the products of the land.

4. The improvement in rural education and culture.

THE TRENDS AND CHANGING CHARACTER OF THE POPULATION

The agricultural situation at any particular time is closely attuned to the general economic condition of the nation as a whole. The economy is sensitive to both short-range and long-term changes in conditions. When the national economy experiences a wave of prosperity, agriculture generally benefits also, although there may be some differences in timing. For example, in the 1920's farm prices began a downward readjustment, while industrial wages still showed little or no decline. In 1948 the prices of many farm products declined months before it was reflected in a low-

159

ering of the cost of living or before the decline in employment or in wages. Farm prices rose again in 1950, but at the conclusion of active warfare in Korea in 1953, the prices received by farmers declined sharply, yet the prices they paid remained high or declined only slightly. At the beginning of the decade of the 1960's the prices received by farmers averaged approximately 6 percent below the prices received 10 years before. In the same 10-year period the prices paid by farmers increased 17 percent.

The unhappy plight of the farmer in respect to prices is a continuing problem. Compared with a price index of 100 for the base period, 1910–1913, the prices received by farmers for their products in 1968 was 267. The farmer, on the other hand, paid in the same year 356 for interest, taxes, and wages as compared with 100 in the same base period. Family living costs were similarly high, 339 in 1968. Production items cost 292 compared with the base period.[1] Farmers and their families are sensitive to these price differentials, and many are leaving the farms and seeking employment in the urban areas where opportunities seem to be more attractive.

The total number of people of all ages that collectively makes up the population constitutes a large domestic market. The high standard of living and particularly the desire on the part of the people to improve their living conditions make the American market almost unequaled from the standpoint of its capacity to consume the products of agriculture and industry.

Not only has the number of people increased steadily, but also there have been internal changes of major importance in the population. The birth rate has displayed significant fluctuations; the death rate has declined steadily; and the national policy in respect to immigration has been subject to important changes. Advances in medicine and nutrition have added greatly to the life expectancy of the people.

The population of the United States, subjected to these internal changes over a long period of time, takes on progressively new characteristics that must be examined critically from time to time so that agriculture and other economic activities can be adjusted to the new situation.

The Population Prospect. The population of the United States can be predicted for a few decades in the future with greater certainty than any other factor affecting American agriculture. This high degree of certainty is related to the fact that a very high proportion of the people now living will be counted by the census taker in 1980 and 1990. The birth rate, the death rate, and the net increase in the population can be predicted with great accuracy from year to year. The factors that may be of major importance in the long-range forecast of the total population include a change in the birth rate, the effect of epidemics on the death rate, a long war, and the policy of the federal government in respect to immigration (Table 1).

Table 1. Population Estimates, 1970 to 1990
(Numbers in Thousands)

	1970	1975	1980	1985	1990
Series A	208,615	227,929	250,489	274,748	300,131
Series B	207,326	223,785	243,291	264,607	286,501
Series C	206,039	219,366	235,212	252,871	270,770
Series D	204,923	215,367	227,663	241,731	255,967

[Source: Bureau of the Census, *Population Estimates,* Series P-25, No. 381, December 18, 1967.]

The projections of the population as shown in Table 1 express in the Series A, B, C, and D four reasonable assumptions in respect to fertility and incorporate data on births, deaths, and immigration in the late 1960's.

[1] These data were reported in *The Farm Index,* Economic Research Service, U.S. Department of Agriculture, November 1968, p. 23.

The projections are also based on the assumptions that there will be no seriously disturbing factors over the next 2 decades, such as an epidemic, a major war, or a significant change in immigration policy.

The most stable of these three factors is the death rate. Birth rates, although variable from year to year, can be forecast for relatively short periods with sufficient accuracy to meet the needs of the school authorities and others interested in the number of children in the population under 5 years of age. There is less certainty about the number of immigrants who will be admitted to this country from year to year. After 1945, the restrictive regulations and other checks were relaxed, and increasing numbers have been admitted to this country. We, as a people, are committed to a policy of selection and consequent absorption of the immigrants so that a degree of homogeneity will result, particularly in respect to an attitude toward American political institutions and traditions. In the middle 1930's, when the decline in the birth rate and the great reduction in immigration became important factors in forecasting the future population, there was a disposition on the part of the forecasters to envision a static, or even a declining, population a few decades hence. Much of this despair in respect to the population was not dispelled by the increased birth rate of the 1940's (Table 2).

The structure of the population in respect to age groups makes significant demands upon the land resources and the general economy of the nation. The relatively low birth rate during the 1920's and 1930's resulted in a reduced number of people requiring first elementary schooling and then high school education through age 17. The still lower birth rate during World War II had a depressing effect on the number of children who would soon be starting school. As soon as the war was over and military personnel returned to their families or married, the birth rate increased notably for a few years and produced

Table 2. Birth Rate and Death Rate, 1940–1967

Date	per 1000 Estimated Population	
	Birth Rate	Death Rate
1940	19.4	10.8
1950	24.1	9.6
1960	23.7	9.5
1965	19.4	9.4
1966	18.4	9.5
1967 *	17.8	9.4

* Provisional.
[Source: *Statistical Abstract of the United States, 1968*, Government Printing Office, Washington, D.C., 1968, p. 47.]

a wave of children who have moved through the elementary and high schools, causing economic stress. New classrooms were required faster than they could be constructed and financed. New teachers had to be recruited from an age group which was small because of the low birth rate 20 years before. The young people born in the immediate postwar years are now in the 20 to 25 age bracket. Many are in college; many are, or have been, in active military service; more have already entered the work force or are seeking employment; and a high proportion are married, have established homes, have one or more children, and collectively constitute a vigorous component of the population. They demand more housing, new furnishings, and all the materials needed to establish a new household. In the year 2000 this age group will be in their fifties and 10 years later will be retiring and increasing substantially the number of people classed as senior citizens.

Military action in Vietnam involving approximately 500,000 service men has led to the separation of families, but the period of service overseas was so brief, usually one year, that the effect on the birth rate cannot be determined with accuracy. However, the losses through death and injury probably will have a slight effect on the future birth rate.

It is not likely that the death rate can be re-

162

duced much more. In fact it may be expected to increase slightly as the population is made up of proportionately more old people whose life expectancy decreases rapidly in the later years.

The lowering of the death rate has increased the number of people in the over-65 group. In 1920 fewer than 9,000,000 people in the general population were 65 or over. In 1963 the number was more than 17,000,000.[2] Near the end of the decade of the 1960's the number of people 65 and over was approximately 20,000,000.[3] This older group in the general population will require housing, and have a special interest in the cost of medical service and the availability of nursing homes and hospitals within their financial means. People in the older age groups have reduced desires for food, clothing, transportation, and expensive housing. The drain on natural resources continues but at a reduced rate.

Farm Population. The farm population, once a vigorous component of the total population, is feeling the impact of a number of conditions that tend to lessen the attractiveness of farm life. The modernization of the farm home with inside plumbing and electricity has lightened the burden of the housewife. Mechanization of agriculture and good roads have made farming an integral part of the national economy. In balancing the factors that tend to hold people on the land against the attractions of urban life, the declining farm population reflects the relative advantages, real or imagined, in the urban areas of the country (Table 3).

In an agricultural community the wife is essential to the success of the farm operations. Her contribution is not that of a wage earner but of a helpmate who shares the work responsibility and rears the family. In the rural

[2] *A Place to Live, The Yearbook of Agriculture 1963,* Government Printing Office, Washington, D.C., p. 45.
[3] U.S. Bureau of the Census, *Population Estimates,* Series P-25, No. 385, February 14, 1968, p. 1.

Table 3. Farm Population

Year	Million	Year	Million	Percent of Total Population
1910	32.1	1961	14.8	8.1
1920	32.0	1962	14.3	7.7
1930	30.5	1963	13.4	7.1
1940	30.5	1964	13.0	6.8
1950	23.0	1965	12.4	6.4
1960	15.6	1966	11.6	5.9
		1967 *	10.8	5.4

* Preliminary.
[Source: *Statistical Abstract of the United States, 1968,* Government Printing Office, Washington, D.C., 1968, p. 594.]

area, although children constitute an important cost, they are also a valuable asset and at an early age can make a contribution to the farm income by helping regularly with the daily chores about the farm and during the vacations may help with the more important farm duties.

In the rural areas the farm produces a large proportion of the food consumed by the family. Self-sufficiency or self-support is a significant feature of the farm economy. In the city, particularly in the larger urban communities, children are unable to make a major contribution to their own support unless the father is engaged in a business where his children may help. On the farm the children are an asset, but in the urban community they are a financial liability.

Under the definition used by the Bureau of the Census the farm population was 15.6 million in 1960 and represented only 8.7 percent of the total population. It is now recognized that many people who live in rural areas derive much or most of their income from sources other than farming. Many may commute to the cities or to nearby industrial plants. Some may have employment on the highways, in the forests, at recreational centers, or in occupations other than farming.

Many farm people may be classed as part-time farmers who find it economically advantageous to derive their income from more than one source.

The Nonfarm Population. In 1960, the Bureau of the Census counted as rural 54 million people, but fewer than one-third of these lived on farms. Many of these nonfarm people lived in towns, villages, and hamlets with a population of under 2500 inhabitants. In these small inhabited places live many people who escape classification as urban, but their activities may be very similar to those of people who live in the larger urban centers. Many professional people, such as teachers, doctors, lawyers, butter makers, and others having similar occupations live in homes not unlike those who live in cities. In these small central places the trading or merchandising functions are carried on as they are in the larger urban communities.

Many other occupations help to classify these people as nonfarm, yet their activities may link them with agriculture. Some people utilizing a small tract of land may run chicken hatcheries; provide a dusting and spraying service to farmers and orchardists; practice custom harvesting, including silo filling; sell crop insurance; operate a small slaughtering plant; and provide many other service activities closely related to the principal agricultural crops and livestock produced on the nearby farmlands.

Approximately 3.6 million of the rural population live in small towns of 1000 to 2500 inhabitants. Included in this number are many people over 65 years of age who have moved from the farm to the nearby village. The farm they have moved from may be rented or sold to a son or daughter who is taking the first steps toward eventual ownership of the land. The older people retain an interest, financial and sentimental, in the farm on which they spent many years of their life. Many people who live in these small towns are basically rural people and their chief interests center around problems of the agricultural community. Most of the residents of the small towns and hamlets have a vital interest in the farming enterprise and will respond to the various programs aimed at maintaining the productivity of the land, the availability of fish and game in easily accessible areas, the development of recreational facilities such as swimming pools and picnic grounds, and the preservation of forested areas. Many of these people may not be directly involved in the action programs to conserve and protect these natural resources, but they can join with the people in leadership positions to encourage the people who own and work the land to practice conservation and protect the land resource from deterioration and destruction.

LAND RESOURCES

"Land" as a term means different things to different people. In some situations land may connote simply space or area. Whereas many people in past decades thought of land in terms of its suitability for agriculture it is in fact utilized for many other purposes. Increasingly land, and some of it good agricultural land, is being occupied by cities and smaller urban communities. Forested lands, once attacked by the pioneer to create a farm for himself, now intermingle with the farms or are spread over extensive areas where the land is largely unsuited for farming. To people who live in cities and work in an economy that provides time and money for recreation land, areas of a variety of dimensions become necessary for recreational purposes. Land is utilized for the building of highways, for wildlife, for mining operations, for reservoirs, for airports, and many other economic purposes. However, it is agriculture that makes the largest demand upon the available land of the nation to meet the needs of the people for food and fiber.

The United States as a nation contains within its national boundaries 2266 million acres of land, or 6.9 percent of the land area of the world. Only the Soviet Union, China, and Canada are larger. The 3,615,123 square miles which make up the area of the fifty states and the District of Columbia contain, in addition to the 2266 million acres of land, 47.5 million acres classed as inland water areas, including lakes, reservoirs, rivers, canals, and coastal waters, such as estuaries, bays, sounds, and lagoons. The land resources distributed widely across the nation differ greatly, depending on climatic conditions, such as the length of the growing season, the amount of precipitation, the relief of the land, the character of the soil, and the nature of the vegetation. Under natural conditions the qualities of the land developed over a long interval of time, but during the period of settlement, human use has altered locally the physical character of the land resource (Fig. 1).

In the early seventeenth century when the first settlers were establishing their homes on the Atlantic seaboard, the natural cover of this thinly occupied land consisted of the following categories of vegetation.

	Million Acres	Percent
Forest and woodland	1065	47
Grassland	726	32
Desert shrub	266	12
Tundra	214	9

After 350 or more years of settlement, clearing, agricultural readjustment, and economic development the categories of cover or land use show some striking changes.

Cropland. Cropland may be defined as the area in harvested crops, crop failure, cultivated summer fallow, soil improvement crops, idle cropland, and cropland used only for pasture (Fig. 2). Each year important areas fail to yield a crop because of winter kill in the case of autumn-sown crops, such as winter wheat, or because other conditions, such as drought, flooding, hail, or wind, make it uneconomical for the farmer to reap a harvest. If the

weather hazards recur too frequently and if crop failure is coupled with continuing low prices, marginal cropland areas may be abandoned. On the dry frontier, land once cropped may be restored to the grassland and range category.

Land classified as cropland is not a fixed number of acres but is subject to change. It required the clearing of 320 million acres of virgin forest and woodland and the plowing up or breaking the sod of millions of acres of grassland to create the cropland. In 1950, the area used for crops was 389 million acres; cropland idle or in cover crops amounted to 22 million acres; and cropland in pasture totaled 69 million acres. In the mid-1960's the areas in these three categories were 335 million acres, 52 million acres, and 57 million acres, respectively. Some of the land earlier converted to cropland has been returned to woodland or to permanent pasture or has been taken over for other uses. Nearly 58 percent of the land area of the fifty states is used for agricultural production: some 19.6 percent is cropland; 28.3 percent is grassland, pasture, and range; and 9.9 percent is grazed forest land.

The discerning observer can note readily the changes that are continually taking place. On an abandoned farm the uncultivated fields may be invaded by weeds, grasses, shrubs, and trees if a source of seeds is nearby and other conditions are favorable. Some of the areas that once were classed as shrub have been converted into pasture and range by removal of the shrubs and the planting of palatable grasses. A wilderness area may be set aside as a game refuge, which is then protected from despoliation by man. In the name of progress it may be necessary to take over high-quality cropland for developing a residential suburb, an industrial community, or a new municipal airport. These and many other changes are continually taking place in those parts of the country that show economic vitality.

Trends in Land Use. During the nine-

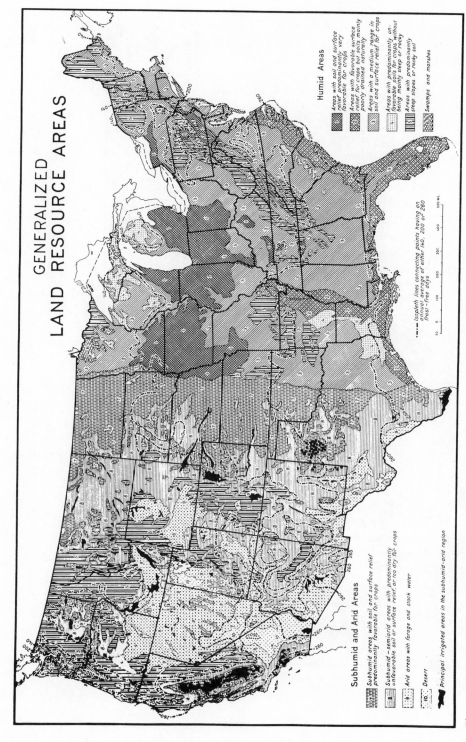

Fig. 1 This map of land resource areas is highly generalized, but it shows the location and extent of ten major land areas and indicates in the legend something of the character of each area in respect to soil, relief, drainage, and climatic conditions. (Economic Research Service and Bureau of the Census.)

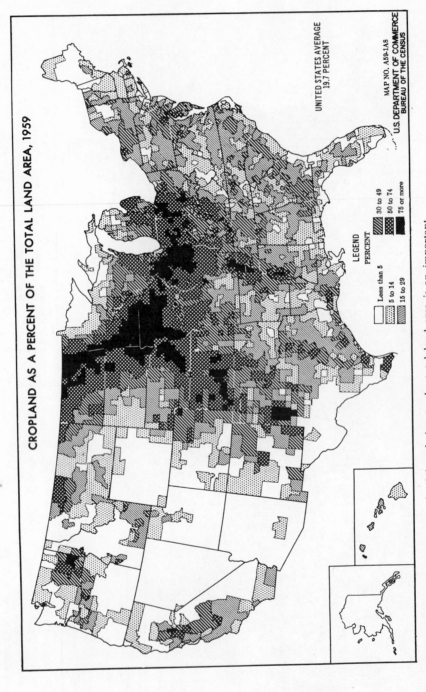

Fig. 2 The distribution of cropland in relation to the total land area is an important means of identifying the sections of the 48 contiguous states that are highly suitable for agricultural use. The corners of the important agricultural triangle are centered in North Dakota, Ohio, and Texas. Other important cropland areas can be identified in the East, in the South, and in the West. (Bureau of the Census.)

teenth century and for the first 2 decades of the twentieth century the number of farms in the contiguous forty-eight states increased steadily, reaching 6,448,343 in 1920. For more than a century farmers and their families advanced across the country taking possession of the land, establishing farmsteads, and becoming at the same time a major force, both economic and political, in the life of the nation.

After 1920, the number of farms began to decrease, and in 1967 it was down to 3,-176,000, fewer than half the number in 1920. After 1959, the data for Hawaii and Alaska were included with the other forty-eight states. In the same period the land in farms continued to increase and reached 1,-206,000,000 acres in 1953 and 1954. In 1967, less than 15 years later, the land in farms decreased to 1,140,000,000 acres. The changes in the number of farms and the area in farms were accompanied by an increase in the size of farms. The average size of a farm in 1967 was 359 acres, more than double the average for 1940. The decrease in the land in farms is related to the need for lands for other purposes, such as land for homes, schools, factories, reservoirs, wildlife refuges, and transportation.[4]

As farmers and their families have abandoned farming and moved into town or to the larger cities their land has been bought up by corporations or large operators. In the case of adjacent farms, fences have been removed so farm machinery could be used economically on the large fields. Many of the older farm buildings if dilapidated and no longer functional have been torn down. The better houses have been retained and provide living quarters for the farm manager and his employees. In the Great Lakes area many dairy farms have been consolidated and converted into livestock farms. Beef cattle have replaced the dairy herds.

The 1950's and the 1960's saw some notable changes in American agriculture. Extensive areas of agricultural land are retained in the cropland category in spite of their low productivity. Areas of low capability cannot be made to yield abundantly without the expenditure of large sums for commercial fertilizer and the practice of farming techniques which in the long run are beyond the means of the farmer. In spite of the fact that large areas of marginal land are still used for agriculture, the lands best suited for farming make up the immense area known as cropland. Anyone concerned about the land resources, especially in relation to their availability and adequacy, should be encouraged by the fact that productivity of the land remains high, while the total population increases and the area in cropland declines. There is no immediate danger that the land resources will be inadequate to meet the needs of the United States for food and fiber.[5]

From the time of settlement to World War I increased agricultural production was related to the expanding frontier and the addition of new increments to the cropland area. Shortly after 1920, the mechanization of agriculture with the related decline of horses and mules freed 70 million acres for the production, even the overproduction, of foods, fibers, and agricultural raw materials. Next to come were the technological advancements that would increase yields.[6] The application of fertilizers, the selection of better crop varieties and seed, continued mechanization, control of plant and animal diseases, more efficient live-

[4] Orville L. Freeman, *Agriculture/2000, Report of the Secretary of Agriculture, 1967*, U.S. Department of Agriculture, Washington, D.C., 1968, p. 55.

[5] Marion Clawson, R. Burnell Held, and Charles H. Stoddard, *Land for the Future*, Resources for the Future, The Johns Hopkins Press, Baltimore, 1960, p. 266.

[6] Chauncy D. Harris, "Agricultural Production in the United States: The Past Fifty Years and the Next," *Geographical Review*, Vol. XLVII, 1957, pp. 175–193.

stock, skilled management, and on occasion higher prices increased notably the productivity of the land.[7]

Increased production in the 1920's and 1930's was related in a large measure to the substitution of mechanical power for horses and mules. Land long needed and used for the production of food for horses and mules became available for other crops. Half the increase in livestock and crops is directly related to the mechanization of agriculture. Increased yields per acre accounted for a third of the increase. In the 1940's, when mechanization was an achievement, less than a quarter of the increase in production can be ascribed to the continued substitution of mechanical power for horses and mules. Much of the gain in production was related to increased yields per acre, which in turn reflected the higher prices that induced the farmers to put forth their best efforts to meet new production goals. In the 1950's, the same factors were operative to increase still further farm output. Mechanization is credited with nearly 20 percent of the increase. Somewhat less than half the gain was derived from increased yields. The increased contribution of livestock accounted for nearly a third of the gain in production.

The Use of Fertilizer. The maintenance of the productivity of the soils of the United States and the upbuilding of soils that are low in plant nutrients require the application of fertilizer materials. Because new lands seemed always to be available as the frontier of settlement moved across the country, the soil resources were allowed to decline by erosion and leaching that insidiously reduced the physical base on which the industry of agriculture was built. Many farmers were slow to realize that their lands had depreciated in quality, and productivity could be maintained only by the application of fertilizer.

The older agricultural areas of Europe and Asia have long been heavy consumers of ferti-

lizers, both organic and mineral. In the United States the fertilizer industry had been expanding and was ready to meet the needs of agriculture when the demand came. During World War II one important contributing factor in attaining high levels of agricultural production was the increased use of mineral fertilizers. Nitrogen, once imported in the form of Chilean nitrates, became available in the form of synthetic ammonia, in by-product ammonium sulfate, and other nitrogen-containing substances. Large sources of phosphates and sulfur were developed to meet the needs for superphosphates. Potash, once imported from Germany, became available from deposits in the Southwest.[8]

The Minor Elements. In addition to nitrates, potash, and phosphates, which may be regarded as the great triumvirate of fertilizer minerals, lime is of great importance, and a number of minor or trace elements are known to be essential in plant and animal nutrition. These minor elements include magnesium, manganese, boron, iron, sulfur, copper, and zinc. Deficiencies of one or more of these elements in the soils have been found to be responsible for abnormalities in both plants and animals that fed on the vegetation. Where the farmers are largely dependent on manures and other organic wastes, the deficiencies of these minor elements are less serious than in the areas where mineral fertilizers are used.[9]

Trade in Agricultural Products. The land resources of the United States in good years and under proper management can produce many crops in such abundance that surpluses are available for export. About one out of every five acres in crop production provides

[7] *Ibid.,* pp. 187–188.

[8] K. D. Jacob and F. W. Parker, *Fertilizer in World War II,* Proceedings of the Twenty-Second Annual Meeting of the National Joint Committee on Fertilizer Application, 1946, p. 38.

[9] Matthew Drosdoff, "The Use of Minor Elements," *Science in Farming, The Yearbook of Agriculture, 1943–1947,* Government Printing Office, Washington, D.C., 1947, pp. 577–582, reference on p. 578.

an exportable surplus of wheat and flour, corn, soybeans, tobacco, cotton, grain sorghum, rice, and many other crops. In 1966, agricultural exports were valued at $6,676,-400,000. Agricultural exports represent approximately 22 percent in value of all products sold abroad.

Many agricultural products must be imported because domestic production is inadequate in quantity or in quality. Leading imports include live cattle, casein, cheese, canned meats, other meats, wool, fruits, sugar, tobacco, and many others. These are classed as supplementary because the United States does not produce adequate supplies to meet the needs of the American people. In 1966 they were valued at $4,668,000,000.

There are many agricultural products which because of climate or labor costs cannot be produced in quantity in the United States. These are known as complementary imports and include silk, wool, cacao, coffee, tea, bananas, rubber, and others. Collectively these complementary products were valued at $1,-786,000,000 in 1966.

The total value of agricultural exports exceeds the value of agricultural imports. This may lead some conservationists to protest the use of land resources to support people abroad. Considering the variety and the quantity of agricultural products imported into the United States the land resources of many countries are being utilized to meet the needs of the United States.

The Agricultural Regions. The practice of agriculture, especially the development of distinctive crop combinations with the associated livestock industries, has resulted in an agricultural regionalism commonly recognized as the major types of farming (Fig. 3). In areas where the predominant type of farming may be feed grains and livestock (Corn Belt) there are farmers who have developed a specialty, such as fruit and vegetable growing. In the Northeast where dairying gives the region its distinctive characteristics there are individual

farmers who may raise poultry or sheep or use their land for other purposes. But in spite of considerable diversity several farm types can be identified in the forty-eight contiguous states.

The distribution of crops in this cropland area reflects the character of the climate, the physical nature of the land in respect to relief, and the productivity of the soil. Economic conditions, particularly market demand and prices, function as important factors in production. The combination of crops and farm animals raised in any area is related to both the physical and economic conditions that give distinctive character to the agricultural regions of the United States.

The chief cropland area of the United States is essentially triangular in shape. A straightline drawn from central Ohio to the 49th parallel in northwestern North Dakota, thence southward into the Panhandle of Texas, and thence northeastward to central Ohio encloses a great triangular area of cropland that is probably unequaled by any other agricultural area in the world. Within this area are included parts of the spring wheat region, the hay and pasture belt, the corn belt, a part of the corn and winter wheat belt, and a small section of the Cotton Belt (Fig. 4). East and west across the central section of the triangle extends the corn belt centered on what Transeau has called the prairie peninsula.[10] Most of this great cropland area was originally an expansive tall-grass prairie of slight relief and under the economy of the Amerinds remained a grassland. The aborigines, by the use of fire, may have helped to maintain the prairie against the encroachment of the forest and may have extended the prairie area locally by the same means. This moot question need not be debated here. It is important, however, that the white settlers came into possession of one of the greatest agricul-

[10] E. N. Transeau, "The Prairie Peninsula," *Ecology*, Vol. 16, 1935, pp. 423–437.

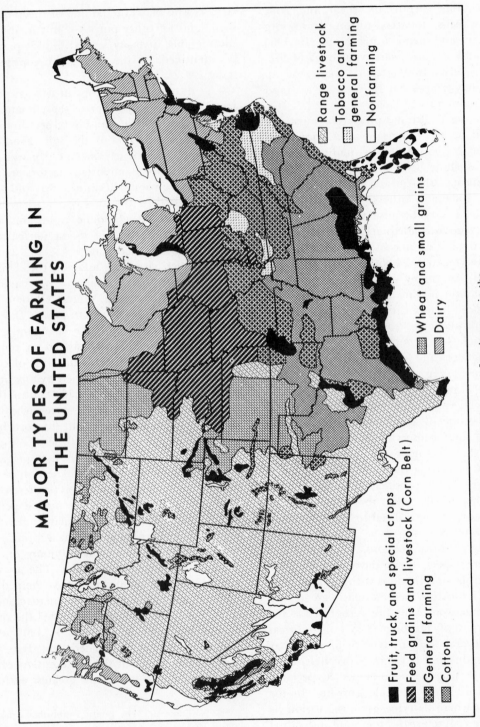

MAJOR TYPES OF FARMING IN THE UNITED STATES

Fruit, truck, and special crops
Feed grains and livestock (Corn Belt)
General farming
Cotton

Wheat and small grains
Dairy

Range livestock
Tobacco and general farming
Nonfarming

Fig. 3 This map shows the eight major types of farming and one nonfarming area in the 48 contiguous states and the location and geographical extent of the several crop and livestock areas. (Economic Research Service and Bureau of the Census.)

Fig. 4 This stand of corn near Eureka, Illinois, is representative of the major crop grown throughout much of the Middle West. The luxuriant vegetative growth and the high yield of corn as a grain give an indication of the favorable conditions, both physical and economic, under which this crop is grown. (Caterpillar Tractor Company)

tural areas in the world as they dispossessed the natives and, in due course of time, broke the prairie and substituted cultivated crops for the natural grasses which for thousands of years had been building the agricultural heartland of America, known as the Middle West.

In certain counties in this great triangular area as much as 75 percent of the total area was classed as cropland in 1959, and locally more than 75 percent of the land was actually in crops.[11] In the areas of slight relief the

[11] *United States Census of Agriculture 1959, A Graphic Summary of Land Utilization*, Vol. V, Part 6, Chapter 1, Government Printing Office, Washington, D.C., 1962, p. 12.

mechanization of agriculture had reached a high stage of development. This is the great granary area of the United States, and in favorable years it can contribute great quantities of food to the hungry peoples of the world.

In the South the irregularity of the terrain, infertile soils, swamps, and other unfavorable factors function collectively to limit the areas suitable for crops. In the more favored areas, such as the inner Costal Plain; the Piedmont; the valleys of the Ridge and Valley Province of the Appalachians; the alluvial lowlands of the Mississippi, Arkansas and Red rivers; and the black prairies of Texas and Oklahoma, the proportion of farmland

Fig. 5 In the South and in the Southwest, where cotton is an important cash crop, the mechanical cotton picker has eliminated the numerous hand laborers who spread across the cotton fields each autumn and gathered in the crop. One man remains to handle the machine. The others have been displaced and must look elsewhere for work. (International Harvester Company.)

devoted to crops locally may exceed 50 percent. This region of heavy rainfall, erodible soils, clean cultivated crops, notably cotton, corn, and tobacco, cultivated by people not fully aware of their responsiblity, is one of the great problem areas of the United States (Fig. 5). The land resource of this area can be saved from destructive exploitation, but the proportion of the land in row crops should be reduced. The agriculture of the South may require many important changes before the area

attains its proper place in the farm economy of the United States (Fig. 6).

Scant rainfall and extensive mountain systems restrict the croplands in the West to local areas of adequate precipitation or with water for irrigation. Large areas in the Great Plains and in the Palouse country are classed as cropland, but the practice of fallow farming reduces the area harvested each year (Fig. 7). The Puget Basin and the Willamette Valley of Oregon carry on agriculture without the benefit of irrigation. The areas where the highest proportion of the lands is in crops include the irrigated valleys of the Columbia and its tributaries, the Colorado and its tributaries, and the Central Valley and coastal valleys of California.

Land for Urban Use. Living in urban communities is an ancient way of life, but in the United States urbanism has taken on some aspects of newness. The spread of home building on the fringe of the older urban communities has produced what many people know as urban sprawl. In 1950, 64 percent of the population in the United States lived in cities of more than 2500. By 1960 the proportion had increased to 69.9 percent and by 1970 may be more than 75 percent. The increasing number of city dwellers makes it necessary for lands to be withdrawn from other uses and converted for urban purposes. The casual observer may get the impression that the areal expansion of cities may reduce substantially the land in other use categories, particularly valuable cropland.

In the inner sections of the principal cities vacant or unused lots are available for future developments. Along the urban fringe urban and rural land may be intermingled to the extent that delineating the urbanized area becomes very difficult. Because the internal lands are not fully used, most urban areas would be able to absorb great numbers of people without expanding their corporate boundaries. Many of the significant features of land use in urban communities have been investigated by Clawson, Held, and Stoddard,[12] and others.

The intensified use of the land for urban purposes has resulted in many unfortunate economic and cultural consequences. In some areas an attractive natural landscape has given way to an unsightly assemblage of man-made structures of doubtful aesthetic quality. Urbanization is inevitable and the expanding city with its attendant problems must be accepted. The major highways and freeways that interlace the countryside and tie the urban communities together attract commercial and industrial establishments and help to create what Gottmann calls a megalopolis.[13] Ribbons or bands of closely settled areas join the suburbs of one town with those of another, and the traveler gains the impression that most of the land has become urbanized. Urban areas expand and engulf rural land and rural people, but the total area occupied by urban communities is only about 1 percent of the land area of the country.[14]

The urban areas of the United States, while requiring only limited areas for their homes, factories, commercial establishments, and the

[12] Clawson, Held, and Stoddard, *op. cit.*, pp. 51–123.

[13] Jean Gottmann, *Megalopolis*, The Twentieth Century Fund, New York, 1961.

[14] Clawson, Held, and Stoddard, *op. cit.*, p. 53.

Fig. 6 This field of Texas oats on sloping ground is protected by a system of low terraces. It is important that these areas, which were originally prairie, be protected from wind and water erosion when brought under cultivation. (Caterpillar Tractor Company)

Fig. 7 On the relatively flat and dry plains of the Dakotas combines are used in harvesting the several small grains such as wheat, rye, oats, barley, and flax. On a highly mechanized farm a small labor force is able to farm extensive areas. The people released are seeking work in other occupations. (International Harvester Company.)

other appurtenances of urban life, make heavy demands on the rest of the country for food, the raw materials of industry, recreational facilities, water supply, power, and other materials and facilities. The urban centers have become great consumers of resources, and at the same time they provide goods and services required by all the people.

MISCELLANEOUS LANDS. Twelve percent of the land area of the United States or 277 million acres classed as miscellaneous lands include marshes, sand dunes, bare rock areas, deserts,

and tundra. It would not be entirely accurate to refer to these areas as wastelands. Expansive areas of desert in the Southwest and the tundra of Alaska may be regarded as wilderness areas, and many people who live most of their lives in crowded urban areas derive satisfaction from viewing or penetrating briefly such wilderness areas. The desert areas of Nevada, New Mexico, and other states in the West have been used as testing areas for both atomic and conventional weapons. The tundra and marshlands are natural refuges and breeding grounds for wild animals and water-fowl. These expansive open areas have utility as do other land areas, but the return may be largely aesthetic.

Land Use in the Years Ahead. It would be difficult to identify and list all the factors and conditions that will operate over the next few years to change the use of land in the United States (see Table 4). By applying science in all its various aspects, the utilization of more fer-

ble to transfer some of the land now in crops to other use categories. Some cultivated land can be restored to grass and permanent pasture. Not only will the additional grassland areas help support the livestock needed to feed the increasing population, but lands planted or restored to grass will protect the land from erosion, prevent excessive runoff, and preserve a basic resource until it is required by future generations.[15]

Table 4. Needed Shifts in Major Land Uses, 1959–1980

	Used in 1959, Million Acres	Shifted to Other Uses, Million Acres	To Be Added from Other Uses, Million Acres	Net Change, Million Acres	Projected Use in 1980, Million Acres
Cropland	458	68	17	−51	407
Grassland pasture and range	633	30	49	+19	652
Forest land	746	32	27	−5	741
Recreational	62	0	23	+23	85
Farmsteads and farm roads	10	0	0	0	10
Special purpose uses	85	0	25	+25	110
Miscellaneous uses	277	11	8	−11	266

[Source: U.S. Department of Agriculture, *Food and Agriculture, A Program for the 1960's,* Washington, D.C., 1962, p. 2.]

tilizer, the selection and use of more productive plants and animals, the selection and use of the most productive farmlands, and by other means the area of cropland required to produce the foods and fibers required by a growing population can be reduced from 458 to 407 million acres. The results of research carried on at the Agricultural Research Laboratories at Beltsville, Maryland, at the regional research laboratories, at the state agricultural colleges, at the state agricultural experimental stations, and at the laboratories of industrial firms engaged in the manufacture of fertilizers, the formulation of insecticides and fungicides, and food processing are available to facilitate the impending readjustments in land use.

Increased yields per acre will make it possi-

GRASSLAND PASTURE AND RANGE. Originally 32 percent of the land area of the United States was classed as grassland and consisted of immense tallgrass prairies of the Middle West and the shortgrass prairies of the Great Plains and other areas in the West. Locally along the Gulf of Mexico coastal prairies can be included with the grasslands. In the long process of converting the land area into cropland large areas of grassland remain in grass. The Census of Agriculture for 1959 showed that 28 percent of the land area of the nation is grassland pasture and range. Woodland pastures, particularly in the South and West, are

[15] For an extended statement in praise of grass see *Grass, The Yearbook of Agriculture, 1948,* Government Printing Office, Washington, D.C., 1948.

utilized for livestock and make a significant contribution to the grassland resources of the country. (For a fuller treatment of the grassland resources see Chapter 17.)

FOREST AND WOODLAND AREAS. When the United States was first settled, 1065 million acres or 47 percent of the land consisted of forest and woodland. In the process of settlement clearing the land for agriculture reduced the forest and woodland to 33 percent of the area, excluding reserved forest lands. Lumbering in the virgin forests followed by repeated harvesting of second-growth timber has reduced the quality of the timber resources of the country. Cutover land where the remaining trees have been reduced to less than 10 percent of the original stand is classed as woodland if the land has not been converted to other uses. Areas that have been planted to trees (afforestation) are also included in the forest and woodland category.

Major tracts of forested land have been set aside as national forests, state forests, and publically owned woodland areas. These forest reserves, the immense woodland areas in farms, and the great forest lands held by private interests make up the forest resources of the nation (see Chapters 18 and 19).

WOODLAND PASTURES. In the United States, including Alaska and Hawaii, 93 million acres of pastured woodland were reported by the Census of Agriculture for 1959. On the cutover lands largely in the eastern part of the country native grasses have invaded the once-forested areas or have been planted in woodland areas to provide pasture for livestock so essential in the agriculture of the nation. In the drier West and along the transitional zone between the forests and the prairie the open forests provide pasture of great value to the ranchers and farmers who are in a position to utilize these pastures chiefly for cattle and sheep. In the West the carrying capacity of the grasslands must be respected to prevent overgrazing. If the grass cover is destroyed or seriously damaged by overgrazing, not only is

a grassland resource reduced in value, but the soil becomes more susceptible to wind and water erosion; also water that might be retained on the land is permitted to flow rapidly to the stream channels, carrying with it a burden of silt that may reach reservoirs and eventually reduce their water-holding capacity.

LAND FOR SPECIAL PURPOSES. Seven percent of the land area or 157 million acres are used for various special purposes, such as highways, railroads, airports, parks, wildlife refuges, farmsteads, urban areas, and other land-requiring developments (Fig. 8). The extension of highways to meet the transportation needs of the nation usually requires that the rights of way be withdrawn from other use categories. The establishment of new parks and recreational areas to serve the people who have leisure to enjoy these facilities requires land that was previously used for some other purpose.

THE LEVEL OF LIVING

The consumption of farm products, particularly the food crops, in the United States depends on (1) the future population of the nation, (2) the per capita consumption of food, and (3) the net exports or imports of edible products. Of these three factors the most important in the immediate future, as in the past, will be the total number of people in the nation. The market for food crops is closely related to the number of mouths to feed. With the present population and the productive capacity of the arable land available for food crops the American people are well fed, but there still remains an important number whose diet is inadequate in some respect. Improving the living standard of this segment of the population will require readjustments in the production of food crops, but the rising level of living will not increase the over-all demand for food as rapidly as will the normal increase in the population.

Fig. 8 The spread of a network of limited-access highways, throughways, parkways, turn-pikes, and tollways across the country requires great strips of land, largely farmland, for the modern highway system. In the open country the two multilane highways may be widely spaced but, in the urban areas, because of the high cost of the right-of-way, the median strip may be very narrow. (Garden State Parkway, New Jersey Highway Authority.)

The Level of Living and the Market for Agricultural Products. The market for agricultural products is related not only to the number of consumers but to the consumption capacity of the population. People with a high standard of living and with a high effective purchasing power can provide a very large market for the products of the land. It is recognized, however, that the consumption of certain foods does not seem to bear any significant relationship to the family income. Certain long-time trends have been established,

and a change in income has little or no effect on the general trend. For example, the per capita consumption of wheat flour averaged 224 pounds in 1880, and for more than 90 years the consumption declined until it reached an average of only 112.6 pounds in the 5-year period, 1963–1967. The general decline in flour consumption continued and reached 112 pounds per person in 1967.

It is clear and significant, from the standpoint of the total economy and the conservation of the basic resources, that the higher the level of living the greater will be the quantity of goods required to satisfy the wants of the people. As long as the people of the United States have available a large and productive acreage for agriculture, have access to large mineral treasures, employ fully the power resources available, and apply intelligence in the development and utilization of resources, the present high level of living can be maintained and improved, particularly for many underprivileged groups in the population. To say that all these things can be done does not mean that they will be achieved immediately. For one or many reasons the economy may fail to make the necessary readjustments, and fear may grip the people. In spite of the opportunities for progress, economic prostration may overwhelm a people, and temporarily a depression may wipe out many of the gains. But when prosperity returns new levels of consumption may be attained, and the stimulating effect of an expanding economy once more may bring hope to the people.

An Adequate Dietary Standard for the People of the United States. Providing an adequate diet for the people of the United States can be examined from a number of viewpoints. The diet of a family reflects somewhat the level of income or the amount of money available for the purchase of essential foods. For many families the inadequacy of the diet can be remedied by increasing the income so that more money will be available in the food budget. But an increase in income will not always provide a solution, for bad food habits tend to persist. Established culinary practices are altered slowly. By education and demonstration, progress can be made, particularly among the young women who may be induced to depart from the outmoded methods of their mothers. It should be a major objective of every family where there is responsible leadership to see that adequate quantities of the essential foods are available.

The farmers generally have a dietary advantage over many of the people who live in the urban communities. Because they are producers of a variety of food products, including dairy products, fruits, and vegetables, the farm families, with many exceptions among the renter class particularly, are well fed. People who live in the major cities have access to the large markets, and if the income is adequate and other conditions are favorable their families may have an adequate diet. The poor farm families, especially the sharecroppers and the farm laborers, usually are inadequately fed, and the cash income of these poor families is often so low that they are unable to supplement in any substantial way their home-grown food crops. Where the land resources are suitable, food production for home consumption should be sufficiently diverse to provide adequate diets. Surpluses of certain farm products may be available for sale in the market so that the cash can be used to purchase other essential foods. The farmers in the poor areas need supplementary sources of income which will permit them to purchase food that cannot be produced locally. In many instances limited land resources could be used to greater advantage if the people were adequately informed about their dietary needs and had sufficient energy and ambition to meet their food requirements.

In the cities the poor, underprivileged families live in the midst of plenty but, because of low income and little knowledge of what constitutes an adequate diet, are ill fed. These people, however, although much too large a group to receive adequate assistance, are the beneficiaries of the good works of the organized charities and the tax-supported relief agencies.

Consumption of Food per Person. The character of the diet consumed by a people greatly affects the area required to feed the population. In the United States in 1964 only 286,708,000 acres of harvested cropland were used to produce the foodstuffs and fibers used by a population of nearly 195,000,000, or approximately 1.5 acres per person. In this are included the areas used to produce fibers and other inedible products and the exportable surpluses.

Because of the high standard of living the area required to supply the various food products is comparatively large. The relatively low density of the population permits the use of extensive areas with relatively low average yields as compared with the older agricultural areas of Europe and the Orient.

The Food Groups. For convenience the several food items that make up the diets of the American people are grouped as follows:

Milk
Potatoes, sweet potatoes
Dry beans, peas, nuts
Green and yellow vegetables
Tomatoes, citrus fruits
Other vegetables and fruits
Meat, poultry, fish
Eggs
Grain products
Fats, oils
Sugar, sweets

These are the foods that in combination provide the inadequate, the staple, and the quality diets of the people. From these the people secure the essential nutrients of proteins, carbohydrates, fats, minerals, vitamins, and the food energy expressed in calories. Slowly and progressively, in peace and in war, in good times and bad, and as greater knowledge of foods becomes available, these several food groups increase or decrease in relative importance.

From the accompanying data it is clear that there has been a number of significant changes in the diet of the American people (Table 5). Generally the changes indicate an improvement in the level of living. Since World War II there have been notable increases in the consumption of meat and poultry products. The carbohydrate content of the American diet has declined, except for sugar.

Table 5. Per Capita Consumption of Major Food Commodities

	1963	1964	1965	1966	1967
Meat	169.3	174.5	166.7	170.5	177.6
Fish	10.7	10.5	10.9	10.6	10.6
Poultry products	30.7	31.0	33.3	36.0	37.2
Eggs (number)	317	318	314	313	324
Fluid milk and cream (milk equivalents)	307	304	301	296	286
Fats and oils	46.3	47.5	47.7	48.5	48.2
Butter	6.9	6.8	6.4	5.7	5.5
Potatoes and sweet potatoes	111.3	110.3	108.1	113.3	115.0
Fresh vegetables and melons	101.0	98.3	98.1	98.0	100.3
Citrus fruits	22.1	26.1	29.0	29.0	31.6
Wheat flour	113	114	113	111	112
Sugar	96.6	96.5	96.4	97.4	96.9

[Source: *National Food Situation,* Economic Research Service, U.S.D.A., Washington, D.C., February 1968.]

Fats and oils have changed little during the past 20 years.

Food Energy. In the United States where the quantity of food is relatively abundant the number of calories per day is high as compared to the standards of other countries. In the 40-year period from 1909 to 1949 the energy represented by the average disappearance of food varied from 3170 to 3560 calories per person per day. The highest totals were attained in the period from 1909 to 1912 when the food energy consumed exceeded 3500 calories per day. A low of 3120 calories was reached in 1935 when economic conditions limited the quantity of food purchased by the American people. In the period just before World War II the foods consumed were equivalent to 3250 calories per person per day. During the war the calories increased slightly to 3370 in 1945. No doubt the number of calories would have been somewhat higher except for rationing which greatly reduced the per capita consumption of sugar. In the late 1950's the average consumption of food expressed in calories was 3200 per person. In 1967 it was 3180 calories.

The high levels of food consumption over a long period of years may be expected to continue as a distinctive feature of the family economy. Although many people may be living and working on diets that are inadequate in some significant way, the energy available from the food consumed is relatively high. A decline in food energy need not be regarded as an unfavorable trend provided the diets are improved in other respects.

The Protective Foods. As knowledge about nutrition has increased in the United States, dietary standards have been established which involve more than calories, proteins, carbohydrates, fats, and oils. It is now recognized that certain minerals, such as calcium, phosphorus, and iron, and vitamins are essential ingredients of a proper diet. Foods that contain these necessary substances are classed as the protective foods, which, if consumed in proper quantities, prevent the insidious deficiency diseases. These protective substances include vitamin A and ascorbic acid (vitamin C) which are available in green and yellow vegetables; thiamine and niacin which are contained in meat, poultry, and fish; and riboflavin contributed by milk. A suitable diet must include the foods that will supply the necessary quantities of protein, carbohydrates, fats, minerals, and the protective substances so necessary to meet the energy requirements of the individual consumer and at the same time maintain his physical well-being over the years.

In planning for a permanent agriculture for the United States many programs and objectives must be considered. But the agricultural use of the land should be so organized that adequate quantities of food are produced to meet the dietary needs of the people.

Food Consumption and Income. There is a significant relationship between the money income of the family and the consumption of food. The people with the lowest incomes are unable to purchase the various food products that make up a quality diet but must be content with the less expensive foods that constitute the so-called staple diet. The more nutritive and protective foods usually require more money in the food budget than the families in the lowest income classes can afford. The relationship between food consumption and money income is characterized by complexities.

The consumption of individual foods differs greatly among the several income classes. After a family receives a sufficient income to purchase adequate quantities of fluid milk, an increase in income does not step up the consumption of milk. The quantity of meats consumed, or at least the money spent, increases with the family income. Not only is there an increase in consumption of meat among families with the large incomes, but there is generally a shift from pork to beef and lamb. In the case of grain products, particularly flour, an increase in the family income usually means a decrease in the consumption of bread. The lowest income classes consume flour and meal because they cannot afford the more expensive quality foods. Families with large incomes do not consume proportionately large quantities of fats. Apparently the level of income does not affect greatly the quantity of fats consumed, but people with larger incomes probably buy the more expensive fats, such as butter. The per capita consumption of butter in the 3-year period from 1947 to 1949 averaged 10.6 pounds per year, but by 1967 consumption had declined to 5.5 pounds. In the same period the per capita consumption of margarine increased from 5.6 to 10.5 pounds.

The dietary use of large quantities of refined sugar has long been a significant feature of American food habits. Between 1935 and 1939 the per capita consumption of sugar averaged 96.5 pounds annually. During the war period the quantity was reduced substantially by rationing and in 1945 was only 73.6

pounds. In 1967, however, the consumption was up to 96.9 pounds. Sugar has long been so cheap in the United States that most families are able to buy the quantities needed. Over half the sugar consumed in the United States is imported from overseas sources, whereas essentially all the wheat and potatoes consumed in the domestic market are produced at home. This situation poses a significant land-use problem, for the continued importation of large quantities of sugar must be counterbalanced by exports. In effect we may be exporting carbohydrates in the form of wheat in order to purchase sugar.

Fruits and vegetables are of major importance in the diet. With an increase in the family income the quantity increases. This is especially true of the protective foods, such as the green vegetables and citrus fruits. Between 1935 and 1939, the per capita consumption of citrus fruits averaged 48.9 pounds annually. The quantity consumed declined to 22.1 pounds in 1963 and then increased to 31.6 pounds in 1967. In the same period the use of canned and frozen fruit juices increased substantially. Much of this increased consumption probably benefited the people of the middle and higher income groups, but these protective foods are available in limited quantities to the families of the lowest income groups.

During World War II when rationing was in effect, meat products were in short supply and it was suggested that grain products, particularly bread, be substituted for meat. Enriched white bread and whole wheat bread could partially replace meat and at the same time maintain high nutritive standards at much lower costs to the consumer. However, when the family income is high, people in the United States prefer more meat and less bread in their diet. Under such conditions it usually is profitable to use the grain to increase the supply of meat which is in demand by the high-income families. In 1967, the per capita consumption of meat was 177.6 pounds.

The federal government through the various activities of the Department of Agriculture and other agencies has made significant progress in advancing nutritional standards of the people. In 1967, 3.1 billion school lunches were served to 18.5 million children in 73,000 schools. Other programs brought nutritional benefits to additional thousands of children. Through the Special Milk Program the federal government reimbursed the participating schools for part of the half-pint of milk served to the school children. Under the Child Nutrition Act of 1966, 80,000 children were served breakfast in a number of selected schools. The Food Stamp Program in 1967 permitted 2.2 million persons to purchase certain foods at greatly reduced prices. The Department of Agriculture annually distributes great quantities of surplus foods to schools, institutions, and needy families. This program includes such foods as meat, oil products, poultry, fruits, vegetables, orange juice, peanut butter, and dry beans. The Department also carries on special compaigns to help the producers to market the foods available in abundance under the Plentiful Food Program.[16]

Nutritionists are aware that many people in our affluent society are not well fed. People on welfare and others with low incomes may be unable to purchase quality foods and as a consequence their diets are high in carbohydrates but low in proteins and the protective foods. Even in families with adequate incomes many may not prepare and consume properly balanced meals. Too many people, especially school children and young adults, are skipping breakfast, snacking at odd hours, and generally making it difficult for the mother to see that her family is well fed. Crash diet programs may remove the excess pounds but leave the dieter undernourished in some respect.

[16] For a more extended statement on these several programs see Freeman, *op. cit.*, pp. 85–100.

RURAL EDUCATION
AND CULTURE

In maintaining the high production on the arable lands of the United States it is important that the people who live on the farms enjoy and share with the city dwellers the comforts and advantages of our material culture. As the farmer assumes the responsibility for extending the cultivated areas by draining the wet lands, clearing the forests, and irrigating the dry lands, he must secure for himself better educational opportunities for his children and improved dental and medical services for his family. Pioneer conditions of living have lasted too long in the farming areas. Farm people are anxious to have the benefits of electricity, running water, indoor plumbing, power machinery, and the automobile, so that life on the farm will be attractive, healthful, and satisfying to all members of the family. The telephone, radio, television, and other means of communication have overcome much of the isolation so long characteristic of life in the country. Farm families can participate in and enjoy the attractions of the city and still retain a strong attachment to the land which is so necessary in a long-range program of soil conservation and the maintenance of high productivity of the land.

Direction of Migration as a Factor. The prospect for rural culture, like that for a high standard of living, depends in large measure on the character, extent, and direction of rural-urban migration. If migration from the farms to the cities continues, there will be important readjustments in the agricultural economy. Except for a brief interval in the mid-1930's and immediately at the end of World War II when demobilization returned many servicemen to the rural areas, the cityward migration has been relatively more important than the movement from the cities to the rural areas. The relatively higher birth rate in the rural areas, particularly in the

poor farming areas, has tended to maintain the more or less steady migration of people from the rural areas to the urban communities.

Although people of all ages are involved in the migration to the city, it is the loss of the youth from the farms that is regarded as most serious both economically and culturally. When whole families including the young children move to the city, they relieve the population pressure on the land. But when the youth from the farms migrate to the cities when they attain the working age the rural areas suffer a serious loss. The farm families and the rural community have shared in the cost of their rearing and their education, and the cities become the beneficiaries without assuming a fair share of the costs. The migration of the farm youth to the cities without a counter movement of city youth to the country results in an important net loss to the rural areas.

The farm areas lose in other ways also, particularly when the farmer and his wife die and the estate is divided among their children. In many instances part of the estate goes to the children who live in the city and part to those who remain on the farm. It usually becomes necessary for those who retain the farm to mortgage the land to pay off the brothers and sisters who have moved to the city. The interest payments represent a further drain from the farm for the benefit of city people.

This regular outflow from the rural areas helps to maintain the general upward trend of the urban population. At the same time it tends to reduce the pressure of population in the rural areas. If high farm incomes as well as production can be maintained, there is an opportunity to improve the standard of living. If the income is not needed to provide the creature comforts of a large family, funds will be available for electrification of the farm, modernization of the home, an automobile, and other labor-saving equipment. Simultaneously, the rural areas with higher fertility can make a significant contribution to the labor force of the urban communities and perhaps secure better living conditions for those who remain on the land.

Rural Electrification. Electricity, like good roads and the automobile, has been one of the most important factors in improved living conditions in rural areas. Electricity in the home means more than better lighting. It lightens the work of the housewife by making available to her many labor-saving appliances. The farmer's work is greatly facilitated by electric grinders, drills, feed mills, and other current-using machines. The operation of a home water system is made possible by the availability of electricity.

In the period of 30 years from 1935 to 1965, electricity became readily available to the rural population. Not all farmers and other people who live in rural areas can afford to use this available electrical energy. After the Rural Electrification Administration was created by Executive Order on May 11, 1935, electrification in rural areas moved forward. Electrical energy is supplied from both government financed and the privately owned utilities.[17] The small generators which many farmers had installed were inadequate to meet their many needs, so they welcomed the electrical service from the large and more reliable central stations. "A quarter century of progress has put electricity at the door of nearly every farmer in America." [18] The Rural Electrification Administration, a somewhat controversial agency, can take some credit for the extension of power lines to the rural areas, but the private utilities are the principal distributors of electric energy to the farmer-consumer.

The Migratory Farm Laborer. The benefits of improved living conditions have been un-evenly distributed among the rural people. The farm owner and the tenant, where tenancy is the first important step to ownership, have made important progress in securing the advantages of electricity on the farm, water systems, an automobile, and labor-saving appliances and equipment. But the poorer tenants, where tenancy is a way of life, and the migratory farm laborers commonly live under primitive conditions. Many of the seasonal farm laborers, often involving whole families, have a very low annual income, are ill housed, and are denied many of the benefits of a well-established community in respect to schooling, medical service, and public relief in case of need. In 1939, John Steinbeck, in *The Grapes of Wrath,* called the nation's attention to the people of the dust bowl who were driven from their land by drought and low prices of the depression years of the 1930's. The seasonal laborer who moves from one strawberry area to another and from one fruit-picking area to another and who moves into the sugar-beet area at peak periods of work has received sympathetic consideration by Carey McWilliams.[19] These migrants as well as the land owners must share in the improved conditions of life that are spreading into the rural areas.

Economic Security. Land ownership, owner-operated farms, and the integrity of the farm family are the foundations of farm life in rural America. From time to time adverse forces have been operative and the stability of the agricultural industry has been in doubt. Farm tenancy has increased alarmingly in many areas. Corporate ownership of farmlands and large-scale operation have become a challenge to the small owner-operated farm. As new patterns of agriculture are introduced into the farming areas, the farmer retains his basic political and human rights to participate in the new developments and movements

---

[17] John H. Pixse, Jr., "Electricity Comes to Farms," *Power to Produce, The Yearbook of Agriculture, 1960,* Government Printing Office, Washington, D.C., pp. 69–75.

[18] *Ibid.*, p. 69.

[19] *Ill Fares the Land,* Little, Brown and Co., Boston, 1942.

and to share with the other citizens the material and cultural benefits that accrue to the nation.

Family living on the farms of the United States has been improved by the Extension work of the U.S. Department of Agriculture. In nearly 3000 county offices the Extension personnel make their services available to the general public, but special attention is given

to the young marrieds, adolescents, disadvantaged, and senior citizens.[20] The programs of the 4-H clubs are developed and expanded with the help of adult leaders in the local communities, releasing the professional Extension workers for general program planning and other essential services.

[20] Freeman, *op. cit.*, p. 96.

References

Ackerman, Joseph, Marion Clawson, and Marshall Harris, editors, *Land Economics Research,* Farm Foundation, Resources for the Future, The Johns Hopkins Press, Baltimore, 1962.

Agricultural Statistics (Annual), U.S. Department of Agriculture, Government Printing Office, Washington, D.C.

Barlowe, Raleigh, *Land Resource Economics,* Prentice-Hall, Englewood Cliffs, New Jersey, 1958.

Brady, Nyle C., editor, *Agriculture and the Quality of the Environment,* Publ. 85, American Association for the Advancement of Science, Washington, D.C., 1967.

Clawson, Marion, *The Federal Lands Since 1956—Recent Trends in Use and Management,* The Johns Hopkins Press, Baltimore, 1967.

————, *Land for Americans,* Rand McNally & Company, Chicago, 1963.

————, *The Land System of the United States,* University of Nebraska Press, Lincoln, 1968.

————, *Man and Land in the United States,* University of Nebraska Press, Lincoln, 1964.

————, *Policy Directions for U.S. Agriculture: Long Range Choices in Farming and Rural Living,* The Johns Hopkins Press, Baltimore, 1968.

Clawson, Marion, R. Burnell Held, and Charles H. Stoddard, *Land for the Future,* Resources for the Future, The Johns Hopkins Press, Baltimore, third printing, 1968.

Clawson, Marion and Charles L. Stewart, *Land Use Information,* The Johns Hopkins Press, Baltimore, 1966.

Crops in Peace and War: The Yearbook of Agriculture, 1950–1951, U.S. Department of Agriculture, Government Printing Office, Washington, D.C., 1951.

Dewhurst, J. Frederic and Associates, *America's Needs and Resources, A New Survey,* The Twentieth Century Fund, New York, 1955.

Economic Policy for American Agriculture, The Research and Policy Committee, New York, January 1956.

Farm Population, Net Migration from the Rural-Farm Population, 1940–1950, United States Department of Agriculture, Statistical Bulletin 176, Government Printing Office, Washington, D.C., 1956.

Food and Agriculture, A Program for the 1960's, U.S. Department of Agriculture, Government Printing Office, Washington, D.C., 1962.

Food, The Yearbook of Agriculture 1959, U.S. Department of Agriculture, Government Printing Office, Washington, D.C.

Grass, The Yearbook of Agriculture 1948, U.S. Department of Agriculture, Government Printing Office, Washington, D.C.

Harris, Chauncy D., "Agricultural Production in the United States: The Past Fifty Years and the Next," *The Geographical Review,* Vol. XLVII, 1957, pp. 175–193.

Haystead, Ladd and Gilbert C. Fite, *The Agricultural Regions of the United States,* University of Oklahoma Press, Norman, Oklahoma, 1955.

Higbee, Edward, *The American Oasis, The Land and Its Uses,* Alfred A. Knopf, New York, 1957.

————, *Farms and Farmers in an Urban Age,* Twentieth Century Fund, New York, 1963.

Irving, George W., Jr. and Sam R. Hoover, *Food Quality,* American Association for the Advancement of Science, Washington, D.C., 1965.

Land, The Yearbook of Agriculture 1958, U.S. Department of Agriculture, Government Printing Office, Washington, D.C.

Mighell, Ronald L., *American Agriculture: Its Structure and Place in the Economy,* Census Monograph Series 1, For the Social Science Research Council in cooperation with the U.S. Department of Agriculture, Agricultural Research Service, and the U.S. Department of Commerce, Bureau of the Census, John Wiley & Sons, New York, 1955.

Ottoson, Howard, editor, *Land Use Policy and Problems in the United States,* University of Nebraska Press, Lincoln, 1963.

A Place to Live, The Yearbook of Agriculture 1963, U.S. Department of Agriculture, Government Printing Office, Washington, D.C.

Protecting Our Food, The Yearbook of Agriculture 1966, U.S. Department of Agriculture, Government Printing Office, Washington, D.C.

Schmid, A. Alan, *Converting Land from Rural to Urban Uses,* Resources for the Future, Washington, D.C., 1968.

Science for Better Living, The Yearbook of Agriculture 1968, U.S. Department of Agriculture, Government Printing Office, Washington, D.C.

Science in Farming, The Yearbook of Agriculture, 1943–1947, U.S. Department of Agriculture, Government Printing Office, Washington, D.C., 1947.

Tisdale, Samuel L. and Werner L. Nelson, *Soil Fertility and Fertilizers,* The Macmillan Co., New York, 1956.

United States Census of Agriculture 1959, A Graphic Summary of Agricultural Resources and Production, Special Reports, Vol. V, Part 6, Chapter 3, U.S. Department of Commerce, Government Printing Office, Washington, D.C., 1962.

United States Census of Agriculture 1959, A Graphic Summary of Land Utilization, A Cooperative Report, Vol. V, Part 6, Chapter 1, U.S. Department of Agriculture and U.S. Department of Commerce, Government Printing Office, Washington, D.C., 1962.

The World's Food Problem, 2 volumes, President's Science Advisory Committee, Washington, D.C., 1967.

Part 3

CARL H. STRANDBERG

Director, Alameda County
Water District
Member, California Water
Pollution Control Association

CHAPTER 8

Water Pollution

INTRODUCTION

Water pollution is emerging as a threat to all mankind, but like an iceberg, only a small tip of the danger which lurks below can be seen on the surface. Environmental pollution, which includes water pollution, could end all life as we know it on earth. The threat of a *Silent Spring,* so vividly described by Rachel Carson, aroused most Americans to the problems which beset us, and showed many for the first time how important water is as a natural resource. Polluted water is water which has been abused, defiled in some way so that it is no longer fit for some uses. Prevention of water pollution is a major challenge confronting mankind and is a major objective of all efforts for the conservation of natural resources.

All of mankind has one great common bond: The male human body is about 67 percent water by weight; the female human body is about 52 percent water by weight. These percentages demand more than halfway cooperation; they demand the best from all of us.

As we shall see, the "dirty world" of water pollution is broad and complex, and just get-ting a grasp on it, so that it can be discussed intelligently, presents problems. We are all different in some way, yet each of us has a need for our "fair share" of water. Since we are different, many of the priorities which we set for use of that "fair share" compete and conflict with the priorities set by others. As a result, the mental images which each of us forms when he thinks of water pollution rarely match with those conceived by others. When compared in discussions with others, they produce, in fact, results much like those which might stem from several blind persons examining, then describing, an elephant.

WHAT IS WATER POLLUTION?

Several definitions of water pollution have been advanced. A definition advanced by the U.S. Public Health Service [1] is: "Water pollution is the presence of any foreign substance (organic, inorganic, radiological, or biological) in water which tends to degrade the quality so as to constitute a hazard or impair the usefulness of water."

[1] U.S. Public Health Service, *Drinking Water Standards,* item 6, 1962, p. 1.

189

A second definition, advanced by the Federal Water Pollution Control Administration,[2] is that pollution includes "discharges of wastes, including radioactive or other substances, actually or potentially harmful to such uses and alteration of the properties of waters in such a way as to be harmful, including temperature, taste, turbidity, or odor." It is further stated that discharges which conform with approved water quality standards are not "pollution." This limitation is generally disagreed with by conservationists and many public health authorities on grounds that it sets double standards for harmful substances.

"Pollution" has been cited in, and accepted by, courts of law as being "any impairment of water quality that makes water unsuitable for beneficial use." [3]

A definition advanced by the United States Senate [4] is more expressive. This definition is that "water pollution is the adding to water of any substance or the changing of water's physical characteristics in any way which interferes with its use for any legitimate purpose." This definition is very broad. Keep it in mind, and we will examine it in detail as we progress into this vital subject.

The term "water quality" is intimately related to water pollution. Polluted water is water which has more "negative" qualities than it does positive ones.

Water quality refers to the physical, chemical, and biological characteristics of water. The physical characteristics of water include temperature, clarity, and similar qualities. Chemical water quality characteristics include the presence, and amount, if present, of organic and inorganic substances in solution,

and the way that these substances are bonded or dispersed within the molecular structure of water. Biological water quality characteristics include identity, impact, and inventory or organisms which are present.

Water quality also includes analyses and evaluation of the ecological characteristics of a given body of water. These characteristics show whether organisms which attack humans can survive in the water being examined. These characteristics are determined, usually, by evaluation of epidemiological criteria, which are based on the presence and number, if present, or Escherichia coliforms (Abbreviated E. coli), which are bacteria of human fecal origin.

"Contaminated water" has a more serious definition. It is water which is so badly polluted that it is toxic to higher mammals, including humans.

THE CONSEQUENCES OF WATER POLLUTION

The American Medical Association has cited eight consequences of water pollution.[5] These are:

1. Disease transmission through infection.
2. Poisoning of man and animals.
3. Detrimental effects on aquatic life.
4. Creation of objectionable odors and unsightliness.
5. Cause of unsatisfactory quality of treated water.
6. Impairment of shellfish culture.
7. Excess mineralization.
8. Destruction of aesthetic values.

This list itemizes only the basic consequences of water pollution. Almost everything we do depends on water in some way, and any im-

---

[2] Suggested State Water Pollution Control Act (Revised), November 1965.

[3] Frank E. Moss, *The Water Crisis*, New York, 1967, p. 64.

[4] United States Senate Select Committee on National Water Resources, Committee Print No. 9, January 1960 (86th Congress, second session), p. 1.

[5] Harold M. Erickson, "The Nature of Water Pollution," *Proceedings of the AMA Congress on Environmental Health Problems*, Chicago, May 1 and 2, 1964, pp. 82–85.

pairment caused by water quality is a "consequence of pollution."

Several attempts have been made to group pollutants into classes or categories. Perhaps the most widely used system is that advanced by the Division of Water Supply and Pollution Control, forerunner of the Federal Water Pollution Control Administration.

This list specifies the following groups:

1. Sewage and other oxygen-demanding wastes.
2. Infectious agents.
3. Organic chemical exotics.
4. Other chemical and mineral substances.
5. Sediments.
6. Radioactive substances.
7. Heat.

This classification appears to cover the five principal types of effects which may stem from different types of pollutants. These include: (1) Contaminating, toxic, or poisonous effects; (2) addition of suspended solids; (3) deoxygenation; (4) addition of nontoxic salts; and (5) heating of water.

WHAT IS WATER?

At first glance, this may appear to be a vapid question, but think about it a bit. Water is one of the most common substances on earth and probably for this reason is one of the most overlooked, misunderstood substances. The physical and chemical nature of water must be understood, though, if one is to understand water pollution. These factors govern the utility of water, and when one or more of them is changed in any way, one or more of the utilitarian functions of water may be interferred with in some way, creating pollutant conditions. Several years ago the engineer Thompson King epitomized the water problem as follows: "Of all substances that are necessary for life as we know it on earth, water is by far the most important, the most familiar and the most wonderful; yet most

people know very little about it." [6] As a substance, water is odorless, colorless, and tasteless. Due to its unique atomic structure, it is paramagnetic. In pure form, it has great dielectric properties. Water may actually be any one of thirty-nine different substances. This is true because water, H_2O, consists of a unique molecular form which combines two hydrogen and one oxygen atoms together. Since there are three isotopes of each, the total number of combinations which may be assembled equals $(3!)^2 + 3$ (3 factorial squared plus 3), or 39. Water is, therefore, a polymer, or substance which has different atomic weights, even though composed of the same percentages of the same elements.

Up until this time, the percentages of each of the several forms of water have remained constant, to the best of our knowledge. There is fear, however, that atomic fusion processes (which are currently being tested for the generation of electric power) may upset this balance. These systems may modify all life as we know it by grossly increasing the quantity of the hydrogen isotope tritium.[7]

The Laws of the Conservation of Matter and the Conservation of Energy are basic to our understanding of water. These Laws may be combined to state that "the total quantity of matter and energy which is available in the universe is fixed."

As a chemical, water is unique. It is a compound of great stability, a remarkable solvent, and a powerful source of chemical energy. Because of its unique atomic structure as shown in Fig. 1, it draws away from most organic substances, but *toward* most inorganic substances. This characteristic affects its ability to assimilate wastes and its ability to be purified. Its attraction to inorganic substances includes

[6] Luna B. Leopold, Kenneth S. Davis, and the Editors of *Life*, *Water*, Life Science Library, 1966, Introduction.

[7] Lamont Cole, "Can the World be Saved?" Annual Meetings of the American Association for the Advancement of Science, December 27, 1967.

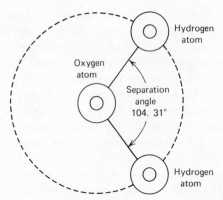

Fig. 1 The molecular structure of water. Water molecules appear out of balance, because the two hydrogen atoms are deeply imbedded and are separated by an angle of 104.31° rather than being positioned on opposite sides of the molecule. Positioned as they are, hydrogen and other atoms struggle to fill the 254.69° region opposite the two hydrogen atoms. The force of this attraction creates the "hydrogen bond," and accounts for much of water's unique solvent ability and other powers, including its paramagnetic properties.

self-attraction, in a way that allows water molecules to cling together more tenaciously than those of certain metals. Water expands on freezing, rather than contracting as do most substances. Because it expands, it becomes less dense, accounting for the fact that ice floats. It can absorb and release more heat than most common substances, which is an invaluable capability industrially. Paradoxically, though, it is the reason why one of the more serious forms of pollution in some areas— thermal pollution—has developed.

HISTORICAL ASPECTS OF WATER POLLUTION AND ITS CONTROL

If we are to gain a good understanding of water pollution as its exists in the United States today, we have to go back into history. We have to gain an appreciation of the water pollution problems which have plagued mankind for years, in this country and in others.

From a settlement standpoint, America is still a relatively "young" country, and many of the problems which we are now beginning to face appeared in Europe and in Asia long ago. Solutions were found for some of the problems which developed; many problems all over the world remain unsolved.

Perhaps the first formal recognition of pollution in the New World stems from an event in what is now California. In 1540, 2 years before what has been recognized as the discovery of California until just recently, a Spanish explorer, Lieutenant Francisco de Ulloa, departed Mexico on a voyage of discovery to the north, toward what is now California. This expedition literally vanished from the face of the earth, and it wasn't until just recently that anyone knew what had happened to it. In 1961, the skeletal remains of twenty-one conquistadors and their Mexican assistants were found in a cave near the U.S. Marine Corps Reservation at Camp Pendleton, near Oceanside, California. This search and discovery culminated more than 30 years of investigation in which, among other things, it had been learned that the members of this expedition had succumbed after drinking bad —"polluted"—water. Only one survivor is known to have returned to Mexico. A fascinating account of this early water pollution tragedy and of the events from which it stemmed entitled, "He Found the Trinidad's Tantalizing Treasure," appeared in the July 1965 issue of *True Magazine.*

Few very early explorers in America reported bad water until after colonization was well established and the early pioneers had begun to trek west. Then tales of bad water began to appear, most of them reporting water which contained salts or alkali which had been encountered in the desert regions in the Southwest.

Most existing water pollution problems stem from human concentration. When our primitive ancestors lived in widely separated family units, human body and household wastes could be disposed of easily. Later, when settlements developed, problems arose rapidly. The Chinese solution was to haul human body wastes out of town in carts, dry them in the sun, and use them for fertilizers. Most pathogenic organisms died this way, and although odors were strong during collection and hauling, they were soon killed by the sun.

The European (and later American) solution was to convert human body wastes into liquid form or fine suspensoids so that they could be drained or flushed away in ditches and gutters along roads. The horrible stench which resulted from these practices was "hidden under the rug," when the wastes were diverted into pipes underground and discharged into the same streams. This solution has proved generally unsatisfactory, and has lead to the development of modern sanitary engineering.

The story of modern sanitary engineering really starts in Europe. Problems along the Rhine River became a matter of major concern early. In 1875, it was reported that more than 100,000 salmon were exported to the Netherlands, but by 1930 the salmon industry had all but disappeared.[8]

Pollution problems were recognized early in England also. During the reign of George III, a member of Parliament reportedly wrote a letter to the Prime Minister complaining about the odor and the appearance of the Thames. He wrote the letter, not with ink, but with *water from the Thames.*

Cholera, typhoid, and other diseases in epidemic proportions led to recognition of the need to protect water resources. In 1865, the Royal Commission on the Pollution of Rivers came into being in England. During this same period in history, the "Genossenschaften"—a combination of public and private corporations with the joint responsibility of supplying water and removing, treating, and disposing of wastes—was organized in Germany.

Epidemiological criteria are based on the type of the bacteria in the waters. This measure of pollution was recognized in the 1880's and will be discussed in more detail later. It is a valid measure of the disease-transmitting aspects of polluted water because the E. coliforms and related organisms which are evaluated are normally found in human feces, and their presence in water indicates human body waste contamination.

Progress in the United States began not long after this. In the 1880's, the State of Massachusetts continued where the English Commissioners left off. In 1881, the Governor of Massachusetts appointed a commission to investigate the drainage from the Mystic and Charles rivers. In 1884, the Massachusetts Drainage Commission was formed. Creation of this Commission marks an important step in the affairs of man in America. Progress has accelerated since then, but much remains to be done—and let us hope that many who read this book will help carry the torch onward. All responsible political and social leaders recognize that the time has arrived for an environmental renaissance, and today's students are going to be tomorrow's leaders—the ones who will bring life to this dream of a better world.

LEGAL BASIS FOR FEDERAL WATER POLLUTION CONTROL

The basic Water Pollution Control Act in the United States, PL84-660 (33 USC 466), has been amended several times in the struggle for a better America. These include amendments of 1961 (PL87), the Water Quality Control Act of 1965 (PL89-234), and the Clean Waters Restoration Act of 1966 (PL89-753). This latter Public Law also amended the Oil Pollution Act of 1924.

In 1950, federal authorities developed a

[8] Walter A. Lyon, "Comparison of American and European Practice in Water Quality Control," National Symposium on Water Quality Standards, University of Michigan, Ann Arbor, July 1966.

"Suggested State Water Pollution Control Act" to aid the states in developing programs. State activity had been accelerated by special provisions of the Water Quality Act of 1965. With the dawn of our new decade every state in the Union has developed and had Water Quality Standards approved covering the interstate waters which originate in or flow through their boundaries.

Our government is charged with the right, duty, and obligation to take such action as is necessary to combat water pollution under the Police Powers. These are the rights of government to regulate the use of privately owned property for the health, safety, morals, welfare, and convenience of the public, with specific limitations. These are that the laws must be (1) uniform in application, (2) nondiscriminatory, and (3) for the general public welfare. Federal jurisidction in setting Water Quality Standards is founded on the Interstate Commerce Clause of the Constitution of the United States and is most directly applicable when streams or bodies of water extend across state boundaries, so that more than one state is involved. Boundary waters, such as those which separate the United States and Canada, are subject. to separate jurisdiction, because of the foreign policy which is inherent in the solution of problems posed. The waters separating the United States and Canada, for example, are governed by provisions of the regulations formulated by both the United States and Canada under the Boundary Waters Treaty signed January 11, 1909. This treaty led to establishment of the International Joint Commission, the agency to which problems, including those concerning water pollution, are referred for solution or correction.

Perhaps the most important words for the preservation of life on earth are contained in Paragraph 3, Section 10 of the Federal Water Pollution Control Act, as amended. These key words are: "Standards of quality established pursuant to this subsection shall be such as to protect the public health or welfare, enhance the quality of water, and serve the purposes of this Act. In establishing such Standards, the Secretary, the Hearing Board, or the appropriate state authority shall take into consideration their use and value for public water supplies, propagation of fish and wildlife, recreational purposes, and agricultural, industrial and other legitimate uses."

The amendments which were made by the Water Quality Act of 1965 authorize the states and the federal government to establish water quality standards for interstate (including coastal) water by June 30, 1967. Standards were, and are, to be formulated by the states. Within the republican form of government, such as is specified by the Constitution of the United States, "gut issue" changes like this should and can be made as close to the using public as possible. Water quality standards, after formulation and approval by the states, must then be reviewed by the Secretary of the Interior.

The approval procedure followed within this Department includes a thorough review of the technical aspects of the water which, although in conformance with the standards of an "upstream" state, does not violate the standards set by the states downstream.

The historical chronicle of water pollution and its control will, we hope, stand as a living testament of the environmental renaissance which continued existence demands.

The standards which are formulated are not rigid, unchanging sets of rules. They are subject to continuous review by all persons and groups who hold a share in the American Dream, and who can and will exercise the supreme power—the vote—to insure that their right to good water is not violated.

WATER QUALITY

The term "Water quality" embraces water pollution and a host of other critical elements which affect the water resources. Essentially, the term means the sum total of the physical, chemical, and biological aspects of natural waters which have an impact on human use and enjoyment of water resources. Man's use may be either direct or indirect. The term is all-inclusive.

Safe, fair, equitable use and protection of America's water resources demands that semantic problems be resolved first, so that rules can be established for the restoration or maintenance of realistic, but high, levels of water purity.

DEFINITION OF TERMS [9]

Water Quality Standards are plans which are established by governmental authority as a program for the prevention or abatement of water pollution. The terminology "Water Quality Objectives" may be used to mean the same thing.

Water Quality Criteria are scientific requirements on which decisions or judgments may be based concerning the suitability of waters to support designated uses. The terminology "Water Quality Requirements" may be used to mean the same thing.

Water Quality Standards consist of three elements:

1. Water Quality Criteria (or Requirements).
2. Water-Use Designations.
3. Implementation and Enforcement Plans.

Achieving water quality goals requires much more than research and data collection. Correction of current progressive deterioration and the restoration of water quality depends on people. America needs alert and responsible administrators at all levels of government and industry; well-trained scientists, engineers, and technicians; sympathetic legislators and stockholders; and an informed public.

The author's underlying purpose in writing

[9] FWPCA, *Water Quality Criteria*, p. vii.

this chapter is to add as many knowledgeable persons as possible to each of the listed groups.

A major step forward was taken when Water Quality Criteria were codified. This huge and complex task was conducted by establishing a special group, the National Technical Advisory Committee to the Secretary of the Interior. This group established criteria to provide guidance for all levels of government, industry, and all other concerned citizens in the war against pollution.

The National Technical Advisory Committee on Water Quality Criteria was organized into five subcommittees to investigate and define criteria for different purposes. These subcommittees were:

I. Subcommittee for Recreation and Aesthetics.

II. Subcommittee for Public Water Supplies.

III. Subcommittee for Fish, Other Aquatic Life, and Wildlife.

IV. Subcommittee for Agricultural Uses.

V. Subcommittee for Industrial Water Supplies.

Additional technical and administrative support was provided by the Federal Water Pollution Control Administration (FWPCA). This agency has since been redesignated the Federal Water Quality Control Administration.

In the sections which follow, each of these water-use designations will be discussed to show how each is impaired by pollution.

I. RECREATION, AESTHETICS, AND WATER POLLUTION

Five kinds of pollutants have the greatest impact on aesthetic value and must be kept out of waters. These are pollutants which: (1) settle and form objectionable deposits; (2) form mats or aggregations of slime, scum, oil, foam, etc; (3) produce objectionable odors, taste, color, or turbidity; (4) are toxic or which produce undesirable physiological responses in human, fish, other animal life, and plants (this category includes radionuclides which alter genetic responses); and (5) substances and conditions or combinations thereof which produce undesirable aquatic life. This group includes substances which remove dissolved oxygen excessively, stimulating growth of sludge worms and other creatures. Excessive phosphates and nitrates are included also. These stimulate eutrophication which is usually accompanied by the wrong kind of "population explosion."

Aquatic recreation embraces swimming, water skiing, and all related water contact sports. Fishing is one of America's most universal forms of recreation. It belongs in this water-use designation category, as well as in category III.

Aesthetics embraces all aspects of human enjoyment which depend on looking at, and thereby enjoying the appearance, odor, and noncontact "feel" of, water and its surrounding natural environment.

Water Pollution Hazards to Recreation. America's headlong "progress from an agrarian to an urban industrial society have altered many concepts and priorities regarding water use. These, in turn, have changed our categorization of pollution.

Outdoor recreation is a preferred form of leisure for millions of Americans, and bodies of water and shore areas serve as focal points for a significant part of this activity. Studies conducted by the Department of the Interior (Bureau of Outdoor Recreation) set forth in the classic report *Outdoor Recreation in America* (1962) report that quantity, accessibility, and quality of water are prime factors in selection of preferred recration areas by 90 percent of all Americans. Of all uses, "walking for pleasure" ranked first, swimming second, and fishing, boating, water skiing, and other secondary water contact activities followed closely. About 30 percent of all Americans

(not counting children under 12) participated in fishing.

Biological, Chemical, and Physical Criteria for Recreation. Epidemiological criteria are very important in setting recreation standards. These show the capability of the water to support infectious organisms. The organisms may, of course, transmit disease, infection, skin rashes, and related human illnesses.

Epidemiological criteria are based on counts (most probable number or MPN) of (E. coli) fecal (human or animal body waste) organisms per 100 milliliters of water. The National Technical Advisory Committee suggested an average not to exceed 2000 MPN per 100 milliliters, with a maximum of 4000 per 100 milliliters. These limits apply, except in specific mixing zones adjacent to outfalls, for any recreational use where participants might consume water, get it in their eyes, or otherwise be exposed to disease or infection.

Surface waters, with specific and limited exceptions, should permit fishing or hunting of waterfowl.

Acidity is an important criterion where body contact is permitted too. The pH should be within the range 6.5–8.3, except where due to natural causes, and in no case should pH be less than 5.0 or more than 9.0.

Have your eyes ever started to burn and hurt when you went swimming in a lake or stream? If so, pollution was probably to blame. Eye irritation characteristics of water are very important indicators of physio-chemical quality. Lacrimal fluid (the liquid comprising human tears) is an amazing substance. Tears are slightly basic (about pH 7.4), but have the capacity of bringing unbuffered solutions into a safe tolerance range (pH 6.3–8.6) from as acid as pH 3.5 to as basic as pH 10.5. Water is a foreign substance in the eyes, and if relatively free of dissolved solids and of low buffer capacity, pH values ranging from 5.0 to 9.0 should not harm the eyes; but even so, swimmers are wise to avoid water which is more acid than pH 6.5 or more basic than pH 8.3.

Water Pollution and Aesthetic Enjoyment. Surface water pollution should not kill life forms which have aesthetic value. As a bare minimum, this includes desirable species of game fish. Ducks, geese, swans, and shore birds should be capable of surviving in and near the water. Periodic ecological disasters, such as fish kills and damage to waterfowl, should not occur. Bad odors, noxious vegetation growths, trash, foam, scum, and similar types of pollution reduce or destroy human ability to enjoy being near the water.

Aesthetic losses extend beyond the periods during which pollution is physically present. If, for example, a body of water stinks at times, potential users will abandon plans for periodic visits. This can, of course, have a stunning economic effect on businesses which cater to tourism. A case history can be found near many dams. Septic conditions develop in the deep-water regions of some reservoirs. When reservoirs are drawn down, dissolved hydrogen sulfide in the septic water may gush forth, deluging surrounding areas with the odor of rotten eggs. Tourists rarely enjoy or return to such areas.

II. WATER POLLUTION AND SOURCES OF PUBLIC WATER SUPPLIES

We all agree that human consumption is the most important use of water. As has been stated, our bodies are largely made up of water. This water requires continuous replenishment and replacement, and it is obviously important that we make sure that drinking water is safe for human ingestion.

It may come as a surprise to many, though, that the "raw" or untreated water from which public supplies can be drawn need not be as clean as is required for some other beneficial uses. This is partly due to our superior tech-

nology in water purification, but primarily it is a tribute to the efficiency and capability of the public servants who give it life. The human body also is quite tolerant. Had our ancestors not been biologically tolerant and adaptive, they would not have survived. Unfortunately, all too few natural bodies of surface water, reservoirs, and almost all flowing streams are too polluted to be used without purification.

Minimum Criteria for Sources of Drinking Water. Table 1 lists the physical, chemical, and bacteriological water pollution limits which must be considered when raw (drinking) water supplies are being evaluated.

III. WATER POLLUTION: FISH, OTHER AQUATIC LIFE, AND WILDLIFE

All forms of aquatic life suffer from water pollution. A very complex problem exists, however. Fresh water, marine, and estuarine organisms vary widely in their ability to tolerate different kinds of pollution. Factors which may be safe for some may be deadly to others. Millions of fish have died in huge "fish kills" in recent years. Most of these have been attributed to pesticides. In addition to fish kills, millions of dollars damage has been caused by DDT contamination of fish. In the spring of 1969, Coho salmon were just beginning to reach the market from Lake Michigan. This step came at the end of a long trek to restore Lake Michigan following the disastrous effects of the lampreys which decimated the lake trout population. Disaster struck again when commercial fishermen attempted to sell the salmon. They had become contaminated with DDT and were considered unsafe to eat by the Food and Drug Administration.[10]

In the following section some of the water pollution problems which threaten fish, other aquatic life, and wildlife are discussed.

[10] *Minneapolis Tribune,* June 6, 1969.

Table 1. Surface Water Criteria for Public Water Supplies

Condition	Permissible Limit	Desirable
Physical		
Color (color units)	75	Less than 10
Odor	Minor	None
Temperature	(See text)	(See text)
Turbidity	(See text)	(See text)
Microbiological		
Coliforms	10,000/100ml	Less than 100/100ml
Fecal coliforms	2,000/100ml	Less than 20/100ml
Inorganic Chemicals (ppm)		
Arsenic	0.05	None
Barium	1.0	None
Boron	1.0	None
Cadmium	0.01	None
Chloride	250.0	Less than 25
Iron	0.3	Virtually absent
Lead	0.05	None
Manganese	0.05	None
Nitrates+Nitrites	10.0 (as N)	None
Zinc	5.0	None
Inorganic Chemicals (ppm)		
Cyanide	0.20	None
Detergent residue (Methylene Blue active substances)	0.5	None
Oil and grease	Virtually absent	None
Pesticides:		
Aldrin	0.017	None
Chlordane	0.003	None
DDT	0.042	None
Endrin	0.001	None

[Source: These data summarize types of pollutants and limits cited in *Water Quality Criteria,* FWPCA.]

Pollutants. Salts are serious pollutants. Salts of various types must be kept out of fresh waters, and changes and alterations of fresh water flows must be closely controlled in estuaries. Industrial wastes which contain toxic materials must be kept out of waters. Even minute amounts of lead, mercury, arsenic, the cyanides, and other substances may be deadly. These substances may obviously be poisonous to humans also. If the water body in question is used as a source of domestic water, an additional reason exists for preventing poisons from being "dumped."

Aquatic organisms are very sensitive to changes in acidity. The carbonate system of the water must be preserved if organic chemical functions are to continue. The accepted acidity range in fresh water is from pH 6.0 to pH 9.0. The survival range in salt water is narrower. Here the range is pH 6.7 to 8.5. Variations in acidity can have a tragic effect on wildlife, too, as will be discussed later.

Thermal pollution has been the subject of much debate. Extensive research has been conducted into both the good and the bad effects of discharging heated coolant water. Various species of fish respond differently to heat. It has been found that 93 degrees F is about the maximum which will support growth of catfish, carp, and other "tough" species. Lake trout, Atlantic salmon, and most other Salmonids require water no warmer than 48 degrees F for spawning and egg development. The State of Maryland conducted tests to determine preferences of game fish in 1960. Special fishing tackle was used which permitted measuring the temperature of the water near the bait when fish struck. It was found that fish schooled in the water downstream from thermal electric generating stations 9 months out of the year (October through June). Tests sponsored by the electric power industry show that oyster production improves when waters are raised somewhat and held constant. Pacific Gas and Electric Company diverted heated coolant water over spawning beds and nursery grounds in Humboldt Bay, where it was found that this practice improved growth of both clams and oysters. Countering this, though, it has been found that pathogenic bacteria like warmer water too. One type, deadly to salmon, threatens all salmon in the Columbia River system.[11] Heated coolant water may prevent ice from blocking areas so that they go septic in the winter in some areas. This beneficial effect has been noted in several northern areas where BOD (biological oxygen demand) loads are high.

Heat exposes a paradox, though, because although *some* heat is good *some* of the time, too much heat is always bad. A major problem caused by excessive temperature is oxygen starvation. Warm water will hold less dissolved oxygen in solution than will cooler water. Rapid changes in temperature can create lethal shock effects. Investigators have found that temperature changes, either increased or decrease, greater than 1 degree F per hour can be deadly to fish. There are many cases on record where fish have been at-

tracted to and become acclimatized to flows of heated coolant water below thermal electric generating stations. Later, when the plants have been shut down for repairs and cold water has replaced the hot water flows, the shock has killed the fish in the discharge zone.

Migrating fish require zones of passage, and if flows of heated coolant water or other pollutants block these passages, the effects create barriers which are as effective as dams in blocking migration.

Dissolved oxygen is vital to survival of most desirable forms of aquatic life. The salmonids (trout and salmon) require more oxygen than do most other species. In general, DO should never be below 6 ppm, where Salmonids are found. More DO is necessary over spawning beds. Here levels should never drop below 7 ppm.

Other types of fish can survive on less oxygen, to an absolute limit of about 2.9 ppm. All game fish require that DO levels remain at least 5 ppm or higher, however.

All types of materials which can be consumed by organisms exert a biological oxygen demand, or BOD, on the water. Those substances which may be reduced by (chemical) oxidation alone remove oxygen. These substances exert a chemical oxygen demand, or COD, stress.

Oil pollution can have a deadly effect on both fresh-water and marine organisms. Extensive data on oil pollution are given in the Industrial Pollution section of this chapter, but it is mentioned here because fish are prime victims of two of the most serious problems caused by oil pollution. A major problem is that oil removes a vast amount of DO (dissolved oxygen). In addition to this, many petroleum products will taint fish flesh. This will obviously reduce their commercial value and lower the recreational desirability of the area. Few sport fishermen will return to areas where the fish which are caught are unpalatable.

Low DO (particularly if hydrogen sulfide is

[11] "Interaction and Interdependence," a Conference on Man and His Environment, Environmental Sciences Institute, San Jose State College, San Jose, California, May 28–29, 1969.

also present) will ruin shellfish too. The gills and mantles of both clams and oysters will turn gray and their shells will turn black. If excessive copper is also present in the water, the gills and mantles may turn green. This will practically destroy their commercial value. Not all "green" oysters are victims of copper pollution, though. Certain diatoms, Navicula in particular, may give their flesh a bilious green color.

Turbidity and water color are serious pollutants for several reasons. One of the most serious impacts is that they block sunlight from reaching algae and aquatic vegetation. The result is that photosynthesis is retarded; when this occurs, a major source of oxygen is lost. Turbidity levels govern the depth of the euphotic zone. This is the depth at which 99.7 percent of the solar energy has been attenuated, absorbed, or scattered. Most of the primary productivity of the oceanic biomass is concentrated in this zone, furnished by phytoplankton. Quantitatively, these organisms are more important than the bottom algae and the rooted aquatic plants for supplying oxygen.

One of the major fears which has been voiced about the widespread use of pesticides is that they might retard or kill off this biomass. If this happened, of course, all life as we know it would cease. About 60 percent of the free oxygen in the air is provided by photosynthesis of green vegetation. The remaining 40 percent is produced by diatoms. DDT levels as low as 4 ppb impair these creatures.

Turbidity can have a drastic effect on clams. In tests which were conducted on hardshell clams (*mercenaria mercenaria*) 3 grams of nontoxic sediment was added to 1 liter of water. In even this dilute concentration, all test animals died.[12]

Turbidity effects often stem from masses of free-swimming organisms. The *Euglenophyta,*

[12] FWPCA, *Water Quality Criteria,* p. 75.

which cause "red tide" conditions, are a good example.

Toxic water pollutants belong in a special category. Any substance in excessive concentration may be toxic. Substances of unknown toxicity should be tested using bioassays. Standard methods have been developed for conducting these, and serious students should undertake studies in this area. Detergents, for example, are very toxic. Concentrations as low as 1 ppm are toxic to fish which are exposed for 24 hours or more. Most of the currently used detergents are "biodegradable," that is, they can be consumed by organisms. The detergents which they replaced used ABS (Alkyl-Benzene-Sulfonate) to create "suds, suds, and more suds," as one of the commercials used to brag. These detergents remained toxic much longer and were subject to biological concentration.

When detergents do decompose and are reduced to the basic inorganic chemical components, they may cause serious additional problems. Detergents contain much phosphorous, one of the most important fertilizers. When added to water, it stimulates algae and aquatic vegetation. These include many in the nuisance category, and these may form dense mats. Photosynthesis is generally accelerated during daylight hours. These processes may stimulate additional heat. While light falls on them, the plants produce oxygen, frequently exceeding 100 percent saturation. The excess free oxygen is added to the air. After sundown, though, these plants and other creatures which live on or near them may deplete all oxygen. Septic conditions may develop and exist just long enough to cause damage (kill fish and other desirable organisms, for example). After sunrise, photosynthesis starts again and oxygen is returned to the water. The damage may have already been done, however.

Additional undesirable results caused by toxic and other kinds of algae and aquatic vegetation are discussed in other sections of this chapter.

Most of the problems which stem from plant nutrients and nuisance organisms are concentrated in fresh water. Some problems extend into estuaries, but none has been reported in the open oceans. In a broad sense, though, the Sargasso Sea, which has been known for centuries as a place of mystery and filled with ocean weeds (actually the alga Sargassum), appears to have a nutrient imbalance.

Nuisance organisms are those which transmit disease (are pathogenic), cause odors, skin rashes, block filter screens, kill fish, or cause other problems. Prime examples are those which create the "red tide" fish kill problems, and the swarms of jellyfish which have plagued Chesapeake Bay for years. Nutrients may have a strong impact on aquatic animals as well as on aquatic vegetation. Given pollutants may kill selectively. The organisms which are killed off may serve as a biological control by maintaining predator pressure on a given desirable species. When this pressure is gone, the controlled species may experience a population explosion, exhaust their food supply, and thereby lead to their own destruction.

Many organisms have the unique ability to ingest and concentrate substances selectively. This capacity permits them to aid in purifying water. The organisms may acquire and carry substantial amounts of toxic material with no apparent harm to themselves. These steps start with minute organisms and are concentrated by "biological concentration." When these small creatures are eaten by larger varieties, toxic materials may be concentrated and the effects they cause magnified. This progression is shown in Figure 2.

The excessive DDT concentrations found in Coho salmon from Lake Michigan were probably acquired this way. Humans also concentrate DDT. Our bodies contain, on the average, about 11 ppm DDT, more than the legal limit for interstate transport of meat. Even more shocking is the fact that DDT compounds are concentrated in human milk so that a breast-fed baby in the United States receives, on the average, five times the U.N. recommended maximum.[13]

Water is the major initial source of the pesticides which are concentrated in our bodies. We (humans) serve as the ultimate concentrator when we eat fish or meat, or drink milk which acquired pesticides at some lower position in the food chain.

Wildlife. Water pollution has a shocking effect on wildlife. Most species which have become extinct within recorded history have done so because their environment has been "modified," usually because of pollution of some sort.

Wildlife requires water of a quality adequate to maintain health. A healthy animal is one which can survive a normal life span, display normal habits and migration patterns, and can reproduce successfully. As used here, wildlife includes all species of mammals, birds, reptiles, and amphibians which are found in a native habitat. Most of these creatures depend on the presence of surface water which is of relatively high quality. The water which will support wildlife is good for most other uses. It is axiomatic, also, that water which will support fish is capable of supporting waterfowl, and that water which will support waterfowl will support most other types of wildlife.

Certain factors—DO, pH, alkalinity, and salinity—deserve further study. They must be considered in their special relationship to the growth, health, and vigor of waterfowl and other wildlife, and their habitat interrelationships.

DISSOLVED OXYGEN (DO). Low DO is associ-

[13] Testimony before California State Legislature, 1969.

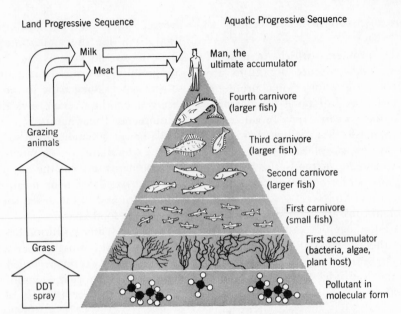

Fig. 2 Biological concentration occurs when relatively indestructible substances (DDT, for example) are ingested by lesser organisms at the base of the food pyramid. An estimated 1000 lbs. of plant plankton are needed to produce 100 lbs. of animal plankton. These, in turn, are consumed by 10 lbs. of fish, the amount needed by a man to gain one pound. The ultimate consumer (man) then, takes in the DDT taken in by 1000 lbs. of the lesser creatures at the base of the food pyramid, when he ingests enough fish to gain one pound. (By the author.)

ated with outbreaks of one of the deadliest killers of waterfowl—botulism. Botulism is caused by the organism *Clostridium botulinium*. This organism is a strict anaerobe. When temperature and organic residue (sludge) balances are right, the spores will germinate and multiply rapidly in the absence of oxygen. These conditions normally occur on the fringes of marshes and lagoons. Although all the factors which govern their production are unknown, it is generally accepted that if proper water circulation is maintained, DO kept high, and "black water" (biological residue, sludge bank, and perhaps low DO alone) conditions prevented, botulism outbreaks will be retarded, if not eliminated.

ACIDITY (PH). Variations in acidity can have a shocking impact on the capability of water to support wildlife. Acid mine drainage (AMD) has destroyed or seriously damaged

the waterfowl value of more than 4000 miles of streams in Appalachia.[14] This value has been destroyed largely because the aquatic plants and organisms upon which the ducks and geese depend for food have been destroyed. In August and September 1963, acidity near Back Bay, Virginia, dropped from the pH 7.7–8.5 range to pH 6.5. When it did, aquatic plant production dropped from 164 to 13 pounds per acre.

In general, submerged aquatic plants which are of greatest value as waterfowl foods (*Potomogeton perfoliatus*, wild celery, etc.) thrive best in waters which have a summer pH range of pH 7.0–9.2.

ALKALINITY. Generally, waters with reasonably high bicarbonate alkalinity are more productive of valuable waterfowl food plants.

[14] FWPCA, *Water Quality Criteria*, p. 94.

Radical fluctuations in alkalinity will upset plant communities drastically. Variations of 50 ppm would probably contribute to unstable conditions. Fluctuations of this magnitude are quite possible through diversion of irrigation waters and related physical changes.

SALINITY. Salt content in water may have a twofold effect on wildlife. It may have a direct effect on the life processes of some species. Salinity may also have an indirect effect by altering the aquatic environment.

Game birds (order Galliformes) are very sensitive to salt, and adult quail prefer dehydration to drinking water which would be deadly to juvenile chickens.

IV. WATER POLLUTION: FARMS AND RANCHES

Pollution can threaten the health and safety of all who work and live on farms. It can also threaten the health of farm crops and livestock, and in this way acts as a potential secondary infection source to all who handle or eat diseased farm foods and products.

Most outdoor recreational activities also take place near farms and ranches (or at least in rural areas). These too are affected by water pollution problems, as has been discussed previously.

Several sources of water are available in rural areas. These sources vary in quality and are susceptible to pollution in various ways. Rainfall provides most of the water which is needed for crops and livestock. Some of this water, particularly that which falls on the southeast sides of cities, on the downwind side of freeways, and through other areas which are subject to air pollution, may be polluted when it reaches the ground. Most of it, though, is relatively pure (except for slight acidity, natural in rainwater, which stems from the minute amount of carbon dioxide which is found in the air).

Cisterns and storage tanks are used to hold some of the water consumed on farmsteads.

The U.S. Department of Agriculture estimates that about three-fourths of the water which is used on farms comes from surface sources (streams, lakes, and ponds) and one-fourth from wells and springs. Water from springs, seeps, and shallow wells is apt to be heavily contaminated with bacteria. This is particularly true in areas where limestone underlies the area. Here, open solution channels, literally "under-ground rivers," may flow and come to the surface miles from the areas of origin as large springs. Since little opportunity exists for suspended and other material in transport or in solution to precipitate or to be filtered out, waste materials which have been picked up far away may be present in the water.

Water from deep wells may contain more dissolved materials. This may detract from the quality of the water which is drawn from them.

The agricultural revolution has brought about vast changes in rural areas. These include changes in farm and food handling procedures. Water pollution can have a far-reaching and dangerous impact on foods which are washed for sale and for delivery to processing plants for canning, freezing, or other treatment.

All water mixed with or used to wash fruits and vegetables should conform to PHS Drinking Water Standards.

Water used to wash milk-handling equipment and for cooling dairy products can have a strong effect on milk quality. Most milk which is sold for human consumption must conform with the USPHS Grade A Pasteurized Milk Ordinance. Conformance requires that water which is used for washing milk-handling equipment meet high standards.

Several types of nonpathogenic bacteria can pollute milk. Many types of algae, diatoms, and protozoa produce odors in water. These are easily transmitted to milk. One type, an iron bacteria, actually feeds on iron pipes. When the piping is washed, a slimy, mucoid layer may develop in it, perhaps partially blocking it. When milk is pumped through pipes which have been exposed to this water, it becomes contaminated and takes on a bad taste. Some organisms which are found around dairy barns are psychrophitic, or "cold-loving." They can survive and flourish in water which is almost at the freezing level. Many of these organisms are very resistant to chlorine and other disinfectants. Many of these organisms cause milk to sour very rapidly. It is obvious from the foregoing that great care must be taken to prevent microorganisms from entering milk.

Livestock Water Supplies. Domestic livestock represent an important segment of the complex, interdependent organization of the living things on earth. Both humans and animals occupy the paradoxical position of both contributing to, and being harmed by, pollutants, which they add to water. Fecal matter from each cow contributes about 5 PE (*Population Equivalents*) of organic waste daily. When (and if) this material is washed into waters it tends to contribute five times the oxygen stress (in BOD) contributed by human fecal matter. The purity of water consumed by livestock has far-reaching implications. Polluted water may kill cows or at least make them sick. This may obviously lower their milk production capability. Further, some substances may affect the quality of their milk in the same way that wild garlic and onion grass will ruin it.

Some elements dissolved in water are very serious pollutants. Selenium is one such substance. Molybdenum is another. It produces an ailment called molybdenosis. This ailment may be partially alleviated by increasing the amount of copper which the cattle consume. This must be done carefully because copper in excessive quantities is toxic in its own right.

Fish serve as valuable water quality indicators for many purposes. They are particularly valuable on farms and ranches where crop-dusting is allowed. Table 2 lists the toxic lev-

Table 2. Toxicity of Fish to Pesticides

Material	Toxic Concentration (ppm)	
Aldrin	0.02	
Chlordane	1.0	(Sunfish)
Dieldrin	0.025	(Trout)
Dipterex	50.0	
Endrin	0.003	(Bass)
Ferban fermate	1.0 to 4.0	
Methoxychlor	0.2	(Bass)
Parathion	2.0	(Goldfish)
Penta chlorophenol	0.35	(Bluegill)
Pyrethrum (Allethrin)	2.0 to 10.0	
Silvex	5.0	
Toxaphene	0.1	(Bass)

[Source: *Water Quality Analysis,* p. 131.]

els of several types of pesticides. If fish can live in livestock watering ponds, pesticides are rarely present, at least in toxic concentrations. This does not confirm that cattle and other farm animals may not act as biological accumulators, and in this way, ingest enough so that in time their flesh will become useless. Table 3 lists the volume of water consumed

Table 3. Normal Water Consumption of Livestock (These Data Indicate Biological Concentration Potential of Various Domestic Animals)

Animal	Water Consumed per Day (Gallons per Head)
Beef cattle	7–12
Dairy cattle	10–16
Horses	8–12
Swine	3– 5
Sheep and goats	1– 4
Chickens (per 100 birds)	8–10
Turkeys (per 100 birds)	10–15

[Source: FWPCA, *Water Quality Criteria,* p. 130.]

by several common farm animals. These data indicate their concentration potential. As has been emphasized, some pesticides are extremely toxic. Considering the volume of water which livestock consume and the fact that they may ingest additional pesticides from food sources, standards based on meat and milk are more valuable than are standards based on the amount present in water alone. It is generally recognized that water serves as a major transmission vector (vehicle) for many diseases (viral, parasitic, and fungal) which affect both animals and man. Water is, fortunately, less critical than food of other contact mechanisms for infection. Most lethal dose (LD_{50}) evaluations are based on mortality of animals to drugs and pollutants of various types. These supply evidence that water is a principal vector of such diseases as colibacillosis, swine erysipelas, leptospirosis, staphylococcosis, salmonellosis, and others. Some of these (salmonellosis in particular) have a strong effect on humans. Many thousands of persons in and near Riverside, California, were made violently ill by this disease in 1967. This epidemic was traced to a contaminated public water supply.

Mineral Pollutants and Livestock. Livestock may be sensitive to many types of natural mineral pollutants. Table 4 lists the suggested maximum concentrations of several pollutants which have been encountered. Let us examine some of these in more detail.

Table 4.

Substance	Suggested Maximum Concentration (ppm)
Arsenic	0.05
Cadmium	0.01
Chromium (hexavalent)	0.05
Lead	0.05
Selenium	0.01

ANTIMONY. Antimony may enter water supplies in the waste water from textile mills and tanneries. It is used as a mordant, or curing

agent, for killing certain bacteria. It is also used for the control of ants and other insects.

ARSENIC. Arsenic has been used for years as a poison. It is used as an agricultural insecticide, and care must be taken that it is not washed into, or does not otherwise enter, water supplies. Arsenate of lead is used for spraying apple trees, and accidents have occurred when spray equipment and tanks were washed and flushed.

BORON. Boron is found in many deserts or former desert areas, and may be a pollutant affecting livestock on the open range. It is very toxic to plants. Serious problems have developed in Southern California affecting irrigation waters. Concentrations of 2500 ppm inhibit animal growth.

CADMIUM. Cadmium salts are found in some waters which flow from areas which contain zinc sulfide deposits. It may also be found in waste water from plating operations, textile mills, and some chemical plants. This material has been associated with a disease which incapacitates zinc miners in Japan, known as osteomalacia (literally "dissolving of the bones"). It may have similar effects on livestock.

Toxic Algae. Some types of algae (especially those of the Blue-Green Division) are extremely toxic to livestock. Those of the Genus *Aphanizomenon flos-aque, Anabaena,* and *Anacystis* have been identified as responsible for numerous animal deaths.[15]

Pathogenic Organisms. The relationship between polluted waters and animal diseases is well established. Water is not as important a vector as food or as direct physical contact with sick or dead animals, but it is serious none the less.

One of the best examples of waterborne disease organisms which affect livestock is *bacillary hemoglobinuria.* This disease is found in

[15] Eugene Jackim and John Gentile, "Toxins of a Blue-Green Algae: Similarity to Saxitoxin," *Science,* November 22, 1968 p. 915.

both western North and South America. This disease may make its appearance when new areas are cleared and irrigated. To avoid this disease, irrigation and stock watering ponds should be managed to avoid cattail marshes, hummock grasses, and other environments of prolonged saturation.

Anthrax, a deadly killer of livestock, is caused by the organism *Bacillus anthracis*. This organism has a low survival rate in water, but animals which wade in water into which anthrax organisms have been washed may catch it.

Leptospirosis is probably the livestock disease most closely related to water today. It is transmitted by contact with water which contains animal urine (from infected animals). Rodents (rats and mice) are probably the primary source. Sheep, cattle, and hogs wading in water which has been infected may splash water on themselves, into their eyes, ears, and noses, or drink from infected sources.

Many types of animal diseases are associated with anaerobic conditions. Mineral content and acidity of water (pH) are undoubtedly important factors too. Many of these diseases cause nervous system derangements; tissue coagulation and liquification; blood hemolysis; and food poisoning. Organisms of the clostridia division are most frequently associated with these diseases.

Viruses. Viruses are classified by size, ether sensitivity, tissue effects, RNA and DNA activation, and other criteria. Viruses cause such recognizable diseases as pox and hog cholera. Ether sensitivity is an important criterion because it indicates the ability of the virus particles to survive in hostile environments, such as water. Small-sized particles which are resistant to ether are able to survive longer in water and are therefore more apt to transmit diseases over greater distances.

Parasitic Organisms. Parasitic organisms may pollute water when part of their life cycles involve a phase in water. Fortunately, very few of these organisms can survive alum

and other precipitants, settling, sand filtration, and chlorination. They may, however, pose a threat in raw water supplies. They threaten man as well as animals. Flukes of various types threaten both man and animals. They generally require snails as an intermediate host. Immature forms leave the snails and enter humans or animals by ingestion in water, or on food, or, in rare instances, by passage through the skin.

Tapeworms in animals do not commonly utilize water as a transmission medium, although those which attack humans do. These types utilize copepods or fish in their life cycles. Tapeworms have been observed by the author in lake trout which were caught in very deep water along the Minnesota-Ontario border. Their presence constitutes a unique form of biological pollution.

Water Quality and Crops. Primitive man's recognition that food plants grew best if they were watered initiated the agricultural revolution. Ancient history is filled with tales of huge engineering works which were designed and installed to irrigate crops in the Tigris and Euphrates valleys, in what is now Iraq. These works established the area as the "Fertile Crescent," and millions of people gained sustenance from the food crops which matured there. But in time, all of this wealth, this vast step forward in human development, withered and died. Great dams once existed in what is now Saudi Arabia and in the Holy Land too. All of the good, in the form of human nutrition, which was provided by these advances in human culture withered and died because of water pollution, primarily salt pollution.

Irrigation exposes two facets to water quality. First, the positive qualities which are needed to water crops. Second, the waste water aspect. "Used" irrigation waters contain salts, pesticides, fertilizers, and silt—anything which can be picked up in the fields where it is sprayed or channeled.

Irrigation Water Quality. Plants are very

sensitive to many substances which may be dissolved in water. Some of these substances improve plant growth, but those which are of major concern to us are those which are harmful.

Salts of various kinds, and various materials which are leached from the soil, or which stem from industrial operations as wastes constitute a dangerous threat to American agriculture in many areas of the country. Salts of various kinds distort the osmotic pressure of the soil solution so that plants may actually starve for water even though substantial quantities may be present. Plants have been observed to wilt in fields which appear to have adequate supplies of water present.

In addition to the effects of total salinity on osmotic soil-plant relationships, individual ions may have an effect on plant growth. Suggested trace element tolerances for various elements in irrigation waters are listed in Table 5.

This section only scratches the surface of the many ways in which water pollution affects farms, ranches, and the people who live on them or who use farm products. I hope that it has opened the door to new avenues of study, research, and action for all readers.

V. WATER POLLUTION AND INDUSTRY

Industry straddles the paradoxical hub of America's water pollution problems. Industry, in general, has more to lose from water pollution and more to gain from its control than does any other segment of Americana. Industry creates more pollution than does any other segment of society, yet it has taken more steps to clean up waste water and must spend more

Table 5. Trace Element Tolerances for Irrigation Waters [Greater Concentrations Are Considered To Be Agricultural (Toxic) Pollutants]

Element	Continuous Use (All Soils), ppm	Short-Term Use (On Fine Soils), ppm
Aluminum	1.0	20.0
Arsenic	1.0	10.0
Beryllium	0.5	1.0
Boron	0.75	2.0
Cadmium	0.005	0.05
Chromium	5.0	20.0
Cobalt	0.2	10.0
Copper	0.2	5.0
Fluoride	No tolerance limits, may be toxic	
Iron	No problems noted	
Lead	5.0	20.0
Lithium	5.0	5.0
Manganese	2.0	20.0
Molybdenum	0.005	0.05
Nickel	0.5	2.0
Selenium	0.05	0.05
Tin	No problems noted	
Tungsten	No problems noted	
Vanadium	10.0	10.0
Zinc	5.0	10.0

[Source: FWPCA, *Water Quality Criteria*, p. 152–154.]

to clean up process water than does the average public facility for production of domestic water.

Industrial water quality demands extend from water which is chemically pure (and therefore "polluted" because it will not sustain life) to "dirty" water which is usable almost regardless of color, temperature, clarity, biological content, or dissolved load. This is true because of the wide range of industrial demands for water.

At the same time, the quality of industrial waste water extends from the near-optimum end demonstrated by Eastman Kodak Company, which raises trout in its effluent water before discharge, to hot, fetid guck which may prove deadlier to downstream "victims" than an atomic bomb. Fortunately, industrialists who permit discharge of liquid filth to attack downstream users' ability to buy their products and services are few and far between now. Strong, properly administered and enforced local, state, and, where necessary, federal laws will soon push even these relics of the robber-baron days off the edge into the past. Industrial pollution, then, is on its way out, and it is up to all of us to try just a little bit harder to get rid of it faster.

Some of the major sources of water pollution from industries are discussed in the following sections. Bear in mind that the major industrial use of water is for cooling, and that the effects of thermal pollution may add to the pollutants which are listed.

Water Pollution and the Textile Industry.
Effluents from textile mills may contain many types of actual or potential pollutants. These include:

1. Fiber.
2. Sizing compounds (usually starches).
3. Bleaches [which may be either alkaline (chlorine) or acid].
4. Dyes (various chemistry).

All of these wastes may become serious pollutants unless proper treatment methods are used. These may include coagulation and settling, filtration, neutralization, and perhaps biological treatment.

Water Pollution and the Logging Industry.
Several types of pollutants may enter waterways from logging. These include preservative sprays, scraps of bark, chips, sawdust, and shavings. These provide BOD and threaten DO. In years gone by, before Americans got wise and stopped using rivers and streams as open sewers, it was customary practice to dump logging residue into streams. Mats and dense beds of sludge from these practices reportedly still clog some streams in Maine and probably in other states as well.

Fortunately, most of these shameful practices have stopped, but some new ones have developed. In many areas it is customary to burn bark, chips, shavings, and sawdust. This may create air pollution problems, of course, and if the ashes are dumped into lakes and streams, nutrient excesses may develop. In summary, many water pollution problems may develop from logging operations, and the only sure way of preventing them is to ensure that spray and wash water does not flush into streams, and that mill residue is not dumped indiscriminately.

Water Pollution and the Pulp and Paper Industry. The pulp and paper industry uses a huge volume of water. In common with many industries who completely change or renovate natural organic materials, many opportunities exist for harming downstream (or subsequent) users if effective action is not taken to stop pollution.

Many miles of the Rainy River, which separates the State of Minnesota and the Canadian Province of Ontario, have been defiled by water pollution. These deplorable conditions have spurred action before the International Joint Commission by both the United States and Canada.[16] Major troubles have devel-

[16] Report of the International Joint Commission on the Pollution of Rainy River and Lake of the Woods, Washington-Ottawa, February 1965.

oped, or lurk just below the danger level, in the Pacific Northwest also.

Problems are not restricted to North America. Major problems appear eminent in Siberia. Major pulp and paper mills have been constructed on the shores of Lake Baikal. Wastes from these mills, coupled with thermal pollution from thermal electric generating stations, threaten the economic wealth and productivity of this huge lake.

In summary, water pollution problems threaten and injure this industry. Other problems caused by this industry may harm downstream water users. The utmost in cooperation, far more than has been evident in years gone by, is both expected by, and demanded from, this industry if our generation is to leave a beautiful America for those who follow.

Water Pollution and the Chemical and Allied Products Industries. A substantial part of all of American industry is included in this category. Included are the manufacture of the following substances:

1. Alkalies and chlorine.
2. Coal tar products.
3. Organic chemicals.
4. Inorganic chemicals.
5. Plastics and polymers.
6. Synthetic rubber.
7. Drugs and pharmaceuticals.
8. Soap and other detergents.
9. Paints and allied products.
10. Gums and wood chemicals.
11. Fertilizers.
12. Explosives.

Numerous opportunities exist for thoughtlessly deliberate or accidental pollution from industries in this category. Intensive research and extensive analyses are required to protect downstream users from the harmful effects of wastes from these industries. Obviously, a broad range of pollutants emerge within this group.

Water Pollution and the Petroleum and Coal Products Industries. The petroleum and coal products industries include all operations starting with finding coal and oil, getting it from the ground, and refining, processing, transporting, and otherwise getting derived products to market. The principal withdrawal of water is for refining. The other operations rely on the use of water but do not use significant amounts.

Discounting oil spills, which are obviously accidental, the major pollutant from oil field operations is the discharge of connate water (salt brine). These brines have been one of the major pollutants afflicting Arkansas for years. Several streams in Texas and Oklahoma are affected this way too. A major pollutant from oil refineries is phenol. Phenols create ugly taints in the flesh of fish and shellfish, even when present in just a few parts per *trillion* in water. Oil pollution itself is another matter.

A thin film of irridescent oil on the surface of a lake, river, or the ocean may not look bad. It may, in fact, look pretty! The play of colors induced by the interference phenomena may give rise to some of the most gorgeous color patterns imaginable—but the effects of the oil can be deadly! Millions of ducks, geese, and other waterfowl have died because of oil pollution. Afloat, even a relatively small quantity of oil goes where the water goes. By nature, oil on water is a seeker. It will move with the surface film of water until it encounters something solid to cling to. When it does encounter such a solid medium, it will cling to it and will not let go readily. Firm support may be provided by a beach, pilings and peers, rocks, and even bathers. The feathers of swimming birds are perhaps the most critical type of anchor, from the standpoint of the conservationists.

Most types of oil will exert a tremendous biochemical oxygen demand (BOD) stress on water. ZoBell reports that one liter of oil will deplete the oxygen from 400 cubic meters of sea water (at saturation O_2, 59 degrees F).[17]

Sea birds and waterfowl of all types are prime victims of oil pollution. Millions of ducks and geese have died as a result of oil spills. A film of oil only 0.0008 inches thick is sufficient to soak through the outer guard feathers, matting the downy layer which provides buoyancy. When their buoyancy is lost, swimming waterbirds will drown, unless they are able to get to shore. If they reach the beach, they usually arrive weakened and sub-

Oil pollution may stem from either natural or cultural sources (Fig. 4). When classed as a natural pollutant, the hydrocarbon must stem from natural sources, such as oil seeps or exposures of oil shale, or from material such as the tar sands in northern Canada or the La-Brea Tar Pits. Natural source contributions are at most very minor, because oil seeps and similar exposures which might pollute waterways are rare, and obviously subject to harnessing and exploitation if large enough to be

Fig. 3 The Lesser Scaup Duck ("Blue Bill") shown above made a fatal mistake. He attempted to land in the Cuyahoga River near where it gushed oil and associated guk into Lake Erie. (Federal Water Pollution Control Administration.)

ject to chilling. In any event, they are easy prey for predators and die in vast numbers. Figure 3 shows an example of the wasteful slaughter of an economically priceless heritage doomed because of a normally preventable type of pollution.

[17] Claude E. ZoBell, *The Occurrence, Effects, and Fate of Oil Polluting the Sea*, Scripps Institute of Oceanography, University of California, La Jolla, California, Advances in Water Pollution Research, International Meeting, Vol. 3, 1962, p. 83.

potentially economically productive. Recent experimental work by the Esso Research Laboratories has shown, however, that oil production commences almost as soon as organisms (algae, plants, phytoplankton, and the higher animals) begin to decay. Some of the minor oil slicks which can be seen in marsh lakes and swamps may be the residue of such production.

True cultural sources (spills from refineries, leaks from pipelines, flushing of ballast tanks at sea, etc.) constitute major sources, closely followed by run-off from city streets, discharge of used, dirty engine oil, and similar sources. The risks of contamination by oil and other hazardous substances are as numerous and as varied as the uses which are made of the many materials involved and the means of transporting them. These risks involve terminals, waterside chemical and industrial plants, loading docks, refineries, tankers, freighters, barges, pipelines, tank trucks, fill-

vessels of 1000 tons or larger. This fleet was supplemented within the United States by approximately 36,000 smaller vessels of many types. These included many thousands of tank ships and barges on American inland waterways. The waterborne commercial fleets are powered almost exclusively by oil, and perhaps one vessel in five is engaged in transporting oil. Thus water transport constitutes a significant pollution threat.[18] The great number of potential sources involved and the fact that

Fig. 4 A typical pocket of dirty oil trapped along the river bank is shown above. (Federal Water Pollution Control Administration.)

ing stations—everywhere that oil is used, stored, or moved. All are subject to mechanical failures compounded by human carlessness and mistakes.

Pumping and transport of oil from boats and barges are particularily vulnerable functions.

With the steady increase in world and domestic commerce, increasing numbers of vessels are being used. In 1965, the world's merchant fleet contained more than 18,000

they are mobile compounds the problems of prevention and control. Both government and industry must give careful attention to pollution control measures stemming from vessels.

Water Pollution and the Primary Metals Industries. This category includes iron and steel production and foundries, copper refin-

[18] *Oil Pollution*, a Report to the President of the United States by the Secretary of the Interior and the Secretary of Transportation, February 1968.

Fig. 5 The source location and visible effects of water pollutants are shown more frequently in color aerial photography than they can be seen by ground observers on the scene. The original photograph used to prepare this illustration was an oblique color infrared photograph. The wastes illustrated stem from coke quenching and other processes in the manufacture of steel at the Bethlehem Steel Company plant at Sparrows Point, Maryland, near Baltimore. Raw sewage is used as source water for these operations. (Photo Science, Inc., Montgomery County Air Park, Gaithersburg, Maryland.)

ing, the aluminum industry, and other mineral industries, including zinc, nickel, chromium, tin, and the precious metals (gold and silver).

WATER POLLUTION AND THE IRON AND STEEL INDUSTRY. As much as 95 to 98 percent of the water which is used by the iron and steel industry can be of very poor quality.

Many strong acids, alkalines, and other substances are ultimately discharged in iron and steel industry process waste water. Included are:

1. Residue from coke quenching.
2. Alkali cleaning materials.
3. Pickling solutions.
4. Plating wastes.
5. Quenching residue (scale, etc).

It was reported in the *Journal of the American Society of Civil Engineers* (December 1967) that these operations included discharge of a vast amount of cyanide into Lake Michigan, near Chicago, from facilities owned by the United States Steel Corporation. Today the steel companies and many others engaged in heavy industries are committed to programs to prevent or reduce air and water pollution.

Figure 5 illustrates the ugly appearance of

the discharge from Bethlehem Steel's facility at Sparrow's Point. In fairness to Bethlehem Steel, it should be pointed out that they use sewage effluent from Baltimore to quench hot steel, which serves to kill much of the bacterial content of the waste water.

Many of the other primary metals operations produce fines and scrap which settle to the bottom. On dissolution (by corrosive, oxyreduction, etc.) these wastes may pollute the benthos and destroy or modify beneficial organisms.

Water Pollution and the Food Canning Industry. Many opportunities exist for pollutants to enter waste water in these operations. First, all of the materials which are washed from unprocessed food enter the discharge flow.

All of the grading, trimming, peeling, pitting, and cutting residue should be removed for disposal as solid waste, but some of this material may enter waste water, particularly from older facilities. Further, solid waste disposal methods may permit wastes to drain or otherwise add liquid wastes to receiving waters.

All additives, such as syrups and brines; disinfectants, such as chlorine; and other materials are potential pollutants. Excess fractions of these materials add to wastes and heat from cleaning, fluming, blanching, and cooling.

Major water pollution problems extending from the food processing industry span the nation. Examples exist in the French Broad Creek, near Ashville, North Carolina (baby food canning); in the Red Lake River between Crookston, Minnesota, and Grand Forks, North Dakota (sugar beet processing); San Jose, California (fruit and vegetable canning); and in Alaska (fish cleaning wastes).

Water Pollution and the Tanning Industry. The objective of this industry is conversion of raw, untreated hides into finished leathers.

Basically, there are only three or four tanning methods (vegetable, mineral, combination vegetable and mineral, and syntans), but many finishing processes.

Discounting bacteria from hides and from the meat and fat which may adhere when the animals are skinned, the major types of pollutants which may stem from this industry are hair, leather scraps, and the chemicals which are used in the tanning process. A substantial amount of organic material has been noted below some tanneries, evidenced by septic water, dense mats of algae, and extensive stands of aquatic vegetation.

This list of industries and the kinds of pollutants which may stem from them could be extended to include every type of industry. As cited in the preferred definition of water pollution, if secondary (or subsequent) use of water is impaired, the water has been polluted.

Most persons in capitalistic societies recognize that healthy, happy people make the best customers. Industry demands good customers for its own survival, and although the lessons about water pollution have been accepted slowly and in some instances grudgingly, they have been learned. The nation's demands and environmental renaissance, and American industry, are moving forward in the war against water pollution.

The Ultimate Solution to Pollution. The quatrain:

"The Solution
  To Pollution
    Is *Prevention*
      Not Dilution"

exposes a dilemma which can be corrected, at least in part, by improved manufacturing processes. The term "industrial symbiosis" may become more widely known and used in the future. This term implies that one industry lives off, or utilizes the waste products of, another. Perhaps the major example of this in the United States is the re-refined oil business. Although poorly devised taxing structure in many areas has almost crippled this industry recently, it has served as a major example of water pollution reducing "industrial symbiosis," since it exists *only* because of the waste products of another industry. About 350,000,000 gallons of used, dirty engine oil must be disposed of from the more than 210,000 gasoline stations every year. A large percentage of this used oil (which never "wears out") is re-refined and sold back to industrial suppliers. The airlines preferred this re-refined oil, and at one time even paid a premium price for it. It was shown that in the course of the first refining, subsequent use in engines, and ultimate re-refining, a greater amount of sulfur and corrosive materials are removed. The lubricating ability of the oil was not impaired, and since most of the corrosive materials were no longer present, engine wear was reduced. Were it not for re-use of this waste oil, it would probably be dumped into sewers or gutters, potentially harming someone downstream.

All Americans have a stake in correcting water pollution problems, and our present governmental systems may have to be restructured to satisfy existing and anticipated problems. Engineering progress has been made in water and waste water treatment. Figures 6 and 7 illustrate two examples of this thriving modern technology.

The Genossenschaften, or quasi-public water supply and pollution control corporations in West Germany, thrive because of a form of "industrial symbiosis." These organizations have pioneered much of the sanitary engineering practice in Europe. The best-known example of these semi-private/public organizations is the Ruhrverband in the Ruhr Valley.

Five rivers run into the Ruhr; one of these is the Emscher. Each of these rivers has been assigned a major function, that of the Emscher being little more than that of an open sewer. Before the murky waste water in the Emscher is discharged into the Ruhr, however, it is transformed into the cleanest, clearest effluent possible within modern German sanitary engineering technology. Every

waste element which has any commercial value is removed and rechanneled into the industrial supply system. Phenol, for example (which if present in water as dilute as 1 ppb will have a serious taste-degrading effect), is required by the plastics industry. Phenol is removed from waste waters and is sold to the German plastics industry at cost. This reduces the tax burden and the materials costs appreciably, while at the same time eliminating a serious pollutant from the effluent.

The German Genossenschaften offer a unique example worthy of emulation by American industrial and governmental bodies. One often hears of the need for a "new" form of industrial economics because of waste disposal problems. The Genossenschaften provide all water supply and waste removal facilities and services within the River Basin regions (usually regions bounded by natural boundaries). All services are supplied at cost, and the re-sale value of the materials which can be recovered from wastes and "symbiotically" fed into the industrial arteries helps defray the cost of water supply and pollution control services which are provided. Reclaimed materials are sold at cost. Their recovery price does not pay for the full cost of their removal from the wastes from which they are extracted, however. Special pro rata taxes are assessed against each industry and community which receives services. The rate of taxation paid by each industry is determined by the volume of material and the cost of treatment afforded by the type of industrial waste which each class of industry generates, reduced by the value of any materials which can be recovered. The ultimate size of the tax bill submitted to each industry reflects how much water is provided and the volume of the waste removed at the rate judged to be fair by a committee representing both industry and government, based on appropriate rate assessment criteria. In this way, improved in-plant practices result directly in lower taxes, stimulating progress.

Fig. 6 Polluted water requires the development and installation of highly sophisticated and expensive water-treatment facilities. This picture shows an industrial water clarification and treatment plant that can treat as much water as the pumping facilities of Cincinnati. This facility, built by Armco Steel Corporation at their Middletown, Ohio, works, can clean, cool, and treat 100,000 gallons of water per minute—much of this water being "used" water from the previous operations of the Middletown works. Armco Steel's control "package," manufactured at a cost of $39,000,000, consists of eight air- and six water-treatment facilities and won for the Corporation an Outstanding Engineering Achievement Award in 1969 from the National Society of Professional Engineers. Upstream polluters cause downstream water users heavy expenditures in providing goods and services demanded by our way of life. Manufacturers must raise prices, and governments must raise taxes; consequently, less money is available to buy goods and services provided by the upstream polluters. (Armco Steel Corporation.)

Almost all refining, mixing, blending, and extraction industrial manufacturing operations produce some waste. This must be removed and transported someplace for subsequent disposal. "Prevention" of pollution could imply that wastes not be produced. Naturally, since raw materials—natural resources—cost money or have some other economic

Fig. 7 Domestic (sanitary) sewage causes many of our worst pollution problems. However, sewage and other oxygen-demanding wastes can be controlled by construction of properly designed sewage treatment plants, provided that they are operated correctly. This photograph shows an advanced secondary treatment facility, incorporating a two-stage biological filtration system. This plant is so efficient that the waste water sludge which concentrates in the digester (the tall structure, upper right) is 18 percent solid material—too thick to be pumped out by normal methods. This facility, located in Salt Lake City, Utah, treats 45,000,000 gallons of sewage a day. (Kennedy Engineers, San Francisco, California.)

value, every effort is made to reduce costs by eliminating waste. Engineers and others in private (capitalistic) industry try to produce products at a profit. To accomplish this, every effort is obviously made to produce products at the lowest cost. This usually means expending the least possible amount of raw material to produce the most valuable product. This obviously implies minimizing waste, and de-

tailed procedures are followed to cut waste to the bone. If wastes were eliminated altogether, the ultimate efficiency would be achieved, theoretically. In the case of mineral extraction and recovery, of course, the reverse condition exists. Refining and extraction systems which permit ores which contain the least possible amount of mineral to be extracted at a profit are considered to be the most efficient. They also leave the greatest volume of residue (rather than waste in a classic sense) which must be disposed of.

Humans, of course, being very imperfect, make mistakes. In this case, this implies accidental spills, and so forth, which may occur in spite of our best efforts. Perfection never seems to be reached, so at least some wastes are produced as long as production continues. Efficient waste treatment is the only solution if pollution is to be prevented.

Pollutants should be considered as "weeds in the garden of industry." Weeds (economically worthless vegetation) have been defined as "plants for which man hasn't found a use —yet," because at one time every vegetable, grain, and forage crop had not been recognized as a valuable commodity from nature's pantry, even though the parent plant species had evolved. Liquid-borne wastes occupy the same position as untested raw material. Those which qualify as pollutants because they harm or impair the water resource in which they are located occupy a special place among solutes, because since they are harmful, it is in the best interests of society to remove them. Engineers and others who find a way to remove harmful substances from water and make a profit while doing so stand on the golden path to fortune and recognition. A brilliant pioneer in the chemical industry, Herbert S. Dow, for example, recognized the potential of removing the "impurities" from saline waters in Michigan, which led to the founding of the Dow Chemical Company, one of the industrial giants in present-day America. Dow removes "pollutants" and produces bromine, magnesium, common salt (NaCl), and many other valuable substances.

SUMMARY

In the preceding sections, water pollution has been defined, and we have shown how almost all of us suffer in some way because of it. We have also shown that water pollution is a relative thing. Most human endeavors depend on water in some way. The preferred definition of water pollution is that it is "the adding to water of any substance or the changing of water's physical characteristics in any way which interferes with its use for any legitimate purpose." This definition, which we suggest is very sound and realistic, emphasizes a paradox. Everyone's needs and uses of water conflict with other personal uses—and these, in turn, conflict with both the competing and noncompeting requirements of others. These conflicts demand that priorities be set and that due weight be accorded each legitimate need for water.

We require water which is usable for all legitimate needs—water which has certain positive "qualities." Water which does not have these positive qualities, but has negative qualities instead, is "polluted."

In our quest for knowledge in this vital field our path has been directed toward those areas which influence most persons most of the time. We have followed a path which starts with recreation and aesthetics, then continues through public (drinking, washing) supplies, fisheries and wildlife, agricultural, and industrial needs. Water which satisfies quality requirements in this order of successive priorities will meet most demands which may be placed on it. Exotic or specialized needs will always demand extra care and treatment. The quality priority schedule which is shown provides "raw" water which can be treated to meet all expected uses.

TO DIG DEEPER

This vital field demands further study, and the following references offer a start. Check daily newspapers and popular magazines too. As more and more persons learn to recognize existing water pollution problems, paths to greater knowledge, better health, and a safer, cleaner, better world will open up to us.

References

Advances in Water Pollution Research, Vols. 1, 2, and 3, Proceedings of the Third International Conference on Water Pollution Research (1963), Permagon Press, Ltd., Long Island City, New York. Distributed in the United States by The Macmillan Co., New York.

Alexander, Gordon, *General Zoology,* College Outline Series, Fifth Edition, Barnes and Noble, New York, 1964.

Biological Science—Molecules to Man (Blue Version), Biological Science Curriculum Study, Second Edition, Houghton Mifflin Co., Boston, 1968. A modern high school biology text.

Bower, Blair T., Gordon P. Larson, Abraham Michaels, and Walter M. Phillips, *Water Management, Generation and Disposal of Solid, Liquid, and Gaseous Wastes in the New York Region,* Regional Plan Association, New York, N.Y., 1968.

Brady, Nyle C., editor, *Agriculture and the Quality of Our Environment,* Publ. No. 85, American Association for the Advancement of Science, Washington, D.C., 1967.

Carson, Rachel L., *The Edge of the Sea,* Houghton Mifflin Co., Boston, 1955. A good basic text on the conditions which exist in the marginal marine environment.

————, *The Sea Around Us,* Revised Edition, Oxford University Press, New York, 1961.

————, *Silent Spring,* Houghton Mifflin Co., Boston, 1962. This book has done much to awaken humanity to the threat of pollution of the environment.

Community Action Program for Water Pollution Control, National Association of Counties Research Foundation, Washington, D.C., 1965.

Dasmann, Raymond F., *Environmental Conservation,* Second Edition, John Wiley & Sons, Inc., New York, 1968.

Erichsen-Jones, J. R., *Fish and River Pollution,* Butterworths, London, 1964.

Farb, Peter, and the Editors of *Life, Ecology,* Time, Inc., New York, 1963. A good basic text; well illustrated.

Fassett, Norman C., *A Manual of Aquatic Plants,* Second Edition, University of Wisconsin Press, Madison, 1957.

Frey, David G., editor, *Limnology in North America,* University of Wisconsin Press, Madison, 1963.

Graham, Frank, Jr., *Disaster by Default, Politics and Water Pollution,* M. Evans and Company, Inc., New York, 1966.

Hutchison, G. Evelyn, *A Treatise on Limnology,* Vol. I, Geography, Physics, and Chemistry, Chapters 1–17, 1957; Vol. II, Introduction to Lake Biology and Limnoplankton, Chapters 18–26, 1966, John Wiley & Sons, Inc., New York, 1957 and 1967.

Hynes, H. B. N., *The Biology of Polluted Waters,* Liverpool University Press, Liverpool, 1963.

Imhoff, Karl, W. J. Muller, and D. E. B. Thistlewaite, *Disposal of Sewage and*

Other Water-Borne Wastes, Second Edition, Plenum Publishing Corp., Inc., New York, 1968.

Klein, Louis, *River Pollution,* Vol. I, *Chemical Analysis* (1959); Vol. II, *Causes and Effects* (1962), Butterworths, London, 1959 and 1962.

Knight, Clifford B., *Basic Concepts of Ecology,* The Macmillan Co., New York, 1695. An excellent introduction to ecology.

League of Women Voters, *The Big Water Fight,* Stephen Greene Press, Brattleboro, Vermont, 1966.

Olson, T. A. and F. J. Burgess, editors, *Pollution and Marine Ecology,* Proceedings of a Conference, Galveston, Texas, March 1966, John Wiley & Sons, Inc., New York, 1967. An excellent reference.

Strandberg, Carl H., *Aerial Discovery Manual,* JohnWiley & Sons, Inc., New York, 1967. The application of aerial photography to the study of water supply and pollution control; extensively illustrated.

The Nation's Water Resources. The First National Assessment of the Water Resources Council, U.S. Government Printing Office, Washington, D.C., 1968.

United States Department of Agriculture, *Water—1955 Yearbook of Agriculture,* Washington, D.C., 1955.

United States Department of the Interior, *Man, An Endangered Species, Conservation Yearbook No. 4,* Washington, D.C., 1968.

United States Department of the Interior, Suggested State Water Pollution Control Act, Revised, FWPCA, Washington, D.C., 1965 (reprinted in 1966).

JOHN H. GARLAND
University of Illinois

CHAPTER 9

Water Supply for Domestic and Industrial Uses

Two old adages combined express very well our situation in respect to water: "Waste not; want not;" and "You never miss the water till the well runs dry." No doubt the universal need for water, its worldwide distribution, and apparent inexhaustibility have led to various human attitudes toward its utilization. It is indeed an anomaly that a resource that not infrequently creates a deluge of extremely destructive proportions needs on occasion to be conserved. Both too little and too much water are, in part, the result of the unwise use of all natural resources. The universal importance of water as a basic necessity of all forms of life makes its utilization a most complicated problem of conservation.

DOMESTIC AND INDUSTRIAL USES OF WATER RESOURCES

The various ways in which water is utilized are such that interests conflict and numerous problems arise. All life is completely dependent on water, which includes drinking water for man and beast, soil water for vegetation, and surface water for the habitat of all types of aquatic life. On the other hand, water is a source of power, an industrial ingredient, a medium of transportation, a waste removal and purification agent, as well as a recreational asset and a marker of boundaries. Of this array, domestic and industrial uses are but a small part, and even these vary widely from place to place. Domestic uses consist of at least two major groups which can be designated as primary and secondary uses. These become manifest in areas of permanent or temporary water shortage.

Primary Domestic Uses. By far of greatest importance is water for human consumption, drinking water, cooking, and the like, without which mankind would perish. Under most dire conditions of water shortage this usage is given first consideration. Closely akin is the use of water for sanitary purposes. The demands of modern civilization for water for personal cleanliness, laundry, and other hygienic needs within the home and within public and private institutions are enormous. In continental United States in 1960, 164,600 million gallons per day were withdrawn from ground and surface water supplies for industrial, public, and rural usage (Fig. 1). Public water systems supplied about 21,000 mil-

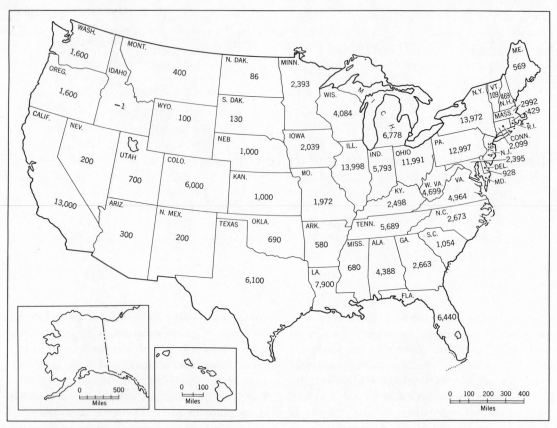

Fig. 1 Million gallons withdrawn daily by states from ground and surface water supplies for industrial, public, and rural uses. (*Water Atlas of the United States,* Water Information Center.)

lion gallons daily to approximately 136,000,000 people with a variation from 100 to 250 gallons per person per day. The average for the nation was about 147 gallons per person per day. Regardless of area or population five states withdrew more than 10,000 million gallons daily, seven withdrew between 5000 and 10,000, and eighteen withdrew between 1000 and 5000 million gallons daily. Only the state of Idaho withdrew less than 1000 million gallons daily.

The figure for each state represents the total amount of water withdrawn from all sources not including irrigation water and the generation of hydroelectric power. It should

be noted that each time water was withdrawn the amount was included in the accumulated total even though the same water may have been re-used by various users. If water was withdrawn and recirculated for re-use in the same system before discharge, it was counted but once. On a national average only about one-fourth of the water withdrawn was actually consumed in the sense that it was not available for re-use.

Secondary Domestic Uses. The distinction between primary and secondary domestic uses of water, in some instances, is difficult to determine. It is obvious that great quantities of water are utilized in the sanitary sewage systems of all towns and cities, most of which has already been utilized as a primary domestic supply. Additional water is necessary to dilute and treat sewage or in many cases to carry the treated sewage away.

Water for fire protection is of greatest importance to towns and cities. Periods of water shortage are always threatened with the danger of a severe fire. Innumerable villages and towns as well as portions of many large cities in this country have been destroyed by fire because their supply of water was insufficient to meet the emergency. The volume of water consumed is not a crucial factor, since it is very small; it is the necessity of having a large flow of water available when needed that is the important factor for fire protection.

Closely associated is the utilization of water to lay dust and wash debris from city streets, as well as to flush accumulations from the catch basins of the storm sewers in periods of dry weather. In the humid portion of the country, the sprinkling of lawns and gardens and the forcing of vegetables by overhead irrigation constitute a domestic type of water utilization (water for commercial irrigation not included).

The air conditioning of stores, offices, and public buildings, as well as apartment buildings and private residences, by water cooling systems has placed an extra demand upon water for secondary domestic purposes. Some systems pump groundwater into the air conditioner and then return the water to a dry well; thus the water becomes groundwater again.

One of the lesser secondary domestic uses of water is for recreational purposes. In the present discussion utilization refers to the direct consumption of water for that purpose rather than the recreational uses made of streams, lakes, and the like. It includes the consumption of water for fountains, public and private swimming pools, and other types of ornamental and recreational uses of water that must come from the water supply. Both indoor and outdoor swimming pools have become users of the domestic water supply (see Chapter 22).

Industrial Uses. Numerous types of manufactures require large quantities of water in their industrial processes other than the water consumed by the employees of the plants. Thus the amount, the quality, and the cost of water are important factors of industrial localization for some types of manufacturing.

The industrial uses of water fall into three broad but somewhat interrelated categories: (1) water is an important ingredient of the finished product; (2) it is used as an agent for cooling, removing impurities, preparing solutions, and the like; and (3) it is important in the diluting and removal of industrial waste.

The several industries using water directly as an ingredient of the finished product include the food canning and preserving industries, the beverage and bottling manufactures, the distilleries, and commercial ice plants. It is also obvious that these industries will require large quantities of water for cleansing, for raw materials, for cooling, and for the removal of waste. The stockyards and meatpacking industries, where water is not important as a direct ingredient, consume millions of gallons of water per day, whereas a modern distillery consumes millions of gallons of water per day for steam, for cooling, and as an ingredient. In the making of one barrel of beer 300 gallons of water are required.

Many other industries, especially paper and pulp making; leather tanning; textile manufacturing; bleaching, dyeing, and printing of cotton textiles; oil refineries; electrical generating plants; coke plants; steel mills; and related types of industries use enormous quanities of water both as cleansing, cooling, or solution media, and to flush away industrial waste. The paper and pulp industries utilize water to wash away impurities as well as to reduce the wood to pulp. In the mechanical grinding process, which produces most of the coarse paper and newsprint, about 15,000 gallons of water are utilized for every ton of paper produced, and in the sulfide and the soda processes as much as 100,000 gallons of water per ton of paper are utilized. A large paper mill uses more water per day than a city of 50,000. To refine 1 barrel of oil 18 barrels of water are consumed, and 10 gallons of water are utilized in producing 1 gallon of gasoline.

The steel industries are tremendous users of water. Twenty-six of the largest integrated steel mills each withdrew an average of 252 million gallons of water daily. This water, drawn mostly from surface sources, is enough to supply a city of almost 2,000,000. About 7.9 percent of the total volume withdrawn is consumed chiefly by evaporation. The consumptive use of water by industry as a whole is about 6 percent; the rest returns to the source and is reused. Cooling, washing scale, reducing dust and gas, and quenching and granulating slag are the basic uses of water. In general, 94 percent of the industrial uses is for cooling.

The associated coke and gas plants also utilize enormous volumes of water to cool gas washers and to clean the gases as well as to quench the coke. As much as 50,000,000 gallons of water are used daily by an individual coke plant. Electrical generating plants are also great consumers of water for cooling and for steam power. For each ton of coal consumed in a steam power plant, 600 to 1000 tons of water are utilized. The estimated daily requirements of fuel-electric power generating plants are about 100,000 million gallons, about one-fourth of which is saline. Thermal generating plants are built where water is available since cooling water for the condensers is the principal demand. About 99.6 percent of the electric generating capacity of Illinois is thermal, but because of the greatly reduced cost with increased size, the Atomic Energy Commission expects 30 percent of the total power to be produced by nuclear energy by the year 2000.

The utilization of water to flush away in-dustrial waste is usually associated with the pollution of streams and rivers. The type of waste varies with the industry, some being more harmful than others. The problem of the disposal of industrial waste, is enormous, and the amount of water used directly and indirectly probably cannot be estimated.

Numerous other industrial demands are made upon the water supply, especially to operate hydraulic mechanisms. The so-called hydraulic water under a pressure of 750 pounds is used in steel mills for the removal of scale as well as for operating hydraulic mechanisms that open and close furnace doors and move other heavy pieces of equipment. Large quantities of water are also used in connection with the pumping of salt, sulfur, and some oil wells, as well as in petroleum refining. Water-flooding is a secondary method of oil recovery in which water is pumped into oil-bearing strata to flush oil toward the well.

SOURCES OF WATER SUPPLY

The amount of water utilized each day for both domestic and industrial purposes immediately raises the question of the supply, its amount, and its quality as well as the probability of an adequate and continuous supply.

With the exception of the connate and magmatic waters, our water supply falls as some form of precipitation. Thus in general the supply is related to distribution of precipitation. The map (Fig. 2) indicates the unequal distribution of precipitation over the United States. In general, east of the 100th meridian the precipitation is adequate, increasing from 20 inches per year on the Great Plains to 50 to 60 inches on the East coast and 60 to 80 inches on the Gulf coast. Westward, except on the Pacific Northwest coast where the rainfall is very heavy, precipitation decreases to desert proportions over much of the intermontane region. Of the precipitation that falls, 71 percent is evaporated from the surface of the ground. The amount thus lost

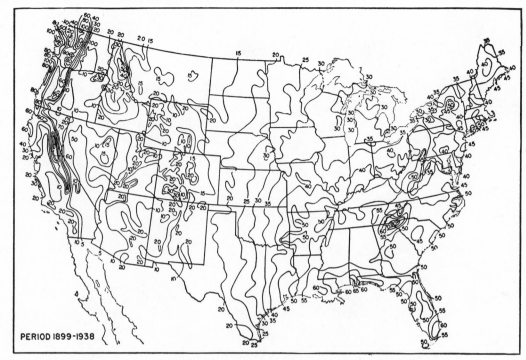

Fig. 2 The average annual precipitation in the United States. With the exception of the Pacific Northwest the average annual precipitation of western United States is inadequate. (*The Yearbook of Agriculture,* 1941, U.S. Department of Agriculture.)

depends on the temperature of the air, the nature of the surface, and the vegetational cover on which it falls. A portion is absorbed by the surface materials of the earth, and a portion drains off to the sea. The water that enters the surface of the earth and the water that flows off or remains on the surface are the two sources of water for domestic and industrial uses. Of the two, groundwater constitutes over 90 percent of the available water.

Surface Water. Surface water or runoff is available in three forms: streams and rivers, lakes, and reservoirs and tanks. The larger the area drained and the heavier the precipitation, the larger is the volume of the master stream. Although steams and rivers are an important supply of domestic and industrial water in the humid part of the United States, most of the large reclamation projects, which

furnish water for irrigation and hydroelectric power as well as domestic water, are in the semiarid and arid portion of the country.

Inland fresh-water lakes, especially the Great Lakes, are outstanding sources of water for the many towns and cities along their shores, as are many of the smaller lakes in the glaciated portion of the United States.

The impounding of water of a tributary stream is a common practice of ensuring a water supply; reservoirs and tanks are used to store runoff, usually referred to as rain or storm water, to supplement the water supply. These range in size from the cistern and rain barrel of humid lands to the large reservoirs designed to impound melting snow and storm water to provide a domestic supply, as well as water for stock and irrigation in the semiarid lands of the West. In the rural areas of the

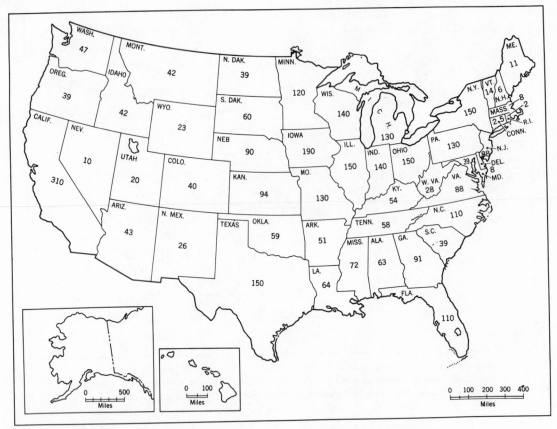

Fig. 3 Million gallons withdrawn per day for rural use. Water from both ground and
surface sources that are not served by public water supply companies. (*Water Atlas of the
United States,* Water Information Center.)

United States, the "drinking" water well and
the cistern or soft-water pump are conspicuous
features of the water supply of each home
(Fig. 3).

Groundwater. The precipitation that soaks
into the earth percolates downward through
the unconsolidated soil and mantle rock and
into the crevices and interstices of the underlying bedrock until a depth is reached where
the density of the rock and the lack of crevices
prohibit any further penetration. The greater
portion of rock porous enough to contain
water is within a few hundred feet of the surface. The groundwater is maintained by the
portion of precipitation that seeps into the

earth. If the water is not of sufficient volume
to fill all the interstices, the upper portions of
the mantle rock may be damp, whereas the
areas below are saturated. The upper limit of
the saturated zone is known as the "groundwater table."

The groundwater table or groundwater
level is not a horizontal surface, nor is it at a
constant depth below the earth's surface. The
water table tends to assume a position between true surface configuration and a horizontal surface. Thus the water table is close
to, or at the surface of, the ground in the valleys and at greater depths from the surface beneath the hills. Similarly, the water table is at

greater depths in subhumid and dry regions or after lengthy periods of drought in humid regions; whereas in humid regions, especially after periods of heavy precipitation, it may be near the surface.

Bedrock formations porous enough to contain groundwater are known as aquifers. These are grouped roughly into three classes: unconsolidated aquifers, consolidated aquifers, and both consolidated and unconsolidated aquifers. In the United States, exclusive of Alaska and Hawaii, their distribution is indicated on the map of Ground Water Areas (Fig. 4). Unconsolidated aquifers are most conspicuous in the lower Mississippi Valley, the Gulf coast, and eastern Coastal Plain. Much the southern Great Plains, the Great Lakes Region, the Southwest, and the valleys of the Far West possess these aquifers. Consolidated aquifers dominate the Dakotas, the Midwest, the Ozarks, Appalachians, southern Coastal Plain, central Texas, and the Columbia Plateau. Much of Florida, as well as scattered areas in the Great Lakes Region, the Great Basin, and the Columbia Plateau have mixed aquifers. Likewise, as indicated on the map (Fig. 5), narrow aquifers are related to the valleys of many rivers, some of them the buried valleys of preglacial streams.

SPRINGS. The location of springs depends on terrain and rock structure in relation to the position of the water table. In its simplest form a valley eroded below the water table is the locus of a series of springs which will cease to flow if drought or other causes lower the water table below the valley floor. A horizontal layer of impervious material, if exposed on a hillside, would allow the water to escape in a series of springs along the hillside. Fault and joint planes are also important features in permitting groundwater to rise to the surface, some of which may have been in contact with igneous rocks of sufficiently high temperatures to produce hot springs and geysers.

Many springs are of such limited volume or of intermittent nature that they are of value as a source of water supply only for individual houses, especially isolated farmsteads, and small villages. There are, however, in the United States several areas of springs of enormous volume. The U.S. Geological Survey [1] has located sixty springs, each with a flow sufficient to supply completely a city of 500,000 inhabitants, and at least six others, any one of which would supply a city of 2,000,000 with all its water requirements. Large springs develop in regions of cavernous limestone and in porous lavas where groundwater from relatively large areas drains into subterranean channels of large capacity. The areas of large springs in the United States are northern Florida, the Ozark Region of Missouri, central Texas, the Upper Snake Plains of Idaho, western Oregon and northern California, and central Montana. The springs of the northwestern portion of the country are largely in the porous lavas, whereas the rest of the large springs are associated mainly with cavernous limestone.

WELLS. A supply of water may be obtained by digging or drilling below the surface of the water table. Dug wells of necessity are shallow and are constructed in glacial drift or other unconsolidated material. The well, although curbed, is open and thus is subject to contamination from the surface. The water is lifted by a windlass, or sweep, or a simple lift pump. Supplies of this type, although numerous, are suitable only for isolated homes in rural areas, and even there, a summer's drought may lower the water table sufficiently to cause the well to go dry.

Dependable supplies of water for towns and cities, and even individual homes are obtained by drilling deep wells, cased against pollution from surface seepage, into the drift or underlying bedrock. Water from most deep wells must be brought to the surface by force pumps.

[1] O. E. Meinzer, *Large Springs in the United States*, Water Supply Paper 557, U.S. Geological Survey, Washington, D.C., 1927.

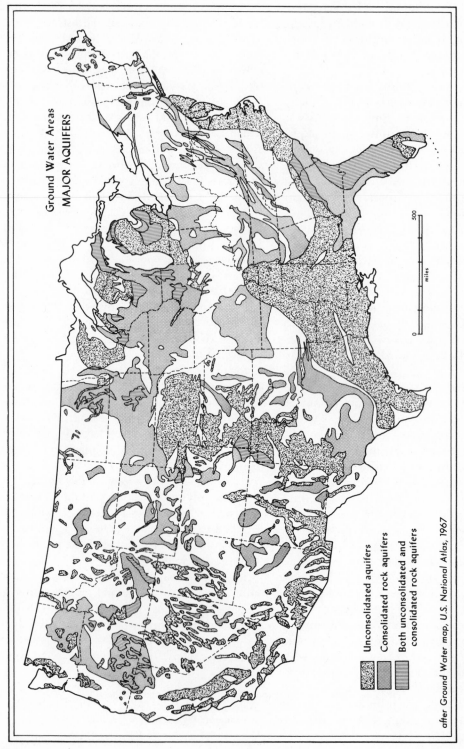

Ground Water Areas
MAJOR AQUIFERS

500

miles

0

Unconsolidated aquifers

Consolidated rock aquifers

Both unconsolidated and
consolidated rock aquifers

after Ground Water map, U.S. National Atlas, 1967

Fig. 4 Aquifers that lie beneath the surface may consist of unconsolidated materials, of consolidated materials, or of a combination of both. Some water-bearing sediments may be near the surface, and others may lie at great depth. Usually, the water at shallow depths is used first, unless it becomes contaminated. Waters at great depth will require deep wells and expensive pumping equipment and, when they are brought to the surface, may be highly charged with salts and other undesirable mineral substances.

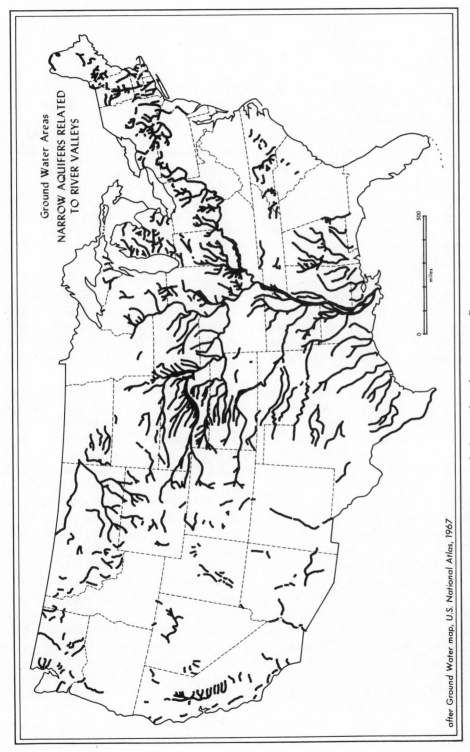

after Ground Water map, U.S. National Atlas, 1967

Fig. 5 Many valleys in the United States were once much deeper than they are now. Partial filling of these valleys with sand and gravel has created a system of long linear aquifers that contain large quantities of water.

ARTESIAN WELLS. Under special conditions large supplies of water are obtained from deep, flowing artesian wells. Hydrostatic pressures develop only under special conditions of terrain, underlying bedrock, and climate. The conditions consist of a porous formation, generally sandstone, exposed to sufficient precipitation to fill it, and gently dipping below a layer of impervious material. If the water-bearing formation is closed off at its lower elevation the water is entrapped and is therefore under pressure. A well drilled into the water-bearing layer from any point on the surface lower than the exposed portion of the porous formation will flow, or at least will rise in the well as a result of the weight of the water in the higher portion of the porous strata.

In the United States artesian wells have been drilled on the Gulf Coastal Plain and on the Great Plains and Central Lowlands to depths of 3000 and some to almost 5000 feet.

In 1900 there was a total of about 155,000 wells in the United States, which was increased to about 436,000 by 1965. In 1945 almost one-fourth of the public water supply, 2.9 billion gallons, came from wells, whereas by 1965 the amount had increased to 8.1 billion gallons or about 34 percent of the public supply. Artificial re-charge using the aquifers as reservoirs for the storage of unusable surface or reclaimed water has led to the drilling of more wells.

Wells producing 72 million or more gallons of water per day are indicated on the map (Fig. 6). The three greatest concentrations of wells are in the Great Valley of California, the Panhandle of Texas, and the desert of southern Arizona, with secondary concentrations in Colorado, Kansas, Nebraska, and Idaho.

SETTLEMENTS AND WATER SUPPLY

It is convenient to think of the population of the United States as being composed of three settlement groups, each of which contains about one-third of the total population. The first group is metropolitan and is made up of cities with populations of 100,000 and over; the second is composed of small cities, towns, and villages; and the third is composed of the rural population. The last two groups depend largely on groundwater, whereas the metropolitan group depends on surface supplies supplemented for secondary domestic and some industrial uses by groundwater.

Metropolitan Group. By far the greatest consumers of water are the metropolitan areas, for it is there that great concentrations of people make a tremendous demand on the domestic supply. Likewise the presence of industry within the cities places an industrial demand on the water supply that in most districts greatly exceeds the domestic use.

Although a variety of systems, both private and municipal, has been developed to supply the water needs of metropolitan areas, the volume required is so large that most urban areas depend on surface water supplemented for certain uses with groundwater. For some large urban districts it has been necessary to transport water long distances at great cost. Interstate conflicts over water rights have arisen in connection with the water supply of some of our large metropolitan areas.

The relationship of population density and distribution to humid climate conditions in the United States is clear. Most of the cities of the metropolitan group are located on rivers or lakes that may be utilized as a source of domestic and industrial water.

Conspicuous among the city groups are those associated with the Great Lakes and with the Mississippi drainage system. Less conspicuous are the associations of the cities with the streams of the Gulf and Atlantic Coastal Plain, and those of the Pacific Northwest and the mountains. Thus only a few of the cities, those in the semiarid portion of the country, such as Los Angeles, San Diego, and Salt Lake City, and those on bays and estuaries along the seacoast, such as Boston and

Ground Water Areas
WITHDRAWALS FROM WELLS

• 72 million gallons per day

after Ground Water map, U.S. National Atlas, 1967

0   400
miles

Fig. 6 The heavy pumping of water from aquifers of high capacity is located in the areas where recharging matches withdrawal. However, in the Great Plains, particularly in the High Plains of Texas, excessive withdrawals have lowered the water table and have reduced the quantity of water available for future use.

New York City, have insufficient surface water supplies in their immediate environs. Although all urban groups have innumerable problems concerning the conservation of their water supply, these cities have the added problem of ensuring an adequate supply.

Los Angeles, the only city of over 1,000,000 outside of the humid section of the United States, is entirely dependent on a water supply from beyond its local area, in part beyond the limit of the state. The Los Angeles River was the original source of water for the first 125

years of the city's existence. By 1908, efforts were being made to increase the water supply, since the growth of the city was limited by the local water supply. In 1914, the Los Angeles aqueduct was completed to the Owens River east of the Sierra Nevadas 238 miles away. At a cost of $25,000,000 the water was brought by canal, siphon, and tunnel across the desert and under the mountains into the Los Angeles Basin. Since one of the conditions by which the water of Owens Lake was obtained was the requirement that all the water be used within the city, Los Angeles enlarged by incorporating 50,000 acres of the San Fernando Valley immediately north of the city. The population of the city increased to more than 500,000 by 1920. Additional water was secured from Mono Lake north of Owens Valley. By 1930, the population of Los Angeles had passed 1,000,000, with another million people in the metropolitan district of the Basin.

In 1934, the Colorado Compact was arranged to secure an additional supply from the Colorado River at a cost of $220,000,000 to the Metropolitan Water District of Southern California, which includes fourteen other communities, including San Diego, and supplies a population greater than 7,475,000. The water from Lake Havasu above Parker Dam, 155 miles below Hoover Dam, is conducted through 241 miles of aqueduct. There are 92 miles of tunnels, and the water must be raised 1617 feet by five pumping stations operated by electric power generated at Hoover Dam. Several new lines, pumping stations, and reservoirs have been added to distribute the water. After about 12 years of legal action the Superior Court ruled against the City of Los Angeles, which was trying to stop Glendale, Burbank, San Fernando, and the Crescent Valley County Water District from pumping groundwater in their areas.

The water table has been lowered to more than 75 feet below sea level. Desalted sea water has been offered as a supply and distant sources have been suggested. No doubt supply will be exceeded by demand by the end of the century.

Within the humid portion of the United States the New York metropolitan district is the largest that must reach out for a sufficient domestic and industrial water supply. The Ringewood system supplies groundwater from an elaborate system of infiltration galleries laid 10 to 15 feet below the water table for 6 miles in the glacial sands of Long Island. New York City Board of Water Supply will build

an underground tank to store 100,000,000 gallons of water in Silver Lake Park on Staten Island where a reservoir is now located.

Wells on Staten Island produce about 10 million gallons per day as compared with 100 million gallons from the Ringewood system. The other systems, which are the main sources, supply surface water impounded in reservoirs. The oldest is the Croton River watershed with twelve storage reservoirs and six impounded lakes with a total capacity of 103 billion gallons, the largest of which is Croton Lake with 34 billion gallons capacity. In Westchester County south of the Croton watershed are the Bronx and Byram rivers, Byram and Wampus ponds, and the 30-billion-gallon Kensico Reservoir. In the Catskill system, the Schoharie Reservoir with a capacity of 20 billion gallons is connected to the Ashokan Reservoir by the Shandaken Tunnel. The Ashokan Reservoir has a capacity of 130 billion gallons and was in use in 1915. The Catskill Aqueduct connects it with the Kensico Reservoir 17 miles north of the city, from which the water comes to the city.

New York State and Vermont entered into a compact in 1966 to manage and control Lake Champlain.

In 1968, the U.S. Geological Survey released the information that Long Island is underlain by water-bearing rocks that contain 60,-000,000,000,000 gallons of water which is replenished at about 800,000,000 gallons per day.

In 1930, the State of New Jersey attempted unsuccessfully to enjoin the State of New York from diverting the water of the Delaware River for an additional water supply for New York City. In 1945, the Delaware-Rondout and Delaware Aqueduct system was developed in the watershed of the East Branch and Neversink, tributaries of the Delaware, and the Rondout, tributary of the Hudson. Because of the water shortage in New York City in 1950, an emergency station with a capacity of 100 million gallons per day was set up to pump water from the Hudson River into the Delaware River Aqueduct. In 1963, drought reduced reservoirs to about one-third their normal supply. Metered water to the three-fourths of the water users now on estimated consumption basis might help conserve the supply.

Boston, having outgrown the supplies of the Framingham and Wachusett reservoirs, receives an additional water supply from the Quabbin Reservoir in the Connecticut Valley. The State of Connecticut filed a bill of complaint with the Supreme Court against the Commonwealth of Massachusetts for planning to divert the waters of the tributaries of the Connecticut from their natural flow into that river.

Other cities on secondary streams have ensured themselves a supply of surface water by impounding the rivers. Those cities on the major rivers and on the Great Lakes pump their water directly from the source with less danger of the supply diminishing acutely. Chicago and Milwaukee draw their water directly from Lake Michigan; Duluth, from Lake Superior; Detroit, from Lake St. Clair; and Toledo, Cleveland, and Buffalo, from Lake Erie, whereas Syracuse takes its water from Skaneateles Lake and Rochester from Hemlock and Canadice lakes.

Wells supply all the water for 150 cities with populations of 25,000; a dozen or more cities including Houston, San Antonio, Miami, Dayton, and Wichita are in the metropolitan group.

The surface supply of New York City; Los Angeles; San Francisco; Indianapolis; Columbus, Ohio; Louisville, Kentucky; Pittsburgh, Pennsylvania; and St. Louis, Missouri, are supplemented by wells.

Second and Third Groups. The remaining population of the United States lives in towns and cities with less than 100,000 population and on individual farmsteads. The water supply for this portion of the population is obtained chiefly from groundwater. On the farms and in the villages individual wells are pumped by hand, windmill, gasoline engine, or electric motor.

In the larger towns and small cities the individual wells have given way to water companies or municipal water systems. As the demand for domestic and industrial water has increased, groundwater has not been adequate, and many small cities have added surface supplies by pumping directly, if they are located on large rivers or lakes, by impounding small streams, or by purchasing water from nearby large cities that already had established an adequate surface supply. Mountain towns depend on the melting snow and rain to keep open reservoirs filled.

Although more than 75 percent of the municipal water systems in the Midwest, lower Mississippi Valley, Gulf Coast, Southwest, and New Jersey and Delaware on the Atlantic coast depend upon groundwater for their source of supply, about 53 percent of the communities with populations of 10,000 or more depend on surface supplies only, 28 percent on groundwater only, and 12 percent on a combination of both. Less than 25 percent of the nation's population supply their own water, with about one-fourth without running water. About 2000 million gallons are for domestic uses and the rest for livestock.

CONSERVATION PROBLEMS

The two major conservation problems affecting water for domestic and industrial purposes are the quantity of water available and its quality for the purpose for which it is to be used. It is upon these two conditions that the entire program of water conservation rests.

As cities have grown and running water for domestic purposes has been made available, the per capita consumption has risen. With urbanization came tremendously increased utilization of water for industrial purposes. Likewise the greater number of people and especially their concentration in urban groupings have caused a problem of sewage disposal which together with industrial waste has helped to pollute many of the existing sources of water supply. The conditions of deforestation, erosion, floods, and declining water tables are also contributing factors in the complete conservation problem.

Pollution. The disposal of sewage and industrial waste is an important problem of water conservation, especially in the metropolitan districts. Great Lakes cities draw domestic water from the lakes and return sewage to them; Chicago discharges sewage into the Sanitary Canal, dilutes it by water diverted from Lake Michigan, and then the Illinois River delivers the city's waste to the Mississippi. River cities draw their domestic supply from the river above the town and return the sewage, partially or entirely untreated, into the river below the city. Industries also withdraw water for numerous industrial uses and return various types of industrial waste. The Ohio, the largest of the interior rivers flowing through the populated, industrial portion of the United States, is our most utilized river. From Pittsburgh at its source to Cairo at the Mississippi confluence, it is lined with industrial and commercial cities and towns, all of which draw their water supplies from the river and return domestic sewage and industrial waste. The tributaries of the Ohio are similarly utilized. The Mahoning River, which flows through the Youngstown, Ohio, steel district, is so extensively used and re-used that the hot, rusty liquid has little resemblance to a river (the temperature of the water sometimes reaches 115 degrees F).

Although pollution has become a problem in the lower Great Lakes concern is also expressed for the upper Lakes. Both Lake Michigan and Lake Erie have become polluted. Because of its size and shallow depth pollution is most serious in Lake Erie. In the Cleveland area conditions are such that bathing beaches are useless. Attempts were made to block off and renovate bathing beaches. It is estimated that Lake Erie could be restored about 90

percent in 6 years because of its low volume, whereas Lake Michigan, if equally polluted, would require 100 years for the same restoration, and Lake Superior over 500 years. It is obvious that they must not be allowed to become that polluted initially.

THE OHIO RIVER VALLEY SANITATION COMPACT. With the industrial and commercial development of the Ohio River Valley, like that of many other valleys in the United States, has come increased utilization of the water in the streams. The Ohio is used for commerce, particularly for a heavy barge traffic in coal, sand, and gravel, and iron and steel products. Many industries require enormous quantities of water in their industrial processes or for cooling.

An average of more than two bills per year concerning water pollution was introduced in Congress in the past century. The Water Pollution Act was adopted in 1948, and on June 30, 1948, the Ohio River Valley Water Sanitation Compact was ratified by Ohio, Indiana, West Virginia, New York, Illinois, Kentucky, Pennsylvania, and Virginia. The cooperation of the several states can do much to reduce the pollution of the Ohio and its tributaries.

Flowing water exposed to sunlight and air tends to purify itself. The problem of pollution has become more complex as domestic and industrial uses have placed an ever-increasing drain on the volume of water. Sewage and industrial wastes have increased enormously; aquatic life has been partially destroyed; silting due to increased erosion has been accelerated; and floods and droughts have become more acute, produced in part by deforestation and improper utilization of the watersheds.

THE WATER FACILITIES ACT. A Cabinet Committee was appointed by President Eisenhower on May 26, 1954, to review all water policies and programs, to assist in the coordination of activities of the various government agencies concerned with water, and to consider national legislation on water. Nearly 3 months later the Water Facilities Act was signed by the President on August 17, 1954.

At the National Conference on Water Pollution in December 1960, it was pointed out that cities were having great difficulties in keeping abreast of the ever-increasing amounts of sewage, while trying to cut the backlog of untreated sewage from existing sewers. Industry was having an even greater problem keeping up with ever-increasing production. In the United States untreated sewage from 22 million people is discharged yearly, over 60 percent of which occurs in the river basins of the Northeast, North Atlantic, Ohio, and the Southeast.

The Committee on Water Resources Research was set up in September 1963 by the Federal Council for Science and Technology. In October 1964, Congress passed the Water Resources Research Act and in 1965, the Water Resources Planning Act. UNESCO sponsored the International Hydrological Decade. In 1965, the Federal Water Pollution Control Act was passed. In 1966, the Federal Clean Water Law, and in May 1966, the Federal Water Pollution Control Authority was established in the Department of the Interior. Under this authority the Water Quality Act set June 30, 1967, as the deadline for the states to set up water pollution controls. The Federal Water Resources Research Program for the fiscal year 1968 allocated $134,000,000 for this purpose.

The 90th Congress (1968) passed legislation providing for a National Water Commission to make a one- to five-year study of the nation's most pressing water problems and to recommend solutions to Congress. The seven commissioners were not to be federal employees but were appointed by the President.

Purification of water and the processing of sewage and industrial waste are two of the important steps in the program of conservation of surface water, since sewage and industrial waste in the rivers and lakes are among the major causes of pollution. Beginnings have

been made to process sewage and industrial waste, returning only harmless residues to the streams and lakes. If these processes are carried to their logical ends—reclaiming usable materials from industrial waste and producing fertilizers from sewage—only pure water would be returned to the streams and lakes, and one of the conservation problems would be solved.

Because most surface water is polluted, domestic supplies taken from streams and lakes are purified according to the nature of the pollution. Because the water of the Great Lakes is potable in its natural state, the cities drawing their water supply from the lakes have placed their intakes far out in the lake in deep water to overcome in part the pollution from sewage and industrial plants along the lake shore. Most rivers have a much higher degree of pollution, and more extensive purification and sterilization processes must be followed than are necessary in the lake cities to ensure clean, tasteless, pure water for domestic use.

Among the numerous processes that have been developed to remove the various undesirable and dangerous substances from water of polluted sources that are intended for domestic consumption are sedimentation, coagulation, filtration, aeration, chlorination, and coppering.

River water is usually turbid or muddy from the amount of material carried in suspension by the flowing water. The more excessive erosion becomes, the greater is the problem of dealing with turbidity, the silting of reservoirs, and the like. Turbidity ranges all the way from 100 to 5000 parts of suspended material in a million in the various rivers of the United States.[2]

Much of the suspended material is removed from turbid water in settling basins, after

[2] As of October 1967, the U.S. Geological Survey reported dissolved and suspended material in milligrams per liter instead of ppm.

which sulfate of alumina is introduced to coagulate organic matter and entangle bacteria. Turbidity is further reduced and harmful bacteria are removed by both mechanical and bacterial filtration. Odor and taste due to the destroyed bacteria are removed by aeration. Coppering prevents the growth of algae, which tend to cause taste and odor in the water. Especially in water that has not been subjected to other processes of purification, chlorination serves as a germicide and effective safeguard.

The water supply for both domestic and industrial purposes of almost all communities must be treated in some way before it is used. Of the communities of 25,000 or more in the United States served by organized water supply systems, all use chlorination processes. Chlorination alone is used in only 26 percent of the communities, filtration is added to chlorination in 29 percent, softening is included in 17 percent, and various combinations with chlorination are used in 28 percent.

Fluoridation has been a source of great controversy in recent years. It is not a problem of destroying impurities in the water but of adding fluorides to the human body.

Mineral Content. Groundwater supplies, especially from deep wells, are less likely to be polluted but usually present two equally perplexing problems. One is the presence of minerals in solution in the water; the other is a diminished supply due to falling water tables. Much of the groundwater, as well as some surface water that has been in contact with calcareous material, contains magnesium and calcium salts and other soluble material in solution in sufficient quantities to cause the water to be hard and therefore less desirable for many purposes. Hardness is a measure of the calcium and magnesium salts in solution in the water. Soft water contains less than 60 parts of salt per million; temporarily hard water contains from 60 to 120 ppm; and permanently hard water contains more than 120 ppm (Fig. 7).

Temporary hardness may be removed by simple softening processes, but permanent hardness cannot be removed without extensive and expensive permutate operations. Municipal or water company softeners are sometimes employed, but in most towns and cities depending on hard groundwater the softening is at the discretion and expense of the user. Soft-water services have been established in hard-water communities, both the softener and the regenerating service being conducted on a rental basis. Since hard water does not permit the proper detergent action of soap, it is not desirable for household purposes or for laundries. Various types of textile mills, breweries, photographic establishments, laundries, and steam boilers also require large quantities of soft water.

Since the development of atomic energy, fallout, especially strontium-90, has become a contamination problem. In excess it is considered harmful to people and detrimental to certain industrial activities. More than 1 ppm exists in the streams of western Texas and Oklahoma and southeastern New Mexico and Arizona. The lowest concentration, less than 0.1 ppm, is in the Pacific Northwest, Central Valley of California, and southeastern United States. The rest has a concentration between 0.5 and 0.1 ppm. The presence of nonradioactive natural strontium complicates the removal of strontium-90 from surface water.

Manganese, iron, sulfur, and sodium chloride are other harmful or undesirable mineral properties of groundwater that affect the taste or odor of the water. Sulfur water and salt water from deep wells are not potable but are suitable for cooling. If the salt water is dense enough, the brine is usable in the chemical industry. Sulfur water is suitable for air-conditioning plants. The spent water, however, is, or should be, returned to a dry well rather than the sewer.

The substitution of chemical detergents for soap has caused problems in water supplies. Since some detergents do not break down as

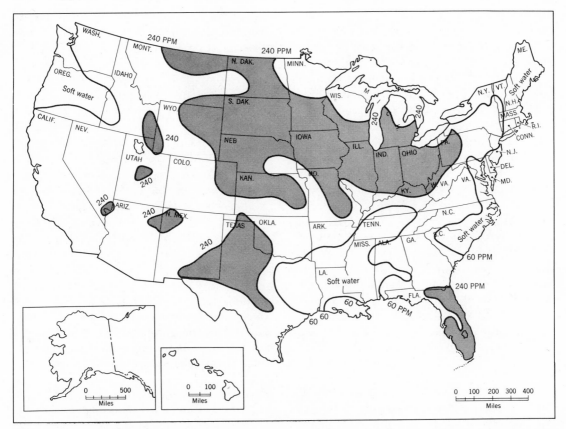

Fig. 7 Hard groundwater. The groundwater of the shaded areas contains more than 240 ppm of CaCo₃ in solution. (*Water Atlas of the United States,* Water Information Center.)

soap does in sewage treatment, great quantities of suds create problems in surface water into which treated or untreated sewage charged with chemical detergents has been discharged. However, the detergent may have certain beneficial effects at the sewage disposal works.

Declining Water Table. One of the conservation problems confronting towns and cities that depend on groundwater as a source of supply is the declining level of the water table. Especially in the dry regions where numerous wells tap the groundwater for both domestic and irrigation water, the level of the water table has fallen a number of feet, making it necessary to deepen many of the wells.

Also in humid areas groundwater is being removed faster than it is being replaced by recipitation. Similarly, the hydrostatic pressure of artesian wells has been reduced until some of them have ceased to flow above the level of the ground.

Any well drilled into the groundwater and pumped continuously lowers the water table in a great cone in the vicinity of the well into which the water must percolate from the surrounding area. If the water-bearing formation is composed of coarse, porous material the water will flow in rapidly, but if it is fine-grained material the replacement will be slow, and it will be relatively easy to pump the well dry temporarily. Thus it is necessary to drill a series of wells at rather widely spaced intervals to ensure an adequate water supply for a town or city entirely dependent on wells. More and deeper wells are drilled as the demand for water increases, and many communities turn to surface water for their supply.

About 70 percent of the population of the United States depends on public water-supply systems that utilize both groundwater and surface water to supply about 21,000 million gallons per day (Fig. 3). Of this group 58 percent of the systems furnishes an adequate supply of water at all times for 51 percent of the people. About 32 percent receives an inadequate supply all the time or must expect periodic shortages and restrictions in water use, and 17 percent depends on an uncertain supply. With the rapid increase of population and the rising industrial demand, adequate water for domestic and industrial uses will be a continuing problem. The quality of water supplies will require continuous attention.

CONSERVATION ATTITUDES

The problem of water conservation is not one that can be solved independently of the conservation of the other natural resources. It is possible to restrict the use of water by various devices of metering, checking leaks, and raising the price. Although desirable and necessary at times and in various places, restricted use is not a solution.

The total volume of water will always depend on the amount that falls as precipitation, whereas the available water depends upon flyoff, runoff, and cutoff, or the relation of evaporation, surface drainage, and groundwater. It has been estimated that if only 1 percent of the 70 percent of the water lost to evaporation from other than irrigated land was saved, that water would meet the needs of our present population of all of our metropolitan regions. It follows then that open reservoirs are wasteful unless protected by evaporation covers of some type. Underground storage, recharging by surface waters through dry wells, and the purification and re-use of water are among the necessary conservation measures. Much progress has also been made in desalinization, both of sea water and of ground water with high concentrates of salts. Several processes have been perfected, but the amount made usable is not great. The reduction of pollution and the purification of surface waters is one of the most urgent needs of conservation today.

Sufficient forest and grass cover will retard runoff and floods, reduce erosion, and raise the level of the groundwater. With a proper balance of evaporation, runoff, and groundwater maintained by adequate reforestation and soil conservation programs an enduring source of water for everything but the most fantastic demands can be ensured.

To complete the conservation program the problem of pollution must be solved by disposing of domestic sewage and industrial waste in a manner that will not contaminate water supplies. The best conservation program to ensure a water supply for domestic and industrial purposes is a good reforestation and natural vegetation program, an intelligent soil conservation program, an adequate flood control program, as well as an enlightened wildlife conservation program, for they are all the same—the intelligent and continuous utilization of our natural resources.

References

Baldwin, Helene L. and C. L. McGuinnus, *Primer on Ground Water,* U.S. Geological Survey, Washington, D.C., 1963.

Beattie, Byron, *Nature's Water Factory,* U.S. Department of Agriculture Forest Service, Washington, D.C.

Blake, Nelson M., *Water for the Cities,* Syracuse University Press, Syracuse, New York, 1956.

Fair, Gordon M. and John C. Geyer, *Water Supply and Waste-Water Disposal,* John Wiley & Sons, New York, 1954.

Ingram, William, and Kenneth M. Mackenthurm, *Biological Field Investigative Data for Water Pollution Surveys,* Superintendent of Documents, Washington, D.C., 1967.

Journal of the American Water Work Association, American Water Work Association, New York.

List of Research Projects Under Title I of the Water Resources Research Act, Washington, D.C., 1967.

Miller, D. W., J. J. Geraghty, and R. S. Collins, *Water Atlas of the United States,* Water Information Center, Port Washington, New York, 1962.

Murphy, Earl Finbar, *Water Purity, A Study in Legal Control of Natural Resources,* The University of Wisconsin Press, Madison, 1961.

Proceedings, First Annual Meeting, American Water Resources Association, Urbana, Illinois, 1965.

Proceedings, The National Conference on Water Pollution, U.S. Department of Health, Education, and Welfare, Public Health Service, Washington, D.C., 1961.

Public Water Supply, Business Report, U.S. Department of Commerce, Government Printing Office, Washington, D.C., 1955.

Thomas, Harold E., *The Conservation of Ground Water,* McGraw-Hill Book Co., New York, 1951.

Water Resources Research Catalogue, Vol. 2, U.S. Department of the Interior, Office of Water Resources Research, 1966.

Water, The Yearbook of Agriculture, U.S. Department of Agriculture, Government Printing Office, Washington, D.C., 1955.

Water and Sewage Works, Vols. 93–103, Chicago, 1946–1956.

Water Newsletter, Water Supply, Waste Disposal, Conservation, Water Information Center, Port Washington, New York.

Water Supply Papers, U.S. Geological Survey, Government Printing Office, Washington, D.C.

LOWRY B. KARNES
Bowling Green State University

CHAPTER 10

Reclamation of Wet and Overflow Lands

The man-land ratio in the United States is not nearly as satisfactory as most people believe it to be; effective conservation practices are absolutely essential if we are to maintain an ever-rising standard of living for an ever-increasing number of people.

The drainage or the protection of overflow lands as a phase of the conservation of the agricultural resources is a rather complex problem. This complexity is indicated by sharp disagreement as to whether the drainage or protection of wet lands is a conservation measure at all.

Water is an indispensable element of the natural environment and only that water which is on or beneath the surface of the land is readily available for use by man. In all parts of the country there is developing an increasingly difficult problem of providing an adequate supply of water for domestic and industrial use. Furthermore, as the per capita acreage of cropland decreases, due to increasing population and other causes, there will develop an increasing demand for water for supplemental irrigation. As the need for water increases the problem of keeping water on the land rather than hastening its removal from the land will become increasingly important. Artificial drainage is only one phase of the major problem of water management, and no drainage project should be undertaken unless it can be demonstrated that the planned operation will be consistent with sound water management. If drainage of new land is to be undertaken as a step toward the wise use of the land, it should be inferred that the need for further extension of arable land is sufficiently great that the benefits to be derived from bringing new land into agricultural use will be greater than the cost of the labor and capital involved.

We hear and read a great deal about the destruction of our land and the increasing needs of the people for food, clothing, and industrial raw materials, but during most of this century, one of the most troublesome problems in the national economy has been overcapacity of agricultural productive facilities. There appears to be no immediate necessity for additional land to supply the needs of the people of the country.[1]

[1] J. Frederic Dewhurst and Associates, *America's Needs and Resources, A New Survey*, New York, 1955, pp. 783–800.

Agricultural drainage refers to the removal, by artificial means, of excess water to improve the condition of land used, or to be used, for agriculture. Excess water either in or on the soil—whether a permanent or a temporary condition—influences farm production, farm income, and farm values. Too much water in the soil adversely affects crop growth and the timely performance of operations such as tillage, seeding, cultivation, and harvesting.

Accumulation of excess water can arise from heavy local precipitation, runoff from upstream areas, low-lying land in depressions, tidal action in coastal areas, impervious subsoil, build-up of a high water table as a result of irrigation or seepage, or from artesian or other underground movement of water.

The question may arise as to the desirability of draining additional land in order to have it ready for immediate use, when needed, to provide food and fibers for our growing population and industrial raw materials for our rapidly expanding industry. There is abundant evidence from all types of land from Michigan [2] to Florida [3] that marshland deteriorates more rapidly after it is drained than it does in its natural state. Several causes contribute to this deterioration, but the most serious one seems to be general subsidence of the land due to settling and accelerated oxidation of the organic matter in the drained soil. Also, fire may completely destroy peat and muck soil, thus lowering the level of the land surface. So long as the water table is maintained at the surface of the ground, little or no deterioration occurs, and the land is more likely to be available for full productive use than it would be if it were drained and thus exposed to the hazards of subsidence and fire.

Although it appears certain that there is no need for additional agricultural land in this country in 1970, it is almost equally certain that the time will come when it will be necessary to bring new land into cultivation. It would be impractical here to attempt to say just when that time will come or to attempt to recount all the means whereby its coming may be postponed.

Importance of Drainage. The drainage of wet lands offers the greatest of all potential sources of additional farmland. Some evidence of the present and potential importance of drainage as a means of adding to, or improving, our agricultural land is derived from the fact that more than 100,000,000 acres of land have been drained, and it is estimated that a comparable amount of additional land is capable of being drained.[4] The acreage of land provided with irrigation is approximately 30,000,000 acres, and the prospects of doubling this figure by additional developments are far from encouraging. Roughly one-fifth of our best agricultural land has been made available or has been improved by drainage, and, at least theoretically, it would be possible to increase the amount of farmland by a similar amount by additional drainage. However, the quality of much of this additional land is questionable.

The conservation of wet and overflow lands has a twofold significance in that it involves the improvement of lands now in use and the reclamation of lands not now used. The common assumption is that unused land is that not being used for crops, pasture, or forestry and that used land includes all in privately owned farms, ranches, and woodlands. However, it must be recognized that a great deal of undrained land has a present value as a habitat for native animal life, as a resting place and a nesting and feeding area for migratory waterfowl, and as a habitat for

---

[2] *State Planning, Review of Activities and Progress,* National Resources Board, Washington, D.C., 1935, p. 156.

[3] Glenn K. Rule, "The Challenging Glades," *The Land,* Vol. XI, 1952, p. 156.

[4] *Land Available for Agriculture Through Reclamation,* Supplementary Report of the Land Planning Committee to the National Resources Board, Part IV, Washington, D.C., 1937.

aquatic life, as well as having scientific value for studying plant and animal life.[5] Also, before an attempt is made to drain new land, there should be recognition of the potential value of the area as a regulator of stream flow and a source of groundwater supply. Drainage is conducive to rapid runoff, and thus may result in erosion, floods, and the deposition of debris.

Drainage projects should not be undertaken without comprehensive knowledge of the ends sought, the values involved, and the probable results. However, there appear to be some circumstances under which the drainage of new land can be thoroughly justified. Landowners paying taxes on unproductive lands may find it advantageous to drain land to protect their investment or to increase their income. Also, it is probable that some farmers now located on submarginal land might advantageously be moved to more fertile land made available by drainage. Nevertheless, before investing heavily in new drainage enterprises the individuals should know that many such undertakings were never completed and that some that were completed have been abandoned as economically unsound. Before new land is drained, its potentialities should be studied thoroughly to determine whether the land would be more valuable for recreational and scientific purposes than if put to agricultural use.

LAND IN DRAINAGE ENTERPRISES

Classes of Wet and Overflow Lands. Wet and overflow lands vary greatly in their productive capacities and in other agricultural advantages and disadvantages.

Wet lands, more or less permanently, have such a high water table that they cannot be farmed profitably. Overflow lands, although not permanently wet, are so situated that inundation is sufficiently frequent that farming is impractical or severely handicapped.

The problems associated with wet and overflow lands are so numerous and they vary so much from place to place that it is convenient to group them into the following classes within which generalizations are possible: (1) the outer Coastal Plain along our Atlantic and Gulf coasts, including tidal marshes; (2) river floodplains, of which the Mississippi River floodplain and delta are the most extensive; (3) glacial lands of low relief and obstructed drainage; (4) alkaline or water-logged areas associated with irrigation enterprises; and (5) wet spots on slopes or flat land where the land surface intersects the general water table or a perched water table. No data are available on the amount of land that has been drained or should be drained in the last class, but undoubtedly the total acreage of such lands would reach into the millions of acres.

Extent of Drained Land. No attempt has been made to estimate accurately the amount of land in the United States that should be drained. Reasonably satisfactory data are available concerning the extent and location of artificially drained land and land in drainage enterprises. In 1920, when the first census of drained land was taken, there were 65,-000,000 acres reported in drainage enterprises.[6] The next decade showed a great increase in acreage (to 84,000,000 acres in 1930) related partly to great activity in drainage enterprises and in part to more complete data. The acreage of drained land increased slowly during the decade from 1930 to 1940 because these years were characterized by drought conditions that lowered water tables, and capital was not available during the depression years

---

[5] *Recreational Use of Land in the United States*, Report on Land Planning, Part XI, National Park Service, Washington, D.C., 1934, p. 55.

[6] All the data for this discussion of the expansion of drainage enterprises were taken from *Drainage of Agricultural Lands*, U.S. Census of Agriculture for 1950, Vol. IV, Washington, D.C., 1952, and from U.S. Census of Agriculture, 1959, Vol. IV, Washington, D.C., 1961.

for desirable improvements. The decade from 1940 to 1950 witnessed renewed intensification of activity in drainage as rainfall returned to normal and as wartime and postwar markets brought prosperity to farmers and increases in land values, enabling them to improve their land. During this decade the reported acreage of drained land increased from 87,000,000 acres in 1940 to 103,000,000 acres in 1950. The actual increase was somewhat greater than these figures would indicate because the 1950 census did not include drainage enterprises with fewer than 500 acres. Furthermore, the 87,000,000 acres reported in 1940 included the entire area of irrigation developments that had their own drainage, whereas the figures for 1950 included only the land in such developments that was actually drained.

The total area in drainage projects serving agricultural lands according to the 1960 census was 101,870,257 acres. This is slightly less than the acreage reported in 1950, but actually represents an increase for comparable categories of land. The 1960 data excluded about 3 million acres of drained irrigated land and about 6 million acres of swamp and waste lands which had been included in the 1950 census. During the decade of the 1950's, drainage was reported as newly established on 5.3 million acres and new works or services on previously established drainage projects amounting to 2.6 million acres. The total cost of drainage works and services during the 10-year period from 1950 to 1959 inclusive was $461,875,000. About 40 percent of this was for new works.[7]

Small-sized enterprises accounted for about 5 percent of the total acreage of artificially drained land reported in 1940. If we can assume that the ratio of land in small drainage enterprises to that in large enterprises was about the same in 1960 as in 1940, it would

appear that slightly more than 5,000,000 acres of land in enterprises of less than 500 acres were drained in 1960. This would bring the total acreage of artificially drained land in organized drainage enterprises to about 107,-000,000 acres. In addition to organized drainage enterprises, there are large numbers of small undertakings which have never been tabulated.

PROBLEMS ASSOCIATED WITH WET-LAND RECLAMATION

Is It Wise to Drain More Land? The need for drainage appears to be local and personal, since there is no need for increasing the national acreage of farmland at present. As a local and personal problem, the principal aim of drainage is to improve the use of the land and thus promote the welfare of the community and the landowner. This certainly cannot be achieved unless the benefits exceed the cost. Thus, it is advisable, before any drainage project is undertaken, to analyze thoroughly the benefits expected and to weigh them carefully against the expected cost of the project and its maintenance. Furthermore, when estimating the costs involved and the probable benefits to be derived, it should be borne in mind that certain costs will be more or less recurrent and permanent. Therefore, in making comparisons between costs and anticipated benefits, it is necessary to add the probable annual cost of upkeep to the initial cost of the enterprise and to determine whether or not the increase in product from the land will be sufficient to amortize the entire cost within a reasonable time and yield a profit. The farmer who undertakes to improve his welfare by the drainage of his land should allow a considerable margin between costs and benefits, or he may find himself losing money during periods of decreasing farm prices.

From a regional or community point of view, the improvement of land through drainage may be expected to yield such benefits as

[7] *Drainage of Agricultural Lands,* U.S. Census of Agriculture for 1959, Final Report, Vol. IV, Washington, D.C., 1961.

increased land values with higher tax duplicates and all the benefits that come from them, the elimination of mosquito-breeding areas, and the addition of land available for homes. Yet the greater share of the cost of any land improvement will, in the long run, be borne by the farmer, and he must be concerned with the money value of the benefits as compared with the cost of the improvement. The farmer is interested in increasing the quantity and improving the quality of his product, and it is very difficult for him to know with certainty just what financial returns these may bring.

Certainly no farmer should undertake a major drainage project until he has thoroughly investigated every phase of the problem involved. He must ascertain carefully the quality and depth of his soil. He should determine as precisely as possible the amount of settling that will follow drainage, the effects of the increased rate of oxidation of organic material, and the possibility of fire if his soil has a very high content of organic matter. He should consider alternate uses of the land that would prove profitable with little or no outlay of capital. The land might be used profitably as it is, or with but little improvement, for pasture or forest. It might be adaptable for rice, cranberries, ducks, or aquatic life. If his land happens to be a resting place for migratory waterfowl, perhaps he could realize a net gain by selling hunting privileges. He might combine a drainage project with the development of one or more farm ponds and thus achieve benefits from the drainage of part of the land and at the same time plan to harvest fish or other aquatic life from the ponds. Many farmers report that, acre for acre, the most productive parts of their farms are their ponds. If he decides to drain his land, crops should be grown that are best suited to the soil and the climate of the area and to the market. This list of problems is not intended to be exhaustive, but it is sufficiently long to demonstrate that the drainage

of additional land is not something to be entered into hastily.

Methods of Drainage. After a landowner has carefully considered his problem from all angles and has decided to drain his land, he has to face the question of which method of drainage will be most advantageous. First he should determine whether a thorough perforation of the subsoil would permit the surface water to sink into the ground fast enough to give him all the drainage he needs. This procedure probably would be the cheapest method, it would get the water off the land without contributing to increased flow of streams, and it would help to maintain the permanent water table.

If the foregoing method is not feasible and actual drainage installations are necessary, the choice will probably be between open ditches and tile. Tile drains have an advantage over open ditches in that they do not take valuable land out of use. However, open ditches are effective as well as cheap and are simple to install; they are much more extensively used than tile drains. In 1960, there were, in the country as a whole, about three times as many miles of open ditches as there were of tile drains. Moreover, the relative popularity of open ditches appears to be increasing: between 1940 and 1950, sixteen times as many miles of open ditches were constructed as of tile drains (9301 miles of open ditches to 581 miles of tile drains). From 1950 to 1960, the comparable figures were 33,543 miles of open ditches and 2192 miles of tile or covered drains. Open ditches seem to be especially favored in the southeastern states, whereas tile drains are more extensively used in the Corn Belt, a fact which is doubtless related to the higher land values of the latter region. Ohio, Indiana, and Iowa have more than one-half of all the mileage of tile drains in the entire country (Fig. 1).

The practice of land grading or smoothing, popularly known as land leveling, is very common in connection with irrigation and

Fig. 1 Ditching has been simplified by the development of adjustable machines that are adaptable to the construction of deep, narrow trenches or broad, shallow ditches which offer little interference with field operations (The John Deere Company.)

the drainage of irrigated land. In recent years this practice has become increasingly popular in the humid eastern states. It is less expensive than tiling, and it offers little or no interference with ordinary field operations. No data are available concerning the amount of land now drained by land leveling, but it is reasonable to expect this practice to increase greatly in the future.

In some cases the success of a drainage enterprise is dependent on pumps. The total area served by pumps in 1950 was just under 1.7 million acres. From 1950 to 1960 the number of drainage pumps in use was approximately doubled, but figures as to the acreage benefited are not available.

It is obvious that pumping should be resorted to where topography is such that grav-

ity alone cannot be made to yield the desired results, but pumping is also advantageous in places where it is especially desirable to control carefully the water table, as is the case with peat and muck lands. In such soils most crops will not grow if the water table is too high. On the other hand, if the water table is lowered too far, the results can be serious. The most common of these serious results of excessive lowering of the water table are fire, wind erosion, and rapid decomposition of organic matter.[8] The most extensive areas of land drained by pumping are located in California,

[8] M. S. Anderson, S. T. Blake, and A. L. Mehring, *Peat and Muck in Agriculture,* Circular 888, U.S. Department of Agriculture, Washington, D.C., 1951, p. 27.

Florida, Louisiana, Illinois. and Missouri.[9] Because of the expense involved in pump drainage, it is especially important to weigh carefully the expected benefits.

THE LOCATION FACTOR

Geographic Distribution of Drainage Enterprises. Although some drainage was reported in every state in the country in 1950, West Virginia, the Commonwealth of Pennsylvania, Alaska, Hawaii, and the New England states did not report any regularly organized drainage enterprises of more than 500 acres in extent.

In the forty states that did report regularly

[9] U.S. Bureau of the Census, *Drainage of Agricultural Lands,* 1959, p. 21.

organized drainage enterprises, the amount of drained land is very unevenly distributed (Fig. 2). The states of Indiana, Michigan, and Minnesota each have approximately 10 percent of the total for the country, whereas Ohio, Illinois, and Iowa together have about 20 percent. Thus six of our north-central states account for about 50 percent of the total acreage of drained land in the country.

The only other states that individually account for as much as 5 percent of the total acreage of drained land are Louisiana, Florida, and Texas, with Arkansas ranking next with about 4.8 percent of the total (Fig. 3). In 1960, Louisiana reported slightly more than 9 million acres in drainage enterprises and thus ranked fifth in the country, with about 9 percent of the total for the country. In contrast to the nine states which report more than 5

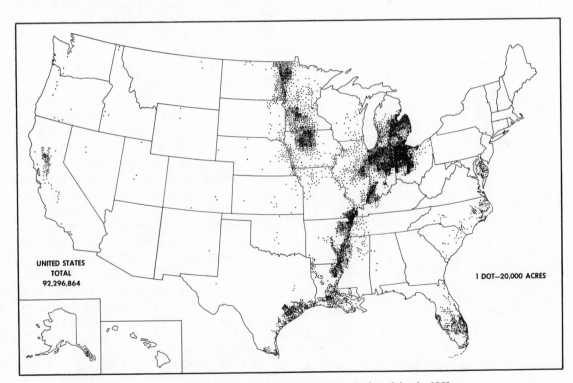

UNITED STATES
TOTAL
92,296,864

1 DOT—20,000 ACRES

Fig. 2 Map of the United States, showing the location of drained agricultural lands, 1960 (U.S. Bureau of the Census.)

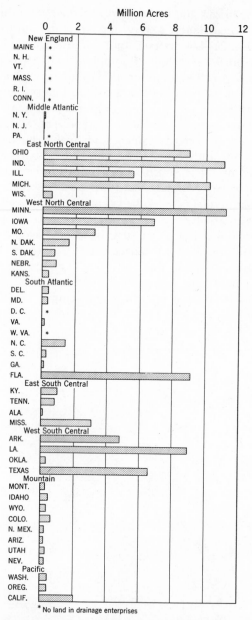

Fig. 3 Land in drainage enterprises by states. (*Drainage of Agricultural Lands*, U.S. Census of Agriculture: 1959, Final Report—Vol. IV.)

million acres of drained land, there are twenty-nine states (including the ten previously mentioned as reporting no drainage enter-

prises) that report less than 500,000 acres each. These are distributed in such a way that at least one such state is found in every census division except the East North Central, in which the State of Wisconsin, reporting 587,-000 acres, passes the half-million mark by only 87,000 acres.

Although maps of drainable wet lands show extensive areas of such lands along our Atlantic coast, there is only one state (North Carolina) which has more than 400,000 acres in drainage enterprises (Fig. 4). North Carolina's 1,498,892 acres in drainage enterprises account for approximately one-half of all the drained land along the Atlantic coast north of Florida. Florida alone has about six times this acreage in drainage enterprises. Most of the drainage in Florida was developed during the 1920's. The acreage of drained land remained relatively static until about 1950, but it has been increased by about 50 percent since then. Many of the principal drainage canals in Florida seem to have been put through without adequate consideration of the capabilities of the land and with insufficient knowledge of the problems involved.[10]

In the semiarid and subhumid western states drainage is not much of a problem except where it is associated with irrigation. In California, which leads all the western states in both irrigated area and land drained, it was estimated, in 1930, that 85 percent of all land in drainage enterprises was also irrigated land.[11] Although census data are not available to verify the assumption, it is reasonably safe to conclude that a similar relationship exists between drained land and irrigated land in California at the present time.

It may be noted also that California leads all states in the acreage of land drained by means of pumps.[12] Much of the pumping in

[10] Rule, *op. cit.*, p. 156.

[11] U.S. Bureau of the Census, *Drainage of Agricultural Lands, 15th Census of the United States, 1930*, Washington, 1932, p. 64.

[12] U.S. Census of Agriculture, 1950, *op. cit.*, p. xvii.

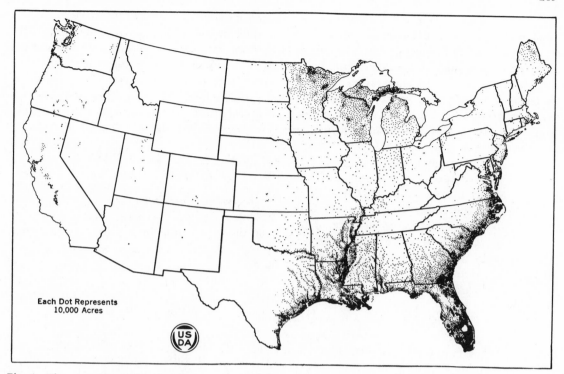

Fig. 4 The approximate location of drainable wet lands. (U.S. Department of Agriculture.)

irrigated areas is so arranged that the water can be pumped back onto the land and used a second, or even a third, time for irrigation.

Regional Appraisal of Drainage Achievements. About one-half of our drained land is in the Corn Belt and the Spring Wheat Region; without artificial drainage, these regions could not have attained the high rank as prosperous farming regions that they now enjoy.[13] However, the success of commercial agriculture has been favored in much of this area by such important factors as naturally fertile soil, topography favorable to machine-type agriculture, a stimulating climate that permits the growth of all middle-latitude

[13] Martin R. Kaatz, "The Black Swamp, A Study in Historical Geography," *Annals of the Association of American Geographers,* Vol. XLV, 1955, pp. 1–35.

crops, the world's finest transportation systems, and unexcelled markets for farm products. All these factors have combined to give the farmers of this region competitive advantages that have enabled them to finance costly improvement of their land at considerable financial benefit to themselves. However, there is evidence that drainage was extended too greatly in the northern parts of Michigan, Wisconsin, and Minnesota by including some land that is better adapted for forest growth, a haven for wild life, or for scientific and recreational purposes. Some adjustments have already been made to correct this, especially in Wisconsin.

Other areas of notable achievement in drainage are located in the states of Arkansas, Louisiana, and Texas. In Louisiana and Arkansas, the artificially drained areas lie chiefly on the back slopes of the levees along the Mississippi and Red rivers. These areas have been relatively easy and inexpensive to drain, chiefly by using open ditches extending down the slope away from the main rivers. The soil is fertile alluvium, and the growing season is so long, especially in Louisiana, that off-season crops can be marketed advantageously in the North. Also, the fact that rice, a major crop in both Louisiana and Arkansas, has relatively little competition and that sugar, a major product in Louisiana, has effective tariff protection contributes to the ability of the farmers to operate profitably in spite of the expense of artificial drainage. The artificially drained lands in Texas lie mostly on the eastern coastal prairie where drainage becomes largely a matter of control of water for rice production.

Florida is the only other eastern state in which artificial drainage is extensive. About one-half of the land in drainage enterprises in that state is in the Everglades. Problems resulting from artificial drainage in this area include subsidence of the land, rapid oxidation of organic matter, and burning of the peat and muck soils when they dry out. These problems are combatted by careful regulation of the water table, which, in many cases, involves pumping water off the land during the wet season and pumping it onto the land during the dry season. The problem of regulation is complicated by the fact that the water table should be higher for some crops than for others, and it should be as near the surface as possible when the land is not in crops so as to retard oxidation. The difficulty of draining the land in the first place plus the costly problem of regulating the water table precisely make farming in the Everglades precarious. Other areas of artificial drainage in Florida include the west central part of the peninsula, extensive areas along the east coast, and the St. Johns River Basin. In all the drainage districts of Florida, there are extensive areas of infertile soil and unreliable rainfall, and in the coastal areas improper drainage sometimes results in infiltration of salt water. Thus the farming of artificially drained land in Florida is costly and precarious, and it has achieved a reasonable degree of success only because of the unexcelled market for off-season and subtropical fruits and vegetables in the northern and northeastern states.

SHALL ARTIFICIAL DRAINAGE BE EXTENDED?

Arguments for Extension of Drainage. No stronger argument favoring extension of artificial drainage can be offered than the fact that, on the whole, the artificial drainage of agricultural land has been highly successful. At least one-fifth of our best agricultural land has been made available for crops or has been improved by artificial drainage. This would seem to indicate the wisdom of proceeding with the drainage of additional land, even if it leads to the abandonment of other land already in use. Much submarginal land is in use that might profitably be retired and be replaced by better land acquired by drainage. This may raise the question of why artificial drainage is the key to the problem of the expansion of agricultural land or of the shift from inferior to more productive land. The answer to this problem is twofold: first, most of the remaining potentially arable land requires drainage; and second, artificially drained land is, with some exceptions, likely to be superior land.

What are some of the advantages of well-drained land which contribute to its superiority? The following advantages are readily apparent.

1. Adequate drainage, by removing surplus water, will lower and stabilize the water table and thus provide a greater depth of the root zone.

2. Well-drained soil warms up earlier in the spring and thus permits earlier planting and germination of crops.

3. Adequate drainage improves the physical condition of the soil, making for a better seedbed and better tillage.

4. On a field that is uniformly well drained, farm work can be done more efficiently.

5. Satisfactory conditions of drainage minimize damage by winter freezing.

6. Effective drainage contributes to improvement of both quality and quanity of crops and thus increases the gross income of the farmer.[14]

In comparing artificially drained land with land that has adequate natural drainage, it may be observed that:

1. The percentage of wasteland on the artificially drained land is relatively low.

2. Erosion is relatively insignificant on artificially drained land.

3. Artificially drained land is less likely to be affected by severe drought than is land that is so situated that it requires no artificial drainage.

4. Artificially drained land is usually so nearly level that labor-saving machinery can be used advantageously.

The student of conservation can doubtless think of additional advantages of artificially drained land, and he may also find exceptions to some of the advantages just listed. However, the list is long enough and reliable enough to suggest that there are sound arguments favoring the artificial drainage of additional land for agricultural use as fast as it can be effectively occupied.

Opposition to Extension of Artificial Drainage. For many years the United States Biological Survey and later the Fish and Wildlife Service pointed out that an undrained marsh might be more profitable than adjacent farmland and that it may provide feeding, breeding, and resting places for birds, fur-bearing animals, and other forms of life. It can yield great quantities of fish, a supply of natural ice, and grasses and other growth that can be used as forage, bedding, rugs, and baskets. It may maintain the water table, promote forest growth, ensure the flow of springs, and reduce runoff, thus reducing floods and erosion. Furthermore, it can provide areas for educational and recreational uses.[15]

Unfortunate experience in land drainage in a number of states has led to the opinion that: "Unused land should be kept under water until it is needed, to avoid subsidence, fire and oxidation."[16]

In recent years, since several large lumber and paper companies have become interested in maintaining forests on a sustained-yield basis, some of them have expressed themselves strongly against the extension of artificial drainage. At an open hearing of the United States Army Engineers in Memphis, an executive of one of the largest southern lumber companies pointed out that the drainage of new land usually leads to elimination of forests which often are of more value than any crops that might be raised on the land.[17] At the same hearing representatives of another large lumber company went so far as to express opposition to the drainage of land adjacent to forests. It was their contention that the lowering of the water table in cleared land adjacent to forests would result in the lowering of the water table in the nearby forests and thus make them more susceptible to destruction by drought.[18]

Another segment of our population, represented by both urban and rural dwellers, that

[14] Report on Land Planning, Part IV, *Land Available for Agriculture Through Reclamation,* Prepared by the Bureau of Agricultural Engineering, U.S. Department of Agriculture, for the Land Planning Committee of the National Resources Board, Washington, D.C., 1937, p. 37.

[15] U.S. Department of Agriculture, *Yearbook of Agriculture,* Washington, D.C., 1926, pp. 313–314.

[16] *State Planning,* Review of Activities and Progress, National Resources Board, Washington, D.C., 1935, p. 156.

[17] *Memphis Press-Scimitar,* April 12, 1955, p. 1.

[18] *Ibid.,* p. 2.

voices strong opposition to the extension of drainage includes the inhabitants of low-lying lands in downstream locations who fear that the speeding up of runoff from lands above them would increase the flood hazard in their own communities.

These examples are sufficient to demonstrate that there are some strongly organized groups who have legitimate arguments against drainage of additional land until it is needed for cropland and pasture, and that any major project is likely to meet with determined opposition until it has been proved to be fully justified.

Eutrophication. The destiny of lakes, particularly shallow bodies of water, is to disappear and the exposed land area to become a lacustrine plain. In the early stages of the evolution of a lake the depth of the water is reduced by sedimentation or the deposition of sand and silts by the tributary streams and by the winds. Along the margins of the lake where the water is shallow aquatic plants, by contributing their organic remains, help in the demise of the lake. The lake becomes smaller in circumference, shallower, and eventually becomes a swamp or a morass consisting of vegetation and water. In some areas a mat of floating vegetation may conceal pools of water beneath the surface. If such a lake receives sewage, either treated or untreated, the vegetation grows luxuriantly, and the conversion from a water area or swamp to a lacustrine plain is accelerated. This final demise of a lake is known as eutrophication.

The gradual transformation of a lake into a lacustrine plain may be hastened if it receives large quantities of sediment deposited by streams that discharge into the lake. The outlet of a lake may deepen its channel, and as a consequence the surface of the lake is lowered. Sediment, both water-borne and wind-blown, and organic debris decrease the depth of the water. The life of a lake may be extended by the use of dams in the headwater areas to reduce the discharge of sediments into the lake;

Fig. 5 Canada geese in flight over Horicon Marsh in southeastern Wisconsin. The northern portion of the marsh is the Horicon National Wildlife Refuge and contains 20,924 acres. The southern section consisting of 10,794 acres is state-owned and is known as the Horicon Marsh Wildlife Area. This expansive marsh has contained a lake area. Parts have been drained, and muck-land farming was practiced briefly. Today it is recognized as a marsh and is being maintained as such. (Wisconsin Natural Resources Department.)

aquatic plants may be destroyed by the use of chemical substances or by harvesting devices. The deepening of the outlet channel may be slowed by the construction of concrete flumes or sills that resist erosion. But the process of eutrophication goes on and eventually lakes become marshes; wet lands become lacustrine plains; and these areas, depending upon the stage of development, may or may not require artificial drainage to convert them into cropland (Fig. 5).

The resurgence of interest in water areas

and wet lands, wilderness areas, and other natural areas is well represented in official and scientific concern for the estuarine areas along the coasts of the country. Where the salt water of the sea mingles with the fresh water from the land the salinity is reduced. With the changing of the tides sea water advances and recedes and as a consequence creates special environmental conditions. The shallow water areas and the adjacent wet lands are important habitats for migrating and nesting waterfowl and for a variety of shellfish.[19]

In such coastal areas a rise in sea level expands the water areas. A recession of the coastline related to the lowering of sea level may result in the creation of coastal plains sufficiently elevated to be drained and cultivated. The current mood of the people is to preserve the water areas of the estuaries and the adjacent wet lands as they are and defer development until the economic needs of future generations are better known.

---

[19] For an extended discussion of coastal waters see George F. Lauff, editor, *Estuaries*, Publication No. 83, American Association for the Advancement of Science, Washington, D.C., 1967.

CONCLUSION

There is no present need for the drainage of new lands to provide food, fibers, and industrial raw materials for the people of our country. There are, however, many individual farmers and some communities that would profit by the drainage and improvement of agricultural lands in local areas.

Wet lands, subject to drainage, constitute the greatest reserve of new land available for use at some future time when our growing population and expanding industry require additional materials. Undoubtedly, the first major step should be the drainage and improvement of land already in farms.

Any major development of a drainage enterprise must be preceded by a thorough study of (1) need, based on accessibility to actual and potential markets; (2) desirability, based on comparative advantage of the use of the land for agriculture in relation to its use for other purposes; (3) physical condition of the land, to determine whether or not it will be permanently productive; and (4) cost, to determine whether or not the undertaking will be sufficiently profitable to pay for itself.

References

Agricultural Conservation Program; Summary, U.S. Department of Agriculture, Agricultural Conservation Program Service, Washington, D.C. An annual report.

Bartelli, L. J. and C. A. Engberg, "Classification of Michigan Lands According to Use Capability," *Papers of the Michigan Academy of Science, Arts and Letters*, Vol. XXXVIII, Part III, Geography and Geology, Ann Arbor, Michigan, 1952, pp. 287–294.

Bourn, W. S. and Clarence Cottam, *Some Biological Effects of Ditching Tidewater Marshes*, Research Report 19, Fish and Wildlife Service, Washington, D.C., 1950.

Clawson, Marion, R. Burnell Held, and Charles H. Stoddard, *Land for the Future*, Resources for the Future, The Johns Hopkins Press, Baltimore, 1960, pp. 432–439.

Darling, F. Fraser and John P. Milton, editors, *Future Environments of North America*, The Natural History Press, Garden City, New York, 1966.

Dewhurst, J. F. and Associates, *America's Needs and Resources, A New Survey,* The Twentieth Century Fund, New York, 1955, pp. 513–574.

Farm Drainage, Farmers' Bulletin 2046, U.S. Department of Agriculture, Washington, D.C., 1952.

Hewes, Leslie, "The Northern Wet Prairie of the United States: Nature, Sources of Information, and Extent," *Annals of the Association of American Geographers,* Vol. XLI, 1951, pp. 307–323.

Hewes, Leslie and Phillip E. Frandson, "Occupying the Wet Prairie: The Role of Artificial Drainage in Story County, Iowa," *Annals of the Association of American Geographers,* Vol. XLII, 1952, pp. 24–50.

Journal of Soil and Water Conservation, Official publication of the Soil Conservation Society of America, Inc., Des Moines, Iowa. A bimonthly periodical.

Kaatz, Martin R., "The Black Swamp: A Study in Historical Geography," *Annals of the Association of American Geographers,* Vol. XLV, 1955, pp. 1–35.

Lauff, George H., editor, *Estuaries,* Publication No. 83, American Association for the Advancement of Science, Washington, D.C., 1967.

Maintaining Drainage Systems, Farmers' Bulletin 2047, U.S. Department of Agriculture, Washington, D.C., 1952.

Peat and Muck in Agriculture, Circular 888, U.S. Department of Agriculture, Washington, D.C., 1951.

Peterson, Elmer T., "Insoak Is the Answer," *The Land,* Vol. XI, 1952, pp. 83–88.

Rule, Glenn K., "The Challenging Glades," *The Land,* Vol. XI, 1952, pp. 155–162.

Saunderson, Mont H., *Western Land and Water Use,* University of Oklahoma Press, Norman, Okla., 1950.

Sears, Paul B., "Comparative Costs of Restoration and Reclamation of Land," *Annals of the American Academy of Political and Social Science,* Vol. 281, 1952, pp. 126–134.

Soil Conservation Service, U.S. Department of Agriculture SCS, *National Engineering Handbook,* Section 16, *Drainage,* Chapter 1, "Principles of Drainage," Washington, D.C. 1961.

Supplementary Report of the Land Planning Committee to the National Resources Board, Part III: *Agricultural Land Requirements and Resources,* Part IV: *Land Available for Agriculture Through Reclamation,* Part VI: *Maladjustments in Land Use in the United States,* Part VII: *Certain Aspects of Land Problems and Government Land Policies,* Washington, D.C., 1935.

Teal, John and Mildred, *Life and Death of the Salt Marsh,* Little, Brown and Company, Boston, 1969.

United States Bureau of the Census, *Drainage of Agricultural Lands, 15th Census of the United States, 1930,* Washington, D.C., 1932.

————, *United States Census of Agriculture,* Vol. IV: *Drainage of Agricultural Land—1950,* Washington, D.C., 1952.

————, *United States Census of Agriculture,* Vol. IV, *Drainage of Agricultural Land, 1959,* Washington, D.C., 1961.

United States Department of Agriculture, *Land, The 1958 Yearbook of Agriculture,* Washington, D.C.

————, *A Place to Live, The Yearbook of Agriculture, 1963,* Washington, D.C.

————, *Soil, The 1957 Yearbook of Agriculture,* Washington, D.C.

————, *Water, The Yearbook of Agriculture, 1955,* Washington, D.C.

United States Department of the Interior, Fish and Wildlife Service, *Wetlands of the United States,* Circular 38, Washington, D.C., 1956.

H. BOWMAN HAWKES
University of Utah

CHAPTER 11

Irrigation in the United States

Daniel Webster once publicly said of the West:

What do we want with this vast worthless area—this region of savages and wild beasts, of deserts of shifting sands and whirlwinds of dust, of cactus and prairie dogs? To what use could we ever hope to put these great deserts and those endless mountain ranges, impenetrable and covered to their base with eternal snow?

A large portion of this western land is still characterized by sparse vegetation, and the "shifting sands and whirlwinds of dust" are still evident, yet this has not prevented the development of an economy that supports over 50 million people. This great national leader, regardless of his wisdom and experience, did not recognize that irrigation could transform the semiarid and arid regions of western America into a suitable home for man.

Irrigation with its many ramifications is complex business; a study of this age-old "institution" can be approached many ways. To know irrigation along the entire spectrum is to have a knowledge of such related fields as agronomy, engineering, hydrology, climatol-

ogy, geology, sociology, economics, history, administration, institutional services, and conservation. Conservation is that encompassing concept that touches all aspects of man and his resources; it is undoubtedly one of the most "elastic" words in the English language. The term implies to most students the avoidance of waste. Yet waste is a relative issue. More specifically, irrigation conservation may be defined as the efforts of man to obtain the maximum returns from the available water inputs on the land. It is within this context that the subsequent material has been prepared.

HISTORY OF IRRIGATION

In the pre-Columbian period irrigation was practiced on a rather limited but effective basis by several aboriginal groups in the American Southwest. Maize, beans, and squash were raised by the natives of this area. The Hopi Indians of northeastern Arizona practiced floodwater irrigation in dry washes; the Zuni and other Pueblo Indians of the Colorado Pleateau engaged in similar practices. The most elaborate system of irrigation was carried on around 500 to 600 A.D. by the Hohokam people who inhabited the Gila and Salt river drainage of southern Arizona. It has been estimated that 200 miles of canals and ditches had been built in the Salt River Valley alone.[1]

The immediate post-Columbian period of American irrigation could be defined as the Spanish era. It was characterized by the activities of the Spanish missionaries operating in the American Southwest and California. The Catholic padres endeavored to establish among the natives an agricultural way of life based upon irrigation. Mediterranean crops, such as wheat, barley, olives, and citrus fruits, were introduced by the Spanish Americans.

The modern period of irrigation began on July 23, 1847, when the Mormon pioneers directed the waters of City Creek on the bench lands of Salt Lake Valley. Other irrigation endeavors by the Anglo-Saxons preceded the 1847 date, such as the irrigation of fields by Protestant missionaries near Walla Walla, Washington, and at Lewiston, Idaho, in 1863 and 1847, respectively. It was not the earlier date, however, but the "institutionalization" of irrigation that gives to Utah claim to the title, "Cradle of American Irrigation." [2]

Irrigation and Public Land Policy. Irrigation in America is inextricably tied up with the development of land policies. It was not until 1862 that Congress enacted the first legislation leading to the settlement of the West. The Homestead Act of 1862 permitted settlers to acquire farms of 160 acres with title to the land to be received when the individual had lived on and improved the farm over a period of 5 years. A large number of homesteads were successfully claimed under this Act, especially in the subhumid and semiarid regions of the West. But it was soon recognized that the Homestead Act was not well adapted to the conditions west of the 100th meridian. If

the land were to be put to use for dry-land farming or grazing purposes, a quarter section or 160 acres would be too small. If it were to be irrigated, it would be too much for an individual to handle with the methods then in use.

One of the first general laws enacted in recognition of the need for extensive works to develop water supplies in the West before settlement could take place was the Act of July 26, 1866, which granted rights of way for ditches and canals on the public lands to acknowledged holders of valid water rights or irrigation. Other bills were introduced at this time to encourage irrigation, but no serious action was taken by Congress.

In time, however, the need for federal assistance to aid in full-scale irrigation development became more and more apparent and received increasingly sympathetic responses in Congress. The Desert Land Act was passed in 1877. Under this Act provisions were made for the reclamation of arid land in the West. The Act authorized the sale of 640 acres of land at $1.25 per acre to any person who would irrigate it within 3 years. There were honest developers who took advantage of the Act, but there were also dishonest speculators and many "irrigation evangelists," who did not comprehend irrigation. Several million acres of land were entered under the Act of 1877, but most of it unfortunately went to build up landed estates.

Because of the many abuses, disappointments, and confusion of ideas about reclamation in the arid West, public sentiment was aroused in favor of state intervention in the irrigation dilemma. The first National Irrigation Congress in Salt Lake City in 1891 and the second in Los Angeles in 1893 went on record as endorsing the cession of public land to the states. The trend culminated in the Carey Act of 1894 which permitted the federal government to donate to the western states an amount of land not to exceed one million acres. The states in turn were to assume the

[1] Omar A. Turney, "Prehistoric Irrigation in Arizona," *Arizona Historical Review*, Vol. 2, 1929, p. 163.

[2] John A. Widstoe, "A Century of Irrigation," *Reclamation Era*, Vol. XXXIII, 1947, pp. 99–102.

responsibility for settlement, irrigation, and cultivation of the segregated areas. Operations under the Carey Act, however, did not produce the results expected; the states were not in a position to take on aggressively the responsibilities that this Act entailed. Ultimately, development under the Carey Act reached about 1.1 million acres of some 4 million acres segregated.

By 1900, a total of 7.5 million acres were under some form of irrigation in the western states. Developments to this date had been rather haphazard, but the evidence available indicated rather convincingly that irrigation was a catalyst in the economic development of the region. At this time much of the best land and the easiest to irrigate had been developed, and westerners were increasingly aware that further irrigation, which was needed to promote economic growth, would require much more in the way of capital investment than had all earlier developments.

Irrigation in the United States as we know it today is closely related to the establishment and development of the Bureau of Reclamation. Probably no one saw the problems and challenges of irrigation with more vision and experience than did Francis G. Newlands of Nevada (Fig. 1). He is considered by many to be the father of reclamation. As early as 1893 he stated:

It is therefore utterly impossible to inaugurate a system of settlement in that region (the west) similar to that which has existed in the Mississippi and other valleys. Individual settlement and individual reclamation cannot obtain generally. It becomes necessary in order to bring larger areas of land within cultivation, to resort to the system of storage, of establishing artificial reservoirs, and of constructing canals and ditches at great expense, covering large areas of land by a comprehensive plan.[3]

Fig. 1 Francis G. Newlands—Founder of the Reclamation Era. (Bureau of Reclamation.)

Furthermore, he argued:

The United States government is the owner of 600 million acres of land in the arid region, of which 100 million acres can be reclaimed by a gradual process of storage. The limit of reclamation and settlement has been reached unless the federal government makes a scientific study of each river and its tributaries and so stores the water as to prevent the torrential flow in the spring and to increase the scanty flow in the summer.[4]

This was the need, the justification, and the means of achieving reclamation in the West as Senator Newlands of Nevada envisioned it. The pendulum of responsibility shifted gradually away from state administration to the federal government.

Reclamation Act of 1902. Numerous bills to establish a federal reclamation program were introduced in the 55th and 56th Con-

[3] Arthur B. Darling, *The Public Papers of Francis G. Newlands*, Vol. 1, Houghton Mifflin, Boston, 1932, p. 56.

[4] *Ibid.*, p. 60.

gresses. Public sentiment in support of federal leadership began to stir. There was ample opposition to reclamation from some of the eastern and midwestern states. Constitutionality was a major issue, cost of project, ability to pay, increased agricultural surpluses, and lower farm prices were claims made by the opposition. But favorable interest seemed to accelerate in spite of the criticism. In 1900, the platforms of the major political parties favored the undertaking by the federal government of reclaiming arid lands.

President Theodore Roosevelt in his message to Congress of December 3, 1901 expressed many ideas with respect to the development of the West and the formulation of a federal reclamation program. He, more than any other person, defended the idea that reclamation would serve to develop and settle the West and thus integrate it with the rest of the nation. And furthermore, he argued, by irrigation developments our nation would become firmly established in the Pacific and prepared to face the new potential of old Asia.

The Reclamation Act or the Newlands Act, which finally succeeded in bringing federal irrigation to the arid West, was passed and signed into law by President Roosevelt on June 17, 1902. Reclamation was administered by the Geological Survey as the Reclamation Service until 1907 when a Reclamation Commission was set up. Finally in 1923, the Bureau of Reclamation was established in the Department of the Interior.

The Reclamation Act put the federal government squarely into the irrigation business and charged the federal officials with the responsibility of solving the problems of water rights, distribution of the water, construction of the system, and settlement of the reclaimed areas. The money for the undertaking was to be derived from a revolving fund which would supposedly be kept alive by the sale of public lands.

The Act of 1902 did not resolve all the problems of irrigation; in the wake of new de-velopments there were always the unforeseen difficulties. From its inception entire reclamation operation was kept under close scrutiny by Congress. Between 1902 and 1923 there were no less than 500 hearings. Finally in 1924, a committee of special advisers on reclamation, known as Fact Finders, was appointed to review the mistakes and successes of reclamation.[5] This committee found that the project costs had far over-run estimates; that the costs to the settlers of farm developments far exceeded expectations; and that inadequate consideration had been given to such matters as soils, project economics, and drainage. The committee also found that there had been a considerable amount of speculation in connection with the sale of private lands within the project area.

Largely on the basis of the committee report, legislation was enacted to alleviate some of the shortcomings. Over $14,000,000 in construction charges were written off; repayment contracts were extended to a maximum of 40 years; and the anti-speculation provision of the reclamation laws was re-enforced. The legislation included numerous other provisions to protect both the government and the settlers, and provided a basis for continuation of the reclamation program until the evolution of multiple-purpose concepts necessitated a revision of reclamation laws in 1939.

Multiple-Purpose Development. The single-purpose irrigation projects were obviously the first to be developed. But with the growth of the West, the demand to use water to serve other purposes increased. First of the major multiple-purpose projects to be authorized was the Boulder Canyon Project in 1928. The intensification of agriculture in California's Imperial Valley and the rapid growth of population in southern California posed several related hydrological problems: the need for flood control and irrigation, the need for hy-

[5] *The Fact Finders' Report,* Senate Document 92, 68th Congress, Washington, D.C., 1924.

droelectric power and municipal water supplies throughout the area, and the need for better protection of the fish and wildlife resources. The challenges which had arisen along with the expansion of the reclamation program made it evident that some overhaul of the basic legislative authority was needed. This was accomplished with the passage of the Reclamation Project Act of 1939 which brought up to date reclamation laws pertaining to multiple-purpose projects, variable payment plans, classification of land as to irrigability and productivity, contracts for the sale of water for irrigation and municipal water supply purposes, and the sale of electric power.

Several multiple-purpose projects were authorized and started under the 1939 Act. World War II forced gradual slowdown in the program, except where hydroelectric power was necessary for defense purposes. Toward the close of the war, Congress became concerned with the possibility of postwar unemployment and authorized multiple-purpose river basin developments so that a backlog of construction projects would be available. Among these was the Pick-Sloan Plan for the Missouri River Basin. This was a comprehensive multi-purpose river basin development program participated in by two governmental agencies: the Bureau of Reclamation had responsibility for irrigation development and the Corps of Engineers was responsible for flood control and power generation.

The end of the war found the Bureau of Reclamation making plans for expanded programs. New projects were authorized and by 1950 the annual appropriation of about $300 million exceeded by three times the prewar maximum. Since then new projects have been authorized and placed under construction with ever-increasing emphasis on multiple-purpose development.

"Multiple-purpose" is a slogan or catchword that has been adopted by many government agencies charged with the responsibility of administering the public land and associated resources. It is a terse, clean-cut symbol, but it is not always fully comprehended. Multiple-purpose planning to the Bureau of Reclamation is the means of obtaining optimum benefits from water resource development. The key words are "optimum benefits," but there can be many interpretations of this expression depending upon the point of view. From an economic standpoint, the essence of multi-purpose planning is that irrigation, recreation, pollution abatement, and other water uses can be realized most efficiently if considered collectively. Multi-purpose planning is unbelievably complex, involving joint design, alternative allocations of joint costs, and various methods of project financing. To these complexities must be added the intangible social parameters expressed in welfare economics. Where intangible benefits are considered important, then additional investments must be made that are not balanced by additional monetary benefits. Or the intangible adverse effects may suggest reduced investment at the expense of monetary benefits. This general principle of weighing into any multi-purpose project the intangibles of social welfare is currently expressed in the literature of all water resources economics, and it is within this important and involved multi-purpose frame of reference that the use of water to serve irrigation is, and must be, placed.

In retrospect it seems that the first third of the Reclamation century (1902–1928) was identified almost exclusively with water for irrigation. The second third (1928–1969) of the century finds the same objectives carried forward but the breadth of planning widened to include multi-purpose developments along a wide spectrum of parameters, including social welfare. Now the last third of the century confronts us. The objectives of the two earlier periods will undoubtedly be brought forward, but what are the challenges for tomorrow?

The Bureau of Reclamation accepts the demographers' estimate of an increase of population in the United States from the present

200,000,000 to 340,000,000 by the year 2000, and in the world from the present 3.4 billion to 6.5 billion by the year 2000. The last third of the century will witness the confrontation between an expanding population with an insatiable appetite for the things of the earth, projected against a finite amount of fresh water. These facts when translated mean that conventional practices of storage and diversion of our rivers and pumping ground water will not suffice. The skies and the oceans must be explored to augment the needed water supply. Programs must be activated that will encourage greater efficiency in using the fresh water already at hand. The 11th Monograph of the Agronomy Series *Irrigation of Agricultural Lands,* published in 1967 by the American Society of Agronomy, voices the same concern. The general forword to this monumental study prepared by 110 scientists states that the research represented in the 1180 pages of the Monograph "comes at a time when the science and application of irrigation practices are crucial factors in areas where a delicate balance exists between the supplies of food and fiber and the demands of an exploding population." [6]

In the best judgment of the world's irrigation specialists, these are the challenges of the last third of the century. In this milieu of problems and challenges irrigation will participate, for if there is to be more food and fiber it must come in large part from an expanded and intensified irrigated agricultural economy.

THE "RIGHTS" TO USE WATER

Irrigation and water rights are inextricably tied up with the acquisition and settlement of the West. The territory ceded to the United States in 1848 through the Treaty of Guadalupe Hidalgo comprised what is now the State of New Mexico. In this territory long before acquisition there was a large number of community *acequias* (ditches) constructed by Indians and Spanish explorers after 1589. These ditches served to carry needed water for irrigation over a considerable acreage. Another part of this ceded territory comprised Utah. In this instance the Mormon colonizers in 1847 immediately took over the streams in Salt Lake Valley and adjacent areas to irrigate the land. California was another area in which water had been diverted and used for mining purposes and for irrigation before acquisition in 1848. The question arose as to what water rights the Indians, Spanish Americans, and Mormons had after the Treaty of Guadalupe. [7]

The national policy of westward expansion encouraged land settlement and private development of land, minerals, and water; the prevailing local customs, laws, and court decisions regarding such resources were respected. This meant that the original users of water had prior rights.

By the end of the 1870's the policy of transferring public lands to private uses was well underway. There was also the beginning of the conflict between the two interpretations of water rights, that is, the eastern adherents of the common law doctrine of "riparian rights" and the western advocates of "appropriation rights."

The essence of the riparian doctrine, which came from England, is that a landowner contiguous to a stream is entitled to have the water of the stream flow by his land undiminished in quantity and unaltered in quality. A strict application of this rule would not permit consumptive use of water from a stream or use of water on lands not contiguous to the stream. This would not be a serious limita-

[6] Robert M. Hagen, *et al.,* "Irrigation of Agricultural Lands," *Agronomy Series, No. 11,* American Society of Agronomy, Madison, Wisconsin, 1967.

[7] Wells A. Hutchins, "Background and Modern Developments in Water Law in the United States," *Natural Resources Journal,* Vol. 2, 1962, pp. 416–444.

tion on the river system in a humid region where the only use of water might be for navigation or recreation.

The appropriation doctrine declares that water belongs to the public, but a right to use it may be obtained by individuals or agencies provided they comply with certain procedures and principles. The doctrine as applied to natural water courses means the exclusive right to the first appropriation. Since the national policy was to obtain the largest practicable use from public land, and the riparian doctrine of the East, with emphasis on benefits only to lands contiguous to the streams, was not well adapted to the West, the system of prior appropriation emerged in Utah, California, and New Mexico.

In Utah the doctrine of prior appropriation has been the law in practice, if not in title, since the Mormons entered Salt Lake Valley in 1847 and directed the water from the stream channel to irrigate the dry alluvial plains several miles away. Brigham Young made it known early that the streams belonged to all people. The code of water ethics was: "Those first in time are first in right but beneficial use is the limit and measure of right." Beneficial use means that the appropriator use only the amount of water needed and the remaining supply be left for someone else to appropriate.

In California it was the placer miners seeking gold in 1848 who directed the water from stream channels to the mining claims some distance away. The California courts recognized the early appropriations of water as valid. In Utah it was simply a matter of no water, no settlement; in California it was no water at the mining claim, no gold. In either case it was the essence of the doctrine of prior appropriation that protected the farmers and the miners from the encroachment of other water users and at the same time permitted them to divert the water from the natural stream channels to where it could be most expeditiously used.

Although the details differed as the prior appropriation system developed in the western states, all forms accorded priority to the earliest water user. His water rights continued regardless of its location with respect to the stream. Thereafter each subsequent appropriation had a priority over all who followed him. The appropriation doctrine is in vogue in seven Intermountain states (Colorado, Idaho, Montana, Nevada, New Mexico, Utah, and Wyoming). In the eight bordering states there is a combination of appropriation and riparian rights which is known today as the California Doctrine. Arizona is an exception; the state belongs geographically to the appropriation block but has modified its water laws in keeping with the California Doctrine. In Oklahoma and Oregon, although a riparian code is on the books, the courts are not upholding these rights. The remaining states adhere with mixed degrees to the rights derived from common law. Where the modified riparian doctrine prevails, it is held that the riparian rights include the right to make use of the water for irrigation.

Figure 2 points up the hard core of the appropriation realm and the adjacent transition zones where both doctrines prevail. Furthermore, the figure portrays the relationship between the areas of deficit rainfall and the doctrine of "first in time, first in right."

The appropriation doctrine has served and protected irrigation developments in the West, but it is certainly not without shortcomings, particularly in the context of modern problems. The following suggestions by Bushy point up some of the weaknesses and a plausible improvement in the system: [8]

1. Provide a means whereby a lawful taking of appropriated water may be authorized under a basic water conservation program.

[8] C. E. Bushy, "Regulation and Economic Expansion," *Water, The Yearbook of Agriculture*, U.S. Department of Agriculture, Washington, D.C., 1955, pp. 666–676, Ref. p. 673.

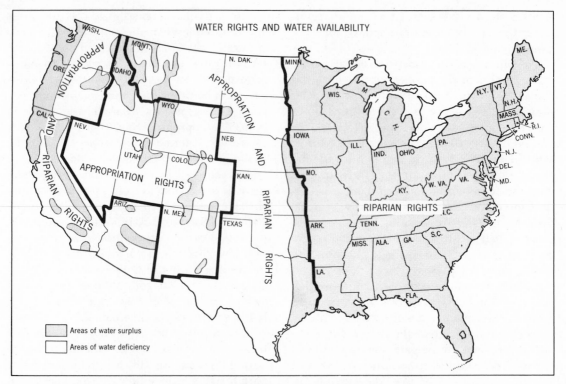

Fig. 2 The relationship between the pattern of water rights and water availability is expressed on the above map; the correlation is striking. The islands of surplus moisture in the deficit areas are expressions of the mountain uplands. These islands serve the most basic function in the irrigated economy, since without them there is no water surplus for storage and irrigation. Even the groundwater in the surrounding valleys is recharged by the streams feeding down the mountain slopes to the adjacent plain. Weather modification operates around and over the mountain masses to increase the rainfall and snowpack in the upland.

2. Reduce or abolish the law of prescription which permits a person who does not have a lawful right to acquire the right without notice by merely usurping for a statutory period.

3. Improve the standards whereby beneficial use may be ascertained.

The suggestions in items 1 and 3 are certainly designed to modify the well-established doctrine of prior appropriations. When irrigation was the major use of water, the doctrine could be easily defended but in the age of multiple-use, some reappraisals must be made.

An essential principle of the doctrine of prior appropriation is application of water for beneficial use, yet despite the authoritative expression on the need for making water beneficial, wasteful practices have been tolerated. For example, the efforts of water users to hold title to maximum quantities of water to which their rights extend, even though this results in excessive use, is wasteful. The rights are valid and the law must be adhered to, but how long should such misuse be ignored?

Thus far the discussion has centered exclusively on "rights" as they apply to water in natural stream courses and lakes. These, of course, are the important sources, but as the demand for water continues to mount, the rights to water under other occurrences will require legal interpretations and state legislation.[9]

1. Who is entitled to use the "diffused surface water" or the water that is associated with precipitation and snow melt but has not found its way into a natural water course? Can the farmer legally intercept the diffused surface water? Does the farmer, who has been deprived of the water, have any recourse? Water users and state legislators need to be alert to such problems.

2. Rights to groundwater are not clearly defined. The common law of groundwater rests on the theory that the landowner has absolute right to everything above and below his land. The mobile nature of surface water is recognized, and therefore the laws grant usufructuary rights to it. In percolation groundwater, however, the courts and legislative bodies have not consistently taken cognizance of the fact that groundwater may also flow from one property to another.

The "strict rule" places no limitation on the nature or extent of use. A landowner can pump until his well runs dry and the "draw down" extends to adjacent property. Recently, a modification of the strict rule, referred to as "reasonable use," has been introduced. In Utah, New Mexico, Washington, and Oklahoma, the doctrine of prior appropriation has been adapted to groundwater with "beneficial use" providing the essence of the right, and with priority in time, the better right.

In California the allocation of a limited supply of groundwater is governed by the doctrine of correlative rights.[10] Accordingly, each landowner, when the supply is short, is entitled to a reasonable proportion of the common supply. The correlative rights for groundwater are an expression of the modified California Riparian Doctrine. It is prompted by a consideration of moral fairness, but the doctrine does not protect the man who came first. Interest in the California line of judicial reasoning has increased as domestic and industrial demands for water have mounted.

3. As yet there are no laws regulating directly the use of water in the air. The few laws that do prevail were set up to license rain making or cloud seeding. If irrigation is defined as the artificial application of water to land for agricultural purposes, then cloud seeding may someday come under that category.

To say that water law is static would be a mistake. The pressure of political, social, and economic forces upon water law changes, and these changes are expressed in a veritable forest of policy declarations. The changes come slowly and painfully, but they are inevitable. Important unresolved conflicts exist within states, between states, and between the federal and state governments which will eventually modify and bring new laws into existence.

IRRIGATION AND MODERN FARMING

The practice of irrigation in the past has been more of an art than a science. There has been much guesswork and haphazardness associated with the endeavor, and the vestiges of yesteryears are still evident. But the trend is toward improved management, and irrigation is becoming an established science.

Irrigation has been largely an agricultural pursuit, and changes in the American agricultural structure will obviously bring changes in the methods of irrigation. Farming has become "big business"; the grinding forces of competition are pushing the less competent farm operators out of the farming business. The impact of changes in agriculture are ex-

[9] *Ibid.*, p. 668.
[10] Roy E. Huffman, *Irrigation Development and Public Water Policy*, New York, 1953, pp. 51–52.

pressed in such features as the increase in size of farm and a decline in farm numbers and farm workers, a move toward greater specialization of crops and selection of crops best suited for local conditions, introduction of chemical fertilizers, and an increase in the availability of agriculture credit. These and other variables will have expression in the extent and methods of irrigation.

The modern farm manager must constantly appraise the several parameters of farm production and manipulate them to achieve the greatest returns for money invested. He must learn to substitute for scarce and high-priced resources, more plentiful or less expensive ones. A primary example is the substitution of capital for labor. In the jargon of the day this process is lumped under the simple term "mechanization." A farmer will install a sprinkler system or an automated irrigation system, which is a form of capital, as a substitute for labor. At the going prices of equipment and the cost of labor the substitute can be a profitable one. Another example would be the substitution of capital for the more expensive resource, such as water. Capital will be represented in the improved mechanical means of irrigation that will enable the farmer to utilize more efficiently the scarce and more expensive water resource.

It would be difficult to ascertain what percentage of the present-day farmers are aware of the economic forces that are shaping the structure of agriculture. The traditional practices of irrigation that have made the "institution" more of an art than a science may still characterize most farms, but the bulk of agricultural production in the United States is from the large modern farms that are under the management of an entrepreneur who knows how best to combine the factors of production—land, labor, capital, and management—to obtain maximum returns. The Census of Agriculture reports that 27.5 percent of all farms in 1964 had gross value sales of $10,000 or more. But these farms ac-

counted for more than 80 percent of the farm products sold. Farms with a gross value sales of less than $2500 comprised 42 percent of the total farms, but they contributed only 2.5 percent of the total value of sales.[11]

The trend toward large, well-managed farms was recognized by the Bureau of Census in preparing the new Census of Agriculture for 1969. They were to use two forms: a detailed report was to be expected from all large operators, but a simplified questionnaire was to be sent to smaller farms. The explanation for the apparent discrimination was an expression of the fact that the small farms contribute so little to the total farm production.

It is noteworthy that some farm management magazines are adjusting their circulation pattern to these trends. For example, the magazine *Big Farmer* [12] is distributed free to farm operators who gross $20,000 or more annually. The publisher and advertisers know full well that it is this group that is actively engaged in the use of innovations in irrigation and other facets of modern farming. The selective circulation enhances the manufacturer's opportunity to seek out and sell to farmers who have a high gross sale each year.

The modern farmer has shortened the distance between the producer of farm equipment and the consumer; they expect the equipment to serve their objectives, that is, reasonable returns for the investment made. The only justification for mechanization is to make money by increasing yields, improving quality of crop, and reducing labor costs. If the investment in mechanical innovations will do this, then there is a place for it on the modern farm but for no other reason.

Irrigation Methods. There are three primary methods employed in irrigation: (1) sur-

[11] James K. Rutter, "The Modern Farm Market," Sprinkler Irrigation Association, *Proceedings*, 1968 Annual Technical Conference, Denver, Colorado, 1968, pp. 28–35, Ref. p. 28.

[12] Big Farmer, Inc., 230 North Michigan Avenue, Chicago.

face irrigation, (2) subirrigation, and (3) sprinkler irrigation.

SURFACE IRRIGATION. Surface irrigation was the method practiced in 500 A.D. by the Hohokam people of the American Southwest; it was the method utilized by the Mormons in 1847; and it is still a widely used method of getting the waters on the land.

In surface irrigation the water is conveyed to the land and finally to the root zone of the plant by a series of large and small "ditches." The largest structure is generally referred to as a *canal;* this ditch transports the water from the reservoir or stream to the general area to be irrigated. Taking off from the canal are the *laterals* that carry the water to the field to be irrigated. They generally follow property lines, fences, and the edges of the fields. Secondary laterals, if present, are more conspicuous, since they wander about the fields to place the water where it can be most advantageously used. The canals and laterals can be open-earth ditches or they may be lined with concrete or other materials to reduce seepage and eliminate transpiration from the *phraetophytes* along the stream course (Fig. 3).

Turnouts are used to direct the water from the lateral to the area to be irrigated. The simplest turnout is a gap cut in the ditch bank; sometimes metal or wooden fixtures are used. Siphon tubes are an innovation that transfers the water over the banks by siphonic action to the furrows; it provides excellent control of the water (Fig. 4).

Surface irrigation can be grouped into two broad methods: border strip or flood, and furrow. In flood irrigation the entire surface is covered with a continuous sheet of water that is held in bounds and directed down a strip between dikes. If the strip to be flooded has a uniform slope of a degree or less and the length of the run is about 400 to 600 feet the method is effective. There must also be ample water to push the wave of water through rapidly, or one end of the field will receive too

much and the other too little water. It is well adapted for close-growing crops, such as hay or grain, or for pastureland.

In the furrow method of surface irrigation, closely spaced ditches or furrows distribute the water laterally across the field and downward to moisten the plant root zone. It is the common method employed for irrigating truck crops, orchards, vineyards, and row crops, such as sugar beets, potatoes, corn, and tomatoes (Fig. 5). If the slope of the land is too great there is always a threat of erosion, since the concentration of water in the small ditches or furrows enhances the erosive capacity of the stream. Soil erosion by water has long been considered a threat to agriculture in humid regions, but the recognition of water erosion as a problem on irrigated lands is relatively new.

A modified type of furrow irrigation is corrugated irrigation. This method is best adapted for close-growing crops, such as hay and grain, on rolling topography. The water is directed down and around the contours of the land by means of many small ditches or furrows that have been scratched into the surface. The water may spill over some from one small furrow to the other, but the net movement will be down and around the contours of the land.

SUBIRRIGATION. Subirrigation is a form of irrigation in reverse; the water is applied beneath the ground rather than at the surface. It is a method of artificially regulating the elevation of the groundwater table to support plant growth. The method is generally associated with existing drainage systems that can be controlled during periods of dryness to hold the water table sufficiently high to supply water for the crops.

Florida has two extensive areas where conditions favor subirrigation: the Everglades and the Flatwoods of the Coastal Plains. Before the introduction of controls in the drainage system these lands were either too wet or too dry. In the Great Lakes Region a practice

Fig. 3 Laterals. (*a*) Before. The lateral on the left side belongs to irrigation that is traditionally more of an "art" than a science but is rather poor "art" at best. The water losses by seepage, evaporation, and transpiration could be as high as 40 percent in a lateral of this nature. The brush along the fence line makes a good home for game birds and animals, but is the price too high?

of "controlled drainage" is used which in effect is subirrigation practice.

Some of the more notable areas in the West where subirrigation is practiced are located in California, Idaho, Colorado, Utah, and Wyoming. Approximately 160,000 acres of low-lying delta lands are subirrigated at the convergence of the Sacramento and San Joaquin rivers. Before diking the area was periodically flooded, but by diking and installing a drainage system the water table can be maintained either by pumping the excess water into the river during the wet season or directing the river water by gravity to the fields during the dry summers. Along the Upper Snake River in Idaho there are 28,000 acres that are subirrigated. The land slopes

uniformly at about 0.2 percent and the extremely permeable soils overly an impervious lava formation. The San Luis Valley of Colorado is one of the most extensive subirrigated areas in the West. Along the Platte River in Nebraska a natural water table greatly favors the production of alfalfa.[13]

SPRINKLER IRRIGATION. One of the most striking changes in the agricultural landscape in the last 15 years has been the appearance of sprinkler systems on farms in both humid and arid regions of the United States. As one drives across the countryside he can see the

[13] Wayne D. Criddle and Cornelis Kalisvaart, "Subirrigation Systems," *Agronomy Series, No. 11*, American Society of Agronomy, Madison, Wisconsin, 1967, pp. 905–921, Ref. p. 915.

graceful arcs and lines of white mist which characterize the sprinkler as it sprays water over the farmlands (Fig. 6). As one flies over many parts of the western states he can see circular crop patterns which are products of one type of sprinkler system—the large rotating sprinkler (Fig. 7). One may also see in some instances as he travels across the country sprinklers used on sagebrush and cedar-covered tracts of rangeland to increase the summer feed for livestock.

There are many types of sprinkler systems, but they can be grouped under three general classes according to portability: (1) portable, (2) semiportable, and (3) stationary or permanent.

In a fully portable system the main lines, laterals, sprinkler, and sometimes even the pumping mechanism is portable. One method is the hand-moved system in which the laterals or irrigation pipes are carried from place to place. This system requires considerable labor, and it becomes tolerable only if lightweight aluminum pipe is utilized. About 63 percent of all sprinklers are of this kind.[14] Another type of portable system is equipped with giant sprinklers and pump attached to a

[14] Wallace McMartin, "Economic Trends and Future Markets for Sprinkler Irrigation Equipment," Sprinkler Irrigation Association, *Proceedings,* 1968 Annual Technical Conference, Denver, Colorado, 1968, pp. 89–98, **Ref.** p. 95.

(*b*) After. The concrete lined lateral would convey 95 percent or more of the water introduced. The efforts of the Soil Conservation Service and the Bureau of Reclamation to educate the small farmer to these facts are commendable, but the resistance to change on the part of the farmer is of considerable magnitude. (Soil Conservation Service.)

Fig. 4 The farmer is using a siphon for each row in this sugar beet field. Notice that the lateral is concrete lined and that metal headgates, designed to fit the contour of the lateral, are used to control the level of the water. For the siphon to operate the water in the ditch must be higher than the adjacent row. The wilted weeds along the sides of the lateral have been controlled by spraying. (Bureau of Reclamation.)

self-propelled engine that will straddle and move along the open ditch providing the water. The entire operation is portable, but in contrast with the hand-moved unit this system is engine-powered.

The semiportable system usually has a stationary pump and stationary main lines but with portable laterals and sprinklers. This system is sometimes identified as irrigation with "water on wheels" (Fig. 8). The laterals can be moved by hand and wheeled sideways

across the field, or they can be pulled lengthwise on wheels or skids. In some instances the lateral rotates on wheels around the supply riser which serves as a pivot. It is estimated that about 21 percent of the sprinklers are of this type.

The initial cost of installing a portable or semiportable system is relatively high. The portable system has the lowest per acre cost, ranging from $60 to $125. The semiportable system will range from $90 to $175 per acre

(1960 estimates).[15] However, the amount of pipe required to cover a single acre can be used to irrigate 15 to 20 acres by moving the system. Furthermore the availability of a portable or semiportable system makes it possible for the farmer to irrigate low-income crops and pastures that otherwise would be too costly.

In the stationary system, sometimes referred to as permanent or solid set, the main lines and laterals are generally buried and only risers and sprinklers appear aboveground. The system is frequently used for high value, water-sensitive crops, such as berries vegetables, orchards, and nurseries.

The stationary system is much more expensive in initial costs than the other methods. Installation and equipment costs per acre will range from $400 to $700.[16] This may account for the fact that only 11 percent of the sprinklers in use are of this nature. But there are advantages that may warrant the investment. The stationary system when properly installed can provide extra-close control of moisture in fields of high-value crops. The water can be placed where and when it is needed, since there are no portable pipes to be put in place. Furthermore, in fields where portable equip-

[15] Claude H. Pair, "Sprinkler Irrigation," Agricultural Research Service, Leaflet No. 476, U.S. Department of Agriculture, Washington, D.C., 1960, p. 3.

[16] *Ibid*.

Fig. 5 Furrow irrigation is used in this field of sweet corn. The crop in the foreground of the picture may be receiving more water than it requires since the rows are lengthy. The slope of the land appears to be almost ideal, but even at best these small furrow streams do carry limited amounts of silt to the far end. (Bureau of Reclamation.)

Fig. 6 The "mist line" of sprinkler irrigation in a wheat field of southern Idaho. Such features are fast becoming a characterizing element in the irrigated landscape of the United States. Other lines can be seen against the hills in the background. This is a portable system; it must be moved by hand or dragged by a tractor to its next location. (Bureau of Reclamation.)

ment is installed, there is always the inconvenience at harvest and cultivating time of moving the pipes out of the way. The buried lines of a permanent system eliminates the labor costs and the inconvenience. The semiportable system may minimize the problem by using a plastic hose that can be easily rolled up and stored around the hydrant during tillage and harvesting, but still such a procedure involves labor that is costly.

Sprinkler irrigation is not new, but the rapid increase in acreages under sprinklers and explosion in the production of sprinkler equipment is recent. Each manufacturer has

something just a trifle different from his competition, and some items do work better than others, but how is the farmer going to know? The sprinkler industry undoubtedly has been its own worst enemy in allowing some systems to be installed under conditions that are not suitable. The system installed may not be able to apply the water at rates necessary for best crop growth, or there may be problems of distributing the water uniformly. The shape of the field can limit the use of certain sprinkler types; the costs may be too excessive for a farmer to assume; the labor requirements may make a certain model impractical. These and other factors should be carefully appraised before a system is installed, and this has not always been the case. Such problems are more common and more acute on the smaller farms, since there is less communication between manufacturer and consumer.

OTHER USES OF SPRINKLERS. There are other activities associated with sprinkler irrigation that are of special interest because they are not directly connected with the use of the system to meet deficiencies in rainfall but to meet extremes in temperature. Surface irrigation for frost control has been practiced for many years in the citrus groves of California and the cranberry bogs of Wisconsin and Massachusetts, but the use of sprinklers to control temperature is relatively new.

In Michigan the sprinklers have been used to protect strawberries from frost damage.[17] When 1 pound of water at 32 degrees F is transformed into ice at 32 degrees F, 144 Btu's of heat are released. If the water surrounds the plant tissue in this transformation from liquid to solid, some of the released heat is absorbed by the plant tissue. The sprinkled plants are protected as long as the freezing process continues (Fig. 9).

[17] John N. Landers and K. Witte, "Irrigation for Frost Protection," *Agronomy Series, No. 11*, American Society of Agronomy, Madison, Wisconsin, 1967, pp. 1037–1057.

Another use of the sprinkler system is to guard against high temperature.[18] It has been found that light sprinkling at intervals during hot days will lower soil and plant temperature and thereby help maintain steady plant growth. During excessive heat, plants transpire moisture at a rate faster than the roots can acquire it, and the plant wilts. Under these wilted conditions blossoms will drop and even some fruit will be lost. The sprin-

[18] American Fruit Grower, "Keep Your Crops Cool," *Reynolds Irrigation Digest*, Spring 1967, pp. 42–44.

kler systems generally operate from the time the temperature reaches 90 degrees F until it returns to 90 degrees F. Information is limited regarding the susceptibility of various crops to heat. For many years it was thought that 100 degrees F was critical for grapes immediately after the new bunch was formed, but through trial and error procedures the viticulturists have identified 95 degrees F as a critical value. In the pole bean fields of the Willamette Valley in Oregon the sprinklers are turned on at 95 degrees F (Fig. 10). In the Great Valley of California 90 degrees F is con-

Fig. 7 Circular fields of sprinkler irrigation. These striking patterns can best be appreciated from an aerial view. They are typical on the Great Plains, particularly in Colorado, Kansas, and Nebraska. The mist line can be easily identified in the fields of sorghum. This is a self-propelled system that rotates about the riser in the center of the circular pattern. In this instance the radius of the circle is one-fourth of a mile. (*Irrigation Age*.)

Fig. 8 "Water on Wheels." This is a self-propelled system irrigating soybeans in Kansas. (*Big Farmer Magazine.*)

sidered critical for walnuts, cherries, and almonds. While the temperature is being controlled by the sprinklers there is a negative feature involved, however, since the constant wetting encourages foliage diseases. This can be controlled in part by the use of fungicides applied through the system.

If irrigation is defined as man's method of partially overcoming deficiencies in the natural pattern of precipitation, then there are practices other than agricultural pursuits that should be identified with irrigation. To the urban and suburban dweller, sprinkler irrigation is a common phenomenon, but it has not been considered in the context of irrigation. But regardless of terminology, putting water on the lawn with a sprinkler is a method of overcoming natural deficiencies in rainfall. What is more important is the fact that such practices are going to expand. As a nation we are becoming more conscious of the need to beautify our surroundings even in industrial

areas. The rise of the city in recent decades has accelerated the recognition of new resources or a reappraisal of old resources. Open spaces and green areas are in demand. There will be an increase in the use of water or, in other words, the irrigation of grounds surrounding public buildings, schools, college campuses, factories, industrial parks, and along highways.

Electronic devices are programmed to water after dark to permit the full use of the parks and recreation areas by the public during daylight hours. In Arizona a rather elaborate automated system has been established and records maintained over a period of 6 years to justify the investment.[19] The park system has been expanded 97 percent in the 6-year pe-

[19] Gene C. Reid, "Conservation and Economy by use of Automation and Sprinkler Irrigation," *Proceedings*, 1968 Annual Technical Conference, Sprinkler Irrigation Association, Denver, Colorado, 1968, pp. 59–64, Ref. p. 60.

riod, yet labor costs to manage the parks have increased only 7.3 percent and actual water usage has increased 30 percent. This savings amounts to 276 million gallons of water—a most convincing argument in favor of substituting capital in the form of mechanization to save labor costs and a limited resource.

Surface Versus Sprinkler Irrigation. Surface irrigation can be used on nearly all irrigable soils and with most crops. The method is inexpensive to operate because of low pressure requirements. Water is usually applied directly to the farmland by gravity flow from the larger canal to the lateral and finally to the furrow. Furthermore, surface irrigation is as dependable as the water supply. The likelihood of having to stop and repair the mechanical sprinkler is nil, and sometimes these periods may be critical for the crops involved. New technology will undoubtedly make surface irrigation more attractive to some farmers. Such developments as automatically controlled surface systems and the increased use of buried pipe for farm laterals would be moves toward mechanization.

The criteria for sprinkler irrigation are dif-

Fig. 9 A close-up of a strawberry plant protected from frost by the spray from the adjacent sprinkler. (Reynolds Metals Company.)

Fig. 10 A stationary system that is irrigating pole beans in the Willamette Valley of Oregon. This system is also used to lower plant and soil temperatures during periods of excessive heat. (Reynolds Metals Company.)

ferent from those of traditional surface irrigation. The importance of such factors as topography, size and shape of field, intake rates, soil texture, and surface drainage will differ between the two systems. Sprinkler irrigation has made it possible to farm sandy soil that 10 years ago might have been classified as marginal. Areas of complex undulating topography are now productive under the sprinkler methods but nonirrigable with a gravity system.

A study in the Columbia Basin Project has provided an opportunity to contrast farm irrigation efficiencies under the conventional method of gravity irrigation with those obtained by the sprinkler method.[20] The Columbia Basin Project, when it commenced in 1947, envisioned the traditional method of gravity irrigation. Later it was decided that

the farmer can, if he so desires, install a pump and irrigate with sprinklers. An intensive study was made in 1959 and 1960 contrasting the two methods. The efficiency was computed by dividing the consumptive irrigation requirements by the actual farm delivery. The average sprinkler irrigation efficiency for the 2 years was 64.3 percent as compared with a 2-year average of 43.4 percent for the gravity irrigated lands. Under sprinkler irrigation approximately 21 percent less water was used to achieve the same returns.

PATTERNS OF IRRIGATION

The patterns of irrigation in the United States have changed in time and in space. The average changes in acreage during the time interval from 1890 to 1964 are presented in Table 1.

During this interim of three-quarters of a century there has been a constant increase in acreage; the only exception took place during

[20] L. R. Swarner and M. A. Hagood, "Irrigation Trends in the Pacific Northwest," *Agricultural Engineering*, Vol. 44, 1963, pp. 304–307.

Table 1. Irrigation Through the Years, 1890–1964

Year	Acreage Irrigated (Millions of Acres)
1890	3.7
1900	7.7
1930	14.6
1935	13.0
1940	18.0
1945	20.5
1950	25.8
1954	29.6
1959	33.2
1964	37.1

[Source: U.S. Bureau of the Census, *Census of Agriculture, 1964*, Vol. II, Chapter 9, "Irrigation, Land Improvement Practices, and Use of Agricultural Chemicals," Washington, D.C., 1968, p. 913.]

the Depression and dust-bowl years of the 1930's.

A closer look at the regional changes in irrigated acreage since 1950 is given in Table 2.

Table 2. Regional Changes in Irrigated Land, 1950–1964

Year	11 Western States and Hawaii (Millions of Acres)	6 Great Plains States (Millions of Acres)	31 Eastern States (Millions of Acres)
1964	23.3	10.0	3.8
1959	22.0	9.0	2.2
1954	20.5	6.4	2.7
1950	20.6	4.1	1.7

[Source: U.S. Bureau of the Census, *Census of Agriculture, 1964*, Vol. II, Chapter 9, "Irrigation, Land Improvement Practices, and Use of Agricultural Chemicals," Washington, D.C., 1968, p. 913.]

It is noteworthy that more than half of the 11.2 million acre increase since 1950 occurred in the Great Plains states. Furthermore, the increase in the eastern states was almost as large as in the 11 western states. The increase in the Great Plains resulted from the expansion of well irrigation in the High Plains area of Texas, Oklahoma, Kansas, and in western Nebraska. The increase in the east is largely from expansion of irrigation in the citrus fruit and truck crop producing area of Florida and rice along the Mississippi Lowland.

In 1964, there were 37.1 million acres irrigated in the United States and every state was represented. The acreage ranged from about 1000 acres in Vermont to over 7.5 million in California. A detailed listing of all states with more than 100,000 acres and the percentage change since 1959 is presented in Table 3. This represents about 98 percent of the total irrigated acreage in the nation.

Table 3. Irrigated Acreage in the United States, 1964 and 1959 (States with More than 100,000 Acres)

	1964	1959	Percentage Change
California	7,598,688	7,395,570	2.7
Texas	6,384,963	5,655,638	12.9
Idaho	2,801,500	2,576,580	8.7
Colorado	2,690,018	2,684,757	0.2
Nebraska	2,169,317	2,077,926	4.4
Montana	1,893,360	1,874,520	1.0
Oregon	1,607,659	1,384,284	16.1
Wyoming	1,571,192	1,469,911	6.9
Florida	1,217,192	413,526	194.3
Washington	1,149,842	1,006,969	14.2
Arizona	1,125,376	1,152,450	−2.3
Utah	1,092,270	1,061,683	2.9
Kansas	1,004,210	762,101	31.8
Arkansas	974,297	711,812	36.9
Nevada	824,511	542,976	51.9
New Mexico	812,723	731,835	11.1
Louisiana	580,687	484,850	19.8
Oklahoma	302,081	197,632	52.9
Hawaii	143,940	141,179	2.0
South Dakota	130,050	115,629	12.5
Mississippi	123,398	99,686	23.8

[Source: U.S. Bureau of the Census, *Census of Agriculture, 1964*, Vol. II, Chapter 9, "Irrigation, Land Improvement Practices, and Use of Agricultural Chemicals," Washington, D.C., 1968, p. 915.]

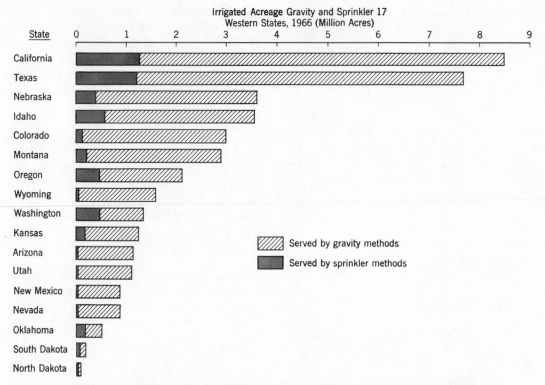

Fig. 11 Irrigated Acreage-Gravity and Sprinkler (17 Western States—1966). The statistics in the bar graph above differ slightly from the tabulations in Table 3. (1) The bar graph in Fig. 12 uses 1966 data; Table 3 uses 1964 data. (2) The graph uses statistics made available by *Irrigation Engineering* and *Maintenance,* Table 3 is based on the Census of Agriculture for 1964, and there are some minor differences in defining irrigated land. (3) The bar graph above is limited to the 17 Western states whereas Table 3 includes all states with irrigated acreage over 100,000 acres. (*Source. Irrigation Engineering and Maintenance,* Annual Directory Issue, August to September, 1967.) (Courtesy of John T. Maletic, Bureau of Reclamation, Denver, Colorado, 1968.)

During the brief interim of 5 years (1959–1964) the acreage of irrigated land increased from 33 million to 37.1 million acres. The most striking increase in percentage (194 percent) and in acres (804,000 acres) was in Florida (Table 3). This pronounced change is related to expanded subirrigation and sprinkler irrigation to produce fruits and vegetable crops, as well as forage for a thriving livestock industry. Texas with a 729,000 acre increase would rank second in total acreage increase. Other states with increases of 200,000 acres or more were Nevada, Kansas, Idaho, Oregon,

and California. All of them except Florida are in the irrigated 17 western states. The slight percentage decrease in Arizona is related to water shortages and drought conditions. Arizona has lagged behind in developing the sprinkler method but recent trends imply marked changes. If and when the Central Arizona Project is completed, the situation in Arizona will be markedly changed.

Although the 21 states listed in Table 3 would include 98 percent of the irrigation in the United States, it is noteworthy that the large percentage increases during the same interim of 5 years are in the East: Rhode Island, 252 percent; Connecticutl, 180 percent; West Virginia, 117 percent; and New Hampshire, 112 percent. Specialty truck crops and tobacco that can profit from sprinkler irrigation account for most of this doubling and tripling of acreage.

Sprinkler Methods in the Total Picture. The pattern of irrigation in the United States is largely an expression of surface or gravity irrigation. This is particularly true in the western states, but sprinkler methods are increasing and future patterns will reflect this development. Figure 11 points up the status of sprinkler irrigation in relation to the total irrigated acreage in 1966. The data indicate that sprinkler irrigation is most widely used in states where the productivity level and returns per acre are high, the areas in subtropical and speciality crops. The states of California, Texas, Idaho, Washington, and Oregon all have 400,000 acres or more under sprinkler irrigation.

The graph also indicates that, although the total acreage under sprinkler irrigation is high in California and the Pacific Northwest, on a percentage basis the Great Plains states of Oklahoma and South Dakota with 20 to 30 percent of all irrigable land using the sprinkler method rank high. For many years it was believed that sprinkler irrigation would not move into the Plains states, because there are relatively few crops that could produce enough to cover costs. But this is changing. With efficient management crops such as silage corn, hay, and even wheat may produce enough additional income to make the installation of a sprinkler system a paying proposition. In 1966, there were only six states (Colorado, Montana, Nevada, Utah, Wyoming, and New Mexico) with 10 percent or less of the irrigated land under sprinklers.

The spectacular growth of the sprinkler method in the 17 western states during the 10 years 1956–1966 is shown in Table 4. The average increase from 1956 to 1966 is about two

Table 4. Irrigated Acreage Using Sprinkler Method, 1956–1966

Western States	Total 1956	Sprinkler	Total 1966	Sprinkler
California	7,750,000	400,000	8,500,000	1,250,000
Texas	6,962,234	577,015	7,700,000	1,205,000
Idaho	2,408,132	130,000	3,569,000	569,600
Washington	947,000	228,000	1,340,000	455,000
Oregon	1,575,000	157,500	2,120,000	420,000
Nebraska	2,012,320	201,230	3,641,000	395,000
Montana	1,890,000	70,000	2,901,078	200,000
Oklahoma	285,000	100,880	498,000	157,000
Kansas	722,575	100,000	1,235,000	155,000
Colorado	2,382,000	33,110	3,003,000	95,000
South Dakota	112,000	20,000	145,000	40,000
Wyoming	1,300,000	8,000	1,595,000	40,000
New Mexico	800,000	3,000	875,000	25,000
Arizona	1,150,000	1,000	1,125,000	20,600
Utah	1,200,000	5,500	1,092,270	18,500
Nevada	700,000	12,000	846,000	16,000
North Dakota	48,000	7,000	81,000	15,000
Totals	32,244,261	2,054,235	40,266,348	5,076,700

[Source: John T. Maletic *Sprinkler Irrigation, Soils, Climate, and Land Classification,* Bureau of Reclamation, Denver, Colorado, February 1968.]

and one-half times, but in some cases, such as in Wyoming, New Mexico, and Arizona, the acreage has increased eight to twenty times. During the 10-year period sprinkler irrigation increased at the rate of 14.7 percent, whereas all irrigation was growing at a rate of only 2.5 percent per year.

The trend in the central and eastern states indicates continued growth. In 1956, there were 1,212,000 acres under sprinklers; by 1964, there was a slight increase to 1,219,000 and then a marked jumped to 1,566,000 acres in 1966.[21] In the so-called humid east a subtle change is taking place, for it appears that rainfall is becoming a supplement to irrigation.

[21] John T. Maletic, "Soils, Climate and Land Classification," Paper presented at the 1968 Annual Technical Conference, Sprinkler Irrigation Association, Denver, Colorado, February 27, 1968, pp. 1–17.

In the ultimate one might say that all land now under irrigation and all new land may potentially be put under sprinkler. The limiting factors will be the availability of water and competition from surface irrigation if new technology can make the traditional method more attractive economically.

The pattern of irrigated land, whether gravity or sprinkler, is spotty, even more so than Fig. 12 suggests. If all of the 37.1 million acres of irrigated land were brought together in one place it would occupy an area a trifle larger than the State of Iowa. The concentration is in special crop areas, such as the cotton, fruit, and vegetable producing areas of California; on the High Plains and in the Lower Rio Grande Valley of Texas; along the Snake River Valley of Idaho, in Oregon, Washington, and Colorado; and on the livestock ranches scattered throughout the West

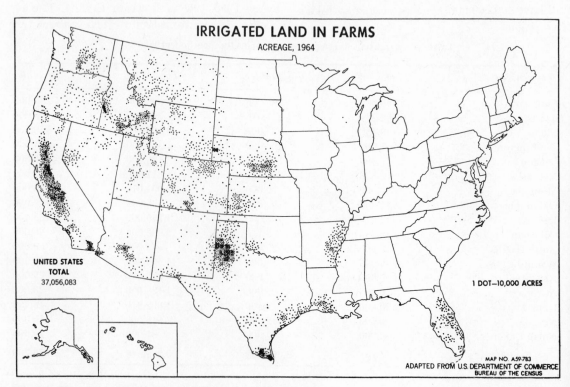

Fig. 12   The irrigated land in farms. (1964 data added by the author.)

where irrigated land produces hay or forage for the livestock industry.

The irrigated acreage devoted to selected crops is presented in Table 5. In terms of acreage alfalfa with 5.2 million acres outranks all other crops grown on irrigated land. If all hay crops where listed, the acreage would be expanded to 8.2 million. The important

Table 5. Acreages Harvested from Irrigated Lands for Selected Fruit and Truck Crops, 1964

	Acres Harvested from Irrigated Land	Percentage
Alfalfa	5,210,000	18.5
Cotton	3,769,000	27.1
Sorghum	3,378,000	22.6
All corn	2,428,000	3.8
Land in orchards	2,203,000	51.8
All wheat	1,964,000	4.1
Rice	1,815,000	100.0
Barley	1,504,000	15.3
Sugar beets	1,099,000	79.9
Irish potatoes	609,000	51.9
Dry beans	601,000	44.9
Soybeans	427,000	1.4
Oats	300,000	1.6
Fruits and Vegetables		
Tomatoes	252,000	64.8
Lettuce	202,000	96.1
Cantaloupe	93,800	75.5
Carrots	72,000	90.1
Watermelon	46,000	18.8
Lima beans	33,500	37.5
Celery	30,800	97.0
Radishes	23,200	76.7
Artichokes	8,800	99.1
Brussel sprouts	6,000	91.8
Parsley	2,400	87.8

[Source: U.S. Bureau of the Census, *Census of Agriculture, 1964*, Vol. II, Chapter 9, "Irrigation, Land Improvement Practices, and Use of Agricultural Chemicals," Washington, D.C., 1968, p. 921.]

theme represented is the close tie between irrigation and the livestock industry as expressed in forage crops.

Table 5 also identifies the specific crops that are dominantly irrigated agricultural products. Rice with 100 percent from irrigated land is exceptional; this subtropical crop grown in the Mississippi Lowland and the San Joaquin-Sacramento delta of California requires flooding for successful production. Sugar beets and Irish potatoes from the irrigated farms of California, Idaho, and Colorado are more representative.

The total acreage devoted to truck crops is diminutive in contrast with the field crops, but the high percentage of these crops grown on irrigated land is striking. Such crops as artichokes, celery, lettuce, Brussel sprouts, and carrots are almost exclusively irrigated products. These are the specialty crops of the irrigated Pacific coast states, the Southwest, and Florida.

FUTURE OF IRRIGATION

The nation is not lacking in irrigable land; the limiting factor is availability of water. There is an enormous land potential in western United States of 60–160 million acres that could be put under irrigation! [22] However, according to the best estimates of the Bureau of Reclamation, water supply competition and current in-basin regulations will limit the development to about 20 million acres. The prognostications of the newly established Water Resources Council are about the same as those of the Bureau of Reclamation. The increase of 20 million acres by the year 2020 over the 1965 acreage of 42 million amounts to the estimated 62 million.[23]

These projections into the next half century

[22] *Ibid.*, p. 1.
[23] *The Nation's Water Resources*, United States Water Resources Council, Washington, D.C., 1968, Part 4, Chapter 4, Table 4, p. 5.

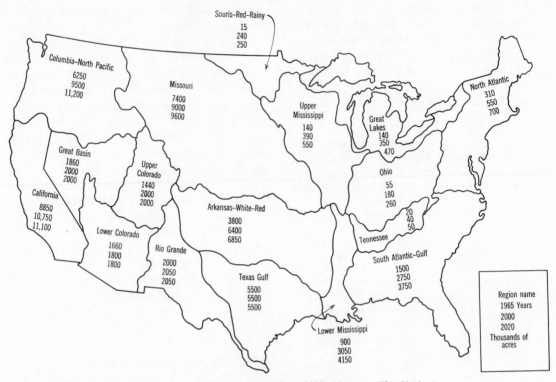

Fig. 13 The regional projection of irrigated lands (1965 to 2020) (*Source: The Nation's Water Resources*, The First National Assessment of the Water Resource Council, Washington, D.C., 1968.)

are based upon trends during the last 25 years as modified by expectations of available water supply. The acreages include the projects authorized and under construction by the Bureau of Reclamation and those which studies show to be economically feasible. For purposes of regional allocations, the Water Resource Council has divided the nation into 18 regions for conterminous United States, plus estimates for Alaska, Hawaii, and Puerto Rico. The anticipated changes in irrigated acreages for the years 2000 and 2020 in the 18 regions are plotted in Figure 13.

The increases in percentage in the East are significant. This will be largely an expression of supplemental irrigation. The limited changes expected in the Texas-Gulf and Rio

Grande regions are related to the receding groundwater levels. The slight increases in the Intermountain area, California, and the Pacific Northwest are related to reclamation programs under construction or authorized. If there are to be additional amounts of water available, they will have to come from new sources or from a more efficient use of the present supply.

New Sources. The total fresh water supply has been estimated to be 33 trillion acre-feet; three-fourths of this is ice and slightly less than one-fourth is groundwater. The remaining amounts are negligible in percentage, but some are important as new sources (Table 6). There are three new water sources worthy of consideration: (1) the sea, (2) the atmosphere,

Table 6. The Earth's Hydrosphere (Estimated Quantities of Water Available)

	Millions of Acre-Feet	Percentage of Fresh Water
Oceans	1,060,000,000	–
Fresh water	33,016,084	100
a. Polar ice, glaciers	24,668,000	74.72
b. Hydrated earth minerals	336	0.001
c. Lakes	101,000	0.31
d. Rivers	933	0.003
e. Soil moisture	20,400	0.01
f. Groundwater		
(1) Fissures to 2500 feet	3,688,000	11.05
(2) Fissures 2500 to 12,500 feet	4,565,000	13.83
g. Plants and animals	915	0.003
h. Atmosphere	11,500	0.035
Hydrologic cycle (annual)		
a. Precipitation on land	89,000	
b. Stream runoff	28,460	

[From Edward A. Ackerman and George O. G. Lof, *Technology in American Water Development,* The Johns Hopkins University Press, Baltimore, 1959.]

and (3) the ground. The implications of salt water conversion are limited as far as irrigation is concerned, but weather modification holds some promise and particularly groundwater development.

FROM THE SEA. The conversion of sea water is a very old method of securing fresh water. What is significant is the increase in production and decline in cost over the last 20 years. This has been made possible through an ever-improving program of technology. The costs of production today range from $1.50 to $3.00 per thousand gallons, which is equivalent to $500 to $1000 per acre-foot. The research scientists believe that with the use of nuclear energy the cost will ultimately be reduced to $.50 per thousand gallons. This is still too costly for most irrigation needs. Even if the water were made available with no cost at seaside, the price of lifting and conveying it to the farms would still make it financially prohibitive in most cases.

FROM THE ATMOSPHERE. It is estimated that 90 percent of the atmospheric moisture passes over the United States without falling to the earth. It is this vast potential source that atmospheric scientists hope to manage through their weather modification program.[24]

A decade ago the idea of utilizing this atmospheric moisture to increase the fresh water supply seemed remote. Recent reports of the National Academy of Science [25] and the National Science Foundation [26] show a change in the prevailing opinion among scientists on the subject of weather modification. In 1961, a program was initiated with an appropriation of $100 million for atmospheric research on increasing rainfall by cloud seeding, and the Bureau of Reclamation was assigned the responsibility for directing this program. Under

[24] *Ibid.,* Part 3, Chapter 2, p. 16.

[25] *Weather and Climate Modification—Problems and Prospects,* Publication No. 1350, National Academy of Sciences, National Research Council, Washington, D.C., 1966.

[26] Report of the Special Commission on Weather Modification, National Science Foundation, Washington, D.C., 1966.

its direction field experiments are currently being conducted in six geographic locations: Colorado River Basin, Missouri River Basin, Bonneville Basin, Pacific Northwest, southern Sierras, and Rio Grande River Basin. In these efforts the Bureau of Reclamation is assisted by other federal agencies. The research at the several field laboratories differs greatly in the nature of the studies, but the over-all goal is to put water on the ground where it can be used. Experiments suggest that under certain meteorological conditions a 10 to 20 percent increase in precipitation yield is possible over areas as large as 1000 square miles.[27] After 15 years of cloud seeding in the southern Sierras the actual stream flow of the area was increased by 8.5 percent. This is not rainfall or snow pack but actual runoff. After cloud seeding experiments, instrumentation development, and applied cloud physics research have progressed sufficiently the accumulated know-how will be applied first to those areas where water problems are more critical. All water users will benefit, including irrigation. Concurrent with the scientific and technical work there are studies concerned with the economic, biological, and legal problems that will follow in the wake of successful weather modification. There is an awareness of these pending dilemmas, particularly those of a legal nature, but the answers are lagging far behind the advancement in the physical sciences.

FROM THE GROUND. Groundwater as a source of additional water for irrigation is most promising. The technological advancements in this field are adaptations of methods used in the successful petroleum industry. There is an immense amount of groundwater available, but larger and deeper wells are necessary. Most of the nation's wells are relatively shallow and the flow meager. Larger investments could be justified if more water were pumped to serve more needs. The "new" water will be secured from depths of 500 to 2000 feet.

Efficient Use of Present Supply. The second set of techniques important in the quest for increasing the availability of fresh water is designed to permit more effective use of the present supply. According to the Soil Conservation Service engineers, the efficiency of water use for agricultural purposes throughout the West is low; in Arizona it ranges from 10 to 50 percent, and in Utah a careful survey indicated that the average efficiency was 18 percent in 1940 but 28 percent in 1960. It will vary from state to state and farm to farm, but the noteworthy issue is that efficiency can be improved by water conservation measures, such as reduction in seepage and evaporation, water salvage, elimination of *phraetophytes*, and mechanization.

When future projections are being made, irrigation, as one among many users of water along a broad spectrum, finds competition increasingly keen. The actual returns on water in terms of production range from $3000 to $4000 per acre-foot for industrial use, $250 for recreation, and $50 per acre-foot for agriculture.[28] In 1965, irrigation was the number one user of water, but in the year 2020 all major users of water will exceed irrigation by far in their projected requirements (Table 7).

In view of these appraisals and allocations it is important that irrigation specialists assume a responsibility to select the land that can sustain maximum profitable returns for water resources expended. Changes in the agricultural economy are going to demand a reappraisal of just what portions of the so-called irrigable land is first class and what portions should be classified as marginal. The answers to these queries are not constant; what is marginal by yesterday's standards may be first class tomorrow. Farmers are getting fewer; fields are much larger to accommodate modern machines; yields are increasing; new

[27] *Ibid.*

[28] Nathannel Woolman, *Value of Water in Alternative Uses*, Albuquerque, 1960, pp. xvii–xviii.

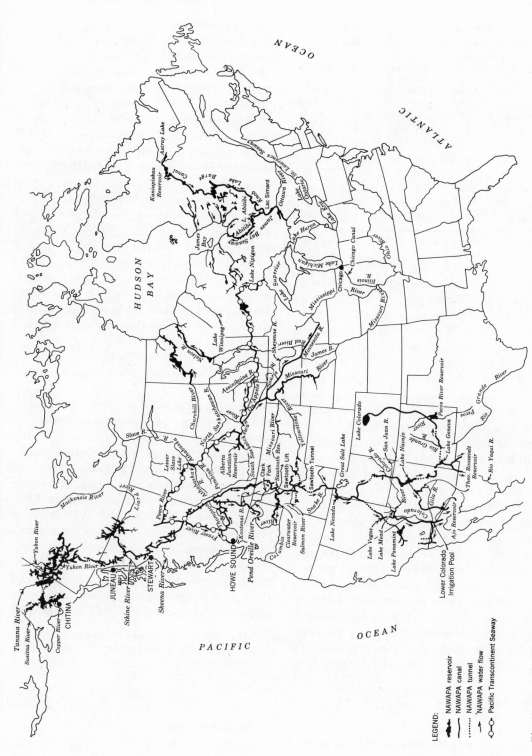

LEGEND:

![NAWAPA reservoir] NAWAPA reservoir

| NAWAPA canal

⋯ NAWAPA tunnel

↑ NAWAPA water flow

—o—o— Pacific Transcontinent Seaway

Fig. 14 The NAWAPA Plan.

Table 7. Estimated Water Requirements,
United States (Millions Gallons Daily)

| Type of Use | 1965 | Projected Requirements | | |
		1980	2000	2020
Rural domestic	2,351	2,474	2,852	3,334
Municipal	23,745	33,596	50,724	74,256
Industrial	46,405	75,026	127,365	210,767
Steam electric	84,538	193,303	470,448	914,093
Agriculture:				
Irrigation	110,852	135,852	149,824	160,978
Livestock	1,726	2,375	3,397	4,660
Total	269,617	442,626	804,610	1,368,088

[Source: *The Nation's Water Resources,* Washington, D.C., 1968.]

hybrid seeds are bing developed; new forms of fertilizer are available; plowing takes place in the fall and crops are planted earlier; a wide choice of weedicides and insecticides are on the market; and plant growth regulators and defoliants are available. These are a few of the innovations underway. It is highly significant to note that all lands will not respond in the same manner and with the same returns to the new inputs, new methods, and new machines. As the demands for greater returns intensify and more capital investment is substituted for labor and water the differences in irrigable soils will become wider.

River Basin Diversion. The present policy of the Water Resource Council will not permit a consideration of river basin diversion beyond the confines of the 18 water resource regions they have identified. This current policy is an in-basin policy and prompted very wisely by the desire to have each water resource region put its "house in order" before looking to neighboring drainage basins. However, in 10 years the policy may be reviewed and interbasin transfer of water on a national

and a continental basis may be encouraged. Under such a program the potential for irrigation would change significantly.

NAWAPA (North American Water and Power Alliance) is a plan prepared by the Ralph M. Parsons Company of Los Angeles for developing the water and power potential of the entire North American continent.[29] The basic idea is to capture the surplus waters of the Fraser, Yukon, and Athabaska river systems and to direct, via an elaborate system of canals, reservoirs, and tunnels, the surplus water to deficit areas in Canada, the United States, and Mexico (Fig. 14). According to NAWAPA 142 million acre-feet of water would be earmarked for irrigation. This amount would bring 60 million acres of land under irrigation with 41 million acres of the total assigned to the American West, which is actually more acreage than the total irrigated today.

NAWAPA is initiated by private enterprise, prompted by a profit motive, and so constituted as to utilize the full spectrum of modern engineering techniques. It reflects the farsightedness and vigor so typical of technological advancement. If the past bears any record to indicate future events, the prediction will be the normal but knotty problems associated with human relations as expressed in prevailing social, political, and economic patterns. There are some "ifs" associated with the project. It will of necessity change to meet technical and human demands. It may even be accomplished someday under another canopy. But it is forward looking and challenging and the idea will undoubtedly be carried forward in some form or another to full fruition.

[29] The Ralph M. Parsons Company, *NAWAPA, North American Water and Power Alliance,* Summary Report, June 1964.

References

Ackerman, E. A. and George O. G. Löf, *Technology in American Water Development,* The Johns Hopkins Press, Baltimore, 1959.

Bushy, C. E., "Regulation and Economic Expansion," *Water, The Yearbook of Agriculture,* U.S. Department of Agriculture, Government Printing Office, Washington, D.C., 1955, pp. 666–676.

Criddle, Wayne D. and Cornelis Kalisvaart, "Subirrigation Systems," *American Agronomy Series, No. 11,* American Society of Agronomy, Madison, Wisconsin, 1967, pp. 905–921.

Darling, Arthur B., *The Public Papers of Francis G. Newlands,* Vol. 1, Houghton Mifflin, Boston, 1932.

Hagen, Robert M., Howard R. Haise, and Talbott W. Edminster, editors, *Irrigation of Agricultural Lands, American Agronomy Series, No. 11,* American Society of Agronomy, Madison, Wisconsin, 1967.

Huffman, Roy E., *Irrigation Development and Public Water Policy,* Ronald Press, New York, 1953.

Hutchins, Wells A., "Background and Modern Developments in Water Law in the United States," *Natural Resources Journal,* Vol. 2, 1962, pp. 416–444.

Landers, John N. and K. Witte, "Irrigation for Frost Protection," *American Agronomy Series, No. 11,* American Society of Agronomy, Madison, Wisconsin, 1967, pp. 1037–1057.

Maletic, John T., "Soils, Climate, and Land Classification," Paper presented at the 1968 Annual Technical Conference, Sprinkler Irrigation Association, *Proceedings,* Denver, Colorado, 1968.

McMartin, Wallace, "Economic Trends and Future Markets for Sprinkler Irrigation Equipment," Sprinkler Irrigation Association, *Proceedings,* Denver, Colorado, 1968, pp. 89–98.

National Academy of Sciences, *Weather and Climate Modification—Problems and Prospects,* National Research Council, Washington, D.C., 1966.

National Science Foundation, Report of the Special Commission on Weather Modification, Government Printing Office, Washington, D.C., 1966.

Ralph M. Parsons Company, *NAWAPA, North American Water and Power Alliance,* Summary Report, June 1964.

Reid, Gene C., "Conservation and Economy by Use of Automation and Sprinkler Irrigation," Sprinkler Irrigation Association, *Proceedings,* Denver, Colorado, 1968, pp. 59–64.

Reynolds Metals Company, "Keep Your Crops Cool," *Reynolds Irrigation Digest,* Spring 1967, pp. 42–44.

Ruttan, Vernon W., *The Economic Demand for Irrigated Acreage: New Methodology and Some Preliminary Projections, 1954–1980,* The Johns Hopkins Press, Baltimore, 1965.

Rutter, James K., "The Modern Farm Market," Sprinkler Irrigation Association, *Proceedings,* Denver, Colorado, 1968, pp. 28–35.

Swarner, L. R. and M. A. Hagood, "Irrigation Trends in the Pacific Northwest," *Agricultural Engineering,* Vol. 44, 1963, pp. 304–307.

Turney, Omar A., "Prehistoric Irrigation in Arizona," *Arizona Historical Review,* Vol. 2, April 1929, pp. 12–52; July 1929, pp. 11–52.

United States Bureau of the Census, *Census of Agriculture 1964,* Vol. II, Chapter 9, "Irrigation, Land Improvement Practices, and Use of Agricultural Chemicals," Government Printing Office, Washington, D.C., 1964.

United States Department of Agriculture, *Sprinkler Irrigation,* Agricultural Research Service, Leaflet No. 476, Government Printing Office, Washington, D.C., 1960.

United States Senate Document 92, 68th Congress, *The Fact Finders Report,* Washington, D.C., 1924.

United States Water Resources Council, *The Nation's Water Resources,* Parts 1–7, Government Printing Office, Washington, D.C., 1968.

Widstoe, John A., "Century of Irrigation," *Reclamation Era,* Vol. 33, 1947, pp. 92–102.

Wollman, Nathannel, *Value of Water in Alternate Uses,* University of New Mexico Press, Albuquerque, 1960.

FRANK SEAWALL

Chico State College

CHAPTER 12

Waterways and Their Utilization

Waterways have served mankind from the earliest civilization to the present. Many of the early settlements were oriented to the navigable waterways. The inhabitants of Babylon used the Euphrates River for transportation, and the early Egyptians were oriented to transportation on the Nile River. Before the Spanish conquests in Latin America, the Incas used rafts on Lake Titicaca.

Ready access to navigable interior waterways continues to be a prime location factor for many of the major coastal cities because navigable waterways serve as avenues of communication with interior areas. New York City has access to the interior of the United States by an inland waterway—the Hudson River and the New York State Barge Canal. Many of the major interior cities are also situated adjacent to navigable waterways. The great majority of interior metropolitan areas in the United States and Canada with populations in excess of one million are located on navigable waters.

Man's earliest mode of mass movement of commodities—by inland water transportation —remains relatively important in our modern urban-industrial society. Inland water transportation presently is highly specialized in the types of commodites transported and in the area which it serves. The transportation of people on waterways, for commercial purposes, remains relatively unimportant, with the exception of a few excursion vessels. These waterways, however, are intensively used; they have the greatest traffic density of all modes of transport, when the comparison is based on ton-miles of traffic per mile of route. Waterways can be readily viewed as a vital natural resource and an essential segment of the transportation system.

When ton-mile of traffic is used as a criterion for measurement, water-borne traffic in the United States has shown a significant increase. The common unit of measurement used to compare the importance of the intercity freight traffic in the United States is the ton-mile, the movement of 1 ton of freight 1 mile. Table 1 shows the relative importance and trends of the various modes of freight traffic for selected years. The total intercity freight has increased almost threefold during the 27-year period included in Table 1. In relation to the other modes of transportation the traffic of the Great Lakes shows a marked decrease; however, the total ton-miles of all modes has increased during this 27-year period, but shipments on the Great Lakes have been relatively stable. The major change in the use of water transportation has been the significant increase in the traffic on the rivers and canals. Much of this increase has been on the Mississippi River and its navigable tributaries, such as the Ohio, Tennessee, and Illinois rivers.

inland waters of the United States (Fig. 1). The navigation clause, Article IV of the Ordinance, "secured absolute freedom of water and carrying places", as that was the only means of effective transportation for commerce between the interior and the eastern seaboard.[2]

The concept of freedom of use of the inland waterways has been challenged periodically. In recent years there have been several proposals to tax waterway users. A tax on fuel oil

Table 1. Distribution of Intercity Freight Traffic in the United States

Year	Total Ton-Miles in Billions	Percentage Distribution					
		Rail- roads	Motor Trucks	Great Lakes	Rivers and Canals	Oil Pipe Lines	Air Carriers
1940	619	61.3	10.0	15.5	3.6	9.6	–
1945	1,027	67.3	6.5	11.0	2.9	12.3	–
1950	1,063	56.2	16.3	10.5	4.9	12.1	–
1955	1,275	49.5	17.5	9.3	7.7	16.0	–
1960	1,314	44.1	21.7	7.6	9.2	17.4	–
1965	1,668	42.5	23.3	6.6	9.1	18.4	0.1
1966	1,763	42.6	23.4	6.4	8.6	18.9	0.1

[Source: Interstate Commerce Commission, Corps of Engineers, U.S. Army.]

Freedom of Use. The tradition of freedom in the use of inland waters for navigation dates to Colonial times with the Treaty of Paris in 1763. By this agreement France and Spain ceded to Great Britain the territory of Louisiana east of the "mid-channel of the Mississippi River (except the Isle of Orleans)", provided for mutual liberty of navigation from the source to the sea, and stipulated that there be freedom from payment of tolls.[1] The Treaty of Paris of 1783, which terminated the American Revolutionary War, re-affirmed this principle of freedom of use of inland waters for navigation. However, Article IV of the Ordinance of 1787 for the government of the Northwest Territory is usually regarded as the basis of the policy for free navigation on the

used by the vessels operating on the inland waterways was recently presented to Congress. To date, no proposal for taxing the use or charging of tolls has been successful for interior waterways. Tolls are charged for vessels using international waterways such as the Panama Canal and the St. Lawrence Seaway.

The United States and Canada traditionally honor 3 nautical miles (3.45 statute miles) as the limit of territorial waters. Merchant vessels of other nations and, in time of peace, warships are granted passage through territorial waters provided these vessels comply with navigation and police regulations during passage. This free passage is not permitted for submerged submarines or for fishing by for-

[1] P. M. Ogilvie, *International Waterways*, New York, 1920, p. 274.

[2] W. J. Hull and R. W. Hull, *The Origin and Development of the Waterways Policy of the United States,* Washington, 1967, p. 5.

eign vessels. Some nations claim jurisdiction over zones in the high seas adjacent to their territorial waters for special purposes. These purposes include fishing protection, sanitary regulations, and security. The United States and Canada claim a 12-mile jurisdiction for fishing privileges.

Advantages of Water Transportation. The major advantage of water transportation for the shipment of selected commodities is low cost. With the use of efficiently designed vessels the power required to move a given weight of cargo on water is less than on land or in the air. This can be illustrated by diesel fuel consumption in the power units used to transport cargo. It requires approximately one-third more fuel per ton-mile to transport cargo by rail than by river barge on the Mississippi or Ohio rivers. Fuel and power requirements per ton-mile movements by truck are more costly than rail shipments. Maintenance and repair costs for equipment are considerably less for barges, towboats, and ships than for rail or truck transportation when the comparison is based on comparable ton-miles. Labor productivity for barge transport is almost three times as great as for railroads when ton-miles per operating employee is used as a base for the comparison. Truck and airline labor costs are much greater than rail costs, but waterways are the lowest of the various modes of transport. Total pipe line transport costs are also relatively low, but the comparison between pipe transportation and the other modes is very difficult. The types of commodities transported by pipe line are limited, and land costs to lay the pipe lines vary greatly, making the cost comparisons difficult.

The cargo capacity of water transportation equipment is usually much greater than the capacity of other modes of transportation, hence the waterways are well suited for large movements of bulky commodities. Mississippi River tows of 35,000 tons are not unusual. A tow of this size would be equivalent to 7 trains containing 100 rail cars with a capacity of 50 tons each, or 1400 trucks, each with a capacity of 50,000 pounds. Most of the vessels presently operating exclusively on the Great Lakes have capacities between 13,000 and 20,000 tons. Generally, when capital expenditures are based on capacity, the investment per ton of capacity for water transportation equipment is less than for rail, truck, or air.

Due to their size and weight, certain commodities must be transported by water. In recent years the size and capacity of railroad freight cars have been increasing, but unusually large or odd-shaped cargoes shipped on rail cars may encounter problems due to cargo overhang on adjacent rail tracks, and bridge and tunnel clearances may prohibit the movement of such commodities. Water transportation is the only feasible method to ship the large Saturn launch vehicle booster constructed in Huntsville, Alabama, to the launching site at Cape Kennedy. Special barges are constructed for certain commodities (Fig. 2). A large, bulky 90-ton cement kiln manufactured in Chicago was shipped by barge to the Bahama Islands, because the kiln was too large to be moved by any other mode of transportation.

Most Hawaiian and Alaskan trade must be shipped by water. Only small high-value goods can bear the high cost of air freight. The volume of air freight is increasing, but the use of air freight for United States foreign trade, excluding Canada and Mexico, is less than 1 percent of the total ton-mile shipments. With our present level of technology, water transportation can be readily considered as a vital segment of the transportation industry.

Water Transportation Problems. It is commonly stated that the major problem in inland water transportation is the limited length of navigable waterways, as many areas do not have access to this mode of transportation. This limitation is evident in Table 2.

The navigable waterways comprise only 1.1 percent of the total length of the national

THE INLAND

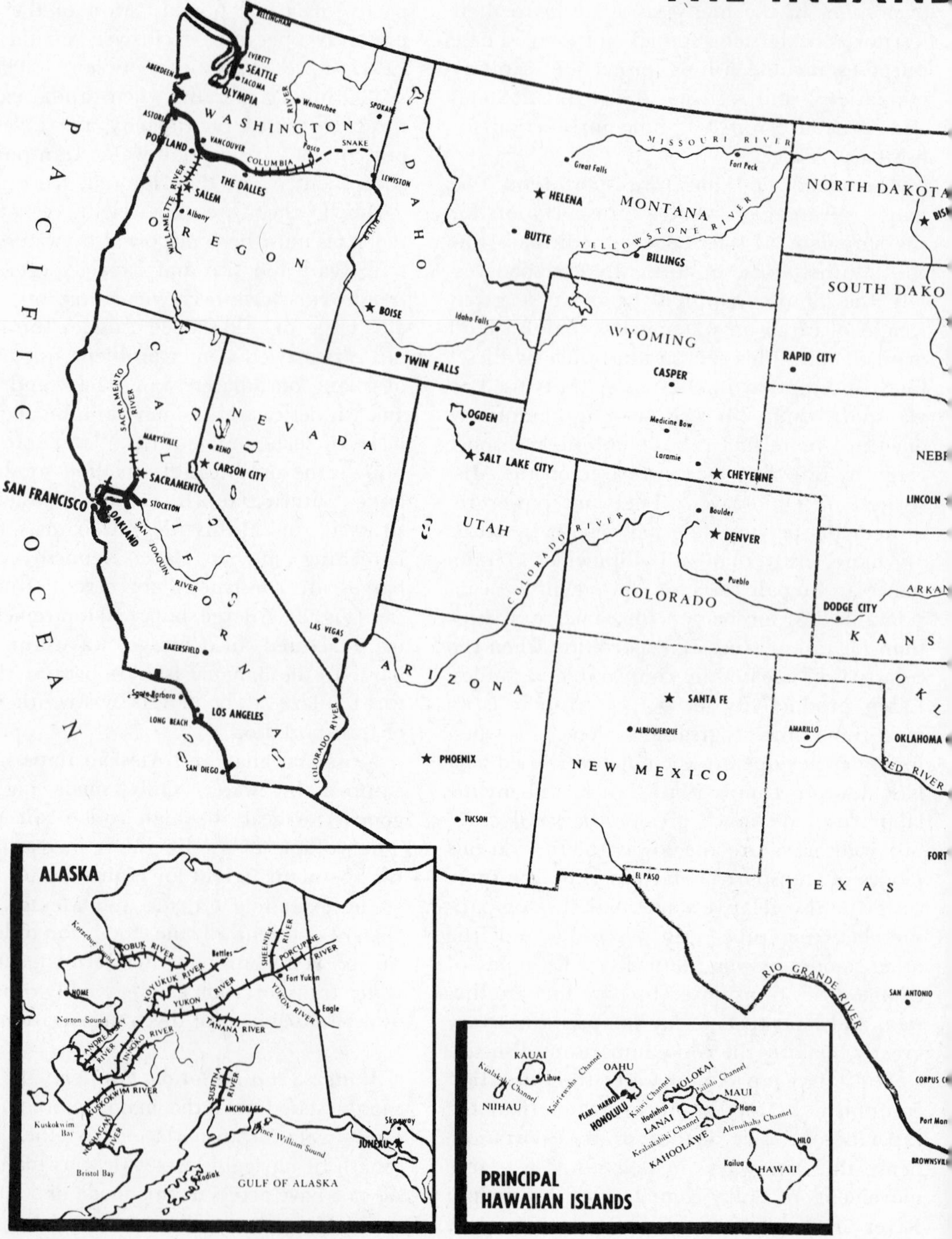

Fig. 1 The commercial inland waterways of the United States. (The American Waterways Operators, Inc.)

COMMERCIALLY NAVIGABLE
INLAND WATERWAYS
OF THE
UNITED STATES

CONTROLLING DEPTHS

9 FEET OR MORE
UNDER 9 FEET
PROPOSED EXTENSIONS

PUBLISHED 1961 BY
THE AMERICAN WATERWAYS OPERATORS, INC.
1025 CONNECTICUT AVENUE N.W., WASHINGTON 6, D. C.

Compiled from Information Supplied by
CORPS OF ENGINEERS, U.S. ARMY

ATLANTIC OCEAN

GULF OF MEXICO

GULF INTRACOASTAL WATERWAY

ATLANTIC INTRACOASTAL WATERWAY

Fig. 2 The unique white barge in the foreground was constructed to transport the Saturn launch vehicle booster from Huntsville, Alabama, to Cape Kennedy, Florida. (National Aeronautics and Space Administration.)

Table 2. Approximate Length of United States Transportation Systems, in Miles

Waterways (excluding the Great Lakes)	26,000
Railroads (mainline, rights-of-way)	212,000
Pipe lines (gas and oil)	290,000
Highways (paved roads)	1,900,000
Total	2,428,000

transportation system; however, this mode of transportation moves approximately 15 percent of the total ton-miles of freight traffic in the United States. In one respect this limitation on length of the inland waterway system is not too severe, as many of the most populous areas in the United States and Canada do have access to water transportation. Twenty of the twenty-two largest cities [3] in the United States are served by either the inland water-

[3] The largest cities are based on the estimated population in 1964 by the Bureau of Census of the Standard Metropolitan Statistical Areas.

ways or ocean transportation, or both. One of the two exceptions, Dallas, Texas, will have access to inland water transport when the Trinity River project is completed. The same general pattern is characteristic of Canada where Montreal, Toronto, Vancouver, Winnipeg, Ottawa, and Hamilton are all located on navigable waters.

Many of the problems associated with transportation in coastal waters differ from those of the inland waterways and the Great Lakes; however, some problems are common to all navigable waterways. The one problem which is characteristic of all modes of water transportation is speed. By comparison with other modes of commercial transport, water is the slowest. If speed of movement is essential, water transportation is not satisfactory, since air, rail, or truck are usually much faster. On inland waterways speed of movement depends on the power of the towboat and the direction of the movement. In many instances vessels have the capacity to move faster than their usual speed, but increasing the speed causes a considerable increase in fuel consumption. Some of the factors which determine the speed of river tows are: the character and condition of the waterway, the number of lockages, the congestion at the locks, the direction of movement (with or against the current), the size of the tow, and the power of the towing vessel in relation to the size of the tow. Some typical transit times for tows under ideal conditions are: Cincinnati to New Orleans, 1380 miles, upstream 10 days and 19 hours, downstream 6 days and 7 hours; Minneapolis to New Orleans, 1731 miles, upstream 13 days and 12 hours, downstream 7 days and 22 hours.[4]

Some of the problems in the use of waterways are the result of the natural environment. River meanders, such as found in mature or old streams, cause some disadvantages. Distances are increased by meandering river channels. In a comparison with rail, pipe line, and highway, the water distance between given places is often the greatest due to meandering river channels. The railway and highway distances are considerably less than the water route between Pittsburgh and New Orleans. Visibility and maneuverability of a river tow is often reduced when vessels meet in the bend of a river. In some instances it becomes necessary to change the arrangement of the barges in the tow because of the meandering and narrow river channel (Fig. 3).

River channel and harbor depths are a critical phase of water transportation, since the depth may limit the amount of cargo carried on a vessel and the size of the vessel. Minimum depths are specified by the Corps of Engineers for all commercial waterways. Some harbors and inland waterways require periodic dredging, because of silting and river deposits, in order to maintain the specified minimum depths. With the increased use of larger

vessels with greater depth requirements, periodic increases in depths of waterways become necessary. Usually, authorization and appropriations from Congress are required before the Corps of Engineers authorizes dredging operations.

The tributary streams to a natural waterway constitute one of the major sources of sediments, and dredging is often required at the mouth or immediately downstream from the mouth of the entering tributaries. When dredging is required in a river or a harbor it is usually dredged to a depth of 2 or 3 feet greater than the minimum specified depth. The extra dredging, beyond the minimum depth, is referred to as an overcut. This reduces the frequency at which dredging is required.

When navigation in a waterway is maintained by navigation locks, it is usually the lock dimensions which fix the depth of the waterway. Lock chambers are fixed concrete structures and thus serve to determine the minimum channel depths.

Exclusive of the Great Lakes, the United States has approximately 26,000 miles of inland waterways for commercial use. Approximately 10,000 miles have less than a 9-foot channel, and nearly 16,000 miles of inland waterways have channel depths of 9 feet or more.

Generally, the deeper the waterway the greater the efficiency. For example, a typical Ohio River tow of 25,000-ton displacement has a barge resistance of 64,500 pounds at 8 miles per hour. When the draught is increased from 8.5 feet to 11 feet the resistance becomes 68,000 pounds and the displacement from the additional loading increases to 33,200 tons. In other words, for 5.4 percent more horsepower the tonnage can be increased by 33 percent at the same speed. Increased channel depths can thus produce a significant increase in efficiency.[5]

[4] *Big Load Afloat*, American Waterways Operators, Inc., Washington, D.C., 1965, p. 15.

[5] Frank Seawall, "Water Transportation on the Ohio River: Its Economic Significance to Appalachia," *Bulletin of Business Research*, Ohio State University, Vol. 41, February 1966, p. 6.

Fig. 3 The Cheatham Lock and Dam on the Cumberland River in Tennessee. (The American Waterways Operators, Inc.)

Ice formation during the winter months limits the navigation season on the Great Lakes, St. Lawrence River, the Upper Mississippi River system, and the New York State Barge Canal. Usually the ice-free period on Lake Superior is slightly over 8 months, extending from early April to December. The entire surface of the Great Lakes is rarely frozen in the winter, but ice formation near the shore and at constricted areas, such as Sault Ste. Marie, prevents ship movements. The Duluth-Superior harbor and the Sault Ste. Marie area often have ice from 20 to 36 inches thick during the winter. The U.S.

Coast Guard sends special ice-breaking vessels through the entrance to the canal at the Sault Ste. Marie and the Duluth-Superior harbor in early April to open shipping lanes. Ice piles near the shore resulting from movements of free-floating ice, termed "pack" or "drift" ice, often prevent the use of some harbors during the winter season.

The length of the navigation season on the Upper Mississippi, the Missouri, and the New York State Barge Canal varies from one year to the next and from one segment of the waterway to another. Ice does restrict navigation on these waterways for a portion of every year.

Occasionally, ice formation on the Ohio River and the Illinois Waterway is sufficiently thick to prohibit navigation for short periods. Drift ice, which appears on the Great Lakes and St. Lawrence Seaway, is also a problem of the rivers, as the influence of river current and wind causes piling of ice near the shore. This creates a problem when drift ice collects in front of the dock areas. Pilings in the river upstream from landings may minimize the effect of drift ice.

Another navigational problem which characterizes some inland waterways is the fluctuations in the water supply. The change in the amount of water in the waterways results from seasonal variations in precipitation and runoff in the river basins. If the water level is unusually low, cargo vessels cannot be loaded to their normal capacity or navigation may be restricted. In the past, variations in water supply were more critical than at present. The construction of water storage reservoirs on tributary streams has minimized the seasonal variations in water supply.

Some navigational problems are created by man. Certain aspects of the design of a bridge can be considered as detrimental to navigation. The vertical distance between the water and the lower level of the bridge is a critical factor, as this distance limits the height of the vessels. Usually it is the towboats which are hampered by the low vertical clearance. Some towboats operating on inland waterways are equipped with masts and pilot houses which can be lowered when passing under fixed bridges with low clearances. The Corps of Engineers stipulates vertical clearance for bridges above the mean water level, but some of the older fixed bridges constructed before minimum clearances were specified are obstacles to navigation. This problem of sufficient vertical space for vessels when passing under bridges becomes more severe during the high water stages on the inland waterways.

The horizontal clearance between bridge supports is also an important dimension which can affect navigation, since it may limit the width of tows and can become a hazard in a meeting situation. The Corps of Engineers currently specifies minimum horizontal clearances, but some older bridges do not meet these specifications. All new bridges and old bridges being re-built are required to meet the current specifications when crossing inland waterways.

Man-Made Improvements. Most of the nation's natural waterways require some improvements to meet the present needs of water transportation. Improvements such as dredging of harbors and river channels can be viewed as temporary, since physical conditions often necessitate repeated corrective action. Locks, navigation dams, and water storage reservoirs, which eliminate the navigation hazards of rapids and waterfalls or control water depths, are characterized as having a greater degree of permanence. Technological changes in vessel design have made some of the older locks and dams outmoded. The efficiency of water transportation has been improved by the use of larger barges, more powerful towboats, and the increased size of ocean vessels. These vessels, which need increased water depths, have required reconstruction of some of the older locks and an increase of channel depths. Without these alterations the present navigation system would be limited.

Most of the financial burden of improvement of waterways has been on the federal government. Congress, in 1818, decided that it had the power under the Constitution to appropriate money for the construction of canals and for the improvement of water courses.[6] During this period a view was held that the states were financially unable to make the necessary improvements in the waterways. Another factor favoring the federal government making the improvements was that individual states might have difficulty in gaining cooper-

[6] *Annals of Congress,* 15th Congress, 1st Session, 1818, p. 1384.

ation to improve the waterways which bordered two or more states. It should be noted that most modes of commercial transportation —the airways, highways, and railroads—have been recipients of some financial assistance from the federal government. Some state and local governments and private organizations have improved and financed some of the commercial waterways.

In the early part of the nineteenth century an intricate network of canals was constructed in the eastern part of the United States. The Erie Canal was constructed by the State of New York. A private company owned and operated the locks and dams on the Monongahela River before their acquisition by the federal government. With the development and expansion of the railroads many segments of the canal system were abandoned. Some of the natural waterways continued to be used commercially, but were not reliable because of the fluctuating water levels.

The first appropriations of funds by Congress was in 1824 to remove sand bars and snags in the Ohio and Mississippi rivers. In the same year another appropriation was made to deepen the channel for the harbor at Erie, Pennsylvania. In the last half of the nineteenth century and the early part of the twentieth century the railroads dominated commercial transportation; thus improvements to waterways were relatively limited until after World War I.

The dredge and the navigation lock and dam are perhaps the most significant developments as aids to inland water navigation. The navigation lock, an invention credited to Leonardo da Vinci, permits vessels to move from one water level to another. Navigation dams control the water flow so that stored water can be released during the low water stage, whereas they permit water to flow unrestricted during the high water stage. With sufficient water storage reservoirs to supplement the water supply during low water periods, water supply at the low water stage is usually

not a severe aspect of the problem; the high water phase of control is usually the most acute phase of the water supply problem. Flooding out of the locks, making them inoperative, may suspend navigation. Traffic can proceed through the locks until the water of the upper pool rises to one-half a foot from the top of the lock walls; however, navigation is usually suspended at somewhat lower stages due to the velocity of the high water current.[7] Navigation may also be suspended because of insufficient clearance between the water level and fixed bridges for the towboat to pass under the bridges.

Most of the lock chambers on the inland waterways are standardized in size, depending on the intensity of use, the size of the vessels commonly used on the waterway, and the water supply in the waterway. The following standard dimensions were established by the Corps of Engineers in 1959 for waterways in the United States:

Lock width 66 feet with length of 400 feet or 600 feet.

Lock width 84 feet with length of 600 feet, 800 feet, or 1200 feet.

Lock width 110 feet with length of 600 feet, 800 feet, or 1200 feet.

Some of the locks constructed before 1959 conform to these standards, but there are locks in use on the inland waterways with divergent dimensions. The large lock chambers, 110 feet by 1200 feet, in use on the Ohio and Mississippi rivers can accommodate 24 standard barges which measure 26 by 175 feet. These barges are usually arranged four wide and six long. Another standard barge size, 35 feet wide and 195 feet long, can be arranged three wide and six long in order to pass through the large lock chamber as a unit. An exception to the standardized locks is found on the Columbia-Snake River system. These

[7] Frank Seawall, "Water Supply for Navigation," *Public Works,* Vol. 91, 1960, p. 109.

locks measure 86 feet by 675 feet. Most lock-ages take from 20 to 30 minutes for one operation. If a tow is too large for a single lockage, the tow is separated and a double lockage is required, thus increasing lockage time.

Major Waterway Projects in Process. Several major navigation projects which will increase the length of the internal waterways are under construction. The completion of some of these new projects is relatively time-consuming. The Arkansas River development was first approved by Congress in 1946, construction was started in 1955, and the scheduled date of completion is 1970. This project will consist of 17 locks and dams to adjust for the 420-foot difference in elevation between the Mississippi River and Tulsa, Oklahoma. When completed, the project will provide a minimum channel depth of 9 feet along the lower 435 miles of the Arkansas River. Estimated annual traffic of 13 million tons is projected for the waterway, with coal, grain, steel, sand, gravel, and cement as the major cargoes. This multi-purpose project will provide elecrical power, additional flood control, domestic and industrial water supply, and recreational sites.

Several other major waterway projects which will increase the nation's water transportation system have been proposed, or authorized, or are in the construction stage. The Trinity River project in Texas will bring water transportation to the Dallas-Fort Worth area. Other projects include an extension of navigation on the Snake River to Lewiston, Idaho; the Cross Florida Canal; the lower Red River in Louisiana; and the connecting Tombigbee and Tennessee River Waterway.

The New Poe Lock which was opened in late 1968 at Sault Ste. Marie is 110 feet wide and 1200 feet long, compared to the old MacArthur Lock which is 80 feet by 800 feet (Fig. 4). As a result new Great Lakes vessels are being constructed to utilize the capacity of the new lock. An ore carrier with a 45,000-ton capacity is under construction. This new vessel is 105 feet wide, 30 feet wider than the vessels currently in use on the Great Lakes. Other current improvements on this waterway include deepening of the channels in the St. Clair and Detroit rivers and the Strait of Mackinac.

Ports and Waterways. The indented coasts of the Atlantic and Gulf of Mexico provide more and better natural harbors than are found on the Pacific coast which has a more regular coast line. New York City, Philadelphia, Baltimore, Boston, and Hampton Roads (Norfolk and vicinity) are all busy, established ports on the Atlantic coast. With the exception of Hampton Roads, which is a major coal exporting port, all the major ports' import tonnages exceed exports. Some of these harbors have required occasional dredging to accommodate the new large ocean vessels. Generally these protected natural harbors have minimal tides and are of sufficient size to accommodate most of the large ocean vessels.

Due to the nature of the commodities— petroleum and petroleum products, chemicals, metallic ores, and grains—shipped and received via the ports on the Gulf of Mexico, these ports record a large volume of traffic. The total tonnage for New Orleans in 1966 was greater than for any other Gulf port. This old established port, New Orleans, has direct access to water-borne traffic from the Mississippi River system and the Gulf Intracoastal Canal. On the western Gulf coast the City of Houston, which is connected to the Gulf of Mexico by the Houston Ship Canal, is the major port. Other southern ports with a large volume of traffic include Baton Rouge, Beaumont, Port Arthur, Corpus Christi, Mobile, and Tampa.

On the Pacific coast four harbors dominate the domestic and foreign water-borne commerce. In 1966, Los Angeles-Long Beach, which had over 55 percent of its shipments of foreign origin or destination, had the greatest volume of traffic. Other Pacific ports which

Fig. 4 The busy locks at Sault Ste. Marie connect Lake Superior, which is 22 feet higher, with Lake Huron. (Lake Carriers' Association.)

have significant trade include the San Francisco Bay ports, Seattle, and Portland.

The Mississippi River, which is navigable from Minneapolis to its mouth, serves as a major north-south artery of water-borne traffic. Another factor which contributes to Mississippi traffic is the navigable connecting waterways such as the Ohio and Missouri rivers, and the Illinois and Gulf Intracoastal Waterways and their tributaries. Of the 30 locks and dams on the Mississippi River 27 locks are located on the upper river, upstream from St. Louis. River depths in the Mississippi as far upstream as Baton Rouge, Louisiana, are suffi-

cient to accommodate large ocean tankers which require a 40-foot depth. A 9-foot channel depth is maintained to Minneapolis, 1837 miles from the mouth of the Mississippi. Five groups of commodities comprise 75 percent of the river traffic. These commodites include petroleum and petroleum products, grain and grain products, bituminous coal and lignite, sand and stone, and iron and steel products.

The Ohio River, which is formed at the confluence of the Allegheny and Monongahela rivers, is navigable for its entire 981 miles. In the early nineteenth century a canal was constructed to by-pass the rapids in the

Ohio River at Louisville. The current Ohio River project includes the construction of 19 locks and dams with 110-foot by 1200-foot lock chambers to replace 46 of the locks and dams built during the period from 1910 to 1929. The new project is creating larger navigation pools (the distance between adjacent locks), and increasing channel depths above the 9-foot minimum. Both of these factors are improving the efficiency of Ohio River transportation. Industrial expansion has characterized the shores of the Ohio River in recent years, creating a demand for river transportation. Since 1965, the annual traffic on the Ohio River has been in excess of 100 million tons. The Monongahela, Kanawha, Tennessee, Cumberland, Kentucky, Allegheny, and Green rivers, all navigable tributaries to the Ohio River, contribute significant traffic to it. Bituminous coal usually comprises about half of the total traffic on the Ohio. When petroleum and petroleum products, sand and stone, industrial chemicals, and crushed limestone are added to the coal traffic, these shipments comprise 85 percent of the river traffic.

The New York State Barge Canal system is unique among the commercial waterways in that it is owned and operated by the State of New York. This waterway, which connects Lake Erie, Lake Ontario, the Hudson River, Lake Champlain, and other lakes, is 522 miles long and has 58 navigation locks and a 12-foot channel depth. Attempts have been made in the State of New York to transfer the Barge Canal system to the federal government for improvements, enlargement, and inclusion into the national system of inland waterways. The cost of maintaining and improving this waterway has been a financial obligation of the state government. In 1967, 53.7 percent of the shipments on the waterway was interstate traffic, and this can be viewed as support for the control and operation of this waterway by the federal government. In recent years total traffic has been decreasing slightly. The 1967 traffic was slightly over 3 million tons, with

petroleum and petroleum products the most important of the commodity groups.

When ton-miles of traffic are used as a criterion of use of the inland waterways, the Great Lakes traffic is more significant than the traffic on either the Mississippi River system or all other inland waterways combined. Iron ores dominate the Great Lakes traffic. As typified by iron ore traffic, the major portion of the Great Lakes traffic is in low-value bulky commodities. The bulk of iron ore traffic originates in the western end of Lake Superior in Minnesota where several ports ship iron ore and taconite pellets, an upgraded processed form of iron ore, to the Chicago area, Buffalo, Detroit, Cleveland, and several smaller Lake Erie ports. This traffic flow has characterized the shipping pattern on the Great Lakes throughout this century. Based on the expanded taconite facilities and the size of the taconite reserves, it appears that this movement will continue to be of major importance in the Great Lakes traffic for a considerable period of time.

Bituminous coal ranks second in ton-miles, with Toledo as the port of origin and Detroit, Toronto, Hamilton, Buffalo, and Duluth as the destination for the coal traffic. Grain traffic has several ports of origin, with Fort William and Port Arthur, the Canadian Lakehead, as the major shipping ports. Within the United States, Duluth-Superior continues to be the major shipping terminal, but shipments of grain from Chicago and Toledo are also noteworthy (Fig. 5). With the enlarged St. Lawrence Seaway operative, Montreal is a major destination. A considerable portion of the grain traffic terminates in Buffalo. The limestone quarries of northeastern Michigan supply much of this traffic, which generally terminates in steel- and cement-producing plants on the Great Lakes.

St. Lawrence Seaway. When Jacques Cartier entered the Gulf of St. Lawrence in 1535, he had expectations that the St. Lawrence River would lead him to the Orient. La

Fig. 5 The Duluth-Superior harbor, one of the Nation's major ports, is well protected from Lake Superior. Grain is shipped from the elevators in the foreground to many foreign destinations via the St. Lawrence Seaway. (Duluth Seaway Port Authority.)

Chine Rapids [8] near the present site of Montreal was the first obstacle. Efforts by subsequent French explorers were successful in gaining access to the Great Lakes via the St. Lawrence Valley. Portages around the rapids and waterfalls were necessary.

The first navigational improvement on the St. Lawrence River was the construction of a canal to by-pass the rapids upstream from Montreal in 1700. Other small canals were completed in various segments of the waterway in the late eighteenth and early nineteenth centuries. A small canal with locks was constructed in 1797 by a fur trading company to by-pass the rapids between Lake Superior and Lake Huron. The Lachine Canal, near Montreal, was deepened to 5 feet in 1825. It was not until 1830 that the first Welland Ship Canal was completed. This canal, which by-

[8] Cartier referred to the rapids as "Sault La Chine" —the rapids of China.

passed Niagara Falls, had a 7-foot depth. In 1855, a canal 9 feet deep was built which permitted access to Lake Superior from Lake Huron at Sault Ste. Marie, Michigan.

Periodic improvements at these critical points in the St. Lawrence River system became necessary as traffic continued to increase and larger, more efficient vessels came into use. The western movement of the population, the increase in grain traffic, and the copper and iron ore production all contributed to the increased lake traffic. By 1900, Canada had completed a navigation system from Lake Erie to the Atlantic Ocean with a 14-foot channel. The St. Lawrence River segment consisted of 22 locks. Some small ocean vessels used this Seaway, but traffic was limited due to the size and depth of the locks. Several attempts were made in Congress in the first half of the twentieth century to approve authorization for the reconstruction of the Seaway, but all attempts failed. The Atlantic and Gulf ports and many of the railroads were opposed to the Seaway. Since the proposals for the Seaway included hydroelectric power development as part of the project the coal interests were also opposed to the enlargement of the waterway.

In 1951, the Canadian Parliament passed the St. Lawrence Seaway Act which authorized the construction of a waterway entirely within Canadian borders. The rich iron ore deposits of Minnesota were being depleted, but a new deposit of high quality iron ore was discovered on the Labrador-Quebec border. The proposed enlarged Seaway could be used to transport this iron ore to the steel mills adjacent to the Great Lakes. In 1954, the Congress of the United States passed the Wiley-Dondero Act which permitted the United States to join Canada in the reconstruction of the St. Lawrence Seaway. The development of hydroelectric power from the project and the recovery of some costs by toll charges were aids in obtaining Congressional approval for the project. Undoubtedly the threat of an all-Canadian Seaway was one of the major factors in obtaining approval from the Congress.

The St. Lawrence Seaway, which includes eight locks in the Welland Ship Canal, has been an asset to water transportation and to selected phases of the Canadian and United States' economy. The Seaway, however, has some problems. One of the major problems is the seasonality of open waters. Due to ice in the winter the Seaway has but an 8-month navigation season. Hence, one-third of the year this Seaway is of no use to man for navigation.

The dimensions of the locks in the Seaway are currently considered a problem and will be a more acute problem as the size of the ocean vessels continue to increase. The water depth of the locks is the most severe limitation. The locks on the St. Lawrence River have 30 feet of water over the lock sills (con-

crete foundations at the lock entries), and the Welland Ship Canal consists of eight locks with a 27-foot depth (Fig. 6). By comparison the Panama Canal, which was constructed over 55 years ago and is considered outmoded, has 39 feet of water over the lock sills. The locks of the Panama Canal are 30 feet wider than the locks on the St. Lawrence River. At present only approximately two-thirds of the world's general cargo vessels and tankers can use the Seaway. There is a pronounced trend toward larger vessels in the future. Labor and operating costs per ton of cargo transported are reduced with larger vessels.

Shipbuilding on the Great Lakes is also handicapped by lock size. Shipbuilding costs on the Great Lakes are at times less than costs on the Atlantic coast due to ready access to steel plates in the steel mills adjacent to the Great Lakes. Many United States Naval vessels cannot be built at the Great Lakes shipyards because the vessels are too wide for the Seaway locks.

Commodity Movements. Total tonnage shipped in domestic water-borne commerce is greater than in foreign commerce for the United States; however, the rate of increase for foreign commerce is greater than for domestic commerce. Based on Corps of Engineers' data, 21 percent of the water-borne commerce in 1948 was foreign; this figure rose to 30 percent in 1957 and to 35 percent in 1966. By 1966, export tonnages were slightly more than double the 1948 exports. During this same period the greatest change in foreign water-borne commerce was the import tonnages, which nearly quadrupled. Nearly 90 percent of the foreign water-borne commerce terminates in the coastal ports. However, the role of the Great Lakes in attracting foreign traffic has significantly changed with the advent of the enlarged St. Lawrence Seaway. Imports from Canada more than doubled the first year that the Seaway was in operation. From 1958 to 1966, water-borne imports from Canada increased threefold. The last year of

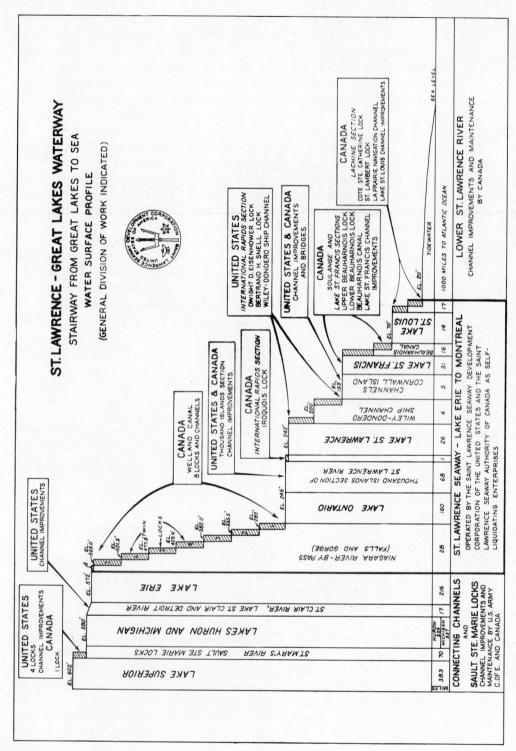

Fig. 6 The St. Lawrence-Great Lakes Seaway provides the interior of North America with ocean transportation. The profile illustrates the difference in elevation between Lake Erie and Lake Ontario. (St. Lawrence Seaway Development Corporation.)

record prior to the completion of the St. Lawrence Seaway was 1958. The big relative change in Seaway imports has been in the overseas traffic which in 1966 was nearly twelve times the pre-Seaway traffic in 1958.

Total export water-borne tonnages for the United States more than doubled between 1948 and 1966. This gain in exports has been reflected in coastal port traffic which increased 2.4 times during the 1948 to 1966 period. Exports via the Seaway to overseas destinations had a nineteenfold increase between 1958 and 1966, whereas water-borne tonnages exported to Canada were practically unchanged during the period between 1948 and 1966.

Total domestic tonnages transported on the inland waterways, which comprise the major segment of water-borne commerce, have had a relatively constant increase. From 1948 to 1966 the total tonnages increased by 37 percent. An examination of the data published by the Corps of Engineers reveals that this change varied between the coastwise, internal waterways, Great Lakes, and local traffic. The most significant increase has been in the internal water-borne traffic; the 1966 tonnages were 2.3 times as great as the 1948 shipments. Coastwise traffic increased by 20 percent during this same period. Domestic shipments on the Great Lakes decreased 6 percent between 1948 and 1966, whereas local, or intraport, shipments within a port area decreased by 13 percent during this period.

Rail and truck carriers transport a much greater variety of commodities than do waterways or pipe lines. Waterway shipments generally consist of low-value bulky commodities which are generally more sensitive to transportation costs, and water movements have traditionally been a low-cost method of shipment. A small change in transportation costs of a low-value bulky commodity may have a significant effect on the total cost of the commodity at its destination. Barge transportation costs on the Mississippi or Ohio rivers average between 2.5 and 4 mills per ton-mile.

Mineral fuels, largely petroleum and petroleum products, and coal and coke, comprise the major portion of the domestic water-borne tonnages. In 1966, these low-value bulky commodities made up over 57 percent of the domestic tonnages on waterways. Petroleum and petroleum products shipments were over 38 percent of the total traffic, and coal and coke comprised nearly 19 percent of this traffic. Sand, gravel, and stone shipments formed over 12 percent, and iron ore and iron and steel products made up nearly 10 percent of this commerce. Other commodities with large tonnages in the water-borne domestic commerce and their portion of the total tonnage in 1966 include: chemicals, 3.6 percent; logs and lumber, 3.6 percent; seashells, 2.8 percent; and grains, 2.3 percent (Fig. 7). All of these commodities, which account for over 91 percent of the domestic water-borne commerce, can be classified as low-value bulky goods.

Many of the major commodities shipped in 1966 in foreign water-borne commerce were the same as in domestic commerce. Mineral fuels comprised 44 percent of the total tonnage, with petroleum and petroleum products forming 33 percent of the total foreign water-borne tonnages. Iron ore and iron and steel made up 16 percent of the total shipments, while grain traffic composed over 11 percent of this traffic. Traffic in chemicals in 1966 was 4.5 percent of the total. These five groups of bulky goods made up slightly over 75 percent of the total foreign water-borne traffic; hence the pattern of tonnage shipments in foreign traffic is somewhat similar to the domestic traffic. The one variation in this pattern is the insignificance of sand, stone, and gravel in the foreign water-borne commerce. In domestic commerce this group of commodities composed over 12 percent of the traffic, whereas in foreign water-borne traffic only 1.2 percent of the total tonnage was in sand, stone, and gravel.

National Defense. The inland waterways are considered as a vital segment of the na-

Fig. 7 A log raft is passing through the Bonneville Lock on the Columbia River. (Portland District, U.S. Corps of Engineers.)

tion's defense transportation system. During World War II the navigable inland waterways were placed under the control of the Office of Defense Transportation. At this time, large quantities of strategic commodities were transported on the inland waters when foreign submarines were harassing coastal shipping lanes and blockading the coastal ports. Transportation of some commodities became integrated as barge transport was used in conjunction with pipe line, rail, and truck. Maximum efficiency of the transportation system was essential to maintain wartime production.

During World War II shipyards adjacent to inland waters constructed and repaired thousands of the smaller ocean-going vessels such as relatively large submarines, destroyer escorts, various landing craft, and auxilliary vessels. In 1945, approximately 140 shipbuilding and repair facilities were operative on the nation's inland waterways. Some of the large ships and boats constructed at inland points were pontooned or floated via the inland waterways to the sea. By floating vessels above the normal water displacement level, a ship requiring 17 feet of water could be moved in a river with a 9-foot depth. The facilities, skills, and materials of many of these shipyards remain intact and presently serve Great Lakes and river transportation fleets. It can be considered advantageous to have these facilities available in case of a national emergency.

By the use of inland waterways for the construction of the smaller ocean vessels, a desirable dispersal of essential defense industries is permitted. This decentralization of shipyards may permit a reduction in ship construction costs. Materials such as steel produced in industrial facilities located in the interior of the nation can be used for ship construction. By the use of these materials construction costs may be reduced as the cost of transporting materials to coastal shipyards is eliminated.

Another national defense aspect of the inland waterways has been previously mentioned and is illustrated by the use of river barges to transport bulky items, such as the Saturn space vehicle boosters from Huntsville, Alabama, to Cape Kennedy, Florida (Fig. 2).

Recreation. With our affluent society and more leisure time, there has been a significant increase in the recreational use of private pleasure craft on the nation's inland waters. This recreational use has been expedited by the construction of small boat harbors, launching ramps, and docking and service facilities by governmental and private organizations. Various levels of government (municipal, county, state, and federal) are participating in recreation development programs. In recent years numerous privately owned pleasure marinas have also been developed for boat owners along our navigable waterways. It is estimated that nearly 10 million pleasure craft are currently in use on the nation's inland waters.

Coastal waters near the populous metropolitan areas are probably those most intensively used by pleasure-boat operators. The Mississippi River system, with its navigable tributaries, and the Great Lakes also provide excellent intensively used facilities for pleasure craft. Relatively long journeys are possible through the use of connecting waterways. The new series of locks and dams on the Ohio River has increased the length of uninterrupted segments of the river, thus making recreational boating more attractive. Other facilities which have been of benefit to the pleasure-boat operators include the dams which impound waters in the headwater areas of tributary streams. These dams on the tributaries are classified as multi-purpose dams since they serve as flood control dams, provide water during the low water stages to the navigable rivers, and conserve water for recreational uses. In many areas the naviagable waters and reservoirs created by dams on the tributary streams also provide facilities for fish and wildlife conservation. These waters form a refuge for the permanent waterfowl and provide flyways during the migration seasons. Fishing in navigable waters continues to be a recreational activity for many sportsmen; however, water pollution of inland waters in recent years has caused the killing of some fish.

The navigable Mississippi River system serves as a route for one of the few remaining steam-powered stern-wheeled passenger vessels. A riverboat, which was built in Scotland and reconstructed in California for service on the Sacramento River in the 1920's, provides passenger excursions on the Mississippi, Ohio, Tennessee, and Cumberland rivers. No freight is transported on this vessel, which can accommodate 200 passengers (Fig. 8). Although this vessel may be decommissioned because of a federal law requiring all passenger vessels to have steel superstructures, it has been serving a unique recreational function on the inland waters.

Role of the Federal Government. Since inland waterways are interstate in nature, much of the regulation and operation of these waters for navigation becomes a function of the federal government. Various agencies and departments of the federal government perform functions related to inland waterways.

THE ARMY CORPS OF ENGINEERS. In 1824, the Congress authorized and appropriated $75,000

Fig. 8 The modernized paddlewheel steam powered *S.S. Delta Queen* continues to operate scheduled cruises on the Mississippi, Ohio, and Tennessee rivers. (Greene Line Steamers, Inc.)

to the Corps of Engineers, U.S. Army, for the removal of sand bars from the Ohio River and sawyers and snags from the Mississippi River. Harbor improvements on Presque Isle on Lake Erie and Plymouth Beach in Massachusetts were authorized with an appropriation in the same year. This Congressional action was the first coordinated effort to improve waterways for navigation.

The Corps of Engineers is responsible for the construction, operation, and maintenance of the nation's waterways for commercial navigation, including harbor improvements. Specifically this includes the following duties:

1. Removal of obstructions to maintain navigability of the waterways.

2. Canalization where locks and dams are required.

3. Providing and maintaining channels at their authorized depth and width.

4. Improving and maintaining harbors, including the provision of protective works such as jetties and breakwaters.

5. Providing means other than lighting and marking of channels for facilitating navigation.[9]

The Corps of Engineers is also directly involved with planning improvements for waterways and harbors. Under planning, the Corps of Engineers' program includes economic analysis, cost studies, engineering feasibility studies, and an over-all justification for development. Many of the Corps of Engineers' projects are classified as multi-purpose, and navigation is but one phase of the program. Other phases of these projects include flood control, hydroelectric power development, and other allied activities. With multiple-purpose projects it is relatively difficult to be precise on costs for an individual phase of a project, due to the interrelationship of the functions of the structures. For instance, a flood control dam may store water to be used to maintain channel depths for navigation, create a reservoir for a hydroelectric project,

[9] *Big Load Afloat*, Washington, D.C., 1965, p. 52.

and develop a lake for recreational use, and as a fish and wildlife preserve.

Water transportation data are collected and published by the Corps of Engineers on inland waterways and all ports. These data show the direction of movement of commodities and passengers and the arrival and departure of vessels. The length of the navigation season and authorized channel depths are also tabulated in the *Corps of Engineers Annual Reports.* This information is of considerable value to the commercial interests of the nation, the government, and others concerned with water transportation.

The Corps of Engineers is essentially a military organization which is one part of the United States Army; however, the Corps serves as an agent of the federal government for a wide variety of civil works, including waterways and harbor improvements. A large staff of civilians is employed by the civil works phase of the Corps of Engineers. Most of the construction and maintenance of navigational projects of the Corps is accomplished through private contractors. The Corps does operate some dredges and barges which are used for certain continuing maintenance and operational work.

Many other functions related to navigation are included as responsibilities of the Corps of Engineers. It is necessary to obtain approval from the Corps before any structures are built over, under, or alongside a navigable waterway which would affect navigation; this includes bridges, tunnels, docks, and moorings. The Corps has authority to restrict the size of tows and the speed of vessels.

With the re-organization of the executive branch of the federal government, some changes in the administration of water transportation activities are possible. It has been suggested that the planning, construction, and maintenance of the inland waterways be shifted, for administrative purposes, from the Department of Defense to the Department of Transportation. Tradition favors the Depart-

ment of Defense, but many people advocate that the Department of Transportation is a more logical location for the administration of water transportation.

INTERSTATE COMMERCE COMMISSION. On February 4, 1887, Congress passed the Interstate Commerce Act to regulate commerce and also created the Interstate Commerce Commission. The purpose of this independent agency of the federal government is to regulate the transportation of passengers and commodities which move from state to state. Discriminatory rate practices by some carriers created the need for government regulation. The original statute was relatively brief; however, the two hundred amendments or modifications have made the present Act relatively voluminous.

Certain conditions exempt some inland water shipments from regulation by the Interstate Commerce Commission. Shipments which originate and terminate within a state are not subject to the Act, as they are not interstate shipments. Exceptions to the Act for inland water transportation also apply for commodities transported in bulk when the cargo space of the vessel in which the commodities are transported is used for carrying not more than three such commodities. Shipments are considered in bulk when the commodities are loaded and carried without wrappers or containers and are received and delivered by the carrier without a transportation mark or count.[10] The Interstate Commerce Commission considers two or more vessels (towboat, tugs, and barges) when operating as a unit, as in a tow, to be a single vessel. The Interstate Commerce Act also exempts from economic regulation water transportation of liquid cargoes transported in bulk in vessels designed for use exclusively in, and certified for, such service.

Most of the commodity movements on inland waterways are exempt from regulation

[10] *The Interstate Commerce Act*, Government Printing Office, Washington, D.C., 1958, Section 303, (b), (c).

under the Interstate Commerce Act. Approximately 92 percent of the inland waterway carriers engage in either exempt for-hire service or in private transportation. The private transporter is the owner of the cargo, or the transporter is a wholly-owned subsidiary of a parent corporation which is the owner of the cargo. A considerable part of the Great Lakes traffic is via private carrier. The exempt for-hire service is referred to as a contract carrier. Cargo transported by contract carrier is exempt from regulation if a shipment is limited to three commodities.

Only 8 percent of the companies operating vessels on inland channels are regulated under the Interstate Commerce Act. Rates and service, which are under jurisdiction of this Act, are published by the carrier.

The water transporters which operate under the Interstate Commerce Commission regulations are referred to as common carriers. This group must have a certificate issued by the Interstate Commerce Commission and is subject to the economic regulations of the Commission. Common carriers are also required to file and publish their tariffs (rates) and issue financial reports.

UNITED STATES COAST GUARD. The basic functions of the United States Coast Guard are directly related to inland water transportation. The origin of the Coast Guard dates back to 1790; but its duties and responsibilities, as known today, date to its re-organization in 1915. The prime function in relation to inland water transportation is to insure the safety of persons and property. To accomplish this objective the Coast Guard has the power of law enforcement and search. Other significant duties of the Coast Guard include the establishment and enforcement of navigation regulations and the establishment and maintenance of navigation aids.

"Rules of the Road" are established regulations enforced by the U.S. Coast Guard governing the operation of vessels. A major problem related to the Rules is that differing sets of "Rules of the Road" apply to different waters. For example, one set of Rules is applicable to the Great Lakes, whereas other rules apply to the Western Rivers, the Inland Rivers, and the International Waters. The last set of rules was established by an international treaty and is honored by nearly all nations. Currently efforts are being directed toward unification of these various "Rules of the Road."

Over 40,000 various navigational aids are maintained and serviced by the Coast Guard on our inland waters. These aids consist of buoys, day beacons, lighthouses, radio beacons, fog signals, lightships, and other facilities.

Coast Guard regulations are directed to the construction and operation of certain vessels, that is, for the transportation of dangerous cargoes. Coast Guard inspection is required of tank barges during construction and for periodic renewal of inspection certificates. Special Coast Guard rules apply to the location of tank barges in relationship to other barges in a tow.

Some regulations for power vessels vary according to the type, size, and use of the vessel. Steam-powered vessels require Coast Guard inspections, whereas diesel-powered vessels operating on inland waters are not subject to the inspection. Both diesel- and steam-powered seagoing vessels of 300 gross tons or over require Coast Guard inspection and certification. All powered vessels used in commercial operations are subject to Coast Guard safety requirements, including the life-saving and fire-fighting equipment.

Licensing of certain personnel employed on commercial vessels is another of the duties of the Coast Guard. If the cargo includes inflammable or combustible liquids in bulk, the towing vessel must have a licensed or certified employee aboard to meet Coast Guard regulations. Officers on diesel-powered vessels operating on the inland waters are not subject to these regulations; however, some companies make licensing a condition of employment.

The Oil Pollution Act of 1924 authorized the Coast Guard to investigate and arrest the person causing pollution of the "coastal navigable waters of the United States". These waters have been taken to include the portion of the sea where United States jurisdiction prevails as territorial waters and inland navigable waters where the tide ebbs and flows. Pollution by unavoidable acts, such as collisions and strandings, are exempt from the Oil Pollution Act.

Ice-breaking operations have been a part of the Coast Guard's duties since 1936. The Coast Guard operates several ice-breaking vessels on the inland waters and the Great Lakes.

The Coast Guard is also directly involved in a program of recreational boating safety. Authorization for this program was granted by the Motorboat Act of 1940 whereby negligent or reckless operators of motorboats are subject to fines. The Federal Boating Act of 1958 provided the Coast Guard with greater powers to promote the safe use of inland waters.

Search and rescue work is a relatively new role of the Coast Guard. In an average year it is estimated that the Coast Guard saves 3000 lives, helps an additional 85,000 persons out of trouble, and saves or helps protect 2 billion dollars of property.[11] Storm warnings issued by the Weather Bureau are displayed, radioed, and published by the Coast Guard, primarily to inform waterway users of the possibility of danger to vessels.

Floating Equipment. As with most material items in our society the vessels used for water transportation have undergone considerable change through time. These changes have affected vessels operating on the internal waterways as well as on the oceans.

[11] *Big Load Afloat,* Washington, D.C., 1965, p. 64.

The ore and grain carriers used exclusively on the Great Lakes have also increased in size during recent years. The largest vessels operating on the Great Lakes as recently as 1958 had a capacity of 15,000 tons. The increased channel depths and the new, wider, longer, and deeper locks now permit the use of Great Lakes' vessels with a capacity of 45,000 to 50,000 tons. Some of these lake bulk carriers are now equipped with self-unloading machinery.

The stern- and side-wheeler steamboats of the Mark Twain era are now mostly replaced by compact, diesel-powered towboats on the internal waterways. Some of the larger towboats have power capacities from 6000 to 9000 horsepower, about six to nine times the power of the old steamboats. These large towboats currently in use are capable of transporting tows of 40,000 to 50,000 tons. By comparison a 6000-horsepower railroad locomotive will haul from 6000 to 8000 tons of freight.

On the protected inland waterways, such as rivers, where the water is naturally calm or where a series of locks and dams create calm waters the towboat pushes its cargo (Fig. 9). The barges are rigidly tied together and to the towboat to form one unit. With the towboat at the rear of the unit, greater speeds and more precise control can be attained by pushing the barges. The large towboats are equipped with two to four screws (propellers) and multiple rudders, allowing greater maneuverability.

Tugboats are designed for towing on open waters such as the Great Lakes, the Intracoastal Waterway, and the open ocean where wind and wave action is more prevalent. The tugboat is a multi-purpose vessel which performs many functions in addition to towing; these include docking oceangoing ships, lighterage work, salvage work, assistance in bunkering, and many other duties.

Generally three sizes of barges are in use on inland waterways. The common sizes are:

Fig. 9 A tow of 40 grain barges (58,000 tons) on the lower Mississippi River near Baton Rouge, Louisiana. (The American Waterways Operators, Inc.)

Length in Feet	Width in Feet	Depth in Feet	Capacity in Tons
175	26	9	1000
195	35	9	1500
290	50	9	3000

Although the dimensions of the barges are somewhat standardized, their appearance differs reflecting their usage. The open barges are used to transport materials which do not require protection from the weather elements. Coal, lumber, sand and gravel, crushed limestone, heavy equipment, and machinery are transported in the open hopper barge. The covered dry cargo barge is used to transport commodities such as grains, soybeans, sugar, dry chemicals, salt, and other commodities which require protection from weather. Liq-

uid cargo barges are used to transport petro leum and petroleum products, alcohol, anc various acids and chemicals. Some tank barge are equipped to transport liquids under pres sure or at controlled temperatures. Other spe cialty barges are also used to transport specia types of cargo.

Oceangoing vessels have also been subjec to great changes in recent years. The most no table change has been in the size of some o the petroleum carriers. As of 1969 there wer more than 65 oil tankers of over 110,000 tons deadweight, involved in the petroleum trade Some of these vessels have deadweight ton nages up to 312,000 tons. Most of these o tankers are registered to nations other tha the United States, but some transport crud petroleum to the refineries in the Atlanti ports of the United States. The large ocean ships are generally the most efficient as low-cost transporters of cargo. As a result there has been an increase in the size of almost all new ocean ships, especially the bulk oil and ore carriers.

Water, a basic natural resource for man, has many essential uses, and it is impossible to state that one use is more basic than another use. However, the waterways of a nation do provide natural avenues for transportation. If man is to utilize the resources that nature has provided, it is only logical that the waterways be used where it is economically feasible. Generally an entire nation benefits from the intelligent use of natural resources.

References

Annual Reports of American Commercial Lines, Houston, Texas.

Annual Reports of the Lake Carriers' Association, Cleveland, Ohio.

Annual Reports of the Mississippi Valley Barge Lines Company, St. Louis, Missouri.

Annual Reports of the Texas Gas Transmission Company, Owensboro, Kentucky.

Annual Traffic Reports of the St. Lawrence Seaway, The St. Lawrence Seaway Authority and the Saint Lawrence Seaway Development Corporation, Queen's Printer, Ottawa, Canada.

Big Load Afloat, The American Waterways Operators, Inc., Washington, D.C., 1965.

Blackwell, Richard B., "Toward Improved Cost Data for Inland Waterway Transportation," Reprinted from Papers—Fifth Annual Meeting, Transportation Research Forum, Urbana, Illinois, published in Chicago, 1964.

Carlson, Fred A. and Frank Seawall, *Coal Traffic on the Ohio River System,* Bureau of Business Research, The Ohio State University, Columbus, Ohio, 1962.

Carter, Richard E., "A Comparative Analysis of United States Ports and Their Traffic Characteristics," *Economic Geography,* Vol. 38, 1962, pp. 162–175.

Draine, Edwin H., *Export Traffic,* Transportation Division, Chicago Association of Commerce and Industry, Chicago, January 1965.

————, *Import Traffic,* Business Research and Statistics Division, Chicago Association of Commerce and Industry, Chicago, January 1962.

Export Traffic, Business Research and Statistics Division, Chicago Association of Commerce and Industry, Chicago, 1959.

"Freight Transportation and Industrial Activity in the United States," *Economic Review,* Federal Reserve Bank of Cleveland, Cleveland, Ohio, July 1968, pp. 14–25.

Great Lakes Commission, *Great Lakes News Letter,* Ann Arbor, Michigan, Bimonthly.

Great Lakes Commission, *Proceedings of the Institute on the St. Lawrence Seaway,* Cleveland, Ohio, March 6, 1964, 44 pp.

Hazard, John, *Potentials and Problems of the Seaway,* Industrial Development Department, Ohio Chamber of Commerce, Columbus, Ohio, 1960.

Howe, Charles W., *Models of a Bargeline: An Analysis of Returns to Scale in In-*

land Waterway Transportation, Krannert School of Industrial Administration Institute, Paper No. 77, Purdue University, West Lafayette, Indiana, 1964.

————, *Process and Production Functions for Inland Waterway Transportation,* Krannert School of Industrial Administration Institute, Paper No. 65, Purdue University, West Lafayette, Indiana, 1964.

Howe, Charles W. et al., *Inland Waterway Transportation: Studies in Public and Private Management and Investment Decisions,* Resources for the Future, Inc., Washington, 1969 (distributed by The Johns Hopkins Press, Baltimore).

Hull, William J. and W. R. Hull, *The Origin and Development of the Waterways Policy of the United States,* National Waterway Conference, Inc., Washington, D.C., 1967.

Inland Water Emergency Transport Planning, Prepared by the Interstate Commerce Commission, The American Waterways Operators, Inc., and Lake Carriers' Association, 1965.

Inland Waterborne Commerce Statistics 1966, The American Waterways Operators, Inc., Washington, D.C., 1968.

The Interstate Commerce Act, Government Printing Office, Washington, D.C., 1958.

Judson, Clara I., *St. Lawrence Seaway,* Follett Publishing Co., Chicago, 1964.

Laws Relating to Interstate Commerce and Transportation, Compiled by Gilman G. Udell, Superintendent, Document Room, House of Representatives, Government Printing Office, Washington, D.C., 1966.

Port Series, Prepared by the U.S. Army Engineers.

"Regional Patterns of Industrial Activity and Freight Transportation in the United States," *Economic Review,* Federal Reserve Bank of Cleveland, Cleveland, Ohio, September 1968, pp. 12–30.

Report of the Chief of Engineers, U.S. Army, Government Printing Office, Washington, D.C., Annual.

Seawall, Frank, "Recent Changes in Water Transportation in the Upper Ohio River Valley," *Annals Association of the American Geographers,* Vol. 55, December 1965, pp. 645–646 (abstract).

————, "Water Supply for River Navigation," *Public Works,* Vol. 91, November 1960, pp. 109–110.

————, "Water Transportation on the Ohio River: Its Economic Significance to Appalachia," *Bureau of Business Research,* The Ohio State University, Vol. 41, February 1966, pp. 1, 6–9.

U.S. Department of Agriculture, *Water, The Yearbook of Agriculture 1955,* Government Printing Office, Washington, D.C., 1955.

Van Hise, Charles Richard, *The Conservation of Natural Resources in the United States,* The MacMillan Co., New York, 1910.

Waterway Economics, Vols. 1 and 2, The American Waterways Operators, Inc., Washington, D.C., 1966–1968.

Wattenberg, Ben, *Busy Waterways, The Story of America's Inland Water Transportation,* The John Day Co., New York, 1964.

Weekly Letter, The American Waterways Operators, Inc., Washington, D.C.

GUY-HAROLD SMITH
The Ohio State University

CHAPTER 13

Floods and Flood Control

The control and useful development of water in our streams constitutes an important segment of the larger problem of water conservation. In the operation of the hydrologic cycle the return of the water to the sea from which it was originally derived provides an opportunity to use the water beneficially and as far as possible to prevent destructive floods. Rivers come into existence as the result of precipitation falling on the land and have as their ultimate destiny the return of the waters to the sea. Because the lands receive their precipitation at irregular intervals and because the amount varies from place to place, the streams resulting from the runoff are markedly irregular in their discharge. In fact, a stream with a uniform flow does not exist.

If all of the precipitation that falls could be absorbed into the earth and then discharged more or less steadily or uniformly, most streams could be confined to their channels. But an important proportion of the precipitation that falls never becomes a part of the reservoir of underground waters but flows quickly to the watercourses, swelling the streams beyond their constraining banks. The placid stream which between rainstorms is so

attractive and useful becomes in times of flood a raging torrent. With its carrying capacity and its competency greatly increased, a river in flood becomes a powerful agent of destruction.

The fertile alluvial lands of the Nile, the Tigris-Euphrates, the Hwang Ho, and the Mississippi—the creations of their respective rivers—have been repeatedly inundated. These and other great rivers are, at the same time, the givers and the destroyers of life and property. The flood problem may be said to have its beginning when the excessive waters derived from runoff and from underground sources spread beyond the banks of the stream channel. On occasion, torrential rains may produce flooding of local areas by the runoff from highland areas to the adjacent lowlands, the water not having reached the channels of either the permanent or intermittent streams. Usually such floods produced by sheet-wash are of short duration and cause little water damage. The principal damage is done by rill erosion and sheet erosion on the slope lands and by burial of the adjacent lowland areas under a layer of sediment. A thin veneer of silt might enhance the value of the land.

FLOOD DESTRUCTION

It is difficult to determine exactly the extent of flood damage and to compare in a satisfactory manner one great flood with another (Fig. 1). This is due in part to the tendency to overestimate flood damage, particularly at the time of the flood. In 1913 the damage from floods along the Mississippi and Ohio rivers was computed to be in excess of $162,000,000. The great flood of 1927 caused a total loss of more than $284,000,000 within the Mississippi drainage basin. The unprecedented flood of 1937 along the Ohio caused damage estimated at $417,000,000, not including soil losses. The "duck drownder" flood along the Mississippi and the tributaries in the St. Louis area in the summer of 1947 caused an estimated damage of $160,000,000 to agriculture alone. The long-continued flooding of the lowlands of the Columbia during the early summer of 1948 caused an estimated damage in excess of $100,000,000.[1]

In 1936 New England suffered from a disastrous flood, the result of heavy rains falling on frozen ground in northeastern United States. The Atlantic slope from New England to Florida is subject to occasional floods which damage riverine property amounting to millions of dollars. Along the coast of Florida flooding also results from the hurricanes, which are accompanied by heavy precipitation and high winds. These strong onshore winds drive the tidal waters inland, causing inundation of low-lying areas.

In mid-August 1955, Hurricane Diane moved northward across North Carolina, Virginia, Maryland, and Pennsylvania and then turned northeastward across northern New Jersey, southern New York, and southern New England. This storm, coming closely behind

Hurricane Connie, dumped an enormou quantity of water into the river basins, and a a result southern New England suffered o August 19–20 and the following few days major disaster (Fig. 2). The damage from Hurricane Diane was estimated by the Army Corps of Engineers to be $1,677,000,000.

Late in 1955, northern and central Califor nia was subjected to serious flooding which re sulted from continued heavy rains in the mountain areas (Fig. 3). Immediately after the floodwaters receded, there were pleas for flood-control projects, which, if approved by Congress and the President, would cost ap proximately $2,000,000,000.[2]

From April to June 1957, many streams in Texas, Arkansas, Kansas, Louisiana, Missouri and Oklahoma flooded the adjacent lowland and caused damage estimated at $105,000,000 Late in June and early July, Hurricane Au drey came ashore along the Louisiana and Texas coasts and produced damage running into millions of dollars. In December 1964 northern California and Oregon were sub jected to heavy rains and extensive flooding and property losses were estimated at $415, 832,000.

In March to May 1965, the upper Missis sippi and Missouri river basins and the Red River of the North were flooded as a result of the rapid melting of a heavy snow cover Property losses were estimated at $181, 325,000. In April 1969, the same area experi enced similar flooding and for the same rea son. The 1969 flood was delayed by the late arrival of spring. This gave communitie along the rivers a little time to make prepara tions for the flood that was sure to come. In spite of the attempts to increase the height of dikes and embankments the defenses in many places were inadequate. Breaks allowed the waters to inundate the lowlands, particularly in urban areas, before the people could evacu ate their homes and save their belongings

[1] Douglas W. Polivka, Chief, Technical Information Branch, Office of the District Engineer, Portland District. Personal communication.

[2] *New York Times*, January 15, 1956.

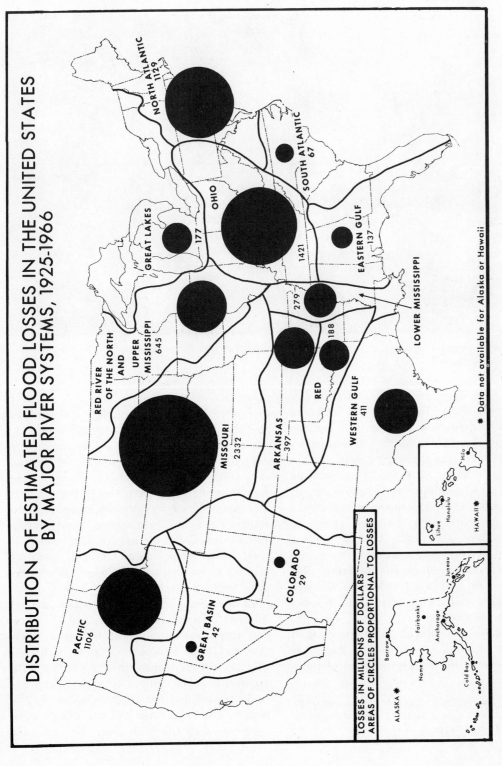

Fig. 1 Distribution of estimated flood losses in the United States, 1925–1966. (U.S. Weather Bureau.)

Fig. 2 Flood damage in Putnam, Connecticut, caused by Hurricane Diane on August 20, 1955. (Corps of Engineers.)

The South Platte basin in June 1965 was subjected to disastrous flooding, and damage was estimated at $415,076,000. In September 7–10, 1965, Hurricane Betsy caused serious flooding and heavy wind and water damage in Florida, Mississippi, and Louisiana. In early June of 1966, Hurricane Alma caused flooding and extensive damage along its course. In September 5–23, 1967, Hurricane Beulah moved westward through the Caribbean and came on shore in the Lower Rio Grande section of Texas and Mexico. Damage was extensive and the grand total of all losses was set at $168,844,000.[3]

Flood damage is difficult to determine with exactness. The U.S. Corps of Engineers usually reports the damage in terms of prop-

erty losses. But there are other losses related to the suspension of business operations. In September 1967, electric service was interrupted for 2 weeks as a result of the destructive winds and floods caused by Hurricane Beulah along the Lower Rio Grande. Manufacturing and services dependent upon public sources of electrical energy could not operate. Income loss to people who could not work at their usual jobs caused difficult financial problems where families were dependent upon regular paychecks.

In late January and early February of 1969, southern California was drenched by heavy and almost continuous rains falling on slopes that had little protective cover to hold back the floodwaters. Brush fires had reduced the vegetative cover, and locally the land had been graded to permit the construction of homes. The loose earth had not become stabilized, so when the rains came the unconsoli-

[3] *Report on Hurricane "Beulah"*, September 8–21, 1967, U.S. Army Engineer District, Corps of Engineers, Galveston, Texas, 1968, p. 261.

dated surface materials became mobile. Mud slides destroyed many homes and the watercourses were heavily loaded with sediments, both fine and coarse, that were removed from the slopelands. The disruption of communication required that the public utilities in the area make heroic efforts to restore service (Fig. 4).

Flood Damage to Transportation Facilities. The predisposition of the people to pre-empt the rich riverine lands for agricultural, industrial, and commercial purposes subjects them to the hazards of recurring floods. Railroad builders found the land adjacent to watercourses nicely graded and therefore well suited for the railway lines, and as a conse-

quence the flood damage to railway property has been high. However, the damage has been lessened by the relocation of the tracks and the redesign of bridges. As data on floods have become available, the railways, in order to protect their large investment, have spent millions on the relocation of tracks and bridges.

Flood Damage in Urban Areas. Many of our large cities, such as New Orleans, Cincinnati, St. Louis, Pittsburgh, and Nashville, were located on rivers when the watercourses were the principal highways of commerce. The utilization of the low-lying lands adjacent to the rivers for industrial and commercial purposes has resulted in heavy damage in

Fig. 3 Break in the levee along the Feather River near Yuba City, California, December 24, 1955. (Division of Highways, California.)

Fig. 4 A helicopter was used to survey the flood damage along the Santa Ynez River in southern California and to string a cable across the river to restore electrical service to the people in the valley in late January 1969. (Pacific Lighting Service and Supply Company.)

times of flood, owing both to the destruction of property and to the suspension of business for periods varying from a few days to several weeks (Fig. 5). Urban areas subject to floods are abandoned only with great difficulty, for industries seeking low land values and people in the low-income group seeking low rentals are likely to locate on these cheaper lands along the river. Usually protection against floods is sought before abandonment is considered. If protective levees, generally built at public expense, prove adequate, property values increase and the utilization of the land is intensified. Then an unprecedented flood overtops or breaks through the levees and causes enormous damage. The increased property damage reported by many cities is due to man's encroachment upon the rivers.

Flood Damage to Agricultural Lands. In agricultural areas the amount of damage de-

pends on the season and whether intensive economic use is made of the land. A winter flood may cause little damage to farmlands, but in southern California where the intensive cultivation of vegetables is an important winter industry, the occasional winter floods may be very destructive. The floods of spring may inundate newly planted fields and delay replanting until it is too late to secure a fully matured crop. The immediate losses in a single season may be offset somewhat by the enrichment of the lowland by the deposition of silts.

PHYSICAL CONDITIONS AFFECTING FLOODS

Causes of Floods. Floods are the result of many conditions working singly or in combination. Usually no single cause can be as-

Ayres, E. and C. A. Scarlott, *Energy Sources—The Wealth of the World,* McGraw-Hill Book Co., New York, 1952.

Commission on Organization of the Executive Branch of the Government, *Water Resources and Power,* 3 Vols., Government Printing Office, Washington, D.C., 1955.

Daugherty, C. R., A. H. Horton, and R. W. Davenport, *Power Capacity and Production in the United States,* Water Supply Paper 579, U.S. Geological Survey, Washington, D.C., 1928.

Federal Power Commission, *Annual Reports,* Washington, D.C.

————, *Estimated Future Power Requirements of the United States by Regions, 1953–1975,* Washington, D.C., 1954.

————, *Hydroelectric Power Resources of the United States, Developed and Undeveloped, 1960,* P-33, Washington, D.C.

————, *National Power Survey,* Parts I and II, Washington, D.C., 1964.

————, *Prevention of Power Failures,* Vol. I: *Report of the Commission,* Vol. II: *Advisory Committee Report. Reliability of Electric Bulk Power Supply,* Vol. III: *Studies of the Task Groups on the Northeast Power Interruption,* Washington, D.C., 1967.

Krutilla, John V., *The Columbia River Treaty: The Economics of an International River Basin Development,* The Johns Hopkins Press, Baltimore, 1967.

Krutilla, John V. and Otto Eckstein, *Multiple Purpose River Development,* Resources for the Future, The Johns Hopkins Press, Baltimore, 1958. Reprinted 1961.

Kuenen, Philip Henry, *Realms of Water,* translated by May Hollander, John Wiley & Sons, New York, 1955.

Landsberg, Hans H. and Sam H. Schurr, *Energy in the United States: Sources, Uses and Policy Issues,* Random House, New York, 1968.

Langbein, Walter, *Topographic Characteristics of Drainage Basins,* Water Supply Paper 968-C, U.S. Geological Survey, Washington, D.C., 1947.

Moreell, Ben, *Our Nation's Water Resources—Policies and Politics,* The Law School, The University of Chicago, Chicago, 1956. See particularly Lecture IV, "Federal Power Developments," pp. 149–188.

National Resources Committee, *Our Energy Resources,* Washington, D.C., 1939.

The President's Materials Policy Commission, *Resources for Freedom,* Volume III: *The Outlook for Energy Resources,* Government Printing Office, Washington, D.C., 1952.

Rayhawk, Arthur L., *The Energy Resources of the United States in Relation to Future Population Developments,* Chapter II: "Water Power," Washington, D.C., 1932, pp. 33–67.

Schurr, Sam H., Bruce C. Netschert, et al., *Energy in the American Economy, 1850–1975,* Resources for the Future, The Johns Hopkins Press, Baltimore, 1960.

United Nations Department of Economic Affairs, UNSCCUR, Vol. IV, *Water Resources,* New York, 1951.

United States Department of Agriculture, *Power to Produce,* The Yearbook of Agriculture, 1960, Government Printing Office, Washington, D.C.

U.S. Energy Policies: An Agenda for Research, Resources for the Future Staff Report, Washington, D.C., 1968.

Young, Lloyd L., *Summary of Developed and Potential Waterpower of the United States and Other Countries of the World, 1955–1962,* Circular 483, U.S. Geological Survey, Department of the Interior, Washington, D.C., 1964.

Part 4

GUY-HAROLD SMITH
The Ohio State University

CHAPTER 15

Conservation of Mineral Resources

The mineral materials which make up the accessible portions of the earth's crust are unlike most of the other natural resources. Their concentration in the earth's crust in sufficient quantity and richness to form ores is the result of geological processes operating over a very long period of time. In terms of human history, the natural resources such as plants and animals can be so managed that production can be maintained and even improved over a long period of time. Even a soil seriously eroded and depleted can be restored by proper management. By reforestation and protective measures, a forest can be restored in quality comparable with the virgin forest, although the association of species may be altered. By restrictions on hunting and fishing and by improving and protecting the habitat, many game animals and fishes may become as abundant as under primitive conditions. But minerals once mined, processed, and put to beneficial use cannot be restored, though a fraction may be recovered. They cannot be replaced or accumulated again at any foreseeable time in the future. The resource has been diminished by use, and the deposit may be completely exhausted.

The situation in respect to minerals is not as gloomy as it may appear from the previous statement. The combustible materials, once they are used, are gone forever. But many minerals, particularly the metals, can be used over and over again, and, as a consequence, metals-in-use become a resource which can be tapped in time of emergency and made to supply important quantities of re-usable metal. Conservation of these diminishing resources can be achieved also by the use of mining and processing methods that result in the least waste and the maximum protection of the unmined portion of the mineral deposits. This may be a means of leaving to future generations their share of the resources. With improved technology, a low-grade deposit of one generation may become a workable ore of the next. It becomes the duty of people now living to use the irreplaceable resources of the earth's crust so that generations yet unborn will get their share of the mineral wealth.

THE HISTORICAL DEVELOPMENT OF MINERAL PRODUCTION

The progressive development of man and his cultural and technological attainments are manifestations of man's mastery over his physical environment. As people advanced culturally, their use of materials about them increased. The use of metals in weapons and tools by the more advanced groups gave them greater mastery over the earth and over the other peoples who had not made similar advances. But when men were able to tap the energy contained in the great fuel resources of the earth and to manufacture the complex power-driven machinery, they possessed a powerful mechanism which could be used to bring great wealth and comfort to millions of people. The development and expansion of the modern mineral-using civilization have made enormous demands upon the earth to supply fuels, metals, and nonmetallic substances in ever-increasing quantities.

Metals in Primitive Societies. Early man, as he took on the cultural characteristics which distinguished him from the lower animals, used whatever was at hand in the way of tools and implements. In time he learned to chip stone, shape bone, and work wood into useful tools or weapons. He had little or no knowledge of metals in the early stages of his cultural evolution. It is believed that gold was the first metal used by man. Copper, like gold, occurs in nature as a native metal and very early became a useful and prized possession of the cultures that were making material progress. Gold, because of its rarity, its softness, its rich brilliant color, and its untarnishable quality, was particularly well suited for jewelry and as a standard of value. Copper was more abundant, and although it was used for decorative purposes, it had great value to early man as an implement or tool and as a weapon. The value of copper to early man greatly increased when by accident or intention tin was alloyed with it to produce bronze. Neither tin nor copper is particularly hard, but when the two metals are combined in an alloy, the resulting bronze is hard and strong. When the Roman Empire extended its frontiers westward to the shores of Britain, the tin of Cornwall was carried back along

with copper from southern Iberica to make bronze; the use of bronze strengthened the legions of Rome.

Primitive man was largely dependent on the metals that occurred in nature in the native or metallic form. Those that are easily smelted, such as tin, were obtained by the application of the metallurgical skills that had been developed. The ores that were more difficult to smelt had to wait until man's knowledge was equal to the task. The great achievement of early man was the smelting of iron ore. When he was able to produce metallic iron in quantity, he was on the threshold of a great technological revolution.

Pure or metallic iron occurs in nature in small quantities, usually in meteorites. In a few places in the world, meteoric iron had been picked up before rust had destroyed it. Primitive man had acquired some knowledge of metallic iron, and small quantities had been accumulated. By repeated experimentation iron was eventually separated from its ore. It is known that the recovery of metallic iron from iron ore dates back to the fourteenth century B.C., but production in quantity had to wait many centuries. The full importance of iron in the cultural history of man had to wait upon other important developments, particularly the invention of the steam engine.

The Industrial Revolution and the Use of Minerals. James Watt invented the steam engine in 1768, only a few years before the United States won its independence. It was the practical use of the steam engine that ushered in the Industrial Revolution. The United States was still in the pioneer stage of its economy. The farms still had to be won from the forests and the prairies. In England the use of steam power had sounded the death knell of the handicrafts and the household industries.

In the United States agriculture continued to dominate the economy, but with the invention of the cotton gin in 1793 and the increased use of machinery in the North, the country began to take on some of the characteristics of an industrial nation.

The abundant resources of coal made it possible for the United States to make rapid progress in the development of the metal-using industries. Late in the nineteenth century the production and use of electrical power marked a notable achievement in the industrial transformation. By 1900, the great mineral resources of the United States were being developed to satisfy the ever-increasing demands for machines, which in turn required increasing quantities of fuel to keep them going.

Rapid Rise in the Use of Mineral Resources. The great increase in the use of minerals as compared with agricultural and forest products is related in part to mechanization. Not only in industry and transportation, but in the home as well, power-driven machines and applicances require both metals and fuels in large quantities to maintain our way of life. These are the so-called fund resources, and once they are used they are gone forever. This is particularly true in the case of the fuels such as coal, petroleum, and natural gas. By secondary recovery many of the metals, at least fractionally, can be re-cycled back into essential uses.

The Future Demand for Earth Materials. To project the curves of production for most of the minerals to 1975 and beyond raises some very disturbing questions. It is clear that the demands for materials drawn from the earth will rise unevenly. Because of the inadequate reserves available to us both from domestic sources and from foreign areas, it may be necessary to shift the demand to more readily available substitutes. Increased use of tin, zinc, copper, nickel, petroleum, tungsten, and aluminum can be expected.[1]

[1] The President's Materials Policy Commission, *Resources for Freedom*, Vol. I: *Foundations for Growth and Security*, Washington, D.C., 1952, p. 9.

The changing character of the resource base results from the depletion of once abundant resources, the discovery and development of new resources, and the changes in technology which bring into use materials that previously had not been available, at least economically. A combination of factors, both physical and economic, affects the availability of materials for economic use in modern society. The physical conditions are generally unchanging in character, but changes in technological and economic conditions may determine whether a mineral deposit can be worked or left untouched (Fig.1).

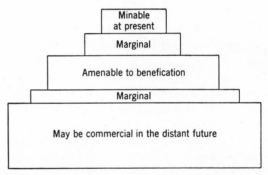

Fig. 1 Mineral deposits and mineral reserves. As costs are reduced and technological advances make possible the mining of leaner ores, the ultimate reserves may be very large.

The Extravagant Use of Materials. The American people have long been accustomed to great abundance of many materials and as a consequence have been extravagant with the bounty of nature. The per capita use of metals, power, fibers, and foods is so high that many other peoples of the world are poor by comparison. The great abundance has made a high standard of living possible for a high proportion of the population. For example, Americans are very extravagant in the use of metals in automobiles. The size, weight, and beauty of our automobiles are not a reflection of need but an expression of abundant materials, high purchasing power, and a desire for an automobile that not only has utility but gives prestige as well.

If it became a national necessity because of a great emergency, the power and the size of passenger automobiles could be reduced. The decorative trim which requires chromium, nickel, aluminum, and other strategic metals could be eliminated or greatly reduced, thus producing great savings. The extravagant use of many metals that are recoverable may have the effect of creating a valuable reserve of metals-in-use which can be re-cycled into essential uses in case of emergency.

Reserves for Posterity. Among the students of mineral resources there are some who believe that a proportion of the known reserves of many minerals should be set aside for future generations. This assumes that discovery and other means of increasing the reserves will not be able to keep pace with the rising rate of use. There are others who believe that each generation, through the development of science and technology, will be able to discover and process the ores required. There may be important minerals in short supply, and others may be relatively abundant. This condition could be expected to exist indefinitely. An ever-expanding economy which seems to be the hope of many people will require larger and larger quantities of minerals. It seems clear that the readily accessible ores of high value will be depleted or will be increasingly difficult to mine. But in the earth's crust there is a variety of minerals that can be made available by the genius of the technologist and the resourcefulness of the businessman. This is the view of the optimist who believes that the future will take care of itself and the present generation need be concerned only with its own problems of supply.

Among geologists and mineral conservationists there are many who have a genuine concern about the problem of supplying the needs of the country with minerals, particu-

larly the metals required to maintain the high standard of living and our national defenses. The realization that mineral deposits contain a fixed quantity of usable metal or material has prompted some conservationists to accept the viewpoint that a reserve of workable ores should be set aside for the future.

The future supplies of minerals or the volumetric dimensions of the reserves are related to the price we can afford to pay for the mineral materials and the metals we need. A substantial increase in the price of ores and the metals extracted therefrom increases the quantity of ores available to the economy. At a new high price the mining operation can be extended to greater depths and leaner ores can be worked economically. There is no assurance that every advance in price, which in effect increases the reserves of mineral resources, can be absorbed by the metal-using industries. If the latter can absorb the increased cost of the metallic raw materials they use by greater efficiencies in fabrication, the high level of use of metals in our economy can be maintained. If the increased costs must be passed on to the ultimate consumer and if the purchasing power will not permit him to pay for the metal products and structures necessary to maintain his high standard of living, the process may be reversed, so that a lower price for ore may actually diminish the reserves.

If an important mineral is in short supply, the rising price may have the effect of limiting its use to absolutely essential purposes. Or, an important rise in price might have the effect of causing a shift to metals of the more abundant minerals in the common rocks. Such metals as iron, aluminum, silicon, and magnesium are available in unlimited quantities. Under such conditions it would not be necessary to set aside important reserves for the future. Perhaps in the more distant future, the metals in the common rocks and in sea water and ceramic materials can be used in place of such metals as tin, lead, zinc, copper, and the ferroalloys which are relatively less abundant.

Prospecting and Exploration. The search for minerals must continue. The prospector of a past age is being replaced by a modern mineral explorer who brings to his task a knowledge of the basic science of geology, including paleontology, stratigraphy, and petrology. The geologist does not work alone but brings to the task of finding new deposits other scientists who are qualified to utilize the most sophisticated techniques of exploration. The sciences of geophysics and geochemistry have been enlisted to press the search for mineral resources.

Exploration transcends its physical aspects and becomes involved with the economic and legal problems related to the addition of newly discovered deposits which, when proved, can be added to the known reserves. The application of new techniques in mining and processing may save an industry from failure, but the economic gains may be offset by an antiquated system of taxation.[2] Further exploration requires the application of modern techniques and an enlightened approach to the economic and legal aspects of the mineral problem.

THE EARTH MATERIALS

Composition of the Earth's Crust. The common materials and the rarer substances of the earth's crust vary greatly in their relative abundance and the degree to which they are concentrated in valuable minerals and ores (see Table 1). The eight most abundant elements—oxygen, silicon, aluminum, iron, calcium, sodium, potassium, and magnesium—make up 98.58 percent of the earth's crust.

[2] See John D. Ridge, "The Problem of Mineral Exploration," *Mineral Industries,* Pennsylvania State University, University Park, Pennsylvania, Vol. 32, November 1962, pp. 1, 3–7.

Table 1. Composition of the Earth's Crust

Element	Weight Percent
1. Oxygen	46.60
2. Silicon	27.72
3. Aluminum	8.13
4. Iron	5.00
5. Calcium	3.63
6. Sodium	2.83
7. Potassium	2.59
8. Magnesium	2.09
9. Titanium	0.44
10. Hydrogen	0.14
Total	99.17

[Source: Brian, Mason, *Principles of Geochemistry,* New York, 1952, p. 41.]

All of the other elements make up less than 1.5 percent of the earth's crust. Because of the very unequal quantities of the minerals, composed of common and rare elements, it is more or less obvious that over a long period of time the most common and most abundant elements and minerals will be used increasingly in a maturing industrial society. In the modern economy, the widely used metals, such as copper, lead, zinc, and the ferroalloys, are in reality relatively rare, and it is only because of their concentration in localized deposits that they can be used at all. If they were uniformly dispersed within the earth's crust, it would be impossible, or at least economically unfeasible, to process the great quantities of material necessary to recover adequate quantities of these metals.

The precious metals, such as gold, silver, and platinum, and the rare metals, such as antimony, tin, mercury, and tantalum, occur in such small quantities that ordinarily their relative abundance cannot be determined with accuracy. They are relatively rare, and again it is only because of their concentration in localized ore bodies that they can be profitably developed and used for a number of specialized purposes.

The Metalliferous Ores. An ore is a mineral deposit that can be mined and processed at a profit. A mineral deposit may contain important quantities of an essential metal, but unless it is economically feasible to work, the deposit may be regarded as rock or at best as a marginal or submarginal ore. An advance in technology, an increase in price, or both may have the effect of making a low-grade ore into a mineral resource of great value. It may be that the success of a mining operation may be related to the scale of operations. If great quantities of the ore can be mined and processed, the unit cost may be so low that the operation shows a profit. Conversely, to reduce the scale of operations might make the mining operation uneconomical.[3]

Aluminum, iron, and the less abundant metals, although widely distributed in the earth's crust, do occur in important ore bodies which have resulted from the operation of long-continued geological process. It is clear, therefore, that the modern economy must rest upon geologic processes of the past; in almost every case, the geologic processes that form ore bodies are not rapid enough to meet the needs of an industrial society requiring large quantities of materials. In effect, at present man is drawing on capital resources accumulated in the past, and in the interests of conservation it is necessary that he understand the nature and dimensions of this great reserve and the rate at which he is using it.

In many cases the ore-forming processes operate at great depth, and the evidences of the existence of ore bodies are not revealed at the surface. Fortunately, many ore bodies formed in the remote geologic past and at great depth have been laid bare or have been revealed near the surface by uplift and long-continued erosion. In the Laurentian Upland of Canada and the Upper Lakes section of

the United States the rich iron ores, believed to be of sedimentary origin, have been down folded in great linear formations and largely covered by a veneer of glacial drift. Continued mining and exploration have revealed the true dimensions of these rich iron deposits.

It is because of the prospect that there remain many undiscovered ore deposits, particularly in areas that have not been thoroughly explored, that many people believe that new deposits will be found when the need arises. When the conservationist expressed the fear that known resources of some important mineral will be exhausted there is the optimist who has an enduring faith in the ability of the prospector and the geologist to find new deposits to take the place of the depleted ores.

The Minerals in the Sea and in the Atmosphere. Both the sea and the atmosphere contain great quantities of certain elements and compounds that can be recovered and used in connection with the mineral materials taken from the earth's crust (see Table 2).

Table 2. Composition of the Ocean

	Percent		*Percent*
Oxygen	85.79	Calcium	0.05
Hydrogen	10.67	Potassium	0.04
Chlorine	2.07	Sulfur	0.09
Sodium	1.14	Bromine	0.008
Magnesium	0.14	Carbon	0.002

[Source: Professional Paper 127, U.S. Geological Survey.]

The sea is known to contain a great variety of elements, but the quantity of each is very small. By processing a large volume of sea water, sodium chloride, magnesium salts, magnesium, potassium, iodine, and bromine are recovered commercially. Calcium carbonate and calcium sulfate also occur in the sea, but calcium salts and the metal, calcium, are usually obtained from limestone and gypsum formations in the earth's crust.

---

[3] For a more extended statement on minerals and ores, see Peter T. Flawn, *Mineral Resources*, Chicago, 1966, pp. 1–7, 9–53.

Not only do the oceans contain minerals of great value but it is known that the bottom of the sea out beyond the area of active sedimentation is covered in many places by nodules containing nickel, iron, manganese, cobalt, and copper. The United States must import 90 percent of its manganese requirements. The strategic position of the nation could be greatly enhanced by the recovery of mineral-bearing nodules in the ocean-bottom areas off the southeast coast of South Carolina, Georgia, and Florida. If it becomes economically feasible to recover these nodules from depths of 5000 to 18,000 feet the known deposits will become a mineral resource of importance in the national economy.[4]

The atmosphere contains such valuable gases as nitrogen, oxygen, and the rarer gases of helium, neon, and argon that are recovered, purified, and prepared to serve the needs of industry. The great reservoir of nitrogen constitutes an inexhaustible source of a vital element used in the manufacture of synthetic ammonia and other nitrogen-containing fertilizers (see Table 3).

Table 3. Composition of the Atmosphere

	Percent		*Percent*
Nitrogen	78.03	Hydrogen	0.01
Oxygen	20.99	Neon	0.00123
Argon	0.94	Helium	0.0004
Carbon		Krypton	0.00005
dioxide	0.03	Xenon	0.000006

[Source: Professional Paper 127, U.S. Geological Survey.]

THE MINERAL SITUATION [5]

Iron. In the period between 1953 and 1957 the production of iron ore in the United States averaged over 100,000,000 tons annually. In 1962, production was under 72,-000,000 tons. The imports of iron ore and of steel have lowered the quantity of domestic ore used in the iron and steel industry. Imports of iron ore rose from an average of 31,-439,000 tons annually between 1957 and 1961 to 46,259,000 tons in 1966. Foreign ores have become increasingly competitive and domestic producers have turned to the beneficiation of taconite and other low-grade ores to hold on to a major share of the market.

Domestic production is centered in Lake Superior area where Minnesota, Michigan, and Wisconsin mined 77 percent of the output in 1966. The northeastern states of New York, New Jersey, and Pennsylvania and the southeastern states of Alabama and Georgia together produced 7 percent, and ten western states, chiefly Utah and Wyoming, produced 13 percent in 1966.

In 1950, imported iron ore represented only 5 percent of the ores consumed in the iron and steel industry. By 1965, the percentage of imported ores had risen to 34 percent. Imported ores came chiefly from Canada, Venezuela, Liberia, Chile, and Brazil (Fig. 2).

Beneficiation Continues Apace. In the Upper Lakes area, in Wyoming, Pennsylvania, California, and Missouri taconite and other low-grade ores are concentrated and pelletized before being shipped to the blast furnaces. In Canada pelletizing plants have been constructed in Ontario, Quebec, and Newfoundland. In 1962, only 15 percent of the ore was shipped directly to the consuming market in the crude form, whereas 78 percent was treated at some type of beneficiation plant before shipment in 1966.[6]

[4] David B. Brooks, *Low Grade and Nonconventional Sources of Manganese*, Baltimore, 1966.

[5] The mining of ores may change significantly from year to year depending upon demand, price, technological developments, economic and commercial poli-

cies, and other factors. Recent data on production can be secured from published sources such as the *Minerals Yearbook* and other publications of the United States Bureau of Mines, Washington, D.C.

[6] United States Bureau of Mines, *Minerals Yearbook, 1966*, Vols. I–II, Metals, Minerals, and Fuels, Washington, D.C., 1967, p. 254.

Fig. 2 The *Ore-Meridian,* a giant ore-carrier shown at the Canton dock area, Baltimore, Maryland. Such ocean-going ore-carriers transport iron ore from Venezuela and other overseas sources to Sparrows Point and other shipping and smelting centers in the Middle Atlantic area. (Curtis Bay Towing Service, Photo by Hans Marx.)

Steel-making capacity in the United States has been built up to a level necessary to maintain a high annual output. Production reached 117,000,000 tons in 1955 and then dropped below 100,000,000 tons in 1958 but by 1966 was up to 134,101,000 tons.[7] Steel is feeling the competition from aluminum, magnesium, structural concrete, titanium, plastics, and resin-bonded wood. Common or carbon steel is being replaced by alloy steels that provide great strength with less weight.

Recent advances in iron and steel technology have altered the proportions of the raw

[7] *Ibid,* p. 264.

materials used. In the blast furnace the use of agglomerated ores, fuel injection, and higher top pressures have increased the consumption of natural gas and lowered the consumption of coke. The recent changes in steel technology, particularly the development of the basic oxygen furnace, have required larger quantities of pig iron, oxygen, and lime in the making of steel. The open hearth furnaces use relatively more scrap than the basic oxygen furnaces, and as a consequence scrap has been relatively abundant. Technological changes in iron and steel making have altered the raw material situation in this major domestic industry.

The steel industry in the United States has been hard pressed to maintain a strong competitive position in the steel markets of the world and at home. In 1950, the substitutes, plastics, and other metals, were bidding for a share of the steel market. In 1959, imports of steel exceeded exports. By the late 1960's, 11,500,000 tons of steel were imported, or 12 percent of domestic consumption.

The steel industry is asking Congress for legislation to protect the domestic industry against foreign competition. The industry claims that national security is served by maintaining a strong and competitive domestic iron and steel industry. The importers of steel claim that the demand for iron ore, coke, and other raw materials is diminished by the importation of foreign steel.

Knowing that tariff protection is no longer possible when the nation is joining with other countries to reduce tariffs and other obstacles to free trade the domestic producers are asking Congress to enact legislation approving a quota system that would have as its objective the reduction of imports. The chief suppliers are Japan and the countries in the European Coal and Steel Community. These two areas supplied over 80 percent of the imported steel in the late 1960's. The remainder came from more than forty suppliers including the United Kingdom, Brazil, Poland, Mexico,

Australia, Sweden, the Republic of South Africa, and others.[8]

On August 1, 1968, the steel companies entered into a new wage agreement with the United Steelworkers of America and almost immediately raised prices on many types of steel. Under pressure from President Johnson there were reductions or rollbacks on steel needed in the defense industries. The increases put into effect by American steel makers were followed by increased prices on imported steel. Parallel action by the manufacturers and the importers probably will have little effect on the importation of steel. If steel imports could be greatly reduced the domestic industry would have to increase the imports of iron ore to meet the needs of the iron and steel industry.

The Ferroalloys. The manufacture of specialty steels requires the addition of small quantities of metals or their compounds to impart to the steel the qualities desired. These are the ferroalloys. They include manganese, chromium, cobalt, molybdenum, nickel, tungsten, and vanadium, and a number of others such as boron, columbium, titanium, and zirconium. Of the principal ferroalloys only molybdenum and vanadium are genuinely abundant in terms of the needs of the nation. The United States is a major producer of molybdenum. Vanadium supplies are adequate, but the metal is recovered as a by-product or co-product in the processing of uranium ores.

The supply situation is particularly unfavorable in the case of manganese, chromium, nickel, and cobalt. Domestic production of manganese represents a relatively small fraction required to meet the needs of the iron and steel industry. In 1966, consumption of manganese ore was 2,163,968 short tons. Only 30,043 tons were of domestic origin; 2,133,925 tons were imported. This is a ratio of 1 to 70. The chief suppliers were Brazil, Ghana,

the Republic of South Africa, and India.

The United States is almost completely dependent upon imported chromite to meet the needs of the metallurgical, refractory, and chemical industries, which consume 57 percent, 29 percent, and 14 percent of supplies, respectively. In 1966, consumption of chromite was 1,461,000 short tons. Imports in the same year totaled 1,864,000 tons, and stocks at year's end amounted to 1,305,000 tons. Chromite is imported from the Republic of South Africa, the Philippines, Zambia, and Turkey.

Mine shipments of tungsten concentrates totaled 8,482,000 pounds in 1966. A total of 8,273,000 pounds were released from government stocks. Imports for consumption amounted to 4,298,000 pounds. And consumption was 17,710,000 pounds. In the period 1957–1961 production averaged 7,630,000 pounds, imports for consumption totaled 6,329,000 pounds, and domestic consumption was 9,286,000 pounds. The supply situation in relation to consumption is strategically unsatisfactory. Important quantities of tungsten concentrates must be imported from Canada, Australia, Bolivia, Peru, and South Korea.

For nickel, the United States is dependent chiefly on Canada, which produces 51 percent of the world's supply. New Caledonia ranks second as a producer of nickel ores with 14 percent, and the United States contributes less than 3 percent. Metallic nickel is also recovered by the processing of scrap metals that contain nickel.

Because of the variety of metals that make up the ferroalloy group and the remoteness of many of the source areas it has been necessary to build up stockpiles of these strategic metals or ores and to take other measures to assure the United States of adequate supplies in case of a national emergency.

The Nonferrous Metals. The metals commonly listed as nonferrous include copper, aluminum, lead, zinc, tin, mercury, antimony, magnesium, and a number of others. The de-

[8] *Steel Facts,* October–November, 1967, pp. 1–2.

gree of self-sufficiency varies greatly among the several metals. For example, the United States must import bauxite, alumina, and aluminum to meet the needs of industry and the national stockpile. Bauxite, totaling 11,-529,000 long tons in 1966, was imported chiefly from Jamaica, Surinam, Dominican Republic, Guyana, and Haiti. Imports entered the United States chiefly through the ports of New Orleans, Galveston, and Mobile. In 1966, metallic aluminum in the crude or semicrude form to the extent of 679,000 tons was imported. Canada supplied 72 percent of the imported metal with Norway, France, and Belgium-Luxembourg contributing most of the remainder.

In 1966, production of copper as reported by the smelters using domestic ores was 1,-353,087 tons. Production from imported ores was 357,897 tons. Consumption for the same year, including both primary and secondary metal, was 2,128,000 tons. The United States is both an importer and an exporter of copper, and in recent years imports of ores, concentrates, and metallic copper have exceeded exports. The United States because of its technological and economic position retains a dominant place in the international copper market (Fig.3).

Aluminum and copper are competitive in the electrical field. A price differential over many years in favor of copper gave copper an

Fig. 3 The Kennecott Copper Corporation's world-famous Bingham Canyon open-pit copper mine, 30 miles southwest of Salt Lake City. (Kennecott Copper Corporation.)

advantage. In recent years the price advantage of copper has been eroded away. The increased cost of mining, smelting, and refining copper, related in part to increased wages, has required the industry to increase prices. For example, in mid-August 1968, the price of copper in the New York metal market was 42.25 cents per pound, whereas aluminum was 26 cents per pound. The average price of copper on the London market averaged 69.04 cents per pound. The copper industry continues to seek new markets for the metal and to urge the expanded use of copper in those industries where its properties are unequaled by any other metal.

The domestic consumption of lead in the United States in 1966 was 1,324,000 short tons derived from domestic production, secondary recovery, and importation. Mine production of lead in 1966 was 318,646 tons. Production of secondary lead was 572,834 tons. Consumption of both primary and secondary lead was 1,323,877 tons. In order to meet the domestic needs of the lead-using industries and the national stockpile the United States must import ores, concentrates, and metallic lead. Domestic production of lead is centered in Missouri, Idaho, Utah, and Colorado. Imports of metal come from Peru, Australia, Mexico, Canada, and Yugoslavia and ores are imported from Canada, Peru, Australia, and Bolivia.

The situation in respect to zinc is similar to that of lead. Domestic production has felt the competition of foreign producers. Stockpiling has provided some support for both metals in the domestic market. Secondary recovery returns large quantities of lead and zinc to the metal market. The production of zinc from domestic ores was 579,558 tons in 1966, mined chiefly in Tennessee, New York, Idaho, Colorado, Utah, and several other states. Imports came chiefly from Canada, Mexico, and Peru. It is hoped that increased research in the use of zinc and zinc-containing products may bring more favorable economic conditions to the zinc industry.

The United States is an unimportant source of primary tin as measured by mine production. Domestic production averaged 12 tons annually for the years 1957–1961. Consumption in 1966 was 85,486 tons, with slightly less than one-third being secondary tin. Most of the remainder in the form of concentrates or metal was imported from Malaysia, Thailand, Bolivia, United Kingdom, and Nigeria. A government-owned smelter at Texas City, Texas, smelted tin ores from Bolivia and other sources for a number of years but was sold to private interests in 1956 and has since abandoned tin smelting. Tin is imported to meet the needs of industry and the national stockpile. If for any reason tin cannot be imported from the Far East imports may be increased from nearer sources, secondary recovery expanded, and substitution increased to meet a national emergency.

Other nonferrous metals, such as antimony and mercury, must be imported. In the case of antimony less than 5 percent is produced from domestic mines. In 1966, secondary recovery amounted to 24,258 tons and imports to 19,712 tons, whereas consumption in the same year was 19,681 tons (does not include antimony recovered from scrap). The major foreign sources include Mexico, Republic of South Africa, and Bolivia. The domestic production of mercury totaled 22,008 flasks in 1966. A larger quantity (34,540 flasks) was imported from Italy, Spain, Mexico, and Yugoslavia. The supply situation in the case of magnesium is particularly favorable because the source materials and the productive facilities are adequate to meet domestic needs.

Metals of Special Importance. The platinum group of metals includes platinum, palladium, iridium, rhodium, and ruthenium. Once used chiefly for jewelry these materials are of major importance in the chemical and electrical fields. Supplies of these metals are imported chiefly from the Soviet Union, United Kingdom, Canada, West Germany, and Switzerland. Domestic production of 51,-

423 troy ounces in 1966 was derived chiefly as a by-product of copper refining.

The situation in respect to uranium is more favorable than for a number of strategic metals. Uranium ores are produced in quantity in New Mexico, Wyoming, Colorado, Utah, and Arizona. A small fraction of United States' needs was met in 1966 by importation of ores from Canada, Republic of South Africa, and France. Vanadium is a by-product or co-product of the uranium-processing industry, and a cutback in uranium production may affect adversely the production of vanadium.

Gold and silver, because of their monetary importance, received increased attention in the 1960's. Gold coinage was abandoned in 1933 but the metal functions as an international standard of exchange and moves from country to country as the trade balances require. Gold production in the United States has trended downward over many years. About one-third of the gold produced in the country is a co-product with copper, lead, zinc, and silver, resulting from the refining of complex metalliferous ores.

The industrial demand for silver and the need for increased coinage of silver-bearing coins combined to force a change in silver content of dimes, quarters, and half-dollars. Laminated sheets of metal are used to produce what are known as clad coins. Silver continues to be an important monetary metal. Domestic production is far below national requirements and as a consequence the metal- or silver-bearing ores must be imported from the major producing countries such as Mexico, Canada, and Peru. Domestic production is centered in Idaho, Arizona, Utah, and Montana.

The several nonferrous metals can be classed as strategic materials and essential to national security. Nearly all must be stockpiled in variable tonnages depending upon domestic requirements and the relative difficulty of securing new supplies in the case of a national emergency. For example, tin, anti-mony, and mercury are long-haul metals, and the lines of commerce might be cut. In the case of copper and aluminum off-shore supplies may be secured with less chance that imports could be cut off. Secondary recovery and the development of substitutes might help lessen the impact of a reduction in imports of these strategic metals. Normally copper is recycled into the market after an average of 35 years. In case of great need the recovery of scrap copper could be speeded up to the advantage of the nation.

The Nonmetallic Minerals. The common earth materials such as stone, sand and gravel, and clay are available in relative abundance, hence there is little reason to be concerned about supplies. Locally there may be shortages, but national supplies are adequate except for architectural stone, rare earths, and other uncommon mineral substances. In the United States the fertilizer minerals and closely related materials are now adequately or readily available to meet the nation's needs. The United States is the leading producer and consumer of sulfur and is both an exporter and importer. In the United States phosphate production exceeds that of any other nation and represents more than one-third of world production. The United States ranks second to East and West Germany (combined) in the production of potash. The expansion of potash production in Canada had made supplies of this valuable fertilizer mineral available to the United States market. In 1965–1966 the United States led in the production of nitrogen compounds, 7,007,000 short tons out of a world total of 25,563,000 short tons. The agricultural and industrial demands can be met from domestic producers who tap the inexhaustible supply of nitrogen in the atmosphere.

A selected number of nonmetallic minerals essential to industry and to national defense must be imported and stockpiled. They include asbestos imported chiefly from Canada and the Republic of South Africa; quartz crystals from Brazil; fluorspar from Mexico and Spain; cryolite from Greenland; mica from Brazil, India, and Malagasy Republic; and graphite from Malagasy and Mexico. These and many other mineral products which the United States cannot produce in quantity and competitively must be imported. Many in one form or another are stockpiled so that a supply will be readily available in case of a national emergency.

Lack of space has restricted the discussion to selected and representative minerals and metals important in the national economy, both present and future. Many other mineral commodities might have been treated briefly. These include such materials as arsenic, barite, bismuth, cadmium, columbium, feldspar, gem stones, iodine, lithium, pumice, rare earths, selenium, talc, thorium, titanium, zirconium, and others. Each has a place in the highly industrialized economy in which we live and in the future may attain national importance.

CONSERVATION IN MINING AND PROCESSING

Open-Pit Mining. Certain mineral deposits occur at the surface or are covered with a thin overburden. If the material which covers an ore body is relatively thin and nonresistant, it can be readily and cheaply removed, making it possible to mine the ore by open-pit methods. In the Lake Superior area, open-pit mining of iron ore has made possible the recovery and shipment of great quantities of ore since the mines were opened. In Bingham Canyon in Utah, in Nevada, and in other localities copper ores have been mined by the open-pit method.

Under such conditions, the ores are readily accessible and mining may be carried on as a large-scale operation. In the more northern latitudes, the cold of winter may interrupt or halt operations. But in spite of obstacles to continuous operations the open-pit method of mining, wherever conditions will permit, is one of the cheapest methods of ore recovery.

More Complete Recovery of Mineral Resources. Important quantities of minerals are left in the ground because of the difficulties in achieving 100 percent recovery. In open-pit mining where the overburden can be completely removed, recovery approaches 100 percent. Underground operations, because of the necessity of providing supporting walls and pillars, may leave as much as half of the ore in a condition that prevents recovery. The recovery of minerals in underground workings may contribute substantially to the reserves by the improvement of mining methods. In the course of time, economic necessity may require that the mineral resources be so developed that a high percentage of the mineral or ore can be recovered.

Block-Caving Method of Mining. Where an ore body lies near the surface but too deeply buried to be mined by the open-pit method, underground methods may be employed to reach and to recover the ore. If the ore occurs as a large mass of considerable thickness but of limited areal extent, the block-caving method may be used to recover a high percentage of the ore at a relatively low cost. In this method of mining, a vertical shaft is cut in the country rock to a level beneath the base of the ore body. Then a horizontal tunnel or drift is extended to a position directly under the ore body. Above this tunnel or haulage way, a system of vertical and inclined chutes are cut in the rock upward to the base of the ore body. Then after the process of undercutting and blasting the ore loose, the broken ore moves downward by gravity so it can be loaded into the cars and hauled directly to the shaft to be lifted to the surface. This method permits the recovery of a very high percentage of the original ore if the caving is carried out so as to avoid the incorporation of the low-grade overburden.

Beneficiation. When commercially workable ores approach exhaustion, means will be sought to process profitably the low-grade or marginal ores. The richer ores are commonly associated with low-grade ores which because of depth beneath the surface, the inclusion of deleterious substances, or for some other reason cannot be worked profitably. These low-grade or marginal ores may become workable at a profit when costs can be reduced or when the price of the ore advances sufficiently to encourage development or exploitation (Fig. 4).

The low-grade ores may become usable by the development of processing techniques which have the effect of enriching the ores or of increasing the metal content of the ore shipped to the smelter. In the Lake Superior Upland, from which the United States has

Fig. 5 This photography shows Jeffery magnetic separators used to upgrade taconite ores. (Jeffery Manufacturing Co., Division of Jeffery Galion, Inc., Columbus, Ohio.)

Fig. 4 An aerial view of the iron-ore pellet plant near Butler, Minnesota. The beneficiated ore is shipped by rail to Lake Superior for transhipment to the Lower Lakes smelters. (The Hanna Mining Co.)

been receiving the major share of its iron ore for more than a half century, the taconite and jasperite deposits are now becoming available to the iron and steel industry by the process of beneficiation. In the case of the magnetic iron minerals in the taconite deposits, the iron-bearing minerals can be separated from the gangue materials by the use of a powerful electromagnet. The low-grade ore after mining must be crushed and pulverized so that the finely divided magnetic minerals can be separated from the remainder of the material. By this means a relatively rich iron ore is produced from the abundant low-grade ores of the Lake Superior area (Fig. 5).

This fine granular material cannot be used directly but requires solidification into pellets of such size that they can become a part of the charge in the blast furnace. Pelletization is an integral part of the beneficiation process and is necessary for the proper functioning of the blast furnace.

The jasperite and other nonmagnetic iron ores must be enriched by other mechanical processes. By these means the very abundant low-grade ores can and will replace the less abundant high-grade ores which are subject to early exhaustion. In the case of iron, which is the fourth most abundant element in the earth's crust, beneficiation has the effect of increasing the relative abundance of iron ore to meet our industrial needs.

In 1966, 70.5 million tons out of a total of 134 million tons of iron ore used by the iron and steel industry were beneficiated.[9]

Sintering. Important tonnages of iron ore occur as a soft powdery material which is not well suited for charging the blast furnace.

[9] *Minerals Yearbook, 1966,* Vols. I–II, 1967, pp. 245 and 254.

The fines that result from the beneficiation process also require treatment before they are satisfactory for a good furnace charge. The mix that is fed into the sintering machines consists of ore (approximately 70 percent), limestone, dolomite, mill scale, flue dust, and coke (Fig. 6). As the material moves forward a sheet of flame in the sintering furnace plays on the material and heats it to incipient fusion (Fig. 7). The hard, resistant sinter as it leaves the machine is cooled and sized. The coarser fragments are ready for the blast furnace, but the fines are returned to the sintering machine. By this means, important quantities of powdery iron ore can be used in the iron and steel industry.

Fig. 6 A sintering plant in Pennsylvania. The three circular structures in front of the large building are the coolers that are used to reduce the temperature of the sinter before it moves on to the storage bins or to the smelters. (Dravo Corporation.)

Fig. 7 A sintering machine used to prepare the fine ores for the blast furnace. The fine ore particles, fluxes, coal, and coke move slowly through the sintering machine in which the ore becomes a clinker-like mass as it moves forward to a breaker which prepares the material for the blast furnace. Remaining fines are recycled back to the sintering machine. (Dravo Corporation.)

CONSERVATION PROBLEMS

Corrosion. The destructive effects of corrosion, chiefly the rusting of iron and steel, are difficult to estimate or determine with accuracy. Large losses are sustained by the railroads, the Navy and the merchant fleet, automobiles, metal structures, and machinery of all kinds. The losses cannot be prevented, but they may be delayed. Each year 3 or more million automobiles are scrapped. Their deterioration in usefulness is related in part to corrosion. Whatever the average life of an automobile, it may be in the best interests of the national economy to scrap the cars as soon as genuine obsolescence sets it and re-cycle the metals back into new products. The auto graveyards and the junkyards of the nation constitute a great reserve of iron and steel and other metals. Rust each year destroys a large tonnage of metals because of the delay in returning the scrap to be re-melted and refined.

Corrosion Control. Most metals which have been freed from the ores with which they were associated in nature tend to corrode or combine with other elements or substances. Iron is more susceptible to rusting or corrosion than the nonferrous metals such as aluminum, copper, lead, zinc, and tin. By the use of protective coverings or alloys the loss from corrosion can be prevented or reduced. Steel structures, such as the great suspension bridges, require almost continuous re-painting to save them from serious deterioration.

The use of enormous lengths of tubing and pipes to carry a great variety of gases and liquids exposes both the internal and the external surfaces to corrosion unless protected by some kind of covering to prevent or delay the rate of deterioration. The losses sustained by failure of metals-in-use may be many times the value of the pipe or tubing required as a replacement. The failure of a major water line may mean that an important section of a city is without fire protection and industries within the area affected may have to shut down for hours. A break or a perforation in the tubing in a chemical plant, a battleship, a petroleum refinery, or a pharmaceutical factory may result in great damage to a plant, but even greater losses may result from the shutdown required to make the necessary repairs. The failure of metals because of corrosion and the measures required to protect them against deterioration become a heavy charge upon the general economy.

Protective Coatings on Metals. If a metal that is normally subject to rapid corrosion can be coated promptly by some substance resistant to weathering and alteration, the useful life of the metal may be greatly extended. The protective coating may be a paint, a lacquer, or an enamel brushed on or sprayed on the metal to be protected. Steel products may be coated with molten zinc (a process known as galvanizing) or by plating steel, copper, and bronze with tin, chromium, nickel, or cadmium.

Rust inhibitors are used in the water that comes in contact with the metal tubing in boilers or the cooling systems of automobiles. The chemical inhibitor reduces the oxygen in the coolant, thus preventing the rusting of the engine block and the clogging of the cooling system.

Alloys. Corrosion of iron and steel may be greatly reduced or largely eliminated by combining small amounts of alloy metals with the metal to be protected. The best-known example is the manufacture of stainless steel by combining nickel and chromium with the molten steel. To give stainless steel certain qualities required for particular purposes, small quantities of other metals such as copper, silicon, titanium, columbium, molybdenum, and other elements may be added. The durability

of steel may be increased manyfold by the addition, in the proper proportions, of these and other alloy metals.

The addition of alloying elements to steel may improve the resulting specialty steels in such a way that great savings are achieved by reducing the amount of steel required for certain purposes. If steel is given great strength and stiffness by the addition of alloying elements such as nickel or vanadium, there is a large initial saving. There is a further saving of fuels where these special steels are used in the manufacture of transportation equipment. The development of a great number of specialty steels for a variety of purposes reduces the quantity of steel required and at the same time permits the selection of exactly the right steel for a particular purpose.

Recovery of By-Products. In order that a mineral resource may make its fullest contribution in satisfying the needs of man, the associated minerals should be recovered. To develop a mineral deposit for a single metal or product may be uneconomical, but the recovery of a single by-product or co-product may mean the difference between failure and success of a mining venture. The waste or tailings may contain small quantities of important minerals, but at one stage in the processing it might not be practical or feasible to recover the metal contained. Later, with improved methods of recovery and increased price of the metal contained in the waste material, it might be economically profitable to re-work what was formerly regarded as waste.

Substitutes. In the event that metals are not available in adequate quantities to meet the nation's needs, other materials may be used as substitutes to a limited extent. It is not to be expected that all metals can be replaced. When there is not enough steel to meet all needs, wood and stone can be used for certain structural purposes. If and when the several ferroalloys are not available in the usual quantities and at fair prices, specialty steels may be made by using the alloys that are in good supply. During World War II it became necessary to reduce the number of specialty steels and concentrate on the production of a few standardized types.

In the United States molybdenum is relatively abundant, for nearly two-thirds of the world's supply is produced in this country. A major share of the world's nickel is produced in Canada, and we can assume that in a national emergency nickel produced by a friendly neighbor would be more readily obtainable than manganese, tungsten, and chromium which must come from more distant sources. Within certain technical limits the use of the ferroalloys may be adjusted in terms of their relative abundance. This may be in effect a substitution of one metal for another in lesser abundance.

During World War II, when copper was not available in adequate quantities to meet the needs of industry, certain uses were curtailed in order that the supply available would be adequate to meet urgent needs. Silver was used in bus bars to free copper for more essential needs. Copper for siding and roofing was replaced by cheaper materials which were relatively more abundant. By these and other means, the available supply of copper could be and was allocated to meet the critical needs of the wartime economy.

The ubiquitous tin can did not disappear completely from the grocer's shelves, but many changes or substitutes were necessary because of the critical shortage of tin in the United States. By making improvements in tin-plating, the amount of tin used per can was decreased slightly. Lacquered cans were used where the contents did not require tin for protection from deterioration. In recent years the aluminum can has become increasingly important.

In order that substitutions may be made with little disturbance in the metal-using industries, research and technological developments should be carried out in advance of need so the new alloys or new materials can

be quickly substituted for the scarce metal.

Shifting from Scarce to Abundant Materials. A change in the relative abundance of a mineral or metal, providing the price differential does not interfere with the change, is the essential first step in shifting use from a scarce to a relatively abundant material. For example, aluminum is a satisfactory replacement for copper in the electrical field, and it can be expected that the relative importance of these two metals in the electrical industry will result in the increased use of aluminum. It is also evident that plastic materials made out of air, water, and other abundant substances can be substituted for metals, thus diminishing the demand for copper, lead, zinc, and other metals which are in short supply.

Re-cycling of Metals in the Economy. It is fortunate indeed that many metals and other materials can be recovered and re-used. Unlike the fuel minerals the metals can be used over and over again. In the case of the precious metals, such as gold, silver, and platinum, today's supply includes metal which was first mined and refined decades if not centuries ago. The wedding circlet worn by the modern bride may at one time have been a part of the ceremonial jewelry of an ancient princess or the loot of pirates. It is important in the conservation of many metals that the supply available for current use consists of both virgin metal produced from ores freshly mined and of secondary or scrap metal being prepared for new uses.

The nonferrous metals, such as copper, lead, zinc, aluminum, and tin, and others which resist corrosion or deterioration in use, may be recovered and used again and again. Whenever a small amount of these metals is widely dispersed in connection with its use, it may be quite uneconomical to recover it, except in a national emergency. During World War II collecting stations were set up to facilitate the accumulation of tin cans which were sent to the de-tinning plants. In the scrap-metal or junk business, machinery and other heavy scrap may be broken up, and the non-ferrous metals recovered through a process of sorting or refining.

Great quantities of metals are lost each year because the form in which they are used makes recovery impossible. The pigments used in paint in the form of lead, zinc, and titanium oxides are so thinly spread on painted surfaces that they are lost forever. Other uses may permit re-use after varying intervals of time. The owner of an automobile generally exchanges his old battery for a new one, and the dealer returns the old battery to the manufacturer who recovers the lead and uses it in the manufacture of new batteries.

The metal that is recoverable in the greatest quantities is iron commonly used in the form of steel. The iron and steel industry is an important producer of scrap. Wherever steel is a major raw material in the manufacture of machinery, new scrap becomes available for re-cycling back into the manufacture of steel. In densely populated areas, particularly where heavy industry is concentrated, the amount of used scrap available is very large.

Some Lessons from World War II. During World War II the junk dealers of America were called upon to speed up the collection and delivery of scrap to the steel makers. In remote and thinly populated areas the derelict auto, the abandoned mowing machine, and a section of oil pipe may never be recovered and re-used because it is uneconomical to collect such isolated quantities of scrap.

The destruction of military equipment in wartime constitutes an enormous loss of valuable resources. On the battlefields and in materiel depots where bombing and military action converted weapons and vehicles into scrap, there can be and usually is some recovery of this spent material. However, the enormous tonnage of steel and other metals in ships sunk at sea is largely lost forever. The merchant ships and naval craft lost in World War II constitute not only a loss of the metals from the original supply, but for every ton of steel which was sunk in the open sea beyond the possibility of salvage, there was also a loss of man power and other materials used in the production of the steel in the first place. The secondary recovery of steel and other metals for re-use in industry represents more than a saving of metals. There is also the recovery or the salvage of the power, the labor, and the capital used in the smelting of the ore and in the manufacture of steel and the other metal products.

Over a long period of time the relatively abundant mineral resources of the United States had been conducive to an attitude of complacency. During World War I and the 1920's, a limited number of shortages served as a warning to conservation-conscious Americans who realized the increased use of metals would eventually mean depletion of some relatively rich but small deposits.

The number of strategic minerals in short supply before World War II was about ten, or a dozen at the most. But during the war the number increased until more than sixty different minerals were imported from more than fifty different countries to satisfy the insatiable war machine. Of the twenty most essential minerals in the wartime economy, eight were imported entirely from foreign sources. For another half dozen, 85 to 100 percent of the nation's needs had to be imported. A continuing high level of industrial activity and a defense program based on the use of large quantities of minerals make clear that shortages of vital mineral resources in continental United States are real and not imagined.[10]

Stockpiling. Late in the 1930's, it became evident that the United States should have been stockpiling a large number of nonperishable but essential materials during the depression years when prices were low. In 1939,

[10] Alan M. Bateman, "Our Future Dependence on Foreign Minerals," *The Annals,* Vol. 281, 1952, pp. 25–32. Reference on p. 26.

when Public Law 117, the Strategic Materials Act, was passed by the 76th Congress, prices had risen and many materials had become scarce. When the United States became involved in World War II, the nation was soon confronted with shortages among the metals and other strategic materials.

After the war was over new legislation in the form of the Strategic and Critical Materials Stockpiling Act was enacted in 1946. At the outset funds were inadequate to finance a comprehensive program of stockpiling. Furthermore, the international situation did not suggest urgency in the stockpiling program. However, the outbreak of hostilities in Korea in 1950 made it clear that supplies of a large number of strategic materials should be built up quickly. But it was impossible to meet the needs of the civilian economy, of the defense industries, and the stockpiling program all in the space of a few years after 1950.

Under the authority of Public Law 520 of the 79th Congress, entitled, "The Strategic and Critical Material Stock Piling Act," approved on August 8, 1946, the national stockpile acquired inventories accumulated under previous authorizations and was extended to include materials deemed necessary to the national defense.[11] Public Law 480 of the 83rd Congress, entitled, "Agricultural Trade Development and Assistance Act of 1954," approved on July 10, 1954, authorized "the barter of surplus agricultural commodities produced in the United States for strategic and critical materials produced abroad." [12] A supplemental stockpile was authorized and material ac-

[11] For a brief review of the stockpiling operations, goals, and problems related to authorization, acquisition, execution of contracts, and disposals of surplus materials see the *Inquiry into the Strategic and Critical Materials Stockpiles of the United States*, Draft Report of the National Stockpile and Naval Petroleum Reserves Subcommittee of the Committee on Armed Services (Senator Stuart Symington, Chairman), United States Senate, Government Printing Office, Washington, D.C., 1963, 126 pages.

[12] *Ibid.*, p. 11.

quired under the "Agricultural Act of 1954" and Public Law 733 of the 84th Congress, entitled, "Domestic Tungsten, Asbestos, Fluorspar, and Columbium-Tantalum Production and Purchase Act of 1956." The establishment of stockpiling policies and goals was chiefly the responsibility of the Office of Emergency Planning and its predecessor agencies. The General Services Administration was assigned the duty of implementing the policies of OEP.[13]

On January 31, 1963, President Kennedy announced that the stockpile program would be reviewed and that the cloak of secrecy would be removed. Accordingly the information on stockpiling was declassified and Senator Symington and his Subcommittee of the Committee on Armed Services, United States Senate, began an extended study of the stockpiling program. The committee recommended among other things that the objectives and goals of the stockpiling program be reexamined and that Congress authorize the orderly disposal of surplus materials.

STOCKPILING FROM DOMESTIC SOURCES. If the capacity to produce minerals and mineral products from domestic sources cannot be expanded quickly to meet urgent defense needs, stockpiles should be built up to such levels as deemed necessary to meet the emergency. Conceivably productive capacity might be damaged or destroyed by sabotage or more direct enemy action. Under such circumstances large stockpiles of ores and other mineral products above ground would be an element of strength in conversion to a war economy when man power and materials generally become scarce. A stockpile of ores and metals built up by the employment of domestic skills and local resources would have the effect of maintaining an operating facility which could

[13] For a more recent statement on stockpiling see Office of Emergency Planning, Executive Office of the President, *Stockpile Report to the Congress*, Washington, D.C., January–June 1968.

be expanded quickly to meet a national emergency.

STOCKPILING FROM FOREIGN SOURCES. Building up the stockpile of strategic materials, particularly the metals, is absolutely essential in the case of those materials that are not available in economically accessible reserves. Certain of the ferroalloys such as manganese, chromium, tungsten, and nickel and the nonferrous metals such as tin, mercury, aluminum, and copper should be purchased abroad and added to the government-owned stockpile. A more or less continuing policy of purchasing supplies regularly would have the effect of maintaining continued production abroad. If the importation of minerals for the stockpile were reduced or abandoned, the economic consequences might be very great. For example, for a copper mining and smelting operation in an area where there is no alternate employment, a shutdown would cause great hardship through the loss of wages and purchasing power of a large number of people. The need of the United States for metals and other strategic materials that must be imported from foreign sources should not lead first to overdevelopment of a mineral resource and then abandonment of the operation. For the greatest security, based on continued accessibility to mineral resources beyond our national frontiers, the mining and processing operations must be maintained, and the routes of commerce kept open if at all possible.

In the late 1960's, the stockpiles were reduced to provide defense industries with essential supplies that were not available chiefly because of long strikes. The threat of increased prices in the aluminum and copper markets induced the President to release supplies of the metals, and an economic impasse was averted. The stockpile may be regarded as a national necessity, and on occasion it may be used to achieve economic stability.

In the case of a nuclear war the conflict may be of short duration and the stockpile may be used, not for the strengthening of the war-making activities of the nation, but for the reconstruction and restoration of communication systems, and the rehabilitation or construction of homes, factories, hospitals, schools and other essential structures in modern economic society. Stockpiling for recovery from a short war may be different than stockpiling for a conventional war of 4 to 10 years duration.

STOCKPILING DIFFICULTIES. In addition to the major objective of establishing an adequate stockpile of the essential strategic materials, it is also important that stockpiling achieve other purposes as well. When federal funds are provided for the purchase of strategic materials, it is important that the funds be allocated and expended in a very businesslike manner. Priorities should be established so that the scarce and inaccessible materials can be promptly built up, deferring until some later time the stockpiling of materials that are less urgently needed.

Purchases for the stockpile should be carried out in such a manner that the government does not compete with private industry for the same materials at the same time. This would have as one consequence an increase in price which in turn would limit the quantity of material the available funds would purchase.

STOCKPILING OF LABOR AND POWER. Whenever strategic materials such as copper, aluminum, tin, and other metals are stockpiled, the labor, power, and transportation used in their production are also stockpiled. For example, 20 percent of the price of metallic aluminum represents the cost of the electrical energy required to separate the metal from the ore. To the extent that the electrical energy was produced from falling water, the stockpiling of aluminum is a means of stockpiling water power which otherwise might have gone to waste. When the stored materials are released from the stockpile, the other constituents are also released (Fig. 8).

RESERVES IN THE GROUND. In the case of pe-

Fig. 8 A stockpile of aluminum bars. Aluminum is one of more than 60 minerals and metals stockpiled in the United States. (Office of Emergency Preparedness.)

troleum, copper, lead, and several other mineral resources, it is important that large proved reserves be known with some exactness. Discovery of new resources or reserves should be well ahead of use so that the reserves will be large enough to permit the rapid expansion of production to meet an emergency. It is not enough to have adequate reserves in the ground. It is also essential that stand-by facilities for expanding mining and smelting be in readiness so that production of strategic metals can be increased promptly to meet the industrial and military needs after the stockpiles have absorbed the first shock of an enemy attack.

DANGER IN STOCKPILING. The stockpiling program of the federal government may have some inherent weaknesses which might be regarded as dangers to the national economy. The goals must be determined a few to several years in advance of achievement. To be genuinely effective the stockpiling program should be continually re-examined to make sure that the objectives are realistic in relation to the military and civilian needs.

The industries that require large quantities of strategic raw materials to carry on their manufacturing activities should be encouraged to build up and maintain substantial inventories so that it will not be necessary for them to draw upon the national stockpile. The inventories of the manufacturing companies and the stockpile of the federal government should jointly be adequate to meet a national emergency extending over a period of years.

There is also the danger that the stockpile may be conducive to the development of an attitude of complacency.[14] It is important that

[14] The President's Materials Policy Commission, *Resources for Freedom*, Vol. I, p. 163.

stockpiling be considered as only one of the means of meeting the material needs of the country in case of a national emergency. Exploration for new supplies of minerals must go on; the search for substitutes must not be relaxed; and technological advances must be sought at every opportunity. Stockpiling must be recognized as only one of the ways of preparing for an emergency.

NATIONAL POLICIES AND INTERNATIONAL CONSIDERATIONS

The Prospect for Future Discovery. In some portions of the world such as northwestern Europe, the United States, and limited areas elsewhere, geological knowledge is reasonably complete. In these areas it is highly improbable new deposits of great value will be discovered. Further exploration, especially at great depth, may have the effect of increasing the known reserves and give the people and the nation a greater sense of security. The deposits that are known at great depth may not be readily accessible because of both engineering and economic limitations.

The greatest hope for new discoveries lies in the exploration of areas that have not been carefully examined geologically. These lesser known areas lie in Asia, Africa, South America, Australia, Antarctica, and limited sections in Europe and North America. Unless new and important discoveries are made in the United States or in areas easily accessible by trade, it is clear that the nation will become increasingly dependent on imported mineral products.

Percentage Depletion Provisions of the Internal Revenue Code.[15] A mineral deposit is a depletable resource and by continued mining will be exhausted in time. The net income

from the mining operation cannot be regarded as profit alone but is in fact a combination of profit and a return of capital. The United States Congress, in drawing up the Internal Revenue Code, recognized the dual character of the income from mining operations and provided that an allowance for depletion of the deposit or resource would encourage the owners to use some of their income for exploration for new deposits or to determine if deposits currently being worked extended to greater depths or extended horizontally into adjacent areas.

The depletion allowances range from 27.5 percent in the case of oil and gas to 5 percent for a number of common earth materials such as sand and gravel, clay (for brick and tile) and shale, mollusk shells (clam and oyster), peat, and pumice. Also the brines, bromine, calcium chloride, and magnesium chloride, if pumped from wells, are included in the 5 percent category.

For sulfur and uranium and many other domestically produced minerals the depletion allowance is 23 percent.

A 15 percent allowance is applied to a number of special clays such as ball clay, bentonite, china clay, metals (other than those enjoying the 23 percent allowance), rock asphalt, and vermiculite.

A 10 percent allowance is applied to the production of asbestos, coal and lignite, sodium chloride, and a number of metals not included in the 23 percent or 15 percent categories.[16]

Removing the Barriers to International Trade. Tariffs and other devices have been

---

[15] For a more extended discussion of depletion allowances see *American Law of Mining*, Vol. 5, Rocky Mountain Mineral Law Foundation, Matthew Bender and Co., New York, 1964, 282 pp.; and Peter T. Flawn, *Mineral Resources*, Chicago, 1966, pp. 205–210.

[16] The Tax Reform Act of 1969 adjusted the tax rate on a large number of natural resources. For example, the depletion allowance on oil and gas wells, sulfur, uranium, and many others was set at 22 percent. The rate on gold, silver, copper, iron ore, and oil shale was fixed at 15 percent. For a full listing of the depletion allowances, see the *Conference Report* to accompany H. R. 13270, 91st Congress, first session, House of Representatives, Report No. 91–782, December 21, 1969.

used in the past to protect American industry from competition from abroad, generally where labor costs are relatively low as compared with the wage scale in the United States. The advantages gained by the use of the protective tariff were matched by disadvantages of higher costs to the consumer which delayed or interfered with the development of the resources in foreign source areas. The lowering of a tariff or its abandonment altogether might not lower prices immediately, especially in those situations where the domestic production is small and where production abroad is under the control of a monopoly or international cartel. But in the long run there should be an effort to reduce tariffs or abandon them entirely.

TARIFFS VERSUS SECURITY. The tariff has been used to protect a domestic industry which as a going concern could give the nation a degree of self-sufficiency in case of a national emergency. But the argument in favor of a protective tariff for security can be challenged. There are other means of achieving national security, such as stockpiling and long-term contracts with domestic and accessible foreign producers of strategic minerals. The tariff on each mineral or metal product should be reviewed periodically to determine if the national interest might be better served by the reduction or elimination of the import duties.

EXPORT QUOTAS AND CONTROLS. By the use of embargos, restrictions, and quotas the free movement of materials in international trade can be controlled. The government in an emergency or in anticipation of an unfavorable situation may, by decree, put export controls into effect. When prices in the metal market tend to stimulate the outflow of essential metals to the extent that the supplies on hand are too low to meet domestic needs, it may be necessary that export controls be used in order to maintain adequate inventories to meet all domestic requirements.

The Concept of Custodianship. Minerals are very irregularly distributed in the earth's crust and over the surface of the earth. The natural division of the earth into great continental land masses has resulted in dividing the mineral wealth unequally among the continents. The further division of the continents among the nations has resulted in great inequality among the countries in material wealth.

Any nation that contains within its frontiers a high percentage of a mineral resource that is widely needed over the world should be under some compulsion to share this bounty of nature with other peoples. A spirit of custodianship should be promoted that would encourage development and exportation of minerals essential to the world economy. Strategic minerals such as nickel, mercury, molybdenum, and manganese may be in high demand when the nations are experiencing industrial expansion or building up their national defenses. To the extent that these and other strategic minerals might be used for carrying on war they may be denied to an aggressor and made available to nations defending their independence. Under wartime conditions the concept of custodianship can be modified to serve the ends of peace.

Foreign Trade—A Necessity. At the close of World War II it became clear that the United States was no longer self-sufficient in certain minerals. For many years some of these had been produced in excess of domestic requirements, and limited quantities were available for export as native metals or in the form of products made from these metals. The changeover from a surplus-producing country to an importer occurred at different dates, depending upon the metal. By the middle 1930's, the United States became a net importer of zinc and copper. It was near the end of World War II that imports of petroleum exceeded exports. It also became clear that increasing quantities of iron ore would have to be imported to satisfy the needs of American industry.

The importation of strategically important minerals may have other beneficial consequences besides supplying the nation with an essential resource. The money necessary to purchase the imports would become available in the country supplying the mineral for the further development of their resources and for the raising of the standard of living of the people. They would be able to make purchases of other materials produced in their own country and in other countries.

In those countries where the standard of living is relatively low and where their industry is in the extractive stage of development, there is a great need for capital, technological help, and managerial skills. The United States, because of its great wealth and technical knowledge, is in a position to provide the capital and skills to develop the resources of certain underdeveloped areas of the world. In return we might secure minerals essential to our national well-being. Trade in minerals becomes a virtual necessity, for no nation, no matter how large or richly endowed, can be entirely self-sufficient in all essential minerals.

Trade Routes and the Accessibility of Mineral Resources. Strategic minerals which must be imported from distant sources make it necessary that the routes of commerce be kept open and, in case of emergency, strongly protected. The United States, because of its enormous demand for a great variety of minerals which cannot be produced in adequate quantities from domestic resources, must maintain a more or less continuous flow of minerals or metals to the American market. This is well illustrated by tin, the production of which from domestic resources is practically nil. This metal or its ores, in order to meet the needs of the country, must be imported from Bolivia or from the more distant producing areas in Malaysia and Indonesia. Minerals that are available in foreign areas which lie adjacent to the United States or in areas which are readily accessible may be utilized to meet the industrial and defense needs of the nation. Relatively short trade routes which lie within areas that can be defended or protected against enemy action are more dependable than the long trade routes that reach out to the more distant sources of strategic minerals. Over the longer trade routes it may be necessary to move essential minerals and other materials in convoys which necessarily move only as fast as the slowest ship and require many types of naval craft to provide adequate protection.

References

Adams, John A. S., James Boyd, and Paul W. McGann, "Exploring for Minerals," Chapter III in *Science and Resources,* edited by Henry Jarrett, Resources for the Future, The Johns Hopkins Press, Baltimore, 1959, pp. 75–112.

Bateman, Alan M., *Economic Mineral Deposits,* Second Edition, John Wiley & Sons, New York, 1950.

Blondel, F. and S. G. Laskey, "Mineral Reserves and Mineral Resources," *Economic Geology,* Vol. LI, 1956, pp. 686–697.

Brooks, David B., *Low Grade and Nonconventional Sources of Manganese,* Resources for the Future, Inc., Washington, D.C., 1966.

———, *Supply and Competition in Minor Metals,* The Johns Hopkins Press, Baltimore, 1966.

Flawn, Peter T., *Mineral Resources,* Rand McNally & Company, Chicago, 1966.

Fontana, Mars G. and Norbert D. Greene, *Corrosion Engineering,* McGraw-Hill Book Co., New York, 1967.

Herfindahl, Orris C., *Mineral Economics* (Three Studies), Resources for the Future, Inc., Washington, D.C., 1961, 63 pp.

Hurlbut, C. S., Jr., *Minerals and Man,* Random House, New York, 1968.

Jarrett, Henry, editor, *Perspectives on Conservation,* essays based on the RFF Forum Lectures of 1959, The Johns Hopkins Press, Baltimore, 1959, 256 pp.

Landsberg, Hans H., Leonard L. Fischman, and Joseph L. Fisher, "Metals," Chapter 16, and "Nonfuel Minerals," Chapter 21, in *Resources in America's Future,* Resources for the Future, The Johns Hopkins Press, Baltimore, 1963, pp. 293–316 and 422–496.

Leith, C. K., "Principles of Foreign Mineral Policy of the United States," *Mining and Metallurgy,* Vol. 27, 1946, pp. 6–17.

Leith, C. K., J. W. Furness, and Cleona Lewis, *World Minerals and World Peace,* Brookings Institution, Washington, D.C., 1943.

Lovering, Thomas S., *Minerals in World Affairs,* Prentice-Hall, Englewood Cliffs, New Jersey, 1944.

Marovelli, R. L. et. al., *Lake Superior Iron Resources,* U.S. Bureau of Mines Report of Investigations No. 5670, Governmental Printing Office, Washington, D.C., 1961.

McDivitt, James F., *Minerals and Men: An Exploration of the World of Minerals and Its Effect on the World We Live In,* The Johns Hopkins Press, Baltimore, 1965, 168 pp.

Netschert, Bruce C. and Hans H. Landsberg, *The Future Supply of the Major Metals, A Reconnaissance Study,* Resources for the Future, The Johns Hopkins Press, Baltimore, 1961.

The President's Materials Policy Commission, *Resources for Freedom,* Vol. I: *Foundations for Growth and Security,* Vol. II: *The Outlook for Key Commodities,* Vol. III: *The Promise of Technology,* Government Printing Office, Washington, D.C., 1952.

Preston, Lee E., *Exploration for Nonferrous Metals: An Economic Analysis,* The Johns Hopkins Press, Baltimore, 1960, 212 pp.

Riley, Charles M., *Our Mineral Resources,* John Wiley & Sons, New York, 1959.

Schurr, Sam H., *Historical Statistics of Minerals in the United States,* The Johns Hopkins Press, Baltimore, 1960, 48 pp.

Staff of the Bureau of Mines and Geological Survey, *Mineral Position of the United States,* Appendix, Investigation of National Resources, Hearings Before a Subcommittee on Public Lands, United States Senate, 80th Congress, May 15, 16, and 20, 1947, Government Printing Office, Washington, D.C., 1947, pp. 165–310.

United Nations Department of Economic Affairs, Proceedings of the United Nations Scientific Conference on Conservation and Utilization of Resources, August 17–September 6, 1949, Vol. II, *Mineral Resources,* United Nations, New York, 1951.

United States Bureau of Mines, *Mineral Facts and Problems* (1960 edition), Government Printing Office, Washington, D.C., 1960.

————, *Minerals Yearbook*, Government Printing Office, Washington, D.C., Annual.

Van Royen, W. and Oliver Bowles, "Atlas of the World's Resources," Vol. II, *Mineral Resources of the World*, Prentice-Hall, Englewood Cliffs, New Jersey, 1952.

Willard, F. W., "Some Aspects of Our Wasting Assets," *Mining and Metallurgy*, Vol. 27, 1946, pp. 583–584.

E. WILLARD MILLER

The Pennsylvania State University

CHAPTER 16

The Mineral Fuels

The United States could not be one of the leading nations today, nor could the citizens of our country have attained the highest standard of living in the world, without its rich heritage in mineral fuels. The economic and military strength of our nation depends increasingly on the capacity to exploit these resources.

To meet the energy needs of the United States two broad groups of potential sources may be utilized. The first are continuous, renewable sources, such as solar, water, wind or tidal energy, and vegetation. At present, these furnish less than one-seventh of our energy requirements, primarily in the form of water power and vegetation.

The second group includes the irreplaceable energy sources, such as the fossil fuels and atomic energy. Of the irreplaceable energy sources, petroleum, coal, and natural gas currently furnish six-sevenths of our total requirements. Atomic energy developments are still in the initial stages, but basic and applied research promises a wide utilization of this energy to supplement the traditional fuels within a relatively few years.

At present mineral fuel production represents about two-thirds of our total value of minerals produced in the United States. The nation in 1968 produced about 23 percent of the world's bituminous and anthracite coal, 25 percent of the petroleum, about 70 percent of the natural gas marketed, and had approximately 40 percent of the electric energy produced.

The mineral fuel reserves are very unequally proportioned (Table 1). A comparison on a uniform British thermal unit basis of reserves of coal and other fuels shows that coal constitutes 80 percent of the estimated total ultimately recoverable reserves, and petroleum and natural gas combined constitute about 9 percent. Oil shale provides about 8 percent of the ultimate recoverable energy reserves, and uranium oxide about 3 percent.

Relative Importance of Energy Resources 1800–1967. During the early days of our country, water and wind power, wood, and work animals provided the principal sources of power. However, between 1800 and 1870, there was a gradual shift from the predominance of nonfuel energy sources to mineral energy sources. About 1830, coal began to be increasingly important as a source of energy

Table 1. Remaining Recoverable Reserves of Fuel in the United States, January 1, 1967

	Known or Proved Recoverable Reserves			Estimated Total Ultimately Recoverable Reserves		
	Standard Units of Measurement [1]	Quadrillion Btu [2]	Percent According to Btu Content	Standard Units of Measurement [1]	Quadrillion Btu [2]	Percent According to Btu Content
Coal	220.0	4,600	80	1,605	33,705	75
Petroleum	31.5	183	3	419	2,430	5
Natural gas	389.3	299	5	2,182	2,252	5
Natural gas liquids	389.3	38	1	65	300	1
Oil in bituminous rocks	1.3	8	–	5	29	–
Shale oil	80.0	464	8	1,000	5,800	13
Uranium oxide (U₃O₈)	380.0	171	3	1,500	675	1+
Total energy in fuels		5,763	100		45,191	100

[1] Coal in billions of tons; petroleum, natural gas liquids, oil in bituminous rocks, and shale oil in billions of barrels; natural gas in trillions of cubic feet; and uranium oxide (U_3O_8) in thousands of tons.

[2] Reserves converted to Btu according to the following heat values: anthracite, 12,700 Btu per pound; bituminous coal, 13,100 Btu per pound; sub-bituminous coal, 9500 Btu per pound; lignite, 6700 Btu per pound; petroleum, oil from bituminous rock, and shale oil, 5,800,000 Btu per barrel; natural gas liquids, 4,620,000 Btu per barrel; natural gas, 1032 Btu per cubic foot; and uranium oxide (U_3O_8), 450 billion Btu per ton.

and reached its relative peak of importance in 1899 when bituminous and anthracite accounted for 89.1 percent of the total energy contributed by both mineral fuels and water power in the United States. In that year oil and gas accounted for only 7.7 percent of the total (Fig. 1).

The relative importance of coal as a source of energy has been declining since the early 1900's. In 1918, the peak production year of World War I, coal supplied 82 percent of the energy resources, whereas petroleum and natural gas supplied 13.4 percent. The relative value of coal as a source of energy decreased rapidly after 1918 to 63 percent of the total in 1929 and to 21.4 percent in 1967. Oil and natural gas have largely replaced coal in domestic consumption and on the railroads. Since 1955, virtually all new locomotives have been powered with diesel engines.

With the industrial development of the twentieth century, petroleum's share of the energy consumed increased from 4.6 percent in 1899 to 34.8 percent from domestic petroleum in 1967, with another 4.5 percent from imported oil. Natural gas has followed the same general trend as petroleum, increasing from 3.3 percent of the total in 1899 to 13.7 percent in 1945 and 31.3 percent in 1967, and 3.5 percent came from natural gas liquids such as propane and butane. The production of water power has increased many times, but has maintained about the same relative position. In 1967, it accounted for 3.9 percent of total energy consumption. Nuclear power provided only 0.1 percent of energy consumed, but it is becoming more important.

Trends in Energy Consumption. The consumption of energy in the United States has been continuously upward. It has risen from 2,354 trillion Btu's in 1850 to 22,975 trillion Btu's in 1922, to a peak of 56,835 trillion

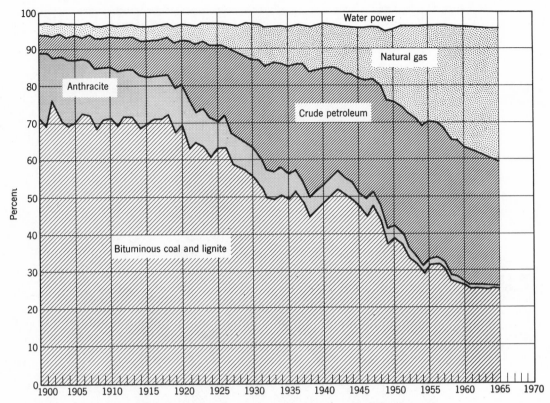

Fig. 1 The relative importance of the power resources of the United States. (U.S. Bureau of Mines.)

Btu's in 1966 (Fig. 2). Between 1965 and 1966, consumption of energy rose by more than 3,000 trillion Btu's. In the past century fuel wood was replaced by coal, which in turn has been replaced by petroleum and natural gas as the dominant sources of energy. To maintain the present rate of increase in the future it is likely that another energy source must be developed to replace petroleum and natural gas. At the present time the most promising future source of energy is nuclear energy.

COAL RESOURCES

Importance of the Coal Industry. Coal was the wonder fuel of the nineteenth century and is still of major importance in providing the comforts and necessities of life. It has been a vital factor in the growth of modern world industry. Although the coal industry has been affected by competition from competing fuels, coal remains the major fuel for heat and process steam in thousands of industrial plants. The annual value of bituminous coal is presently over $2,400,000,000.

The transportation of bituminous coal from mine to market is the largest bulk-handling industry in the United States. Over 292,000,000 tons of coal were transported by railroads, 173,000,000 tons by water transportation, and 47,000,000 tons by truck in 1967. In the same year, 12 percent, or more than $1.1 billion, of the nation's railroad freight revenue came from the movement of coal. To

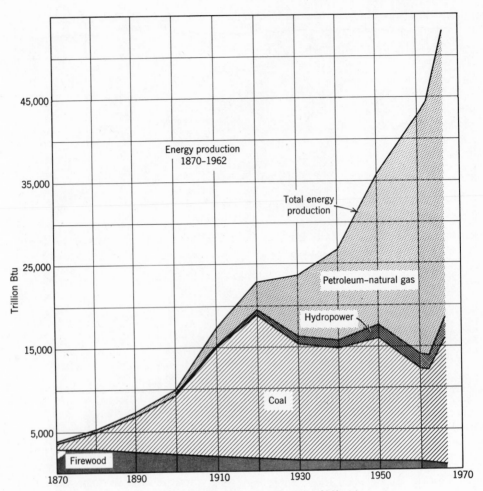

Fig. 2   Energy production in the United States, 1870 to 1966. (U. S. Bureau of Mines.)

meet competition the railroads have developed the unit-train concept for volume movement. Basically, the unit train consists of perhaps 100 or more high-capacity cars which carry a single commodity. A unit train generally carries 4000 to 10,000 tons of coal, although some run as high as 15,000 tons. During 1967, railroads put 16,275 new or rebuilt coal cars into service, and another 11,726 were on order as of January 1, 1968. The unit train has aided coal in maintaining a stable price and retaining its position as a leading source of energy.

Coal is a major supporter of economic life in many regions and is of great importance in others. In West Virginia the number of coal miners is nearly double those employed in the chemical and allied products industries, and the coal industry of Pennsylvania employs twice the number in the metal-working machinery industry.

Origin and Nature of Coals. Coal is a combustible earth material composed of fixed carbon, volatile matter, moisture, and ash originating from the alteration of plant life. In every geologic age since the Precambrian period, great swamps have existed in which layer upon layer of vegetation accumulated to form peat bogs. Peat developed into coal in a number of stages. The vegetational material was first compressed under successive layers of vegetation. Later as marine or continental deposits covered the coal swamps the accumulated weight of sediments compressed further the plant materials and caused a progressive decrease in volatile matter and moisture. It is estimated that it takes 100 years to form 1 foot of peat and from 3 to 8 feet of peat to produce 1 foot of coal. Pressure, therefore, is one of the great factors in coal development. Lignites are characteristically found where burial is shallow and where there is little crustal distortion, whereas anthracite and high-carbon coals are formed by great compression related largely to crusted disturbances.[1]

Fixed carbon gives the black color to coal and burns with a short flame giving almost no smoke. The volatile matter, consisting of compounds of carbon and hydrogen, is important because of its high heat content and the number of by-products that are obtained from it in the destructive distillation of coal in coke ovens.

Besides fixed carbon and volatile matter there are a number of waste materials in coal. The moisture content of coal varies from as little as less than 1 percent in anthracite to more than 40 percent in lignite. The ash in coals comes from foreign matter in the original plant material or from sediments washed into swamps as the peat was formed. The ash content in different coals varies from less than 1 percent to as much as 55 percent. Ash and water are diluting substances, so they are an economic waste factor in storage, handling, transportation, and consumption.

Ranks of Coal. Rank indicates the differences in the progressive evolution of coal from lignite to anthracite. The alteration is marked by a decrease of volatile matter and an increase in fixed carbon from the low- to high-rank coals. This change is a function of weight of original overburden, age, and local deformation. It does not refer to grade or quality, which is primarily a function of the amount of ash and sulfur in the coal.

The standard classification of coal by rank in use in the United States was established by the American Society for Testing and Materials[2] (Fig. 3 and Table 2). The basic scheme of classification is according to fixed carbon and heat efficiency (expressed in Btu's) calculated on a mineral-matter-free basis. The higher-rank coals are classified according to fixed carbon on a dry basis and the lower-rank coals according to Btu's on a moist basis. Agglomerating and slacking indices are used to differentiate between certain adjacent groups.

Lignite, frequently called brown coal, is the lowest rank. It is characterized by a moisture content of 30 to 43 percent and a fixed-carbon content of 30 to 55 percent. The structure is fibrous and woody. It disintegrates readily on exposure and must be stored carefully to prevent spontaneous combustion.

Sub-bituminous coal is black and may be dull or lustrous, but it still retains the woody appearance of lignite. Its moisture content also may be high, ranging from 2 to 40 percent. Fixed carbon varies from 35 to 60 percent. On weathering it slacks and has a tendency toward spontaneous combustion. Sub-bituminous coal has a fairly high heat value and is consumed locally in the United States.

Bituminous coal is the most important industrial and heating coal in the world. It may be dull black to highly lustrous. The moisture content is low, and the fixed-carbon content varies between 48 and 86 percent. This coal stores well and burns with a yellow flame, fre-

[1] Wilfred Francis, *Coal: Its Formation and Composition,* London, 1961, Chapters 2, 4, and 5.

[2] *Classification of Coal by Rank,* ASTM Standards, Part 8, American Society for Testing and Materials, Philadelphia, Pennsylvania, 1961, pp. 1227–1232.

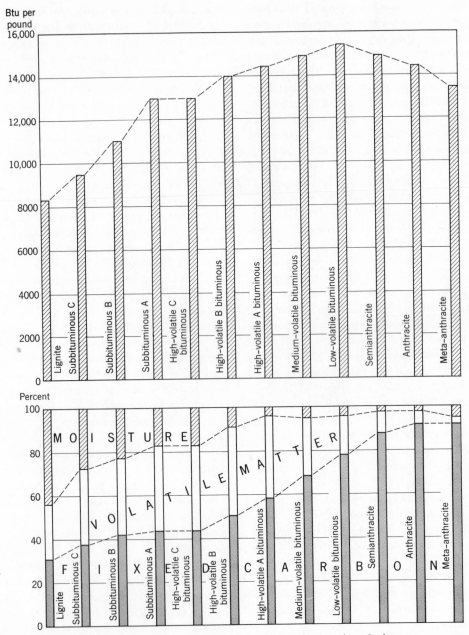

Fig. 3 Heat efficiency and the composition of different types of coal. (American Society for Testing and Materials.)

Table 2. Classification of Coals by Rank (FC=Fixed Carbon, VM=Volatile Matter, Btu=British Thermal Units)

Class	Group	Limits of Fixed Carbon or Btu Mineral-Matter-Free Basis	Requisite Physical Properties
I. Anthracite	1. Meta-anthracite	Dry FC, 98 percent or more (dry VM, 2 percent or less)	
	2. Anthracite	Dry FC, 92 percent or more and less than 98 percent (dry VM, 8 percent or less and more than 2 percent)	
	3. Semianthracite	Dry FC, 86 percent or more and less than 92 percent (dry VM, 14 percent or less and more than 8 percent)	Nonagglomerating
II. Bituminous	1. Low volatile bituminous coal	Dry FC, 78 percent or more and less than 86 percent (dry VM, 22 percent or less and more than 14 percent)	
	2. Medium volatile bituminous coal	Dry FC, 69 percent or more and less than 78 percent (dry VM, 31 percent or less and more than 22 percent)	
	3. High volatile A bituminous coal	Dry FC, less than 69 percent (dry VM, more than 31 percent); and moist Btu, 14,000 or more	
	4. High volatile B bituminous coal	Moist Btu, 13,000 or more and less than 14,000	
	5. High volatile C bituminous coal	Moist Btu, 11,000 or more and less than 13,000	Either agglomerating or nonweathering
III. Sub-bituminous	1. Sub-bituminous A coal	Moist Btu, 11,000 or more and less than 13,000	Both weathering and nonagglomerating
	2. Sub-bituminous B coal	Moist Btu, 9500 or more and less than 11,000	
	3. Sub-bituminous C coal	Moist Btu, 8300 or more and less than 9500	
IV. Lignitic	1. Lignite	Moist Btu, less than 8300	Consolidated
	2. Brown coal	Moist Btu, less than 8300	Unconsolidated

[Source: *Classification of Coals by Rank*, ASTM Standards, Part 8, American Society for Testing and Materials, Philadelphia, Pennsylvania.]

quently giving off a penetrating odor. There are many varieties of bituminous coal distinguished by high, medium, and low volatile matter.

Semianthracite differs from anthracite only in that it is more friable. It has a fixed-carbon content of 86 to 92 percent and is thus a smokeless fuel with a high heat value, is free from soot, and burns slowly, making an excellent domestic fuel when used with a stoker system.

Anthracite is a hard dense coal with the highest fixed carbon and lowest hydrocarbon content of all coals. It is characterized by a jet black color, freedom from ash and moisture, excellent coherence, and burns with a short blue flame. It was consumed principally as a domestic fuel because of its smokelessness and steadiness in burning.

Coal Reserves of the United States. The nation's coal reserves are extensive but are unevenly distributed and highly variable in quality and accessibility. The remaining reserves of coal in the United States, computed by the United States Geological Survey as of January 1, 1967, are placed at 3,197,097,000,000 tons of bituminous, sub-bituminous, and lignite. This is in addition to 12,969,000,000 tons of anthracite. Of this amount about 2,872,961,000,000 tons lie between 0 and 3000 feet beneath the surface, and an additional 337,105,000 tons are known to lie between 3000 and 6000 feet. At present there is no coal mine in the United States as deep as 3000 feet.

The estimates of reserves are based on a combination of factors. Primary sources include detailed geologic maps showing the outcrops and correlations of the individual coal beds and geologic reports giving detailed measurements of the coal, augmented locally by data from exploratory and development drilling and from operating mines. Because of the tremendous reserves, many coal-bearing areas in the United States have not been mapped geologically. As a result many areas which are known to have coal have been omitted from the estimates because of lack of information.

In estimating reserves the minimum thickness of coal that could be mined commercially is placed at 14 inches for bituminous and anthracite, and 30 inches for sub-bituminous and lignite. All coals with an ash content up to 30 percent are included. The average specific gravity of anthracite was estimated at 1.47, bituminous coal 1.32, subbituminous coal 1.30, and lignite 1.29, and tonnages were computed on this basis.

If it is assumed that 50 percent of the coal can be recovered—and that is quite a low estimate since 57 percent is presently recoverable —the total mineable reserve would be 1,429,996,000,000 tons. The following illustrations give the magnitude of the United States coal reserves. The reserves would fill a train of 45-foot-long, 70-ton-capacity freight cars that would circle the world 905 times. If that train traveled at an average speed of 50 miles an hour, you would have to wait more than 2400 years at a grade crossing for it to pass. Stated in other terms, if all the reserves were gathered into a stack of coal 3 feet square, it would reach 601,850,000 miles high, or 6.5 times the distance from the earth to the sun. There can be no doubt that reserves of coal will last many generations under any conceivable rate of production.

Regions of Production. The coal areas, located in thirty-six coal-bearing states, have been classified into seven major provinces: Eastern, Interior, Gulf, Northern Great Plains, Rocky Mountain, and Alaskan (Fig. 4). In Canada there are two leading provinces: Atlantic and Prairie.

EASTERN PROVINCE. The Eastern Province, containing the Atlantic coast, the Anthracite, and the large Appalachian region, is the oldest mining area in the United States. The Atlantic coastal region in Virginia and North Carolina is of little importance. The Anthracite region of northeastern Pennsylvania is the most important in the country, producing 98

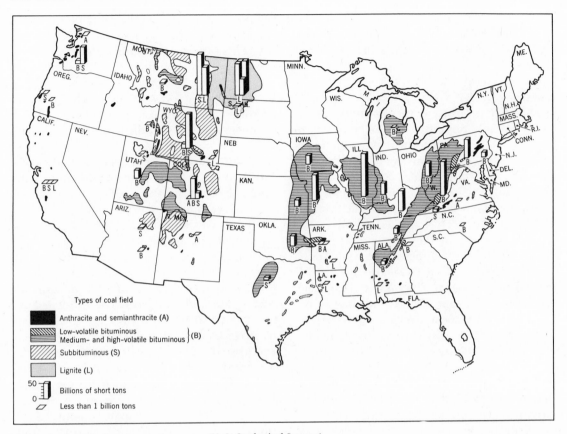

Fig. 4 Coal producing areas and reserves. (U. S. Geological Survey.)

percent of our anthracite and containing 80 percent of our reserves.

The Appalachian region is one of the largest areas of high-grade bituminous coal in the world. An area of approximately 50,000 square miles is underlain with coal. In 1966, the area produced 381,524,000 tons of coal, or 71 percent of the national total. West Virginia, with an output of 149,681,000 tons of coal in 1966, has led the nation in coal production since 1928, followed by Pennsylvania and eastern Kentucky.

The region has a large number of coal seams. Of these the famous Pittsburgh coal seam of western Pennsylvania, eastern Ohio, and northern West Virginia is one of the world's largest single deposits of high-volatile bituminous coal. It supplied the coal for the beehive ovens of Connellsville which were the primary source of coke in the early development of the iron and steel industry of the Pittsburgh region.

INTERIOR PROVINCE. This province consists of four regions: Eastern, Western, Northern, and Southern. The coal of the Interior Province is largely bituminous, but the quality is not as good as in the Appalachian fields. The coal of the Eastern region, Illinois, Indiana, and western Kentucky, has been mined most extensively, and has been a leading source of fuel and power for the industrial development of the Central Lowlands. In 1966, the Eastern region produced 123,087,000 tons of coal, or 23 percent of the nation's total. Illinois, with

77 percent of its area underlain by coal with 239,756,000,000 tons of reserves, has the greatest reserves of bituminous coal in the United States. Due to good-quality coal and large regional markets, Illinois is the fourth largest producing state.

The coal deposits of the Western region, which extends from Iowa to Oklahoma, are large but are mostly low-rank bituminous which burns with considerable soot and smoke. It has little coking value, but it does have a high heat content and is therefore used locally for domestic heating and as a steam coal for industry. Only limited mining activity is carried on in the Northern region of Michigan and the Southern region of Texas.

GULF PROVINCE. The Gulf Province, which extends from southern Arkansas and northern Louisiana to southern Texas, has mostly lignite. The lignite is in a region of young, undisturbed rocks so that the coal has remained of low rank. The lignite is of highest quality in northern Texas and southern Arkansas, but deposits remain essentially unexploited. Because the coal has a high volatile content it has a potential use in coal hydrogenation.

NORTHERN GREAT PLAINS PROVINCE. This province includes all the coals of the Great Plains of the United States and extends into the Prairie Provinces of Canada. This province has tremendous quantities of lignite and sub-bituminous coal. Montana and Wyoming, ranking first and third, respectively, in reserves of sub-bituminous coal, have about 56 percent of the United States total of proved reserves of 428 billion tons. North Dakota has 350 billion tons of proved reserves of lignite of the total United States reserves of 448 billion tons. Although the Northern Great Plains states possess huge quantities of coal, these reserves are largely of low-rank coals with only about two-thirds of the heating value of bituminous, and the coals are essentially noncoking. The province produces less than 1.5 percent of the national total.

ROCKY MOUNTAIN PROVINCE. This area is composed of a large number of noncontiguous fields extending from Montana to New Mexico. The province contains all ranks of coal from lignite to anthracite. The coal was formed in great basins, and the rank depends largely on crustal disturbances. The province produces less than 2.5 percent of national production because of the small regional market.

PACIFIC PROVINCE. The coal of the Pacific Province occurs largely in Washington, with minor deposits in Oregon and California. Although Washington has a substantial reserve of bituminous and sub-bituminous coal, mining is limited because the rocks are folded and faulted in many places and subsequently were covered by thick deposits of glacial drift.

ALASKAN PROVINCE. The coal deposits of Alaska are widely distributed. Estimated reserves total 265 billion tons, of which about 85 percent are sub-bituminous. At the present time two fields are under exploitation. The Matanuska Valley coal field is a good grade bituminous. The Nenana field (or Healy River field) in the interior southwest of Fairbanks produces a high-grade lignite. Two-thirds of the state's production comes from the Nenana field. Strip mining produces between 85 and 90 percent of the Alaskan coal. The scattered deposits, lack of accessibility, complex geologic conditions, and small local markets have handicapped development.

The nation's best coals are being depleted at a rapid rate. The famous Pittsburgh coal bed has an estimated life of less than 100 years. The reserves in beds thicker than 42 inches in the fields of southern West Virginia have an estimated life of less than 75 years at present extractive rates.

ATLANTIC PROVINCE. The coal fields of the Atlantic Province are located in Nova Scotia and New Brunswick. The coal is bituminous, and some is of excellent metallurgical coking quality. This area, with approximately 75 percent of the Canadian bituminous reserves, has an output of about 5,000,000 tons annually.

Although the number of coal miners is only about 5000, the mining industry forms the basis for the economy of several important urban centers. On Cape Breton Island a coal field extends for about 30 miles along the shore of the Atlantic Ocean, and a large portion of the coal mined comes from submarine workings which lie as far as 2½ miles off shore. The total reserves of the area are estimated at more than 10,000,000,000 tons.

The Canadian coal industry has experienced difficulties in recent years. The weak competitive position is caused by several factors, but is mainly due to high production costs because of low productivity. Mining is entirely underground, and labor costs are high. The coal deposits are great distances from the industrial markets so that high costs of moving coal long distances from Nova Scotia and New Brunswick to the industrial centers of Ontario and Quebec have retarded development. Mechanization of production, underground and surface coal preparation, and efforts to control quality through coal sampling and analyses have aided the industry to supply higher-quality coals at reduced costs.

The federal and provincial governments have aided the industry through research programs. The Dominion Coal Board, established in 1947, advises on all matters relating to production, importation, distribution, and use of coal in Canada. Its research program investigates systems and methods of mining coal, physical and chemical characteristics of coal, the position of coal in relation to other fuels, cost of production and distribution of coal, and the co-ordination of the activities of government departments relating to coal and other carbonaceous deposits.

PRAIRIE PROVINCES. The coal fields of the Prairie Provinces of Canada are an extension of those in the Great Plains of the United States. The coal deposits of Saskatchewan and Manitoba are largely lignite. The coal of Alberta is mostly bituminous, but there are small quantities of sub-bituminous and anthracite. The proved reserves of Alberta are estimated at 48,000,000,000 tons, those of Saskatchewan at about 24,000,000,000 tons, and Manitoba 100,000,000 tons. Alberta is the leading producer with an output of 3,400,000 tons of bituminous annually. Saskatchewan produces about 2,000,000 tons of lignite by stripping operations.

Several small coal fields are also exploited in British Columbia and the Yukon.

Production Trends and Problems of the Coal Industry. Coal in the United States was first mined in the early Colonial period, but the modern coal-mining industry began only about 1820. Although the relative growth was rapid, total output remained small until after the Civil War. In 1840, production was 2,070,000 tons and by 1860 only 14,610,000 tons. Anthracite exceeded the production of bituminous until 1869, and until 1873 the United States imported more coal than it exported.

From 1850 to 1910, with the great industrial expansion of the United States, coal production virtually doubled every 8 or 9 years (Fig. 5). This rate of gain was maintained almost unabated until 1910, but after that there was a tendency toward retardation. From 1890 to 1900, the gain was 91 percent, but from 1910 to 1920 only 36 percent. Production rose to 579,385,000 tons in 1918.

Although there were annual fluctuations in production, the general trend from 1919 to 1938 was downward. World War II once again created tremendous demands for coal. In 1944, a total of 619,576,000 tons of bituminous coal were produced. Production declined temporarily at the close of the war, primarily as a result of prolonged strikes in the industry. However, in 1947, the bituminous production of 630,623,000 tons was an all-time peak, partly due to a large export market. From the 1947 high, production declined to a low of 402,977,000 tons in 1961. Since then production has increased annually to a high of 551,000,000 tons in 1967. The expanding

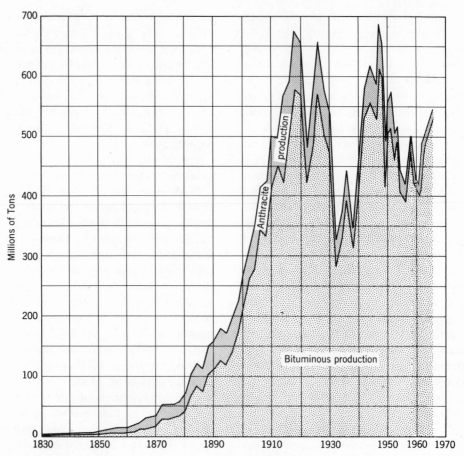

Fig. 5 Coal production of the United States, 1830 to 1966. (U.S. Bureau of Mines.)

economy of the 1960's required coal in greater quantities.

Production trends in the anthracite industry have generally paralleled those of the bituminous industry. Anthracite production reached its peak in 1917 when 99,611,000 tons were produced. Although production declined gradually in the next quarter of a century, the drastic drop from 63,701,000 tons in 1944 to 12,139,000 tons in 1966 has placed this branch of mining in a particularly precarious position. The mining of anthracite is no longer an important aspect of the economy of northeastern Pennsylvania. After a long period of economic depression the economy of the area

has been revitalized by the introduction of a diversified industrial economy.

The number of coal miners in the bituminous and anthracite branches of the industry has declined even more than production. In the bituminous industry the number of workers declined from a high of 704,793 in 1923 to a low of 128,698 in 1964. This was a decline of 576,095, or 81.7 percent. With increased production the number of coal mines increased to about 133,000 in 1967. The number of workers in the anthracite industry has declined from a peak of 165,386 in 1926 to 9282 in 1966. This was a decrease of 156,104 workers, or about 94 percent.

The plight of the coal industry is due to a number of causes. The encroachment of oil and gas is the basic reason for the decline in production of both bituminous and anthracite fuels. Contributing factors include greater efficiency in home heating and conversion to mechanical energy. The decrease in employment is due not so much to a decrease in total coal output but to greater efficiency in mining coal. The mechanization of the underground mine and the growth of surface strip mining have been major factors in increasing productivity. The output of bituminous coal per man per day was 4.28 tons in 1923. At that time 68.3 percent of the coal was cut by machines, 31.7 percent was cut by hand, and underground mechanical loading was virtually unknown. In 1966, 51 percent was cut by machines, 45.8 percent was mined by continuous mining machines, only 3.2 percent was cut by hand and shot from the solid seam, and 91.7 percent was mechanically loaded. In 1966, 33.7 percent of the coal was produced from strip mines compared to 2.1 percent in 1923. In 1965, the average daily output per man in underground mines was 14.00 tons, strip mines 31.98 tons, and in auger mines 45.85 tons.

Principal Uses of Coal. Most of the 45,-000,000 tons of bituminous coal produced monthly in the United States is consumed in the nation's electric power utilities, coke ovens, manufacturing plants, and by retail consumers. The consumption of coal in the electric power utilities has increased from 12 percent of the total in 1945 to 56 percent in 1967. Coal now generates about 53 percent of the nation's electricity and 65 percent of the power produced in plants where steam drives a turbine generator.

The manufacturing industries take about 20 percent and the coke industries about 19 percent of the nation's coal output. Coal used for domestic heating has declined from 25 percent of the total in 1945 to about 15 percent in 1955 and only 3.5 percent in 1967.

This same trend has occurred in coal used by railroads, with a decline from 22 percent of output in 1945 to 7 percent in 1955 to less than 1 percent by 1960. In recent years nearly 10 percent of bituminous coal output has been exported.

COAL CONSERVATION PROBLEMS

Mining Practices and Losses. There are two principal methods of mining coal—underground workings and open pit or stripping. Auger mining, which began about 1952, is still of little importance with 2.9 percent of total production. The percentage of total coal recovered in mining varies to a considerable extent. In individual mines as much as 80 to 90 percent of the coal in the area actually being mined may be recovered. From the total resource point of view, however, recoverability appears to apply to only about 57 percent of the coal in the ground.

A number of causes lead to underground mining losses. Present mining methods, utilizing only the best coals, leave millions of tons of coal in the thinner and impure seams untouched in the ground in a condition that makes future recovery unlikely, even at a markedly higher price. Coal left on the roof and floor, in rooms, in entries, and in panel pillars causes other losses.

Formerly, the greatest loss in mining came from coal left in pillars to support the roof of the mine. Modern methods employing the long-wall or panel system avoid much of the loss, for the coal is mined in retreat and the roof allowed to fall as soon as the coal is recovered. Other wastes involve coal lost under buildings, transportation routes, in boundary pillars, in cemeteries, and around oil and gas wells. Coal may also be wasted in handling and in its preparation. Economic pressure and insufficient margin between the cost of mining and the selling price of coal are other reasons for leaving large areas of the less desirable coal seams unmined. The suspension of mine operations at times of strikes and shutdowns frequently results in great loss of coal, especially on pillar lines. A continuously operated mine will aid materially in the conservation of available coal still left in the ground.

Since the early 1930's strip mining has increased greatly in importance. Coal stripping began before World War I but was relatively unimportant until large power shovels were developed. Before 1926, the largest stripping shovels had a dipper capacity of only 1 to 3 cubic yards. The largest shovels now hold more than 75 cubic yards, and it is possible to dig with them to a depth of 120 feet. The amount of coal mined by stripping has risen rapidly from 1 percent of the total in 1917 to about 33 percent in 1967. The U.S. Geological Survey estimates that the United States has 108 billion tons of coal which can be recovered by strip mining, at a depth not greater than 100 feet. This is 28 times as much coal as strip mining has produced in the nation, and 600 times the amount strip mined in 1967.

The economic advantages of strip mining are many. In 1967, the average surface miner produced more than twice as many tons of coal per day as the subsurface worker. Although investment in stripping machinery is high, the salvage value of the equipment is much greater than that of subsurface equipment. The danger in strip mining operations is minimal. The recovery of coal is from 75 to 95 percent of the original reserve.

The great problem of strip mining is the restoration of the land after the power shovels have worked to remove the coal. The great furrows of rocky materials, commonly called spoil banks, have often become major areas of desolation. Most states and many local communities have passed legislation requiring that the land be leveled and improved. However, restoration to the original contour is now questioned. Usually the cost of such oper-

ations is prohibitive. The leveling processes often pack the soil so firmly that seedling trees do not survive. In many situations it has been found that the best restoration is the planting of trees on the original spoil banks. In many mines the last open cut can be made into small lakes with excellent recreational possibilities. In hill country the furrows, which are usually on the contour, hold the runoff water effectively and are thus highly beneficial to the growth of trees. Excellent timber stands have been developed in Illinois, Ohio, and Pennsylvania on the banks. In some instances the income from the land is greater after such treatment than it was before the stripping operations. However, no two spoil bank areas can be subjected to the same treatment. Some spoil banks have high lime content and can support various grasses and deciduous trees. Pasture and forage use is usually limited because the strip slopes prevent cultivation. Other banks are highly acid and will support only conifer plantings at best. Nevertheless, because of its many advantages, strip mining will remain until the surface deposits are exhausted.

Production of Coke. The processing of coal into coke resulted in tremendous losses when the beehive oven was employed. With the introduction of the by-product coke oven in the early 1900's these losses have been largely eliminated. A ton of bituminous coal coked in a beehive oven will yield about 1300 pounds of metallurgical coke, whereas the same amount of coal, coked in a by-product oven, will yield 1500 pounds of coke as well as 22 pounds of ammonium sulfate, 9 gallons of tar, 2.5 gallons of light motor oil, and 10,000 cubic feet of gas. In 1905, less than 10 percent of the coke was produced in by-product ovens. In 1966, of 95,892,000 tons of coal consumed in the production of coke, 93,523,000 tons of coal were converted in by-product ovens.

Conservation in Consumption. There has been a remarkable gain in efficiency of coal utilization by the principal consumers. This substantial reduction in consumption of coal per unit of work is an important form of conservation, for it increases the potential usefulness of our coal resources. These improvements have been due largely to the following advancements: (1) growth of knowledge of the composition and properties of coal; (2) improvement of the physical processing of coal for specific uses; (3) introduction of economies in conversion of coal to heat energy; (4) introduction of economies in conversion of coal to mechanical energy; and (5) reduction of energy required for a given purpose.

Research and Development in the Coal Industry. Coal is a highly complex substance which is the source, in part, of thousands of products from aspirin to dyes. Of the coal laboratories, Bituminous Coal Research, Inc., a National Coal Association affiliate, is in the forefront of the industry's effort to develop new products. Other agencies working on improving the utilization of coal include the United States Geological Survey, the Bureau of Mines, and the American Society for Testing and Materials.

The rapid development of pilot plants, process development units, and prototype installations gives evidence of the expanding utilization of coal. A pilot plant at Cresap, West Virginia, developed by the Consolidated Coal Company under a $20,000,000 contract with the Department of Interior's Office of Coal Research, processes 20 to 25 tons of coal daily, producing 50 to 75 barrels of synthetic petroleum. Other pilot plants are producing high-quality building bricks made mostly of coal ash, and they are also proving that coal is an effective, low-cost filter in municipal sewage treatment. A process development unit of the Bituminous Coal Research laboratories has a gas generator research and development unit that has a coal-to-gas reactor with a capacity of 100 pounds of coal an hour. The goal is to convert coal to synthetic or raw gas that can easily be upgraded without further compression to pipe line gas.

Physical Processing of Coals for Specific Uses. Coal as it comes from the mines usually has impurities and is not the best size for efficient utilization. Nearly all the anthracite and nearly two-thirds of the bituminous in 1966 was sized and cleaned before it was marketed. Mechanical cleaning means cleaning raw coal with mechanical devices that separate out the impurities, usually by differences in specific gravity. In 1966, from the 435,089,000 tons of raw coal cleaned, there were only 340,625,000 tons of cleaned coal. Refuse amounted to 94,-414,000 tons, or about 21 percent of the total.

The washing of coal to reduce its ash and sulfur content developed about 1920. The keen competition with other fuels and the introduction of mechanical methods of mining have encouraged this development. The percentage of coal washed has increased from 5.3 percent in 1927 to nearly two-thirds in 1966. The cleaning of coal is a conservation measure, for it permits the crushing of lumps of impure coal and the recovery of a considerable portion of the coal.

After the coal is washed, the problem of removing surface moisture is critical. Removing the moisture is necessary in order to avoid freezing difficulties and to facilitate handling the coal during shipment and transfer to the firebox; to reduce the heat wasted in evaporation of surface moisture of the coal; to decrease transportation costs; to improve the coal so that it may be used for specific purposes, such as producing coke and briquets; and to facilitate dry cleaning. The three principal methods of removing surface moisture from coal are gravity drainage, mechanical dewatering, and thermal drying. Thermal drying is generally used on coals that cannot be easily dried by gravity drainage or mechanical means. Thermal drying became important in the late 1950's, and by 1966 thermally dried bituminous coal and lignite amounted to 70,619,000 tons, or about 13 percent of total production in the United States.

Conversion of Coal to Heat Energy. Most modern home furnaces are inefficient producers of heat energy. Efficiency tests by the Battelle Memorial Institute in Columbus, Ohio, have revealed wide variations in effective utilization, summarized as follows: 45 percent efficiency for hand-fired bituminous, 55 percent for stoker-fired bituminous, 50 percent for hand-fired semibituminous, 70 to 75 percent for natural gas, and 60 to 70 percent for oil. The greatest losses are due to escape of heat in dry flue gases, ranging from one-third to two-thirds of the total. Other losses are from moisture, carbon monoxide gas, and unconsumed carbon in the ash.

Most of the present losses can be prevented by improving firing methods. Stoker firing gives higher efficiency and eliminates a large percentage of smoke. In hand firing, efficiencies depend to a large extent on the personal factor. The public needs to be educated in the handling of coal furnaces. The schools of the nation can contribute greatly to the saving of coal by educating the coming generations in the most economical and efficient manner of using the particular coal available in the different parts of the country. Maximum efficiency, as great as 90 to 92 percent, can be attained by proper firing of pulverized coal in stokers.

Conversion of Coal to Mechanical Energy. Efficiency when coal is converted to mechanical energy has been increasing steadily, but still needs improvement. By 1920, the most efficient steam engines consumed a little more than a pound of coal per horsepower hour, and by 1967, this figure had been reduced about 50 percent. The electric-utility power plants have made significant gains in fuel efficiency. From an average in 1902 of 6.4 pounds of coal per kilowatt hour, the level was reduced to 1.30 pounds in 1942 and 0.87 pounds in 1966. The quantity of coking coal consumed per ton of pig iron was reduced

from 3194 pounds in 1918 to about 1700 pounds in 1967, a decrease of over 45 percent.

Coal-burning steam turbine plants have been able to attain an efficiency of only 31 percent, and mercury-vapor plants have a maximum efficiency of 38 percent. Industrial boilers have an efficiency of between 60 and 65 percent. One of the great needs is for more extensive and better utilization of insulation materials to eliminate these wastes.

Air Pollution and Coal Utilization. Because air pollution is becoming a major problem in many areas, the sulfur content of coal becomes increasingly important. In many urban areas sulfur removal from either the fuel or the stack gases is becoming mandatory at various levels of concentration. Because removal is costly a strong research program is now under way to study the problem. A pilot plant at Seward, Pennsylvania, sponsored by Bituminous Coal Research and twelve electric utility companies, is studying the removal of pyritic sulfur from coal during pulverization and before combustion. Laboratory tests reveal that 60 to 70 percent of the total sulfur can be removed by existing coal-cleaning processes. In 1966, the National Coal Association and the Electric Research Council established a multi-million-dollar research program for control of sulfur pollution. Current research on control of sulfur in stacks stresses the principle of injecting limestones and dolomites into combustion gases to combine with sulfur oxides and remove them from the gas stream. In order to minimize the problem of air pollution coals that have a low sulfur content or have a high cleaning potential are now sought. In a recent study by the U.S. Public Health Service's National Center for Air Pollution Control of thirty samples of coal from Ohio, Pennsylvania, and West Virginia, only one sample showed pyrite reduction of less than 70 percent and the bulk promised reduction of 80 to more than 90 percent (see Chapter 6).

Water Pollution and Coal Mining. Water pollution control from mine waters has been a

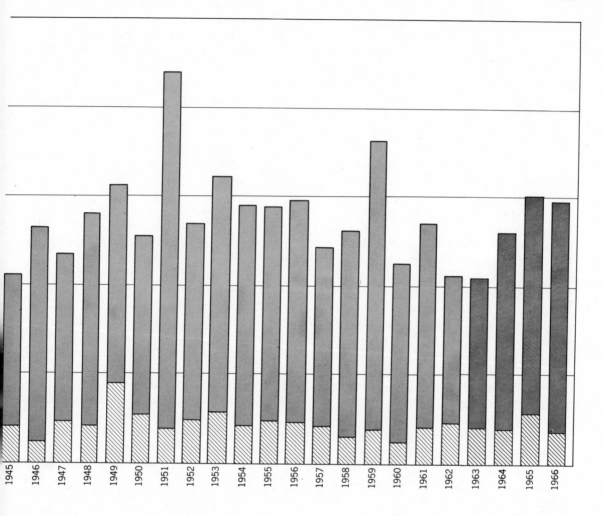

geophysical methods in 1915. The main purpose of geophysical exploration is to determine subsurface geology in likely petroliferous areas.[4] One of the earliest procedures was the refraction seismic method developed by German scientists. In this method, scientific use is made of the fact that seismic or earth waves, caused by a charge of explosive detonated at or near the surface, will travel with greater speed through dense rocks than through the surface formations between the starting and recording device. The refraction method was successful in locating a large number of salt domes on the Gulf coast.

American scientists developed the now widely used reflection seismic method. In the reflection method the depth and configuration or deeply buried beds are determined from records of waves that originate at the blast and are reflected back to the surface, similar to the

[4] Harrison T. Brundage, "Gas and Oil Finding Methods Must Depict Geology Clearly," *World Oil,* Vol. 166, February 15, 1968, pp. 85–92.

echoes that result from reflection of sound waves. The results have been phenomenal, and the method is used today in practically all oil-producing countries. Seismic mapping is the most precise of geophysical methods, and applies to the widest variety of geological conditions.

The gravitational method of exploring for oil, which by means of a torsion balance measures local variations in the intensity of the earth's gravitational field, was introduced in the early 1920's. It is based on the principle that as the density of the rock varies, so does the gravitational attraction at the surface. Thus the pull at the surface of a thick limestone bed in an anticlinal structure is greater over the crest than where the limestone is more deeply buried. Gravitational changes are very small so that the instruments must be of great sensitivity. The gravimeter, however, has the advantage of being small, weighing as little as 5 pounds. It can also be used under water. This instrument has been particularly helpful in discovering salt domes and for reconnaissance surveys.

An indication of subsurface structures can also be obtained by measurement of changes in the intensity and directions of the earth's magnetic field brought about by certain mineral deposits as a result of the conductivity or resistivity, and other electrical properties of rocks constituting the earth's crust. The method is useful in determining depths of the magnetic igneous basin and thus assists in the mapping of sedimentary basins. The most significant advance in magnetic surveying was the development of the airborne magnetometer. This instrument is normally towed behind the aircraft, and recordings are made of the total magnetic field along a series of grid traverses. The magnetometer is principally used for reconnaissance surveys.

Another important exploration method is geophysical borehole logging. This procedure entails making measurements at various levels in a well by means of such techniques as electrical resistivity, radioactivity, and acoustic logging. The use of electrical logging is based on the fact that the resistivity of a rock layer is a function of its fluid content. Oil-filled sand has a very high sensitivity. The natural radioactive properties of many oil-bearing rocks have made it possible to use nuclear radiation detectors in the borehole to aid in oil exploration. Acoustic logging uses electric pulses instead of explosives as in seismic work to detect differences in formation porosities. Finally, density can be logged with a new technique utilizing radioactivity. The rock formation is bombarded with gamma rays. The degree to which the radiation is absorbed is a function of the density of the rock.

Test well sampling is another important method used in oil exploration. Data secured from various depths of the borehole are of considerable value in exploratory work. The samples can be cores or chips taken from the hole. The objective is to identify various strata and compare them with standard stratigraphic sequences of the sedimentary basin. The analysis is both physical and chemical.

Geochemical mapping has become an important tool in petroleum exploration. This technique is used for mapping the chemical composition of rocks and their fluid contents. Such maps may show the surface distribution of the hydrocarbons, the hydrocarbon waxes, or the bacteria that utilize hydrocarbons. If there are concentrations of these at the surface, the inference is that there is a leaking oil or gas pool below. Hydrocarbon concentration maps, sometimes called soil analysis maps, are actually maps of micro-seepages. A serious problem in producing these maps is the extremely low hydrocarbon content of normal rocks, which is usually measured in parts per million or parts per billion. Other geochemical maps may be produced from data supplied by cores and drill cuttings taken from wells. Some oil pools show high hydrocarbon content in the shales overlying the reservoir rock, and discoveries of oil pools have resulted from encountering shales with high hydrocarbon values.

The use of aerial photographs is advancing rapidly in oil exploration for interpretation of structural features such as anticlines, faults, and other features. Plane-table mapping still is of value, but aerial photographs present a direct view of the terrain and make it possible to establish easily the exact position of objects. Aerial maps can be made with a contour interval of approximately 1 foot; they are equal in accuracy to transit and plane-table surveys.

Computers have become an important tool in both geophysical and geological applications to petroleum exploration. As a result of both past and present activities most explored regions have a vast amount of data accumulated. One of the principal uses of the computer is rapid retrieval of these data. A specific type of data may often be plotted directly on maps, saving the geologist endless hours in assembling and recording information. The use of the computer is in an initial stage so that many advancements can be expected in the future.

RESULTS OF PLANNED EXPLORATION. The development of geophysical and other methods of surveying has greatly increased the possibilities of discovering oil. The problem of finding additional oil for our expanding market demands an active exploration program. The industry is now spending several million dollars a year in research to develop new techniques and improve old ones.[5] Some of the current studies involve direct oil findings by geophysical and geochemical methods, application of the seismic method, the origin of petroleum, and intensive studies of subsurface data collected from old and new wells.

Drilling. TREND TOWARD DEEPER DRILLING. Drilling advancements, which have permitted the penetration of all types of formations at ever-increasing depths, have been significant factors in extending the life of the petroleum industry.[6] The pioneer wells were exceedingly shallow, many not exceeding several hundred feet. Gradually the depth increased. By 1890, the deepest well was over 5000 feet, and by 1925 it was nearly 8000 feet. In 1938, a test well in California reached a depth of 15,004 feet, and in 1958 a new record was established with a well 25,340 feet deep in west Texas. The deepest producing well drilled in 1965 is 22,032 feet, also located in west Texas.[7]

Deeper drilling has been responsible for the discovery of new sands underlying oil-producing fields in which the existence of such sands, if known, was previously considered beyond the limit of drilling. It is estimated that the ultimate recovery from reservoirs already discovered at 5000 feet or more in depth will be in excess of 12,000,000,000 barrels, or about 10 percent of the total ultimate recovery from fields discovered up to 1968.

IMPROVEMENTS IN EQUIPMENT. The outstanding change in drilling technology, directly responsible for reaching greater depths, was the shift from the cable tool method to the rotary method. Greater speed is an important advancement of the rotary drill. It is not uncommon for a modern rotary rig to drill as much as 1000 feet of soft formation in 1 day. As a result of the development of "hard-rock" bits and hard-surface alloys, the rotary system has been adapted to practically all formations.

The success of the rotary system has been due to scientific control of the circulating mud fluid and the ability to drill a hole of uniform size. The mud coats the walls of the hole, so that the water sands are sealed without using numerous strings of steel casing. Thus in rotary drilling a hole of uniform

---

[5] Harrison T. Brundage, "Modern Exploration Methods and Field Applications," *World Oil*, Vol. 158, February 15, 1964, pp. 109–131.

[6] Jerry C. Funderburk, "Drilling Improvements," *World Oil*, Vol. 166, February 15, 1968, pp. 77–80.

[7] "Deep Drilling" *World Oil*, Vol. 166, May 1968, pp. 58–84.

size can be maintained to any depth, whereas with cable tools the hole gets progressively smaller, eventually leading to "running out of hole," a condition that prohibits further drilling.

Other major advancements in drilling include improvements in cements and cementing techniques and development of methods to control high subsurface pressures and temperatures. The application of directional drilling has made it possible to develop offshore fields, such as those in the Gulf of Mexico and along the California coast, where the derricks are on the shore and the oil reservoirs underlie beach resorts or deep water. There has also been significant advances in the floating rigs so that offshore deposits can be drilled.

There has been a general improvement in the design, strength, and power of drilling equipment. With increased depth the trend has been to heavier rigs. The cable tool derrick has increased in height from 64 to 122 feet, and rotary derricks vary from 122 to 178 feet. Efficient gas-pressure control equipment has been invented which permits drilling in high-pressure areas. The development of these drilling techniques has added thousands of square miles of prospective oil area and has added substantially to our crude oil reserves.

Petroleum Production. The techniques of producing oil from wells have been revolutionized. A scientific analysis of traditional methods has indicated many desirable modifications, for the life of an oil field depends to a large extent on its method of development. Improvement in well spacing, efficiency of reservoir operations, increased importance of production engineering, and secondary recovery methods have enabled constantly larger proportions of the oil and gas in the underground reservoir to be recovered.

Reservoir Management. Oil is found in a variety of reservoir conditions. Consequently production techniques must be adapted to specific reservoir conditions. Among the important variables in a reservoir are (1) the

chemical and physical properties of the fluids and gases in the reservoir, (2) the porosity of the formation, (3) the permeability of the formation, (4) the reservoir pressure, (5) formation temperatures, (6) presence of connate water, (7) presence or absence of a "water drive" or "gas cap," and (8) degree of saturation of the reservoir rock with oil, gas, and water.[8]

Oil is produced by penetrating the impermeable cap of the reservoir and creating a lower pressure in the well bore than in the formation. Efficient oil recovery involves utilizing the natural driving forces in the reservoir initially, but as these are depleted artificial drives become essential. Oil production is thus a displacement process.

Reservoir management entails the control of the three basic "drives": a dissolved-gas drive, a gas-cap drive, and a water drive. A dissolved-gas drive occurs when the gas is dissolved in the oil. The gas-cap drive develops when a cap of gas occurs on top of the oil in place. The water drive is similar to the gas-cap drive except that water is the displacement agent. In most reservoirs a combination of drives is present. In order to secure maximum production optimum pressure maintenance is a necessity.

Unitized Development. It is universally recognized by engineers that the most efficient way to develop a reservoir is as a single producing unit. Because oil moves readily throughout active reservoirs, it is the reservoir that becomes the basic unit of production rather than the well. Because the long-established "rule of capture" in oil and gas regions gives the owner of an oil well the right to produce all oil that flows into a well, efficient operation of a pool cannot be secured unless a method is developed whereby individual producers can pursue common objectives and secure resultant economic benefits.

[8] Wallace F. Lovejoy and Paul T. Homan, *Economic Aspects of Oil Conservation Regulation*, Washington, D.C., 1967, p. 60.

In the past the fact was largely ignored that oil and gas pools are single units and to secure maximum production they should be developed and operated without reference to surface property lines. In hundreds of our oil fields thousands of needless wells have been drilled because of the competitive character of the American oil industry. The greatest disadvantage of uncontrolled drilling is maximum production within a short period of time with resultant loss of the reservoir pressure and consequently a low ultimate recovery of the oil.

No general rule of well spacing has been devised, for each pool must be considered separately.[9] The wells should be so spaced that the most efficient drainage is secured. Besides this major factor, the interests of the small-tract owner, the property rights of tract owners, and the investment costs of development must be considered as well as economic factors which influence the desired rate of production.[10] The problem of well spacing is directly related to regulatory practices, where the conflicting interests of the industry are focused. In recent years there has been a tendency toward wider well spacing. During the 1940's, the federal government required a spacing of one well to 40 acres. At present there is a tendency toward a spacing of up to 600 acres per well.

Secondary Recovery. By primary production methods as much as 50 to 90 percent of the original oil remains in the oil sand when the wells are abandoned. As a result processes have been developed by which a greater recovery of oil can be obtained after the free flow has ceased and pumping is no longer profitable. Secondary recovery practices are growing in importance, and the application of these techniques has been the most significant development in oil recovery technology in recent years. Consequently, millions of barrels of additional oil have been added to our reserves.

Secondary recovery projects are designed to augment the natural forces of the reservoirs and thus increase the total recoverable reserves. When the natural reservoir pressures are exhausted they must be artificially created by either a water or gas drive.[11] As a result of pressure differences the water or gas invades the oil-saturated portion of the reservoir, pushing the oil ahead of the drive into a producing well. A natural water drive normally requires vast quantities of water, although water produced with oil can be reinjected. Recovery efficiency, as a rule, is considerably higher for water drives than for gas-cap or dissolved-gas drives. Recovery as high as 80 to 90 percent of the oil in place has been indicated.

Secondary recovery is now practiced in all oil-producing states and Canada. In northwestern Pennsylvania production on certain leases has been increased more than 1000 percent by water drives. In the Bartlesville field of Oklahoma the original reservoir pressures yielded a total of 4000 to 6000 barrels per acre over a period of 20 years. With the introduction of a gas drive an additional output of 1000 to 1500 barrels per acre has been recovered for a period of more than 10 years. In Texas in 1968, there were approximately 3000 secondary recovery projects of which about three-quarters used water, one-fifth gas, and the remaining water and gas as the type of injection fluid. New secondary recovery projects are being added in Texas at the rate of more than 300 annually. Secondary recovery projects now account for about one-third of Texas crude oil production. These projects

[9] J. W. McKie and S. L. McDonald, "Petroleum Conservation in Theory and Practice," *Quarterly Journal of Economics,* Vol. 76, February 1962, pp. 98–121.

[10] M. A. Adelman, "Trends in Cost of Finding and Developing Oil and Gas in the United States," in *Essays in Petroleum Economics,* Colorado School of Mines, Golden, Colorado, 1967, pp. 54–91.

[11] A. G. Ostroff, *Introduction to Oilfield Water Technology,* New York, 1965, Chapter 1.

have increased the estimated reserves by 20 percent, or approximately 3,000,000,000 barrels.

Tertiary Recovery. After the application of primary and secondary processes most oil fields still contain large quantities of oil that is not recoverable by these methods. For example, according to the Interstate Oil Compact Commission, only 26.5 percent of the original oil in California can be recovered by primary and conventional secondary recovery methods. As a consequence tertiary recovery techniques are essential for the future of the industry. One of the most promising of the new tertiary recovery methods is that of using in-situ combustion, commonly known as fireflooding. The basic principle of this process is to heat the oil sufficiently to decrease the viscosity so that it can, under pressure, be moved to a producing well. This process is particularly important in regions of heavy oil. It is estimated that fireflooding could add 4,-100,000,000 barrels to the recoverable reserves of California. Known results indicate that fireflood production can create certain difficulties, including safety problems. The safety problems include disposal of toxic, explosive gases resulting from the combustion process; the handling of high-pressure air equipment necessary to sustain combustion; the handling of high-voltage electricity if an electrical ignitor is used; and protection against well blowouts caused by high pressures induced by combustion.

Maximum Oil Production Through Conservation Laws. Because the petroleum industry developed under the "law of capture," overproduction, exemplified by the East Texas Field, became so devastating by the 1930's that the individual states recognized that cooperative action was necessary to regulate the industry. Thus, as a consequence of wasteful overproduction and the deterioration of the market, the science of modern petroleum conservation began to crystallize.

Although efforts to control production by proration began in the 1920's, particularly in Oklahoma, action was sporadic until the creation of the Interstate Oil Compact in 1935.[12] This is basically a treaty, sanctioned by Congress, entered into by oil-producing states for the purpose of assisting the various states in the formulation of sound oil and gas conservation programs and for the purpose of public education in the necessity and methods of oil and gas conservation. The Interstate Oil Compact establishes no collective power of enforcement, and membership is entirely voluntary. However, each state, in assuming membership, pledges its efforts to enact and enforce laws, rules, and regulations that may be required to bring about the conservation of oil and gas produced in its own jurisdiction. These regulations are to accomplish within reasonable limits the prevention of: (1) the operation of an oil well with an inefficient gas-oil ratio; (2) the drowning with water of any stratum capable of producing oil and gas; (3) the avoidable escape into the open air or the wasteful burning of gas from a natural gas well; (4) the inefficient, excessive, or improper use of the reservoir energy in producing any well; and (5) the drilling, equipping, locating, spacing, or operation of a well so as to bring about physical waste of oil.

Thirty-one states have become members or associate members of the Compact. Each state appoints one representative to the Commission. Action by the Compact members is for the explicit purpose of preventing waste. The Compact specifically prevents control of production for the purpose of stabilizing or fixing prices. The participation of the federal government is not mentioned in the Compact. All members have enacted conservation laws and have issued rules and regulations under such laws. Because of its dominant position as an oil producer, Texas plays a unique role among the oil-producing states as a vital force

---

[12] *The Compact's Formative Years, 1931–35*, IOOC, Oklahoma City, 1955.

in the conservation movement. The position Texas takes in regulation of production influences all other oil-producing states and even many foreign countries.[13]

Refining. ADVANCES IN REFINING. The technological advances in refining in the twentieth century have also added millions of barrels of oil to our reserves. The greatest advancements have occurred since 1913, beginning with the development of the cracking process, by which heavy hydrocarbon molecules are broken into lighter fractions by the application of comparatively high temperatures and pressures. By this method the amount of gasoline from a barrel of crude oil has been increased from 5 to 18 percent to 38 to 54 percent of the total yield. With the development of catalytic cracking, the yield of gasoline has been increased to 65 percent, and could be increased beyond this figure. In 1965, the average product yield was: gasoline, 45 percent; kerosene, 6 percent; gas oils and distillants, 23 percent; residual fuel oil, 8 percent; and other products, 18 percent.[14]

If it were not for the increased yield of motor fuel made possible by cracking and such later techniques as catalytic polymerization, alkylation, hydrogen reforming, and continuous catalytic cracking and reforming, two or three times more crude oil would be needed to supply the present demands. Besides lengthening the life of petroleum resources, the conversion of the heavy fractions of petroleum to gasoline has tended to retard the extent to which coal has been replaced by oil as an industrial fuel.

Modern refining processes not only increase the quantity of gasoline but also its quality. With thermal cracking, gasoline as high as 80 octane could be obtained. Then through auxiliary processes and catalytic cracking, high-oc-

tane ratings have evolved. Polymerization, the first of the auxiliary catalytic processes developed in 1934, yields gasoline of about 90 octane. Alkylation, another catalytic process based on refinery gases, made possible the production of 100-octane gasoline. Catalytic cracking, which came into widespread commercial development during World War II, produces gasoline with 88 to 90 octane and gives as high yields as thermal cracking. Even with these processes, refineries would have difficulty in fulfilling the demands for high-octane fuels if it were not for a development called catalytic reforming in which low-octane gasolines are upgraded to gasolines which, on addition of tetraethyl lead, have an octane of 95 to 100.

The conservational effects of these developments are tremendous. Also, because of better fuel, the modern internal combustion engine is more than twelve times as powerful, weighs about one-quarter as much per horsepower, and has more than forty times as great thermal efficiency as those used in 1920. Thus refining technology has increased our reserves and at the same time made available a product of greater efficiency.

Synthetic Liquid Fuels. As the natural petroleum supplies are depleted, substitute liquid fuels can be produced to supplement the declining crude oil reserves. This supply can come from a number of sources, such as (1) alcohols from vegetable matter, (2) conversion of natural gas by the gas synthesis process, (3) liquification of coal or lignite by the hydrogenation process, (4) conversion of water gas from coal by the Fischer–Tropsch synthesis process, and (5) by-product oils and tars from coking coal. Because of the vast quantities of petroleum available in recent years only limited attention has been given to the development of synthetic fuels.

Alcohol, distilled from vegetable matter, has proved satisfactory when blended with motor fuels. At present its production cost is greater than that of gasoline from petroleum,

---

[13] Erich W. Zimmermann, *Conservation in the Production of Petroleum*, New Haven, 1957, p. 142.

[14] William F. Bland and Robert L. Davidson, editors, *Petroleum Processing Handbook*, New York, 1967, pp. 1–6.

but if the price can be lowered, its use may increase greatly.

Natural gas can be converted to liquid hydrocarbon by first changing it to carbon monoxide and hydrogen, which are the raw materials for the gas synthesis process. Small commercial plants have operated in Kansas and Oklahoma for more than a decade. Although gas reserves are fairly large, natural gas is usually considered too valuable as a gas to use it to supplement the petroleum reserves.

In the manufacture of coke and coal gas, 10 to 12 gallons of tar and 3 gallons of light oil are obtained in the high-temperature carbonization of 1 ton of coal, and 20 to 35 gallons of tar are obtained in the low-temperature carbonization of 1 ton of coal. Much of this tar is now used as a liquid fuel at the steel plants. At present, however, this is not a practical method to produce large quantities of liquid fuels, for the yield of oil is too low in relation to the quantity of coal consumed.

Two processes for the direct production of synthetic fuels from coal or lignite have been developed. These are the coal hydrogenation, or Bergius–I. G., process and the gas synthesis, or Fischer–Tropsch, process. Liquid fuel is the primary product of both processes, with combustible gases and waxes as by-products.

In the coal hydrogenation process the large reserves of high-volatile coal of Ohio, Indiana, western Kentucky, and Illinois, and the sub-bituminous and lignite of the Great Plains are potentially of value. Sub-bituminous coal is the only grade that can be used at present until improved processes are developed. One ton of high-volatile bituminous coal will yield from 1.43 to 1.79 barrels of gasoline, 1 ton of sub-bituminous coal will yield approximately 1.11 barrels of gasoline, and 1 ton of lignite will yield 0.8 barrel of gasoline. Coal can be hydrogenated directly to gasoline, but it is possible to produce diesel fuels as well as some grades of lubricating oil and

wax. By conventional high-pressure hydrogenation, a gasoline of 70- to 75-octane rating can be produced in 20 to 25 percent yield.

The gas synthesis, or Fischer–Tropsch, process has a much wider application to greater varieties of raw materials, including coal, coke, lignite, coal gas, natural gas, charcoal, and wood. The yield of gasoline from bituminous coal is about 2.3 barrels per ton and from sub-bituminous about 1.7 barrels. The gasoline from American reserves of coal alone would be approximately several thousand billion barrels. The straight-run gasoline, constituting about 60 percent of the total, would have an octane number of about 50 to 55. Other products include diesel fuels, lubricating oils, and waxes.

Petroleum Consumption. In consuming petroleum and its products, motorists frequently forget that they are using an irreplaceable natural resource. Largely because of the cheapness of cars and motor fuels, the United States has become the world's greatest per capita consumer of petroleum. Motoring within the United States and Canada during 1968 was equivalent to about 25,000,000 trips around the earth. It is commonly known that greater mileage per gallon of gasoline can be obtained if the speed is only moderately fast. Through reasonable reduction of speed it is estimated that 10 percent of the more than 75,000,000,000 gallons of gasoline consumed in 1967 could have been saved.

It is also estimated that another 10 percent could have been saved by eliminating much needless driving, such as short drives in cities and seeking a parking place, and by keeping pleasure riding within reasonable limits. About 15,000,000,000 gallons of motor fuel would be saved for worthwhile projects. It is also common practice for filling station attendants to destroy oil that has motor sludge and dirt in it. This oil has nearly as much fuel value as new oil and should be used in heating plants and incinerators. Most carburetors on American cars are inefficient utilizers of gas-

Fig. 2 Close up of the mixed grass prairie shows that it is made up of a mixture of taller grasses, in this case needle-and-thread and western wheatgrass, with shortgrasses such as blue grama grass forming a dense cover close to the surface of the ground. About twenty-five grass and forb species would be present in a square yard of this prairie. (North Dakota Agricultural Experiment Station.)

lion acres, it still is found on almost 200 million acres of grazing land in the northern and southern Great Plains (Table 1).

The mixed prairie portion of the type lies between the shortgrass on the west and the tall-grass on the east and is characterized by dominants from both. The bluestems and tall needlegrasses are of considerable importance, but its true character is shown by the mixture of grasses of intermediate height, called midgrasses, with the shortgrasses (Fig. 2). Important midgrasses include western wheatgrass (*Agropyron smithii*), needle-and-thread (*Stipa comata*), green needlegrass (*Stipa viridula*), and prairie Junegrass (*Koeleria*). By far the most important shortgrasses are blue grama grass (*Bouteloua gracilis*) and buffalo grass. Associated with these are several short sedges, a number of forbs, and in some places an appreciable to heavy development of shrubby species. In the southern area, blue grama and galleta grass become characteristic. The shortgrass portion is considered by some to be a disclimax, caused by overgrazing of the mixed prairie. This phase is most strongly developed in the western and southern portions. The mixed prairie portion is considered to form a transitional strip about 100 miles wide on the east, extending from central Saskatchewan to northern Texas, whereas the shortgrass phase extends from the mixed prairie westward about two-thirds of the way across Montana and one-fourth of the way across Wyoming and Colorado, through the panhandles of Oklahoma and Texas, with outliers westward across New Mexico and into Arizona.

SEMIDESERT GRASSLAND. The semidesert grassland, or desert-plains grassland, extends from central and southwestern Texas across southern New Mexico to southern, western, and northern Arizona and is the driest of the true grassland associations. It resembles the shortgrass type because of its short but more open growth, and indeed some of the species from the shortgrass type are important in the semidesert grassland. The chief dominants are several species of grama grass, especially black grama (*Bouteloua eriopoda*), three-awn grasses (*Aristida*), and curly mesquite (*Hilaria belangeri*). Tobosa grass (*Hilaria mutica*) and alkali sacaton (*Sporobolus airoides*) are important in low sites which are alternately wet and dry. Many desert shrubs, small trees, cacti, and yucca are scattered throughout the type, frequently becoming abundant.

About 89 million acres of this grassland type remain, and despite the much increased abundance of woody species, the semidesert grassland is one of the better yearlong ranges in the country.

PACIFIC PRAIRIE (CALIFORNIA). The Pacific prairie is here considered in two parts because the dominants in the original vegetation of the California prairie and the northern bunchgrass were appreciably different from the vegetation that exists now. The California prairie formerly covered extensive areas in the valleys and foothills of California and Lower California, with the main body of the type occupying the great interior valley. The original dominants were bunchgrasses with purple needlegrass (*Stipa pulchra*) and nodding needlegrass (*S. cernua*) especially important. Associated with these grasses were wildryes (*Elymus*), prairie Junegrass, melic grasses, and a vast number of annual and perennial forbs.

On the portions of the prairie not converted to cultivation, the former bunchgrass dominants have been largely replaced by annual grasses and forbs, mainly of exotic origin. Included among the annual grasses are such species as wild oats (*Avena fatua*), soft chess (*Bromus mollis*), ripgut (*Bromus rigidus*), red brome (*Bromus rubens*), and the fescues (*Festuca megalura, F. myuros*). Important annual forbs include bur clover (*Medicago hispida*), filaree (*Erodium*), Span-

ish clover (*Lotus*), several mustard species, and many others. Major growth of this type begins in late winter or very early spring, and the forage is usually mature and dry by late April or early May. The annual grassland occupies about 10 million acres now, mainly in the foothills around the Central Valley and in the Coast Ranges. It appears almost impossible, and perhaps not desirable, to attempt to restore the original vegetation. Over most of the millions of acres occupied by annual plant species, it seems best to aim at maintaining and using the annual-plant cover in its most productive condition.

PACIFIC BUNCHGRASS (PALOUSE). The northern Pacific bunchgrass, or Palouse prairie, at one time occupied extensive areas in eastern Washington and Oregon, northern Utah, and southern Idaho, with extensions in south central Montana, southwestern Wyoming, northern Nevada, and western Alberta. The type attained its best development in what is now the wheat-producing area of eastern Washington known as the Palouse country. This type resembles the California prairie in that it is a bunchgrass type with a spring growth pattern, but the dominants are different. The chief dominant of the type is bluebunch wheatgrass (*Agropyron spicatum*). Other important grasses are Idaho fescue (*Festuca idahoensis*), Sandberg bluegrass (*Poa secunda*), western wheatgrass, needle-and-thread, big bluegrass (*Poa ampla*), and prairie Junegrass.

The portions of the type that have not been converted to agricultural production have very often been seriously overgrazed. Consequently, much of the remaining 32 million acres of northern bunchgrass has been extensively invaded by big sagebrush (*Artemisia tridentata*) and annual grasses, particularly cheatgrass (*Bromus tectorum*). The annuals have grazing value for only a short period in the spring, and on drying in early summer present a serious fire hazard. The invasion of sagebrush and the large-scale conversion of the grass cover from perennials to annuals has reduced markedly the grazing capacity of this type.

SAGEBRUSH-GRASS. The sagebrush-grass type is the largest of the western shrub types, and it is believed that originally the grass component of the cover in this type was much more important than it is now. The type has increased in area from about 90 million acres to 96.5 million acres in the last 100 years. Most of this increase has been at the expense of the northern bunchgrass in Oregon and Washington and the shortgrass in Wyoming. As the grass component of the cover has thinned out, the sagebrush has thickened, but the type is important to the grazing industry because it provides practically the only source of spring-fall range in the central and northern Great Basin. The type extends from eastern Wyoming to northeastern California and from central Utah and Nevada over the southeastern third of Oregon and the southern half of Idaho. It is also important in east central Washington, and outliers extend from Colorado, New Mexico, and Arizona to eastern Montana.

The principal shrubs in the type, big sagebrush, rabbitbrush (*Chrysothamnus*), and greasewood (*Sarcobatus*) have little forage value, but the understory perennial grasses, bluebunch wheatgrass, squirreltail (*Sitanion hystrix*), Indian ricegrass (*Oryzopsis*), galleta grass, needle-and-thread, and western wheatgrass provide excellent grazing. Cheatgrass has invaded the understory throughout the range of the type.

SALT-DESERT SHRUB. The salt-desert shrub is closely associated with the sagebrush-grass type and is of major importance in Utah and Nevada. The saltbushes (*Atriplex* spp.) winterfat (*Eurotia lanata*), and black sagebrush (*Artemisia nova*) provide good winter forage for sheep, and the type is primarily valued for its palatable shrubby species. However, there is a thin grass understory that provides considerable forage. Important species here are Indian ricegrass, sand dropseed (*Sporobolus cryptandrus*), squirreltail, galleta grass, blue grama, and saltgrass (*Distichlis*).

SOUTHERN-DESERT SHRUB. The southern desert shrub has very low grazing value, the shrubs themselves being largely unpalatable and the grasses occurring only at higher altitudes and in areas where water accumulates, as in drainage ways or depressions. Low and undependable rainfall combined with high temperatures make this area essentially a desert. The grasses found in the area are principally those from the semidesert grassland. In favorable years a very heavy growth of winter and spring annuals may occur, and some grazing use is made of this crop.

OPEN FORESTS OF THE WEST. The open forests of the West provide a great forage resource for summer grazing by cattle, sheep, and big game animals. Grazing in these forests is on an understory of grasses, forbs, and shrubs beneath rather widely spaced trees or on open parks, mountain meadows, and subalpine grasslands. Open forest types extend on the higher elevations and the mountains from western South Dakota to western California, and from central New Mexico and Arizona to Canada. The ponderosa pine forests are especially important as a grazing resource, and the Douglas fir-aspen forests of higher altitudes also provide good grazing. In the alpine spruce-fir zone the grazing season is very short, but cattle and sheep find the grasses and forbs of these high ranges both palatable and nutritious. The wheatgrasses, fescues, bluegrasses, needlegrasses, pinegrasses, oatgrasses, and a number of sedge species provide much of the forage on these timbered ranges. Numerous palatable forbs and a wide variety of brush species such as serviceberry, snowberry, cliff rose, and mountain mahogany provide additional grazing.

MISCELLANEOUS TYPES. The *pinon-juniper* type lies below the ponderosa pine primarily in Colorado, New Mexico, Arizona, Utah, and Nevada, although it has extensive outliers to the south, northwest, and west of this area.

The short coniferous trees that characterize this type have little value as timber, and it is primarily a spring–fall or yearlong range on which wheatgrasses, needlegrasses, grama grasses, and a variety of shrubs and forbs provide grazing for cattle, sheep, and big game, especially deer. The type has been seriously depleted over extensive areas by heavy grazing use.

Chapparal and *Woodland* types occupy fairly extensive acreages in the central and southern portions of the western range area. Their value for grazing is variable, depending primarily on the relative openness of the woody vegetation cover. The true chapparal is a close-growing, evergreen shrub type largely confined to California and parts of central and southern Arizona. Where fairly open, the understory cover is composed largely of the same annual grasses and forbs that have replaced the perennials in the Pacific prairie. At the higher altitudes and in southern California the dense brush growth may be nearly impenetrable, and the type is unfit for grazing.

Oak woodland types occur throughout the foothills of the southern Rocky Mountains and the intermountain area. Low-growing oak types known as "shinnery" occur in the southern portion of the mixed-grass prairie, and scrub oak types of varying species composition and degree of woody cover are found from Missouri and east Texas to the California coast ranges. Where the tree cover is fairly open, a good understory of grasses and forbs frequently supplies good spring–fall or yearlong grazing.

A mountain brush type occurs frequently as a narrow transition zone between grassland and coniferous forest along the southern end of the Rockies and on the higher elevations of the basin and range province through New Mexico, Arizona, Utah, and into California. Many of the brush species are themselves palatable to livestock, and often the type is open enough to have a good understory of grasses and forbs.

SOUTHERN FOREST RANGES. A number of forest-grazing types occur on about 182 million acres of land in the area from east Texas and Oklahoma to Virginia, the Atlantic coast, and Florida. The open and cutover forests of both pines and hardwoods provide good grazing, and much of the land throughout the area has been cultivated and abandoned. In this forested area the associated grasses which provide the bulk of the forage include bluestems and broomsedge (*Andropogon* spp.), wiregrass (*Aristida*), dropseeds, panicums, paspalums (*Paspalum* spp.), Bermuda grass (*Cynodon*), carpet grass (*Axonopus*), and others. Switchcane (*Arundinaria tecta*) is an important source of forage in the bottomlands and swamps.

GRASSLANDS OF HAWAII. The range lands of Hawaii include roughly about one-fourth of the total area of the islands and are nearly all permanent pastures. Some of the land included in pastures is arable and may be plowed and reseeded at intervals of several years. Much of the existing pastureland was once heavily forested, and trees and shrubs are still of considerable importance in the cover. The types of pastures are mainly related to altitudinal zones, with most of the pastured areas lying below 8000 feet.

At the present time introduced species are far more important than the native grasses. Giant grasses such as Guinea grass (*Panicum maximum*) and Napier grass (*Pennisetum purpureum*) are important at lower elevations, along with Bermuda grass and Dallis grass. A native leguminous shrub, Koa haole (*Lucaena*) and Kiawe, a tree related to the mesquite, are also important here. Intermediate and higher altitudes support such grasses as orchardgrass (*Dactylis*), Yorkshire fog (*Holcus*), ryegrasses (*Lolium*), and bluegrasses (*Poa* spp.). Kikuyu grass (*Pennisetum clandestinum*) and Pangola grass (*Digitaria*) are important at both low and intermediate altitudes. Pili grass (*Heteropogon contortus*) is the only indigenous grass of consequence in the cover.

GRASSLANDS IN ALASKA. The native grass-

grassland did not begin until well into the nineteenth century. The development of the grazing industry on the western range was based on the free use of public lands, and such lands were still in existence on the northern plains until after the end of the century. There are still a few men alive who actually took part in the final movement of livestock into the largely unoccupied ranges of the northern plains.

The final slaughter of the great herds of bison on the plains in the 1870's and 1880's was accompanied by the invasion of the cattlemen. Initially many of the cattle came from Texas in the well-known "trail drives." The cattlemen soon recognized the importance of taking possession of streams and springs for watering their stock and thus securing control of adjoining public rangeland. The private land owned by some of the early cattle "barons" formed a fantastic pattern as it followed a meandering stream. Various and devious methods were used to secure title to such streamside "homesteads." As the news spread throughout the eastern states and in Great Britain of the huge profits that could be realized from "free grass," there was a tremendous boom to invest in the cattle business, reminding one of the "gold rushes" to California or Alaska. Sheepmen also appeared on the range, and conflicts occurred between them and the cattlemen. The grasses were nutritious the year round; it was not considered necessary to put up hay for the winter; little or no shelter was provided; expenses were small. It was a bonanza. No wonder the industry expanded by leaps and bounds. But droughts came; the grass was short; ranges were overstocked; no hay was available. Disaster was not long in coming.

Disaster. The winter of 1885 was very severe in the southern Great Plains. Losses of livestock were unusually heavy, and in the following summer large numbers of cattle were moved to the already heavily stocked ranges of the northern plains. The cattle were in poor condition in the winter of 1886–1887. The cold came early; storm followed storm; the mercury went lower and lower. Temperatures of 60 degrees below zero were reported. The oldest resident had never remembered experiencing such severe conditions. There were no reserves of feed on the range or in the stack. Livestock losses were terrific. More than 90 percent of the livestock died on some individual ranges. Many operators did not even bother to make the spring roundup. With the coming of spring, most of the operators in this region faced bankruptcy. The days of careless management were over. The summers of 1934 and 1936 and the winter of 1948–1949 were reminiscent of the extreme conditions of the earlier years. Drought conditions on the plains in the 1950's served again to emphasize that the need for careful management is a constant feature of range use on the plains.

Mismanagement Continues. Undoubtedly, many stockmen realized that the boom was over, and that those who continued in the business would have to work out proper management methods. There were, however, many difficulties to contend with. The grassland resources had been badly damaged, and new difficulties were arising from the westward march of farmers. They were invading the rangelands. The homestead laws favored acquisition of land by the farmers. Many secured 160- to 320-acre homesteads in areas that were so deficient in soil fertility and soil moisture, had such a short growing season, and were at such a great distance from the market that the only use the land could be put to was grazing. Many of them used ideas and methods of farming that they brought with them from the East or Midwest, not realizing that differences in climatic and soil conditions would not permit their use. After a year, or at the most a few years, during which many depended on the cattlemen for a living, they had to leave their homesteads. But much damage had been done to the grasslands. Small areas were necessarily heavily grazed.

The plowing of such rangeland is best expressed by the wondering Indian who remarked, "Wrong side up." The truth of his remark is realized now when one sees so much of the range country still scarred and notes the invasion of numerous weeds and insect pests.

The presence of the farmers in the range country made it difficult for the stockmen to prevent further deterioration of the range. Too often the stockmen did not realize how much damage had already been done by too heavy stocking, by grazing too early and too late in the season, and by failure to distribute stock properly on the range. It was not entirely the fault of the stockman. He had no pattern, guides, or rules to follow. There was no science of range management; grassland ecology was unknown. The first effects of overgrazing are so slight that only careful observations or measurements will reveal them. Often it is difficult to distinguish between the effects of overgrazing and subnormal moisture conditions.

Overuse and mismanagement of the grasslands and the associated shrubby and forest grazing types in the West were not confined to the Great Plains area by any means (see Fig. 3). Serious range deterioration was reported from nearly all areas by the early 1900's. The first really quantitative estimate of the status of the western rangelands, however, was the classic report of the United States Forest Service in 1936.[4] This report showed that mismanagement had resulted in the depletion of most of the grassland in the range country, with a considerable decrease in grazing capacity. In its report the Forest Service estimated that the forage on about 55 percent of the range area was so depleted as to have less than half of its original grazing capacity. Another 30 percent was not so seriously depleted,

but the forage on this area had far less than its normal grazing value. On only about 15 percent of the total range area was the forage in reasonably good condition. An over-all estimate placed 93 percent of the total range area as being depleted to some extent.

During World War I, because of the need for grain crops, much rangeland was again turned wrong side up, and during the droughts of the 1930's, grasslands, especially those that had been overgrazed, deteriorated considerably. The great dust storms during this period originated in large part in certain mismanaged parts of the range country. The planting of grain in the range country was widespread again during World War II, and after the war, there were serious droughts, especially in the Southwest.

There has been no complete comprehensive report on the status of western rangeland since the 1936 report of the Forest Service. However, the *National Inventory of Soil and Water Conservation Needs*[5] has provided important information on the physical condition of the land and cover in 1958 on about 417 million acres of privately owned range and permanent pasture in the seventeen western states. Federally owned range was not included in the inventory. The results of the survey showed that nearly 75 percent of the privately owned western rangeland (over 307 million acres) was in need of some type of conservation treatment. On the other hand, the survey showed that over 109 million acres had received conservation treatment and were in a generally improved condition. Conservation treatments have been applied to an increasing extent throughout the range area. The Soil Conservation Service, U.S. Department of Agriculture, reported that in 1967 range conservation practices were applied to over 93 mil-

---

[4] *The Western Range*, Senate Document 199, Government Printing Office, Washington, D.C., 1936, 620 pp.

[5] Summarized by T. A. Neubauer, "The Grasslands of the West," *Journal of Range Management*, Vol. 16, 1963, pp. 327–332. Information for a new *Inventory of Conservation Needs* for 1968 has been assembled, but the publication is not yet available (January 1969).

with an estimated 51 percent depletion and 87 percent still trending downward. The National Forest ranges were considered to be 30 percent depleted, with only 5 percent of the area involved showing a downward trend. For purposes of this survey, range depletion was defined as the loss in forage values from virgin range conditions. It seems likely that the estimates of depletion, made during a period of nearly continuous severe drought, may have been influenced somewhat by the current condition of the forage resource. It should be remembered, too, that the true grazing capacity of our ranges in the virgin state is not known.

The principal difficulty in arriving at a reliable statement on the current status of our grassland resource is that adequate survey data on present condition and potential productivity are not available. Such data as are available are generally fragmentary and unreliable, and in fact do not even provide accurate estimates of the acreage of the various range vegetation types. A comprehensive reevaluation of the status of our native vegetation grazing lands is badly needed. In the absence of the factual data that would be provided by such a survey the degree of range improvement since the 1930's can only be postulated. Without doubt there has been a marked improvement in the condition of the range forage resource over almost all of the range area during the last 40 years. This improvement has taken place despite the fact that livestock numbers in the seventeen western states have increased substantially during this period. This is not to imply that all range has improved in condition. There are acreages of both public and private rangeland that are still deteriorating, and certainly very little of the rangelands of the West would be considered to be in excellent condition. Thomas and Ronningen [8] estimate that pro-

ductivity of our rangelands could be doubled or even tripled. Such an increase could not be attained by a stabilization of our range capabilities at their present level. Rather an all-out effort at range improvement must be made to achieve the goal of more than doubling production from our natural grazing lands. There should not be many acres of range remaining in critical condition by the end of the next decade, but the problems of improving deteriorated grassland and forested ranges will be with us for a long time.

Statistical reports indicate that there has been an over-all increase in grassland pasture and range in the western states since 1959, but the acreage of forested grazing land has decreased. On a national basis the combined acreage of all types of pasture and range has been continuing on a decreasing trend since 1950. The increase in grassland pasture and range in the western states has been the result of conversion of cropland to pasture and of land-clearing activities. These changes have been particularly marked in the southern plains, where over 9 million acres of grassland pasture and range have been added since 1959. Despite the conversion of appreciable amounts of cropland to pasture in the western states that has taken place over the last decade, the long-range outlook would seem to be for a relatively small but continued decrease in the amount of land available for use as pasture and range.

The major possibility for increased grazing capacity of western ranges lies in better management of our present range resource. The primary approach to improvement is through the adjustment of range stocking to the capabilities of the vegetation in relation to (1) intensity of use, (2) season of use, and (3) uniformity of use. Coupled with careful grazing management must be the physical improvements involved in erosion control, water de-

[8] Gerald W. Thomas and Thomas S. Ronningen. "Rangelands—Our Billion Acre Resource," *Agricultural Science Review*, Vol. 3, Fourth Quarter, 1965, pp. 11–17.

velopment, reseeding, control of noxious and poisonous plants, and fencing. The magnitude of the improvement task is indicated by the data obtained from the National Inventory of Soil and Water Conservation Needs. In 1964, it was estimated that of the 417 million acres of privately owned range in the western states about 307 million acres (75 percent) were in need of conservation treatment. Erosion was a problem on 217 million acres; 46 million acres needed reseeding; improvement of plant cover by means other than general reseeding was needed on another 84 million acres; better regulation of stocking to prevent overgrazing was needed on 157 million acres; and control of noxious woody plants was needed on 53 million acres.

In 1960, Congress passed the Multiple Use–Sustained Yield Act applicable to the National Forest lands. The Bureau of Land Management was made a multiple-use land management agency by act of Congress in 1965. The U.S. Forest Service had long been managing its lands on a multiple-use basis, and the passage of these acts served to confirm and extend this principle of public land management. Under these acts the western public lands are to be managed with consideration being given to the values of the various resources, "and not necessarily to the combination of uses that will give the greatest dollar return or the greatest unit output." Recreational use thus becomes one of the major uses of these lands along with wood, water, wildlife, and forage production (Fig. 5). Under the programs implementing the Act lands which have particular recreational value have been classed as recreational areas or sites and are being developed for recreational use.

No doubt there will be some shift of rangelands to recreational use in the years to come. Present indications are that much of this shift will take place on the forested ranges at higher altitudes, whereas the principal recreation pressure on the open grasslands at lower altitudes probably will be for hunting. The

Fig. 5 Mule deer in dense grassland cover. The range is a home for many kinds of wildlife, and recreational use of rangelands is increasing rapidly. The grasslands not only provide opportunities for the hunting and viewing of wildlife, but also provide for the simple enjoyment of uncluttered space. (Ed Bry, North Dakota Game and Fish Department.)

tremendous increase in recreational use of rangelands is indicated by the experience of the Forest Service. In 1957, the Forest Service estimated that by 1975 recreational visits to Forest Service lands would total 135 million annually. This number of visits was actually reached in 1964. Forest Service estimates now indicate 250 million visits by 1976 and 630 million visits by the year 2000.[9]

It is becoming increasingly apparent that major recreational pressures are developing on both publicly owned and privately owned rangelands to a much greater extent than had been anticipated. Fortunately recreational uses and grazing uses can be harmonized in a concept of multiple-use land management. It can be expected that areas of conflict will arise, however, and in some cases recreational use and wildlife production will take prece-

[9] Marion Clawson, *The Federal Lands Since 1956*, The Johns Hopkins Press, Baltimore, Maryland, 1967, p. 9.

dence over other uses. Many farm and ranch operators in the western range area are already finding it profitable to use parts of their land for income-producing recreation, especially hunting.

PRINCIPLES AND METHODS IN GRASSLAND RESTORATION

Plant Succession. Grazing introduces a factor that greatly alters and modifies the competitive relations of species in the grassland complex. Defoliation generally results in reducing the carbohydrate reserve needed for the formation of new growth of roots and tops. Grassland species are tolerant of certain degrees of grazing, for grasslands and grazing animals followed the long path of evolution together, but excessive grazing, resulting in repeated defoliation, will greatly reduce the vigor of the plants and the herbage yields and may finally result in death.

The grazing by livestock or game animals on grassland containing a mixture of species is seldom, if ever, uniform either in relation to geographical distribution of grazing, time of grazing, degree of grazing, or species utilized. Usually the most palatable and most desirable species suffer the greatest grazing pressure and are the most likely to be seriously weakened or even eliminated from the cover. Thus differential grazing may result in the reduction of one or more of the more valuable species, whereas undesirable species, such as weeds or poisonous plants, may gain the advantage over the other species. These competitive relations have been utilized as the basis of classifying plants into three groups, according to their reaction to continued grazing pressure: (1) decreasers, (2) increasers, and (3) invaders (Fig. 6). Under continuous overgrazing, the most desirable forage plants may decrease rapidly, whereas undesirable and unimportant kinds that are already present in the area, or that may invade, increase rapidly. Under moderate or no grazing, the reverse processes may take place, but if overgrazing has continued for a long time, recovery will require a long time.

The determination of the competitive rela-

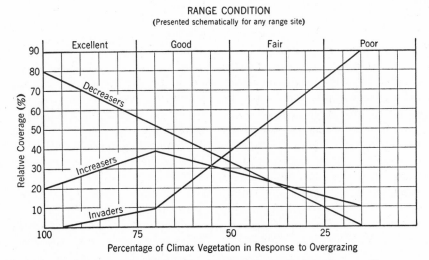

Fig. 6 Diagrammatic presentation of the relationships between groups of plants in natural vegetation classed as increasers, decreasers, and invaders in four range conditions. Percentages will differ from place to place in relation to the type of vegetation and the prevailing grazing conditions. (By E. J. Dyksterhuis, A. and M. University of Texas.)

tion of plants under grazing is properly an important field of study in the ecology and management of ranges and pastures. Much information on the general trends of plant succession under grazing in range and pasture grasslands is now available, but many of the intricate relationships of individual species to associated species and to environmental conditions remain to be determined.

RANGE CONDITION. In the management of natural grasslands, it is important to determine the condition (successional status) and trend (direction of successional change) of the vegetation in each area being grazed. Management and stocking recommendations are based on the condition or successional status of the vegetation and, where trend can be determined, on the apparent direction of the successional processes currently taking place on the range area. Forage production and conservation values parallel rather closely the condition status of the vegetation. A system for expressing the successional status of the range vegetation on a given site was first developed by Dyksterhuis[10] and his associates. This system, with various modifications, has been widely adapted by federal and state agencies involved in the management of grazing and the classification of vegetation on both public and private rangelands.

A range-condition classification essentially represents a statement of the degree of departure of the existing vegetation from the potential climax or near climax vegetation possible for that site. It also represents an approximate statement of the grazing value of the vegetation and the extent of improvement possible as successional processes advance under proper management. In order to determine range condition, a thorough knowledge of the present vegetation as well as the potential climax vegetation is essential. The composition

and productivity of climax vegetation can be learned only by careful study of "relict" areas or remnants of the climax vegetation that have survived from earlier days; such areas are invaluable for determining the relative positions of decreasers and increasers in climax or near climax vegetation on many different sites. As these relict areas are discovered throughout the grassland area, their location and a careful description of the vegetation should be permanently recorded. Every effort should be made to preserve these relicts for future study and observation.

Range trend in many ways is more difficult to determine than range condition. Differences in rainfall from year to year or differences in grazing use may reverse the trend from one year to the next. Long-range trends either upward or downward will eventually show themselves in the condition status of the range. The condition status will change more slowly than will the trend. In fact, it is possible for the current trend on a range to be downward while the condition status is improving. The interpretation of trend factors is thus very difficult. To arrive at a sound interpretation of trend and to detect relatively small changes in condition, it is necessary to observe small, permanently marked sample areas of the vegetation from year to year. Such observations will give answers to many questions, such as: What is the condition of the plants this year compared to previous years? (Best measured by height and area of plant clumps.) Are the most desirable forage plants increasing or decreasing? Are the less desirable forage plants increasing or decreasing? Are new plants invading and are they desirable or undesirable? This procedure may be considered as taking annual inventory of the chief resource of the ranch—the grassland. The range condition survey and the estimate of trend applied to the specific grazing operation are the primary tools for adjusting grazing use to the capability of the vegetation.

Reseeding. Natural revegetation through

---

[10] E. J. Dyksterhuis, "Condition and Management of Rangeland Based on Quantitative Ecology," *Journal of Range Management,* Vol. 2, 1949, pp. 104–115.

CHARLES A. DAMBACH *

The Ohio State University

CHAPTER 20

Conservation of Wildlife

Environmental degradation of the nation's air, land, and water has profoundly affected its wildlife resources. Restrictions in the use of wildlife are no longer adequate alone to assure its continued availability at present levels of abundance. The conservation of wildlife means the wise use and management of non-domesticated animals for the benefit of all the people. Both game and nongame species and those that sometimes are inimical to man's interest are included in this definition. Game and fish management are specialized branches of the field of wildlife conservation. Their objective is the maintenance of an adequate supply of game, fish, and fur to meet the demands of those who seek wild animals for sport and profit.

Nongame species of wildlife have received little attention in the past from the state agencies charged by their respective legislative bodies with holding wildlife in trust for all the people. Their welfare is largely dependent on the efforts of interested individuals, private organizations, and such government agencies as the United States Fish and Wildlife Service

* Professor Dambach died October 30, 1969.

and the National Park Service, which are supported by funds available through taxation. An increasing number of state wildlife conservation agencies, however, are developing programs to protect this resource.

IMPORTANCE OF WILDLIFE RESOURCES

Early History. Native wild animals are an integral part of our American heritage. Their utilization for food, clothing, and barter was vital to the success of the colonists and later to the opening of the West. They made possible the establishment of many pioneer settlements. Many of the early explorations and discoveries which opened up the interior of the United States were made by trappers seeking new sources of fur for foreign trade. Wild animals were an important source of food for man as recently as the westward expansion of the railroads during the 2 or 3 decades following 1830. During this period, for example, about 250,000 bison were killed annually, largely to supply meat for crews building the railroads. Deliberate reduction of buffalo herds was also practiced to deny to Indians an important source of food and shelter, thus weakening their capacity to resist the westward march across the continent.

Food. We have long since passed the time when wild animals were of importance in meeting our food or clothing needs. Although the annual kill of present-day game species is enormous in the aggregate, it falls far short of meeting annual food needs. The dressed weight of all big game animals taken annually in continental United States is estimated to be 1 pound per person. The white-tailed and mule deer account for three-fourths of this total. The dressed weight of all small game is estimated to be less than a pound per person, and much of it is wasted.

Fish for Food and Pleasure. The fishes taken from the seas and inland waters, however, add significantly to the food supplies of the nation. Commercial landings by United States fishermen aggregate nearly 5 billion pounds annually.[1] Before processing, the value of these fishes is nearly $500 million. Shellfish represent approximately 50 percent of the value of all fish landings but less than 20 percent of the volume of the catch. More than half of the total United States commercial catch is utilized for human consumption. Current per capita consumption of commercially caught fish is approximately 11 pounds. Fishes not used for food supply a wide variety of needs for our modern society. This includes great quantities, nearly 300 million pounds annually, for bait and animal food and nearly 2 million pounds for meal, oil, and fish solubles. Commercial fishing provides a livelihood to more than 128,000 fishermen operating a fleet of 12,000 or more vessels of over 5 tons. Although the United States catch of fishes has increased 17 percent in the past decade, it has delined in relation to population growth. In

the same period fish and fish product imports have increased substantially and now represent nearly 50 percent of the total United States supply. This country continues, however, to rank fifth among the fishing nations of the world, being preceded by Peru, Japan, China (mainland), and the U.S.S.R.

The principal fisheries industries are located along our Atlantic and Pacific coasts and the Gulf coast. The Pacific region and Alaska alone produced 82 percent of the canned fish pack. The Atlantic coast produced 16 percent, and the Gulf states 2 percent. Our fresh-water fisheries exclusive of the Great Lakes are of importance primarily for recreational fishing.

Fur. Wild furs, although no longer a home necessity, still provide a modest source of income for thousands of trappers and part-time income for many farm boys. The aggregate value of wild trapped fur from reporting states in 1966 was $16,400,000.

Wild trapped furs prior to World War II made up 85 percent of the total raw fur value. Subsequently the fur market became glutted with long-haired furs, such as foxes, wolves, skunks, and raccoons. Prices on these species dropped to such low levels that few trappers troubled to catch them. Prices on short-haired furs, such as muskrat and mink, have remained fairly steady.

Populations of long-haired fur-bearing animals, particularly fox and raccoon, have reached high levels throughout much of their range. Other species, notably otters, martens, and fishers, remain relatively scarce and command good prices. Beaver, at one time the backbone of the wild-fur trade, are again becoming common in areas where they had been absent for decades.

Fur prices fluctuate greatly as styles, economic conditions, and supplies have changed and as acceptable substitutes have been developed. Increased knowledge of genetic principles and nutritional requirements of fur-bearing animals has made fur farming a profitable

---

[1] Charles H. Lyles, *Fishery Statistics of the United States,* U.S. Department of the Interior Statistical Digest 59, U.S. Government Printing Office, Washington, D.C., 1967.

venture for persons skilled in this field. It is probable that commercial fur farms may within a few decades become the principal source of raw furs for the American market.

Since the end of World War I, the United States has been the leading producer of furs among the countries of the world and is now the center of the fur industry. The retail fur trade in the United States which results from processing native and imported furs annually exceeds $300,000,000.

Biological Value. Modern insecticides, rodenticides, and herbicides, such as DDT, malathion, methoxychlor, and parathion for insects; 2-4D for weed control; and ANTU for rodents, have made possible some control of pests heretofore reduced largely by natural enemies. Forest insects, such as the spruce budworm, larch sawfly, and bark beetles, have been brought under control by use of new insecticides.

Many of the native and introduced wild animals consume great quantities of injurious insects, weed seeds, and rodent pests. The U.S. Biological Survey, the forerunner of the present U.S. Fish and Wildlife Service, made, prior to 1940, extensive studies of the pest consuming capacity of birds and encouraged similar studies throughout the country. The reported contributions of birds to insect control were convincing. For example, Forbush estimated that birds in 1921 reduced the cost of insect damage in this country by $444,-000,000 annually.[2] Bryant credited the meadowlarks in the Sacramento Valley of California when feeding their young with the daily consumption of 193 tons of insects.[3] McAtee estimated that on a single North Carolina farm native finches daily ate more than 900,-

000 aphids during an outbreak of these insects.[4] During their lifetime, insect-eating mammals, particularly moles and shrews, also consume great quantities of insects.

Many of our hawks and owls feed primarily on such destructive rodents as house mice, rats, meadow mice, ground squirrels, and gophers. Larger mammals, such as foxes, skunks, and weasels, also feed extensively on these injurious animals, as do some kinds of snakes. Unfortunately some of these predators occasionally feed on beneficial species of wild animals and domestic livestock, particularly poultry.

Although many birds feed extensively on weed seeds, it is doubtful if they are as valuable in destroying the seeds as are field-inhabiting rodents, which thoroughly grind their food before swallowing it. The seeds of such plants as red cedar, dogwood, and hackberry, for example, pass unharmed through the digestive tract of birds and may in this manner become established in places where they are unwanted.

Injurious Habits. Not all wild animals are beneficial to man. House mice, rats, and other rodents are charged with an annual destruction of $1,000,000,000 worth of property in the United States. On a worldwide basis it has been estimated that nearly 4 percent of bread grains and rice in storage are lost to rodents each year. Predatory animals take their toll of livestock also. Throughout the country, poultry farmers suffer from raids by rats, weasels, mink, skunks, foxes, and predatory birds. The cattle and sheep men of the western plains and mountain ranges suffer losses from large predatory animals, including coyotes, wolves, mountain lions, and an occasional marauding bear. Because of their burrowing habits, muskrats are sometimes responsible for breaks in dams and levees; ground hogs, badgers, go-

[2] Edward H. Forbush, *The Utility of Birds*, Massachusetts Department of Agriculture, Bulletin 9, Boston, 1921.

[3] Harold C. Bryant, *Economic Value of the Western Meadowlark in California*, University of California Agricultural Experiment Station, Bulletin 236, Berkeley, 1913, p. 12.

[4] W. L. McAtee, *Yearbook*, United States Department of Agriculture, Washington, D.C., 1912, pp. 397–404.

phers, and prairie dogs cause considerable damage by digging dens in crop fields, pastures, and road fills.

A problem of increasing concern in some areas is the damage to grain crops by blackbirds, bobolinks, crows, wild ducks and geese, and to fruit by starlings and other birds (Fig. 1). Estimates of losses attributable to birds are difficult to assess. A recent publication of the U.S. Fish and Wildlife Service [5] places such losses at between $50 million and $100 million annually.

Wild animals are known to serve as reservoirs of disease for both man and domestic livestock. Probably the best known is tularemia or rabbit fever, a sometimes fatal disease contracted by human beings from infected rabbits or other wild animals.

Recreational Value. According to a national survey hunters and fishermen annually spend within the United States nearly 4 billion dollars in the pursuit of their sport.[6] The significance of these expenditures is apparent. More is spent on hunting and fishing than for any one of such necessary services as household use of electricity, home telephone and telegraph service, physicians' services, or for radio and television receivers, and records. Expenditures for hunting and fishing are much greater than those estimated for all spectator amusements including movies, theater, concerts, and sports.

The survey showed that more than 33,-000,000 persons 12 years of age or older in the United States enjoy hunting or fishing or both, and the number is growing. It has increased by 3,000,000 since a similar study was conducted in 1960. The $4 billion expended

Fig. 1 Wildlife, including such species as the red-winged blackbird, the bob-o-link, and certain diminutive warblers may under some circumstances do damage to crops. Ripening corn, as shown in this photograph, is often attacked by red-winged blackbirds, skunks and raccoon, and other animals also may cause serious damage to this crop. Under such conditions control measures are necessary. Wildlife management thus necessitates practices to regulate the abundance of wildlife so that it is beneficial and not harmful to man's interests.

[5] U.S. Department of the Interior, Fish and Wildlife Service, *Some Blackbird and Starling Problems in the United States and Proposals to Deal with Them,* Washington, D.C., March 1966.

[6] U.S. Department of the Interior, Fish and Wildlife Service, Bureau of Sport Fisheries and Wildlife, *National Survey of Fishing and Hunting,* Resource Publication 27, Washington, D.C., 1966.

annually in pursuit of these sports was divided as follows: For bait, guides, and other expenses, 24.7 percent; for auxiliary equipment including tents, canoes, etc., 22.5 percent; for fishing and hunting equipment, 17.8 percent; for transportation, 14.8 percent; for food and lodging, 14.3 percent. License fees which are largely earmarked for managing the hunting and fishing resource totaled 3.5 percent, and privilege fees to enjoy wildlife on private lands and waters totaled 2.4 percent. A national recreation survey conducted by the

Bureau of Outdoor Recreation in 1965 tallied 8 million bird watchers and 3 million wildlife photographers. Many of the bird watchers and wildlife photographers live in the rapidly expanding suburbs where wildlife can safely be "shot" with a camera and its behavior spied upon with the aid of binoculars. Such use of wildlife appears to be of growing importance in the metropolitan areas of the United States, Canada, and Latin America. It has long been established as a pleasant form of recreation in the many municipal parks of Europe.

Many persons enjoy wildlife for aesthetic reasons only and gain their pleasure through observation and study. This interest provides a market for the makers of photographic equipment and supplies; for the binocular, field-glass, and telescope manufacturers; the publishers of natural history books; the manufacturers of outdoor clothing; and many other businesses large and small that are dependent on wildlife resources in part, at least, for marketing their services and products.

INVENTORY OF WILDLIFE RESOURCES

The Past. The first white men to set foot on what is now the United States entered a country that abounded with wild animals of many kinds. They found in the eastern seaboard areas an abundance of white-tailed deer, elk, wild turkey, and such smaller animals as ruffed grouse, heath hen, and gray squirrel, which provided food in quantities. A like abundance of fish in the streams and natural lakes also provided food for those who sought to take them by net, spear, poison, and hook. Wild ducks of many kinds, geese, and shore birds frequenting the waterways during their spring and fall migrations and their nesting season afforded another source of food. Inhabiting the waterways and wilderness areas were fur bearers, such as beaver, otter, fisher, marten, muskrat, and mink, whose pelts were shipped

in great numbers to European ports in exchange for goods needed by the early colonists. Also present were bears, mountain lions, wolves, wildcats, lesser predatory animals, and rodents, which raided the herds of livestock and ravished the gardens and fields of the pioneers.

Under these conditions, a public attitude developed that wildlife resources were limitless, that they could be utilized fully without restraint or concern for the future, and that wildlife inimical to the interests of man was to be eliminated by the most effective means at hand. This pattern of unrestraint was repeated again and again as civilization spread westward. When the Ohio Valley was reached, large numbers of grouse, wild pigeon, waterfowl, and the furs of beaver, otter, muskrat, and other animals were sent to the eastern markets. The supply appeared to be limitless.

Pushing still farther westward, the pioneers found on the great prairies and plains in the heart of America an abundance of grass-feeding animals. American bison in great droves extended as far as a man could see; estimates of their numbers ranged from 15,000,000 to more than 50,000,000. Prong-horned antelope lived on the plains in numbers equal to, if not greater than, the bison. Elk, deer, and small game including quail, prairie chicken, and sharp-tailed grouse were present the year around. In the sloughs, marshes, and waterways, vast flocks of waterfowl and shore birds congregated. This vast abundance of wildlife was quickly reduced by killing for food, sport, and clothing. Grain production and grazing also contributed to the loss until the region is now one of the poorest big-game areas in all North America (Fig. 2).

The wilds of the western mountains were opened and exploited before the vast herds of buffalo and antelope had been reduced on the plains. Here animals were fewer but more varied than on the plains. There were elk, mule deer, black and grizzly bear, mountain sheep, mountain goat, wild turkey, grouse, beaver,

Fig. 2 Packing in for a big-game hunt. Four billion dollars are spent annually in the United States for guide services, equipment, transportation, lodging, meals, licenses, and other costs related to utilizing fish and wildlife resources for recreation. (Photo by Don Domenick. Courtesy of the Colorado Game, Fish and Parks Department.)

many kinds of squirrels, and other lesser animals, and large predators such as wolves and mountain lions wherever deer herds were found. In the desert regions game was scarce except for trout in some of the cold streams which had their sources outside the desert area and except for vast flocks of waterfowl in marsh areas. As the westward expansion reached the Pacific Ocean, the last remaining virgin populations of wild animals were tapped. The trout of high mountain streams, the salmon of coastal rivers, the waterfowl of the Pacific flyway, and the sea otters and seals of the Pacific coast were rapidly exploited.

The Vanished and the Survivors. The heavy heel of civilization crushed deeply into our once vast stores of wildlife resources. Among the victims of our expansion were the great auk, the Labrador duck, the heath hen, the Carolina paroquet, the passenger pigeon, the Pennsylvania bison, several races of the grizzly bear, the Audubon big-horn sheep, the big plains wolf, the big sea mink, the Gull Island meadow mouse, and probably the Eskimo curlew, and the Cape Sable seaside sparrow.

The Endangered Species Preservation Act of 1966 provided for an official listing of native fish and wildlife threatened with extinction. At the present time 28 kinds of mammals, 50 kinds of birds, 39 kinds of fish, 4 reptiles, and 3 amphibians are considered to be endangered species or so rare that further loss of required environmental conditions would threaten their survival. The key deer, for example, is believed to have been reduced to 300 in number. Whooping cranes, despite near heroic efforts to protect them, in 1965 were down to 32 adults and 10 young. Mammals of the sea (whales, seals, manatees) account for 11 of the rare and endangered mammals. Predatory animals such as the grizzly bear and timber wolf account for 8 of the mammals in this class. Only 4 large ungulates sought for food are in this group. Seventeen of the endangered birds frequent the continent's waterways; 6 are predatory species, and 23 are in that group classified as song birds. Four species which were subject to hunting for food and sport are among the rare and endangered species. Seven of the endangered and rare fishes were at one time sought commercially, and 10 are game species sought by angling.

In a few species, the trend has been reversed. Prong-horned antelope, white-tailed deer, fur-seals, and egrets are examples of animals that have partially or wholly recovered from low population levels.

No single cause can explain the decline of all American wildlife. Market hunting was probably the chief cause for the decline of gregarious birds like the passenger pigeon, Eskimo curlew, and many species of ducks. Passenger pigeons were killed by the thousands in their roosts at night. Eskimo curlews were killed in great numbers during their spring and fall migrations. Ducks and shore birds were killed with specially constructed guns capable of bringing down dozens of birds at a

single shot. The great buffalo herds were decimated by hunters seeking the hides for sale or the choice parts for food. Many were killed merely for sport. The whaling, sealing, and fishing industries accounted for the decline of fish, seals, whales, and manatees, and fishermen along the North Atlantic coast were responsible for wiping out the colonies of the great auk and the Labrador duck. Plume hunters nearly caused the extinction of the snowy egret and the reddish egret and reduced many other species before their activities were outlawed. Aquatic resources declined because of the pollution of streams and lakes by industrial and mine wastes, raw sewage from cities, silt from eroding farm fields, and over-fishing of some species. Draining of swamplands, clearing of forests, and the development of grasslands so altered the environment that animals unable to adjust to the changes could not survive. Misuse of the land accelerated erosion and intensified the effects of floods and drought. As a consequence, the capacity of the soil to support both human and wildlife populations was reduced. These factors are of equal or greater importance than the more evident ones previously considered (Fig. 3).

Although the toll of wildlife that fell before the guns, clubs, nets, and traps of man was enormous, not all of it was wasted. Much of the kill was used in helping to meet the food needs of a growing nation and in aiding the development of commerce. We must recognize also that the vast herds of bison which roamed the plains, the deer, elk, bear, wild turkey, the grouse of the eastern forests and central hardwood region, and the mule deer, panthers, and grizzly bear of our western forests could not, even with complete protection, exist now under intensive cultivation and grazing of land necessary to our civilization.

The appearance of the book, *Silent Spring*, by Rachel Carson [7] focused attention on an

[7] Rachel Carson, *Silent Spring*, Boston, 1962.

Fig. 3 The beaver house, once common on streams and natural lakes in early America, is now found principally in remote areas. Recently, however, under rigid protection, they have returned to some well-populated regions.

insidious threat to wildlife which has generated considerable controversy. A panel of eminent scientists named by President John F. Kennedy to study the problem reported in 1963 that "many kinds of insect-control programs have produced substantial mortalities among birds and other wildlife. Some fatalities have been the result of carelessness or nondirected use: others have followed programs carried out exactly as planned. Mortalities among birds have approached 80 percent in areas heavily treated with DDT for Dutch elm disease control, with heptachlor for imported fire ant control, and with aldrin or dieldrin for controlling the Japanese beetles. Fish losses have been extensive even with lower rates of application in programs such as spruce budworm control using DDT."[8]

Pinpointing sources of insecticides harmful to wildlife is especially difficult. Some organisms in the food chain of higher animals may not be harmed by ingestion and accumulation of DDT in their bodies at higher levels than found in the environment. "At Clear Lake, California, for example, waters containing 0.02 parts per million of TDE produced plankton containing 5 parts per million."[9] Fish which fed on the plankton accumulated hundreds to thousands of parts per million of the insecticide in their fatty tissues. Grebes which fed on these fish died.

Annual synoptic surveys of chlorinated hydrocarbon pesticides conducted by the Federal Water Pollution Control Administration[10] indicate that these compounds or their decomposition products are widespread in the nation's waterways. However,

[8] U.S. President's Science Advisory Committee, *Use of Pesticides*, The White House, Washington, D.C., May 15, 1963.

[9] *Ibid.*

[10] Richard S. Green, Charles G. Gunnerson, and James J. Lichtenberg, *Agriculture and the Quality of Our Environment*, A.A.A.S. Publication 85, Washington, D.C., 1967.

concentrations large enough to cause damage to wildlife appear to result most frequently from accidental spills or carelessness and to be local in nature. Extensive educational campaigns appear to have reduced the frequency of such accidents. Threatened restrictive legislation and legal enjoinment of the use of pesticides in recent years have focused attention on necessary research and education programs to assure use of these materials in a manner which minimizes their threat to wildlife, while we enjoy the benefit their use brings to mankind.

Present Wildlife Resources. Despite the decline of many species, the wildlife resources of the United States are still vast, and some species are more plentiful today than at any time in recorded history, especially on farms and ranches. The several races of cottontail rabbits, quail, muskrats, field-inhabiting songbirds (Fig. 4), and introduced game birds (pheasants and Hungarian partridges) have been benefited by the clearing of the forests and the development of mechanized agriculture. More than 80 percent of the land available for wildlife production in the entire United States is farm or ranch land.[11] We probably now harvest annually most of the surplus crop of upland game, much of which previously went unharvested for lack of interest or need. Some animals are still being overused, whereas others are not utilized sufficiently to keep their numbers within the capacity of their environments to support them. Big-game mammals, such as deer and elk, under too rigid protection soon overpopulate their range.

Known wild vertebrate animals total more than 35,000 species.[12] Of these about 18,000 are fish; 5500 are reptiles and amphibians including frogs, toads, and salamanders, snakes, lizards, and turtles; 8600 are birds (Fig. 5); 3500 are mammals. The North American fauna, especially that of the United States, is unusually rich in number of species. Even in the intensively farmed and highly industrialized midwestern states, the variety and abundance of wildlife is surprising. The State of Ohio, for example, is known to have at least 171 kinds of fish, 32 kinds of frogs, toads, and salamanders, 39 kinds of reptiles, 180 kinds of nesting birds, and at least 65 kinds of mammals. On a single well-managed 100-acre farm in the same state, we can expect to find 50 to 60 kinds of wild animals totaling 2000 to 3000 individuals.

Fig. 4 Many native woodland birds, like this chicadee, have become accustomed to urban areas and utilize man-made facilities for nesting places. They may be found in many residential districts, as well as in parks and remaining natural woodlands. Although there are no available statistics on the subject, it is probable that more people enjoy observing wildlife of this kind than participating in hunting and fishing.

[11] J. Paul Miller and Burwell B. Powell, *Game and Wild-Fur Production and Utilization on Agricultural Land,* U.S. Department of Agriculture Circular No. 636, Washington, D.C., 1942.

[12] Ernst Mayr, "The Number of Species of Birds," *The Auk,* Vol. 63, 1946, pp. 64–69.

Fig. 5 Migratory birds, including song, insectivors, waterfowl, and shore birds are protected by federal laws. Some of these birds, like the woodcock shown in this photograph, are especially subject to decimation in areas where earthworms have accumulated toxic levels of insecticides applied for injurious insect control. Other earthworm-eating birds like robins may also be affected in such areas.

Farm Wildlife. Our present wildlife resources can probably best be understood by considering the abundance and variety of animals in relation to the class of land that they occupy. Of first importance in this classification is farm wildlife, which provides approximately 68 percent of the total game kill.[13] The principal kinds of farm game are the cottontail rabbit, squirrels, bobwhite quail, the ring-necked pheasant, and the Hungarian partridge. These species annually provide the bulk of the recreational hunting throughout the country. Farm wildlife also includes many of our songbirds and other nongame animals which are enjoyed by great numbers of people and such fur bearers as opossums, skunks, and weasels. Farm game animals primarily occupy land owned privately and managed for profit

[13] Miller and Powell, *op. cit.*, p. 29.

and are often only a by-product of farming operations.

As increasing areas of farmland are taken over for urban purposes the composition of the wildlife population is subject to changes. Rabbits and squirrels may continue to occupy the same areas, but as dogs become more numerous as the urban area is more closely settled the rabbit population diminishes. Squirrels may continue to be relatively abundant in certain sections of a city, providing that nut-bearing trees are abundant and other habitat conditions are favorable. The suburban areas, especially where food is provided, may have a variety of birds including the cardinal, the mourning dove, robins, the mockingbirds, and many others, depending on the geographical location of the area.

Wildlife of the Forest and Range. Forest and range wildlife includes most of the important big-game animals: white-tailed deer (Fig. 6), mule deer, black-tailed deer, antelope, and black bear (Fig. 7). Nearly one-half of the total are white-tailed deer, one-half of which are in eastern states (Table 1). Forest and range wildlife also includes wild turkey, sharp-tailed grouse, ruffed grouse, sage hen, western quail, and gray and other squirrels. The coyotes, wolves, gray foxes, bobcats, and black bears that enter the fur trade come largely from forest and rangeland. Although they and the big-game animals are principally

Fig. 7 Prong-horned antelope. These graceful big-game animals have been restored on many once depleted ranges by good game management. (Photo by E. P. Haddon. Courtesy U.S. Department of the Interior, Bureau of Sport Fisheries and Wildlife.)

species of forest and rangeland, they are relatively abundant on land that is used in part for agricultural purposes. These areas provide about 21 percent of the total annual game kill.

Fig. 6 The white-tailed deer is the most important big-game animal in the United States. They are becoming more abundant in areas recently retired from agricultural use. Where such areas border land used for agriculture, deer damage to crops frequently results. (Photograph by E. E. Good, The Ohio State University.)

Table 1. Big-Game Kill in the United States

Species	1961	1966
White-tailed deer	867,764	1,273,007
Mule deer	814,977	593,558
Black-tailed deer	158,253	154,320
Elk	77,905	84,804
Prong-horn antelope	75,645	57,569
Wild turkey	75,398	93,461
Black bear	20,430	23,424
Moose	13,363	8,605
Peccary	5,643	6,893
Grizzly	515	1,350

[Source: Wildlife Leaflet 446, 1962 (for 1961 figures); Wildlife Leaflet 477, 1967 (for 1966 figures), U.S. Fish and Wildlife Service, Bureau of Sport Fisheries and Wildlife.]

The Wilderness Refuge. Wilderness wildlife includes those animals that occupy relatively remote and inaccessible areas like the high mountain ranges and unexploited forested or swampy land. They are greatly restricted in distribution and are nowhere abundant. Among the better-known species are elk, grizzly bear, moose, mountain sheep, mountain goat, ivory-billed woodpecker, and trumpeter swan, and such fur bearers as the lynx, fisher, marten, and wolverine.

Migratory Wildlife. Migratory wildlife inhabits all classes of land. It includes most of our common song and insectivorous birds and such game species as shore birds, ducks, geese, and doves. Although providing only about 11 percent of the total annual game kill, these game birds, because of their spectacular migratory flights and the national and international problems involved in their management, often attract more interest than more abundant species. Various species of waterfowl nest in the wet prairies and marshes of northern United States or Canada and winter in the coastal marshes of southern United States, Mexico, and Central America. Thus at least three countries are frequently involved in the production, protection, and utilization of a single mobile resource. Four well-established flyway routes are followed by these birds in their flights to and from breeding and wintering grounds: the Atlantic flyway along the Atlantic coast, the Mississippi flyway through the Mississippi Valley, the Central flyway through the Great Plains, and the Pacific flyway along the Pacific coast (Fig. 8).

Unless drained, the nesting and wintering grounds of waterfowl and shore birds are usually of little or no agricultural or industrial value. Many millions of acres of former duck marshes have been drained and put to agricultural use, with a resultant decline in the area available for breeding and wintering grounds.

Resident Aquatic Wildlife. Resident animals which inhabit our swamps, marshes,

Fig. 8 Sandhill cranes, Monte Vista National Wildlife Refuge, Colorado. These birds will be used to restore wild sandhill crane breeding populations in areas where they were formerly native. (Photo by C. Eugene Knoder. Courtesy U.S. Department of the Interior, Bureau of Sport Fisheries and Wildlife.)

sloughs, lakes, ponds, streams, and ditches include some of the most important fur-bearing animals. To this group belongs the muskrat, which is the most remunerative fur bearer in the United States. Beaver, mink, otter, and raccoon also occupy waterways and, like the muskrat, do much of their feeding either along the margins of water areas or in the adjacent agricultural land. Two of these animals (muskrat and the introduced nutria) make up two-thirds of the total annual fur production in the United States, which amounts to about 15,000,000 to 20,000,000 pelts.

BASIC PROBLEMS IN WILDLIFE CONSERVATION

Problems of Ownership. Present concepts of ownership and legal title to wildlife were established during our early history when nearly all wild animals were produced and harvested on publicly owned land. Now more than 75 percent of the annual harvest of game and fur comes from privately owned agricultural land. One of the basic problems in the management of wildlife stems from this change in land ownership. By common law the states hold wildlife in trust for all the people, and the people have the right to use wildlife subject only to restrictions set up by the states and the federal government for migratory species. Thus the responsibility for the welfare of wildlife rests not with each individual but with the government which has practically no opportunity to act beyond limiting the time and manner in which animals can be sought and the number that can be taken. In effect, the government can enforce regulations designed to distribute fairly the wildlife crop among the citizenry, but it can do little directly to improve the crop size since it is produced mainly on land in private ownership, primarily farms and ranches.

Farmers and ranchers have the best opportunity to provide for the welfare of wildlife but have little or no incentive to do so. The farmer who encourages wildlife production on his land runs the risk of abuse by rowdy hunters, personal inconvenience occasioned by even the most considerate hunter, and damage to livestock and crops by both hunters and wildlife; yet he has no greater legal right to use the wildlife he produces than the city sportsman. The only means at his disposal to protect himself from the hunter nuisance is to exercise his trespass rights by closing his land to hunting, trapping, or fishing. A growing number of farm and ranch operators use this means to prohibit hunting on their property. Some farmers charge a nominal fee for hunting privileges. This income often is used to assure better property protection than state game and fish law enforcement provides. This movement has developed because the public attitude until recently had not generally supported enforcement of trespass laws adequate to afford the farmer the protection to which he feels he is entitled.

Unfortunately many sportsmen still feel that holding of a hunting or fishing license entitles them to full pursuit of their sport wherever they may find it as long as they abide by the regulations pertaining to bag limits, seasons, and legal manner of taking game.

The problem of wildlife ownership is further complicated by the fact that nearly all the state game and fish departments are financed largely by money received from the sale of hunting and fishing licenses. To enforce trespass rights with game protectors or wardens paid from these funds would in effect lead to the closing of more land to hunting and thus to a decline in the number of license-buying hunters. This conflict of interest between sportsmen and landowners is of considerable and increasing importance.

A paradoxical situation exists in that a crop produced by the landowner is widely advertised to the sportsmen by business interests which profit from the manufacture and sale of sporting goods or services. The number of paid hunting license holders has increased from nearly 6 million in 1935 to nearly 15 million in 1967. They paid over $80 million in license fees during the latter year. These funds, together with sales of fishing licenses and federal aid in wildlife restoration funds, are the principal sources of support for state wildlife agencies.

Thus we have a growing army of hunters and fishermen who annually buy more and more equipment and seek places where it can be used. Economic and social changes leading to fewer working hours, the short workweek, more and longer vacations, and better transportation facilities have all influenced this trend.

Hunting Pressure. The resulting pressure on wildlife and the land is particularly great in heavily populated states. Twelve states have less than 50 acres of total huntable area for each hunting license sold.

Most public designed recreation lands (85 percent) are open to some form of hunting. Most of this land (75 percent) is in the West. The West also has over 95 percent of the public domain lands. Although most of the public hunting land is in the West, most of the hunters (84 percent) are in the other regions. (See Tables 2 and 3.)

For the country as a whole, there are only about 115 acres of potentially huntable land per licensed hunter.

These data do not take into account the many thousands of hunters who do not buy licenses, such as farmers when hunting on their own land, exempted veterans in states granting this privilege, and local people in rural areas in those states where hunting law enforcement is lax. The figures also do not reflect the relative amount of game available per unit of area. The abundance of game is a direct function of the productiveness of the land, and for this reason more game is produced per unit of area in the Midwest than in the rougher and less fertile parts of the country. In few, if any, areas is the supply adequate to provide every hunter with all the game his license permits him to take.

In general, hunting pressure is greatest where the population is highest, but the percentage of the population that hunts and

Table 2. Number and Acreage of Nonurban Public Designated Recreation Areas Open to Hunting, by Level of Government and Type of Managing Agency, Forty-Eight Contiguous States, 1960

Level of Government and Type of Agency	Areas Open to Hunting		Acreage Open to Hunting, in Thousands of Acres	
	Number	Percent of Total	Acres	Percent of Total
Federal	(424)	(17)	(165,818)	(88)
National Park Service	5	(*)	1,787	1
U.S. Forest Service	200	8	158,002	83
Fish and Wildlife Service	80	3	3,590	2
Bureau of Reclamation	18	1	124	(*)
Corps of Engineers	121	5	2,315	1
State	(2,034)	(79)	(21,217)	(11)
Park agencies	223	9	818	(*)
Forest agencies	369	14	15,571	8
Fish and Wildlife agencies	1,407	55	4,693	2
Water-development agencies	4	(*)	51	(*)
Transportation agencies	5	(*)	4	(*)
Special authorities	20	1	60	(*)
Other	6	(*)	20	(*)
Local	(95)	(4)	(2,334)	(1)
Park agencies	26	1	17	(*)
Forest agencies	35	1	2,232	1
Water-development agencies	1	(*)	–	–
Special authorities	2	(*)	28	(*)
Other	31	1	57	(*)
Total, 48 states	2,553	100	189,369	100

* Less than 0.5 percent.

[Source: U.S. Outdoor Recreation Resources Review Commission, *Outdoor Recreation for America,* A Report to the President and to the Congress, Study Report 1, Washington, D.C., 1962.]

Table 3. Summary of Acreage of Public Land Open to Hunting, by Regions, Forty-Eight Contiguous States, 1960

| Region | Public Land Open to Hunting in Thousand of Acres | | | |
	In Designated Recreation Areas	Public Domain	Defense	Total
Northeast	8,066	—	111	8,177
North Central	23,740	343	230	24,313
South	15,660	—	1,978	17,638
West	141,903	148,320	1,443	291,666
Total, 48 states	189,369	148,663	3,762	341,794

[Source: U.S. Outdoor Recreation Resources Review Commission, *Outdoor Recreation for America*, A Report to the President and to the Congress, Study Report 1, Washington, D.C., 1962.]

fishes is in inverse ratio to population density. This suggests that the quality of hunting declines as hunting pressure increases.

Although it is becoming increasingly apparent that hunting pressure is not the chief factor affecting the abundance of most species of wildlife, some species are especially susceptible to reduction by this means, particularly wilderness-inhabiting species and those that are intensively sought because of their superior sporting qualities or high trophy value.

Waterfowl, too, are subject to drastic population reduction by overshooting because of the high-quality sport they provide and because of their gregarious and migratory habits. During the droughts of the early 1930's the North American waterfowl population dropped to the dangerously low level of 30,-000,000 birds. With stringent hunting regulations and the return of favorable weather, the waterfowl population rose to about 140,-000,000 during World War II, when hunting pressure was low.

A rise in duck license sales of a little less than a million to a total of nearly 2.5 million in 1956 raised concern lest ducks again be reduced below the average annual increase and below the carrying capacity of their breeding grounds. Following the imposition of more stringent hunting regulations and higher fees the number of such license sales has dropped to pre-1956 levels.

Pollution. Fortunately, the reproductive capacity of most kinds of fish is so great that their numbers are seldom seriously depleted by ordinary recreational fishing, although commercial fishing reputedly has reduced some once abundant fish of both coastal and inland waters. However, the rendering of streams and lakes uninhabitable for fish because of pollution is a problem of considerable magnitude. Many of our streams are now inhabited only by species of fish such as the carp which is tolerant of the sewage the streams carry.

The chief sources of pollution affecting fishes are agricultural chemicals, domestic sewage, industrial and mine wastes, and fine particles of soil washed from farms. Oxidation of domestic sewage exhausts the water-borne oxygen necessary to fish life and results in the production of materials toxic to fish. Industrial and mine pollution results from the emptying into bodies of water of waste products which may poison fish directly or interfere with their respiration, thus causing death. Minute quantities of such waste materials may be sufficient to kill fish directly or indirectly by destroying their food supply. For example, phenol, a waste product of gas plants and oil refineries, is toxic to trout at concentrations of but 5 ppm of water; and potassium cyanide, a waste product of coke ovens, at concentrations as low as 0.1 to 0.3 ppm. Silt in streams covers up spawning beds and bottom-inhabiting organisms which fish feed upon and also reduces light penetration below that necessary for plant growth.

Although some kinds of pollution have been alleviated, the problem still exists on a large scale in many states. Chemicals from coal mines in the principal coal-producing states and the wastes that drain into streams from iron, copper, lead, and other mines, and industrial plants have made hundreds of streams uninhabitable to fish. The treatments necessary to render pollution harmless to animal life are often expensive and imperfectly developed. For this reason, many states are slow to enforce pollution-abatement measures because they fear loss of important industries to states where pollution laws are less strict. Passage of the Federal Water Pollution Control Act in 1948 opened the way for the states to attack this problem cooperatively. The effect on fishes of modern chemicals, especially detergents and agricultural chemicals used for insect, disease, and weed control, is the subject of much controversy. Significant kills of fishes in streams have resulted from careless use of insecticides, and excessive amounts of detergents in streams do create unsightly conditions. The use of these materials appears to be necessary to our economy, but caution in their use is also necessary to protect fish and other wildlife resources.

The Federal Water Pollution Control Law of 1948 (Taft-Barkley Act) was extended in 1951 and again in 1953. It was strengthened by amendment in 1956 which authorized more generous grants-in-aid for the construction of community sewage-treatment plants, federal financial assistance in the working of local pollution-control programs, research and advice to communities, and enforcement after investigation and hearings in interstate pollution cases upon request of either state concerned.

In 1961 there was evident an unmistakable lag in local enforcement effort. The law was therefore changed to transfer the responsibility for initiating action from the Public Health Service to the Secretary of Health, Education, and Welfare, but the Public Health Service retained its operating functions. When it became apparent in 1965 that enforcement records were not improved legislative action

separated pollution-control activities from the Public Health Service, and in February 1966, President Johnson directed their transfer to the Department of the Interior.

The Water Quality Act of 1965 requires standard setting and enforcement by the states and permits strong federal action if the states do not act.

The family farm with its small fields, thick hedgerows, and woodlot and undisturbed lowland areas was long a haven for many kinds of wildlife. The number of farms in the United States declined from 6.5 million in 1920 to a little over 3 million in 1967. Meanwhile, the average size of farms increased from 147 acres in 1920 to nearly 360 in 1967. During the same period, forest and woodland on farms declined 30 percent, and millions of miles of hedgerows were removed to make larger fields which could be more efficiently handled with modern farm equipment. The over-all effect has been a great reduction in the abundance and variety of wildlife on the nation's farmlands.

Land Use. Among other conditions affecting the welfare of wildlife are overgrazing of forested lands and burning, both intentional and accidental, of forest, range, swamp, and other wildlife habitats. Unwise drainage of vast marsh and swampland areas has also been a factor contributing to the decline of some species. Tractor-powered mowers, binders, combines, and other farm machinery have greatly increased wildlife mortality in crop fields during the reproductive season. Roadside mowing during the same period has also caused severe losses. The electric fence and effective weed-killing chemicals have further accelerated the removal of brushy fence rows which often are the only permanent source of wildlife cover on farms. Decline in productivity of land due to overcropping and erosion has also had a profound effect on reducing wildlife production over large areas of formerly good game lands.

Public Apathy. Prejudice, tradition, misunderstanding, and selfishness are other important problems in wildlife conservation. Many sincere people lacking basic biological knowledge still cling to management of our wildlife resources by outmoded and biologically unsound programs of predator control, bounty payments, "vermin-control" campaigns, introduction of exotic species, and artificial propagation and release of originally wild stock. Vociferous minorities of such uninformed persons sometimes prevent state conservation departments from putting sound wildlife conservation programs into effect. Some states, for example, continue to provide protection to female deer during the hunting season in the face of overwhelming evidence that the herd is becoming too great for its food supply.

Because many state fish and game departments are still subject to political maneuvering by the party in power, it is expedient for them to practice programs of appeasement. However, those fish and game departments that operate under the guidance of truly nonpolitical conservation commissions are generally undertaking farsighted programs of wildlife management based on sound biological concepts and principles.

Lack of technically trained personnel on the staff of conservation agencies is also a problem. A tendency to improve this situation by employing college-trained men for permanent positions carrying moderate salaries has become evident.

MANAGEMENT OF WILDLIFE

Three Basic Concepts. The three basic concepts on which any sound program of wildlife conservation must be built were set forth by Gabrielson,[14] formerly director of the United States Fish and Wildlife Service:

1. Soil, water, forest, and wildlife conservation are only parts of one inseparable program.

[14] Ira N. Gabrielson, *Wildlife Conservation,* New York, 1942, p. vi.

2. Wildlife must have an environment suited to its needs if it is to survive.

3. Any use that is made of any living resource must be limited to not more than the annual increase if the essential seed stock is to be continually available.

It should be clear from these concepts that wildlife is primarily a by-product of land use. For this reason, its management must be integrated with, and largely subordinate to, the management of land for agricultural, forest, and mineral use. Management under these conditions requires intimate knowledge of the habits and living requirements of all forms of wildlife.

The basic living requirements of all wild animals are food, water, cover, and a climate to which they are adapted. The particular kind of food, water, and cover required by different animals is usually a fixed characteristic of each species. For example, quail feed primarily on seeds of grain and weeds, fruit, and insects, whereas many birds, such as the warblers and vireos, feed almost entirely upon insects and near relatives of insects.

Food Requirements. To be adequate, not only must the food supply be of the right kind, but also it must be available at all seasons of the year and within the daily traveling range of the animal. This problem is particularly acute on the western range where deer, elk, and antelope find abundant food in high mountain ranges during the summer months but are often unable to secure sufficient food to ward off starvation when driven by heavy snows to the valleys where they must compete for food with domestic livestock (Fig. 9).

On many of our farms and ranches today there is a greater abundance of food suitable for small animals like quail, pheasant, other seed-eating birds, rabbits, ground hogs, and ground squirrels than was present when the land was covered with forests or unbroken grassland, because of the growing of grain and forage crops, which are utilized by these ani-

Fig. 9 Winter feeding elk. Concentrations of elk on winter feeding grounds sometimes are so great that emergency winter feeding is necessary to prevent starvation. Regulated hunting is recommended by game managers to keep herds of elk and other big game from becoming overpopulated on the available range. (Photo courtesy of Washington State Department of Game.)

mals. Although most of these crops are grown for domestic purposes, large quantities of waste grain, forage plants, and weed seeds are left in the fields. For example, mechanically harvested corn fields may contain several bushels of grain and a hundred or more pounds of weed seeds per acre after harvesting is completed. In such areas, lack of cover is frequently the most important factor limiting abundance of wildlife.

Cover Requirements. The specific cover requirements of many animals are varied and complex. Thus the introduced ring-necked pheasant requires for nesting over much of its range open herbaceous cover, such as sweet clover, alfalfa, and bunchgrasses; dense thicket cover into which it may escape when pursued by natural enemies; tall corn, small-grain stubble, or weeds in which it may feed unmolested; weedy or thicket roosting cover; and exposed ground where it can pick up grit. The common bluebirds and wrens of our farms and gardens, for example, are limited by the availability of such nesting sites as holes in trees and fence posts and artificially constructed bird houses.

An important aspect of the cover needs of wild animals is its distribution in relation to available food and water. To be fully effective, cover must be so distributed that it can be utilized during travel to and from sources of food and water and as refuge which can be quickly reached if an animal is threatened with attack.

Water Requirements. The water needs of aquatic or semiaquatic animals like fish, frogs, ducks, geese, and swans are readily apparent. Not so apparent, however, are the needs of individual species.

Trout require clear, cool water with high oxygen content, whereas bullheads, catfish, and carp are tolerant of silt-laden, moderately warm water. Muskrats are most abundant in shallow water in which cattail, bur reed, and other aquatic plants grow profusely. Waterfowl also favor shallow waters where puddle ducks such as the mallards obtain food by probing the stream or lake bottom with their bills, and where fish-eating birds such as the mergansers and herons find an abundance of small fish. Nearly all species of animals that live in or on bodies of water are dependent upon water that is clean, free from toxic substances, and sufficiently rich in mineral nutrients to support a high population of plants and animals (Fig. 10).

Many terrestrial animals like deer, elk, and moose require clear, open water for drinking.

Fig. 10 The lush feeding grounds created by the six Upper Mississippi Headwaters Reservoirs attract numerous waterfowl and game fish. In the autumn thousands of sportsmen flock to the northern Minnesota areas to hunt ducks and rest and relax at resorts and camp sites adjacent to the reservoir waters. In 1961 more than two and a half million hunters and tourists visited the area and the number is increasing. (U.S. Army Corps of Engineers.)

Others like quail and pheasant are able to meet their water needs from dew and by eating available succulent plants and fruits.

The absence of suitable water the year around is often the most important factor limiting the abundance of wildlife in areas of low rainfall, particularly in marginal areas where an occasional drought wipes out populations built up during periods of normal or heavy precipitation. Ducks and geese which nest in the marshes of north central United States and the Prairie Provinces of Canada suffer great losses when such droughts occur. In contrast, wildlife of the more humid regions sometimes suffers from an excess of precipitation, especially when it occurs during the nesting season. During such a period, the eggs and young of many ground-nesting species become chilled from drenching rains or are drowned by floodwaters.

Capacity to Reproduce. The biotic potential or reproductive capacity of most kinds of wild animals greatly exceeds the carrying capacity of the environment they occupy. If all lived and reproduced, the potential progeny from a single pair of adult bobwhite quail would in 3 years' time number at least 1000 individuals. Even deer which per year produce but one to three young may overpopulate their available range under suitable conditions: theoretically, a density of one pair of adult deer per square mile (640 acres) may in only 15 years result in a population of one deer per acre. Although truly phenomenal increases in population occasionally occur, it is doubtful if the full biotic potential is ever attained under natural conditions.

Decimating Factors. Full attainment of the biotic potential of wild animals is prevented in part by one or more decimating factors: diseases, parasites, predation, starvation, accidents, and hunting (Fig. 11). The importance of each factor varies with respect to species, environmental conditions, and human activities; frequently one factor or a combination of factors is more important than any of the oth-

Fig. 11 The porcupine with defenses peculiarly his own continues to survive in spite of hunting pressures and changes in the habitat.

ers. Thus ducks are generally more subject to losses from overshooting and disease than are raccoon, which suffer from inadequate woodland habitat. Bobwhite quail and deer are subject to losses from starvation during severe winters. Because of their nesting in hay and grain fields, ring-necked pheasants are subject to high mortality from accidental encounters with mowing machines, grain binders, and combines.

Wildlife Management Practices. The primary responsibility of the wildlife technician is to determine whether the decimating and welfare factors are in proper balance with the needs of the species and, if they are not, to devise ways and means of correcting them. This necessitates carefully conducted research into the life history and habits of animals with respect to their natural and potential environment. Although only a beginning has been made in this field of investigation, a considerable body of information useful in prescribing guiding principles is now available.

Regulating the Use of Wildlife. Since Biblical times, limiting the harvest of wildlife to not more than the annual increase has been recognized as a management measure. This is the fundamental purpose of all hunting laws and other regulations restricting the use of wild animals the world over. To accomplish this purpose, various methods have been employed ranging from simple tribal taboos against disturbing the female during the breeding season to the complex regulations in force in the United States at the present time. Although regulations vary greatly from state to state, all are largely based upon limiting the period when animals can be taken to the nonbreeding season (open season); limiting the length of time during which they can be taken (length of season); limiting the number that can be taken in a day (daily bag limit) and in a season (season bag limit); and regulating the manner in which they can be taken (restricting caliber and load of gun, preventing use of decoys, bait, ferrets, fire, snares, nets, and dynamite).

All states now require separate licenses for hunting and fishing or a combined license for both sports. Some states require special licenses of commercial fishermen, live-bait dealers, fur dealers, and game-farm operators. In some states scientific collectors and taxidermists also are required to have permits.

The federal government is responsible for fixing regulations protecting migratory species of wildlife and requires the purchase of a federal duck stamp for hunting waterfowl. The United States has entered into international treaties for the protection of migratory species of wildlife. One of the most important federal laws protecting the welfare of wildlife is the Lacey Act of 1900, prohibiting both the importation of any foreign wild animal without approval of the Department of Agriculture and the interstate shipment of the dead bodies of illegally killed wild animals. The latter provision virtually ended the market hunting of wildlife and the wild-bird feather trade which were threatening extermination of many species. Federal protection of migratory species is authorized under the Migratory Bird Treaty Act of 1918, which replaced the Migratory Bird Act of 1913.

Predator Control. Destruction of animals that prey upon game species and domestic livestock has long been a duty of private game managers and of public employees charged with the welfare of wildlife. Many state game law enforcement officers spend much of their time killing hawks, owls, crows, foxes, coyotes, and other predatory animals in the belief that the welfare of desirable species is thus promoted. Some states encourage the destruction of predators by paying bounties for each animal killed.

Scientists have accumulated convincing evidence that these efforts not only fail sometimes to promote the welfare of wildlife generally but may actually be harmful. For example, destruction of predators was an important contributing factor in the increase of the Kaibab deer herd in Arizona to the point where it exhausted the available food supply, resulting in starvation of much of the herd, serious damage to young trees, and decline in the capacity of the range to support future deer populations.

Unfortunately, our knowledge of prey—predator relationships is not adequate for a satisfactory solution of the many problems involved in this controversial subject. It is common knowledge that predatory animals do kill many desirable species. It is also well known to biologists that a limited amount of predation may be beneficial to some kinds of wildlife by killing off diseased individuals, by preventing overpopulation, by encouraging wariness, and by holding in check less valuable species that may compete with desirable animals for food, shelter, and water. Effective predator control should be directed only at those species and those individual animals actually known to be doing harm.

Artificial Propagation and Introduction of Exotic Species. Since historic times, man has been interested in exotic animals and has attempted to substitute them for native animals displaced by his occupancy of their environment. Of the many attempts to introduce exotic game species into this country, only the introduction of the ring-necked pheasant and the Hungarian partridge can be termed successful. Although the ring-necked pheasant has declined somewhat, it seems to be a permanent addition to the farmland of the nation, particularly in the Midwest, the northern Great Plains, and parts of the Pacific Northwest. Filling with foreign introductions gaps left by declining native species does not appear to present a very promising solution to the problem.

In some instances, foreign introductions have caused considerable harm and unexpected displacement of native species. The European starling and the English sparrow, introduced to control certain injurious insects, not only have failed in that mission, but also have become a pest of city and country alike where they occupy nesting sites of bluebirds, woodpeckers, and other hole-nesting birds. The common carp, introduced as a food fish, roil the water in many of our lakes and streams, making the habitat unsuitable for other species.

Closely allied to the introduction of exotic game animals are attempts to increase by artificial propagation their numbers and that of native species. In the United States it has been used both to secure exotic or native stock for establishing new areas or replenishing areas thought to be overshot or overfished and to supply stock for bird-dog field trials, for commercial hunting and fishing preserves, and for sale as food. Because of the increasing frequency of fish kills due to pollution and such disasters as the decimation of lake trout

in the upper Great Lakes by the sea lamprey, artificial stocking has been necessary to restore depleted populations or to provide a substitute species. Many state conservation departments operate one or more game and fish farms and spend as much as one-fourth or more of their total income for this purpose. Ring-necked pheasants and native quail are the game birds generally raised for stocking purposes. Trout, several kinds of bass, bluegills, walleyes, and a number of other fish are commonly reared in artificial ponds for restocking. Most of these are planted in natural bodies of water as fry (recently hatched fish) or fingerlings (fish with one season's growth). Some states attempt to provide public fishing by stocking streams with hatchery-reared adult fish.

Artificial propagation, particularly of upland game species, is an expensive way of providing public recreation. Artificial stocking of fish is usually practical only in new bodies of water. Unfortunately, much of the artificially reared game and fish are released in already adequately stocked areas or in areas not adapted to occupancy by the species released. For many years, artificially reared ring-necked pheasants were distributed equally in all Ohio counties in response to demands by local sportsmen groups. Despite these repeated plantings, huntable populations of pheasants have developed only in the intensively farmed, glaciated parts of that state. A similar approach to stocking fish has been followed in many states. Millions of fry and fingerling fish have been stocked in waters to which they were not adapted or in waters already overpopulated with adapted species.

Wildlife Preserves and Refuges. A few states, Pennsylvania and Michigan, for example, have set aside large areas of publicly owned land for public shooting grounds; many states have also acquired and developed lake sites to provide public fishing waters. Some extensive preserves in this country are privately owned by wealthy persons or by clubs with exclusive memberships. Frequently these areas encompass the finest hunting territory, such as the Lake Erie marshes which are largely controlled by gun clubs for waterfowl shooting. Various systems of leasing exclusive hunting rights on farms in the best hunting areas have also become popular. This practice has been highly developed in the southern and southeastern states and is gaining headway in the good pheasant hunting areas of the Corn Belt.

The development of any system of paid hunting has been opposed by organized sportsmen and conservation departments because they fear that it will restrict hunting privileges to those with better than average incomes. Landowners in general, however, have organized paid hunting preserves more for protection from hunter abuses than for profit. The fees charged amount to but a few cents per acre of huntable land.

Unlike preserves, refuges are developed primarily for wildlife preservation. Their history in the United States is of comparatively recent origin, although a few such private areas were probably in existence when the first official refuge was authorized by the California legislature in the 1869–1870 session. The first federal wildlife refuge was established by presidential order on March 17, 1903, when Pelican Island in Indian River, near the east coast of Florida, was set aside for the protection of a waning population of brown pelicans.

Under the dynamic leadership of Theodore Roosevelt, Gifford Pinchot, E. W. Nelson, William T. Hornaday, and, more recently, Jay N. Darling, Aldo Leopold, and other conservationists, the refuge movement has so developed that the United States has the greatest wildlife refuge system in the world: 272 federal wildlife refuges, aggregating 17,409,968 acres in continental United States and Alaska. The greatest number of areas (184) is for protection of migratory waterfowl; more than half of the land (10,601,364 acres in sixteen

tracts) has been acquired for big game. Other purposes of federal refuges are the protection of nongame birds that nest in large colonies, wildlife in general, and research.

The states, too, have developed a system of wildlife refuges, although the intent has often been to preserve breeding stock of huntable species to establish on adjacent overshot areas. This has proved to be a most useful management method to maintain huntable populations of game in areas of intense hunting pressure, but it is practical for only a few species, such as waterfowl, deer, and pheasant, which are able to spread out quickly into the surrounding territory, are tolerant of crowding, and can be maintained on cheap land.

Two outstanding private waterfowl refuges are the Andrew Clark Refuge at Santa Barbara, California, and the W. H. Kellogg Bird Sanctuary at Battle Creek, Michigan. Other refuges of outstanding importance are Lake Merritt maintained by the city of Oakland in California, Hawk Mountain Sanctuary in Pennsylvania, Bird City at Avery Island in Louisiana, and the extensive system of refuges maintained by the National Audubon Society. The most important of the last group are located in Florida with eight refuges and in Texas with seventeen refuges where colonies, chiefly of herons and ibises, are protected.

Management of Food, Cover, and Water. The foregoing wildlife management measures are designed to control those factors that decimate wildlife populations. Except in relation to refuges, they have little to do with providing the food, water, and cover necessary for these animals to live and reproduce. The wise solution of this problem is the key to the future recreational use of the wildlife resources of our farms and ranches (Fig. 12).

A partial solution to the problem lies in the fact that good soil, water, and forest conservation contribute greatly to the welfare of wildlife. Permanent reservoirs developed for farm and ranch water supplies, for flood control, and for urban use also provide water for fish,

Fig. 12 Seeding range land by helicopter to improve food and cover for wildlife. (Photo courtesy of Utah Department of Fish and Game.)

waterfowl, and the many animals that inhabit streams, lake margins, and the shallow fringes of impounded waters. Only profitable forest management can assure the future of the farm woodlot, which is the permanent home of much farm wildlife and the safe retreat of other kinds. All these measures are vital to the economic security of the farmer and rancher, and they are carried out because it is profitable to do so.

Fortunately a vast program of soil and water conservation has already been initiated on the nation's farms under the leadership of the United States Soil Conservation Service. This agency, working through locally organized soil conservation districts and with the aid of the state agricultural extension programs, has helped thousands of farmers and ranchers to conserve and restore their soil and water and to make their woodlots more productive. As these practices are extended, wildlife will benefit proportionately.

Additional measures are needed, however, to develop fully the potential wildlife productivity of land in agricultural ownership. But other measures of considerable value to wild-

life will probably not be carried out on a significant scale unless it becomes profitable for the farmer to undertake them or unless he is safeguarded against the inconvenience and abuse that often attend hunting on his land.

According to estimates made by the Soil Conservation Service, at least 100,000,000 acres of land in continental United States are best adapted to wildlife use, of which at least 33,000,000 acres are in farms and ranches. About one-half of this area is now making its maximum contribution to wildlife and will continue to do so if it is not disturbed by fire, grazing, or cultivation. The remaining area, in need of some improvement to make it fully productive, includes 6,500,000 acres suited for marsh management, 1,000,000 acres of ponds, 1,000,000 acres of streambanks, 3,000,000 acres of crop-field borders, 6,000,000 acres of oddly shaped fields unsuited to other uses, and 250,000 acres of spoil banks resulting from various surface mining operations.[15]

Careful management of the wildlife areas

[15] Edward H. Graham, *The Land and Wildlife*, New York, 1947, p. 52.

on the nation's farms can establish the cover necessary to hold a wildlife population adequate to utilize fully the food supply that is so often produced as an incidental by-product of highly mechanized agriculture. Such areas are the only land on farms that can be justifiably managed solely for wildlife. They offer the best opportunity for providing the three basic welfare factors of food, water, and shelter which, together with control of the important decimating factors, are the building stones of any successful wildlife conservation program.

Management of food, water, and cover are equally important on other lands if wildlife is to be benefited. Timber production, for example, is given first consideration on both public and private forested land; yet modification of timber management practices can be employed to increase materially forest-wildlife

production. These modifications include the leaving of den trees for squirrels, raccoons, and other tree-dwelling animals; the favoring of desirable seed- or fruit-producing trees; the selective or group-harvest method of cutting timber to provide a variety of forest growth from small seedlings to large trees; and the leaving of open areas in reforestation projects for the securing of mixed stands of natural growth and planted trees.

WILDLIFE CONSERVATION PROGRAMS AND RESPONSIBILITIES

The development of a sound national program of wildlife conservation is dependent on three basic steps:

Fig. 13 Canada goose leaving artificial nesting structure. Through modern wildlife management, breeding flocks of Canada geese and other kinds of wildlife are being reestablished in various localities over the country. (Photo by Frederick C. Schmid. Courtesy U.S. Department of the Interior, Bureau of Sport Fisheries and Wildlife.)

1. An adequate research program to establish the status of important wildlife species, their needs, and measures necessary for their continued welfare under predicted use (Fig. 13).

2. An educational program to acquaint the citizenry with the basic needs of wildlife and with the biological, social, and economic problems involved in its use and to train adequate personnel to administer and manage this resource.

3. An action program to provide the food, water, cover, and protection from decimation needed by wildlife.

Wildlife management is now a well-established profession for which more than fifty colleges and universities in the United States offer training at either the undergraduate or graduate level or both.

The states, through their divisions of conservation, spend for wildlife management purposes the annual revenue from sale of fishing and hunting licenses. Nearly $135 million were collected in 1967 from such sales. This amount is supplemented by federal appropriations to the states from an excise tax on arms and ammunition and sport fishing equipment. In recent years these funds have averaged $20,000,000 per year. Approximately 30 percent of this amount is expended for research, 30 percent for development projects, 35 percent for land acquisition, and 5 percent for administration of the fund.

The United States Fish and Wildlife Service is the federal agency charged with responsibility for migratory species of wildlife and the federal wildlife refuge program. It conducts important wildlife researches in fields ordinarily untouched by state and private institutions. It also participates in a cooperative research program with the American Wildlife Management Institute, state universities, and state divisions of conservation.

Other federal agencies play a leading part in the management of wildlife resources. Of these, the National Park Service and the Forest Service work entirely on public land, whereas the Soil Conservation Service through its technicians develops programs for wildlife restoration on farms managed for soil and water conservation.

Among the many private organizations that contribute to the welfare of wildlife are the National Audubon Society, the Wildlife Management Institute, the National Wildlife Federation, the Sport Fishing Institute, and the Izaak Walton League of America. These and other agencies carry on the educational work of informing the general public of wildlife problems and act as the watchdogs of governmental activities which affect the well-being of our wildlife resources.

SUMMARY

Wildlife is a renewable resource which is subject to management by man. The basic needs of wild animals are adequate food, water, and cover to meet their specific requirements and protection from decimating factors

Fig. 14 A farmer and his family watching Canada geese feeding on farmland near Horicon Marsh in southeastern Wisconsin. (Wisconsin Natural Resources Department.)

which reduce their numbers. These needs can be met only by proper management of the land upon which they live and by control of such decimating factors as overhunting and predation (Fig. 14).

Although many species formerly common or abundant are now rare, the aesthetic value of those remaining is great. Public demand for recreational use of wildlife exerts enormous pressure on the supply and in some species necessitates complete protection and drastic restrictions on the use of others to ensure their welfare.

Most of the recreational use of wildlife is provided by agricultural land where the proper incentives for adopting practices beneficial to wildlife are often lacking. Widespread application of soil and water conservation practices may in part fulfill this need. Where these measures are not feasible or adequate, other inducements must be provided if wildlife production is to be maintained at a high population level.

Considerable advancement has been made in the field of wildlife management. Further progress is dependent on continual research and sound educational and action programs unhampered by political interference and the clamor of uninformed or selfish pressure groups.

References

Allen, Durward L., *Our Wildlife Legacy,* Funk and Wagnalls Co., New York, 1954.

Allen, Glover M., *Extinct and Vanishing Mammals of the Western Hemisphere,* American Committee for International Wildlife Protection, New York, 1942.

Beard, Daniel E. et al., *Fading Trails: The Story of Endangered American Wildlife,* The Macmillan Co., New York, 1942.

Connery, Robert H., *Governmental Problems in Wildlife Conservation,* Columbia University Press, New York, 1935.

Fisher, James, Noel Simon, and Jack Vincent, *Wildlife in Danger,* Viking Press, New York, 1969.

Gabrielson, Ira N., *Wildlife Conservation,* The Macmillan Co., New York, 1942.

———, *Wildlife Refuges,* The Macmillan Co., New York, 1943.

Graham, Edward H., *Natural Principles of Land Use,* Oxford University Press, New York, 1944.

———, *The Land and Wildlife,* Oxford University Press, New York, 1947.

Henderson, Junius, *The Practical Value of Birds,* The Macmillan Co., 1927.

Henderson, Junius and Elberta Craig, *Economic Mammalogy,* Charles C. Thomas Co., Baltimore, Maryland, 1932.

Jackson, Hartley H. T., "Conserving Endangered Wildlife Species," *Transactions of the Wisconsin Academy of Sciences, Arts, and Letters,* Madison, Wisconsin, Vol. 35, 1943, pp. 61–89.

Jarrett, Henry, *Environmental Quality in a Growing Economy,* The Johns Hopkins Press, Baltimore, Maryland, 1966.

Leopold, Aldo, *Game Management,* Charles Scribner's Sons, New York, 1933.

Lyles, Charles H., *Fishery Statistics of the United States,* Statistical Digest 59, Government Printing Office, Washington, D.C., 1967.

Miller, J. Paul and Burwell B. Powell, *Game and Wild-Fur Production and Uti-*

lization on Agricultural Land, Circular 636, U.S. Department of Agriculture, Washington, D.C., 1942.

Mueller, Eva and Gerald Gurin, *Participation in Outdoor Recreation: Factors Affecting Demand Among American Adults,* Outdoor Recreation Resources Review Commission Report 20, Government Printing Office, Washington, D.C., 1962.

Murphy, Robert, *Wild Sanctuaries, Our National Wildlife Refuges—A Heritage Restored,* E. P. Dutton & Co., New York, 1968.

National Resources Board, *Planning for Wildlife in the United States,* Part IX of the *Report on Land Planning,* Washington, D.C., 1935.

National Survey on Fishing and Hunting, Publication 27, Fish and Wildlife Service, U.S. Department of the Interior, Washington, D.C., 1966.

Outdoor Recreation Resources Review Commission, *Sport Fishing—Today and Tomorrow,* Report 7, Government Printing Office, Washington, D.C., 1962.

————, *Hunting in the United States—Its Present and Future Role,* Report 6, Government Printing Office, Washington, D.C., 1963.

Palmer, T. S., *Chronology and Index of the More Important Events in American Game Protection 1776–1911,* Biological Survey Bull. 41, U.S. Department of Agriculture, Washington, D.C., 1912.

Trippensee, R. E., *Wildlife Management,* McGraw-Hill Book Co., New York, 1948.

Troutman, Milton B., *The Fishes of Ohio,* The Ohio State University Press, Columbus, Ohio, 1957.

United States Senate, *The Status of Wildlife in the United States,* Report of the Special Committee on the Conservation of Wildlife Resources, U.S. Senate Report 1203, Washington, D.C., 1940.

Walford, Lionel A., editor, *Fishery Resources of the United States of America,* Fish and Wildlife Service, U.S. Department of the Interior, Washington, D.C., 1945.

GUY-HAROLD SMITH
The Ohio State University

DONALD W. LEWIS
The University of Toledo

CHAPTER 21

Fishery Resources for the Future

The United States with its unmatched land resources has been able to supply a high proportion of the nation's needs for food, feed, fiber, and other industrial raw materials, except for a number of tropical products such as sugar, coffee, and rubber. More than 225,000 people who are engaged in the marine fisheries industries make an important contribution to the food supply and to the national economy.[1] Most agricultural operations are carried out on land that is privately owned. Fish in the open ocean belong to fishermen of any nation who can catch them. Increasingly in the late 1960's fishermen of the United States have been confronted with foreign competition on the fishing grounds where fleets of fishing vessels from the Soviet Union, Japan, Poland, Norway, and other countries have fished in the waters of the northwestern Atlantic and the eastern Pacific. They have also been confronted with the fact that the value of imported fish exceeds the value of the fish supplied by domestic fishermen.

The United Nations Food and Agriculture Organization reported that the United States had dropped to sixth place in 1968 among the fishing nations of the world. Peru was in first place, Japan second, the Soviet Union third, mainland China fourth, and Norway fifth. The total catch in 1968 was reported to be 64 million metric tons.[2]

FISHERIES AS COMMON PROPERTY RESOURCES

Fisheries, like other natural resources, are utilized by man to satisfy human wants and needs. Most resources are owned by the individuals or firms engaged in their exploitation. By acquiring title to the resource, the owners are assured exclusive utilization rights and can manage it as they desire. A basic characteristic of all fisheries is that they are common property natural resources. Like the atmosphere and outer space, wildlife and game, outdoor recreational resources, flowing streams, and large bodies of water, fish popu-

---

[1] *Food for Us All, The Yearbook of Agriculture, 1969*, United States Department of Agriculture, Washington, D.C., 1969, p. 15.

[2] Press release of the Food and Agriculture Organization. Published in the *Columbus Dispatch*, December 8, 1969.

lations can be utilized simultaneously by more than one individual or economic unit. No single user has exclusive rights to the resource, nor can he prevent others from sharing in its exploitation. An increase in the number of users affects each user's enjoyment of the resource.

Fishery resources remain common property because of the difficulty of acquiring and maintaining exclusive rights to them. Fish stocks are highly mobile, ranging over large areas of the aquatic environment. The cost of maintaining exclusive ownership usually exceeds its potential benefits. In addition, prevailing laws and customs often prevent the exclusive ownership of fishery resources. It has been a firmly based American tradition that all citizens should have the right to go fishing, whether for commercial gain or recreational enjoyment.

The concept of the common property resource is fundamental to an understanding of the economic behavior of fishing industries and the problems inherent in the management and regulation of fisheries. In the utilization of a solely owned resource, such as a forest or mineral deposit, the user is able to adjust his rate of exploitation to the differential between production costs and the price of the commodity produced. When the profit margin is large, production can be increased, and when it is small, the harvest can be reduced, deferring production until some future time when the relationship between costs and prices will be more favorable. In this way resources can be managed profitably by the owner to produce long-term, sustained yields for his own benefit, as well as that of society.

One of the unique features of common property fishery resources is that the rate of utilization is not subject to the restraints that govern the exploitation of solely owned resources. The individual or firm engaged in fishing is competing with others to harvest as large a share of the available fish as possible. The individual producer is unwilling to re-

strain his efforts unilaterally, since fish he does not catch will be taken by other fishermen. A fisherman may realize, for example, that fish stocks would be improved if fish were allowed to grow larger before capture, but any attempt by him to increase yields by reducing his fishing efforts simply results in a larger catch by his competitors. Under these circumstances, the economically rational fisherman continues to harvest fish as long as they are available for capture. In addition, there is no limit on the number of individuals or firms which can participate in the fishery. Anyone is free to enter the fishing industry, subject only to licensing. If there are potential profits to be gained, there is a tendency for additional boats, fishing gear, and fishermen to enter the industry until costs and prices approach equality. Under these conditions, with strong market demand for fish and the lack of proper controls, it is almost inevitable that fish populations will be depleted. Furthermore, it is likely that the fishing industry will be unprofitable and many individuals and firms within it will approach bankruptcy. In order to prevent biological as well as economic collapse of fisheries, strong governmental controls are needed to restrict the amount of fish harvested and entry of men and equipment into the fishery. Since most of our important fisheries overlap the jurisdictions of states and nations, interstate and international agreements are often necessary to ensure the proper management of fishery resources.

THE OPEN OCEAN

Great expanses of the open ocean are not particularly rich in fishery resources except for particular species such as tuna. This means that the relatively abundant fish in the waters of the continental shelf attract fleets of fishing vessels of many nations. Off New England and eastern Canada the broad continental shelf extends far beyond 12 miles, the generally recognized territorial limit of both countries. For example, in November 1967, forty-six foreign vessels fished off New England. In this count by the Coast Guard, Polish and East German freezer-trawlers were included. At other times fishing fleets from the Soviet Union, Rumania, Norway, and other countries have fished on Georges Bank off New England. If the fishery resources of this offshore area are to be protected from depletion an international agreement with adequate compliance is essential.

The Continental Shelf. The fishing industry is of major importance in those parts of the ocean that lie upon the margins of the continents. By the erosive action of the waves headlands are cliffed and the shoreline advances inland. The sediments loosened by wave action may be moved farther out to sea, increasing the width of the continental shelf. The erosional section of the continental shelf is relatively small when compared with areas that have been built up by the deposition of sediments derived from the land and carried into the sea by streams, especially the large streams such as the Mississippi, the Amazon, the Rhine, the Nile, the Hwang Ho, and others.

It is believed that the continental shelves of northwestern Europe and off the eastern shore of the United States were once above sea-level and were extensions of the coastal plains along the seaward margins of adjacent land masses. When these areas were above sea level rivers such as the Hudson, Delaware, Susquehanna, and many others flowed across the plains to reach the sea. As the sea moved inland and covered large sections of the coastal plain the valleys of these rivers were submerged, but they are still identifiable as channels or submarine canyons.

Northeast of New York the former coastal plain has been largely submerged. To the south a part of the continent of North America is emergent as the Atlantic and Gulf Coastal Plains. Extensive areas are submerged and provide a very satisfactory habitat for the marine life of the coastal waters.

The continental shelves on both sides of the North Atlantic received extensive deposits of glacial debris when the glaciers from the adjacent land areas advanced into the sea. On the European side of the Atlantic the North Sea and the waters off Norway received glacial deposits. Off New England and eastern Canada the shallow waters from Georges Bank to the Grand Banks off Newfoundland are related in part to glacial drift on the continental shelf. Waves and currents have smoothed the glacial deposits and created a watery environment for the bottom fish of the coastal waters. East of Long Island and northeastward along New England and the Maritime Provinces of Canada only a few offshore islands rise above the surface of the sea. These include Block Island, Martha's Vineyard, Nantucket, and Sable Island.

The sea bottom areas of the continental shelves are the feeding and breeding grounds of bottom fish, and it is important that these areas be preserved as major fishing grounds. The dumping of harmful wastes into these waters may in time diminish or perhaps destroy the fishing resource.

The Seashore. Where the sea makes contact with the land is sufficiently indefinite in many places that it is difficult for marine hydrologists and cartographers to mark precisely the location of the shoreline. The sea extends inland in estuaries, fiords, bays, lagoons, and other water features. The land projects into the sea in the form of headlands, offshore islands, and offshore beaches. The seashore is in effect a zone. When the tide is in the shoreline moves upward and inland. When the tide recedes the shoreline is lowered and moves seaward.

It is in these coastal waters that many marine animals such as shellfish and many species of fin-fish live and may be caught by an individual fisherman seeking food for his family. It is in these same waters that pollutants from the land have already affected adversely the living resources of the close-in waters.

These waters receive not only silt and other particulate materials but untreated or partly treated sewage and other organic materials that use the available oxygen in their decomposition. The reduction of the oxygen content of the coastal waters diminishes the quality of the environment of the aquatic animals that live permanently or temporarily in this coastal zone. Liquid wastes from industrial plants that are not adequately diluted may be discharged into the coastal waters in concentrations too great for the survival of fish, shellfish, and other aquatic animals such as waterfowl. Along the Middle Atlantic the tidal flushing is not sufficient to cleanse adequately the estuaries and lagoons. It is in these coastal areas that pollution control is a major concern of conservationists.

The Properties of Seawater. The water that fills the ocean basins, floods the margins of the continents, and encircles islands is an enormous marine environment, a medium, for numerous life forms to be born, to flourish, and to die. The plants and animals that share this environment are involved in food chains and make up bio-systems of larger eco-systems of the sea.

The sea is also a depository for more than half of the known elements. Most of these in combination with other elements are held in solution temporarily or for very long periods of time. For example, calcium carbonate derived by the solution of limestones on the land is brought to the ocean by the streams that discharge into the sea. Over long periods of earth history calcium carbonate has been removed from seawater and used in the shells and structures of marine organisms, which at the end of their life cycle, have left these inorganic parts at the bottom of the sea.

Salinity of the Sea. Seawater varies in salinity depending upon local rainfall conditions, the discharge of great quantities of fresh water from streams that reach the sea, and other conditions. In the polar areas the salinity of the surface waters is lessened by the melting of snow that falls on the pack ice of the Arctic Ocean and from the icebergs from the Greenland icecap that melt in the sea. The great flat icebergs from the Ross Ice Barrier of Antarctica freshen the surrounding waters as they melt. Where great rivers discharge into the sea the upper layers of the sea have a lowered salinity because of the continuing supply of fresh water from the continents. The sea near the mouth of the Mississippi, the Amazon, the Rhine, and other great rivers reflects the effects of dilution of the seawater by the infusion of fresh water.

Oceans that lie in areas of dry climates or are blown over by winds that yield little rainfall will have a relatively high salinity. The trade winds or trade-wind belts, as far as this characterization is applicable, are relatively dry areas. Evaporation generally exceeds precipitation, and as a consequence the surface of the sea loses water but retains the salt. The increase in salinity also means an increase of density, and the water of high density tends to sink or pass beneath waters of lower density. Desert conditions of the Sahara of Africa extend westward into the Atlantic in the area of the Sargasso Sea, an area of high salinity. Elsewhere around the world the waters beneath the trades are relatively more saline than the ocean areas that receive moderate to heavy rainfall. The Mediterranean Sea, lying as it does on the northward margin of the Northeast Trades especially in summer loses more water by evaporation than it receives in the form of fresh water from precipitation and from the fresh-water streams that discharge into it. As a consequence there is an exchange of water in the Strait of Gibraltar. An inward current moves into the Mediterranean at the surface. A lesser quantity of more saline water flows into the Atlantic beneath the surface current.

Currents. Ocean currents are caused chiefly by the winds and by the difference in density of the water. The wind impinging upon the surface of the water drives the water before it.

The Coriolis force acts at right angles to the direction of movement and the ocean currents are deflected to the right in the northern hemisphere and to the left in the southern hemisphere.

The warm waters of the North Equatorial Current of the Atlantic are driven westward by the Northeast Trades. Some of the water enters the Caribbean between the several islands of the Lesser Antilles and then into the Gulf of Mexico. This mass of warm water flows out through the Straits of Florida and moves northward off the coast of southeastern United States where it is known as the Gulf Stream. Off the New England coast this great stream of relatively warm water is deflected to the right and the westerly winds drive the waters eastward in a broad expanse across the North Atlantic as the North Atlantic Drift where Spain, other headlands, and the British Isles deflect some of the water southward as a relatively cool Azores Current off the coast of northwest Africa. The more northern branch of the North Atlantic Drift moves northeastward into the Norwegian Sea between Iceland and Scotland–Scandinavia and on into the Barents Sea north of Scandinavia and west of Novaya Zemlya. The warm water, cooling as it moves into the Arctic basin, keeps the sea open and relatively free from floating ice as far north as Svalbard (Spitzbergen).

The Arctic basin contributes an outflow of water as the cold East Greenland Current between Iceland and Greenland. This current follows the coast of Greenland and flows into Baffin basin through Davis Strait between Greenland and Baffinland on the west. The outflow of water, bearing icebergs in the period between February and June, moves southward off the coast of Labrador and Newfoundland and into the section of the western Atlantic that covers the Grand Banks. This is the cold Labrador Current that brings icebergs and fog to the shipping lanes of this section of the western Atlantic. The Coriolis force deflects the cool waters to the right and

as a consequence the coastal waters as far south as Cape Cod are good for fishing but not for swimming. The cool waters also contain the basic ingredients of a rich fishery. The water contains oxygen and carbon dioxide which support the plankton in quantity, which in turn support fish that have attracted, and continue to attract, fishermen from many parts of the world.

Cool water from the Arctic basin is also discharged southward from the Bering Sea into the Sea of Okhotsk, the Sea of Japan, and the waters off the northern and eastern shores of Hokkaido and northern Honshu. The fishery resources of these cool waters are abundant and have been highly exploited by the fishermen from the Soviet Union and Japan.

Off the southern coast of Japan (Kyushu, Shikoku, and southern Honshu) the warm Japanese Current (Kuroshio) flows eastward across the north Pacific to a point off the Strait of Juan de Fuca and Vancouver Island where it divides. One current flows northward along the coasts of British Columbia and Alaska into the Gulf of Alaska. The other branch of the Japanese Current flows southward along the coast of Washington, Oregon, California, and Baja California and is known as the California Current. Because of the operation of the Coriolis force the water is deflected to the right. This causes an upwelling of relatively cool waters offshore from Washington to Lower California. By the time the Japanese Current has crossed the Pacific it has lost so much of its heat energy that it is no longer a warm current, but the water still contains enough heat energy to keep the coastal waters open in the Gulf of Alaska.

The cool waters of the northwest Pacific and the eastern Pacific as far south as the Tropic of Cancer contain dissolved oxygen and carbon dioxide in sufficient quantities to support the phytoplankton and zooplankton which in turn support the fish and other animal resources of the sea.

Off Antarctica a cold current driven by the

westerly winds and known as the West Wind Drift encircles the continent. The leftward deflection brings great masses of cool or cold water to the latitude of the southern tip of South America, of South Africa, and southwest Australia. Along the coast of Chile and Peru relatively cold water moves northward and northwestward. Traditionally the current west of Chile has been known as the Humboldt Current, honoring one of the great explorers of the early nineteenth century. Farther north it is called the Peruvian Current. Upwelling brings cool waters to the coastal areas as the current is deflected to the west. In these waters a rich fishery resource has attracted millions of birds that feed and have fed upon the abundant fish. Their droppings and remains, known as guano, accumulated on the desert shore and the offshore islands in great quantities. The guano, rich in nitrogen and phosphorus, was so abundant that great quantities were shipped to the agricultural lands of northwestern Europe. Lesser quantities are still removed and used as an organic fertilizer.

The cool waters off the coast of Peru support an abundant resource of phyto- and zooplankton fed upon by the young anchovies and other small fish which become the principal food of the cormorants and other sea birds native to this area. The coastal islands are now bird sanctuaries and the removal of the guano is a regulated industry.

Fishermen from Chile and Peru carry out their operations and catch great quantities of fish. Peru, on the basis of their catch, is a leading fishing nation of the world.

The cool waters of the Benguela Current off southwest Africa are not as extensive as the Humboldt–Peruvian Current nor are the biological resources comparable in quantity and value. However, the lobsters of South Africa taken in the coastal waters at the southern tip of the continent are distributed in the United States and northwestern Europe where frozen fish products are sold.

THE OCEAN HABITAT

The living resources of the sea have evolved over a long period of time, and their abundance and distribution are related to the dimensions of the several parts of the ocean environment and the internal characteristics of the water, such as temperature, clarity, movement, mineral content, dissolved gases, and other essential conditions. The sea covers 70.8 percent of the surface of the earth, and it may be said that the total quantity of water in the sea is too great for the oceanic basins, and as a result the margins of the continents are flooded by seawater. If the land area could be smoothed so the surface would be uniform in height the ocean would cover the land to a depth of 8800 feet. If the earth–sea relations could remain essentially static while the great ice sheets of Antarctica and Greenland melted it has been estimated that sea level would rise more than 325 feet.

Plankton, a Basic Marine Resource. In the oceans microscopic and larger forms of life collectively known as plankton constitute a marine resource of major importance. Plankton float or drift with the currents; nekton can swim against the current; and benthos are attached to the sea floor or can move about on the bottom. These tiny forms of life may be primitive plants (phytoplankton) or minute animals (zooplankton). Some, such as the foraminifera, have shells or hard parts consisting of calcium carbonate. Others, such as diatoms and raiolaria, have silica shells.

The waters of the sea contain, in addition to calcium carbonate and silica, mineral nutrients such as nitrates and phosphatic minerals essential to maintenance of the plankton as a basic food resource of higher orders of marine life. By photosynthesis the carbon dioxide and the inorganic salts such as nitrates and phosphates are converted into organic materials.

Food Resources of the Sea. The capacity of

the ocean, particularly regions of limited extent, to produce unlimited quantities of fish is an unrealistic view of the oceanic areas as a source of food to support the human population of the earth. Great quantities of fish are consumed by fish themselves and other creatures of the sea and are, in fact, links in the food chain. At the same time it is true that enormous numbers of fish reach full maturity in their marine environment, escape being caught, and die, contributing their remains to the bottom deposits where their skeletons and other hard or resistant parts become a part of the marine sediments.

The productivity of the sea has been estimated to be 1.5 to 1.8×10^{10} tons of carbon-fixed per year.[3] The conditions that affect the availability of fish of commercial value include the presence of cool waters continuously available in certain latitudes from the polar area or from the upwelling of cool water where deflective force of the earth's rotation causes the currents to drift away from the land. Along the coasts of California, Peru, northwest and southwest Africa, and along Antarctica, upwelling creates a favorable environment for plankton and the numerous small fish such as anchovies, herring, and sardines.

Great expanses of the ocean, perhaps as much as 90 percent, are virtually biological deserts.[4] These oceanic wastes can contribute little toward meeting the needs of a food-hungry population.

The offshore waters that cover the continental shelves, especially the cool waters rich in plankton and other organic resources and in mineral nutrients such as nitrates and phosphates, are now and potentially the major source areas for foods of marine origin. Ryther has estimated that the areas of upwelling water represent "no more than about one-tenth of 1 percent of the ocean surface (an area roughly the size of California) [but] produce about half the world's fish supply." [5] If management techniques and processes are to be effective in maintaining and enhancing the productivity of the major fishing areas they should be applied where fish are and where natural conditions are most favorable.

All life in the sea is nourished by solar radiation, oxygen, carbon dioxide dissolved in seawater, chlorophyll, trace elements, and water. By photosynthesis the phytoplankton and more complex plant forms produce carbohydrates, protein, vitamins, oil, and other organic substances. In the process the nitrates and phosphates are utilized. Oxygen is released and becomes available in the seawater to support the zooplankton and higher animal forms that feed upon the simple plants known as phytoplankton. The plants and animals together make up the rich pastures of the sea upon which the higher life forms feed.

Ryther has estimated that 240 million tons of fish (in the round) are produced annually in the sea.[6] This high figure includes the fish consumed by birds, other fish, and mammals. The consumption by these animals collectively may be as great as the fish caught and utilized by man. Chapman has estimated that the annual catch was 50 million tons a year in the middle 1960's.[7] In spite of the fact that certain waters have been overfished and that certain species have declined the fishing industry has continued to increase.

The large number of mature fish in the sea has permitted a catch of 60 million tons (1967). Over the past 25 years the increase in the catch has averaged approximately 8 percent each year.[8] Many fishing grounds have

[3] John H. Ryther, "Photosynthesis and Fish Production of the Sea," *Science*, Vol. 166, 1969, pp. 72–76 (reference on p. 72).

[4] *Ibid.*, p. 75.

[5] *Ibid.*, p. 75.

[6] *Ibid.*, p. 76.

[7] W. M. Chapman, "Potential Resources of the Ocean" Serial Publication 89–21, 89th Congress, First Session, Washington, D.C., 1965, page 132–156 (reference on p. 147).

[8] Ryther, *op. cit.*, p. 76.

been overfished, and regulations must be adopted and enforced so that the productivity of these areas can be restored. If fishing is to endure over a long period of time and contribute regularly to the food needs of hungry people the principle of sustained yield must be adopted. Further expansion of the fishing industry must come from species not now fully exploited and from areas not yet developed.

Fish Protein Concentrate (FPC). Many hungry people in the world are underfed or inadequately fed because their food lacks one or more of the essential ingredients of a well-balanced and nutritious diet. People who depend too heavily on rice, potatoes, bread, or other foods high in starch may be consuming a diet adequate in calories but deficient in protein and the protective foods. There is worldwide interest in upgrading the quality of the diet of millions of people by introducing additional protein into the foods they consume or by providing high-protein foods as a dietary supplement. This movement has the support of the Food and Agriculture Organization (FAO) of the United Nations, the Food for Freedom Program of the United States, and similar programs of other countries.

Fish protein is known to be a highly nutritious food, and it has been recommended that a fish protein concentrate or a marine protein concentrate be prepared and distributed to those countries where it is known that a protein deficiency exists. Fresh fish even with refrigeration deteriorate rapidly. Frozen fish may be stored for several weeks to a few months, but transportation and distribution to remote consumers is restricted because of the lack of refrigeration enroute or at the destination. It is suggested that a fish flour made under sanitary conditions and sealed in sterile containers can be shipped without refrigeration to distant hunger areas. Fish flour can be added to bread, cookies, pasta, tortillas, soups, and other foods as a protein supplement. Fish

protein concentrate is made in the Republic of South Africa, southeast Asia, Scandinavia, Germany, Canada, and other countries.

In the United States the Food for Peace Program was 15 years old in early 1969. It had its beginning in the Agricultural Trade Development and Assistance Act of 1954 in President Eisenhower's administration. Over the years other slogans have been proposed and used. Currently War on Hunger is appealing and is widely used.

Generally the United States approaches the problem of hunger at home and abroad by seeking ways of disposing of surplus agricultural products such as wheat and flour, the feed grains, oil seeds and products, animal products, fruits and vegetables, rice, tobacco, and cotton. In the United States where fish are now imported to meet domestic needs the prospect that fish protein concentrate will be produced in quantity for the hunger areas of the world is not good. Instead a competing food supplement, CSM (corn–soy–milk), is manufactured out of surplus agricultural products and distributed in India where it is used in chapati, in tortillas in Mexico and other Latin American countries, in gruels, soups, soft breads, and other preparations. However, fish protein is an abundant and highly nutritious food, and when the technological and economic problems have been resolved it may be used more widely in the war on hunger.

The United States Catch. Since 1940, the quantity of fish and shellfish caught or taken by United States fishermen has generally exceeded 4,000,000,000 pounds, and in 1956, 1959, 1961, and 1962 it exceeded 5,000,000,000 pounds (Fig. 1). Since the early 1960's the catch has declined (Table 1). The fishing industry has been unable to maintain a strong competitive position in the market because of the importation of increased quantities of fish.

The fishing grounds in nearby, offshore areas are being increasingly exploited by fishermen from the Soviet Union, Japan, Canada,

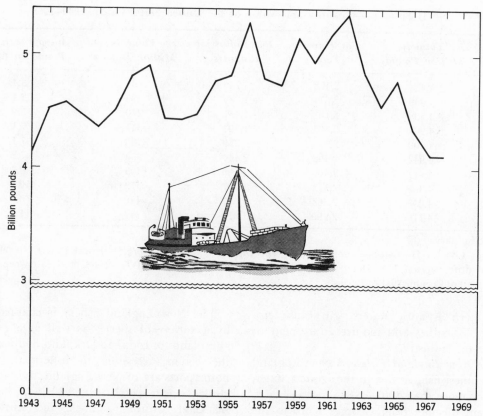

Fig. 1 The United States catch, 1943 to 1968. In this 25-year period the catch exceeded 5 billion pounds in 1956, 1959, 1961, and 1962. Since 1962 landings have declined and in 1968 was 4.1 billion pounds. (After *Commercial Fisheries Review* with data for 1968 from the Bureau of Commercial Fisheries, U. S. Fish and Wildlife Service.)

Norway, Poland, Rumania, and others. Generally the fishing craft stay outside the 12-mile limit, but many fishermen of the United States feel that their fishing grounds are being overfished and in time the resources will be depleted or at least substantially reduced. The rich fishery off the East coasts of Canada and the United States has attracted fishermen from western Europe and other areas for more than 3 centuries.

The capital required to engage in the fishing industry has placed a burden on the fishing companies because of high interest rates. Labor costs have also increased. The fisher-

men who go to sea feel that they deserve a wage that reflects the hazardous life they lead, and increase in the cost of living for their families who remain on shore. The processing of fish on the waterfront of the leading fishing ports, such as Gloucester, Boston, New Bedford, Baltimore, Mobile, San Pedro, San Francisco, and Seattle, requires a large investment of capital, labor, and managerial skills, and the economic welfare of the industry depends upon the maintenance of an adequate and continuing income from their operations (Fig. 2). A substantial decline in the catch of a single species, such as the catch of haddock

Table 1. Fisheries—Quantity and Value of the United States Catch: 1930–1968

Year	Total in Million Pounds	For Human Food	For Industrial Products	Value in Million Dollars	Average Price per Pound in Cents
1930	3,224	2,478	746	109	3.4
1940	4,059	2,674	1,385	99	2.4
1945	4,598	3,167	1,431	270	5.9
1950	4,901	3,307	1,594	347	7.1
1955	4,809	2,579	2,230	339	7.1
1960	4,942	2,498	2,444	354	7.2
1965	4,777	2,587	2,190	445	9.3
1966	4,366	2,572	1,797	472	10.8
1967	4,055	2,368	1,687	440	10.8
1968 *	4,116	2,296	1,820	472	11.5

* Preliminary.

[Source: Charles H. Lyles, *Fishery Statistics of the United States, 1966,* Statistical Digest No. 60, Fish and Wildlife Service, U.S. Department of the Interior, Washington, D.C., 1968, and later reports of the Bureau of Commercial Fisheries.]

in western Atlantic waters, can cause economic difficulties and require adjustment in the fishing industry.

The New England Fishery.[9] New England is the oldest fishing area in the United States, and for more than 300 years the watery environment offshore from Georges Bank to the Grand Banks south of Newfoundland has provided the New England fisherman with a product that could be marketed at home and abroad. In the early years cod fish, dried, salted, pickled, or processed by other methods, was the stand-by of the fishing industry. In time the catch of cod declined, and haddock became the leading fish taken in the waters off New England and eastern Canada. In recent years other species have been caught in great numbers (Fig. 3). Flounders caught in 1967 amounted to 113 million pounds, valued at $14,000,000. These data apply to the United States as a whole, but flounders and other flat fish such as sole were in first place in New England.

[9] Edward A. Ackerman, *New England's Fishing Industry,* Chicago, 1941. This is a highly useful study of the New England fishery before 1940.

The New England fishery is characterized by a variety of species as well as a relative abundance of cod, haddock, and flounders. In the waters accessible to fishermen, whose home ports are in New England, the catch includes ocean perch (rosefish), sea herring, mackerel, whiting, pollock, and scup. The area is also famous for shellfish, including lobsters, sea scallops, and clams (Fig. 4).

Sport fishing in adjacent waters attracts fishermen who have little or no interest in the economic value of the fish caught. Bluefish, striped bass, and flounders are caught, but the fisherman may have to be satisfied with his catch of scup, an edible but less favoried variety. Lobstering is generally restricted to licensed fishermen who must comply with restrictions limiting the number that may be taken in a specified time interval and the size permitted under the state regulations.

The Middle Atlantic Area. The fish caught or taken in Middle Atlantic waters were valued at $23 million in 1967, with fin-fish valued at $6 million and shellfish at $17 million. From New England southward the coastal waters are fished for menhaden, flounders, whiting, scup, and scallops. Menhaden is regarded as a rough fish and is processed for fish meal, fish oil, and other products.

In the Mid-Atlantic Bight from Cape Cod to Cape Hatteras overfishing by the Soviet Union and other countries including the United States interfered with the movement of certain species, such as red hake and whiting, to their usual spawning grounds. The United States and the Soviet Union entered into a 1-year agreement (November 25, 1967) to suspend fishing in a 9-mile contiguous zone and reduce thereby interference with spawning in this protected zone. This agreement was experimental in nature, but it demonstrated the kind of international cooperation that is necessary to maintain a fishery in international waters.

Chesapeake Bay and Adjacent Waters. The value of the Chesapeake Bay fishery resembles that of the Middle Atlantic area. In 1967, the catch was valued at $36 million, divided unequally between fin-fish at $8 million and shellfish at $28 million. The fish caught in Chesapeake waters include menhaden, alewives, croakers, sea trout, scup, and sea bass. The shellfish taken include oysters, crabs, and clams. The shellfish industry has been restricted because of pollution. The oyster industry has been largely limited to public and private areas where oyster farming or aquaculture is practiced in order that an edible product can be sold in the retail market where consumers have become increasingly skeptical about the edibility of oysters.

Oyster production reached its peak in the United States in 1910. The decline in the in-

Fig. 2 The *Santa Maria* with its nets, dory, radar scanning device, and other gear aboard is typical of the hundreds of fishing boats that fish in Atlantic waters off New England. Boston, Gloucester, New Bedford, and other coastal towns are home ports for these fishing boats. (Bureau of Commercial Fisheries, U. S. Fish and Wildlife Service.)

dustry reflected over- and unreasonable harvesting, uncontrolled pollution, and a decline in consumer confidence in the quality and edibility of the shellfish. If the shellfish industry is to survive in estuarine waters and be restored to its former importance the quality of the waters must be greatly improved; the industry must comply with federal, state, and industry standards; and the shucking and packing plants must be operated under acceptable sanitary standards.

The South Atlantic Fishery. The value of the fishery of the South Atlantic at $25 million in 1967 was less than the value of fish caught in the Chesapeake Bay states. Fin-fish were valued at $11 million and shellfish at $14 million. Menhaden, alewives, sheepshead, red snappers, mullet, sea trout, and mackerel were the chief species caught. The shellfish

consisted of sea scallops, shrimp, and crabs. Along the Atlantic seaboard menhaden are caught in such quantities as to give this species the lead in pounds landed (1381 million pounds in 1968). The value was only $10 million and was outranked by salmon, tuna, and flounders among the fin-fish, and by all of the major shellfish including shrimp, crabs, oysters, lobsters, and clam in that order.

The Gulf of Mexico. The fishery of the Gulf of Mexico has been dominated by the rapid development of the shrimp industry. In 1967, the total catch of fish was valued at $128 million, with fish accounting for $24 million and shellfish $104 million. The fin-fish caught include menhaden, sheepshead, red snapper, and mullet. In addition to shrimp other shellfish of commercial importance include oysters and crabs. The development of major ports

Fig. 3 The *Seafreeze Atlantic* is a modern freezer trawler that is able to spend two months at sea before returning to port. The catch is taken aboard, sorted, cleaned, prepared for the market, and quick frozen. The inedible parts and trash fish are converted into fish meal and fish oil. The vessel carries a crew of 54 in air-conditioned quarters: 10 fishermen, 28 processing personnel, 7 in the engine-room, and 9 officers. (Bureau of Commercial Fisheries, U. S. Fish and Wildlife Service.)

Fig. 4 A lobster catch in the North Atlantic. This crustacean of the cool waters off New England and Canada is a highly prized seafood. To preserve the fishery requires international cooperation to prevent overfishing and the enforcement of size limits to prevent the taking of lobsters under a prescribed size. (Bureau of Commercial Fisheries, U. S. Fish and Wildlife Service.)

along the Gulf coast and the extension of the petroleum industry into the offshore waters have caused a deterioration of the coastal and estuarine waters for the shellfish industry. The shrimp industry is farther offshore, but major oil spills can affect the industry adversely.

THE FISHERY RESOURCES OF THE PACIFIC

The Pacific coast fishery from the standpoint of landings is shown in Table 2.

Other fish caught in the Pacific (beside those listed in Table 2) include hake, abalone clams, Pacific oysters, squid, and other fin-fish and shellfish. Space will permit reference to only the principal species and the problems—biologic, economic, and political —associated with them.

THE SALMON FISHERY OF THE PACIFIC

One of the most abundant fishery resources of the northern and eastern Pacific Ocean is the salmon. Every spring and summer from the Golden Gate to Bering Sea the streams that discharge into the sea are sought out by salmon returning to the upstream section of the river where they were hatched several years before. Minor obstacles such as bars, shallows, rapids, and low falls do not prevent the salmon from seeking out their spawning beds. The high dams on the Columbia and several other rivers have made it next to impossible to reach the spawning sections of the headwater areas. Fortunately fish ladders and lifts have been provided to assist the mature salmon to negotiate these major barriers

Table 2. The Principal Kinds of Fish Caught in Pacific Waters in 1966

Fish Landed	Weight in Pounds
Salmon	387,512,000
Tuna	255,851,000
King crabs	159,202,000
Anchovies	62,280,000
Mackerel, Jack	40,899,000
Halibut	40,326,000
Dungeness crabs	39,718,000
Shrimp	34,438,000
Rock fish	25,529,000
Herring	24,107,000
Ocean perch	21,864,000
Bonito	19,148,000

[Source: Charles H. Lyles, *Fishery Statistics of the United States, 1966*, Statistical Digest No. 60, Fish and Wildlife Service, U.S. Department of the Interior, Washington, D.C., 1968.]

across the rivers. Grand Coulee Dam, because of its height and its upstream location, is an effective obstacle which the salmon cannot negotiate.

Anadromous Fish and the Fishing Industry. Anadromous fish, if their numbers could be greatly increased, would contribute to the further development of the fishing industry. These fish, such as the Pacific and Atlantic salmon, return to fresh-water streams to spawn. Even during the few years they spend at sea their offshore habitat is not far removed from the streams of their birth. At maturity when they return to spawn they are concentrated in the streams where they were born (hatched). Unless the streams are blocked by dams, especially those without fish ladders and elevators, the salmon may swim great distances upstream to their spawning areas. If the salmon population is to be maintained at a high level it is important that spawning in the headwater sections of fresh-water streams be facilitated, not impeded. The Pacific salmon die shortly after spawning. The Atlantic salmon may return to the fresh-water streams for spawning as many as three or four times.

In the spawning section of the stream the female deposits her eggs in a shallow basin where they are fertilized by the male. After approximately 2 months the eggs hatch and the small fry emerge from the nest. After spending several months to 1 or 2 years in fresh water they migrate downstream to the sea. These anadromous fish then mature in salt water, the process requiring 2 to 6 or 7 years when they seek the fresh-water streams where they were hatched and repeat the reproductive cycle of their ancestors.

The mature fish after they have spawned are destined to die and drift downstream with the current. For them their life cycle has been completed, but before dying they have established a new generation of their kind. The catching of salmon in the streams and the adjacent waters and the conservation of this important resource must recognize these facts of biology.

The Pacific salmon industry of the United States and Canada can be divided into four major sectors. The Alaskan salmon industry, because of the nature of the island-fringed coast of the southeastern part of the state, the length of the shoreline, and the suitability of the water courses for spawning, was and still remains, in spite of a decline in the catch, one of the major centers of the salmon industry. British Columbia, from Vancouver Island northward to Alaska (54°40′), is the Canadian sector of the salmon fishery. Puget Sound and the Strait of Juan de Fuca jointly make up a major sector of salmon industry of the State of Washington. From the Straight of Juan de Fuca to the Golden Gate and including the waters of the Columbia River system stretches a section of the Pacific coast long identified with the catching, freezing, canning, and processing of salmon.

Species of Salmon. The salmon of the Pacific waters of North America include five species: sockeye or red salmon, chinook or king salmon, pink or humpback salmon, silver or coho salmon, and chum or keta. The life cycles of the five species vary in detail, but they are all anadromous, migrating from the sea to fresh water to spawn and to die. The flesh of the salmon deteriorates rapidly, and as a consequence the canneries, freezers, and processing plants must be close-by, either onshore or on board the large freezer ships at sea.

Alaskan Salmon Fishery. The salmon fishing and canning industry of Alaska from the beginning has been isolated from market, from its labor supply, and from essential service facilities.[10] The once abundant fishery in Alaskan waters has suffered depletion, and production has generally declined since the 1930's. In 1936, the catch was 643.7 million pounds. In the 1960's, the catch averaged

[10] James A. Crutchfield and Guilio Pontecorvo, *The Pacific Salmon Fisheries,* Baltimore, 1969, p. 53.

under 300 million pounds annually. In this same time interval of slightly more than 30 years the real price of salmon rose from an average of 4.2 cents per pound in the late 1930's to 15.5 cents per pound in the 1965–1967 period.[11] There was a similar gain in the total vlaue of the catch.

The Alaskan fishery has suffered from other difficulties related to the labor force, absentee control of the industry, and inadequacy of governmental regulation when Alaska was a Territory of the United States. In the early days the labor force employed in the canneries was recruited in Seattle and San Francisco and included whites and a number of orientals. Later native Alaskans, both whites and nonwhites, were able to find employment in the industry.[12] From the late nineteenth century to the late 1960's the fish canneries in Alaska have been owned and operated by a number of large corporations or associations. These organizations have brought some order to the industry, but they cannot control the market. They find themselves in competition not only with other corporations but with the foreign producers, particularly Japan and Canada.

The Puget Sound Fishery. The configuration of the shoreline in northwest Washington, Vancouver Island, and British Columbia delineates major fishing grounds in Puget Sound, the Strait of Juan de Fuca, and the Strait of Georgia. These waters once became alive with salmon in the spring, summer, and autumn when several species of salmon were seeking out their spawning rivers (Fig. 5). Both commercial and sport fishermen have been attracted to these waters. The sockeye or red salmon head for the Fraser River inland from Vancouver, British Columbia. The other species search for the smaller streams where they were hatched. From year to year the salmon runs vary in the time they come in

Fig. 5 A purse seigner used to brail pink salmon caught in Dungeness Bay on the Washington side of the Strait of Juan de Fuca. (Department of Fisheries, State of Washington.)

from the Pacific and their transit of the entrance to the fresh-water streams.[13]

As in Alaska it has been necessary to bring the salmon fishery under study and supervision. Unrestricted fishing with all kinds of gear soon demonstrated that the salmon fishery was susceptible to depletion. It has been necessary to establish a closed season to prevent depletion. Selected areas along the shore of the Strait of Juan de Fuca and of Puget Sound have been set aside as salmon preserves. Some types of gear have been banned. Puget Sound is under the jurisdiction of the State of Washington and foreign fishing fleets are excluded. It is entirely possible that the salmon fishery of the Pacific coast could be seriously harmed if fishing just outside the 12-mile limit were greatly intensified by the fishing fleets of Japan and the Soviet Union. In spite of various protective measures there is the ever-present danger that overfishing will seriously deplete the resource.

Because of the joint interest of the United States and Canada in the Fraser River fishery the two countries, after repeated attempts to

[11] *Ibid.*, p. 203.
[12] *Ibid.*, p. 55.

[13] *Ibid.*, pp. 123–126.

reach agreement, signed a treaty creating the International Pacific Salmon Fisheries Commisssion.[14] It was ratified in 1937. It has been amended from time to time, but it is still operative. It was first concerned with sockeye salmon that reach the Fraser by way of the Strait of Georgia and the Strait of Juan de Fuca. In 1958, pink salmon were brought under the jurisdiction of the Commission.[15] This international agreement demonstrates that two friendly nations can and do cooperate to restore and maintain a resource that has already suffered serious depletion.

Strait of Juan de Fuca to the Golden Gate. Salmon fishing was an early development on the Columbia River and the coastal areas north to the Strait of Juan de Fuca and south to the Golden Gate. The waters of these areas have been accessible to sports fishermen, and as a result reliable data on the size of the catch are not abundant. The fishery is valuable as a source of food, and at the same time recreational fishing attracts thousands of fishermen each year. In 1967, sport catches of chinook salmon on the Columbia numbered 63,750, coho salmon 250,000, and pink salmon 2100.[16] Commercial fishing is now a regulated industry. Open seasons in late February, late April and early May, and mid-June to mid-July consist of a total of 69.75 days.[17] The fishery can be extended by reduced catches permitting thereby the escapement of a sufficient number of mature salmon to reach the spawning sectors in the headwater areas. Hatcheries are also in use to augment the natural biological process. In this old salmon-fishing area management practices are necessary to conserve a valuable resource. Fishing on the Columbia requires that Washington, Oregon, and Idaho develop and enforce similar regulations and cooperate on projects sponsored by the federal government (Fig. 6).

The Tuna Fishery. In the eastern Pacific from south of the equator to California and westward to Hawaii tuna in great numbers are caught and landed chiefly at California ports of San Diego, San Pedro, and San Francisco. The landings in California consisted of yellowfin, albacore, and skipjack tuna and totaled 328,980,000 pounds in 1967.[18] Tuna are also landed and processed in Hawaii.

In 1967, tuna landings in the United States totaled 329,000,000 pounds valued at $45 million. Tuna ranked second to menhaden in pounds landed, and were third in value, being outranked by shrimp and salmon.

Fishing for tuna in the eastern and central Pacific has become a highly competitive industry. The danger of overfishing has become a reality. Fishing boats or fleets of Canada, Mexico, Costa Rica, Panama, Colombia, Ecuador, Peru, Chile, Japan, Cuba, and the United States fish for tuna in the Pacific waters. In 1950, the Inter-American Tropical Tuna Commission (IATTC) was organized, and the Convention involving the United States and Costa Rica entered into force. Panama became a member in 1953, Ecuador in 1961, Mexico in 1964, and Canada in 1968. Ecuador withdrew in 1968.[19] The Commission has carried on biological research on the tuna, has tried to restrict fishing by establishing closed seasons, and has set quotas for the three principal species, yellowfin, albacore, and skipjack, to be taken by the fishing nations involved. Success has been limited because several of the countries are not members of the Convention, and enforcement of quotas is dependent upon voluntary compliance.

Recent studies have shown that tuna are

[14] *Ibid.,* p. 141.

[15] *Ibid.*

[16] Washington State Department of Fisheries, 1967, *77th Annual Report,* Olympia, Washington, pp. 32–33.

[17] *Ibid.,* pp. 44–45.

[18] *The California Marine Fish Catch for 1967,* State of California, Department of Fish and Game, Fish Bulletin 144, Sacramento, 1968, p. 11.

[19] *Annual Report* (1968), Inter-American Tropical Tuna Commission, La Jolla, California, 1969, p. 5.

Fig. 6 A view of Noyo harbor on the Mendocino Coast about 130 miles north of the Golden Gate. The troll fleet consist of salmon and albacore boats which fish in the off-shore waters of northern California. (California Department of Fish and Game.)

available in numbers sufficient to support commercial fishing in the tropical Atlantic, particularly in the Gulf of Guinea. In order that the tuna resources may be developed in an orderly manner several countries sent representatives to an International Convention for the Conservation of Atlantic Tuna at Rio de Janeiro, May 2–14, 1966. Delegates from Argentina, Brazil, Canada, Cuba, the Democratic Republic of the Congo, France, Japan, Portugal, Korea, the Republic of South Africa, Senegal, Spain, the Soviet Union, United Kingdom, United States, Uruguay, and Vene-

zuela met to consider the measures necessary to prevent overexploitation of the Atlantic tuna fishery.

The Halibut Fishery. In the north Pacific the halibut fishery requires continuing research to determine the dimensions of the area where halibut are abundant, where the spawning areas are located, and how many may be caught each year without depleting the resource. The International North Pacific Fisheries Commission, at its thirteenth annual meeting held in Vancouver, British Columbia, November 7–11, 1966, recommended that a section of southeastern Bering Sea be closed as a halibut nursery. Canada and the United States agreed to release all halibut caught in this area. Japan proposed to release all halibut under 26 inches in length. By these and other means the Commission and the adherents to the Convention hope that the measures taken will maintain the halibut fishery at a satisfactory level. In the 3-year period, 1965–1967, the annual catch was 40 million pounds. Over fishing could reduce the landings in future years.

King Crabs. In 1963, United States fishermen landed 79 million pounds of king crabs in Alaskan waters and adjacent sections of the Gulf of Alaska and Bering Sea. In the following year, the catch amounted to 86 million pounds. There is evidence that the catch cannot be greatly expanded without the threat of reduced catches in future years. The United States and the Soviet Union have exchanged publications, statistics on catches, and research data on king crabs in the eastern Bering Sea. This may be the first step toward a bilateral, or multilateral, agreement on regulation of the fishing industry and the conservation of this choice food resource. There is evidence of the diminishing size of the crabs caught.

Other Fish Caught in Pacific Waters. In addition to the abundant species such as salmon, tuna, and halibut other fish of great value are caught in the eastern Pacific Ocean by United States fishermen. These include sablefish, striped bass, hake, jack mackerel, bonito, ocean perch, herring, anchovy, and many others. Shellfish including shrimp, abalone clams, crabs, oysters, and others are also taken. Space limitations do not permit an extended discussion of these important fishery resources of the Pacific.

FUR SEALS

Fur Seals of the Pribilof Islands. The fur seals of the north Pacific bear their young on the rocky Pribilof Islands of the Bering Sea. With the onset of the winter season the seals swim far south in the Pacific, but in the early summer they return to their home rookeries on the Islands. For many decades before 1911 seal hunters posted themselves offshore and killed seals indiscriminately and in great numbers. As a consequence the herd of fur seals was depleted and endangered. In the early 1890's the United States sought sole jurisdiction over sealing in the Bering Sea to conserve this valuable resource.

In 1911, the United States, Russia, Japan, and Great Britain (for Canada) negotiated a treaty known as the North Pacific Sealing Convention. Pelagic or open-sea sealing was prohibited, and the United States was awarded responsibility for their protection, management of the herd, and the harvest of sealskins. In 1941, Japan withdrew from the Convention. A new agreement known as the Interim Convention on Conservation of North Pacific Fur Seals was negotiated in 1957. The signatory powers were Canada, Japan, the United States, and the Soviet Union. They amended the Interim Convention by signing a Protocol in 1963. The international agreement on the fur seal industry of the Pribilof Islands is a flexible instrument for adjusting the harvest of sealskins to the dimensions of the basic resource. The United States was, and continues to be, charged with the management of the rookeries on the Pribilof Islands and the conservation of the resource. Generally only mature males are killed each year, but in certain years females are also taken to keep the herd in check. For example, in 1963 a total of 85,254 seals, 34,217 of which were females, were killed. In 1967, the kill included 55,638 males and 10,034 females. This was regarded as a normal harvest in terms of the number of seals in the herd. However, the harvest in 1968 was only 40,970 skins.

The skins are divided among the signatory powers, with Canada and Japan each receiving 15 percent of the harvest. The United States and the Soviet Union divide the remainder. The net receipts representing the United States' share of the sealing operation are further divided. The State of Alaska receives a "statutory 70 percent share of net proceeds." [20] In 1967, Alaska received $322,256.

WHALING

Since the early nineteenth century whales, the mammoths of the marine environment, have been hunted so ruthlessly that there is danger that the number will be so diminished that there is genuine doubt about their survival. Because whales have been sought by the hunters or whalers of several nations using modern equipment and factory ships to utilize fully these marine mammals of great value, the prospects for their survival to reproduce their kind is not favorable.

Whaling for many decades of the last century was largely confined to the cool waters of the north Atlantic and the ice-free portions of the Arctic Ocean. Whales were numerous also in the north Pacific and the Bering Sea. However, in the early 1800's, New England whalers were searching for whales in the waters around Antarctica.

After the whales of the north Atlantic and north Pacific had been overhunted and the resource had been seriously depleted the search for whales shifted to the Antarctic where limited hunting over many decades permitted the herds to maintain themselves. Unlimited hunting from the early 1900's until after World War I greatly reduced the herds in the Antarctic waters. It became imperative that the problem receive an international solution.

The International Whaling Convention. An international convention for the regula-

tion of whaling was concluded at Geneva on September 24, 1931. It entered into force on January 16, 1935. The Convention provided for an International Whaling Commission (IWC) which would serve as the agency to give effect to the regulations set forth in the schedule of regulations. Soon whaling in the open seas suffered disruption because of World War II. The original convention was signed by sixteen countries, but only a few were able to become first-order whaling nations.

After the war a Protocol to the Convention was concluded on December 2, 1946, signed at Washington on November 19, 1956, ratification advised by the Senate on August 8, 1957, ratified by the President on August 30, 1957, proclaimed by the President on May 14, 1959, and entered into force on May 4, 1959.[21] The long interval of time between negotiation of the Protocol and the date it entered into force was related to difficulties in getting sixteen different nations to ratify the agreement. In the meantime whaling was largely an unregulated industry, except that prudent whaling was recognized as necessary to preserve the resource.

When the Convention of 1931 and the Protocol of 1946 were in force the IWC was able to give effect to the seventeen items listed in the schedule of regulations. The schedule contains too many items to report here, but a number may be listed. Inspectors were to be placed on factory ships and at land stations to see that the catch of whales was not in conflict with regulations. Gray or right whales were not to be killed except to feed the aborigines. Female whales with suckling young and calves were not to be killed. Legal lengths of 35 feet for sperm whales to 70 feet for blue whales were established. The Commission set limits

---

[20] *Report of the Bureau of Commercial Fisheries, for the Calendar Year, 1967,* U.S. Fish and Wildlife Service, United States Department of the Interior, Washington, D.C., 1969, p. 33.

[21] United States Department of State, *Treaties in Force, A List of Treaties and Other International Agreements of the United States in Force on January 1, 1969,* Publication 8432, Washington, D.C., 1969, pp. 362–363.

on the number of each species or subspecies that might be taken by the nationals of the whaling nations. Closed and open seasons have been prescribed. Whaling has been restricted to certain sectors of the seas that encircle Antarctica. Other regulations, quotas, and prohibitions have been prescribed but not adhered to strictly because the whales are a common property resource and enforcement of the terms of the Convention and the many regulations set forth in the schedule of the International Whaling Convention is dependent upon voluntary compliance.

The plight of the whales is such that the IWC has recommended lower and lower quotas to save certain species. For example, in 1966, the Commission suggested that the killing of blue whales be banned in the southern hemisphere instead of south of 40 degrees as previously recommended. However, working regulations and quotas are more generous than the strict recommendations.

Whales—A Common Property Resource. Whales, like fish, are a common property resource. They range widely in the open ocean and may be caught by whalers who have the equipment to find them, factory ships or shore stations to process the carcasses after they have been captured and killed, and the technical and managerial skills to prepare and market the various products such as the meat, oils, meal, whale bone, and other materials and by-products.

If whales are to be saved in sufficient numbers so that whaling can be maintained on a sustained-yield basis the support of conservationists must be enlisted to strengthen the International Whaling Commission. Charles A. Lindberg has been concerned about the decline in the whale population. Many leaders in conservation need to join in this movement to conserve an international resource.

GREAT LAKES FISHERIES

The Great Lakes system has a water area of 95,000 square miles, with 65 percent within the borders of the United States and 35 percent in the Province of Ontario, Canada. Lake Superior is the largest and deepest of the lakes, followed by Lake Michigan, the only one totally within the United States, and Lake Huron. The three lakes, often collectively referred to as the upper Great Lakes, are deeper, colder, and of higher environmental quality than Lakes Erie and Ontario, the lower Great Lakes. From an average elevation of 600 feet above sea level on Lake Superior, the waters of the Great Lakes descend to about 246 feet on Lake Ontario before flowing through the St. Lawrence River system to sea level at the Gulf of St. Lawrence.

The Great Lakes region represents a major concentration of population and industry for both the United States and Canada. The eight states bordering the Great Lakes on the United States side had a population of 70 million in 1960, representing 37 percent of the nation's total. Ontario, on the Canadian side, contained over 6 million people in 1961, or 34 percent of the national total. Although already containing over 75 million people, the Great Lakes region continues to increase in population at the rate of 25 percent per decade. From the point of view of fisheries, the concentration of population in the region represents a mixed blessing. On the one hand it represents a large and growing market for fishery products, but it also poses the threat of water pollution from industrial and municipal water-borne wastes which can seriously, and perhaps permanently, damage the aquatic environments of the Great Lakes.

The Great Lakes fisheries are small compared to the marine fisheries of the United States. In 1967, the United States catch in the Great Lakes was 82 million pounds, compared to a total national catch from all fishing areas of over 4 billion pounds. Though relatively small in production, the Great Lakes remain the most important source of fresh-water fishery products in the nation. Some Great Lakes fish, such as whitefish, yellow pike, lake trout, and the recently introduced coho salmon, are considered gourmet food items, selling for high prices in consumer markets.

Fishery production from the Great Lakes has been declining since about 1920. The most important factor in the decline of fishing in the upper Great Lakes has been the invasion of the sea lamprey. Native to the North Atlantic, the lamprey became landlocked in Lake Ontario and in 1921 entered the other Great Lakes through the Welland Canal. After passing through Lake Erie, which it found inhospitable, the lamprey exploded in great numbers in Lakes Huron, Michigan, and Superior. The sea lamprey is a parasite which attaches itself to adult fish and feeds on their blood and other body fluids. Within the decade of the 1950's, it nearly eliminated the highly prized lake trout and whitefish populations of the upper lakes which were the mainstays of the fishery. In response to the crisis, the Great Lakes Fishery Commission developed a selective chemical treatment to kill lamprey in its spawning streams. The treatment program has already controlled lamprey in Lake Superior and is being applied in Lakes Huron and Michigan. Intensive restocking programs are being undertaken to restore lake trout and whitefish to their former abundance.

In the lower Great Lakes, changes in the aquatic environment produced by water pollution appear to be the most important factor in the decline of the fishery. Selective overfishing of high-value species has also operated as a parallel, detrimental influence. The three fish species upon which the lower Great Lakes fishing industry was traditionally based are now so scarce as to be commercially insignificant. The lake herring disappeared after 1925 and the blue pike and yellow pike followed in the 1950's. Unfortunately, the fishery problems of the lower Great Lakes are not so easily solved as those of the upper Great Lakes. Although some progress has been made in water pollution abatement, the scale of effluent inputs and the cost of adequate waste treatment make dramatic improvements in the water quality of Lakes Erie and Ontario unlikely in the near future. Similarly, the overfishing problem is complicated by the fact that fishing regulations are fragmented among four states in the United States and one Canadian province. Uniform fishing regulations over an entire lake have been impossible to achieve thus far.

Of the five Great Lakes, Lake Michigan and Lake Erie comprise the most important fisheries. The combined United States and Canadian catch in the Great Lakes in 1967 was 128 million pounds, of which Lake Michigan and Lake Erie contributed 46 and 38 percent, respectively. The chub became the most valuable commercial fish in Lake Michigan following the decline of lake trout and now accounts for about half of the value of the catch. A small fish, the alewife, has recently undergone a population explosion in Lake Michigan and forms the basis for a newly developed industrial fishery. Using mechanized trawling gear, fishermen harvested over 40 million pounds of this plentiful, low-value fish for processing into fish meal, oil, and pet foods in 1967. This fishery is the most modern and efficient in the Great Lakes. On Lake Erie, a vigorous and competitive Canadian fishing industry has successfully challenged American fishermen and now dominates the fishery. Traditionally, the U.S. catch was twice the size of Canada's, but since the early 1950's, the Canadian industry has modernized and expanded, whereas decline and obsolescence characterize the American side of the lake. By 1967, the Canadian catch in Lake Erie was triple that of the United States. Yellow perch and smelt are presently the most important species in the Lake Erie fishery. Like Lake Michigan, Lake Erie is known to contain large populations of low-value fish, but an industrial fishery has not yet developed.

In addition to its commercial fishery, the Great Lakes comprise one of the nation's most important sport fisheries. The lakes contain a variety of sport fish and are within easy driving distance of more than 50 million people. Although reliable data on the sport fishery are lacking, it is likely that the harvest of fish by sportsmen approaches that of the commercial fishing industry. A recent, spectacular development in the sport fishery has been the introduction of the coho salmon to the Great Lakes. Native to the Pacific Northwest, the anadromous coho were first planted in Lake Michigan in 1966. The salmon have adapted successfully to their new environment and now attract sportsmen by the hundreds of thousands during annual spawning runs. The rapidly growing salmon feed primarily upon alewives, converting this abundant resource into a valuable recreational product. Based upon the success of the Lake Michigan stocking program, coho and other species of salmon are being planted in the other Great Lakes.

MISSISSIPPI RIVER FISHERIES

The Mississippi River fisheries region, comprised of the drainage basin of the Mississippi River and the basins of other streams which flow directly into the Gulf of Mexico, represents the nation's second ranking fresh-water fishery. The volume and value of the Mississippi River catch nearly equals that of the Great Lakes, but is comprised of different species and is spread over a much larger area, including all or part of twenty-eight states. The most important item in the regional catch is mussel shells which are exported to Japan for use in the cultured pearl industry. A small fragment of mussel shell is implanted in the pearl oyster to form the nucleus around which the pearl is formed. Mussel shells suitable for this purpose are found nowhere else in the world except in the Mississippi region. Demand for mussel shells is increasing rapidly, causing a corresponding expansion of the industry. Unfortunately, overfishing poses a threat to the long-term stability of the fishery.

Buffalo fish, carp, catfish, and bullheads are also important species harvested by the Mississippi River fishing industry. These fish are utilized both for human consumption and for processing into fish meal and pet foods.

Other Fresh-Water Fisheries. Since the drought years of the 1930's the development of farm ponds has been promoted by the Soil Conservation Service and other federal, state, and local agencies. The ponds, created by constructing a dam across a small stream or across a dry run, served to control or delay the flow of water to the larger streams, thereby lowering flood crests and reducing the damage along the main streams. Many of the small farm ponds, particularly in the dry sections of the country, dried up during the summer. Larger ponds which are fed by springs or perennial streams conserve water and at the same time provide a favorable habitat for several species of fresh-water fish.

The construction of large dams for generating hydro power, for irrigation water, and for domestic and industrial water supplies also usually created a choice recreational area. If the water was needed for domestic or household use swimming was usually banned. The reservoirs, when filled and when food supplies were adequate, became a favored fishing area. It is estimated that at least one out of five fishermen in the United States fishes in farm ponds and man-made reservoirs. Fishing is a recreational activity of major importance, and the fish caught make an important contribution to the food supply. Many poor people who are unemployed may live near a reservoir, a river, a pond, or along the seashore and with luck they may bring home enough fish for the principal meal of the day.

AQUACULTURE

Early in his history, perhaps in response to population pressures and a need to expand his food supplies, man developed agriculture by domesticating and cultivating selected plants and animals which he had previously hunted and gathered. A later development in the Far East and Europe was the raising of fish in ponds to supplement scarce meat supplies in peasant societies. Pond culture marks the beginning of agriculture's companion industry, aquaculture. Recently, due to shortages of certain valuable species of fish and shellfish, there has been renewed interest in aquaculture and the development of commercial fish farming in the United States.

Three-dimensional aquatic environments are inherently more productive than two-dimensional terrestrial environments, thus a greater biomass of fish can be supported per acre of water than of meat animals per acre of grazing land. In addition, fish are more efficient converters of feed to meat than land animals. Most animals require more than 10 pounds of feed to produce 1 pound of meat, and even the chicken, man's most efficient meat animal, has a feed-to-meat ratio of 8 to 1. Shellfish, such as shrimp, need an average of only 6 pounds of feed to produce 1 pound of meat, whereas catfish have a feed-to-meat ratio of less than 2 to 1.

Basically, aquaculture seeks to apply the productive practices of agriculture to marine animals. Within enclosed areas of the continental shelf, in small lakes, or in artificially constructed ponds, "weed" fish, which prey upon desired species or compete with them for food and living space, can be eradicated, thus increasing the populations of desired species. Within this closed aquatic system, fertilizers may be applied to increase the growth of plankton upon which the fish may feed. Finally, through biological research and selective breeding, more productive species of fish and shellfish can be developed. Through the application of these techniques, per acre yields of desirable species can be achieved which are several times those of natural fishing grounds.

Commercial aquaculture began in the United States with oyster farming in Chesapeake Bay and other shallow inlets on the Atlantic coast and has since spread to the Pacific coast of Washington. Soft-shelled crabs are cultivated on the coast of Virginia. A recent development has been shrimp farming in Florida, in response to the expanding domestic shrimp consumption and a relatively stable catch by the U.S. shrimp fleet. Shrimp can be raised in coastal embayments with yields of 800 to 1000 pounds per acre and in specially constructed tanks. In Japan, where tank culture for shrimp was developed, yields average 1500 to 2400 pounds per acre.[22] In fresh-water aquaculture, catfish is the most important crop. In Mississippi, Arkansas, and Louisiana yields average 1400 pounds per acre on more than 19,000 acres of ponds. Production of pond-reared catfish totaled 12,000,000 pounds in 1968, compared to a conventional catch of 36,000,000 pounds, and is growing at a rapid rate as demand increases for this popular southern delicacy. Trout farming in Colorado and the raising of buffalo fish in fallow rice fields in Arkansas provide additional examples of the growing trend toward aquaculture in the United States.

As the preceding examples indicate, commercial aquaculture is now devoted mainly to the production of high-value fish for high-income markets. It is to be hoped that in the future the development of a more efficient aquaculture can help to supplement the dietary deficiencies of poor people around the world.

Transplanting Fish to New but Similar Environments. The transplanting of species from their native environment to an area where conditions are similar may prove successful as a means of making fuller use of the marine environment. If the balance of nature is not disturbed the new species, when well established, may become an important source of a

[22] "How to Raise a Shrimp Cocktail," *Business Week*, No. 2090, September 20, 1969, pp. 184–186.

highly digestible protein. Trout from North American waters have been successfully transplanted in lakes and streams of the high Andes and have become well established. Oysters from Japan and from the Atlantic coastal waters have been transplanted in favorable locations in sheltered coastal waters of the Pacific states. One species of salmon has been transplanted in New Zealand waters; another species has been introduced into the Arctic streams of the Soviet Union and the species has spread westward to Norway, Iceland, and Greenland.[23]

FISHERIES FOR THE FUTURE

International Obligations. Action to protect, conserve, and enhance the fishery resources of the open seas require international cooperation. The United States is currently a party to a number of bilateral and multilateral agreements dealing with resources of the marine environment. The United States and Canada have a joint interest in the fishery resources of the Great Lakes, and as a consequence both countries are parties to a bilateral agreement signed in Washington, September 10, 1954. It entered into force on October 11, 1955, and was amended on April 5, 1966, and again on May 19, 1967. The United States and Canada are parties to six other agreements concerned with fishing and sealing.

Multilateral agreements are necessary in waters fished by three or more nations. The United States in recent years has been a party to twenty or more international agreements dealing with the taking of salmon, tuna, shrimp, halibut, whales, seals, and other bio-

logical resources of the sea. On January 1, 1969, the United States was a party to twelve conventions, including amended agreements, protocols to international conventions, and declarations of understandings regarding conventions.[24] It can be expected that earlier and current agreements will be renegotiated and that new conventions will be required to get international cooperation to conserve and manage the resources of the sea.

The several agreements must be renegotiated from time to time. Renegotiation, ratification, and finally compliance by the signatory powers may require several years, and during this time overfishing may deplete an important marine resource. Usually each treaty provides for an international commission that tries to establish quotas for each country, delineate reserves where spawning areas are off-limits to fishermen, prescribe the type of gear that fishermen may use, fix fishing seasons, and make other recommendations for the guidance of the fishing fleets of the several nations involved. Compliance, of course, is voluntary, and violators go unpunished unless the fishing craft enter territorial waters where they are subject to seizure and confiscation of fish caught and the gear used. In spite of the limitations of international agreements they are necessary as the most important means of protecting and preserving a highly valued marine resource.

Research in Oceanography. Knowledge of the seas has been accumulating ever since man tested his ability to master the watery environment that washed the shores of the lands he inhabited. Because of the great area, depth, and internal characteristics of this three-dimensional body of water much knowledge of the sea remains unknown or obscure to man. There has been a resurgence of interest in the field of oceanography in recent years. This renewed interest should be encouraged and sup-

[23] National Oceanographic Council, *Hearings before the Committee on Commerce,* United States Senate, 89th Congress, First Session, on S. 944, Appendix D, "Preliminary Plan for Expansion of Oceanographic Research as a Contribution to the Peacetime Economy of the United States under Continuing of a Cold War Thaw," Washington, D.C., 1965, pp. 162–163.

[24] *Treaties in Force,* January 1, 1969, *op. cit.,* pp. 286–287, 343, and 362–363.

ported by the scientific community and especially by the Congress, which has the power to finance a large number of research projects proposed by the colleges and universities, by research institutes, and by other private and public agencies.

Marine Ecology. In addition to support for projects having as their goal increasing man's knowledge of the physical characteristics of the marine environment, it is also necessary that the living resources be investigated. The research must extend beyond life histories of individual species and subspecies; it must be concerned with marine ecology. Fish and other marine animals live, grow, reproduce, and die in an environment that is both physical and biological. The studies in the field of ecology should be focused on interaction and interrelations in an oceanic setting. Such studies may require more biological laboratories onshore and more floating laboratories at sea.

Economic Future of the Fisheries. The fishing industry of the United States is being confronted by a variety of economic problems including low prices for its products, competition from imports, obsolete fishing vessels, high interest rates, high labor costs, competition by foreign fishing fleets, and many others.

The solutions cannot be provided on a short-run basis but will require action extending over many years and will require the cooperation of federal and state agencies and the fishing industry as well.

Vice-President Spiro Agnew is Chairman of the National Council on Marine Resources and Engineering Development. The Council was created to prepare short-range programs which would give the Congress time to find and develop the long-range programs that seem to be necessary. The Council has already announced administration support for five programs. These include: (1) Coastal Zone Management including the Great Lakes; (2) Establish Coastal Laboratories; (3) Pilot Technological Study of Lake Restoration; (4) International Decade of Ocean Exploration; and (5) Arctic Environmental Research. Under these headings there are subsidiary recommendations. While these programs receive early attention of the Congress, financial aid is available as in the past to support research and other activities related to the fisheries. If fish is to continue as an important component of the diet of the American people the fishing industry will need financial support beyond the earnings from the industry.

References

Alexander, Lewis M., editor, *The Law of the Sea*, Proceedings of the 3rd Annual Conference of the Law of the Sea Institute, Kingston, R.I., 1968, University of Rhode Island, Kingston, 1969.

Baker, Ralph C., Ford Wilke, and Howard Baltzo, *The Northern Fur Seal Circular 169*, United States Bureau of Commercial Fisheries, Department of the Interior, Washington, D.C., 1963.

Baldwin, Norman S. and Robert W. Saalfeld, *Commercial Fish Production in the Great Lakes, 1867–1960*, Great Lakes Fishery Commission, Technical Report No. 3, Ann Arbor, Michigan, 1962.

Bardach, John, *Harvest of the Sea*, Allen & Unwin, London, 1969.

Behrman, Daniel, *The New World of the Oceans*, Little, Brown and Co., Boston, 1969.

Biological Conservation, An International Journal, edited by Nicholas Polunin (Geneva, Switzerland), printed in England, Quarterly, First issue published, October 1968.

Boyle, C. L., "Oil Pollution of the Sea: Is the End in Sight," *Biological Conserva-tion*, Vol. 1, 1969, pp. 319–327.

Carson, Rachel L., *The Sea Around Us*, Oxford University Press, New York, 1951.

Chapman, W. M., "Potential Resources of the Oceans," Serial Publication 89-21, 89th Congress, First Session, 1965, Government Printing Office, Washington, D.C., 1965, pp. 132–156.

Christy, Frank T., Jr., and Anthony Scott, *The Commonwealth in Ocean Fisher-ies*, The Johns Hopkins Press, Baltimore (for Resources for the Future, Inc.), 1966.

Cotter, Charles H., *The Physical Geography of the Oceans*, American Elsevier Publishing Co., New York, 1966.

Cowen, Robert C., *Frontiers of the Sea*, Doubleday & Company, Garden City, New York, 1960.

Crutchfield, James A. and Giulio Pontecorvo, *The Pacific Salmon Fisheries, A Study in Irrational Conservation*, Resources for the Future, The Johns Hop-kins Press, Baltimore, 1969.

Daniel, Hawthorne and Francis Minot, *The Inexhaustible Sea*, Dodd, Mead & Company, New York, 1934.

Engel, Leonard and The Editors of Life, *The Sea*, Life Nature Library, Time Inc., New York, 1961.

Ericson, Nicole and Goesta Willin, *The Everchanging Sea*, Alfred A. Knopf, New York, 1967.

Federal Aid in Fish and Wildlife Restoration, 1968, Bureau of Sport Fisheries and Wildlife, United States Department of the Interior, Washington, D.C., 1968.

Firth, Frank E., editor, *The Encyclopedia of Marine Resources*, D. Van Nostrand Co., Princeton, New Jersey, 1969.

Fisher, Joseph L., "New Perspectives on Conservation," *Biological Conservation*, Vol. 1, 1969, pp. 111–116.

Frick, Harold C., *Economic Aspects of the Great Lakes Fisheries of Ontario*, Fisheries Research Board of Canada, Bulletin No. 149, Ottawa, 1965.

Gordon, H. Scott, "The Economic Theory of a Common Property Resource: The Fishery," *Journal of Political Economy*, Vol. 62, 1954, pp. 124–142.

Great Lakes Fishery Commission, *Annual Reports* 1956–.

Hobbs, Carl L. and Karl F. Lagler, *Fishes of the Great Lakes Region*, University of Michigan Press, Ann Arbor, 1965.

International Pacific Salmon Fisheries Commission, *Annual Report 1968*, New Westminister, Canada, 1969.

Johnston, Douglas M., *International Law of Fisheries*, Yale University Press, New Haven, 1965.

Koo, Ted S. Y., editor, *Studies of Alaska Red Salmon*, University of Washington Press, Seattle, 1963.

Lewis, Donald W., *The Decline of the Lake Erie Commercial Fishing Industry in Ohio*, Natural Resources Institute, The Ohio State University, Columbus, 1967.

Lyles, Charles H., *Fishery Statistics of the United States,* Bureau of Commercial Fisheries, U.S. Fish and Wildlife Service, Department of the Interior, Washington, D.C., Annual, 1918–.

Maury, Matthew Fontaine, *Physical Geography of the Sea,* Harper and Brothers, New York, 1856.

McKee, Alexander, *Farming the Sea,* Thomas Y. Crowell Co., New York, 1969.

Molluscan Shellfish, Hearings of the Committee on Merchant Marine and Fisheries, 88th Congress, First Session, October 2 and 3, 1963, Serial No. 88-13, Washington, D.C., 1963.

National Fisherman Yearbook Issue, 1969, Camden, Maine.

Netboy, Anthony, *The Atlantic Salmon,* Houghton Mifflin Co., Boston, 1968.

The Ocean, a *Scientific American* book, W. H. Freeman and Company, San Francisco, 1969.

Oda, Shigeru, *International Control of the Sea,* A. W. Sythoff, Leyden, Netherlands, 1963.

Olson, Theodore A. and Frederick J. Burgess, editors, *Pollution and Marine Ecology,* Interscience Publishers, New York, 1967.

A Plan for Marine Resources of the Atlantic Coastal Zone (To accompany Folio 18 of the *Serial Atlas of the Marine Environment*), American Geographical Society, New York, 1969.

Spinner, George P., *The Wildlife Wetlands and Shellfish Areas of the Atlantic Coastal Zone,* Folio 18, *Serial Atlas of the Marine Environment,* American Geographical Society, New York, 1969.

Rogers, George W., *Alaska in Transition, The Southeast Region,* Resources for the Future, The Johns Hopkins Press, Baltimore, 1960.

State of California, Department of Fish and Game, Sacramento, *Annual Reports.*

The State of World Fisheries: World Food Problems, No. 7, Food and Agriculture Organization of the United Nations, Rome, 1968.

Stroud, Richard H. and Robert G. Martin, *Fish Conservation Highlights, 1963–1967,* Sport Fishing Institute, Washington, D.C., 1968.

Sverdrup, H. U., Richard Fleming, and Martin W. Johnson, *The Oceans,* Prentice-Hall, New York, 1942.

Teal, John and Mildred Teal, *Life and Death of the Salt Marsh,* Little, Brown & Co., Boston, 1969.

Thompson, W. F., *The Effect of Fishing on Stocks of Halibut in the Pacific,* University of Washington Press, Seattle, 1950.

Thompson, W. F. and N. L. Freeman, *History of the Pacific Halibut Fishery,* Report 5, International Fisheries Commission, Vancouver, B.C., 1930.

Tomasevich, Jozo, *International Agreements on Conservation of Marine Resources, with Special Reference to the North Pacific,* Food Research Institute, Stanford University, California, 1943.

Turekian, Karl K., *Oceans,* Prentice-Hall, Englewood Cliffs, New Jersey, 1968.

United States Bureau of Commercial Fisheries, *Great Lakes Fisheries, 1967,* Washington, D.C., 1969.

United States Fish and Wildlife Service, Bureau of Commercial Fisheries, *Com-*

mercial Fisheries Review, Department of the Interior, Washington, D.C.,
Monthly.

United States Fish and Wildlife Service, Bureau of Commercial Fisheries, *Fishery
Statistics of the United States,* Department of the Interior, Washington, D.C.,
Annual, 1918–.

Walford, Lionel A., *Living Resources of the Sea,* The Ronald Press Company,
New York, 1958.

Washington State Department of Fisheries, *Annual Reports,* Olympia, Washington.

Part 7

MARION CLAWSON
Resources for the Future, Inc.

CHAPTER 22

Recreational Resources

The demand for outdoor recreation is booming, and public attention to recreational resources has increased greatly in the past decade. One need only look at any popular park on a pleasant summer Sunday afternoon for dramatic evidence; or one may look at the statistics of visits to various kinds of outdoor recreation areas.[1] The park shows a comparatively large number of people, often filling to overflowing the facilities available for them; outdoor recreation area visits show a steady upward trend in the figures. Today people demand and get much more outdoor recreation than they demanded and got 20 years ago.

Why do people seek outdoor recreation in such large and growing numbers? What kinds of natural resources are most in demand for outdoor recreation use? How are these natural resources used for this purpose? These are some of the questions to which this chapter is directed.

A Few Preliminary Definitions. In the voluminous literature about outdoor recreation, there is often confusion and apparently divergent conclusions, arising in no small part from the lack of commonly accepted definitions of some of the chief terms. In the hope of avoiding some of this confusion, we give three definitions as basic to this chapter[2]:

1. *Recreation* means activity (or inactivity) undertaken because one wants to do it. As such, it contrasts with work, done primarily to earn money or otherwise to provide the "necessities" of life, or what have come to be so considered, for one's self and one's family. It also contrasts with the mechanics of life, such as eating, sleeping, operations to keep house, dishes, clothing, and person clean, whether these are for one's self or for his or her family. There is not a sharp line between recreation and all other activities. The same

---

[1] A basic reference source in this field is *Outdoor Recreation for America,* a Report to the President and to the Congress by the Outdoor Recreation Resources Review Commission, Government Printing Office, Washington, 1962; and the 27 Study Reports prepared under the direction of the Commission and published by the Government Printing Office subsequent to the Commission's report. These reports contain a wealth of detail and references to many related publications.

[2] Marion Clawson and Jack L. Knetsch, *Economics of Outdoor Recreation,* The Johns Hopkins Press, Baltimore, 1966.

activity may sometimes be work and sometimes recreation. Cooking, dressmaking, embroidery, furniture-making, and many other specific activities may fall into either classification.

The distinguishing characteristic of recreation is the attitude with which an activity (or inactivity) is undertaken, not the specific nature of that activity. If undertaken because one wants to do it, with no feeling of compulsion or "ought to," then it is almost surely recreation. In the modern complex world, recreation is often a major opportunity for self-expression. Since one more freely chooses his recreation than he does his job or his necessary chores of living, his choice is more nearly a personal one and less a socially determined one.

Recreation is closely related to leisure. If leisure is taken to mean time in which activities (or inactivity) consciously decided on are undertaken, then the relation of recreation and leisure is very close. On this basis, mere idleness is neither leisure nor recreation.

2. *Outdoor recreation* is simply those kinds of recreation typically undertaken in the outdoors.

3. *Resources* for outdoor recreation include areas of land, bodies of water, forests, swamps, and other natural features which are in demand, or likely to become so, for outdoor recreation. The physical characteristics of these natural elements of the landscape affect their use for outdoor recreation, but they become resources for outdoor recreation only as they are useful for this purpose. Land, water, forests, and other natural features which for any reason are not or cannot be used for recreation are not part of the outdoor recreation resource. In this respect, outdoor recreation is no different from farming, forestry, grazing, mining, or any other use of natural resources. There is nothing inherent in the physical landscape or features which makes it a recreation resource; it is the combination of the natural qualities and the ability and desire of

man to use it which makes a resource out of what otherwise may be a more or less meaningless combination of rocks, soil, and trees.

The Statistical Record. The statistical record for every major kind of public outdoor recreation area, and most individual parks or other kinds of areas, shows a mounting use year after year. For most areas, the annual increases are a relatively constant percentage of the number of visits; the higher the level of visits, the greater the absolute size of the increase. The more people enjoy outdoor recreation, the more they want it, it seems.

Actual data on usage of public outdoor recreation areas are rather poor—they are available only for recent years for many areas, and their accuracy is not always above criticism. The best data relate to the postwar years. An upward trend in visits is evident in these data as it is in data for the prewar years. For the national parks, data are available since 1910, and the earlier data show the same tendency toward a constant percentage increase from year to year. The tendency toward increased usage leveled off somewhat during the severe depression years of the early 1930's, but showed growth again before the war. During the war, visits to the national park system and to national forests declined by about two-thirds, for travel restrictions and other wartime situations inhibited the usual recreation developments.

Since the war, a marked upward rise in recreation has occurred on each major type of outdoor recreation area (Table 1). Total visits to all units of the national park system more than doubled from 1946 to 1955, and more than doubled again from 1955 to 1965; total visits to the national forests increased more than twofold in the earlier period, but by threefold in the latter period. Large increases were shown on the reservoirs constructed by the Corps of Engineers—about double in the 10 years from 1955 to 1965. TVA reservoirs and all state parks generally experienced similar increases in visits (Fig. 1). The increase in use was apparently least for city parks, but it is also true that our data are poorest for these, and perhaps the actual increase in visits was much more than these data suggest.

Although the trend varies somewhat from one kind of area to another, and even more from one specific park to another, and also somewhat from year to year, the rate of increase is remarkably close to a median figure of 10 percent annually. A constant percentage increase of this magnitude means a doubling in about 8 years. It can be seen that this rate was actually reached or exceeded in several of the instances in Table 1. No constant percentage rate of increase can go on unchanged forever; in time, the figures reach astronomical heights. If the past percentage trend in visits to Corps of Engineers reservoirs continued un-

Fig. 1   The TVA lakes are widely used for recreational purposes. Recreational facilities and improvements valued at more than $192 million have been placed on lakes and lakeshores by states, counties, cities, and private individuals and companies as well as by the Authority. Boats kept on TVA lakes now number more than 52,000. The lakes are popular for boating (including sailing), water skiing, and fishing. (Bureau of Outdoor Recreation, Department of the Interior.)

Table 1. Annual Visits to Major Public Recreation Areas, 1946, 1955, 1960, and 1965 (Millions of Visits)

Kind of Area	1946	1955	1960	1965
National park system	22	50	72	133
National forests	18	46	92	160
Corps of Engineers reservoirs	1	63	109	129
TVA reservoirs [2]	7 [3]	28	42	49
All state parks	93	232	263	421
City parks [4]	503	724	1	1

[1] No data available; visits to Corps reservoirs totaled 26 million in 1952.

[2] Visitor days in 1947 and 1955; visits in other years.

[3] 1947.

[4] Visits to selected facilities only; data unavailable for total use of city parks.

[Source: 1946 for all areas and 1955 for TVA and city parks, *Statistics on Outdoor Recreation*, by Marion Clawson, published by Resources for the Future, Inc., Washington, D.C., 1958; 1955 (except as noted), 1960, and 1965, *Recreation and Park Yearbooks;* 1961 and 1966, National Recreation Association and National Recreation and Parks Association, respectively.]

changed to the year 2000, every man, woman, and child in the entire nation would be spending 2500 days annually at Corps reservoirs! Some leveling off in past growth rates simply must take place sometime; but when, and from what level of use? This is a question to which we shall return later in this chapter.

One additional point should be borne in mind in considering the figures in Table 1. The number of specific areas and the total acreage of each kind of area increased during the years under consideration. This was especially marked for the Corps reservoirs. A major part of the increased visitation record is probably the result of this larger number and acreage. However, changes in the acreage and number of national forests during this period were minimal; yet recreation visits to them increased almost as much as to any other kind of area. It is by no means clear that all the visits to a new area are a net addition—some may be merely a diversion to this area of visits that otherwise would have occurred on one of the older areas. The future trend in total outdoor recreation activity will depend in part on the acreages available and their location. If relatively few overcrowded areas are available, the visits will not rise as much as will be the case if many new areas are provided.

Basic Factors Underlying Recreation Trends. Although various factors may be operative in particular situations, four basic factors seem to be generally operative and to underlie the large and continuing increases in outdoor recreation activity: population changes, income changes, increased leisure, and improved transportation. These deserve a closer look.

One of the most persistent and pervasive forces in American history has been the steady growth of population. From less than 4 million persons in 1790, when the first Census was taken, we have increased to over 200 million today. There has apparently never been a year in our national history when total population declined. The annual rate of growth was roughly 3 percent, until about the middle of last century; then it declined slowly to a low of roughly 0.75 percent during the 1930's; and it has since risen to about 1.7 percent. Many countries have experienced long secular declines in population growth; ours is one of the few, if not the only one, that has experienced a reversal of such a long-term trend. The death rate has declined steadily; although additional modest declines seem probable in the future, no spectacular changes seem possible. The big and erratic variable has been birth rate. Although this is somewhat responsive to prosperity and depression, and to war, it has changed in the past in ways not easily understood or predictable. The consensus among experts is that the rate of population growth for the next generation will not differ very greatly from the present rate; this means a total population in excess of 300 million by the year 2000.

Although changes in total numbers of people has been the major population change, yet changes in the rural–urban relationship merit comment, as affecting outdoor recreation.

There has been a steady move from rural to urban areas for a long time in the United States, but in recent decades it has reached such proportions as to mean an actual loss of people in many rural areas. During the decade of the 1950's, while total United States population was increasing by 18.5 percent, more than half of all countries lost people, and many additional rural areas did also. Within the large urban complexes, the move has been away from the city center, toward the suburbs. City people, on the average, patronize public outdoor recreation areas far more than do rural people; hence a move of people from rural areas to cities is likely to mean increased demand for outdoor recreation.

Real income per capita has also trended upward in the United States for a long time. However, this trend has been somewhat irregular, being broken by major depressions and becoming steeper in periods of rising prosperity. Moreover, the basic trend has often been obscured by changing price levels. However, in terms of constant prices real income per capita has doubled from the mid-1920's to over $2000 now. For the past several decades, the average annual rate of increase in per capita income, measured in constant dollars, has been nearly 2 percent—roughly the same as the present rate of increase in total population. The best outlook today is for a continued rise in real income per capita, at roughly the present rate. Average per capita incomes, measured in present-day dollars, may well reach $4100 annually by the year 2000.

Another aspect of this rising income situation has special importance to outdoor recreation. Although expenditures for the so-called necessities of life—food, shelter, and clothing—tend to rise as real incomes rise, yet a larger and larger portion of total income falls into the "discretionary" class. People have more choice about how to use some of it. As a matter of fact, as nearly as we can tell from rather unsatisfactory data, the percentage spent on outdoor recreation has risen considerably since the war. A rising percentage of a rising average income obviously means a lot more money spent for this purpose. Total expenditures for outdoor recreation in the year 2000 may well reach six times what they were in 1960.

There has been a rising trend in total leisure in the United States for several decades. This has been manifest not merely in shortened average or typical work weeks, which indeed have become shorter over a long period, but also in other factors. At one time, many men and women worked 7 days a week and most of the others worked 6; now most work 5, with some 6, and some shorter. At one time, 10- and 12-hour days were common; now 8 is typical. As recently as the end of World War I, steel workers were on an 84-hour work week: 12 hours a day, 7 days a week. The work week has shortened irregularly—a good deal in the 1930's, but with some lengthening during the war, and no major trend in recent years away from the prewar situation.

Other changes have been taking place. One dramatic change has been the rise in the paid vacation. Once the privilege of some white-collar workers, it is now nearly universal in union labor contracts and common among many other classes of workers. The length of the paid vacation has also increased. The number of older retired persons has increased, as has the proportion of young people not yet in the labor force, and there is, of course, a great increase in their actual numbers. Whereas boys often began work at 15 years or even younger in an earlier day, today few begin before 18 and some not until older. These older and young people often demand far more outdoor recreation than they would want if they were working.

The fourth major force has been the improvement in travel facilities. When travel was predominantly by public transport or by horse and buggy, as before World War I, a trip to a park only a few miles away was a major undertaking. The great rise in private automobile ownership and the concomitant improvement in highways have opened great opportunities to average persons for convenient, comfortable, and relatively inexpensive travel. Total travel for all purposes has increased from about 500 miles annually before World War I to about 6000 miles per person annually today. Although we do not know how much of this travel is for recreation, it seems probable that a larger percentage is for this purpose today than was true in an earlier time. Many a family today drives 1000, 2000, or even 5000 miles while on their vacation trip. Few areas are inaccessible any longer. The supply of outdoor recreation has opened up greatly to the individual, while at the same time the demand for any area has increased greatly.

Interestingly enough, the upward trend in each of these four major factors has been at nearly the same rate (Fig. 2). That is, the annual growth in each has been somewhat less than 2 percent, as far as our somewhat imperfect data will permit us to calculate. This is to be contrasted with the upward trend in use of many outdoor recreation areas of about 10 percent annually, which we noted earlier. It seems highly probable that these four basic factors have interacted, so that the upward trend in one has reinforced the upward trend in another. For instance, had the improvement in roads and automobiles occurred without any rise in real income per capita—an improbable situation, because roads and autos improved in large part as a result of the demand created by the higher incomes and were financed out of those higher incomes—it is probable that people would have been unable to afford to travel to outdoor recreation areas in the great numbers that actually did. As a matter of fact, during the war when travel was restricted but incomes were high, the number of visits to national parks and national forests declined by more than half. Even if incomes

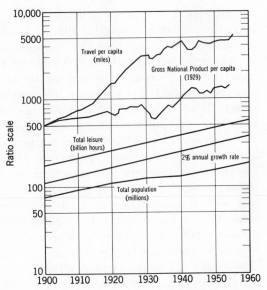

Fig. 2 Four important factors explain the continued growth in outdoor recreation activities since 1900; more people have enjoyed more leisure, higher income, and greatly improved travel facilities. (*Land and Water for Recreation,* Rand McNally and Company, Chicago, 1963.)

had risen and transportation had improved, use of outdoor recreation areas would not have risen as much as it did if working hours had remained at their level of a generation ago. It has been the combination of factors which has been most significant.

The best current prospects are that the upward trend in each of these basic factors will continue. In the year 2000, we shall probably have from 300 to 350 million people, compared with 200 million now; average per capita incomes, in terms of present prices, will then average about $4100, compared with over $2000 now; paid vacations will be longer and more common, typical work weeks somewhat shorter, more people will be retired, and otherwise total leisure in the whole society will be greater; and as transportation will be improved more and more, people will typically travel considerably more.[3] All of this

[3] See report of Outdoor Recreation Resources Review Commission, *op. cit.,* p. 45. See also Hans H.

will lead to a materially higher level of demand for outdoor recreation. The Outdoor Recreation Resources Review Commission estimated that total demand in the year 2000 would be three times what it was in 1960; the author has estimated that in 2000 it would be ten times what it was in 1956 (which is equivalent to about six times what it actually was in 1960).[4] As we have noted earlier, present trends simply must flatten out sometime, somewhere; but we cannot be sure where or at what level this will occur. Almost everyone at all familiar with the recreation scene agrees, however, that future demand for outdoor recreation will be much greater than present demand. Outdoor recreation is, and will continue to be, a growing use of natural resources.

Programmatic Response to Recreation Demand. The persistent and rapidly increasing public activity in outdoor recreation since the war required, and has secured, numerous programmatic responses, both public and private.

The establishment of the Outdoor Recreation Resources Review Commission in 1958 was really the first such response. Its creation constituted an important Congressional, Presidential, and general public recognition of the growing importance of outdoor recreation. Its report, published in January 1962, was a landmark in the field.[5] Several specific public actions have grown directly out of that report and subsequent discussions.

First, the Bureau of Outdoor Recreation has been established in the Department of the Interior to provide a degree of coordination of all federal programs affecting outdoor recreation, as well as to perform other functions described later. A Presidential Council on

Landsberg, Leonard Fischman, and Joseph L. Fisher, *Resources in America's Future,* The Johns Hopkins Press, Baltimore, 1963.

[4] Commission report, op. cit., p. 47; and Marion Clawson, R. Burnell Held, and Charles H. Stoddard, *Land for the Future,* The Johns Hopkins Press, Baltimore, 1960.

[5] *Ibid.*

Recreational and Natural Beauty, composed of Cabinet officers and other high officials, was established; also, a Citizen's Committee to advise on the same subject.

A more tangible result, perhaps, was the establishment of the Land and Water Conservation Fund. Certain federal revenues from disposition of surplus property, from gasoline taxes on motor boats, and from admission charges to certain federal recreation areas were pooled to provide a Fund for purchase of recreation land for federal agencies and as a system of grants to states. By the summer of 1966, nearly $30 million had been spent to acquire federal lands and about $145 million had been apportioned to the states, but much of the latter had not been spent by that date. With a continued and rather severe escalation in prices of recreation land, the Fund was proving inadequate for its purposes, and in 1968 new legislation provided additional sources of financing, up to $200 million total in the Fund annually.

One result of this system of federal grants to states has been the development of comprehensive outdoor recreation plans by the states, since the Bureau of Outdoor Recreation is required by law to make such federal grants available only in states where such plans exist. Although many of these plans are less complete or less imaginative than might be desired, their very existence is evidence of great forward steps in recreation planning.

The Bureau of Outdoor Recreation has commissioned a number of studies, and now publishes a number of reports periodically. One of these is *Outdoor Recreation Action,* which discusses current actions in the outdoor recreation field; another is a selected bibliography; and others deal with other aspects of outdoor recreation.

Another development has been the consolidation into one organization, the National Recreation and Park Association, of a number of previously separate private organizations. This new organization has both professional and lay members, and publications directed at

each. One of the latter is a recreation research journal, begun in the fall of 1968.

In the past decade, a considerable number of conferences of professional workers in outdoor recreation have been held in various parts of the country. Although annual or other meetings of professional workers have long been held, some of these more recent conferences have dealt with research, education, and other aspects of outdoor recreation that previously had had little attention.

The Nature of the Recreation Experience. In order to understand the use of natural resources for outdoor recreation, one must consider carefully the nature of the recreation experience. Every outdoor recreation experience consists of five rather clearly identifiable phases, as follows (Fig. 3):

1. *The anticipation or planning phase.* This takes place before the family or other recreation group leaves home. This is when the decision is made as to where to go, when, how long to stay, what equipment to buy, how much to spend, and the like. It seems probable that more than half of all money spent for outdoor recreation is spent at this time, in the user's hometown.[6] This planning may be careful or careless, informed or uninformed; in any case plans may be modified as the experience later unfolds.

2. *Travel to the recreation site itself.* The length of the trip and the distance traveled vary according to the kind of area visited, but it is not uncommon for as much time and money to be spent in this phase as is spent later at the site itself. Some people regard this travel phase as enjoyable because some people travel for the pleasure of traveling itself; but it seems probable that others regard this with less enthusiasm, as something necessary in order to reach their destination, but not enjoyable for itself alone. The travel may take a few minutes, to visit a nearby park, or a few

[6] Marion Clawson, "Private and Public Provision of Outdoor Recreation Opportunity," in *Economic Studies of Outdoor Recreation,* ORRRC Study Report 24, Washington, D.C., 1962.

and this in turn leads to planning for next trip.

In anticipation of an outdoor recreation experience, a family plans where it will go and what it will do, and buys equipment and supplies.

Back home again, the family recalls its recreation experience, often with great pleasure. Memories may be an important part of the whole experience.

In order to reach the outdoor recreation area of its choice, a family must travel. Considerable expense is involved in such travel, and often as much time is consumed in travel as later on the site. Travel is often not as pleasurable as experience on the site.

When the activities at the site are through, the family must travel back to its home. Often tired, frequently in a hurry, sometimes broke, the family is in a different mood than when it travelled in the opposite direction.

When it arrives at the recreation site, the family may engage in many activities. Bodies of water are especially valued for outdoor recreation. The activities at the site generally provide the basic purpose for the whole experience, even when they occupy less than half the time and require less than half the total expense.

Fig. 3 Phases of the whole outdoor recreation experience: anticipation, travel to recreation area, on-site activities, the return trip, and recollection. (*Land and Water for Recreation,* Rand McNally and Company.)

hours for an all-day outing, or several days for a longer vacation(Fig. 4).

3. *On-site experiences.* This is a part of the whole experience that most persons think of when outdoor recreation is mentioned; it is indeed the chief reason for the whole experience and the chief user of natural resources; we shall consider it in more detail later in this chapter. But the on-site part of the whole experience is only a part of the whole—whether one considers time required or used, money spent, or satisfactions obtained. The range in activities at the site is very wide, and we shall consider some of them in detail later.

4. *Travel home again.* Although the end points of this journey are the same as travel to the site, the intermediate route may be different. Moreover, the recreationists are quite probably in a different mood now—their vacation is gone, their money has been spent, they may be tired, and, for the moment, at least, they may be in a much less buoyant mood than when they ventured forth on this recreation experience. Nevertheless, consider-

Fig. 4 The Yakima Project, Washington, provides fine picnic and camping sites along the shores of Kachess Reservoir. Many tourists as well as local people find here conditions favorable for quiet relaxation. (Photograph by Rasmussen, Bureau of Reclamation.)

able time and money must perforce be spent on this phase of the whole experience.

5. *Recollection is the last major phase of the whole experience.* Back home again, the family or others who went on the trip tell of their experiences to the stay-at-homes, neighbors, friends, co-workers, and others. The memories may not exactly coincide with the experience itself—the fish get bigger, the mosquitoes more fierce, the camping more primitive, etc. It is probable that very often more satisfaction is achieved in this phase than in any other. Less money is spent here, and the time requirement is not rigid. Perhaps most important, it is the nature of the recollections of one experience which do most to determine the timing and the character of the next experience.

These five phases are indispensable parts of the whole experience; none can be omitted ordinarily, although the time and money spent in each might vary considerably. The costs of all phases must be included as part of a package; so must the satisfactions and annoyances of all parts. What happens enroute may affect users' attitudes toward a park fully as much as what they find on the site itself.

Systems of Outdoor Recreation Areas. Recreation areas of different kinds and in different locations form highly complex systems. In this, they are not unlike the plants and animals in an ecosystem. Each has its particular role or function; the relationships between different units may be complementary, competitive, or partly each. When people go to one lake or water body, they may thereby be reducing their recreation use of other ones. But the presence of more than one lake or water body may lead recreationists as a group to develop more water sports than would be the case if there were but one lake. The amount of use a particular area receives is likely to depend to a large extent on the availability of alternative areas for the same users and their families.

There are so many different kinds of outdoor recreation areas that it is helpful to group them into a few broad classes. Some loss in detail is more than offset by greater simplicity for readier understanding. Classifications can be based on one or more of various factors. The Outdoor Recreation Resources Review Commission classified areas largely on the basis of their management problems and objectives.[7] These classes were established: (1) high-density recreation areas, (2) general outdoor recreation areas, (3) natural environment areas, (4) unique natural areas, (5) primitive areas, and (6) historic and cultural sites. Criteria for evaluating each were established, and management guides set forth for each.

A different basis of classification is according to economic characteristics.[8] A threefold grouping of user-oriented, intermediate, and resource-based areas has been established on this basis (Table 2). User-oriented areas must be located near where people live, are used typically after work or after school, consist individually of rather small tracts, and are often city parks. Intermediate areas can lie farther from where people live, but should ordinarily be within 1 or 2 hours driving time. They are typically used for day-long outings and are often part of a state park system. Within the restrictions of distance, they should be on the best sites available. Resource-based areas include the outstanding mountain, shore, swamp, or other natural features, and are often located relatively far from where most people live. They are often visited during vacations. National parks and national forests fall into this category.

Outdoor recreation areas could be grouped according to the type of natural resources included. Thus extensive water surfaces, shores,

---

[7] *Ibid.*

[8] Marion Clawson, R. Burnell Held, and C. H. Stoddard, *Land for the Future,* The Johns Hopkins Press, Baltimore, 1960.

Table 2. General Classification of Outdoor Recreational Uses and Resources

	Type of Recreation Area		
	User-Oriented	*Resource-Based*	*Intermediate*
1. General location	Close to users; on whatever resources are available	Where outstanding resources can be found; may be distant from most users	Must not be too remote from users; on best resources available within distance limitation
2. Major types of activity	Games, such as golf and tennis; swimming; picnicking; walks and horseback riding; zoos, etc.; playing by children	Major sightseeing; scientific and historical interest; hiking and mountain climbing; camping, fishing and hunting	Camping, picnicking, hiking, swimming, hunting, fishing
3. When major use occurs	After hours (school or work)	Vacations	Day outings and weekends
4. Typical sizes of areas	One to a hundred, or at most, a few hundred acres	Usually some thousands of acres, perhaps many thousands	A hundred to several thousand acres
5. Common types of agency responsibility	City, county, or other local government; private	National parks and national forests primarily; state parks in some cases; private, especially for seashore and major lakes	State parks; private

streams, forests, mountains, caves, and many other natural features could be grouped separately. In practice, many recreation areas contain more than one kind of natural resource; sometimes it is the combination of resources that makes an area most attractive. Within some limits, resources can be created for recreation use. Trees can be planted to create forested areas, or dams may create artificial lakes to provide for water sports.

Whatever the basis of classification, there is, in fact, a continuum from one extreme to another. If one element of the classification system is distance from users, then there are obviously areas ranging from the nearby local park to the most distant wilderness area. Or if size of the tract is the basis of classification, parks run from an acre, or at least from a very few acres, up to a million or more acres for large national parks. Even the ORRRC management classification system has intermediate types—an area may be somewhat intermediate between a general outdoor recreation area and a natural environment area, for instance. This continuum from one type to another facilitates transfers of use from one area to another; if one area is crowded, part of its potential use load is likely to be diverted to another somewhat similar area.

This continuum among recreation areas, and the interchangeability in use within limits, emphasizes the system aspect of all the areas. If a new park or area is added, it not merely offers some use, it also affects the use of many others, directly or indirectly. In this respect, the various parks in a general area or region are somewhat like the different dams along a single river; the operation and value of each dam are affected by the existence and operations of all the others.

Characteristics of Public Recreation Areas.
The areas of mass use for outdoor recreation are often publicly owned, as are many areas which have relatively light use. Our information about publicly owned areas is better than it is about privately owned areas, and so we shall take up the public areas first.

Among the resource-based publicly owned outdoor recreation areas, the national parks are outstanding. Beginning with Yellowstone National Park, which was set aside in 1872, a number of areas have been established over the years as national parks. Each has been outstanding in one or more respects, and each has had national, as contrasted with local, importance. Several include outstanding mountain scenery; Yellowstone, Mt. Rainier, Mt. McKinley, Glacier, Yosemite, Rocky Mountain, and others include large mountain areas. Grand Canyon is noted for its tremendous canyon, the Everglades are a great swamp, Sequoia has its famous trees, etc. Most, if not all, contain many natural features. In them, all commercial uses are excluded (with minor exceptions) and each area is for outdoor recreation in the broadest sense of the word. The national parks average nearly 500,000 acres each. To these national parks have been added national monuments, historic areas, and other units. The total area of the national park system in 1965 was about 27 million acres, or slightly over 1 percent of the total land area of the nation. The average intensity of use of this whole system is about five visits annually per acre, but this average conceals great variations, often within the same park. Some parts are intensively used, others have scarcely any visitors. As we have noted earlier, the trend in use has been upward at about 10 percent annually. The long-run future of many of these areas may be in jeopardy as a result of this use trend; it is difficult to see how the national park system can absorb ten to twenty times its present volume of visitors, which the present trends will bring in 30 or 40 years, without serious damage to

the areas themselves.[9] Although a number of proposals are pending now for additions to the national park system, it cannot possibly be extended indefinitely simply because there is not an unlimited supply of suitable additional areas.

Another major resource-based kind of public recreation area is the national forests. These are multiple-use areas; recreation is only one use, sometimes not the major use. Relatively limited areas have been set aside for exclusive or chief use for recreation; the remaining areas are nearly all open for this purpose. Although the national forests were started somewhat later than the national parks, their area has long been larger, about 180 million acres at present. On the average, national forests have about 1 million acres each. On the average, their use is about one visit per acre annually, but they, too, have some intensively used tracts and relatively large areas used very little indeed. Timber production and harvest are the chief purpose on much of the national forest area, and livestock grazing on other large areas. Recreation is an increasingly important use of many national forests, and today is a far more important objective of multiple-use management than formerly. Although the national forests probably will not expand greatly in total area, because of rather general opposition to large increases in federal land holdings, the acreage set aside for outdoor recreation within them could be increased greatly.

The federal wildlife refuges provide a unique kind of resource-based outdoor recreation area. Wildlife today has little economic value beyond its recreation value. The area in all federal wildlife refuges actually exceeds the area in the whole national park system, but this includes several huge game ranges in Alaska and in the West, where relatively few

[9] F. Fraser Darling and Noel D. Eichhorn, *Man and Nature in the National Parks—Reflections on Policy,* Conservation Foundation, Washington, 1967.

Fig. 5 Burr Oak Lodge in southern Ohio. This recreational facility, consisting of 2152 acres, can accommodate a limited number of people at the lodge. It operates the year-round and in season provides areas for camping, swimming, fishing, and boating. (Ohio Department of Natural Resources, Division of Parks and Recreation.)

visitors can or wish to go. Average rate of visitation on wildlife refuges is only half that on the national forests, but many refuges get large numbers of visitors each year. Other uses are subordinate to the main purpose of protecting wildlife. Some expansion in this system is desirable for strictly wildlife purposes, and additional recreation use of the whole system can and undoubtedly will be made.

Of the intermediate type of recreation areas, state parks are the most popular publicly owned kind (Fig. 5). Although some

states have had parks for a long time, the system as a whole got a major boost during the 1930's. Many states, in order to qualify for employment programs financed out of federal funds, substantially added to their park acreage then. More than half of the whole state park acreage is included in a few very large (over 50,000-acre) state parks: Baxter in Maine; Adirondacks, Catskill, and Allegany in New York; Porcupine Mountains in Michigan; Custer in South Dakota; and Anza Desert and Borrego in California. More than a third of all the state parks are less than 50 acres each, and 60 percent are smaller than 250 acres. In 1965, total visits to state parks exceeded visits to all kinds of resource-based public recreation areas. Visits per acre in 1965 averaged about 80 per acre—more than fifteen times the average rate of use of national parks and eighty times the average rate of use of national forests. State parks offer the greatest possibility for increase in acreage of any major kind of public outdoor recreation area. Their acreage could be increased tenfold or more by converting suitable areas to this use and by improving other areas for this purpose. In the past half dozen years, New York, New Jersey, Pennsylvania, Wisconsin, California, and Washington have embarked on major programs to increase their state park acreage. All states have shown notable progress, due in considerable part to the federal grants provided by the Land and Water Conservation Fund.

Reservoir areas and surrounding lands of reservoirs built by TVA and the Corps of Engineers are another kind of public owned intermediate type of outdoor recreation area. These reservoirs are built for flood protection, navigation improvement, and hydroelectric power production primarily, but recreation is coming to be an increasingly important by-product. The total area of this type is somewhat greater than the total area of all state parks, but use is definitely less, so that average use per acre is around thirty visits annually. Partly because of increasing areas in Corps reservoirs, and partly because of the tremendous increase in popularity of water sports, use of these areas for recreation grew extremely rapidly after the war until about 1960, but the rate of growth in use has now slowed down to about that on many other public recreation areas. The same purposes underlying present reservoirs are almost sure to lead to the construction of many more reservoirs in the years ahead, and they probably will be used as recreation areas even more extensively. More-

over, construction of moderate-sized reservoirs primarily for recreation and only secondarily for the traditional uses of reservoirs is likely to become common in the future.

City parks are the chief kind of user-oriented, publicly owned outdoor recreation area. They began in the latter part of the nineteenth century, and their acreage has expanded roughly in proportion to the growth in city population. As we have noted, the prime requisite of such parks is a location close to where people live. Individually, most such parks are small, averaging less than 40 acres each, and with many less than 10 acres. The total area in all city parks is less than 1 million acres. We lack accurate data on the number of visits to them, but it probably exceeds those to all other public areas combined. The extent of use probably exceeds 1500 visits per acre annually, on the average. Like the other areas, this average includes some tracts used much more widely and some much less. Although ample land exists in the expanding suburban areas where city parks might be developed, the big problem is to see that it is reserved for this purpose before it becomes covered with houses. With the almost certain large and continuing growth in urban population, major increases in city parks will be required in the future, and their provision will be a major resource management problem.

Use of Private Land for Public Recreation. We have much less data, especially historical statistical data, about use of privately owned land for recreation purposes than we have for public land. Various situations exist.[10] A common one involves the man who owns a piece of land for the use of his family and perhaps a few friends, but who on occasion may rent it out to others. Although we do not know precisely how many private tracts are owned primarily for such recreation, the number may

[10] Marion Clawson, "Private and Public Provision of Outdoor Recreation Opportunity," ORRRC Study Report 24, *Economic Studies of Outdoor Recreation,* Washington, D.C., 1962.

well run more than a million, for there are more than a million very small forest holdings, many of which must be owned primarily for recreation.

Many landowners permit hunting and fishing by the public on their lands, sometimes without charging a fee, sometimes only on payment of fees, which in some areas may be rather large. In the more thickly settled parts of the country, private land is increasingly being prohibited from private hunting, at least without the permission of the owner. Many landowners have had unfortunate experiences by allowing hunting on their land, such as fences cut, gates left open, livestock shot, and machinery damaged. Sportsmen's groups and others have sought to promote better hunters' manners in the woods and on the farms.[11] In less thickly settled parts of the country, most private land is open to hunting.

Other private landowners permit other recreational uses of their land, sometimes providing considerable facilities for doing so.[12] Large lumber and other timber-owning companies, in particular, have provided camping and other facilities. So have some large electric utility companies. These landowners have also had unfavorable experiences from their lands being used privately, but they recognize that the public wants to use large, extensive, forested areas and they have sought to make such lands available.

In some cases, clubs or other private groups own land that they use for their own enjoyment. A group can own a larger tract, and develop it more fully, than could an individual. Most clubs are on a nonprofit base; their land and facilities are generally available only to their members and guests. Such recreation developments include a wide range of activities, from swimming pools and golf courses to hunting lodges in relatively inaccessible territory.

In still other instances, owners of land conduct major businesses to provide outdoor recreation opportunity to the general public.[13] We have no data on the total extent of such activity. Many of these are located on water bodies and offer water sports of different kinds to patrons. Others offer camping, horseback riding, and other extensive land-use activities. These various operations go by many different names, which sometimes accurately describe their chief activities: resorts, dude ranches, campgrounds, commercial beaches, yacht and boat clubs, shooting preserves, vacation farms, etc. Particularly noteworthy has been the great rise in privately owned campgrounds catering to the general public, especially since 1960. Many private areas are so located that their guests or patrons can also take advantage of publicly owned areas; a boating club is on the shores of a public lake, for instance, or a dude ranch is near or actually within a national park or national forest. Scattered private holdings within the latter are often the basis for a recreation business.

Many problems are connected with this type of business. One major one is that so much of it is highly seasonal. Buildings must be maintained on a year-round basis, and even some staff is maintained year round when most or all the business is confined to a season of 3 months or less. Another obstacle is that so much public recreation area is open without charge or for a very low fee. Although the private providers often charge primarily for the service they render, rather than for their resources as such, the competition from public areas is certainly a factor. The American public, or at least a large part of it,

[11] The Izaak Walton League has put on a campaign to this end, for instance. See *Outdoor America,* June 1958, August 1959, September 1960, October 1960, and January 1961.

[12] *Recreation on Forest Industry Lands,* results of a survey by American Forest Products Industries, Washington, D.C., 1960.

[13] *Private Outdoor Recreation Facilities,* ORRRC Study Report 11, Washington, D.C., 1962.

has become accustomed to free or low-cost outdoor recreation and does not realize the value of the resources it so obtains. But there are many business problems in this type of enterprise also, just as there are in the running of hotels, motels, and other businesses catering to the general public.

There are also great opportunities for greater public use of private land for outdoor recreation. After all, more than two-thirds of all land in the United States is privately owned and much of it has a large recreation potential. Since the early 1960's, the U.S. Department of Agriculture has been active in helping farmers and other rural landowners to establish outdoor recreation enterprises, for profit. The large amount of probable future demand for outdoor recreation makes it probable that public areas will not expand fast enough to satisfy this demand. Recreation could well develop as the dominant use for some private areas or as one use among several on larger areas.

Outdoor Recreation Activities. Americans engage in various activities outdoors which are termed recreation. The simple ones of pleasure riding in automobiles, walking for pleasure, picnicking, and swimming are the most popular, whether we judge by the numbers of people who engage in them or by the numbers of days spent at them.[14] More than half of the total population apparently engage in riding, walking, and picnicking. Boating, canoeing, fishing, hunting, camping, and other relatively common activities are participated in by fewer people for fewer days per year. So are still others, such as horseback riding, water skiing, sailing, and ice sports. In addition to these reasonably common activities, there are many in which far fewer people participate and for relatively few days in total —mountain climbing, cave exploring (spelunking), and many other specialized activi-

ties. Some are too expensive or too strenuous for mass participation or lack general appeal, but they still have ardent devotees. There are, of course, many kinds of participator sports also, but these we exclude from this consideration of outdoor recreation.

Most people take their vacations in the summer season or during the warmer months of the year. Many older people follow the sun and spend their vacation time in the South. Florida, the Gulf coast states, New Mexico, Arizona, and California have become the destination of thousands of people every winter. Some, particularly the older people, are seeking comfort in the sun; others are seeking the diversion, the excitement, and the entertainment available in these resort areas. But there are people who seek recreation in the cooler latitudes and higher altitudes where there are opportunities for hunting, ice fishing, skating, skiing, ice sailing, and other winter sports (Fig. 6). The development of ski resorts with suitable slopes, lifts, lodges to accommodate the guests, and other necessary facilities requires an investment of many thousands of dollars. The tourists themselves must spend considerable sums to be properly outfitted and equipped to participate in the sports programs. In recent years the use of ice machines has brought skiing and skating to warmer latitudes and lower altitudes than was thought possible a few years ago.

It is impossible in this chapter to attempt to describe these activities in any detail. The essential fact to keep in mind is that "outdoor recreation" is not a single activity, but many, with different groups interested in each, with different and sometimes conflicting demands for natural resources. The fisherman and the water skier may have divergent interests in their use of a body of water, as will the most ardent hunter and the rancher for using grazing land, for instance. Some outdoor recreation activities appeal primarily to one age group or another; hunting, for instance, is primarily an adult male activity. However, very

[14] ORRRC report, *Outdoor Recreation for America,* op. cit.

Fig. 6 Winter scene at Squaw Valley high in the Sierra Nevada Range in east-central California. The view shows the 5000-foot KT-22 double chair lift. This famous winter sports area averages 450 inches of snow annually. (Bureau of Reclamation.)

often, the family goes as a group to outdoor recreation areas. In this case, there must be something at the site to appeal to each member of the family. Dad and the older boy go fishing, the younger children swim and play on the beach, the tots use the playground equipment, mothers sit quietly in the shade, etc. Many activities require water bodies or are more enjoyable near water. This fact, plus the need for a variety of activities, lends special importance to the presence of attractive water bodies in outdoor recreation areas.

Effect of Socioeconomic Factors. Not everyone participates in outdoor recreation to the same degree; part of the differences is because of personal preferences, but a considerable part depends on easily observable socioeconomic characteristics (Fig. 7). As people get older, they participate less in outdoor recrea-

tion, on the average, and the kinds of activity also change. Persons over 65 indulge in about half the total activity of persons 18 to 24.[15] Swimming declines rapidly with age, whereas nature and bird walks increase with age. Total recreation activity rises with family income, at least within the range up to $10,000; over that level, outdoor activity per family seems not to rise and may actually decline a little. Even more striking are the variations in kinds of activity with changes in income; in general, those activities involving comparatively high costs increase much faster as income rises, whereas the less expensive kinds increase less or actually decrease.

Total outdoor recreation activity also rises with education, at least up to the point of finishing high school. People with more education participate more in outdoor recreation, but this may not be a simple cause and effect relationship; those personal qualities which lead someone to get an education may also be the qualities which make him enjoy the outdoors. Total recreation activity also rises with amounts of paid vacation; an even greater response is evident for those kinds of activities which can well be carried on only during vacation, mountain climbing, for instance.

All the foregoing are net relationships. That is, older people of the same income level will engage less in outdoor recreation than will young people; but older persons sometimes have higher incomes and their effect may more than offset the effect of greater age, so that one group of older persons may participate more in outdoor activity than a particular group of younger persons. The wide variations in individual tastes should always be kept in mind also. Thus it is very difficult to predict what a particular individual will do, even if we know his age, income, education,

[15] See Marion Clawson, *Land and Water for Recreation*, Rand McNally and Co., Chicago, 1963, where data from ORRRC Study Reports have been summarized.

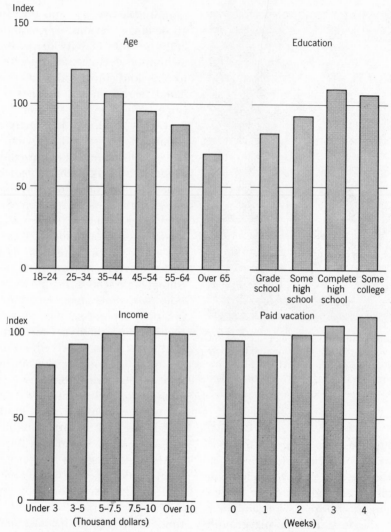

Fig. 7 Net effect of various socioeconomic factors on relative participation in all forms of outdoor recreation. (*Land and Water for Recreation,* Rand McNally and Company.)

and other characteristics; but we can estimate what the average participation of a group will be, depending on these same factors.

Resource Characteristics for Outdoor Recreation. The characteristics making for a good outdoor recreation area depend on the kind of use the area is planned for.

A resource-based outdoor recreation area re-

quires, by definition, unusual natural qualities. These may be outstanding mountains, lakes, swamps, sea or lake shores, geologic formations, or other kinds of areas. They must be truly outstanding by national, not by local, standards. It is not easy to define "outstanding" in quantitative or objective terms, so that every observer would arrive at the same judgment. But anyone who has seen Grand Canyon, or the Yellowstone geysers, or the Yosemite Falls, or any one of numerous other areas set aside in the national park system or included within some of the national forests will agree that these are superlative by any standards.

The same is true, generally, of historic sites. We all agree that Independence Square in Philadelphia is a part of the basic history of the United States. Again, the standard of national, rather than local, interest must apply.

The difficulty with these two classes comes with many areas that are on the borderline. In the Great Plains, where mountains are lacking, the Black Hills are a most unusual feature. Parts of them deserve recognition, as they have achieved in the Custer State Park of South Dakota, even if they lack national significance. The same is true of many historical sites.

When it comes to the intermediate-type outdoor recreation area, attractive water areas, woods, and related natural resources are important, but now *location* becomes more significant. We have noted earlier that good intermediate recreation areas should be within 2, and preferably within 1, hours driving time from where people live. But in most cases this locational requirement gives a rather large range for exercise of choice. Within that range of choice as to location, natural qualities should dominate. The importance of water bodies for recreation has been mentioned. An attractive lake or stream permits swimming, boating, fishing, water skiing, and other water sports, singly or in various combinations. A fairly high degree of water quality is often necessary for these uses; in the future, avoidance of water pollution in order to permit recreation will often be a major resource management problem. Trees for shade or for general enjoyment are also important; so are some areas of modest topography for picnicking, camping, and other uses.

One characteristic of intermediate outdoor recreation areas is that they can often be *made*—they need not be only found, as is true with the resource-based areas. Attractive lakes can often be made by constructing dams with fixed overflow outlets, so that the shores develop the characteristics of natural lakes. An adequate, but not excessive, watershed is required. Trees can be planted; even beaches can sometimes be constructed by filling with sand. Worn-out or relatively unproductive farm or forest land, somewhat uneven in topography, can be converted into quite attractive parks by relatively modest expenditures of money and a few years time. Thousands of suitable sites exist in the United States. The possibilities of expansion are better for intermediate-type recreation areas than for any other.

When it comes to the user-oriented areas, location is all-important. By and large, people live where they do for reasons other than the availability of local recreation—and largely independent of the availability of other types also. The user-oriented recreation must be moved to where people are, and not require people to travel far for it. For neighborhood parks and playgrounds a distance of a quarter to a half mile is as far as people will go; other kinds of local parks can be a little farther away. Obviously, the choice of an area is now sharply limited, and is actually limited still further by the present buildings on each tract. With very limited exceptions, we have not been willing to spend the money to clear dwellings or other buildings from sites in order to make them into parks or playgrounds. Most user-oriented recreation areas require modest topography and medium soil conditions for their best use and development. Some areas, however, have been developed on lands too steep or too swampy for dwellings or other buildings, or on areas too subject to flood overflow. Some excellent local parks have been made on sites abandoned for other purposes, such as abandoned quarries. If the space exists in the proper location, modern earth-moving and other technologies can often convert odds and ends of land into attractive local parks.

The foregoing has made it clear, we hope, that it is difficult to judge the recreation usefulness of a tract of land merely by looking at it. One can come nearer doing this for resource-based areas than for others; but even here, it is how this area compares with others of somewhat similar characteristics which may be decisive. For other kinds of areas, where location is more and more important, one must look beyond the specific tract to form a judgment about it. Tracts can be, and have been, used for recreation when a view limited to the specific tract would reject it as entirely unsuitable for the purpose. If something better is unavailable, we shall often make the best of what does exist, for the demand for outdoor recreation is usually quite strong.

The Role of Government. As we have noted, outdoor recreation takes place on both public and private lands and waters. In the latter cases, the value of an area often depends on the availability of public areas reasonably nearby. Thus the role of government in providing outdoor recreation is very great, often crucial.

Public recreation areas are provided by almost every level of government. The federal government provides national parks and related areas, national forests, various reservoir areas, and wildlife refuges. The states provide parks, forests, highway waysides, and various recreation services to local government and to citizen groups. Cities and other units of local government provide parks, school forests, and various recreation services. There is no clear, sharp line separating the activites of these various kinds of government, although there are general fields of interest or specialty. One of the major policy questions in the recreation field, to which we shall return later, is the proper role of government at different levels.

This has concerned many persons in recent years; the Outdoor Recreation Resources Review Commission gave attention to this problem, among many others.

In considering this matter, it is helpful to realize that government (at any level) may and usually does operate in two rather distinctly different roles. On the one hand, it is an "entrepreneur"—a planner who acquires, develops, and manages a particular area for outdoor recreation purposes. Only government can carry out this role adequately in many cases. Government can consider the needs of all people for outdoor recreation, not merely the needs of those who can afford to pay well; it can use its legal powers to acquire needed land, when private individuals often could not acquire the same land at any reasonable price or even at all; and the large capacity of many recreation areas makes it imperative that they be managed for relatively large groups of people, which often government can do very well. For all these reasons, government has a special, although not exclusive, role to play in the outdoor recreation field.

The other role that government usually plays is that of financier of outdoor recreation. Funds are raised by various means of taxation, to buy, improve, and manage recreation areas. By and large, until now, users have paid very little of the costs through charges levied on each use. There has been no correspondence between the taxes one paid to help provide outdoor recreation and the use which he got out of the public recreation areas. One reason many people have pushed for public outdoor recreation is that it is "free"; obviously, of course, it is not free, because someone must pay for it some way. The costs are submerged in the general tax bills.

However, there has been a marked trend toward the collection of user fees and special charges for special services in federal and state recreation and park areas, especially since the establishment of the Land and Water Conservation Fund. The private suppliers of out-door recreation obviously charge for this serv-ice. They and the public agencies are finding much less resistance from the public to the payment of such fees and charges than was feared, some years ago, might be the case.

The two roles of government could be sepa-rated largely or wholly. This could be done if the government, which planned and devel-oped the recreation area, required its users to pay all the costs, through entrance fees or other charges based on use of the area. There may be good reasons of public policy why we wish to provide free outdoor recreation to some groups in the population who cannot af-ford to pay. However, in practice, most of the public outdoor recreation areas have been provided for the groups who can afford to pay entrance fees sufficient to pay the costs in-volved. This seems clearly true for those types of recreation where the users must incur sub-stantial other costs to visit the areas anyway —the resource-based and intermediate areas, in general. But even in cities parks have been provided far more liberally in the higher-in-come sections where people can afford modest charges than they have been made available in the lowest-income neighborhoods where the capacity to pay is much lower.

Outdoor recreation in Canada. The discus-sion in this chapter has been primarily in terms of the recreation situation in the United States, but nearly all of it applies equally well to Canada. Canada has a total population of about 10 percent that of the United States, and in many respects its economy is roughly 10 percent that of the United States; in total land and water area, of course, Canada is very large.

The same recreation demand factors of larger population, higher real incomes per capita, more leisure, and better travel facilities apply in Canada, and with about equal force. Attendance at public park and recreation areas has been mounting in Canada since the war, and roughly parallel to the increases in the United States. Although Canada has a very large area of both land and water, its population is closely grouped along its south-ern border, and much of its potential recrea-tion land is remote from most of its popula-tion. Popular nearby parks are crowded in Canada, as in the United States.

Canada has national, provincial, and local parks, as well as many private outdoor recrea-tion areas, in these ways also being similar to the United States. In recent years there has been a growth in research on the problems of outdoor recreation, and many professional conferences have been held in Canada.

Some Canadians come to the United States for outdoor recreation; this is particularly marked in New England, in the Pacific Northwest, and in some of our southern areas in winter. Canadians come to the United States in comparatively large numbers as tour-ists, for whom our outdoor recreation areas are one attraction. Americans, in turn, go to Canada in large numbers for outdoor recrea-tion, visiting many areas from Newfoundland and Novia Scotia, across Quebec and Ontario, to Alberta and British Columbia. We like to canoe, camp, fish, and hunt in Canada, as well as be sight seers at their attractions. In outdoor recreation, as in so many other as-pects of life, the two nations have many simi-lar and common interests, each learning from the other.

Some Problems for the Future. We may well conclude this chapter by raising briefly a few of the questions about outdoor recreation that are almost sure to rise in the future.

First, how might our country become better coordinated, but not centralized, in planning for outdoor recreation? We have noted that outdoor recreation is one function of many units of government, at federal, state, and local levels, and also of many private organi-zations. None can adequately plan its pro-gram without taking into consideration the plans and programs of all the others, but there is no mechanism whereby this can be done. It is most unlikely—and this author would argue, undesirable as well—that we will have highly centralized planning in this field. Americans simply resist such centralization. But there is a very real problem here that will demand attention as the use of outdoor recreation areas grows.

Second, how might we estimate, with reasonable accuracy, the future demand for outdoor recreation, and the areas of land and water required to meet those demands? As we have noted, it is not easy to estimate future demands. We cannot simply extend past trends indefinitely, for they lead to ridiculous figures; but we are far from sure as to what should be substituted for such trend extensions. Even if we knew how many million visits there would be, in some future year, to a particular kind of outdoor recreation area, we are still not fully certain as to how much land and water are required to meet this demand properly. We may be forced to accept heavier use ratios in the future than we have thought desirable in the past, and yet there is surely some point at which satisfactions from outdoor recreation decline because of overcrowding.

Third, how can we encourage greater public use of private land for outdoor recreation? Most land is privately owned, especially in the densely settled regions of the nation. Some of this land can be used for recreation, either as the major use or as one use which is not incompatible with other uses. But there are many difficult problems, for the recreationist and more particularly for the landowner. Can we devise better and fairer arrangements whereby the wishes of the one can be satisfied while protecting the legitimate rights of the other? This is a field for research and experimentation.

Last, how can the money necessary for the provision of the public areas best be raised? There will almost surely be considerable resistance to a greatly increased use of general tax revenues for this purpose. The fact that some people rarely use outdoor recreation areas, while others often use areas located outside the political units in which they pay taxes, raises serious problems of equity. One way to avoid these problems would be to raise more of the necessary money from entrance fees or other charges levied on those actually using the recreation areas. But this is strongly opposed by still other groups in the population, who firmly believe that outdoor recreation should be free to all who seek it. This is obviously a political issue which will have to be settled by argument and votes, as are many social issues in this country.

These and other problems that could be posed are another way of emphasizing that outdoor recreation is a rapidly growing activity in the United States. Unless something very drastic, such as a thermonuclear war, intervenes, we shall surely see outdoor recreation continue to grow as a human activity and as a user of natural resources.

References

Beauty for America, Proceedings of the White House Conference on Natural Beauty, Government Printing Office, Washington, D.C., 1965.

Brightbill, C. K., *Man and Leisure: A Philosophy of Recreation,* Prentice-Hall, Inc., Englewood Cliffs, New Jersey, 1961.

Brockman, Christian Frank, *Recreational Use of Wild Lands,* McGraw-Hill Book Co., New York, 1959.

Butler, George D., *Introduction to Community Recreation,* McGraw-Hill Book Co., New York, 1949.

Clawson, Marion, *Land and Water for Recreation,* Resources for the Future Background Series, Rand McNally and Co., Chicago, 1963.

Clawson, Marion, R. Burnell Held, and Charles H. Stoddard, "Land for Recreation," Chapter 3 in *Land for the Future,* Resources for the Future, The Johns Hopkins Press, Baltimore, 1960, pp. 124–193.

Clawson, Marion and Jack L. Knetsch, *Economics of Outdoor Recreation,* The Johns Hopkins Press, Baltimore, 1966.

Langton, Clair Van Norman, *Principles of Health, Physical Education, and Recreation,* The Ronald Press, New York, 1962.

McClellan, James C., *Recreation on Forest Industry Lands,* American Forest Products Industries, Washington, D.C., 1962.

McCune, Ellis, *Recreation and the Parks,* Haynes Foundation, Los Angeles, 1954.

Meyer, Harold D. and Charles K. Brightbill, *State Recreation: Organization and Administration,* A. S. Barnes and Co., New York, 1950.

Miller, Norman, *The Leisure Age: Its Challenge to Recreation,* Wadsworth Publication Co., Belmont, California, 1963.

The President's Council on Recreation and Natural Beauty, *From Sea to Shining Sea,* Government Printing Office, Washington, D.C., 1968.

School of Natural Resources, University of Michigan, and Bureau of Outdoor Recreation, U.S. Department of the Interior, *National Conference on Outdoor Recreation Research,* Ann Arbor Publishers, Ann Arbor, Michigan, May 1963.

United States Department of Agriculture, *Outdoors USA, Yearbook of Agriculture,* Government Printing Office, Washington, D.C., 1967.

United States Department of the Interior, *Community Recreation and the Public Domain,* Government Printing Office, Washington, D.C., 1963.

United States National Park Service, *Water Recreation Needs in the United States, 1960–2000,* Government Printing Office, Washington, D.C., 1960.

United States Outdoor Recreation Resources Review Commission, *Outdoor Recreation for America,* A Report to the President and to the Congress, Washington, D.C., 1962.

LAWRENCE A. HOFFMAN
The University of Toledo

CHAPTER 23

The Conservation of Man

Natural resource problems have recently been viewed more and more in terms of what they mean to people, indicating increased recognition that the country's greatest resource is people.

The strength of the nation lies less in numbers than in quality. Excellent health, high skills, and effective institutional organization taken together are fully as important as any of the other factors of production, that is, material capital, management, government, and natural resources, in effecting large per capita production and great national power.

Conservation of man may be interpreted to mean the avoidance of waste in reproduction and in rearing and educating children, together with the maintenance at minimum cost of good health and high productivity in the adult working population and the aged. With all our failings, we have become relatively low-cost replacers of life. Compared with the past, we are also relatively efficient in maintaining life and health among both children and adults. Our treatment of the aged may be inferior to that of past generations in nonmaterial considerations. Our educational efforts and our use of the average adult worker are probably intermediate in quality: better than previous generations, but still mediocre compared with present and prospective needs.

Most of our knowledge relating to past efforts to conserve man comes from aristocratic societies, in which treatment of the majority of people was mainly ignored in assessing deficiency and progress. Therefore we really have no dependable base points for purposes of accurate comparison, and pessimism is easily attainable by those forgetful that living in the first stages of a quantitatively comprehensible world can easily lead to erroneous comparisons between today's median accomplishments and yesterday's best accomplishments.

PROBLEMS OF POPULATION REPLACEMENT

The two major changes that shape population change in a nation are mortality and fertility. The growth of our population would not be affected much by reduction of infant and child mortality, for infectious diseases are essentially under control. We might still lengthen life expectancy by reducing mortality among adults through learning how to control degenerative diseases.

Waste in Population Replacement. The wastage of life in replacing each generation is very low in our society. Infant mortality is now only 2.1 percent.[1] Mortality among older children is even less; thus at current rates of survival more than 95 percent of those born will at least reach age 15.[2] More than 60 percent will live to age 65.

Progress in medical science, hospital deliveries, and prenatal and postnatal care have largely taken the hazards out of childbirth, with the maternal death rate now less than 0.1 percent, only a fifth of the rate a generation ago.[3]

Eliminating most premature deaths has led to a rising median age: it was only 19 years a century ago, had risen to 23 half a century ago, and is now 29.

The major determinant of our population change is now fertility, or the trend in birth rate. The events of the past generation have made this very difficult to forecast with precision, with the chief variables being the following:

1. The long-run surge in the number of families being formed.[4] In the 1940's an aver-age of 0.5 million new households were formed each year; in the 1950's it was about 1 million; and passed 2 million by 1968.

2. The married proportion of the adult population is now over two-thirds of all 14 years of age and over.[5] Even by age 40 only 8 percent of the men and 6 percent of the women are still single (this is but half the proportion at the turn of the century).

3. Only a tenth of young married couples are now childless, compared with double that proportion before World War II. (However, if all families are considered, some two-fifths have no children at home.)

4. Women are starting childbearing while young, the result partly of the lowering of the average age at marriage (23 years for men, 21 years for women in 1967).

5. Families remain small (3.7 persons per average family). Of the some 30 million families with children at home, roughly a third have one child, another third have two children, and the last third have three or more children. There is no evidence of an abandonment of the small-family system by any appreciable group, and the number of very large families is dropping.

6. The 3.6 million births in 1968 represented a lower birth rate than the low of the Depression years of the 1930's. The baby boom from 1947–1957 was caused partly by older women who married during the Depression and delayed their families until better times, and partly by young people whom World War II had forced to postpone marriage. Today women in childbearing years are a smaller part of the total population than a generation ago, although this is changing as postwar babies mature. Recently the birth rate of women in their 20's has dropped (they contribute 60 percent of all births), but it is still not clear if this means smaller families or

---

[1] However, the poor have a rate of over 2.5 percent, about double the rates of the middle and upper classes. Half of this differential comes from significant differences between white and nonwhite infant mortality in all but three states.

[2] Although accidents are largely amenable to control, they outrank every disease as a killer among children and young adults.

[3] Even when only women in the reproductive ages are considered, maternity causes less than 4 percent of all deaths at those ages (accidents take three times as many lives among them as childbearing). By region, the same general pattern of maternal mortality exists today as 2 decades ago (that is, much higher than the national average in the rural South and rural West).

[4] The Bureau of the Census defines a family as two or more people living together who are related by blood, marriage, or adoption.

[5] Over 70 percent of young women between 20 to 24 years are or have been married, compared with fewer than half in 1900.

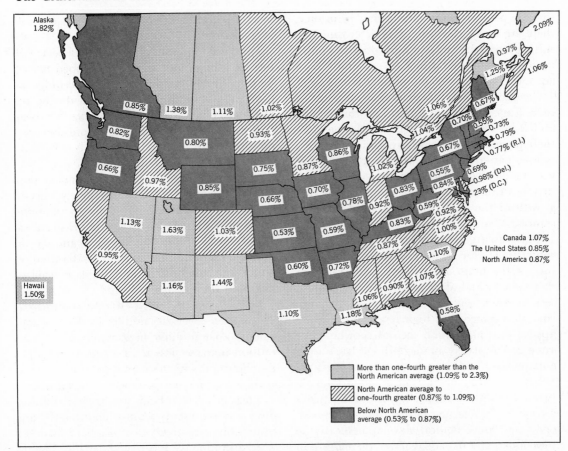

Fig. 1 United States and Canada: percent natural increase in population by states and provinces, 1967. (Public Health Service, U.S. Department of Health, Education, and Welfare and Dominion Bureau of Statistics.)

is a matter of spacing children more widely.[6]

There is still a very uneven distribution of fertility in both the United States and Canada, although less so than during the 1930's.

[6] Fertility is still much higher than necessary for replacement. If the average wife were to have 2.27 babies, the population would be stationary in a few decades. But wives in their early 30's are expected to have an average of 3.3 children by the time they have completed their families. Among wives in their early 30's, all large groups exceed the necessary number:

White wives	2.6	urban wives	2.5
nonwhite wives	3.1	rural wives	3.3

Figure 1 shows the pattern of crude natural increase in 1967, with higher than average rates mainly found in the South, Southwest, and Mountain West, and in the Canadian Maritimes and Prairies. Both countries had birth rates of 1.8 percent, with the Canadian lower death rate (0.2 percent less than the U.S. rate) accounting for the slightly higher Canadian natural increase rate.

In both countries, big families are becoming rare. Only 1 percent have more than six children, and 15 percent have four or more children. Because over two-thirds of such families are poor or lower-middle class in income, there are some who fear "genetic erosion" resulting from the smaller reproductive contribution from the wealthier or culturally most advanced segments of the population.

Genetically there are few valid reasons for such fears. We cannot measure the mental ability of children through measurement of their parents. Every newborn child receives a unique pattern of genes, and the only reliable way to discover how good this new pattern may be is to measure directly the intellectual growth of the child under favorable circumstances.

There is a good correlation between environmental factors and intelligence. The structure of the brain allows for a wide range of delivered mental ability. A child born into a secure family, sent to a good school, and continually exposed to a high level of aspiration approaches maximum mental power. The same child placed in degrading, frustrating situations will approach a minimum of its potential because of the cultural impoverishment. Thus mental efficiency or intelligence is a product of inherited factors, the age, experience, and physiological development of the individual, and the adequacy of the culture in which he grows up.

It follows from all this that the key to fuller utilization of human resources is to provide more enrichment and to give each person the best possible education in the widest sense of that term. A differential birth rate might pose a social danger in a caste-organization society, but in one where the superior classes' culture is continually being diffused to the lower socioeconomic classes, the danger of genetic erosion would seem to be minor.

Cost of Population Increase. Throughout its history, the United States has not only replaced its population, but increased it. During the past century, the American population increased more than sixfold, whereas the world's population only doubled. The national average annual rate of increase was al-

most 2 percent, whereas the world as a whole averaged only 0.75 percent.

However, our rate of growth has been falling, as a long-range trend. It dropped from 3 percent yearly in the decade preceding the Civil War to a low of 0.7 percent during the Depression of the 1930's, but since has been increasing from double the depression rate (and of World War II until early 1960's) to half again that rate (since 1965).

Figure 2 shows the change in resident population during the 1960's. Obviously, certain states and provinces profit from net in-migration: the St. Lawrence Valley and eastern seaboard, the Gulf and Pacific coasts, and several other areas, while most states and provinces either lose much of their natural increase or just hold their own.

In 1970, North America's population passed 226 million (over 205 million in the U.S. and a tenth that number in Canada). Of the 2.5 million increase, less than a fifth is from net in-migration, which has dropped off in recent years much like natural increase has dropped.

The period of infancy and early childhood obviously represents a drain upon family and community resources, an investment made toward a productive return in later life. The demographers, Dublin, Lotka, and Spiegelman, assume that for the United States this nonproductive phase of life extends to the age of 18, on the average, and estimate the investment in a child up to that age at some 4 years' average-family income. In agricultural areas and those in which child labor still persists, the child begins to be productive at a much earlier age. It would probably be safe to estimate, however, that up to the age of 15 years the investment made in a child greatly exceeds its economic return, even in rural areas.[7]

---

[7] Per confinement, the average private expenditure is over $300, not including lost income from inability to work. On the average, American couples spend over $600 on a child during the first year of its life, a sum which mounts, apparently by geometric progression,

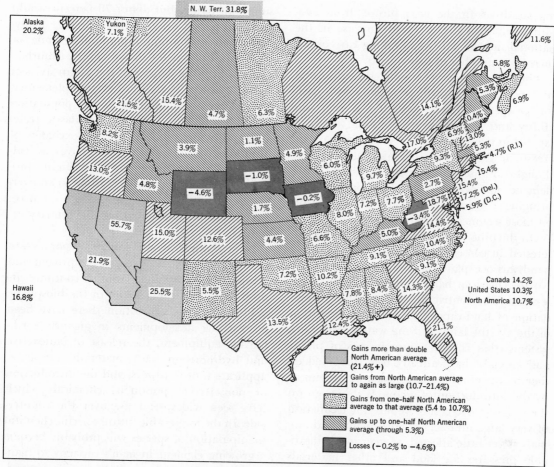

Fig. 2 United States and Canada: percent change in total resident population between 1960 and 1967, resulting from natural increase and net migration in the 7-year period, and includes persons stationed in the Armed Forces in each area. (Bureau of the Census, U. S. Department of Commerce and Dominion Bureau of Statistics.)

Premature death represents a net economic loss to society from about $1000 at birth to perhaps $25,000 at young adulthood.[8] A death at the age of 40, on the other hand, represents a net economic gain to society, whereas one at 65 represents a net gain to society of more than twice what was invested in that individual.

The whole economy is under pressure because of the rapid growth in the two groups at the extreme ends of the age scale. The number of young and aged dependents is growing three times as rapidly as is the group between. The percentage of these dependents compared to the productive age groups is ris-

---

with each succeeding year. The $600 income tax deduction per child saves about $120 in actual tax for most families, or about 33 cents a day, hardly enough to meet the needs of a growing child.

[8] The Institute of Life Insurance estimates that it now costs the average family about $25,000 to rear a child to age 18 (college-age).

ing steadily.[9] In the near future, from two-fifths to half of the expected increase in the national income will go to taking care of the increasing number of dependents.

There are many who hold the idea that such population growth provides a firm basis for prosperity. Their reasoning is that our ability and willingness to consume tends to lag behind our productive potential. An increase in the number of consumers is thus thought to offset this tendency by stimulating demand for personal consumption, through bringing continuous pressure for expansion on most sectors of the economy.

On the other hand, ecologists and others interested in conservation fear that, as man expands his occupancy and varies his use of the North American habitat, he will do so heedlessly, and so contribute to the further degradation of landscapes (for example, pollution of the air, the land, and the water). Most ecosystems (that is, native associations of plants and animals) have already been modified either by the elimination of essential species or by the introduction of aliens. If things go on the way they are going, we face the extinction of very large numbers of both plants and animals as yet little affected, as man in his insatiable pressures for food and other materials and of recreational space absorbs additional wilderness and turns it into agriculture or other altered landscape.

Although the size and continuous growth of population is among the most important stimuli to environmental change, even with stable population the desires for a better life will continue because of poverty and changing pressure of standards, continuously changing landscapes. Recent studies among taste-makers indicate that only 5 percent want to live in urban areas, about 10–20 percent will accept

suburban living, but about 70 percent would prefer dispersed urban styles of living, involving about 100 persons per square mile or about one-quarter the density of the suburban and one-fifth the density of the urban styles of living. If such ideals were ever implemented on a large scale, even a stable population would gobble up land on a fantastic scale, and nullify any tendency for the exchange of unproductive or poorly productive agricultural and related areas for more highly productive ones, thus possibly leading to an overall reduction of the areas of intensive environmental change in use by primary activities.

Even though North America's population growth continued to decline, the present and prospective technology would continue its push to exploit every niche in the biosphere. Within the past generation there have been far-reaching developments in gigantic earth-moving equipment, the release of radioactive and hydrocarbon waste materials, the aerial application of fertilizers, and the introduction of nonselective poisonous chemicals which have seen widespread use over the countryside. In the foreseeable future, specific chemical manipulation of species will probably become a growing element in man's capacity to manage the environment, and changes in domestication pattern and manipulation of genotypes to expand areas of tolerance will continue to culturize ecosystems (perhaps preserving or renewing some, but more likely endangering or destroying them if present attitudes continue).

In sheer quantitative terms it appears highly probable that for the remainder of this century there will be no general running out of raw materials or the natural resources from which they are derived. Therefore, one traditional avenue of rationale for the preservation, restoration, and wise management of the biophysical environment will be weakened. Substitute rationales may have to play up the need for environmental parameters to the achievement of physical and mental health

---

[9] When the dependent age groups—persons under 18 and those 65 and over—are lumped together, they constitute about the same proportion of the total population as was the case at the beginning of the century.

and human happiness (for example, open space, living space scaled to man, quiet, order, variety, and beauty). The greater mobility of man, coupled with more leisure time for outdoor recreation and a desire to relax in natural surroundings, has increased public use and appreciation of relatively undisturbed land, which is of high conservation value because it contains the main reserves of wildlife surviving in fairly natural conditions.

Human population control is inevitable, mainly for reasons other than habitat conservation, but such a goal (still decades away) will not preserve the things that are endangered now. Even to let the natural environment alone now requires positive protective action. The convergent effects of the triple explosions of science, technology, and population make comprehensive environmental administration inevitable in the long run. Changes in attitude and in institutional grasp so as to increase necessary economic-overhead and social-overhead investments [for example, wider use of secondary and tertiary sewage-treatment, increase in protected areas (of unusual habitat and biotype interest), increase in more strictly controlled land use—zoning codes, etc.] will probably be more fruitful than crash programs to stabilize or reduce the human population in the near future.

Trends in Education. An outstanding social achievement of the past half century has been the raising of the general educational level of North Americans. For some 30 percent of the population, education is a full-time occupation or a time-consuming avocation. Total costs (public and private) amount to 6 percent of U.S. gross national product and 7.5 percent of Canadian GNP, more than double the fractions allotted a generation ago.

There is still incomplete coverage in our educational system. Currently, only half of the adults 25 years and older have completed a high school education, and less than 10 percent have completed 4 or more years of college. Even at the appropriate younger age

groups, two-fifths fail to complete high school, and only a seventh complete 4 years of college.[10]

In the 1960's, Canada had swiftly narrowed its gap between potential and reality. In the early 1950's, only half of the potential high school enrollment stayed in school, now it is over 80 percent, and by the early 1970's it is expected to be about 90 percent. Only 5 percent of the college-age group were in school at that earlier date, now it is 15 percent, and soon it will reach 20 percent.

The expanding program of secondary education in the United States has practically reached its possible limits. Some 95 percent of adolescents in the 14–17 age bracket engage in full-time schooling, compared with only 40 percent in England. Over 70 percent of U.S. boys and girls graduate from high school, and 40 percent enter college, while only 13 percent in England complete 12 years of full-time schooling and only 6.5 percent enter institutions of higher education on a full-time basis.

The remainder of the twentieth century bids fair to see higher education become nearly as common as secondary education is today. Already nearly all middle-class and upper-class youth enter college, although only half complete 4 years and receive a baccalaureate degree. Of the top several percent of high school graduates in terms of academic

[10] One of the weakest links in our educational system is the failure of present methods to reach about 20 percent of big-city children. They never learn what they should, even the 3 R's. Vocational schools generally spend 50 percent of the time on academic subjects and 50 percent on shop subjects, so those who cannot handle the first are not allowed to attempt the second. To compound the problem, traditional apprenticeship systems in the United States are dying fast, being strangled by shortsightedness on the part of unions and disinterest on the part of industry, by nepotism, and by racial prejudice. The "dropout problem" is a great waste not because of the inability of nongraduates to perform the more or less menial tasks in society, but because most employers will not hire dropouts even for low-grade jobs if they can possibly avoid doing so.

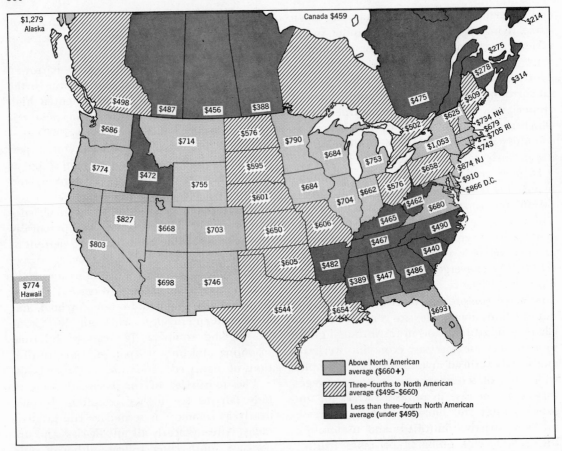

Fig. 3 Estimated expenditures per pupil in average daily attendance in public elementary and secondary day schools by states and provinces. (U. S. Office of Education and Dominion Bureau of Statistics.)

achievement practically all go to college, but from there on down family income is the main determinant of who does. At the moment, for groups with very low incomes, failure to be academically prepared and motivated for college is even more of a problem than finding the money to pay for it. Only about 5 percent of the campus population is nonwhite, and poor whites are relatively no better represented.

Figure 3 shows that regional inequalities in public education are still impressive. The U.S. Southeast, the Canadian Maritimes, and several other areas stand out, although relative

to their income and governmental expenditure they are making greater efforts than the wealthier areas. In general, education in rural areas is inferior to that in urban areas, especially outside the Northeast and West coast, although there appears to be a narrowing of the gap between rural and urban school systems (partly because of difficulties in urban ghetto schools). With some exceptions, the quality of education for nonwhites is somewhat inferior to that for whites, although narrowing the gap has been a major objective in the 1960's (the nonwhite dropout rate has dropped sharply, but in terms of quality the average nonwhite in the final year of high school is performing at a ninth-grade level, so much remains to be achieved before true equality is reached). Only 56 percent of nonwhite school children complete the eighth grade, as against 73 percent of their white classmates. Less than 40 percent of nonwhite teenagers finish high school, compared with 62 percent of whites.

CONSERVATION PROBLEMS IN THE ACTIVE ADULT POPULATION

Much of the increased human conservation in the United States in the past generation is related to the phenomenon of millions of families being lifted from poverty to middle-class levels of consumption. In one way, it can be said that one important new American frontier has been opening up the purchasing power of the poor.

However, poverty restricts the amount of welfare that the poorest American family units can afford. The share of the nation's income going to the top one-fifth of families is 45 percent; the share of the poorest fifth is some 5 percent. The remaining half of the nation's income goes to middle-class families (those in the $4000 to $10,000 annual income range), making up three-fifths of all families.

Obviously, the poorest fifth of all families will include the overwhelming number of families requiring subsidization. That fifth includes 30 million people in families, and 5 million unattached persons. The per capita disposable income of the 35 million Americans in the lowest fifth of the population is under $1000 (compared with the national average disposable income of nearly $3000). It would take $15 billion to bring all poor families up to the $3000 level, which is now considered the minimum to sustain lower middle-class status.

Of the poor families, 47 percent live in the South, 25 percent in the Middle West, 17 percent in the East, and 11 percent in the West. Over a third of all nonwhites are poor, and 40 percent of all farm families are poor; in both categories, such families are mainly concentrated in the South and in the nonwhite West (Fig. 4).

More than 11 million children live in families whose incomes are less than $3000 yearly. The heads of more than 60 percent of all poor families have received only a grade school education. A third of all poor families are headed by a person over 65 years of age. More than 3 million unattached persons (mostly elderly) had incomes below $1000 yearly. The poor unattached individuals are mainly older workers and retired persons widely scattered in both rural and urban areas.

Not all adult problems are caused by poverty, but most that are not so caused are intertwined in complicated cause-effect interrelationships. This is especially true of illness, accidental death, physical handicaps, and disability related to ethnic prejudice, assessed more in the following sections.

Cost of Illness. Morbidity and premature death cost the nation a staggering total each year. According to Ewing, premature death, total disability, and partial disability each costs the equivalent of about 5 percent of the national income yearly, whereas short-term illness costs the equivalent of about 2 percent of the annual national income.[11] On any one day, about 5 percent of the total population is so disabled by illness or by physical or emotional handicaps of some kind as to be unable to go to work. Minimum cost of this short-term illness is estimated at some ten billion dollars annually, of which a fifth is accounted for by prolonged illness.

[11] O. R. Ewing, *The Nation's Health: A Report to the President,* Washington, D.C., 1948. A 1967 estimate for direct and indirect costs of sickness, disability, and death of $75 billion is some 12.5 percent of GNP, two-thirds of the earlier estimate.

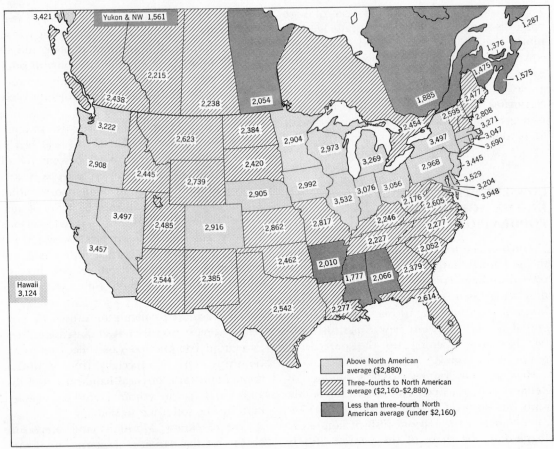

Fig. 4 United States and Canada: per capita personal income in dollars by states and provinces, 1966. (Office of Business Economics, U. S. Department of Commerce and Dominion Bureau of Statistics.)

The U.S. health bill in 1969 was some 7 percent of the gross national product (double the 1930 share) and is expected to reach 15 percent eventually, when ideal standards of hospital, surgical, and other medical services are implemented for the entire population according to need.

By 1967, over 85 percent of the civilian, noninstitutional population under 65 were covered by some form of hospital expense protection (nearly 60 percent by insurance companies, nearly 40 percent by Blue Cross-Blue Shield plans, with several percent pro-

tected by independent plans). Most of the remaining 15 percent include the indigent, near-indigent, and dependents of military personnel, which persons are eligible for comprehensive health care coverage under the provisions of Medicaid and the Dependents Medical Care Act. People over 65 are covered by Medicare.

Hospital expense protection and surgical and regular medical expense protection are somewhat less comprehensive, although these are increasing at faster rates than hospital expense coverage (which is near total coverage).

Some 95 percent of those persons with hospital expense insurance are also covered for surgical expenses, and some 75 percent are covered for regular medical expenses.

Of the total cost for health care, about half is spent by persons without insurance, or was spent on items which are not prescribed by a physician as medically necessary (for example, nonprescribed drugs, luxury accommodations, etc.), or on items optional in nature. On the other half of the expenditures covered by health insurance, roughly half was recovered via the insurance (more than 75 percent of hospital expenses, more than 65 percent of surgical expenses, and smaller fractions of regular and major medical expenses).

As of July 1, 1968, Canada had in effect a national medical care program which permits socialized payment of medicine. It is a shared-cost program in which the federal government pays half of the costs of provincial medicare schemes that meet federal criteria (that is, comprehensiveness, universality, and provincial acceptance of administrative costs). By 1970, 7 of the 10 provinces had joined.

Everywhere the deficiency in medical personnel and institutional facilities falls more heavily on the rural population. Doctors tend to avoid small communities, and good hospitals require medium-sized cities (for example, hospitals with fewer than 350 beds are usually too small to justify adequate laboratory, x-ray, and diagnostic facilities).

Accidental Death. Although accidents are largely amenable to control, they account for nearly 7 percent of all deaths each year. They are among the first five causes of death at every age period, and outrank every disease as a killer among children and young adults. Motor vehicle deaths account for half of all accidental deaths, with a tenth of the loss among those under 15 years of age, about three-quarters of the loss in the productive age period (15–64), and the remaining among persons 65 years of age and over.

The accidental death rate at all ages combined is over twice as high among males as among females, reflecting not only greater exposure to occupational and recreational hazards, but also greater daring.

Motor vehicle mishaps are dominant at every period of life under age 65—at the older ages they are outranked only by falls. Among males, motor vehicle accidents account for about a third of all accidental deaths in every age group (at ages 20 to 24 they account for two-thirds of all such deaths). Among females, motor vehicle deaths are relatively more important than among males during the greater part of life—however, in terms of actual death rates, females consistently have the more favorable experience.

Neglect in Using Handicapped Adults. Nearly one of every ten Americans in the productive age group has a disability that substantially limits activity: there are about 5 million with heart disease, another 5 million with ambulatory problems; hearing difficulties affect 6 million; and 7 million have arthritis, to mention just the largest groups. About 7 million draw paychecks; those who do not collect more than $0.8 billion annually in public assistance payments. Since the government, in cooperation with business and labor, began an intense promotional campaign about 15 years ago, over 4 million handicapped workers have been placed in jobs (including 1 million rehabilitated and retrained, and about 0.6 million disabled veterans of World War II and the Korean conflict helped to obtain private employment).

About 2 million workers are injured each year in job accidents, of which 75,000–85,000 suffer permanent disability. There is a backlog of some 2 million workers with handicaps incurred in past years.

The Office of Vocational Rehabilitation, one of five major programs in the U.S. Department of Health, Education, and Welfare, aids financially state agencies to help place the handicapped in jobs. Some 0.2 million are now placed yearly under this program. However, of the severely handicapped (for example, by blindness, loss of a limb, tuberculosis, epilepsy, and other crippling diseases), only a relatively few are permanently employed.

Cost of Prejudice. The Negro and other nonwhite people throughout the United States have advanced along many fronts in recent years: (1) their longevity has increased, (2) their educational level has been raised, and (3) their social and economic status has been measurably improved. However, the Negro's economic gains have not come up to his dramatic progress in the political and social fields. On the farm there has been little, if any, improvement. Off the farm, at least in the South, the Negro man has not done much better than hold his own, if you first discount the gains that industrialization has brought to the population as a whole.

The white man has had two reasons for discriminating against the Negro since he brought him to the United States. The first was economic; the second was social.

Only a third of Negro families are still poor by the government's official definition,[12] compared with 10 percent of white families. Some 75 percent of Negro families earn less than the $8000 median annual income of white families—Negroes are 11 percent of the total U.S. population, but earn only 7 percent of the total national income, or a median annual family income just under $5000. About 3 percent of Negro families have a median annual income of over $15,000, compared with 10 percent of white families.

In some ways, the problem of the Negro is still mainly concentrated in the South, where 55 percent still live, but where Negro median family income is only half of the white median in the region (see Fig. 5). Considered as a whole, the South was more than one-third Negro at the turn of the century, was less than one-fourth Negro in the early 1950's, and is now less than one-fifth Negro (the Southeast is now about one-fifth Negro, with the Southwest under 15 percent). The Northeast, which is one-tenth Negro (mainly concentrated in the Middle Atlantic southern half), has Negro median family income some 60 percent that of the regional white median, whereas the Middle West and West (with some 5 percent Negro population, higher in a few middle western states but only several percent or less in most states) have Negro median incomes some 75 percent that of their regional white medians.

The foundation of the Negroes' economic progress is the fact that large numbers have left farm and domestic work and have gone into industry and the professions since the cessation of massive European immigration in the 1920's. Of the Negro farm work force before World War II, a majority have been pushed or pulled off the farm. Only 5 percent of all Negroes still live on farms, with another 20 percent in small towns. In large central cities, Negroes are now some 20 percent of the population, although in the suburbs of such cities their numbers drop to less than 5 percent of the total. Of the 75 percent urban population, nearly two-thirds are in the North and West.[13]

---

[12] In 1969, the federally set poverty line ($3743 for a nonfarm family of four; 15 percent less for a farm family; and half as much for an individual) included about 11 percent of the American population. Ten million Americans (5 percent of the total population) were on welfare rolls: 1 percent of these were men physically and mentally employable; 15 percent were working-age mothers; 86 percent were dependent children and dependent aged. Thirteen million Americans (6 percent of the total population) were in families of the "working poor" not yet benefiting from welfare (although many would under the projected guaranteed annual income of $2460 for a family of four). Such poverty is in relation to present middle-class ideals, rather than in relation to world standards or to historic U.S. standards up until mid-twentieth century.

[13] Washington, D.C., and Newark, New Jersey, are already over half Negro. If present trends continue, Negro majorities in central cities elsewhere will occur as follows: New Orleans and Richmond, Virginia, by 1971; Baltimore, Maryland, and Jacksonville, Florida, by 1972; Gary, Indiana, by 1973; Cleveland, 1975; St.

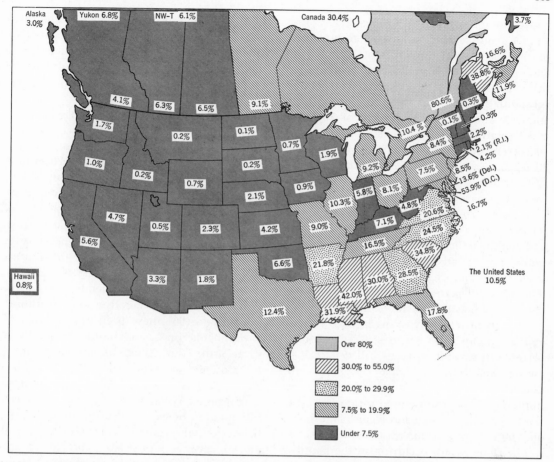

Fig. 5 United States and Canada: percent of Negroes in the states of United States and of French Canadians in the provinces of Canada. (Census of Population for 1960, U. S. Department of Commerce, and the Census of Canada for 1961, Dominion Bureau of Statistics.)

With increasing urbanization and improving levels of living, the gap between the Negro's and the white man's life span is narrowing, but there is still a gap, reflecting inferior environmental and medical conditions. The life expectancy at birth is now 68 for white males and 75 for white females, as compared with 56 for Negro males and 67 for Negro females. The difference narrows with increasing age, but averages 5 years less for Negroes at age 25, 4 years less at age 35, 3 years less at age 45, and 2 years less at age 55.

Improvements in housing come slowly. About a third of northern Negroes (who total 40 percent of the total) live in slums; equal fractions rent good to passable housing and own their own homes. Nearly half of Negro housing in the South is substandard (three-quarters in rural and small-town areas).

The vast majority of the nation's 8 million

Louis, 1978; Detroit, 1979; Philadelphia, 1981; Oakland, California, 1983; and Chicago, 1984. After 1985, other cities likely to be added include Dallas, Pittsburgh, Buffalo, Cincinnati, Harrisburg, Louisville, Indianapolis, Kansas City, Missouri, Hartford, and New Haven.

Negro workers are massed in low-paying jobs. Despite considerable occupational advances in the 1960's, over two-fifths of Negro men and three-fifths of Negro women workers remain in service, laboring, or farm jobs—substantially more than twice the proportion among whites. About 35 percent of all farm and nonfarm laborers are Negro, as are over 40 percent of private household workers and 20 percent of "other services" (mainly protective services and the categories of waiters, cooks, and bartenders). Industrial workers are now nearly 20 percent Negro, although the fraction drops to 5 percent among foremen and highly skilled craftsmen. Among professional and related technical workers and among sales and clerical workers, Negroes are now about 10 percent of the total (about the same fraction as their share of the total population). In the category of managers, officials, and proprietors, the Negro share drops to 3 percent. In general, Negroes still get less pay for the same education, have a higher unemployment rate (especially among the young unmarried), and a substantial income gap (national median income for Negro families is only 60 percent that for white families).

The changes now occurring in the South—urbanization, out-migration, and the breakdown of social isolation—are rapidly narrowing the differences between the South and the North and West. Eventually, this will probably not only improve race relations in the South, but render them much improved in the North and West as well (as out-migration from the South becomes adjusted to opportunity elsewhere rather than to refugee-type outpouring).

Although Canada has 2 percent nonwhite population, they in no way correspond to the 11 percent nonwhite minorities in the United States. About two-thirds are Native Indian and Eskimo, who are the majority population in most of northern Canada—although poor and subject to certain other disabilities, they are better off (partly due to geographic isola-

tion) than their U.S. equivalents. The other one-third are Asiatics, for the most part (Negroes are only 40,000 in number), and like their U.S. counterparts subject to subtle social prejudice although economically fairly well-off.

Canada's only major social crisis is that based on languages and related cultures, on whether it can remain bicultural or will face secession by Quebec. Of Canada's 20 million people, about 58 percent have English as their mother tongue, 28 percent French, and the remainder other languages. Only 12 percent of Canadians speak both English and French, and these are found mainly in Quebec (over four-fifths French-speaking) and other areas with numerous French speakers (see Fig. 5). Proposed constitutional amendments by the Commission on Bilingualism and Biculturalism (in late 1967) have been well received by governments, press, and public. In its 4-year study of the ethnic causes of national disunity, the Commission proposed that: (1) English and French be established as equal official languages everywhere in Canada; (2) official bilingualism be extended to legislatures, public services, and courts—in federal Parliament and in legislatures of Quebec and New Brunswick now, and to other provinces as their French-speaking minorities reach 10 percent of the population; (3) bilingual districts of areas within provinces should be created where the linguistic minority is substantial and judicial and administrative services should be made available in both languages; and (4) provincial governments be required to provide education through high school in both languages in bilingual districts, with discretion left to parents as to the language of instruction. While the suggestions for official bilingualism may well mollify expatriate Quebecois living in other provinces, it will do little for those French-Canadians living in Quebec except redress their grievance over the status of their language and culture elsewhere in Canada. The Union Nationale (conservative) government in Quebec is more interested in wresting economic and political powers from the federal government, thus making Quebec a semiautonomous political entity within the Canadian confederation. Power is the real issue between such leadership and that elsewhere in Canada, and the policy of bilingualism is of importance mainly in convincing French-Canadians that their destiny should lie not in withdrawing into an independent Quebec, but in participating in the development of the riches of all of Canada throughout which their rights of language and culture are respected. If they are not convinced, they may follow the suggestions of certain leaders who advocate political independence for Quebec in a common market-style economic partnership with the rest of Canada.

PROBLEMS OF MAINTENANCE AMONG THE AGED

Under mortality conditions prevailing in 1850, the expectation of life at birth was less than 40 years. For more than a decade, the figure has been 70 years (over 67 years for all males, and 74 years for all females). The average American who now reaches age 25 has nearly double the years of life before him than did the average newly born baby at the turn of the century. The average American who now reaches age 55 has over a score of years presumable life expectancy left.

This remarkable longevity record is the result of many factors: (1) The striking advances achieved in the medical and allied sciences have been made widely available throughout the country. (2) At the same time, official and voluntary public-health agencies have multiplied in number and broadened the scope of their activities. (3) In addition, our health and general well-being have benefited greatly from the rapid rise in the level of living.

The extraordinary progress made in prolonging life during the past century reflects,

in the main, the effective control gained over the communicable diseases, such as pneumonia and influenza, tuberculosis, diarrhea, nephritis, etc. Three out of ten children born in 1900 were all that could expect to reach the age of 70; four out of ten children born in 1925 were expected to reach 70; five out of ten children born since 1950 will live to be 70. Future gains will be more difficult to achieve because they will depend largely upon reducing the toll from diseases which, in the present state of knowledge, are for the most part of obscure or unknown origin.[14] Yet there is reason to believe that some advances will be made in fending off such causes of mortality as the medical and sanitary sciences continue to develop new knowledge and to make more effective use of what is already known.

Neglect of Older Workers. The nation has made less and less use of its older citizens in the past half century. As compared with over two-thirds of the men 65 years of age or older counted in the labor force then, only one-third are now employed. One reason for the decline is the shift of the population from the farm to the city, where it is more difficult for an old man to keep working, either full-time or part-time. A second reason is the development of social security and other pension systems which encourage retirement at 65.[15] A third reason is the premium which our present industrial system puts on younger workers.

The number of persons in the population

[14] If it were possible to prevent all deaths before age 40, expectation of life at birth would be increased about 5 years. Substantial gains in the future will be dependent largely on our success in preventing or postponing the cardiovascular-renal diseases and cancer, which are the preponderant causes of death in the middle and later years of life. The difficulties are indicated by the fact that, in the past generation, the expectation of life at age 60 has increased 1 year for white men and 3 years for white women.

[15] Among males aged 60–64, three-quarters of all separations from the labor force are due to retirement, and only one-quarter to death.

of the United States age 45 or older is now over 50 million, and by 1975 may make up approximately half of the adult population.

For the most part, the prejudice against older workers goes back to a period when physical effort was relatively more important in the labor force than at present. Actually, younger men and women are better only in physically exhausting jobs, the type of job where the machine is more and more substituted for human effort. In more highly skilled jobs, there is a tendency for skill and judgment to increase with experience. The older workers have greater "know-how," display greater patience, cause less waste, and are less frequently absent.

Economics of the Aged Dependent. The problem of the aged, once dealt with adequately on the family or local level, has become a national problem affecting economic, social, and political affairs. The growing number of aged affects the economy by altering the consuming market, influencing union demands, making an impact on finance through investments of insurance and pension funds, and by possible development into a cohesive, special-interest political group.

During the past half century, the number of people over 65 has been increasing twice as fast as the general rate of population growth. This group of retired or retirable now constitutes about 9.5 percent of the total population (see Fig. 6). As a bloc, this group is growing older, is predominantly white, is predominantly female, and is commonly no longer part of a family group. Since the majority of such people are not wholly self-supporting, they represent a burden on society already faced with increasing pressure from young dependents.

The arithmetical average income per person over 65 is now about $2500, only a sixth below the national average. However, much is obscured by the term "average"; the median is little more than half that figure, and the distribution is much more revealing. Actually, one in five has an income under the poverty definition, and half have less than the national median yearly income, with only 5 percent having an annual income over $7000. Only one in five has liquid assets equal to $7000 or over. About two-thirds owned their own houses, but the value was usually small; a single long illness could wipe them out financially (those over 65 use twice as much medical care as those under 65, and Medicare only bears part of the bill).

In 1967, the Social Security program had revenues equal to 3.94 percent of the gross national product (a tenfold increase over the 1940 fraction). Some 75 million employees and self-employed are now covered (employee and employer each contribute 4.4 percent on taxable earnings up to $7800 and self-employed contribute 6.4 percent), 93 percent of all workers in the country.

Over 19 million Americans are now over 65 years of age and practically all of them, plus some widows and others under 65, receive benefits. In 1967, the average retired worker received $85.11 per month; the average surviving widow of retirement age received $74.59 monthly; the average disabled worker received $98.27 monthly; the average payment per claim under hospital insurance was $649; and the average bill paid under medical insurance was $62.

Some 3 percent of the nation's elderly have been forced to give up the fight for self-reliant existence and have entered one of the thousands of institutions for the aged that range from expensive, private maintenance to public squalor. Over-all, 90 percent of the elderly who do not live with their children receive no cash contributions at all from members of their family.

About half of the elderly citizens' income is from private sources. Less than 10 percent receive payments from private pension plans, and these account for less than 5 percent of total monetary income of the aged. The remainder of the income is from social security, railroad, and civil service pensions.

Although older dependents are increasing

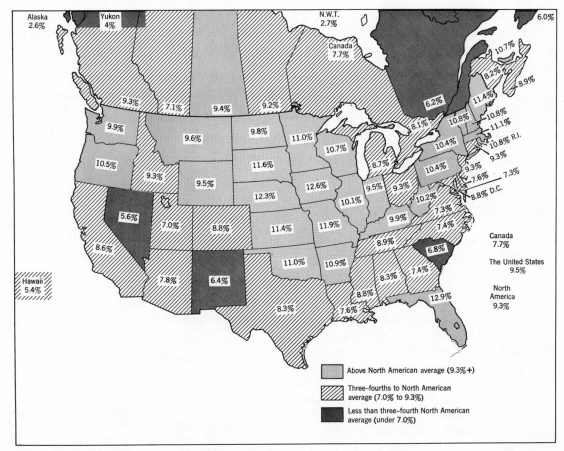

Fig. 6   United States and Canada: percent of the population at age 65 and over, by states and provinces, 1967. (Bureau of the Census, U. S. Department of Commerce and Dominion Bureau of Statistics.)

rapidly in total numbers, the fraction of total population is not increasing, with the post World War II babies now maturing and beginning to rear families. Smaller families, more working women, and perhaps greater use of older workers may provide larger amounts of private income for the elderly. With the gross national product likely to rise even faster than the increase in numbers of old people, it might cost a smaller fraction to provide for the aged. Even if the quantity and quality of welfare for the aged should be greatly improved, maintenance is unlikely to rise above 5 to 6 percent of the GNP, about twice the present fraction.

PERSPECTIVE

Gradually, American society is providing protection against the five major hazards of economic security: unemployment, sickness, disability, old age, and death. More and more it is accepted that a healthy and prosperous society cannot be established and maintained by constituent members handicapped by overwhelming burdens of poverty, disease, and ignorance.

Progress made in the health sciences during the past half century has made it clear that the heavy burdens of disease can, in large measure, be lifted by the application of scientific knowledge already available, and each year the results of health research are broadening the areas of possible control. Future advances in health and reduction of mortality should give us a growing pool of older workers who will add greatly to our potential of manpower and experience.

From the point of view of economic productivity, the age distribution of our population is such that an increasing proportion of our workers will be old, so much depends on our making effective use of our older workers. The working population possesses high skill and initiative, has excellent technical and management leadership, and is tooled with the most productive industrial machine in the world. The average level of formal education and occupational training has risen constantly during the past half-century, and the trend suggests that it will rise to much higher levels in the future. We still have a growing population, and the ratio of the labor force to the total population is still capable of expansion, mainly because technical progress is continually relieving older women from routine household tasks and excessive childbearing so that they can work outside the home if they wish.[16]

[16] Today's average American woman marries at 20, has her first child at 22, the last (second or third) child by 30, and can expect to live nearly half a century after that, which leaves her 30 useful years even after her children grow up. Some 45 percent of all women now work, more than double the 1900 fraction

We are not exploiting sufficiently the intellectual resources of the nation. Much more can be done to identify the brightest youngsters, encourage them to plan on higher education, offer them opportunity to work in their chosen fields, give them financial and moral assistance when necessary, and give them the kind of education that will allow them to go ahead rapidly to take their places among the intellectual elite.

We are not using to the best advantage the judgment potentialities of our older people. We do not wish to have a social framework in which the elders and old traditions are inviolate, nor a situation in which oldsters become beggars, or suffer from social isolation. New ways of maintaining economic solvency and self-respect for the old people will have to be worked out as an increasing segment of our population becomes aged.

who worked outside the home. Women in the labor force are increasing at a rate half again faster than men. However, some 75 percent of working women are in routine (clerical, sales, or factory) jobs, and average only 60 percent of what men earn. Although a majority of the population, women earn only a third of B.A.'s and M.A.'s and a tenth of Ph.D.'s. While 85 percent of all elementary school teachers, and nearly half of all secondary school teachers, are female, women are less than 5 percent of the elite professions. Supportive services are necessary to attract more women into full-time jobs (for example, day-care centers, so mothers can participate in society outside the home; nonprofit-making food-preparation centers conveniently located in all communities).

References

Alma College Perspective (Special Issue containing the background papers, speeches, and final report of the Alma College American Assembly on the Population Dilemma held on the College campus April 6–9, 1967), Alma, Michigan, Vol. 3, No. 2, Spring 1967, 72 pp.

Berelson, Bernard, *Family Planning and Population Programs,* University of Chicago Press, Chicago, 1966.

Boorstin, Daniel J., *The Americans: The National Experience,* Random House, New York, 1965.

Clark, Colin, *Population Growth and Land Use,* St. Martin's Press, New York, 1967.

Darling, F. Fraser and John P. Milton, editors, *Future Environments of North America,* the record of a conference convened by The Conservation Foundation in April 1965, at Airlie House, Warrenton, Virginia, The Natural History Press, Garden City, New York, 1966.

Dominion Bureau of Statistics, Ottawa, Ontario, *Vital Statistics* (Cat. No. 84-001, Monthly), *Estimated Population of Canada by Province* (Cat. No. 91-201, Annual), *Population: Ethnic Groups* (Cat. No. 92-545, Vol. I, Pt. 2), *Estimated Population by Sex and Age Group, For Canada and Provinces* (Cat. No. 91-202, Annual), *Survey of Education Finance* (Cat. No. 81-208, Annual), *National Accounts Income and Expenditure* (Cat. No. 13-201, Annual).

Dublin, L. I., A. J. Lotka, and M. Spiegelman, *The Money Value of a Man,* The Ronald Press, New York, 1946.

Fine, Benjamin, *Under-Achievers: How They Can Be Helped,* E. P. Dutton & Co., New York, 1967.

Gentilcore, R. Louis, *Canada's Changing Geography,* Prentice-Hall of Canada, Ltd., Scarborough, Ontario, 1967.

Health Insurance Council, *The Extent of Voluntary Health Insurance Coverage . . . ,* New York, 1967, Annual.

Journal of Human Resources, Quarterly. Published under the auspices of the Industrial Relations Research Institute, the Center for Studies in Vocational and Technical Education, and the Institute for Research on Poverty, University of Wisconsin Press, Madison.

Maddox, James G. et al., *The Advancing South: Manpower Prospects and Problems,* Twentieth Century Fund, New York, 1967.

Metropolitan Life Insurance Company, *Statistical Bulletin,* New York, Monthly.

Perlman, Mark and associates, *Human Resources in the Urban Economy,* The Johns Hopkins Press (distributed for Resources for the Future), Baltimore, 1963.

Population Association of America, 1967 Meeting April 27–29 at Cincinnati, 19 sessions of papers abstracted in the July–September *Population Index,* 1967.

Population Reference Bureau, Inc., *Population Bulletin,* Washington, D.C., 8 times yearly.

Schultz, Theodore W., *The Economic Value of Education,* Columbia University Press, New York, 1963.

Scientific American, "Human Resources of the United States," Vol. 185, 1951, pp. 27–116.

United States Department of Agriculture, Economic Research Service, *Recent Population Trends in the United States with Emphasis on Rural Areas* (Agricultural Economic Report No. 23), Washington, D.C., 1963.

U.S. Department of Commerce, Bureau of the Census, *Population Estimates,* Government Printing Office, Washington, D.C., 1967 (P-25, Nos. 380, 375), 1968 (P-25, No. 384).

United States Department of Commerce, Office of Business Economics, *Survey of Current Business,* Washington, D.C., Monthly.

U.S. Department of Health, Education, and Welfare; Public Health Service, National Center for Health Statistics, *Monthly Vital Statistics Report,* Washington, D.C., 1968.

U.S. Department of Labor, Bureau of Labor Statistics and U.S. Department of Commerce, Bureau of the Census (joint report), *Social and Economic Conditions of Negroes in the United States,* Government Printing Office, Washington, D.C., October 1967 (BLS No. 332, P-23 No. 24).

U.S. Government Printing Office, First Session of the Subcommittee on Foreign Aid Expenditures of the Committee on Government Operations, U.S. Senate, *Population Crisis* (S.1676, Parts 5-A & 5-B; Appendix, Part 4), Washington, D.C., 1966.

Young, Louise B., editor, *Population in Perspective,* Oxford University Press, New York, 1968.

Zelinsky, Wilbur, *A Prologue to Population Geography,* Prentice-Hall, Englewood Cliffs, New Jersey, 1966.

Part 8

JAMES A. SPENCER
The University of Tennessee

CHAPTER 24

City and Regional Planning

We are an industrial urban nation. Unprecedented demands are being made on the national resources, and the environment in which most of us live is being altered by the expansion of cities and the accumulation of urban by-products.

The growth of cities reflects two trends: the increase of over-all population and the movement of greater proportions of the population to urban areas. The U.S. population increased from 151,135,000 in 1950 to 200,700,000 in mid-1968.[1] Most experts believe that the 50 years between 1950 and 2000 will see a greater national increase than occurred in all the years before 1950. No one can be sure, but many estimates indicate a population of about 300,000,000 by the year 2000. Moreover, the urban population grows faster than the total population. In 1900, only 40 percent of the U.S. population lived in urban areas. Today seven out of ten people live in urban areas. Families who live in rural America and actually earn their living from agriculture make up less than 7 percent of the population.

The effects of industrialization and urbanization are enormous. Water and air pollution are commonplace. The consumption of resources spirals upward. The U.S. Department of the Interior has estimated, for example, that demands for water will increase from 325 to 900 billion gallons per day between 1965 and 2000. Although such volumes are within the capacity of national resources, the concentrated demands of large cities are often beyond the capacity of local supplies. Metropolitan areas require, on the average, 110 gallons of water per day for each resident.[2] That is why California was busy in 1965 constructing an aqueduct over 400 miles long to carry water from the Sacramento River to Los Angeles.

Land is also greatly affected by urbanization, but again, the impact is local or regional rather than national. Only 1 percent of all land in the United States is classified as urban.[3] A doubling of this requirement by the year 2000 does not seem like a matter of

[1] U.S. Bureau of Census, *Population Estimates: Current Population Reports*, Series P-25, No. 393.

[2] Hans H. Landsberg, *Natural Resources for U.S. Growth*, The Johns Hopkins Press, Baltimore, 1964, p. 126.

[3] *Ibid.*, p. 169.

much consequence on a national scale. But the local effects on the environment in which people live are direct and forceful. Every six persons added to a city population require the conversion of an acre of land from nonurban to urban use.[4] Farmlands and forests give way to highways and residential subdivisions. Marshlands may be drained and converted into shopping center sites or industrial parks. Trees and other vegetation are replaced by asphalt, rooftops, and lawns. The hydrological cycle is affected, wildlife disappears, surface water drainage increases in volume; and the environment is permanently altered.

The impact of urban growth on the surrounding countryside is magnified by the scattered pattern of fringe-area development. Technological developments, such as the automobile, refrigerator, radio, and telephone, permit nonfarm families to live further from work and shopping facilities than in earlier times. Subdivisions and shopping centers are scattered over the countryside far from the city core, often with little attention to adequate sewage or solid waste disposal, water supply, or other urban services. Large industrial parks, seeking cheaper land and room for off-street parking or expansion, may be located many miles from the center city.

The urban sprawl, as this scatteration of city growth is called, tends to blur the boundaries between city and country. As the fringes of adjacent cities mingle, vast continuous networks of urban communities called conurbations are formed. Roughly 40,000,000 people now live in the conurbation which stretches from north of Boston to northern Virginia. Similar developments are occurring in the Great Lakes region and on the Pacific coast.

All too frequently this scatteration lacks any kind of order. Its inhabitants are urban creatures, but development is so scattered and

disorganized that the effects of urbanization are spread over larger portions of the country than are actually used for urban purposes (Fig. 1).

A HISTORIC PERSPECTIVE ON PLANNING

Men have tried for centuries to develop human settlements which were harmoniously integrated with the natural environment. Mohenjo-Daro, a city founded in the Indus River Valley about 2500 B.C., was far ahead of its time in providing a high standard of development for its inhabitants. Streets were paved, parks and fountains graced the palace grounds, and underground sewers carried away storm drainage and sanitary wastes. But the city was devastated repeatedly by floodwaters of the Indus River. Hippocrates, in a treatise on "Air, Water and Places," urged the ancient Greeks to select sites for cities which had access to pure water, to avoid marshy places, and to orient streets and buildings to take advantage of cooling winds while avoiding the summer sun.

The survival of ancient cities was directly dependent on a successful adaptation to the physical environment. The surrounding countryside had to provide a sufficient food supply; a steep hill or cliff served as a defensive stronghold in time of attack; and a nearby stream or lake provided a water supply and the primary transportation route. With the advent of technology men have begun to conquer nature instead of adapting to it.

Planning in the United States. A few of our early cities were planned. L'Enfant laid out the nation's capital as a monumental city with public buildings to occupy strategic sites at the intersections of grand boulevards. William Penn laid out his "green country town," Philadelphia, between the Delaware River and the Schuylkill with a central open space and smaller public squares in each quadrant of the city. In establishing Savannah, Georgia,

[4] Marion Clawson, R. Burnell Held, and Charles H. Stoddard, *Land for the Future*, The Johns Hopkins Press, Baltimore, 1960, Table 16, p. 108.

Fig. 1 Saarinen's 630-foot Gateway Arch, which replaces shabby warehouses along the Mississippi, suggests that the traditional vigor of the country may now find its expression in rebuilding cities. (Photo courtesy of The Chamber of Commerce of Metropolitan St. Louis.)

James Oglethorpe devised a system of public squares within a grid street system which guided the development of that city until 1856 and today makes it one of the most delightful urban areas in the nation. But, such imaginative examples were the exception.

Most cities developed with a simple gridiron street plan, usually with little attention to the topography or the needs of the inhabitants. In 1811, a three-man commission culminated 3 years of deliberation by proposing a rigid gridiron street pattern for the undeveloped portion of Manhattan. The plan ignored the features of the landscape and provided only one substantial park. It was defended and implemented on the grounds that it provided a convenient system for the subdivision and sale of property. Real estate speculation and emphasis on maximum im-

mediate profit have continued to play a major role in city development throughout our history.

The World's Columbian Exposition held in Chicago in 1893 was a major stimulant to urban planning. Its Court of Honor featured classical white buildings grouped harmoniously around a formal court with pools, fountains, and sculpture. Visitors, accustomed to the chaotic development and drabness of their own cities, were awakened to the possibilities of urban design. In 1909, Daniel Burnham, one of its chief designers, prepared a plan for Chicago. In addition to proposing major improvements to the street system and waterfront, Burnham pointed out the need for control of development beyond the city limits. During that same year the first National Conference on City Planning was held, and Harvard University offered the first academic course in city planning.

The next 2 decades witnessed an increase in planning activity, primarily the development of plans in the "city beautiful" tradition inspired by Burnham. Few of the plans were implemented, however. Their proposals for monumental civic centers and great boulevards did not take into account other pressing needs or the limitations of the municipal treasury. A more realistic approach was taken by the planners who prepared the *Regional Plan for New York and Its Environs*. The ten-volume document, completed in 1929, was based on detailed surveys and analyses of the physical, social, and economic conditions of the region. Its proposals for a broad range of public improvements took into account the needs and abilities of the governmental units within the region. It was comprehensive in scope: including proposals for rational land use, improvements to the transportation system and public facilities, and the establishment of desirable standards for neighborhoods. Many of its recommendations were carried out, and it influenced the direction of city planning across the nation.

Planning for states and large regions lagged behind urban planning until the Depression. Early efforts of the states were directed toward encouraging more effective local planning. Massachusetts led the way in 1913 by requiring all cities having a population of 10,000 or more to create a town planning board. In 1928, the U.S. Department of Commerce published *A Standard City Planning Enabling Act* which served as a model for state planning legislation.

The National Resources Planning Board stimulated state planning activity in the early 1930's by offering consulting services to states having appropriate state planning boards. Over forty states established planning boards and requested assistance almost immediately. The demand for services was far beyond the capabilities of the few trained and experienced people available. As a result, state planning efforts did not reach maturity before World War II. By the end of the war many states had allowed their planning boards to wither, or had redirected their efforts so as to reduce the importance of planning. The National Resources Planning Board did, however, succeed in altering the direction of planning. The Depression had dramatically demonstrated the inadequacy of the civic design emphasis of past efforts. The grand plan, however attractively published, had little chance of success unless it reflected government policy and could be put into effect on a continuing basis. Moreover, no plan for physical improvements would be valid unless it took into account relevant economic and social factors.

The Tennessee Valley Authority, created in 1933, proved to be a more durable model for planning large regions. Charged with a range of responsibilities, including flood control and navigation potential on the Tennessee River, the TVA attacked the problems of an underdeveloped region on a broad basis. Its planning has been noteworthy in two respects. First, it has planned comprehensively, a reflection of the multipurpose goals of the agency. For example, over thirty dams have been constructed to achieve flood control, navigation, and power production objectives. But extensive soil surveys alerted the engineers to a menace. Soil erosion loaded the streams with silt and might fill a reservoir in only a few years. In addition, the loss of topsoil lowered farm production and, ultimately, farm income. The problems were attacked in several ways. TVA research workers developed a method for low-cost production of phosphate fertilizers, an element identified by the soil surveys as being badly needed. Demonstration projects were initiated to educate farmers to the value of fertilizer application, contour plowing, crop rotation, and other soil-conserving methods. TVA foresters also educated farmers on how to profit from reforesting upland slopes with mulch-producing trees, another contribution to reduction of soil erosion. Thus the goal of silt reduction in reservoirs was pursued in a broad context which conserved and restored depleted resources, augmented local industries, and raised farm incomes.

The second noteworthy aspect of TVA planning can also be seen in the foregoing illustration. TVA combined the power to plan with the power to act. Unlike most large-region planning, including early state planning, TVA integrated the planning process with the process of decision making, rather than setting it apart in a purely advisory role.

Recent Trends. Cities and city problems grew rapidly after World War II. Interest in urban planning was revived in the face of this challenge and stimulated even further by federal legislation. The Housing and Home Finance Agency was established. Shortly thereafter the Housing Act of 1949 declared that every American family should have a decent home in a suitable living environment and required that all urban redevelopment plans conform to over-all community plans. Subsequent housing legislation has strengthened the role of planning and provided major financial assistance to state and local governments for planning purposes. The elevation of the Housing and Home Finance Agency to cabinet-level status in 1965, as the Department of Housing and Urban Development, signified national recognition of the scope of urban problems and the importance of healthy urban areas to the well-being of the nation.

Recent increases in planning activity have been accompanied by shifts in the character of planning. Traditional physical concerns for rational land use, adequate public service facilities, and efficient transportation systems have been broadened to include a greater concern for the quality of the total environment. The involvement of planning agencies in studies of air pollution, refuse disposal, and natural resource conservation is an indication of this trend.

Achievement of social and economic objectives is increasingly given more importance in urban planning. Poverty, unemployment, racial strife, and similar problems have made it evident that physical plans must take these problems into account and be effectively coordinated with the programs designed to combat them.

What is Planning? Every person plans his activities to some extent. Time is reserved for study before an exam. Clothing is selected, cleaned, and pressed in anticipation of an important engagement. In hundreds of ways we design our actions to satisfy present or future needs. The general concept of city or regional planning can thus be easily grasped by everyone. But precise definitions are difficult. As we have seen in the foregoing material, planning for cities and regions has been an evolving practice in which changes continue to occur. It is concerned with the environment, but is also aware of the interplay of social and economic problems as well. Although we may never devise a completely satisfactory definition, we can, with some oversimplification, describe its essential characteristics. City and regional planning, as now practiced, is, or seeks to be:

1. *Systematic.* It is carried on in an organized fashion by trained personnel.

2. *Comprehensive.* It seeks to coordinate all the factors which affect the development of its region. Engineers may design highway plans which would be in direct conflict with recreation specialists' proposals for open-space preservation. Planners seek to identify and resolve such conflicts.

3. *Government oriented.* City or regional plans are usually prepared by or for some unit of government: a city, a county, or a state. Although planners seek to educate and influence many private decision makers, it is government which is most susceptible to having decisions influenced by planning, and government decisions greatly alter the environment—by constructing freeways, impounding streams, etc.

4. *Long range.* Planners seek to anticipate

the needs and problems of the future as well as to identify those of the present. Long-range plans are necessary because of the long-term effects of decisions. A decision to dredge a new river channel or build a dam will be felt long after the decision makers are gone. Even the narrow streets in a downtown area probably follow routes laid out by an early settler who never envisioned the space needs of automobiles or the concentration of people which skyscrapers can produce. There is no set figure for "long term." In 1961, the National Capital Planning Commission published a *Plan for the Year 2000* for Washington, D.C. Most plans attempt to work on the basis of a 20-year span or more.

5. *Flexible.* Planners have no mystical powers to divine the future. Public desires change, and new inventions change the patterns of living. Communities are sometimes altered by events which are difficult to anticipate, such as the decision of a manufacturing firm to erect a major new plant on the fringe of a small city. The plan must be sufficiently flexible to accommodate adjustments to all kinds of unforeseen circumstances.

6. *Ongoing.* As plans are continuously altered and adjusted to fit new situations they are, in effect, new plans. Early planning efforts, in the 1920's, gave emphasis to a plan document, a Master Plan. Increased emphasis has been given in recent years to the process of planning. The plan tends to become a constantly evolving document, frequently amended and updated. We are never finished in the task of building the environment in which we live.

ORGANIZING FOR PLANNING

The twenty-two-county New York Metropolitan Region is home to about 16 million people. The problems of providing clean water, regular garbage collection, an efficient transportation system, and the numerous other services which city dwellers require would be difficult under the best of circumstances. Simultaneously, the constant processes of urban growth and redevelopment must be regulated so as to promote an orderly and satisfactory environment, without unduly restricting individual actions. In the face of such demands, the most dynamic urban area in the world governs itself by means of over 1400 separate political entities—cities, counties, boroughs, towns, school districts, water districts, the Port of New York Authority, and many others—each having power to tax the public and provide specific services in a limited area, often without regard for the effect of its actions on other service agencies or adjacent communities.

New York provides an extreme example, but one typical of the kinds of problems found in almost all large cities. The situation begs for planning and coordination. The kinds of planning agencies which have been organized vary widely, having been adapted to the needs of particular situations, but they have much in common.

Most city and regional planning is carried out under a planning commission, a planning staff, or a combination of both. A planning commission is a citizen board, usually unpaid, appointed by a mayor or other chief executive, which serves on a part-time volunteer basis. The commission usually has authority under state law to exercise direct regulatory power in a limited number of ways. For example, in many cities, plans for new subdivisions must be approved by the planning commission before the developer can build streets and sell lots. Its primary duty, however, is to act as an adviser to the executive and legislative heads of the government.

The planning staff is composed of trained personnel who devote full time to the planning process. The staff usually has only advisory powers. It prepares plans and recommendations for the planning commission or works directly with the chief executive. In recent years the growing complexity of planning problems and the increasing expertness of trained planners have tended to enlarge the influence of the staff. A few staffs have been given direct power previously reserved to the planning commission or a government official. Private consulting firms are also available to provide special skills to augment a local staff.

City and regional planning is a convenient label, but it hardly describes the variety of situations in which planning functions. The traditional divisions of government into local, state, and federal have been blurred in recent years as numerous special kinds of governmental relationships have been created.

City Planning. Planning may be carried on by a city and confined to its corporate boundaries. In the case of large cities, satellite suburban communities may also carry on planning activity within their individual boundaries. Such arrangements tend to be unsatisfactory. The development of the central city cannot be divorced from its surrounding region. Moreover, the satellite suburbs need to coordinate their decisions with each other and the central city in order to fashion a sensible over-all transportation plan, avoid unnecessary duplication of services, etc. Planning should be comprehensive in terms of territory as well as function.

A variety of arrangements have been devised to overcome the limitations of planning to the city limits. Some states authorize cities to plan and exercise limited control over development beyond the corporate limits. In Tennessee this extraterritorial power extends up to 5 miles beyond the corporate limits. Other communities have sought to achieve coordination by establishing metropolitan planning commissions which are supported by, and provide services to, the central city, satellite cities, and the county. It is not uncommon to find several planning agencies functioning in the same area. In Dayton, Ohio, the City of Dayton obtains planning services from its own staff, while the Montgomery County Planning Commission operates in that portion of the county outside the Dayton corporate limits, and the Miami Valley Regional Planning Commission does general over-all planning for a five-county area which includes Montgomery County.

Planning organization has been simplified in a few cities where numerous local governments have been consolidated into a single unit. Dade County, Florida; Nashville, Tennessee; and Toronto, Canada, are outstanding examples of metropolitan area governments.

Many metropolitan areas have sought to provide better cooperation, without giving up the identity of the various units of local government, by establishing coordination agencies. Metropolitan area *councils of government* have been encouraged by federal legislation to attack problems on a coordinated regional basis rather than as individual municipalities, villages, or townships.

Regional Planning. The boundary between city and regional planning is not precisely defined. The exercise of extraterritorial power and county planning are kinds of regional planning. But here the urban area tends to be the focus of attention. In larger-scale regions the cities are seen in a broader context along with the hinterland and its resources.

Large-scale regions may be defined by a variety of criteria. For comprehensive physical planning a watershed is a popular unit, as in TVA.[5] Although it tends to provide a unit which is convenient for purposes of physical analysis and planning, the watershed region has limitations. It does not, for example, coincide with political subdivision boundaries. Thus a plan for coordinated treatment of an area may be easier to secure than the intergovernmental cooperation necessary to put the plan into effect. States or counties would not generally want to be uncooperative with each

[5] For special research, regions might be defined on the basis of a single common feature, such as predominant soil type or timber cover.

other, but they tend to have different financial capabilities, different goals, and different local political pressures. In addition, the physical characteristics of the region may dictate a plan which tends to favor one locality with greater benefits than another.

Other kinds of planning regions are being fostered by federal legislation. The Appalachian Regional Development Act recognized the need for a coordinated attack on a large underdeveloped region which is bound together by its common social and economic problems as much as by common physical characteristics. In similar fashion, the Public Works and Economic Development Act of 1965 encouraged creation of multi-county regional planning and development boards for coordinated public action in areas characterized by low income and high unemployment.

Since the power to implement a plan is usually vested most directly in government, governmental boundaries are often used for planning. Counties, groups of counties, or states commonly have planning agencies.

State planning has enjoyed a moderate resurgence since World War II. Near the close of that war most states assigned to their state planning boards the task of preparing plans and programs to assist in the transition from a wartime to a peacetime economy. These activities had run their course by 1950, and the agencies redirected their efforts. In addition to physical planning, attention was also given to industrial development and fiscal planning.

In recent years state planning has tended to divorce itself from advertising and promotional activities. One or more agencies of state government are usually performing the following activities.[6]

STATEWIDE PLANNING. The preparation of a general plan for the development of a state is a substantial task. Some states have approached the job by developing plans for regions within the state. The sum of all these plans would then constitute the over-all state plan. Other states have prepared statewide plans for specific facilities. State park and recreation plans are especially popular.

Few states have attempted preparation of a comprehensive general plan for the entire state. But *The General Plan for the State of Hawaii* was completed in 1961.

COORDINATION BETWEEN PROGRAMS AND BETWEEN AGENCIES. For years cartoonists and newspaper editors have exposed the waste which occurs when a new street is torn up to install underground utilities. Obviously, money could have been saved by scheduling the underground work first, and the public would not be saddled with a patched street. The same kind of conflicts can occur in state programs when agencies are uninformed about activities of other state departments. In one state a forestry department was notified that the planning agency had not approved plans for a fire tower. The tower had unknowingly been designed for construction directly in the path of a proposed new highway.[7] The simple task of coordinating activities between the two departments resulted in a saving of several thousand dollars.

PLANNING ASSISTANCE TO OPERATING AGENCIES. Some state operating departments conduct statewide planning activities within their own agencies. State highway departments, for example, are constantly studying future highway needs and developing plans to meet them. The state planning office can assist such work by providing data, such as population projections for the state and its regions, or by making available personnel who would have special planning skills not found within the operating department.

[6] The author is indebted to Harold V. Miller, Executive Director of the Tennessee State Planning Commission, for his summary of state planning functions in previous editions of this book.

[7] F. A. Pilkin, "State Planning and Development—What They Are and What They Serve," *State Government*, May 1950, p. 93.

SERVICE AS FEDERAL–LOCAL INTERMEDIARY. Federal grants-in-aid now constitute a major source of revenue to state and local governments. Other federal government activities not in the form of aid have direct impact on the development of localities in which they operate. These activities emanate from a wide variety of federal agencies, each having its own purposes, guidelines, and standards. State agencies and local government officials have, on occasion, been swamped in the resulting confusion and paperwork. State planning agencies have responded to this situation in two ways. First, they have often served as a local source of information on federal programs to state operating agencies and local governments. Second, they have sought to ensure that federal programs were not being used for cross purposes at the state level. The federal government has given increasing recognition to the latter problem. Many federal programs for assistance to local communities and states now require that an appropriate planning agency review the application for federal participation and certify that the proposal is not in conflict with the comprehensive plan for the area in which it would be operative.

STAFF ASSISTANCE TO THE GOVERNOR. As the volume and scope of state government activities have mushroomed, governors have found the need to rely increasingly on a state planning staff. The Governor must formulate programs for submission to the legislature, must formulate and execute the budget, and has final authority for coordinating the work of state operating agencies. The Council of State Governments has suggested that each state establish an Office of Planning Services in the office of the Governor or coequal with the budget office in an integrated Department of Finance to:

1. Assist the Governor in developing objectives for current and emerging trends.

2. Compile an inventory of current basic data and undertake research in various problems of state government.

3. Review and suggest means for coordinating the plans of state agencies.

4. Suggest to the Governor alternative courses of action, indicating the consequences of each course.

5. Assist the departments in their planning efforts.[8]

Enabling Legislation. Planners are not at liberty to undertake whatever form of planning they deem advisable. The authority to plan is a grant of power from the state. Local governments and the state itself must operate within the specifications of the enabling legislation. It specifies the manner in which the official planning bodies may be established, sets forth their duties, and defines their powers. The language of enabling legislation is sometimes sufficiently general to permit a variety of interpretations, as in its charge to promote the health, safety, morals, order, convenience, prosperity, and welfare of the people. But the legislation can also be highly restrictive, as when it fails to grant planning bodies the authority necessary to carry out plans. Florida has been notable for its lack of legislation authorizing control over subdivision development. A planning body needs guiding principles and limits beyond which it cannot go.

The lack of adequate planning legislation has been a matter of some concern, particularly in urban centers whose state legislatures were controlled by unsympathetic rural interests. The reapportionment process which has gone on steadily since the *Baker versus Carr* decision is expected to alter that situation.[9]

[8] The Council of State Governments, Planning Services for State Government, Chicago, March 1956, p. 42.

[9] Epic Supreme Court decision (1962) holding that federal courts have jurisdiction over lawsuits challenging the apportionment of legislative districts on the ground that malapportioned districts may violate the equal protection clause of the Fourteenth Amendment.

THE PLANNING PROCESS

City and regional planning is an organized attempt to improve the quality of the environment. It is an on-going process. We never achieve the perfect environment nor would we want a static society. Human desires change; technology introduces new problems along with new products; and the population increases and changes composition (Fig. 2).

The planning process

Fig. 2 A schematic organization of the essentials of the planning process.

The planning process may be envisioned as cyclical in nature. The accompanying illustration and the following description are somewhat oversimplified. The reader should not imagine that the world always permits the tidiness of textbook illustrations. Goals may have to be re-thought after the inventory and analysis indicate that they are unrealistic, or the plan may have to be altered without detailed evaluation when it becomes evident that implementation of particular proposals is not possible.

Goals. Community goals are usually expressed in very general terms. Everyone agrees on the need to improve the quality of the environment and to promote the health, safety, and welfare of the public. Many plans have stated goals in this general fashion. Some have simply assumed that everyone understood the goals and neglected to state them at all. It is specific goals that give us trouble.

Specific goals are necessary if the plan is to be addressed to the true needs of a community. They give it focus and provide a test of its relevance. But they are difficult to state. Who has the authority to define the community goals? Who can speak for the unborn future citizens of the community? There are no easy answers to such questions. But attempts are being made to establish meaningful goals in ways consistent with democratic traditions.

The Chicago Department of Development and Planning published a report in 1964 on *Basic Policies for the Comprehensive Plan of Chicago.* It was distributed to public libraries, schools, newspapers, television stations, public officials, and hundreds of individuals. Regional policy discussion meetings were held throughout the city. The policies were then revised to take into account the public response and were used as guidelines for preparation of *The Comprehensive Plan.* In Tuscon, Arizona, the Mayor and Council appointed a Community Goals Committee to "determine the aspirations and potentials of the Tuscon community and to define the steps that should be taken to fulfill those aspirations." [10]

The Tuscon goals are both general and specific. General statements were formulated for social, physical, economic, and governmental goals. Specific goals were then formulated to support each general goal. The general physical goal stated that "the Tuscon community should create conditions which will make the city healthful, pleasant, efficient and prosperous, and which will provide those special qualities which identify it as unmistakably Tuscon." [11] One of the specific physical goals for air and water conservation suggested that the community "conserve and develop those natural resources upon which the future well-being and indeed existence of the community are dependent, and take immediate steps to

[10] Citizens Committee on Community Goals, *Tuscon Community Goals,* Tuscon, 1966, p. 3.

[11] *Ibid.,* p. 9.

prevent either undue depletion or pollution of these resources." [12]

Inventory. There must be a clear understanding of the condition of the existing community before plans can be formulated for its future. This requires the collection of a wide variety of information. The distribution and characteristics of the population, traffic volumes, trends in wholesale and retail trade, and numerous other statistical data are required. Much of the physical information lends itself to presentation in map form. Maps showing soil classifications, topography, vegetation patterns, streams, and floodplains provide an overview of the physical environment. Maps showing land use, street locations, and building conditions give an indication of how the environment is being used. Public facilities such as parks, schools, and utility systems must also be inventoried to determine their adequacy.

Analysis. Collecting data is not an end in itself. They must be studied before they can become a useful foundation on which to build a plan. The analysis should reveal several kinds of knowledge.

The identification of major problems is one of the most obvious tasks of data analysis. Problems are usually evident before the inventory, but systematic investigation can provide a precision in problem identification which is lacking in casual observation. Moreover, the analysis would seek to identify the cause of the problems. The knowledge that a stream is polluted is relevant to development of a plan, but that knowledge becomes useful when it is known that the pollution results from the discharge of particular industrial wastes at a particular upstream location.

The analysis also seeks to discover potential assets which are not being utilized. If the analysis shows that a certain site has superior and unique potential for development as a park, plans for transportation facilities and

housing developments may also be shifted to make the site useful from the standpoint of convenience and to protect it from development for other purposes.

A primary purpose of the analysis is to identify present and future needs. For example, a knowledge of the number of inhabitants in the area 20 years hence is necessary before one can anticipate how much additional land will be required for housing, how many new schools will be required, etc. Future employment patterns will affect the need for public transit, the demand for industrial park acreage, and other things. The analysis will not identify future needs with certainty. Continued restudy and revisions of estimates are required.

Plan Formulation. A comprehensive plan has three basic elements: a land-use plan, a transportation plan, and a community facilities plan. It must be emphasized that these elements are intimately related. A change in any one has a direct effect on the other two. They must be designed to support each other in order to form a complete over-all plan (Fig. 3).

Plans may vary in focus and format. *The Plan for the Year 2000* is primarily a policies plan. It attempts to identify the best urban form for the Washington, D.C., area and provide a framework within which the center city and its surrounding areas can prepare harmonious individual plans. When going beyond policies and generalized proposals plans may specify the intended use of all land, proposed highway improvements, sites for new schools, and matters of similar detail. At the scale of a small city or a neighborhood, plans may be detailed to the point of recommending the use of individual parcels of land (Figs. 4 and 5).

LAND-USE PLAN. The rational use of lands is a key to building good communities and improving the quality of the environment. The land-use plan, taking into account the problems and potentials of an area, proposes

[12] *Ibid.,* p. 50.

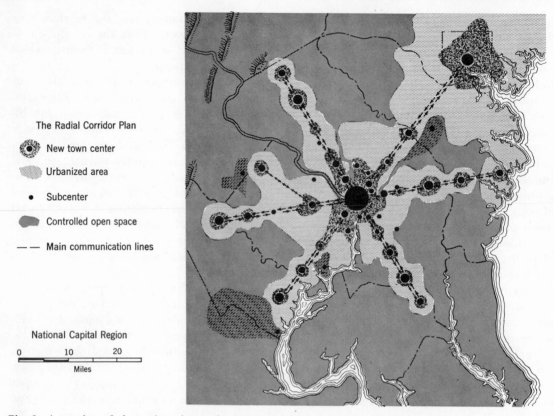

The Radial Corridor Plan

New town center

Urbanized area

• Subcenter

Controlled open space

— — Main communication lines

National Capital Region

0   10   20
Miles

Fig. 3 A number of alternative schemes for accommodating metropolitan growth were evaluated before the recommendation of this scheme for the Washington, D.C. area. (National Capitol Planning Commission.)

the use to be made of land now and in the future. In urban areas the plan provides space for housing, shopping facilities, industry, and parks. In regional schemes attention is given to such things as forests, prime cropland, grazing land, and potential mining areas.

Many factors must be taken into account in developing the plan. Adequate space must be provided to satisfy the needs of the future population. The number of new inhabitants will determine the amount of land required for new housing developments. This, in turn, will influence demands for additional playgrounds, school sites, and neighborhood shopping facilities.

The plan must also be designed to relate

the various land uses to each other in a harmonious way. Employment centers should be within easy access of workers' homes, yet housing should be protected from the noise and smoke of industrial areas. Shopping facilities should have access to major thoroughfares and be convenient to the residential areas they serve.

Finally, the plan should insure that land is used for purposes for which it is suited. On a regional scale this may involve recommendations for conversion of substandard agricultural lands to forestry. In an urban area it might involve protection of a marsh that has important effects on the water table from drainage and conversion into a housing development, a use which could utilize other lands more effectively.

TRANSPORTATION PLAN. We are a nation on the move. The economy of our cities and our nation depends on the efficient movement of goods and materials. Highway systems have been described as the skeleton of a city.

The proposed transportation system should be designed to serve the proposed system of land uses and public facilities. The city core, industrial centers, and regional shopping centers must be served with major highways. The various areas of the city must be intercon-

nected in ways that provide for easy movement.

As a practical matter, streets sometimes become masters instead of servants. In the constant fight to relieve congestion and move traffic more effectively officials may lose sight of the impact of their road-building decisions on the other features of an area. The extension of a freeway into the fringe of a metropolitan area may stimulate housing developments which soon feed new traffic onto the freeway and raise congestion to its previous levels. More lasting benefits could result if

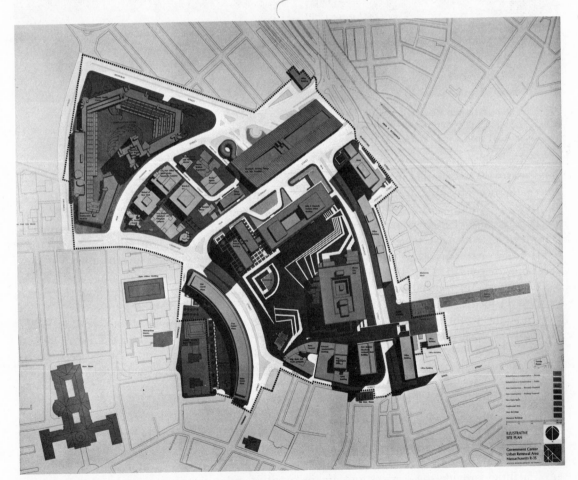

Fig. 4 The site plan of the Boston Government Center Urban Renewal Area illustrates detailed planning for a portion of a city with a consideration of architectural as well as land-use factors. (Photo courtesy of the Boston Redevelopment Authority.)

Fig. 5 The new Boston City Hall is a key item in the Government Center Urban Renewal Area. The pie-shaped building in the right foreground can be seen in the lower center of Figure 4. (Photo by J. McDevitt, courtesy of the Boston Redevelopment Authority.)

land uses were distributed in a way which reduced the necessity for travel.

Street and highway locations are also important because of their relative permanence. The uses of land may change, new buildings replace old ones, but streets often retain their locations for centuries.

Other forms of transportation are also important elements of the plan. Airports, rail and pipeline facilities, and water transportation are especially important at a regional scale.

Provision of adequate terminal facilities is an integral part of transportation plans. A man who cannot park his car is almost as helpless as one who can't walk.

COMMUNITY FACILITIES PLAN. The land-use pattern and transportation system give the community an over-all organization. Community facilities provide the services and amenities which are necessary for satisfactory living. Utility systems, parks, schools, fire stations, and a host of other things are required for satisfying the needs of urban and, to an increasing extent, rural dwellers.

The careful coordination of community facilities with land use and transportation systems enhances their utility and economy. For example, the land-use plan indicates the location and density of new residential developments, thereby making it possible to determine in advance the need for school facilities. Sites can be acquired in advance of actual need, when the cost is low, and streets can be designed to provide adequate access while minimizing traffic hazards to children. The building can be designed with a specific capacity in mind by knowing in advance the area and density of population that will have to be served.

Implementation. Comprehensive plans for cities and regions are not put into effect overnight. Instead they move toward completion by the accumulation over a long period of time of public and private development decisions which adhere to the recommendations of the plan.

Broad citizen support is the key to effective implementation. Plans must be publicized, must be understood, and must reflect the aspirations of the public. Support may be manifested by approval of referendums on bond issues for major public improvements suggested in the plan, such as a new regional park. In San Francisco the people voted to tax themselves in order to build the Bay Area rapid transit system and save their city from being cut up by numerous freeways. Other support

can come from lending institutions which insist that developers respect the plan when developing new subdivisions. Some large corporations will check to see whether a city has a plan before building a new plant. They want their plant investment protected, and they realize that a chaotic and cluttered city may have to raise taxes repeatedly in order to overcome problems which could have been prevented.

There is little hope that a plan will have citizen support unless the affected units of government also adhere to the plan. Government construction projects for dams, high-

Fig. 6 Historic Independence Hall was crowded by drab and uncomplimenting buildings until Philadelphia began restoring vitality to its core. (Photo by Lawrence S. Williams, Courtesy Philadelphia City Planning Commission.)

Fig. 7 Urban renewal can be used in the central cities to restore grace and beauty to a historic area. Compare this photograph to Figure 6. (Photo by Alois K. Strobel, Philadelphia City Planning Commission.)

ways, airports, schools, and other things are a major force in shaping a community. An over-all plan can provide the basis for effective coordination among the many different units of government which are usually found in metropolitan areas.

Experience has shown that land-use plans are not effectively implemented by persuasion and voluntary compliance. Public controls have been developed which restrict the uses of land so that the plan can become a reality. Zoning is a law enforced by a city or other local government which regulates the way land is used. Some areas are restricted to residential uses, some to commercial, some to industrial. Rural zoning can be used to preserve agricultural and forest lands, but care must be taken to avoid controls which are so stringent that they become confiscatory. In each zone the urban ordinance also establishes maximum building heights and lot coverage standards to preserve adequate open space. Subdi-

vision regulations establish minimum standards for the design and construction of new subdivisions. They are usually enforced by a planning commission.

In addition to the preventive measures which the foregoing tools provide, it is sometimes necessary to correct defects in the environment. The central business district of many large cities is surrounded by large areas of dilapidated and obsolete buildings. In these areas industries are often intermixed with housing, streets are too narrow, and parks nonexistent. Urban renewal is a mechanism for rebuilding such areas.

In the years when urban renewal was first initiated, blighted areas were often cleared of all old structures. Land not needed for public use was then sold for private housing, shopping, or industrial uses. Clearance has tended to give way to neighborhood conservation and rehabilitation. When the neighborhood is not completely decayed, it is often possible to raze the worst buildings and restore the remaining structures to standard condition. This process has been used in many cities to conserve areas of historic or architectural significance. The improvement of the area around Independence Hall in Philadelphia is a dramatic example (Figs. 6 and 7).

Evaluation. The words of the poet Robert Burns continue to remind us that the best laid plans often go astray. None is perfect. Many are crippled by partial and half-hearted implementation. Unforeseen events may create problems and opportunities which were not considered when the plan was developed. These situations require the constant rethinking of a plan.

Evaluation leads to a variety of responses. Poor public support may indicate that there was not adequate citizen participation in development of the plan or that the benefits of the plan have not been adequately publicized. Implementation may break down when the various units of government fail to cooperate.

Even when a plan enjoys great success the

planning process must continue. The needs of the future continue to be before us.

PLANNING FOR CONSERVATION

The conservation of natural resources is one among many concerns in city and regional planning. The signs of our failures in adapting to the environment are abundant. But there are also some signs of progress.

Obvious improvement is evident at a relatively small scale. Cluster subdivisions, in which houses are moved closer together and the resulting open space is pooled for com-

mon use, are being built with increasing frequency. A number of privately developed *new towns* have been designed with careful attention to preservation of trees, open spaces, and watercourses (Fig. 8). Reston, Virginia, has succeeded in making the natural features of the town site an important visual asset and functionally useful for recreation. Columbia, Maryland, another new town, is demonstrating that good community planning is an asset rather than a liability for the developers.

Transportation plans can also demonstrate a sensitivity to nature. Interstate 80 was realigned in Pennsylvania to preserve a recrea-

1 VILLAGE GREEN
2 DISPLAY HOUSES
3 SCHOOL SITES
4 APARTMENTS
5 OFFICES
6 REGIONAL SHOPPING CENTER
7 PARKS
8 RESEARCH PARK
9 LIGHT INDUSTRY

Fig. 8 Useable open space was made an integral part of the living environment in Crofton, Maryland, by planning housing around a golf course. (Courtesy of the Crofton Corporation.)

tion area. In other locations special highway overpasses have been built which allow wildlife to follow normal migration routes.

Conservation values are also evident in more and more comprehensive plans. The State of Wisconsin has done outstanding work in identifying the significance of environmental amenities on a regional scale. The Door County, Wisconsin, comprehensive plan gives detailed attention to the natural resources of the area and suggests specific ways in which they may be enhanced through orderly development. The Miami Valley Regional Planning Commission, with headquarters in Dayton, Ohio, prepared an inventory of natural resources in its five-county region to assist in more effective consideration of ecological factors in local planning. The Regional Planning Committee of San Mateo County, California, prepared a detailed survey of its physical setting before revising its General Plan. Countless other examples exist.

But problems of great magnitude persist. Air and water pollution, discussed in other chapters, plague both large and small cities and affect increasingly larger regions.

Perhaps the most conspicuous failure is in the inability to shape the over-all form of cities and arrest urban sprawl. The effort to fit various kinds of urban development into physical settings which are best suited for them is a story of meager success. The real estate market and property tax laws frequently have more to do with development trends than a plan. The use often does not fit the highest capability of the land, but the planner is busy trying to prevent the worst from happening rather than promoting the best.

New ways are being found to preserve open space in urban areas, a prime objective in the fight against urban sprawl (Fig. 9). The federal government has encouraged acquisition of open space by providing grants, contingent upon the purchase being compatible with the comprehensive plan. Leaseback and resale arrangements have also been devised in which

Fig. 9 This view in Crofton demonstrates that there are alternatives to the unimaginative sprawl of subdivisions across the landscape. Here natural amenities have been integrated with an urban housing form to create a pleasant scene while saving valuable land. (Photo by Robert de Gast, courtesy of the Crofton Corporation.)

the city acquires open land, then leases or sells it back to individuals with the provision that it continue to be used for agriculture, forestry, or other approved purpose.

Urban sprawl is a difficult problem because its control is at odds with a basic goal of most communities. Cities tend to grow; they are in competition. Growth provides more than the opportunity for civic boasting. It means more jobs and a larger market for the businessman. To halt urban sprawl without providing suitable alternative forms for growth or compensation for those who are damaged by controls is not feasible.

The conflict in goals lies near the heart of many resource problems in urban areas. The land developer is motivated by a desire for profit. He incurs extra costs when he takes special care to preserve trees or leave a scenic brook undisturbed. This cost must be recovered in higher prices for the land when it is sold. If buyers are not willing to pay the difference the resources suffer the consequences. The owner of a marshland which is strategically located for development as a shopping center site may be assailed by nature lovers who value the wildlife and vegetation which are so scarce in the metropolis. But the property owner wonders why he should bear the financial burden of not developing the land in order to secure a public benefit, particularly when that benefit has many intangible values. Who pays the costs for conservation and how are they equitably distributed? These issues will not be settled by planners. The public must be made more aware of the general benefits of resource conservation, especially in our great urban areas. And more specific research must be carried on.

"The bays, the river valleys and the hilltops, the forests and the fields, perform essential hydrological, climatic, and other functions which we have scarcely begun to define and measure. They maintain and control the flow of water essential to the civilization of the urban area. In many areas they moderate the climate, purify or humidify air, and in other ways maintain thermal controls in the metropolitan area. We can guess, though we cannot prove, that filling San Francisco Bay would raise the temperature of the metropolitan area by 5 to 10 degrees, and blanket it with a layer of smog which would cost tens of millions annually. But these arguments will command little support until they can be scientifically demonstrated and measured." [13]

[13] William L. C. Wheaton, "Form and Structure of the Metropolitan Area," *Environment for Man,* Indiana University Press, Bloomington, 1967, pp. 175–176.

References

American Institute of Planners, Washington, D.C., *Journal,* Quarterly.

American Society of Planning Officials, *Newsletter,* Chicago, Monthly.

Chapin, F. Stuart, Jr., *Urban Land Use Planning,* Second Edition, University of Illinois Press, Urbana, 1965.

Chicago Department of Development and Planning, *The Comprehensive Plan of Chicago,* Chicago, 1966.

Churchill, Henry S., *The City Is The People,* W. W. Norton and Company, New York, 1962.

Citizens Committee on Community Goals, *Tuscon Community Goals,* Tuscon, 1966.

The Editors of *Fortune, The Exploding Metropolis,* Doubleday and Company, Garden City, New York, 1958.

Eldridge, H. Wentworth, editor, *Taming Megalopolis,* Frederick A. Praeger, New York, 1967.

Ewald, William K., Jr., editor, *Environment for Man,* Indiana University Press, Bloomington, 1967.

Gallion, Arthur B. and Simon Eisner, *The Urban Pattern,* D. Van Nostrand Company, New York, 1963.

Goodman, William I., editor, *Principles and Practice of Urban Planning,* International City Managers Association, Washington, D.C., 1968.

Gottmann, Jean, *Megalopolis,* Twentieth Century Fund, New York, 1960.

———, *Megalopolis, The Urbanized Northeastern Seaboard of the United States,* The Twentieth Century Fund, New York, 1961.

Hawaii State Planning Office, *The General Plan for the State of Hawaii,* Honolulu, Hawaii, 1961.

Higbee, Edward, *The Squeeze: Cities Without Space,* William Morrow and Company, New York, 1960.

Kent, T. J., Jr., *The Urban General Plan,* Chandler Publishing Co., San Francisco, 1964.

Mayer, Harold M. and Clyde F. Kohn, *Readings in Urban Geography,* The University of Chicago Press, Chicago, 1959.

McHarg, Ian, *Design With Nature,* Natural History Press, Garden City, New York, 1969.

Miller, Harold V., *Mr. Planning Commissioner,* Public Administration Service, Chicago, 1954.

Mumford, Lewis, *The City in History,* Harcourt, Brace and Co., New York, 1961.

Regional Planning Committee of San Mateo County, California, *The Physical Setting of San Mateo County,* 1968.

Schmid, A. Allan, *Converting Land from Rural to Urban Uses,* Resources for the Future, Inc., Washington, D.C., 1968 (Distributed by The Johns Hopkins Press, Baltimore).

U.S. Department of Agriculture, *A Place to Live, The Yearbook of Agriculture,* Government Printing Office, Washington, D.C., 1963.

United States National Resources Planning Board, *State Planning,* Washington, D.C., 1942.

Walker, Robert A., *The Planning Function in Urban Government,* Second Edition, University of Chicago Press, Chicago, 1950.

GUY-HAROLD SMITH
The Ohio State University

CHAPTER 25

National Planning and the Conservation of Resources

The national government, by its legislative acts, administered by the chief executive and tested in the highest tribunal of the people, provides equal opportunity for all the people of the United States. Since the founding of the Republic the Congress has given attention to the needs of the nation, but inevitably certain acts of Congress have been advantageous to selected groups or particular areas. But in the government there have always been men of high principles whose great ambition has been to contribute to the general welfare of the nation.

The Responsibility of Congress. In the Congress, both in the House of Representatives and in the Senate, the members in general may be said to entertain two major objectives. As would be expected, these elected representatives of the people are the protectors of the interests of the people whom they serve. At the same time they are aware of the needs of the nation, and their legislative actions reflect their interests in the national welfare.

The improvement of rivers and harbors, the reclamation of lands requiring irrigation, the control of floods, the development of power, the protection of coastal areas against erosion, the conservation of the soil resources, the preservation of the dwindling forest resources, the conservation of the mineral treasures, and provisions for recreation have received Congressional attention.

Inequality in the Distribution of Resources. The abundant resources of the country have not benefited all the people equally. Many people have been enriched because they have been successful in securing control over the material resources of the country. Others in humble circumstances have not shared in the great wealth of the nation. Certain pioneers settled the new farmland when the rich prairies were available. At a later period the settlers were not so fortunate, for the richer lands were gone. The abundant timber and mineral resources were developed and exploited by private capital, and a fortunate few were enriched. Other people came into possession of poor land and found it difficult to earn a decent living. The material resources distributed unequally over the country have benefited the people unequally.

Private Enterprise and National Planning. Concurrently with the political growth of the

United States private enterprise and personal initiative were responsible in a large measure for the development of the natural resources. Because of great abundance, rapid and wasteful use of resources became a characteristic feature of the national economy. From the time of settlement and particularly after the frontier moved westward beyond the Appalachians, there was for many decades a prodigality about the exploitation of the great resources of timber, grass, water, coal, iron, oil, and natural gas. But two world wars with their enormous wastefulness and a great economic depression have made us aware of the necessity of husbanding our resources. Planning among other things must be directed toward the wise use of resources and the ordering of the economy in the best interests of all the people. Planning is both a public and a private responsibility. People as property owners, whether as private citizens or as shareholders in large corporations, must join with the federal government in reducing or avoiding the wasteful exploitation of natural resources.

There have been brief periods of economic stress with widespread unemployment and insecurity. Fear has replaced hope, and people have entertained doubt about the stability and the soundness of the national economy. The American economy, characterized by its great capacity for production, has been unable to achieve by itself certain necessary reforms and attain stability and full employment; as a result the federal government has participated increasingly in the economic life of the nation.

THE NATURE OF NATIONAL PLANNING

Planning on a Nationwide Basis. It is not always evident that certain acts of Congress may change in a significant way the utilization of natural resources. The tariff regulations or duties applied to imports may affect all the

people in much the same way. The import duty on foreign sugar increases the price of sugar everywhere in the United States. The duty on wool has a similar effect on the price of all woolen products whether they are made of imported wool or wool of domestic origin. In these instances the government was not primarily concerned with the increased price of sugar and wool to all the people but in the protection provided for the domestic producers of these products.

Although certain acts of Congress may operate selectively for the benefit of the few, many laws have nationwide application. The Pure Food and Drug Act, the insuring of bank deposits, the establishment of uniform postal rates, the operation of the Federal Reserve System, and many other acts and regulations apply more or less uniformly to all the people (Fig. 1).

Benefits or disadvantages may accrue selectively to certain people, but the national welfare requires on occasion that the federal government take definite action. No doubt the best interests of the people were served when the federal government endorsed stockpiling of strategic materials. During World War II and during hostilities in Korea, a large number of resources and industrial materials were brought under control of the federal government. The jurisdiction of the government extended from production and procurement through processing and allocation to civilian and military agencies. This was well illustrated by rubber, the ferroalloys, copper, aluminum, and a great number of products. In times of national stress the participation of the federal government in the economic affairs of the nation is greatly expanded in the best interests of all the people.

However in times of peace and international calm the federal government, depending on the party in power, may encourage private interests to take on a larger responsibility in ordering the national economy.

National planning is regarded by many as a

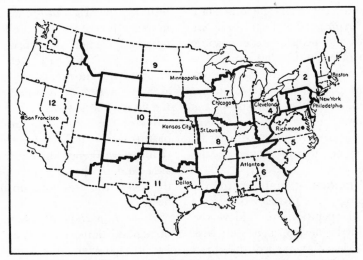

Fig. 1 The Federal Reserve Board: Districts. These divisions were originally set up to serve the banking and financial interests of the country. The boundaries are essentially political and arbitrary in character. (National Resources Committee.)

step toward a kind of totalitarianism which is in conflict with free enterprise and personal liberty. The states that pay more into the federal treasury in taxes than they receive in benefits are disposed to complain about inequities. Generally it is accepted as good governmental planning to use the greater wealth and resources of richer and more fortunate states for the benefit of the poorer areas.

In the broad field of planning for the security and the defense of the nation, and planning for the security and health of the people individually and by groups, the federal government must be concerned with the physical or material resources that are fundamental in security planning. The government extends its protection to all the people and otherwise recognizes the nationwide application of its laws and regulations. The conservation and wise use of the material heritage of the nation require vigilance and dynamic action against waste of the physical base of the national economy.

Government Must Take the Long View. In the long-range development of the economy of

the United States the material resources have been or will be depleted unequally. Certain industrial raw materials occur in such great abundance that there is little danger of immediate exhaustion. The use of enormous quantities of iron and petroleum, on the other hand, has threatened our ultimate supply of these basic resources. The heavy demand for lead, zinc, and copper has made us aware of the possibility of exhaustion of these essential metals.

The federal government and other agencies, both private and public, are giving attention, through research, to extending the productive life of many of the raw materials so necessary in the complex economy of the United States and the world.

Standard of Living and Resource Utilization. The high standard of living attained by the people of the United States is related to a number of factors. The volume and value of material resources in relation to the number of people are favorable to the development of a high standard of living. The capacity of the people, with an urge to improve their physical well-being and raise their cultural standards, has been an important factor. The inventive genius of the people made possible the development of machines that can utilize the great power resources of the country for the welfare of the people. In spite of an imprudent drain upon the material base of the nation the economic and political leadership has been equal to its opportunity to bring favorable conditions of life and security to the American people.

Planning, a Definition. Planning is the development of a program of ultimate objectives and a schedule of operations to achieve the desired results. In the development and wise use of resources a clear statement of the objectives to be attained is essential to the execution of a plan. It is also very important that the several operations in the plan be scheduled so that the key projects are given priority. This simple statement encompasses most of the essentials of planning, whether local, state, regional, or national.

Planning is not regimentation nor need not be. In the United States democratic planning should emerge from community or national discussion of issues that require collective action. Planning should be continuous, or at least there should be a periodic review of previous plans so that obsolete objectives may be abandoned. Also it may be necessary to reschedule the projects in terms of recent developments. A long-term plan characterized by rigidity instead of flexibility may be doomed to failure. It is important that planning, as a community program, should be responsive to the will of the people.

REGIONAL PLANNING

In an area as large as the United States where the geographical diversity is so great, it was inevitable that resource development and use would be distinctly regional in character. For example, the harvesting of the great white pine forest of the Great Lakes states placed upon the lumber markets one of the finest

building materials in the latter decades of the nineteenth century and the first decade of the twentieth. When this harvest was consumed the lumber industry moved on to other forests, and the cut-over lands became a problem area. In a similar manner the grasslands of the Great Plains were first the natural grazing lands of the indigenous buffalo. Then overpasturing and the breaking of the sod for agriculture weakened the natural defenses of the area, and in the dry years of the 1930's and the 1950's the area took on dust-bowl characteristics.

What Is a Region? There are many kinds of regions. Some regions are essentially physical in character, such as soil regions, physiographic regions, climatic regions, and drainage basins. Others are cultural regions, such as language areas, regions with a dominant religion, and areas with a particular mode of government. Whether physical or cultural a region must have one or more distinguishing characteristics that are more or less co-extensive with the area, and it should be set apart from other regions with distinct or arbitrary boundaries.

Many easily recognized regions in the United States have emerged because of certain dominant characteristics. A region, to have validity and usefulness as a planning area, may or may not have exactly defined boundaries or enumerated common characteristics. For administrative convenience it may be useful and desirable that regions, whether physical or cultural, have boundaries that are easily identified and demarcated.

Most Americans are familiar with such regions as New England, the Piedmont, the South, the Middle West, the Great Plains, the Upper Lakes area, the Columbia Plateau, the Great Basin, the Yukon basin, and many more restricted areas or regions such as the Mohawk Valley, the Delta country, the Tennessee Valley, Appalachia, the Salt Lake oasis, the Central Valley of California, or the Puget basin (Fig. 2). Some of these are physical regions or were originally, but have taken on

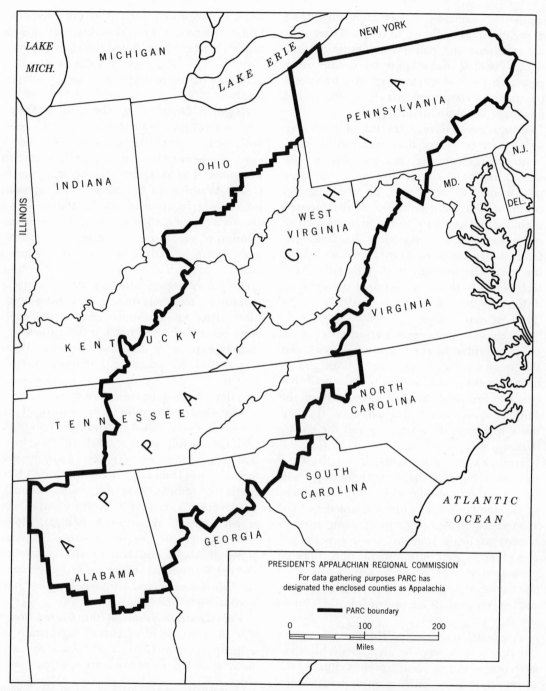

Fig. 2 Appalachia as delineated for the purpose of gathering and assembling data that may be useful in planning programs will require action by the Congress and approval by the President. (Area Redevelopment Commission, U.S. Department of Commerce.)

639

composite characteristics reflecting something of the natural conditions in combination with the economic and cultural attributes. People living, working, and shaping the destiny of an area give to it characteristics that transcend the natural conditions which at the outset may have been dominant.

Most regions have a central or core area which may be regarded as the type location. However, the core may not represent all the characteristics of a large area or in the same proportion. No small area in New England could be truly representative of the forested highlands of northern Maine, the truck farming area of the Connecticut lowland, the sandy beach areas of Martha's Vineyard, or the industrial community of Worcester, Massachusetts. With all its regional or sectional differences New England is a region in the minds of most people.

In regional planning, which in effect is national planning by regions, it is necessary that the areas set up as planning regions should have something of the unity of spirit that characterizes New England, the South, or the Middle West. From this sense of regional unity will come the leadership and the energy that will achieve results.

Frederick Jackson Turner, historian of the frontier, recognized the importance of pioneer life as a significant force in the development of the fundamental political character of the United States. Although the moving frontier tended to bring some common experiences, the pioneers were adventuring into different geographical regions. Sectionalism was from the outset a concomitant characteristic of the settlement and development of the United States.

Regionalism or sectionalism in a narrow provincial sense may be an undesirable characteristic of the national economy. But regionalism, if it is a unifying force which transcends the restricted limits of a small area, may be a vital factor in the development of national character. Out of the diversity of states and regions a spirit of national responsibility emerges. "The diversity of regions rather enriches the national life than impoverishes it . . ."[1] Regional planning is in effect national planning expressed or developed areally.

Regional Divisions of the United States. The federal government has found it desirable, and in particular cases almost a necessity, to decentralize or regionalize certain functions. The concentration of many agencies in Washington has been looked upon as undue centralization of administrative activities in a single urban center. The rapid expansion of governmental agencies in wartime and during the difficult Depression years placed a heavy burden upon the metropolitan area of Washington. Housing for government employees, transportation to and from work, office space for personnel, and related problems became the insuperable difficulties of a rapidly expanding metropolitan area. There was no time for planning, but it was obvious that decentralization of certain governmental functions was an urgent necessity.

The Census Divisions. The Bureau of the Census has established nine arbitrary, but statistically useful, regions. Each of these divisions includes states that have many characteristics in common. They include New England, Middle Atlantic, South Atlantic, East North Central, West North Central, East South Central, West South Central, Mountain, and Pacific groups of states. The new states of Alaska and Hawaii are included in the Pacific division. These regions have statistical convenience and through long use have become well established.

Functional Divisions of the United States. For the purpose of decentralizing certain administrative functions of the government a number of agencies have a regional pattern of

[1] Donald Davidson, "That This Nation May Endure, The Need for Political Regionalism" in Herbert Agar and Allen Tate, *Who Owns America?*, Boston, 1936, p. 116.

organization. This is well illustrated by the United States Circuit Court of Appeals which consists of ten Circuit Districts and the District of Columbia. These regions or districts are judicial areas and serve this function only.

In 1914, during the administration of President Woodrow Wilson, the Congress enacted the legislation that created the Federal Reserve System. For the purpose of carrying out the provisions of the Act the United States was divided into twelve Federal Reserve districts, each consisting of a number of states or parts of states and each having a Federal Reserve bank to serve the banking, industrial, and commercial interests of its area.

Many other agencies of the federal government have been organized on a regional basis, or have established outpost or field offices to facilitate their administrative activities.

Planning Regions. The establishment of regions for the planned development and use of resources emerges as a necessary concomitant of national planning. Certain steps have al-

ready been taken and may indicate the nature of the regions that are most suitable for planning and developmental programs. It is obvious that no single type of region will be suitable for all purposes. Several kinds of regions, differing in dimensions, overlapping perhaps in certain instances, and encompassing a number of vital activities, may be necessary to achieve the several objectives of a well-balanced program of national development.

The Watershed as a Planning Region. It has been recognized that the hydrographic basin or watershed is an appropriate and manageable planning area. In many of the drainage basins of the United States the principal problems that require constructive action are closely related to the river in each watershed. The control of the master stream becomes the key project in a basinwide program of resource development which will, under proper management, extend to other problems not directly related to the river (Fig. 3).

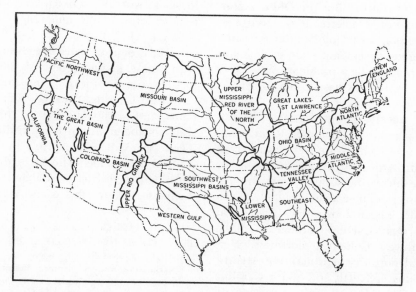

Fig. 3 Major drainage basins of the United States. Drainage basins are naturally well suited for water planning, but in spite of their limitations they have been considered appropriate for the more inclusive regional planning programs. (National Resources Planning Board.)

The Tennessee River basin, developed under the administrative jurisdiction of the Tennessee Valley Authority, may be regarded as the model drainage-basin planning region. Other watersheds have been designated as well suited for regional development. These include the Ohio Valley, the Missouri Valley, the Colorado Valley, the Columbia Valley and others.

Before the need arises for immediate action comprehensive surveys can be made so that plans will be ready *when* the need arises. As an integral part of the plans a schedule of projects should be developed. It may be necessary to proceed immediately with certain plans for a region or watershed and reserve for later periods the completion of the project. That is well illustrated in the signing of the Ohio River Valley Water Sanitation Compact at Cincinnati, Ohio, on June 30, 1948. Navigation on the Ohio has long been a part of the program of river development. Floods remain a great menace, and many years will be required before the excess waters can be brought under control. But the Ohio is more than an artery of commerce. It is a source of water for millions of people, and at the same time it is a great sewer. Sanitation in the Ohio Valley continues to be a problem.

Planning by regions has shifted somewhat over the past 4 decades. The TVA has become a successful operating organization. The Columbia River basin, the Colorado River basin, and the Missouri Valley are well advanced in development. Other areas are receiving or may receive increasing support from the federal government. These areas include Appalachia, the New England area, the Upper Great Lakes, the Ozarks, Four Corners (southeast Utah, southwest Colorado, northwest New Mexico, and northeast Arizona), the Atlantic Coastal Plains of North and South Carolina and Georgia, and other areas of varying dimensions. Planning for these areas requires the integration of plans for areas of different dimensions and the resolution of a variety of jurisdictional problems.[2]

Groups of States as Planning Regions. Other types of areas have been suggested as suitable for regional development. The New England area consists of a group of states rather than a number of drainage areas; yet the water problems of the several major streams such as the Connecticut and the Merrimack require a number of multiple-purpose projects to meet the situation.[3] The Middle Atlantic area, similar to New England, is largely a group of states extending from New York to North Carolina and fronting on the Atlantic. It is an area with many problems, but it lacks the regional consciousness so characteristic of New England.[4] This is a region highly developed industrially and commercially, and many of the most urgent problems of today are related to the lack of careful planning in the past. Urban blight and the related ills of the industrial communities require plans and programs of action that will rehabilitate the unfortunate people who live in such areas and redesign the land-use pattern in terms of the long-range needs of the urban areas.

Other groups of states have been considered appropriate planning regions. Some of these include the Southeast, consisting of South Carolina, Georgia, Florida, Tennessee, Alabama, and Mississippi. Part of this area is already included within the jurisdiction of the Tennessee Valley Authority. In spite of industrial developments in the Piedmont, in the Birmingham district of Alabama, and in the Tennessee Valley, this is also an agricultural

[2] Harvey S. Perloff, "Key Features of Regional Planning," *Journ. Amer. Institute of Planners*, Vol. 34, May 1968, pp. 153–159.

[3] National Resources Planning Board, *Development of Resources and Stabilization of Employment in the United States, Part II. Regional Development Plans,* Washington, D.C., 1941, p. 14.

[4] *Ibid.,* p. 29.

area with some of the agrarian problems associated with the cash crops of cotton and tobacco.[5]

The Mountain states planning region consists of Colorado, New Mexico, Wyoming, and parts of several other states in the Rocky Mountain area. This large area, because of the character of its resources, has been exploited rather than developed. Minerals have been mined until the rich treasures have been exhausted; grasslands have been overgrazed to supply meat products to the eastern markets; and in many areas the limited timber resources have been cut so that watershed protection has been reduced. The scant rainfall, in most places inadequate for either forests or agriculture, becomes a resource of great importance in the watercourses where the water is available for power and for irrigation. The coordination of the several water-use projects is the major regional problem of the mountain states.[6]

The Pacific Southwest and the Pacific Northwest regions are similar planning regions because each consists of a number of states and parts of states. In both areas large tracts of dry land without adequate water are characteristic, though the Southwest has less rainfall than the Northwest. The Southwest has access to the power and the water of the Colorado, whereas the Northwest taps the resources of the Columbia.

In the Pacific Southwest water is the universal need. "Cities, farms, mines, and factories depend directly on perpetuation of their water supplies, which must often be brought from distant sources. The desert is ever striving to recapture the territory that has been wrested from it." [7] In such an area the individual, whether he is a farmer, a miner, or a city dweller engaged in activities that seem to

bear little relationship to the basic industries, may be unmindful of the fact that he is in a large measure dependent upon projects sponsored and developed by collective action.

The Pacific Northwest as a planning region consists approximately of the three states of Washington, Oregon, and Idaho, though the regional limits have not been sharply defined. The several problems related more or less directly to the natural resources include the settlement and reclamation of arable lands, the utilization of water for irrigation and power, flood control, the establishment of the sustained-yield principle in the lumbering industry, forest protection and rehabilitation, and the preservation and development of the scenic resources.

NATURAL RESOURCES AND NATIONAL SECURITY

The basic raw materials so necessary in maintaining the highly developed economy of the United States are available in very unequal quantities. Fortunately America is richly endowed with most of the essential raw materials of industry, but there are notable exceptions. The rapidly expanding economy has increased greatly the demand for raw materials and hastened the exhaustion of certain resources initially in short supply. A people mindful of the real or ultimate scarcity of the resources that are essential to the national economy should take the necessary steps to attain security. The economy of peace should be convertible to war in all possible haste in times of emergency. Whether the United States is a neutral or belligerent, the nation's best interests will be served if the economy is based upon adequate supplies of essential raw materials.

Complete independence in respect to the basic resources of industry is an impossibility for the United States. Dependence upon resources imported from other countries is, and

[5] *Ibid.*, p. 50.
[6] *Ibid.*, p. 174.
[7] *Ibid.*, p. 198.

has been, a significant feature of the American economy. Staley has stated clearly and forcefully, "There is no escape from international raw material interdependence . . ." [8] and this applies to the United States as well as to the less richly endowed countries.

New Discoveries. The available supply of many important resources will be increased by new discoveries if the history of mineral exploration can be used to forecast the future. In spite of the prospect that new discoveries will add substantial supplies of many resources to the total available for industrial use, there is also the grim truth that the rate of discovery will fall below the rate of use. National security is related to the continued search for additional supplies of essential resources and to an expanded program of research designed to make available industrial raw materials from deposits now known.

During World War II it was recognized that private mining interests would not be able to carry out the necessary exploration for, and development of, new mineral deposits rapidly enough to meet the needs of a nation at war. As a consequence the federal government by various means became involved in the exploration for new mineral resources and the expansion of the mineral processing industries. For example, the United States Geological Survey and the Bureau of Mines carried out investigations of domestic deposits of strategic minerals, such as chromite, mercury, and manganese.

Direct Subsidies. In addition to the scientific work of the Bureau of Mines and the Geological Survey and the loans made by the Metals Reserve Company, direct subsidies were paid to the high-cost producers of copper, lead, and zinc amounting to several hundred million dollars in the period, 1942 to 1947. Both by indirect methods and direct subsidies financial assistance can be used to

[8] Eugene Staley, *Raw Materials in Peace and War,* New York, 1937, p. 238.

increase production of a material in short supply.

Energy Resources and the Strength of the Nation. The fuel and power resources of the United States have made possible the high development of power-driven machines and have been responsible in a large measure for the highly productive facilities that have brought material conveniences and comforts to the American people. Inanimate energy released by the consumption of coal, petroleum, gas, and water power has multiplied manyfold the energy of human hands. The continued use of these power resources should give the United States a material civilization of a high order (see Chapters 14 and 16).

It is difficult to state just what fraction of the total power produced in the United States will be developed from uranium and from other nuclear sources by 1975 or the year 2000. Power plants using nuclear fuel are in operation, and a small contribution is being made to the total supply of electrical energy available. Others are under development or are being planned. The ultimate importance of atomic energy as a power resource is related to a number of significant factors including the relative cost of the power resources, the continued availability of adequate quantities of uranium-235 and other nuclear fuels, and the relative importance of the weapon's program to the plans for the peaceful use of nuclear materials in medical science and in industry.

The Metals in a Power-Using Economy. Because the United States is the major consumer of metals and many other mineral products, it is essential that every effort be made to assure the nation adequate supplies from both domestic and foreign sources. The United States normally uses more than half of the world's aluminum, cadmium, beryllium, cobalt, lead, molybdenum, the platinum-group metals, and a number of others. Consumption varies between a quarter and a half of the world's production of antimony, copper, iron ore, magnesium, manganese, mercury, nickel, tin, and others. Important quantities of these strategic materials are imported currently and in the future will have to be secured from foreign areas. As a consequence the Congress and other agencies of the federal government will carry a large responsibility for national and international planning designed to maintain the flow of essential metals and minerals to the United States. (See Chapter 15.)

As the supplies of metals are drawn increasingly from foreign sources privately owned mineral industries will be unable to assume full responsibility for assuring themselves of sufficient supplies of metals and minerals to meet the requirements of peace, the necessities of national defense, or the emergency of war. The maintenance of adequate reserves, stockpiling of strategic materials, and the development of substitutes become, in part at least, a responsibility of the national government.

It is also important that the stockpiling operations of the national government do not permit a number of companies or individuals to profit unduly. President Kennedy, at a news conference held on January 31, 1962, reported that he had reviewed the stockpile program and that it was apparent to him that the storage of costly materials has been "a potential source of excessive and unconscionable profits." [9] Senator Symington and his committee examined the situation as it had developed over the years, and in a number of instances the committee's findings seemed to support the President's contention.

Resources of Organic Origin. The United States is normally dependent on imports for an important list of products of organic origin. During World War II fats and oils were in short supply. The expansion of the production of peanuts and soybeans offset in large measure the loss of coconut and palm nut oil

regularly imported from the Far East. The cordage fibers such as henequen, Manila hemp, and jute are not only important in civilian industries but are essential in time of war. Other fibers such as kapok, bristles, and wool are imported to meet domestic requirements.

The list of materials of organic origin can be extended to include timber and wool pulp, condiments, tanning materials, rubber, and hides and skins. Our dependence upon overseas sources may be reduced by the development of substitutes, particularly rubbers developed from petroleum and alcohol. The increased use of plastic wood, resin-impregnated woods, wallboard, and preservatives may extend greatly the forest resources of the country.

Unlike the nonperishable mineral resources these organic materials cannot be stockpiled without danger of deterioration. Stockpiling requires continual renewal of supplies to meet or offset withdrawals from the nation's hoard of essential materials.

PLANNING BY FEDERAL AGENCIES

Both the legislative and executive branches of the federal government recognize their high responsibility for the long-range planning for the general welfare of the people and the security of the nation. Their objectives have been achieved by legislative action by the Congress authorizing the creation of agencies, prescribing and limiting their functions, and finally, after their functions are no longer necessary, terminating their activities. The President may, under legislative authority and by executive order, establish agencies whose responsibilities may be related to long-range planning in the areas of resource use and national security.[10]

---

[9] See Draft Report of the National Stockpile and Naval Petroleum Reserves Subcommittee (Senator Stuart Symington, Chairman), Washington, D.C., 1963.

[10] *United States Government Organization Manual, 1968–69,* Government Printing Office, Washington, D.C., 1968.

In the executive branch of the federal government several agencies are concerned with natural resources—their availability, their use, and their conservation. The several Departments, each with a cabinet-level officer in charge, have major or lesser jurisdiction over resources. Other agencies, advisory to the President and other branches of the national government, such as the Bureau of the Budget, Office of Emergency Planning, and Atomic Energy Commission, exercise great power in the field of natural and human resources.

The President has access to a number of agencies whose function it is to keep him fully informed on developments in the nation's economy and security. The Council of Economic Advisers must be ready at all times to keep the President knowledgeable about the conditions and trends in the national economic situation.

Bureau of the Budget. The Bureau of the Budget was established on June 10, 1925, and has become a powerful and useful agency in the Executive branch of the federal government. Its chief functions include a close scrutiny of the budgets of the major departments, divisions, offices, services, and other branches of the federal government.

The Nationl Security Council. By Congressional action the National Security Council was created in 1947. The National Security Act has been amended to change slightly the composition of the Council which presently consists of the President, the Vice-President, the Secretary of State, the Secretary of Defense, and the Director of Emergency Planning. The Special Assistant to the President for National Security and an Executive Secretary are officials rather than members of the Council. This important agency has as its chief functions the integration and interpretation of all domestic, foreign, and military policies that have significant bearing on national security.

Office of Emergency Planning. The Office of Emergency Planning, with twenty or more important offices, divisions, and centers, is one of the most important agencies concerned with, or involved in, the field of national planning. This important agency of the federal government stands ready to advise the President and Congress on the capacity of the nation to convert the peacetime economy to a wartime footing if this became necessary. If a serious international situation should require a quick appraisal of the material resources available to meet the challenge, the Director of the National Resource Analysis Center, the Chief of the Stockpile and Requirements Division, the Chief of the Resource Management Division, and the officials of several other offices and divisions could, under the leadership of the Director of the Office of Emergency Planning, present strong and meaningful recommendations to other agencies of the federal government concerned with national security.

Central Intelligence Agency. Created by the National Security Act of 1947 the Central Intelligence Agency has as its principal purpose the coordination of all the intelligence activities of its own organization as well as similar activities of several departments of the government. Naturally, much of the work of this agency is classified and is not readily available to the public.

Atomic Energy Commission. The Atomic Energy Act of 1946 created the Atomic Energy Commission. This Act as amended in 1954 set forth the purposes of the Commission and established in general as well as specific terms the nature of its activities and the areas where it has jurisdiction. In essence the purpose of the Act was to bring control of nuclear energy under the jurisdiction of the federal government so that this enormously important source of energy would be used to serve the interests of national security, world peace, and the general welfare. The Commission must be concerned with the use of atomic energy in the development of a weapons system, the use of isotopes in medical science and in industry, and the allocation of nuclear fuels for use in the generation of electricity.

The Commission encourages the participation of private industry in the development and use of atomic energy. It also must provide for the safety of the public where nuclear materials are used.

The Department of the Interior. No other department has a larger interest in resources and their conservation than the Department of the Interior. There have been informal suggestions that its name be changed to Department of Conservation, but its present name is particularly fitting. Furthermore, it would be next to impossible to transfer to its jurisdiction agencies and activities concerned with resources and conservation without disturbing long-established operations in other departments, divisions, and agencies.

Some of the divisions of the Department of the Interior that are vitally concerned with resources include the Fish and Wildlife Service, Bureau of Commercial Fisheries, Bureau of Sport Fisheries and Wildlife, Office of Oil and Gas, Oil Imports Administration, Office of Coal Research, Defense Electric Power Administration, Office of Water Resources Research, Office of Saline Waters, Federal Water Pollution Control Administration (Water Quality Act, 1965), National Park Service, Bureau of Mines, U.S. Geological Survey, Bureau of Reclamation, Bureau of Outdoor Recreation (1962), Bureau of Land Management, Bonneville Power Administration, Southeastern Power Administration, Southwestern Power Administration, Alaska Power Administration (1967), Office of Ecology (1967), and others.

Other Departments and Agencies Concerned with Resources and the General Welfare. The Department of Agriculture, because of the geographical dimension of its jurisdiction, also has a major interest in conservation. Agencies such as the Forest Service, Soil Conservation Service, Rural Electrification Administration, Commodity Credit Corporation, Agricultural Stabilization and Conservation Service, Rural Community Development Service, and Economic Research Service can be listed. These agencies, as do many others, function in cooperation with agencies in other departments, boards, committees, and commissions. For example, the Commodity Credit Corporation, in disposing of surplus agricultural products, has accepted payment in local credits. These funds instead of being converted into dollars have been used to purchase strategic mineral resources such as manganese for stockpiling in this country.

In the Department of Commerce the Economic Development Administration, the Environmental Science Service Administration (particularly the Weather Bureau), the Coast and Geodetic Survey, and the Area Redevelopment Administration are concerned with resources as well as service (Fig. 4). The list of government agencies involved in resource development include the Corps of Engineers of the Department of the Army, the Office of Naval Research in the Department of the Navy, and many independent agencies such as the Appalachian Regional Commission; Atomic Energy Commission; the Delaware River Basin Commission (a Federal-Interstate Compact); Federal Power Commission; New England Regional Commission; Ozarks Regional Commission; Tennessee Valley Authority; Advisory Board on National Parks, Historic Sites, Buildings, and Monuments; President's Council on Recreation and Natural Beauty, and the Water Resources Council.[11]

PLANNING IN THE PRIVATE SECTOR OF THE ECONOMY

In these times of big government, big business, and big labor unions, planning for the future development and use of resources is a widespread concern of the people. The large corporations, whether they are primary crea-

[11] *Ibid.*

Fig. 4 A view of the major highway connecting Kansas City, Missouri (in the background), and Kansas City, Kansas. One of the major problems confronting the nation is the development of a transportation system that will link the cities with the suburbs, the rural areas, and other cities. (Photo courtesy Armco Steel Corporation.)

tors of wealth such as mining companies and lumber companies or whether they are involved in the later manufacturing processes such as the making of automobiles or chemical products, must have both short-range and long-range plans for the future. In the larger firms a division may be assigned the responsibility of maintaining adequate reserves of raw materials so the parent company can continue in business over an extended period of time. A petroleum company as a producer, a manufacturer of petroleum products, and a distributor must carry on more or less continually the search for new deposits. A firm using timber and other products of the forest must be prepared to utilize the resource fully and move on to other areas that have not been exploited or to adopt a schedule of forest harvest and reforestation which will maintain the lumbering and wood-processing industries over a long period of time. On occasion the responsible officials in a company may yield to short-range goals to keep the firm in a competitive position, but at every opportunity the long-range plans of the company will receive careful attention.

It is important that the federal government and the large resource-using industries carry on research and planning programs that are mutually advantageous. The federal government can hardly be expected to develop an important fishery resource by restocking an area, by reducing pollution, and by other means to improve the resource situation and then without restrictions permit private enterprises which have little concern about the future to overfish the area and actually deplete a fishery that should be managed productively. The long-range interests of the government acting in behalf of all of the people and the commercial interest of a private company may be served by cooperation and mutual understanding.

National Problems That Lie Ahead. As the United States has become increasingly an urban and industrial nation a number of problems emerge that require attention. Many people have been concerned about the demand for additional rural lands to meet the needs of the urban communities for living space. Many manufacturing plants are a part of the urban sprawl, and extensive areas of agricultural land have been taken over to serve the needs of industry. Careful studies of this problem seem to indicate that highly productive land is entirely adequate to meet the needs of the nation for several decades for food, fibers, and other agricultural products.

National and local concern about the continued availability of adequate supplies of potable water and unpolluted air has focused attention on two problems that will require the attention of national, state, and local governments in the immediate future. As much as 97 percent of the water of the earth is in the sea. If potable, agricultural and industrial water is to be developed from this source the desalinization program will have to be greatly expanded. In the immediate future the solutions to the problem of inadequate water sup-

plies will include greater storage of surface waters, reduction of pollution, filtering and processing water to make it re-usable, the reduction of waste in use, slowing the return to the sea, recharging the aquifers, improving the cover and soak-in in the headstream areas, and other water-conserving measures.[12]

INTERNATIONAL CONTROL OF NATURAL RESOURCES

The federal government, by treaty and by other kinds of international agreements, participates in the partial control of a number of resources. This is well illustrated by the Migratory Bird Treaty Act of 1918 (see Chapter 20).

Beginning in 1933 and continuing at intervals of 3 or more years, the United States has been a participant in a number of international agreements relating to wheat. The United States is a major producer of wheat and certain readjustments in acreage allotments have been related in part to the establishment of export quotas and prices by the members of the conference which draws up the terms of the International Wheat Agreements. The operation of the Acreage Reserve Program of the Soil Bank of 1957 is related to the problem of agricultural surpluses.

Because of the danger of depleting an important marine resource, the principal whaling nations are now adherents to an international convention which limits the take of whales in the Antarctic waters. The International Whaling Commission meets at regular intervals and establishes quotas for the several signatory nations.

As the United States participates increasingly in international affairs it may be expected that agreements will be entered into involving the international control of other

[12] Abel Wolman, Chairman of the Water Resources Study, *Water Resources*, Publication 1000-B, National Academy of Sciences, National Research Council, Washington, D.C., 1962.

activities or materials. In addition to wheat, coffee, sugar, seals, whales, migratory birds, and minerals, other resources are likely to be subject to international agreements.

RESEARCH AND THE PROBLEM OF DIMINISHING RESOURCES

In the conservation of the natural resources of the nation one of the great hopes of the future is the intensive search for the solution of the problems related to the exhaustion or decline of the material wealth long so abundant and easily available to us. Organized research must be brought to bear upon this problem, and human talent must be mobilized so that the security of the nation will never be in doubt for want of the essential raw materials.

Individual Research. It is traditional that the individual scholar at work in his laboratory or in his study represents scientific progress in a free society. Scientists working alone in their laboratories or in the field have found ways of utilizing more fully or more cheaply our material resources. The scholar in isolation has become relatively less important, but his work should be encouraged and supported.

Industrial Research Laboratories.[13] Over a period of many years industries intent upon maintaining their competitive position have established research laboratories and employed a staff of scientists to carry out their investigations. Initially these research laboratories or divisions were largely concerned with practical problems related to the industry that supported them. But industrial research has become both practical and fundamental. The federal government, in addition to financing research activities in many agencies of the government, has contracted for research by the industrial research laboratories, research

foundations of many universities, and a variety of private research organizations.

Several hundred industrial research laboratories both large and small have been involved in research for the federal government. Some of the best known are the large corporations such as Allied Chemical Corporation, American Telephone and Telegraph Company, E. I. du Pont de Nemours and Company, General Dynamics Corporation, General Motors Corporation, International Business Machines Corporation, the 3 M Company, and Standard Oil Company of New Jersey.

Many of the smaller business organizations with small research staffs and facilities have offered their services to the federal government.[14] Many of the problems are of such complexity that they require research talent and facilities that only the large companies can offer.

The private or quasi-independent research laboratories have drawn heavy support from the federal government and in turn have rendered an important service. These include Arthur D. Little, Inc., Battelle Memorial Institute, Mellon Institute, The Rand Corporation, Stanford Research Institute, and many others. These laboratories are in a position to carry on highly technical research because of the specialized talents of their scientific personnel and the highly sophisticated equipment available. For example, the development and testing of metals and ceramic materials for use in the space programs are necessary if the nation is to meet the challenges of the future.

Private industry, particularly the large companies that depend upon the availability of large reserves, must make a serious effort to maintain a source of supply over many years. The petroleum industry must carry on explo-

---

[13] William W. Buchanan, editor, *Industrial Research Laboratories of the United States,* Twelfth Edition, Bowker Associates, Inc., Washington, D.C., 1965.

[14] Small Business Administration, *A List of Small Business Concerns Interested in Performing Research and Development,* 1963 edition, Washington, D.C.

ration year after year to discover extensions of known oil fields or to find other sources of supply. A mining company faced with the exhaustion of a known mineral deposit must develop methods of using low-grade ores at a profit or find new ore bodies where development will be economically feasible. The paper and timber industries have become aware of the necessity of providing for their own future. After harvesting the resources of the forest, seedlings are planted on the cut-over land, and in time a new forest crop can be harvested. Many private industries are providing for their own future.

Research in Colleges and Universities. Research in the major educational institutions of this country has been overshadowed by the great industrial research organizations. In fact research in the universities is in many instances indistinguishable from the research in industry. Many universities receive support from industry for their research programs, and generally the achievement of practical results is a major objective. In the universities there can be a detachment that is conducive to long-range research of fundamental character where practical application is not immediately envisioned. The universities are peculiarly well suited for this type of research.

It is appropriate that certain research programs in the universities should be concerned with the many aspects of the resource problem. In the physical and biological sciences, in political science, and in economics both the scientific and the social aspects of natural resources may be investigated with scholarly objectivity.

Many of the large universities have highly developed research laboratories with highly trained scientists and technical staffs and have engaged in research for the federal government over a period of many years. Some of the best known are Massachusetts Institute of Technology, Harvard University, Columbia University, Cornell University, the Big Ten Universities, University of North Carolina, Lou-

isiana State University, University of Texas, University of California at Los Angeles and at Berkeley, Stanford University, and the University of Washington. In recent years there has grown up something of a revolt against the identification of the universities with the military–industrial complex that President Eisenhower warned against in his Farewell Radio and Television Address to the American People on January 17, 1961.

The Government and Research. The federal government and to a lesser extent states and municipalities have conducted and supported research activities over a long period of time. During World War II and in the postwar period research in agencies of the federal government has been greatly expanded. In a similar manner research in the universities and in private research organizations has been generously supported by the federal government. Much of the research is related directly or indirectly to the problem of national security and in one way or another is concerned with the resource situation.

The Agricultural Experiment Stations, the Bureau of Mines, the Soil Conservation Service, the Bureau of Animal Industry, the Forest Service, the regional laboratories and the Agricultural Research Center of the Department of Agriculture, the Office of Naval Research, the Research and Development Board, and many other bureaus and agencies of the federal government are devoted to research programs which will lead eventually to a wiser use of our basic resources.

In a nation of diminishing material resources there are still new frontiers to be explored. New lands are no longer available to challenge the pioneering spirit of the youth of America, but the new frontiers of science present an opportunity for adventure and achievement for those who would serve the needs of their country. Through the resourcefulness of the people in making full and appropriate use of the more abundant materials, a high standard of living for the people and security of the nation can be achieved. Out of the materials of the earth people create resources.

The science of ecology, the study of the relation of organisms, both plant and animal, to each other and to the environment, has experienced a revival of interest. In the schools—elementary, secondary, and higher institutions—increasing attention is being given to ecology. The general public is learning about ecology and its relevance to environmental quality, and as a consequence people may understand their responsibilities as citizens and as public officials in meeting the challenge of the deterioration of the environment. In January 1967, Congress established the Office of Ecology in the Department of the Interior. The Director of the Office serves as Adviser to the Secretary on environmental quality and reports to him through the Office of the Science Adviser.

The preservation of wilderness areas where the influence of man is excluded or held to a minimum provides models in ecology. From these untouched and unspoiled areas future generations may learn something of the primeval conditions that the pioneers had to contend with in carving a home out of the wilderness. From the ecology of these natural areas the new generation may gain insights into the operation of the modern economic system.

National planning in the 1930's was planning for a nation in despair. Economic chaos gripped the nation. In the 1940's, planning to defeat the nation's enemies and to provide for national security required the energies of all the people. Military action in Korea in the early 1950's and in South Vietnam in the 1960's and the economic stresses in intervening years have required a continuing effort to maintain a strong nation, conserve resources, aid other nations less fortunate, and reorient the nation's posture in relation to the needs of the 1970's and the remaining years of the twentieth century.

New Directions in Conservation. The rapid deterioration of the environment has caused a nationwide crusade against pollution; wasteful exploitation of resources; the fouling of beaches, parks, and roadsides with waste products; and other acts that have altered unfavorably the human habitat. In many ways the public's concern is being expressed. The Congress has appropriated funds for the purchase of wetlands chiefly for the conservation of migratory waterfowl. The National Wildlife Refuge System has acquired additional lands. The coastal waters such as estuaries, marshlands, bays, sounds, lagoons, and other adjacent wetlands and water areas are in danger of deterioration by pollution, landfill, and industrial and commercial development. The Department of the Interior in cooperation with the Corps of Engineers, other federal agencies, and the several states may recommend to the Congress the need to protect, conserve, and restore estuaries and other coastal waters of the United States.[15]

It will require herculean efforts to prevent further deterioration of the physical environment. A new plant in a rural area, the expansion of an already-established industry, or any major operation to develop a natural resource will result in some deterioration of the environment. Additional pollutants may be discharged into the atmosphere, surface streams and even groundwater may be polluted, and solid wastes may accumulate or create a disposal problem. In more than 300 years since the natural environments of the United States began to be occupied great changes have taken place. Future requirements for living space and resources are certain to produce many changes in the regional character of the United States and its neighbors.[16]

[15] For an extended report on estuaries see George H. Lauff, editor, *Estuaries,* American Association for the Advancement of Science, Washington, D.C., 1967.

[16] F. Fraser Darling and John P. Milton, editors, *Future Environments of North America,* Garden City, New York, 1966.

References

American Society of Planning Officials, *Planning*, Annual.

Buchanan, William W., editor, *Industrial Research Laboratories of the United States*, Twelfth Edition, Bowker Associates, Inc., Washington, D.C., 1965.

Darling, F. Fraser and John P. Milton, *Future Environments of North America*, The Natural History Press, Garden City, New York, 1966.

Eisenhower, Milton S., "Federal Responsibilities in Total Conservation," *Conservation of Renewable Resources*, University of Pennsylvania Bicentennial Conference, University of Pennsylvania Press, Philadelphia, 1941, pp. 175–189.

Gaus, John M., Jacob Crane, Marshall E. Dimock, and George T. Renner, *Regional Factors in National Planning and Development*, National Resources Committee, Government Printing Office, Washington, D.C., 1935.

Journal, American Institute of Planners, Bimonthly.

Landsberg, Hans H., *Natural Resources for U.S. Growth*, The Johns Hopkins Press, Baltimore, 1964.

Landsberg, Hans H., Leonard L. Fischman, and Joseph L. Fisher, *Resources in America's Future*, Resources for the Future, The Johns Hopkins Press, Baltimore, 1963.

Lilienthal, David E., *TVA, The March of Democracy*, Harper and Brothers, New York, 1944.

Lorwin, Lewis L., *Time for Planning*, Harper and Brothers, New York, 1945.

MacKenzie, Findlay, editor, *Planned Society, Yesterday, Today, Tomorrow*, Prentice-Hall, Englewood Cliffs, New Jersey, 1937.

Millett, John D., *The Process and Organization of Government Planning*, Columbia University Press, New York, 1947.

National Planning Association, Committee on New England, *The Economic State of New England* (Directors of research and editors: Arthur A. Bright, Jr. and George H. Ellis), Yale University Press, New Haven, 1954.

National Planning Association, *Long-Range Projections for Economic Growth: the American Economy in 1970*, Washington, D.C., 1959.

National Referral Center for Science and Technology, *A Directory of Information Resources in the United States, Physical Sciences, Biological Sciences, Engineering*, Government Printing Office, Washington, D.C., 1965.

Odum, Howard and H. E. Moore, *American Regionalism*, Henry Holt and Co., New York, 1935.

Rodgers, Cleveland, *American Planning*, Harper and Brothers, New York, 1947.

Shah, K. T., *National Planning, Principles and Administration*, Vora and Company, Publishers, Ltd., Bombay, India, 1948.

Small Business Administration, Research and Development, *List of Small Business Concerns Interested in Performing Research and Development*, Government Printing Office, Washington, D.C., 1963.

Stanley, Timothy W., *American Defense and National Security*, Public Affairs Press, Washington, D.C., 1956.

Terral, Rufus, *The Missouri Valley,* Yale University Press, New Haven, Connecticut, 1947.

United States Government Organization Manual, 1968–69, Government Printing Office, Washington, D.C., 1968.

United States National Resources Committee, *Regional Planning,* Government Printing Office, Washington, D.C., 1936–1939.

———, *Research—A National Resource, 1: Relation of the Federal Government to Research,* Government Printing Office, Washington, D.C., 1938, 255 pages.

———, *Research—A National Resource, II: Industrial Research,* Government Printing Office, Washington, D.C., 1940, 369 pages.

United States National Resources Planning Board, *Industrial Locations and National Resources,* Government Printing Office, Washington, D.C., 1943.

Wootton, Barbara, *Freedom under Planning,* University of North Carolina Press, Chapel Hill, N.C., 1946.

Wriston, Henry M., *Goals for Americans,* Prentice-Hall, Englewood Cliffs, New Jersey, 1960.

General Works on Conservation

A Committee on Resources and Man, Division of Earth Sciences, National Academy of Sciences—National Research Council, *Resources and Man,* W. H. Freeman and Co., San Francisco, 1969.

Allen, Shirley Walter and Justin Wilkinson Leonard, *Conserving Natural Resources,* Third Edition, McGraw-Hill Book Co., New York, 1966.

Arthur, Don R., *Man and His Environment,* American Elsevier, New York, 1969.

Barnett, Harold G. and Chandler Morse, *Scarcity and Growth: The Economics of Natural Resource Availability,* The Johns Hopkins Press, Baltimore, 1963.

Brady, N. C., editor, *Agriculture and the Quality of Our Environment,* Publ. No. 85, American Association for the Advancement of Science, Washington, D.C., 1967.

Bromfield, Louis, *Out of the Earth,* Harper and Brothers, New York, 1950.

Brown, Harrison, *The Challenge of Man's Future,* Viking Press, New York, 1954.

Burton, Ian and Robert W. Kates, editors, *Readings in Resource Management and Conservation,* University of Chicago Press, Chicago, 1965.

Callison, Charles H., editor, *America's Natural Resources,* Second Edition, The Ronald Press Company, New York, 1967.

Ciriacy-Wantrup, S. V., *Resource Conservation,* Revised Edition, Agricultural Publications, University of California, Berkeley, 1964.

Clawson, Marion, *Natural Resources and International Development,* Resources for the Future, The Johns Hopkins Press, Baltimore, 1964.

Clawson, Marion, R. Burnell Held, and Charles H. Stoddard, *Land for the Future,* The Johns Hopkins Press, Baltimore, 1960.

Clepper, Henry Edward, editor, *Origins of American Conservation,* for Natural Resources Council of America, The Ronald Press Company, New York, 1966.

Conservation Foundation, *Annual Reports,* New York.

Conservation—In the People's Hands, American Association for the Advancement of Science, Washington, D.C., 1964.

Conservation of Renewable Natural Resources, Proceedings of Inter-American Conference, U.S. Department of State, Publ. 3382, Denver, Colorado, 1948.

Coyle, David Cushman, *Conservation: An American Story of Conflict and Accomplishment,* Rutgers University Press, New Brunswick, New Jersey, 1957.

Darling, F. Fraser and John P. Milton, editors, *Future Environments of North America,* The Natural History Press, Garden City, N.Y., 1966.

Dasmann, Raymond F., *A Different Kind of Country,* The Macmillan Co., New York, 1968.

————, *Environmental Conservation,* Second Edition, John Wiley & Sons, Inc., New York, 1968.

DeBell, Garrett, editor, *The Environmental Handbook,* Ballantine Books, Inc., New York, 1970.

Dewhurst, J. Frederic and Associates, *America's Needs and Resources, A New Survey,* The Twentieth Century Fund, New York, 1955.

Ehrenfeld, David W., *Biological Conservation,* Holt, Rinehart and Winston, New York, 1970.

Ehrlich, Paul R. and Anne H., *Population, Resources, Environment: Issues in Human Ecology,* W. H. Freeman and Co., San Francisco, 1970.

Environment, Office publication of Scientists' Institute for Public Information. Published ten times a year by the Committee for Environmental Information, St. Louis, Missouri.

Fairchild, Wilma Belden, "Renewable Resources: A World Dilemma; Recent Publications on Conservation," *Geographical Review,* Vol. 39, 1949, pp. 89–98.

Firey, Walter, *Man, Mind and Land, A Theory of Resource Use,* The Free Press of Glencoe, Illinois, 1960.

Flynn, Harry Eugene and Floyd E. Perkins, *Conservation of the Nation's Resources,* The Macmillan Co., New York, 1941.

Franklin D. Roosevelt & Conservation, 1911–1945 (4 Vols.), compiled and edited by Edgar B. Nixon, General Services Administration, National Archives and Records Service, Franklin D. Roosevelt Library, Hyde Park, New York, 1957.

Frontiers in Conservation, Proceedings of a Meeting, Fort Collins, Colorado, August 1969, Soil Conservation Society of America, Ankeny, Iowa, 1970.

Glacken, Clarence J., "The Origins of Conservation Philosophy," *Journ. Soil and Water Conservation,* Vol. II, 1956, pp. 63–66.

Graham, Edward H., *Natural Principles of Land Use,* Oxford University Press, New York, 1944.

Gustafson, A. F., C. H. Guise, W. J. Hamilton, Jr., and H. Ries, *Conservation in the United States,* Third Edition, Comstock Publishing Company, Ithaca, New York, 1949.

Hatt, Paul K., editor, *World Population and Future Resources,* American Book Co., New York, 1952.

Hays, Samuel P., *Conservation and the Gospel of Efficiency, The Progressive Conservation Movement, 1890–1920,* Harvard University Press, Cambridge, 1959.

Herfindahl, Orris C. and Allen V. Kneese, *Quality of the Environment,* The Johns Hopkins Press, Baltimore, 1965.

Higbee, Edward, *American Agriculture, Geography, Resources, Conservation,* John Wiley & Sons, Inc., New York, 1958.

Highsmith, Richard M., J. Granville Jensen, and Robert D. Rudd, *Conservation in the United States,* Rand McNally and Co., Chicago, 1962.

Huberty, Martin, R. and Warren L. Flock, editors, *Natural Resources,* McGraw-Hill Book Co., New York, 1959.

Jacks, G. V. and R. O. Whyte, *Vanishing Lands: A World Survey of Soil Erosion,* Doubleday, Doran and Co., New York, 1939.

Jarrett, Henry, editor, *Environmental Quality in a Growing Economy,* The Johns Hopkins Press, Baltimore, 1966.

————, editor, *Perspectives on Conservation,* The Johns Hopkins Press, Baltimore, 1958.

————, editor, *Science and Resources: Prospects and Implications of Technological Advance,* The Johns Hopkins Press, Baltimore, 1959.

Kauffman, Erle, *The Conservation Yearbook,* Monumental Printing Company, Baltimore, 1956.

Kerr, Senator Robert S., *Land, Wood and Water,* edited by Malvina Stephenson and Tris Coffin, Fleet Publishing Corp., New York, 1960.

King, Judson, *The Conservation Fight, from Theodore Roosevelt to the Tennessee Valley Authority,* Public Affairs Press, Washington, D.C., 1959.

Kreps, Juanita Morris, editor, *Our Natural Resources,* The Reference Shelf, Vol. 22, No. 2, H. W. Wilson Company, New York, 1955.

Krug, J. A., *National Resources and Foreign Aid,* Report of the Secretary of the Interior, Government Printing Office, Washington, D.C., 1947.

Landsberg, Hans H., *Natural Resources for U.S. Growth,* The Johns Hopkins Press, Baltimore, 1964.

Landsberg, Hans H., Leonard L. Fischman, and Joseph L. Fisher, *Resources in America's Future, Patterns of Requirements and Availabilities, 1960–2000,* Resources for the Future, The Johns Hopkins Press, Baltimore, 1963.

Lyons, Barrow, *Tomorrow's Birthright,* Funk and Wagnalls, New York, 1955.

Margalef, Ramón, *Perspectives in Ecological Theory,* University of Chicago Press, Chicago, 1968.

Marine, Gene, *America the Raped, The Engineering Mentality and the Devastation of a Continent,* Simon and Schuster, New York, 1969.

Marsh, George P., *Man and Nature; or Physical Geography as Modified by Human Action* (1864), Revised Edition, *The Earth as Modified by Human Action,* Charles Scribner's Sons, New York, 1884.

Mather, Kirtley F., *Enough and to Spare,* Harper and Brothers, New York, 1944.

Mayda, Jaro, *Environment and Resources, From Conservation to Economanagement,* School of Law, University of Puerto Rico, Rio Piedras, 1968.

Mouzon, Olin T., *International Resources and National Policy,* Harper and Brothers, New York, 1959.

National Resources Committee, General reports and publications on regional planning, state planning, public works, land planning, and water planning (see also the reports of the National Planning Board and the National Resources Board), Government Printing Office, Washington, D.C., 1934–1943.

Natural Resources Journal, Published four times a year by The University of New Mexico School of Law, Albuquerque, New Mexico.

National Resources Security Board, Reports and press releases, Government Printing Office, Washington, D.C., 1948–1953.

Ordway, Samuel H., Jr., *Conservation Handbook,* New York, 1949.

————, *Prosperity Beyond Tomorrow,* The Ronald Press Co., New York, 1956.

————, *Resources and the American Dream,* The Ronald Press Co., New York, 1953.

Osborn, Fairfield, *Our Plundered Planet,* Little, Brown and Co., Boston, Mass., 1948.

————, *The Limits of the Earth,* Little, Brown and Co., Boston, Mass., 1953.

Parkins, A. E. and J. R. Whitaker, *Our Natural Resources and Their Conservation,* John Wiley & Sons, New York, 1936 and 1939.

Parson, Ruben L., *Conserving American Resources,* Second Edition, Prentice-Hall, Englewood Cliffs, New Jersey, 1964.

Patton, Donald J., *The United States and World Resources* (Van Nostrand Searchlight Book No. 39), D. Van Nostrand Company, Inc., Princeton, New Jersey, 1968.

Perloff, Harvey S., Edgar S. Dunn, Jr., Eric E. Lampard, and Richard F. Muth, *Regions, Resources, and Economic Growth,* The Johns Hopkins Press, Baltimore, 1960.

Pinchot, Gifford, *The Fight for Conservation,* Farmers Bull. 327, U.S. Department of Agriculture, Washington, D.C., 1909.

Potter, Neal and Francis T. Christy, Jr., *Trends in Natural Resource Commodities, Statistics on Prices, Output, Consumption, Foreign Trade, and Employment in the United States, 1870–1957,* The Johns Hopkins Press, Baltimore, 1962.

The President's Materials Policy Commission, *Resources for Freedom,* Vol. I: *Foundations for Growth and Security,* Vol. II: *The Outlook for Key Commodities,* Vol. III: *The Outlook for Energy Sources,* Vol. IV: *The Promise of Technology,* Government Printing Office, Washington, D.C., 1952.

President's Science Advisory Committee, *Restoring the Quality of Our Environment,* Report of the Environmental Pollution Panel, The White House, Washington, D.C., 1965.

Raushenbush, Stephen, "The Future of Our Natural Resources," *The Annals,* Vol. 281, 1952, pp. 1–275.

Renewable Resources, A Report to the Committee on Natural Resources, National Academy of Sciences—National Research Council, Publications 1000 and 1000-A, Washington, D.C., 1962.

Renner, George T., *Conservation of National Resources,* John Wiley & Sons, New York, 1942.

Report of the National Conservation Commission, Senate Document 676, Vol. 1, 60th Congress, 2nd Session, Government Printing Office, Washington, D.C., 1909.

Resources for the Future, *Annual Reports,* Reprints, Monographs, etc.

Resources for the Future, *The Nation Looks at Its Resources,* Report of the Mid-Century Conference on Resources for the Future, December 2–4, 1953, Washington, D.C., 1954.

Reuss, L. A., H. H. Wooten, and F. J. Marschner, *Inventory of Major Land Uses in the United States,* Misc. Publ. 663, U.S. Department of Agriculture, Washington, D.C., 1948.

Roosevelt, Nicholas, *Conservation: Now or Never,* Dodd, Mead & Company, New York, 1970.

Schulz, William F., Jr., *Conservation Law and Administration, A Case Study of Law and Resource Use in Pennsylvania* (Sponsored by the Conservation Foundation and the University of Pittsburgh School of Law), The Ronald Press Co., New York, 1953.

Schurr, Sam H. and Bruce C. Netschert, *Energy in the American Economy, 1950–1975,* The Johns Hopkins Press, Baltimore, 1960.

Scott, Anthony, *Natural Resources: The Economics of Conservation,* University of Toronto Press, Toronto, Canada, 1955.

Sears, Paul B., *Deserts on the March,* Revised Edition, University of Oklahoma Press, Norman, Oklahoma, 1947.

Skinner, Brian J., *Earth Resources,* Prentice-Hall, Englewood Cliffs, N.J., 1969.

Smith, Frank E., *The Politics of Conservation,* Pantheon Books, A Division of Random House, New York, 1966.

Staley, Eugene, *Raw Materials in Peace and War,* Council of Foreign Relations, New York, 1937.

Stewart, George R., *Not So Rich as You Think,* Houghton Mifflin Company, Boston, 1968.

Straus, Michael W., *Why Not Survive?* Simon and Schuster, New York, 1955.

Thomas, William L., Jr., editor, *Man's Role in Changing the Face of the Earth,* University of Chicago Press, Chicago, 1956.

Udall, Stewart, *The Quiet Crisis,* Holt, Rinehart, and Winston, Inc., New York, 1963.

United Nations Department of Economic Affairs, Proceedings of the United Nations Scientific Conference on Conservation and Utilization of Resources, August 17—September 6, 1949, United Nations, New York, 1951. Vol. I: *Plenary Meetings,* Vol. II: *Mineral Resources,* Vol. III: *Fuel and Energy Resources,* Vol. IV: *Water Resources,* Vol. V: *Forest Resources,* Vol. VI: *Land Resources,* Vol. VII: *Wildlife and Fish Resources,* Vol. VIII: *Index.*

United States Department of the Interior, *Conservation Yearbook,* Government Printing Office, Washington, D.C., 1965, 1966, 1967, 1968, 1969.

United States Congress, House of Representatives, *A Program to Strengthen the Scientific Foundation in Natural Resources,* House Document 706, 81st Congress, Second Session, A Supplemental Report to Accompany Hearings on H. R. 6257 and H. R. 6900, Government Printing Office, Washington, D.C., 1950.

United States Congress, House of Representatives, Interior and Insular Affairs Committee, *The Physical and Economic Foundation of Natural Resources,* I. *Photosynthesis, Basic Features of the Process,* II. *The Physical Basis of*

Water Supply and Its Principal Uses, III. *Groundwater Regions of the United States—Their Storage Facilities,* IV. *Subsurface Facilities of Water Management and Patterns of Supply—Type Area Studies,* Government Printing Office, Washington, D.C., 1952.

University of Pennsylvania Bicentennial Conference, *Conservation of Renewable Natural Resources,* University of Pennsylvania Press, Philadelphia, Pa., 1941.

Van Hise, Charles Richard, *The Conservation of Natural Resources in the United States,* The Macmillan Co., New York, 1910 and 1921.

Van Hise, Charles R. and Loomis Havemeyer, *Conservation of Our Natural Resources,* The Macmillan Co., New York, 1935.

Vogt, William, *Road to Survival,* William Sloane Associates, New York, 1948.

Wales, H. Basil and H. O. Lathrop, *The Conservation of Natural Resources,* Laurel Book Co., Chicago, 1944.

Watt, Kenneth E. F., *Ecology and Resource Management,* McGraw-Hill Book Co., New York, 1968.

Whitaker, J. Russell and Edward A. Ackerman, *American Resources,* Harcourt, Brace and Co., New York, 1951.

White, Gilbert F., "Toward an Appraisal of World Resources: New Views of Conservation Problems," *Geographical Review,* Vol. 39, 1949, pp. 625–639.

Wilbur, Ray Lyman and William Atherton Du Puy, *Conservation in the Department of the Interior,* Government Printing Office, Washington, D.C., 1932.

Zimmermann, Erich W., *Introduction to World Resources,* edited by Henry L. Hunker, Harper and Row, New York, 1964.

Zurhorst, Charles, *The Conservation Fraud,* Cowles Book Co., Inc., New York, 1970.

Index